SHAIVISM

in the light of
Epics, Purāṇas and Āgamas

N. R. Bhatt

ÍNDICA

Cover illustration: Naṭarāja, temple of Kaḍambeśvara at Raṭṭihaḷḷi, Karnataka.

1st Edition 2008
2nd Edition 2020

Published by
Indica Books
D 40 / 18 Godowlia
Varanasi - 221 001 (U.P.)
India
Email : indicabooksindia@gmail.com
Website : www.indicabooks.com

ISBN: 81-86569-70-7

Printed in India by
Sadhana Press, Varanasi.
Mob.: 9336838939

Table of Contents

CHAPTER VI. **Forms of Śiva Worship and Ritual in the South 309**

CHAPTER VII. **The Ancillary Cults** . . **457**

APPENDICES:

Table of Figures

Abbreviations

AB	Aitareya Brāhmaṇa
ABORI	Annals of the Bhandarkar Oriental Research Institute, Poona
Ait. Up.	Aitareya Upaniṣad
ALB	Adyar Library Bulletin (Brahmavidyā), Adyar
AO	Acta Orientalia, Ediderunt Societates Orientales Batava Danica Norvegica, Leiden
AP.Gs.	Āpastamba Gṛhyasūtra
AŚP	Aghoraśivācāryapaddhati
AV	Atharvaveda
BDCRI	Bulletin of the Deccan College Post Graduate Research Institute, Poona.
Bṛh.Up.	Bṛhadāraṇyaka Upaniṣad
BRMIC	Bulletin of the Ramakrishna Mission Institute of Culture
Ch.Up.	Chāndogya Upaniṣad
CUR	Ceylon University Review
ERE	Encyclopaedia of Religion and Ethics
HIL	History of Indian Literature
HOS	Harvard Oriental Series
IC	Indian Culture
IHC	Indian Historical Congress
IHQ	Indian Historical Quarterly, Calcutta Oriental Press, Calcutta
JA	Journal Asiatique, Paris
JAS	Journal of the Anthropological Society, Bombay
JBORS	Journal of the Bihar and Orissa Research Society
JBU	Journal of the University of Bombay

JBRAS	Journal of the Bombay Branch of the Royal Asiatic Society, Bombay
JGJRI	Journal of the Ganganath Jha Research Institute, Allahabad
JORM	Journal of Oriental Research, Madras
JRAS	Journal of the Royal Asiatic Society of Great Britain and Ireland, London
JUPH	Journal of the University of Poona (Humanities Section)
Kauś.Up.	Kauśītaki Upaniṣad
MBh	Mahābhārata
MS	Maitrāyaṇī Saṁhitā
NR	The New Review, Calcutta
PO	Poona Orientalist, Oriental Book Agency, Poona
Pr.Bh.	Prabuddha Bhārata (Awakened India), Calcutta
QJMS	Quarterly Journal of the Mythic Society, Bangalore
Rām.	Rāmāyaṇa
RPVU	Religion and Philosophy of the *Veda* and Upaniṣad
ṚV	Ṛgveda
ŚB	Śatapatha Brāhmaṇa
SBE	Sacred Books of the East
Śv.Up.	Śvetāśvatara Upaniṣad
ŚŚS	Śāṅkhāyana Śrauta Sūtra
TB	Taittirīya Brāhmaṇa
TC	Tamil Culture
TS	Taittirīya Saṁhitā
Tait.Up.	Taittirīya Upaniṣad
Up.	Upaniṣad
YV	Yajurveda

Preface

Indian philosophy provides the profound concept of *cit*. The school of Śaivasiddhānta defines the essence of *cit* as universal action and knowledge. It conceives an entity which is none else than pure *cit* and gives it the name *śiva*, word of neuter gender denoting auspiciousness and purity. This is an abstract entity, beyond the grasp of human senses, speech and mind. Truly, the human being is endowed with the same *cit* of same universal faculty of action and knowledge. The difference between the supreme and the mundane beings is achieved by another entity, a universal power of obscuration, to which the figurative name of *mala*, 'stain', has been given. The supreme Śiva is free of *mala*. The mundane soul is bound by it and undergoes drastic limitations of its faculties of *cit*: one cognition, one action at one time, accomplished with the ever-changing tools of mind and body of limited faculties in a material world, but with a background of consciousness limited to that cognition or action only. Whatever is the cognition, whatever is the action, there is always the same background of consciousness. This is the indication of the presence of the fundamental essence of *cit*, inherent in every individual, partially and temporarily unveiled from the obscuration of *mala*.

The idea of a pure essence and a bond to impure, limitative matter is a basic component of many currents of Shaivism, the foundation of the quest for liberation of the bond, which characterizes all religious preoccupations. The being made of pure *cit*, eternally free from *mala* is God, the bound being is man. In fact, Indian thinkers have often used the same name for both: *puruṣa*. That reflects the concept of a fundamental identity of man and God by their common essence of *cit*, their common faculty of consciousness. Man is the bound *puruṣa*, God the eternally unbound *puruṣa*. That brings in a relation of a lower being *versus* a supreme one. The former is called *paśu*, 'bound soul', the latter Paśupati, 'Lord of bound souls'. This relation commands the religious activity, itself based on awareness of the supreme, devotional attitude, quest of ways of approach, aspiration to liberation from the binding obscuration of consciousness. There are two currents of doctrines about the ways of approaching the supreme, preference being given either to the resource of the knowledge faculty, either to that of action, gnosis *versus* ritual, both remaining complementary. The school of Śaivasiddhānta has given emphasis to the ritual, other schools to gnosis. The site for conducting rituals is of several types: the home of the worshipper in the wake of worldly life, the monastery (*maṭha*) of those who opt for a more secluded mode of life, the temple open to all. The temple is the most important and the most original creation of Indian culture. A parent of the royal palace, it is a complex organization of structures adapted to all activities centered on the worshipped deity: purification, consecration, homage, festivities, services for the deity and for the worshippers.

In the religious sphere, the proper name of the Supreme Being is Śiva. With this name we enter in the vast world of mythology. The supreme entity, which is formless, is characterized by its propensity to manifest itself in multiple forms, many human forms with supernatural adjuncts, some half way between the formless and the human form. This is told as a threefold character of Śiva according to the degree of his manifestation: *avyakta*, 'unmanifested', *vyaktāvyakta*, 'manifested-cum-unmanifested', *vyakta*, 'manifested'. The medial one is the Liṅga, the last one is an embodiment in a figure acting heroic feats, offered to the worship of the seekers of liberation.

The core of Shaivism is a vast corpus of philosophical and theological concepts, of myths, of rituals. The present book by Pandit N. R. Bhatt introduces its presentation with the doctrine of Śaivasiddhānta and, after a long narration of numerous myths and an elaborate description of rituals, ends with a list of remarkable temples of south India. Thus it encompasses the whole gamut of the aspects of the religion. This book has a history, which is the life history of its author, and in a way the history of Indological studies of Shaivism. Indology of scientific spirit is born with the nineteenth century, which has been the century of Vedic studies. The twentieth century has opened a new domain in the history and archaeology of Indian religions, with the study of Shaivism and Tantrism. The first half has been that of discovery by pionneers like Bhandarkar, Gopinath Rao, Banerjee, Jouveau-Dubreuil, Hopkins, Marshall, etc. The second half has achieved considerable progress in the knowledge of texts and monuments, by surveys of temples and icons, critical editions of *Mahābhārata* and *Rāmāyaṇa*, of *Purāṇas* and *Āgamas*. The vast domain of Hinduism, of the limitless literature of Tantras, Śaiva or Śākta, as well as Vaiṣṇava, Bauddha, etc., of the countless temples, medieval and modern, has been entered for thorough investigation. It is a giant step and it achieves considerable progress in our knowledge of Indian religions.

Pandit N. Ramachandra Bhatt (born in 1920 in Mudbidri, South Kannara) has been one of the main artisans of this progress. His life has been entirely devoted to research. After his Sanskrit studies in the traditional manner in Tirupati, at the Venkateshvara Sanskrit College, in 1939, he entered the team of researchers of the Adyar Library and Research Centre, which Alain Daniélou (1907-1994) joined years later. There, he acquired a good knowledge of the bibliography and theories, sometimes quite speculative, of the pioneers of the history of Shaivism. He worked with Daniélou on texts of musicology as well as philosophical and religious texts, *Upaniṣads*, *Purāṇas* etc. Daniélou, during a long stay in India, had elaborated personal views on Indian mythology and religion, which he presented in a book entitled *The Myths and Gods of India, Hindu polytheism*. N. R. Bhatt could not share the same ideas. He had a deep knowledge of texts and a preference for literality in interpretation. He was too reluctant to speculation to accept Daniélou's ideas. In spite of such disagreement, an enduring friendship was established between them.

In 1955, Jean Filliozat, my father, established a French Institute in Pondicherry. He invited Alain Daniélou to his Department of Indology to work in the field of Sanskrit musicological texts. Daniélou came with Pandit N. R. Bhatt, who could be appointed at the same time and to whom Jean Filliozat entrusted the main project of his new institution: to collect manuscripts of Śaiva texts of rituals, i.e. Śaivāgamas, survey the relevant literature and prepare critical editions with translations. A new career started for N. R. Bhatt. In the span of nearly fifty years he built a collection of some fifteen thousand manuscripts from temples and gurukkal families of Tamilnadu. He directed a team of pandits to organise an Āgamic library, to collate manuscripts. He could publish several major texts of Āgamic literature, *Rauravāgama*, *Ajitāgama* etc. Thus he has brought to light a large documentation and made accessible a lot of information on Śaiva rituals, architecture, organisation and iconography of Śiva temples. He has constituted a precious tool for researchers of the 21st century, which will be the century of Tantric studies in the history of Indology.

The present book is the result of his full, life-long career in research. It starts with a detailed review of the works and ideas of the pioneers of the first half of the last century. Then, it presents the results of its author's innovative research in the field of Āgamas. We have thus a complete survey of the progress achieved in the knowledge of Śaivism during the past century. This is not an individualistic view of the religion, a personal interpretation of a chapter of its history. This is a view based on an ancient tradition, a tradition of ritualistic performance and literary composition, which N. R. Bhatt has received from the environment in which he is born and lives. This is a view founded on his advanced erudition, intelligently directed, rooted in his own experience of religious practice as a Brahmin follower of the faith. This is Śaivism seen from outside and inside. Thus, we have a picture of it which represents authentically the knowledge and the religious feelings of millions of worshippers in this modern world.

To complete the history of this book, I have to tell my link with its author and my participation in its elaboration. In 1956 I began to learn Sanskrit under the guidance of N. R. Bhatt. From the time of the first lesson was born between us a life-long friendship. I have worked with him for many years, especially on Śaivasiddhānta works, and we collaborated in the English version of *Ajitatantra* (IGNCA,

Delhi, 2004). A few years after the demise of Jean Filliozat in 1982, Alain Daniélou had entrusted to N. R. Bhatt the project of writing a general survey of Śaivism. His intention was to have it published in France. I was entrusted to translate the English work into French, then requested to do a few abridgements to comply with the project of a popular edition. Unfortunately the book could not be printed before the demise of Alain Daniélou. It was finally published in French in 2000 by Āgamāt Publisher, under the supervision of Bernard Bouanchaud. The complete original English version is now coming in print, thanks to the initiative of Shri Alvaro Enterria of Indica Books Publishers. He laboured a lot to digitalize and format this long text. May he find here the sincere expression of my hearty gratitude. We extend our thanks to Bernard Bouanchaud who kindly gave the authorization to reproduce tables, charts and photographs from his publication.

Yādavagiri
Āṣāḍhamāsa, Kṛṣṇapakṣa, caturthī
Kṛṣṇarājamuḍi-puṇyotsava

Pierre-Sylvain Filliozat
Membre de l'Institut

Foreword

Contribution of the Śaiva Āgamas to Śaivism

The religious history of India has a long and continuous tradition. On the basis of archaeological and literary evidence, it is possible to show that the religion persisted in India without a break at least from the pre-vedic times up to the present day. Studies on the Mohenjodaro period show that there was a profound civilization of religion and culture. Further research on the rites, rituals and religious practices of the living religions must be made.

From time immemorial, Hindu Society has been dynamic and progressive. While the externals of the practices remain unchanged, internal changes were allowed to take place. The rituals and practices found in the *Āgamas* are not found in the *Vedas*, yet they are not anti-vedic. The *Vedas* are not to be seen as an encyclopaedia describing every aspect of life in that society. There must have been many concepts and practices which were not recorded in the *Vedas*. On this basis, the *Āgamas* which deal with them cannot be treated as anti-vedic. The same holds for the philosophical background of the *Āgamas*, which arose out of the explanations for rituals.

Two types of literary works portray the religious faiths which are very close to those prevalent today among the people of India. It is in the Epics and *Purāṇas* or the *Āgamas*, and not in Vedic *Saṁhitās*, the *Brāhmaṇas* and the *Upaniṣads*, where we must search for Rāma and Kṛṣṇa, Gaṇeśa and Skanda, or Śiva and Pārvatī. The Hindu religion of today is for the most part constituted by popular sects which have one or another of these gods at their head. Due to the great importance of the Epics, the *Purāṇas* and the *Āgamas* as documents portraying for the first time the history of Indian religion, the popular faiths of the people is thereby well established. Compared to the views of the Vedic period, the conception of Śiva, Viṣṇu or Śakti of the Epics, the *Purāṇas* or *Āgamas* is definitely closer to the present day Hindu concept of those gods. The forms of worship indicated in these texts bear a close resemblance to the forms of worship which are prevalent today, and the other religious practices also continued to be more or less identical. Thus being the case, a study of the Epics, the *Purāṇas* and the *Āgamas* would be very helpful for a thorough understanding of the Hindu religion. It may also be pointed out that the Āgamic Śaivism and Viṣṇuism have been deemed, in more senses than one, a direct continuation of the indigenous Śiva or Viṣṇu religion of the pre-vedic times and thus form a connecting link between the later religion and the religion of the modern followers.

Religion has always played a prominent part in ancient cultures, and this is all the more so in the case of India. On the basis of a thorough investigation of the artefacts discovered in the Indus Valley, Marshall in his book *Mohenjodaro and Indus Civilization* (p. 76) has come to the conclusion that the religion of that period was a composite one and that many cults existed side by side and continued to flourish with neither influence nor hindrance upon one another. Of these religious cults, the cult of the Mother Goddess and the Śiva cult must have been most widely prevalent — a fact which is attested by the abundance of relevant materials unearthed in the Indus Valley. In the later religious history, those two cults are seen to have developed into the two parallel religions of Śaivism and Śaktism. The cult of the Mother Goddess is also seen to have been merged into the Śaiva cult, so that the Goddess or Śakti began to be represented as the consort of Śiva. Other once-distinct minor cults, like tree worship and the worship of inanimate objects were later integrated into the major cults. For example, the worship of serpents and trees, of which traces are found in the Indus period, had been absorbed by Śaivism and Vaiṣṇavism of the Epic and Puranic periods. The serpent becomes the couch of Viṣṇu; Śiva wears a serpent as *yajñopavīta* and as ornaments. Tulasī and Bilva are considered as sacred to Viṣṇu and Śiva respectively. Every temple in south India has its sacred tree under the designation *sthalavṛkṣa*.

Within the religious history of India, no religion has had such a long and continuous tradition as Śaivism; few living religions can boast of such a long and unbroken history. The very antiquity of Śaivism implies that this religion must have gone through various vicissitudes in the course of its long history. A study of Śaivism implies the study of the ancillary cults as well. In south Indian traditions, Śiva is always represented with other subordinate divinities, and we can trace the gradual evolution of this group associated with Śiva. Gaṇeśa, Devī, Skanda and Sūrya are installed in the places duly assigned to them in the South Indian temples; even Viṣṇu has a place duly assigned to him. Colossal in structure and long-celebrated in history, these temples stand as grand monuments of religious traditions which they have preserved intact. These temples have helped to further the growth of several fine arts, such as architecture, sculpture, music and dance. For many generations, they preserved for us traditions of worship and ritual which are of great importance. Thanks to the religious generosity of many South Indian kings of old, who not only established these temples but who also made endowments for their proper maintenance, the ancient traditions of worship and ritual have been preserved more or less unchanged, through the agency of the continuous lines of priests who have been hereditarily associated with these temples. Thus, we see that on account of the munificence of the ancient kings on the one hand, and the interconnection of music, dance and architecture with religious practices on the other, the old religious traditions have been preserved in South India almost in their original form up to this day.

The temples are the most glorious institution of our country. They are the true abodes of the Divine. Much more than any other establishment, it was the temples that brought about unity in religion in the whole of the country. They are the true symbols of the cultural unity of India, assembling within them all types of devotees. Even now, in these temples we can observe religious or philosophical discourses, chanting of the *Vedas*, *Purāṇas*, Tevaram and Prabandam, and performance of music and dance. These devotional events are supplementary activities in a temple in which the prescribed rituals of the consecrated gods are the primary ones. This fact could be easily ascertained if one goes through the authoritative texts, namely the *Āgamas*, which deal with each and everything pertaining to temples — architecture, consecration, rituals, priests, devotees and philosophy. The Śaiva *Āgamas* are the sole authority for the Śaivite temples, as are the Pāñcarātra and the Vaikhānasa *Āgamas* for the Vaiṣṇava temples. The rules have been laid down in these texts; from selection of the site for the temple, up to the installation of the Divinity, the daily, occasional, yearly and expiatory rites to be conducted in such temples, and the requirements concerning the persons who are to conduct all these rituals — all are explained in these *Āgamas*. As such, the best and the most reliable literary sources for an investigation into the religious practices are certainly the *Āgamas*.

A science which comes from teacher to disciple from time immemorial is called an *Āgama*; *Āgama*, *Tantra* and *Saṁhitā* being synonymous terms. For example, the same texts are quoted as the *Raurava Tantra* or the *Rauravāgama*, the *Mṛgendra Tantra* or the *Mṛgendrāgama*, the *Santāna Saṁhitā* or the *Santānāgama*, the *Kāmikatantra* or the *Kāmikāgama* and so forth.

As the *Vedas* come down from teacher to disciple, they also could be termed *Āgamas*. In order to distinguish them from the well known *Āgamas*, the *Vedas* were called by the special name *Nigamas*. As both the *Vedas* and *Āgamas* are coming down by oral tradition, they are called *śruti*. Kullūkabhaṭṭa in his commentary on the *Manusmṛti*, *adhyāya* II verse 1, states that the *śruti* or revealed literature is of two kinds, Vedic and Tantric.

These *Āgamas* or *Tantras* are grouped into three varieties: Śaiva, Vaiṣṇava and Śākta. Those which accept Śiva as supreme and deal mainly with his worship are *Śaiva Āgamas*, and those which describe Śakti or the Goddess as supreme are called *Śākta Āgamas*. The *Śākta Tantras* are traditionally enumerated as 64 but the number now found is much higher. They are grouped into two categories, Dakṣiṇa and Vāma: the right-hand school and the left-hand school. The Vaiṣṇava *Āgamas* are subdivided into Vaikhānasa and Pāñcarātra. The *Āgamas* revealed by Sage Vikhanas to his disciples Bhṛgu, Marīci, Atri, etc., and disseminated by them into the world are the Vaikhānasa *Āgamas*. The Pāñcarātra *Āgamas* are threefold, namely (1) *Divya*, revealed directly by Lord Nārāyaṇa, such as the *Pauṣkara Saṁhitā*, the *Jayākhya Saṁhitā* etc. (2) *Munibhāṣita*, handed over by the sages, such as the *Bharadvājasaṁhitā*, the *Pārameśvarasaṁhitā*, etc., and (3) *Āptamanujaprokta*, written by men whose knowledge is trustworthy. The total number of Pāñcarātra *Āgamas* is enumerated traditionally as 219 or 223 but only a few are presently available.

The Śaiva *Āgamas* are fourfold: Kāpala, Kālāmukha, Pāśupata and Śaiva. The last one is of two kinds: Kashmir Śaiva and Siddhānta Śaiva. Kashmir Śaivism is mainly followed in North India, and Siddhānta Śaivism is only in vogue in South India. There are 28 basic texts in the Siddhānta school. Each of these *Āgamas* has some supplements called the *Upāgamas*, the total number of which comes to 207. Sadāśiva, the Sakala form of the supreme Parama Śiva, revealed the first 10 of the 28 *Āgamas* to 10 Śivas such as Praṇava and the later 18 to the 18 Rudras such as Anādirudra. So, the first group of ten are called Śivabheda and the second group Rudrabheda. In each of these *Āgamas*, a chapter called the Tantrāvatāra Paṭala gives details of these *Āgamas* and *Upāgamas*, their extent, the teachers, disciples, the tradition, and so on. A table giving all these details is appended to our edition of the *Rauravāgama*, Vol. I.

The main topic of the *Āgamas* is the worship of deities and especially the image worship in temples, as well as all other matters related to temples. They also deal with all the civil and moral codes, initiation, purificatory ceremonies, consecration, daily routine of the Śaivas and Śaiva philosophy. These topics are dealt in the four *pādas* of the *Āgamas*: *Vidyā* or *Jñānapāda* (philosophy), *Kriyāpāda* (rituals), *Yogapāda* and *Caryāpāda* (moral codes).

Orthodox Indian religion and philosophy derive their authority from the *Vedas* and *Āgamas*. Still, we have no real evidence to state that there was image worship in the Vedic tradition of ancient times. The ancient *Gṛhya-sūtras* which prescribe the daily rites for the community mention *devayajña*, which is to be done by offering sticks into a sacred fire. The deities worshipped were Sūrya, Agni, Prajāpati, Soma, Vanaspati, Indra, Heaven, Earth, Dhanvantari, the Viśvedevas and Brahman. There are five *yajñas*: *deva* (gods), *ṛṣi* (sages), *pitṛ* (ancestors), *manuṣya* (men) and *bhūta* (semi-divinities). The *yajña* for *ṛṣi* and *pitṛ* is performed by offering water (*tarpaṇa*), for *manuṣya* by offering food, and for *bhūta* by offering *bali* (rice-oblations). How this *devayajña* in the form of a *homa* (fire ritual) was replaced by *devapūjā* (worship of gods) is a matter for investigation. However, it seems that image worship existed prior to Pāṇini, who speaks of two kinds of images, one for personal worship and the other for sale (see sūtra *jīvikārthe cāpaṇye* 5, 3, 99). The images which were used by persons for their personal maintenance by attending on them or for the purpose of *pūjā* were called by the name of the deity, namely Śiva, Skanda, etc., but those for sale were called Śivaka, Skandaka etc. From the commentary of Patañjali on this *sūtra* we would know that the Mauryas, out of greed for gold, were making images for sale. Sir R.G. Bhandarkar states (*Collected Works*, Vol. IV, p. 4.): "In his comment on Pāṇini IV, 3, 98, Patañjali distinctly states that the Vāsudeva contained in the Sūtra is the name of the 'worshipful', i.e. of one who is pre-eminently worshipful, i.e. God. The worship of Vāsudeva must be regarded to be as old as Pāṇini."

Temples of different divinities are mentioned in the *Mahābhārata* and the *Rāmāyaṇa*; also, Kauṭilya's *Arthaśāstra* (25, 22, etc.), *Sāmavedīyaṣaḍviṁśabrāhmaṇa* (VI, 10, 2), *Kāṭhakagṛhyasūtra* (18, 3), *Bodhāyanagṛhyasūtra* (II, 2, 13), *Mānavagṛhyasūtra* (II, 15, 6),

Kauśītakīgṛhyasūtra (III, 11, 15), *Śāṅkhāyanagṛhyasūtra* (IV, 12, 15), *Agniveśyagṛhyasūtra* (II, 4), *Gautamadharmasūtra* (I, 9, 66), *Bodhāyanadharmasūtra* (II, 8, 2) refer to temples and images. So, one could deduct that image worship was known to Vedic tradition as early as the 5th century BC. This would refute the theory that image worship developed from the Buddha's images, because there could not have been any images of Buddha before the 5th century BC. However, one can see that the importance given to Devapūja in later times is not seen in the early stage of Vedic literature.

There have been different views on this question of the incorporation of image worship into the Vedic religion. So far, the majority of scholars seem to hold the view that first sacrifices were prevalent, but owing to the Buddhist influence of *ahiṁsā* and the Upanisadic philosophy, the cult of the worship of images replaced the sacrifices. Already there were descriptions of deities in human form in the Ṛgveda, largely theoretical; this might have later developed into concrete images. Medieval digests of the Dharma Śāstra have described image worship in great detail. Many *Purāṇas*, such as *Matsya*, *Agni*, *Vāyu*, *Viṣṇu*, *Śiva*, *Brahmāṇḍa*, *Viṣṇudharmottara*, etc., have chapters on images.

However, the works which detail everything related to temple construction, images, deities, consecration, ritual, expiation, etc., are the *Āgamas*. They have their own philosophy, yoga systems, daily ritual (*nityānuṣṭhāna*), conduct (*ācāra*) and religion. In the earlier stages, there seems to have been some controversy between the Vedic and Āgamic systems, similar to the dispute between the Śaivas and the Vaiṣṇavas in later times, wherein each denounced the other. Later, there seems to have been some compromise made, both accepting that, as all comes from Śiva or Nārāyaṇa, both have the same essence, the *Āgamas* being but the essence of the *Vedas*. If one views these statements historically, it would perhaps be better to conclude that there existed in India two independent different traditions, the Vedic and the Āgamic, which over the course of time influenced each other. Though there is no historical evidence congruent with the western study of history, we still have a history as recorded in our *Purāṇas*. The Indian history of different times is compiled in various *Purāṇas*. None of them are written by a single author, nor can one state that every *Purāṇa* was compiled by a single person. It is not also wise to give a definite date for any *Purāṇa* because each is a compilation of stories of different epochs. This is why in the same *Purāṇa* one can find conflicting accounts of traditions and cultures which really might have belonged to different times. Thus, in the *Purāṇas*, one could see a divergence of ideology, evidenced in both censure as well as praise of Āgamic systems. As Vedic influence became stronger, the Āgamic schools had to give way and accept the Vedic authority. Later, as time passed, the past was forgotten and everything was considered to belong to the Vedic school. The Vedic school thereby was not able to preserve its purity, but brought into it almost all the parts of Āgamic ritual, philosophy, yoga and other things to such an extent that today, people — including scholars — know very little about the ancient history of these *Āgamas*.

Hindu religion declares the aim or goal of life of mankind (*puruṣārtha*) as fourfold: *dharma* (duty), *artha* (wealth), *kāma* (attaining desire) and *mokṣa* (liberation). Of these four, *artha* and *kāma* must strictly conform to *dharma*, and *dharma* ultimately leads man to liberation. The *dharma* of righteous duty is not perceptible and hence derives its authority from the *śruti* (traditional or revealed literature). There are two kinds of *śrutis*; the Nigamas or *Vedas*, and the *Āgamas*, *Saṁhitās* or *Tantras*. *Veda* means 'knowledge', and the *Āgamas* are also called *jñāna* (knowledge). Naturally, if one goes through the abundant literature of the Vedic school, one could find reference to the *Veda* alone when they quote *śruti*, because naturally that branch derives its authority from the *Vedas*. But that does not restrict the domain of *śruti* to *Vedas* only. Even sages of the Vedic school knew that by the word '*śruti*' one could also indicate the *Āgamas*. For example, Hārīta in the beginning of his *dharmaśāstra* states that *dharma* has for its authority *śruti*, and that *śruti* is of two kinds, Vedic and Tantric.

Both of these literatures are considered to be revealed and to come down through the tradition of teacher to disciple — it is therefore natural that the *Āgamas* are also defined to be *śruti* and are accepted as an authority for *dharma*.

The *Vedas* are divided into two sections, *pūrvakāṇḍa* and *uttarakāṇḍa*; the first explains rituals such as sacrifices through which one obtains *dharma*, *artha* and *kāma*, and the other describes the Supreme which leads to liberation. These divisions are also called *sādhyadharma* (because *dharma* is to be attained by performing rituals) and *siddhadharma* (the *dharma* which is established as their object), or *karmakāṇḍa* (the section of rituals) and *jñānakāṇḍa* (the section on knowledge, i.e. the *Upaniṣads*). Through Vedic rituals one can obtain temporary happiness either in this world or in the other world; the fruit obtained by the merit of the rituals can be enjoyed to a limited period, namely until the earned merit gets exhausted, like earned money is spent. But the knowledge of the *jñānakāṇḍa* will lead to liberation, i.e. complete happiness. In the *Āgamas* there are also separate sections dealing with *jñāna* and *kriyā*, but unlike in the *Vedas*, there is no separate utility for each of them; rather, by performing *kriyā* according to *kriyāpāda* with a complete knowledge of *jñānapāda* and *yogapāda*, and by strictly following the rules prescribed in *caryāpāda*, one will obtain all the *puruṣārthas* of *dharma*, *artha* and *kāma* which come under the category of *bhukti* or *bhoga*. After enjoying the desired *bhogas*, one could attain *mokṣa* with no need to return to a mortal body. This is the main difference between the two *śrutis*.

Thus, though we have two schools of *śrutis* and a subsequent literature based upon them, and although their object is the same, their scope and subject matter is completely different. The *karmakāṇḍa* of the Vedic school mainly describes the sacrifices, and the *jñānakāṇḍa* explains the philosophy. The *Āgama* literature mainly deals with the personal and temple rituals and those concerned with them. Here in the *Āgamas* we find a legend describing a fight between Brahmā and Viṣṇu, which in the end establishes the supremacy of Śiva. This is worthy of note: if one goes through the Śaiva Āgamic ritual, it is very difficult to find any sort of attempt to show an enmity between Śiva, Brahmā and Viṣṇu. In fact the *liṅga* is described as having three portions, the lower part assigned to Brahmā, the middle to Viṣṇu and the upper to Rudra. Śiva the supreme in Sadāśiva form is the object of meditation conducted above the *liṅga*. The *liṅga* is only a representation of the cosmic world of which Rudra, Viṣṇu and Brahmā are the lords of their respective divisions, and they act according to the desire of the Supreme. Devotees are free to worship any of these deities if they desire to attain that world governed by them. This type of attainment is called *bhoga* (enjoying happiness in the desired world).

So, in the early stage we do not find any dispute regarding the question of supremacy of deities in the basic *Śaivāgamas*. But later, probably when under attack from the Pāñcarātra sect, those legends that describe the supremacy of Śiva or Viṣṇu found a place in the Śaiva and Vaiṣṇava *Purāṇas*, and then from there they were sometimes included in the *Āgamas*. This may be perhaps one of the reasons that we presently find 64 forms of Śiva images, though in the early, basic *Āgamas* only 14, 24, or 25 forms have been described. Many of the later additions seem to be based on the legends found in the *Purāṇas* describing the supremacy of Śiva. However, the *liṅgodbhava* form seems to be one of the earliest forms of the Śiva image, (as *liṅga* worship existed from ancient times), and from this legend is born the *liṅgodbhava* form, the definition of which we find described in the *Pratimālakṣaṇa-vidhipaṭala* of the *Āgamas*.

Though we find topics such as architecture and iconography in the *Āgamas*, one cannot hope to therein find the complete details; rather, the *Śilpaśāstras* describe them in full. When something relates to the temple or the images, some kind of ritual is prescribed for each step which could be done only by a Śaiva priest. So those portions of architecture and fine art have been dealt with in passing in the *Āgamas*. Furthermore, the building of the temple and the making of images is to be done by *śilpins* in collaboration with the priests who know the art; in case of doubts, the priest's decision is final. So a priest is supposed to have thorough knowledge of both *Āgamas* and *Śilpa-śāstra*, without which he cannot claim authority to give any conclusion. In any event, the main purpose of those topics found in the *Āgamas* is ritualistic performance. The details relating to the rituals of every stage — from the selection of a site for a temple to the consecration of the *liṅga* or image, the occasional (*naimittika*), daily (*nitya*), beneficial (*kāmya*), expiatory (*prāyaścitta*) and propitiatory (*śānti*) rituals, temple festivals (*utsava*) and special baths (*snapana*) which were only described in the *Āgamas* in ancient times — part by part found their way into the *Purāṇas*, which are actually ancient Indian historical encyclopaedias, and then to the texts prescribing the rituals of the Vedic school, such as the digests of the Dharma Śāstra and the supplements (*pariśista*) to the *Gṛhyasūtras*. Nowadays they have penetrated into the rituals of the Vedic school to such an extent that at a first glance one could not guess that these two schools were distinct from one another at one time in our civilization. Similar is the case for the *Āgama*, digests, in which Vedic hymns or formulas have been prescribed for rituals. In any event, reading the early *Gṛhyasūtras* (the texts which deal with the rites and rituals of the Vedic school), it is easy to observe that nowhere are temple rituals described. Even the daily *pūjā* finds no place there, even though the temples in ancient times seemed to have been centres of religious activities, and daily worship seemed to have always had an important place in daily rites.

In any event, one could easily observe that, while some Vedic hymns and even some other rituals were incorporated in the later abridged versions of the *Āgamas*, the whole corpus of temple rituals and personal worship found its way into the later texts that prescribed the rules and rites for the followers of the Vedic school (see for example the *Pūjā Prakāśa* of Vīramitrodaya).

Religion is popularly defined as superior power, either for attainment of divine life or for avoiding the evils of the worldly life. The essence of religion consists of worship. This is the most important subject matter of the *Āgamas*.

For example, let us take one aspect of this worship called *devapūjā*, which may help us in our investigation of the earliest source of the Hindu religion. We find texts belonging to three schools: the Vaidika *pūjā*, in which hymns of the *Vedas* are prescribed, the Kalpa *pūjā*, in which appropriate Sanskrit verses are used, and the Āgamic *pūjā*, in which formulas or specific mantras are used. Texts dealing with the Vaidika and Kalpapūjā are well known; as for the Śaiva Āgamic school, thanks to Mrs. Helène Brunner we have an excellent study in the form of a critical edition of a digest named the *Soma-śaṁbhupaddhati*, with a French translation and extensive notes. If we just make a comparative study of the texts belonging to three schools, it may not be difficult to arrive at the conclusion that the Āgamic school could have been the earliest source and the Kalpa and Vaidika school texts were later evolutions of this original one.

This is just an example. At present, almost all the Āgamic rituals and other related matter, including philosophy, have found their counterpart in the later Vedic digests, and this fact can be proved by a comparative study.

While in North India temples rituals are conducted according to the digests belonging to the Vedic school still available in print, the rituals prescribed in *Āgamas* are still in practice in the temples in South India. These rituals are conducted without much change, and have come down to us through the tradition; that which now continues conforms to the digests. In case of the Śaiva ritual, a digest named the *Kriyākramadyotikā* by Aghoraśiva of the 12th century is the one which is mostly followed with little change. This digest deals with all aspects of Śaiva ritual and is based on basic *Śaivāgama* texts. Initially there were some differences among the different texts, but to avoid difficulties and disputes the great Aghoraśivācarya, learned in all the *Śaivāgama* texts, extracted their essence and wrote this manual. In present practice, it is possible to observe that this digest is completely followed in all the Śaiva temples.

Thus, for practical study the digests are very important; it is also important to study the original sources of these digests, the root or *mūla Āgama* texts. They are as important as the *Vedas* which are considered as the authority for the digests of the Vedic school.

The *Vidyāpāda* or the *Jñānapāda* of the *Āgamas* deal with the metaphysical basis of the *Āgama* system. It provides the philosophical truths underlying the system and expounds their origin, their rationale and their goal. The subject matter of the *Vidyāpāda* varies among the *Āgamas*, according to their various approaches to the subject. All of them deal with the definition of *pati* (Lord), *paśu* (soul) and *pāśa* (the bonds), their relationship, and the means for the *paśu* to obtain release from bondage and obtain liberation.

The supreme Śiva, the all-knower (*sarvajña*), independent (*svatantra*), pure (*amala*), above everything (*sārvādhika*) who is pure intelligence and who is *niṣkala* (having no form and undefinable), is the instrumental cause of the world. From the state of dissolution, God causes the world to re-emerge from Māyā through his Śakti, the power or energy with which he is in complete union. This creation is motivated by his desire to give an opportunity to the souls to obtain their goal: enjoyment in the different worlds, followed by liberation. The actions of the Supreme through his five powers are fivefold: *sṛṣṭi*, to manifest the world which was absorbed into himself by his desire; *dhvaṁsa*, dissolution of the world; *saṁrakṣaṇa*, to protect and to allow the souls to enjoy in their worlds; *anugraha*, leading souls who are in bondage to liberation by his grace; and *janma*, to incarnate souls into different kinds of bodies in the worlds, according to the fruits of their previous actions.

The cosmic creation is divided into thirty-six categories of realities named *tattvas*. These are: (1) Śiva, (2) Bindu or Sadāśiva, (3) Īśvara (the governor), (4) Śuddhavidyā (pure knowledge), (5) Māyā (illusion), (6) Kalā (action), (7) Vidyā (knowledge), (8) Rāga (passion), (9) Kāla (Time), (10) Niyati (regulation), (11) Puruṣa (cosmic man), (12) Prakṛti or Avyakta (the non-manifested), (13) Guṇa (qualities), (14) Buddhi (intelligence), (15) Ahaṁkāra (ego), (16) Manas (mind), (17) Śrotra (ear), (18) Tvak (skin), (19) Netra (eyes), (20) Jihvā (tongue), (21) Ghrāṇa (nose), (22) Vāk (speech),

(23) Pāṇi (hand), (24) Pāda (feet), (25) Pāyu (anus), (26) Upastha (genitals), (27) Śabda (sound), (28) Sparśa (touch), (29) Rūpa (form), (30) Rasa (taste), (31) Gandha (smell), (32) Ākāśa (ether), (33) Vāyu (wind), (34) Agni (fire), (35) Ap (water), (36) Pṛthivī (earth).

These *tattvas* are grouped within five main *kalās*: *Nivṛtti*, *Pratiṣṭhā*, *Vidyā*, *Śānti* and *Śantyatītā*. *Nivṛtti kalā* governs only one *tattva*, namely *Pṛthivī* (No. 36); *Pratiṣṭhā kalā* governs the *tattvas* up to *Prakṛti* (Nos.12 to 35); *Vidyā kalā* governs the *tattvas Māyā* to *Puruṣa* (Nos. 5 to 11); *Śānti kalā* governs the *tattvas Śuddhavidyā*, Īśvara and Sadāśiva (Nos. 2 to 4) and *Śantyatīta kalā* governs the Śiva *tattva* (No. 1). The 224 different worlds are distributed within these different *tattvas*.

The *tattvas* 1 to 4 (Śiva, Sadāśiva, Īśvara and Śuddhavidyā) are described to be the pure *tattvas* and the rest as impure.

The Supreme through his Śakti manifests the Śaiva *Āgamas*. The Śakti assumes a pure body made of mantras called Sadāśiva and teaches these *Āgama* texts to Ananteśvara, the liberated soul, who passes them to the Vidyeśvaras, who govern the group of liberated souls called the mantras. These mantras, under the direction of the Supreme, help the bound souls obtain liberation.

Among the liberated souls there are two groups; one is completely released from all bondage and as such rests in actionless bliss. The other group, though liberated, has some desire to govern (*adhikāramala*) and thereby act for the liberation of souls in bondage. Each word of the mantra (mystic syllable) recited denotes one of these liberated and governing souls; this is why the recited mantras are called *vācaka* and the souls indicated by them are *vācya*. Similarly, the *Āgama* texts which deal with the Supreme are called *jñāna* (knowledge) and *Śabdabrahma*, and the subject is known as *Arthabrahma* or *Brahman*. These texts are also perceived to be the body of the Supreme.

The syllables of the mantras are formed from the letters of the alphabet, called *mātṛkā*, which is produced from the letter *Auṁ*, which denotes the Supreme. Thus, even the letters of the alphabet have a special significance and play their part in ritual. Mantra is thus explained: the letter 'ma' indicates *manana*, meaning all-knowing, and the syllable 'tra' indicates protection of the bound souls. The mantras, which actually are liberated souls graced by Śiva through his Śakti and who act under their direction, are the meanings of the words recited as mantras. These mantras are governed by Mantreśvaras, and they again by Mantramaheśvaras or Vidyeśvaras; Ananteśvara governs all of them under the direction of the Supreme. The pure world is created by the Supreme through his power and the rest of the world is created by Ananteśvara.

There are seven crore mantras. The main mantras used are Īśāna, Tatpuruṣa, Aghora, Vāmadeva, Sadyojāta, Hṛdaya, Śiras, Sīkhā, Kavaca, Netra and Astra, which comprise a group of eleven main mantras named *samhitā mantras*, and *vyomavyāpi padamantra*, a mantra which contains either 81 or 94 words, according to different schools.

The Supreme, the souls and the bonds are eternal. The first two are conscious and the bonds are unconscious. The Supreme alone is independent and acts through his powers of will, action and knowledge (*icchā*, *kriyā* and *jñāna*). Though the fully liberated souls have the same qualities as the Supreme, they nonetheless merely enjoy the supreme bliss and do not act, out of respect to the Supreme through whose grace they have obtained complete liberation.

According to the *Āgamas*, the animate and inanimate world passes through the cycle of evolution, maintenance and dissolution. The Supreme, who is the agent of creation, is also the agent of maintenance and dissolution. All this is done to enable the souls to free themselves from their bondage.

The bondage which binds the souls and suppresses or hides the true nature of pure consciousness is called *pāśa*. Bondage is of three kinds. One is called *mala*, the impurity which is natural (*sahaja*) to all the bound souls. The second is the action and the fruit of actions which is called *karman*; the third one is Māyā, the illusion caused by the power of the Supreme which veils his true nature of pure knowledge.

The one who is bound by *mala* alone is called Vijñānākala; the one who is bound by both *mala* and *karman* is called Pralayākala and the one bound by all the three is called Sakala.

Mala is one but has limitless powers to bind many souls separately yet simultaneously. It is eternal and has the power of pervasion (*vyāpaka*). *Karman* is action, both right (*dharma*) or wrong (*adharma*), which is unique for each soul, and which they do to obtain some fruit they desire. Māyā is of two kinds, pure and impure. It is called Māyā because it absorbs the world into itself during dissolution and manifests the same during creation (*māty asyāṁ jagat pralaye, sṛṣṭau vyaktiṁ yāti*). As each soul enjoys the fruits of its own action, each is individual and distinct from one another. Therefore souls are different and eternal as per this school.

The soul must enjoy the fruits of its actions (*karman*) here in this world. The fruit of good and bad actions are the cause of its next birth, in which it must enjoy or suffer. Even the fruits of good actions will not help to obtain liberation; it will be reborn to enjoy them. But when the fruits of good and bad actions are found to be equal, and when the grace of God falls on the soul, the fruit of those actions will be destroyed. He will then be fit to obtain initiation (*dīkṣā*) from Śiva or through the intermediation of his guru and will be able to obtain liberation.

The soul who is called *siddha* (one who has obtained his desires) is the one who is supreme by obtaining enjoyments in superior worlds. The experiences of the other worlds are of different kinds. The soul will either be the lord of those worlds to which he desires to go, or will merely dwell in them.

The soul who is called *mukta* (fully liberated), for whom the powers of all the *pāśas* have ceased to act, will not come back to this world during next creation. His natural qualities, which are equal to the qualities of the Supreme, will reappear in him. But he will remain without any action as the Supreme no longer directs him.

There is another kind of liberation, *aparamukti*, which is inferior, in which the soul will be either a mantra or a lord of mantra and will remain under the direction of the Supreme Śiva. The reason for this is that such souls still have a sort of *mala* called *adhikāramala* (the desire to govern) and as such will not obtain the status of equality with Śiva, but will perform those duties assigned by the Supreme. After the proper completion of their duties, they will obtain the supreme liberation after the dissolution of the world.

Further details relating to the *Āgama* texts, the different mantras, the details of the tattvas and the worlds within each *tattva* are explained in the Vidyāpāda.

The *Āgama* texts always follow a natural path of evolution in detailing with the four *pādas*. The first simple stage, *caryā* (daily routine), helps each individual to follow the right path prescribed in the texts. The *yogapāda* teaches one to fix one's mind to the feet of his Guru and the Supreme. The *kriyāpāda* deals with the observance of advanced ritualism. Finally, to perform the rituals prescribed in the *kriyāpāda*, one has to be well-versed with the subject matter of the *vidyāpāda*. To be fit to be a member of the Śaiva religion and practice the rituals, one should conform to the rules laid down in the *caryāpāda*. Thus, in this Āgamic school, the subject matter of all the four *pādas* is interrelated. This is stated clearly in the *Mṛgendrāgama Vidyāpāda*, p. 68:

Iti vastutrayasyāsya prākpādakṛtasaṁsthiteḥ |
Kriyācaryāyogapādair Viniyogo 'bhidhāsyate ||

"The three subjects — namely *Pati*, *paśu* and *paśa* which have been explained in the previous *pāda*, namely the Vidyāpada — their utility will be described in the next three *pādas* which are *kriyā*, *caryā* and *yoga*."

Liberation is the main fruit of the knowledge in the Vidyāpāda and practice (*jñānād anuṣṭhānācca*) and, incidentally, other desired fruits (*bhoga*) could also be obtained. So, as far as *Āgama* texts are concerned, rituals (*kriyā*) and knowledge (*vidyā*) must go together and one may not obtain liberation by knowledge or rituals alone.

Normally, all the rituals pertaining to the personal cult as well as to the temple cult are explained in the Kriyāpāda. Temple worship derives its authority from the *Āgama* texts. The images installed in the temples are considered to be gods personified or incarnated, and as such elaborate rituals are prescribed, from the selection of the site for the construction of the temple up to the installation of the image called *karṣaṇādi-pratiṣṭhānta*. After installation, daily (*nitya*), occasional (*naimittika*), optional (*kāmya*), and expiation (*prāyaścitta*) ceremonies or rituals, as well as festivals (*utsava*), to be conducted for the deity installed, are prescribed in this section. Also, the rituals to be personally performed every day by the priest to make him fit to perform the temple rituals, as well as the most important ceremony, the initiation (*dīkṣā*) which makes one eligible for performing these rituals, are explained in detail.

For the initiation (*dīkṣā*) ceremony, one must draw a specific diagram. In this diagram one should contemplate the Supreme pervading the existence of the whole cosmic world with its divisions of the five *kalās Śāntyatītā*, *Śānti*, *Vidyā*, *Pratiṣṭhā* and *Nivṛtti* as well as the thirty-six *tattvas*. One should meditate that Śiva's head pervades *Śāntyatītakalā*, His face as pervading *Śāntikalā*, His chest as pervading *Vidyākalā*, His genitals as pervading *Pratiṣṭhākalā*, His knees and feet as pervading *Nivṛttikalā*, the hair of His body as pervading each of the different worlds, His skin as pervading the letters of the alphabet, His blood as pervading the mantras, His flesh as pervading the words of the *Vyomavyāpipadamantra*, and His bones as pervading the *tattvas*. Thus Śiva is to be perceived as pervading the whole cosmic universe from the *pṛthivītattva* up to the Śiva *tattva* on this diagram.

The guru is to hang on the body of the disciple a string which should hang from his head to his toes. The string represents both the *suṣumṇānāḍī* and the bondage (*pāśa*) — a dwelling of all the enjoyments which are the fruits of the past actions, but which have not yet started to yield their result. The actions or *karman* is of three kinds: *sañcita*, collected in past births, *prārabdha*, the actions which have begun to give fruits, and *āgāmi*, actions to be done in the future after initiation. During the *dīkṣā* ceremony the *sañcita* and the *āgāmi* karmas are destroyed, but the *prārabdha karman*, by which the present body has been obtained and continues to exist, is not destroyed and one must receive the fruits of those actions even after initiation. On this string the guru is to invoke all the bondages of *mala*, *karman* and *māyā*, and during the initiation ceremony this string is to be beaten (*tāḍana*) and cut (*cheda*), representing the removal of the different bonds. The five *kalās* are also to be invoked on this string. During the initiation ceremony the guru is expected to purify all these *kalās* together with the corresponding *tattvas*, mantras, worlds, letters of the alphabet, and words of the Vyomavyāpipadamantra. This procedure is technically called *ṣaḍadhvaśodhana*: the purification of the six paths.

Before starting any ritual one is expected to purify one's own body. During this procedure, the soul is to be elevated from the body and placed into Śiva, who is above the head — twelve inches above (*dvādaśānta*) — and then, by recitation of different mantras and through a prescribed regulation of breath and other yoga procedures, the gross body is supposed to be burnt, then by the sprinkling of the nectar from above the head (*bindu*), a new purified body is re-constructed. The soul is then brought back from Śiva and is placed in the heart of the new pure body.

The mantras which are to be used during rituals also must be purified. Such purification is performed by reciting those mantras in different pitches called *kalā*. The main mantra, which is called *Prāsāda mantra*, is to be recited with sixteen *kalās* — recitation with different pitches starting from the navel up to the head, and then up to *dvādaśānta*. These *kalās* are named *medhā*, *ghoṣā*, *viṣa*, *bindu*, *ardhacandra*, *nirodhī*, *nāda*, *nādānta*, *śakti*, *vyāpinī*, *vyomarūpā*, *anantā*, *anāthā*, *anāśrita*, *samanā* and *unmanā*. The texts describe the pervasion, duration (*mātrā*), length (*aṅgula*), form, colour, *tattvas* and presiding deity for each *kalā*. In his yogic practice, the practicioner takes the power of the mantra to each stage and there has the corresponding vision. This is called *Ṣoḍaśakalā prāsāda mantra*. The normal mantras are recited up to *bindu*, *nāda* and Śiva in *dvādaśānta* to obtain purification.

During daily worship, one is expected to prepare a seat for the Supreme in the *liṅga*, image or any other representation. This seat is to be contemplated as starting from the *śakti* at the bottom (*ādhāraśakti*) up to the *śakti* at the top, *bindu śakti*. One must have the knowledge of all the *tattvas* to worship properly.

When one worships the Supreme in his own body (*antar-yāga*: inner worship), the devotee contemplates his body as the cosmic universe and the seat of the Supreme. In the same way, if the worship is performed in an outside being or image (*bahiryāga*: outer worship), the *liṅga* or the image is contemplated as the cosmic universe. Śiva the Supreme is above this body, the *liṅga* or the image — again, 12 inches above (*dvādaśānta*).

These are just few examples of some rituals. All the rituals detailed in the Kriyāpāda cannot be properly understood and performed unless one is proficient with the details of the Vidyāpāda and of the Yogapāda. In order to be fit to perform the rituals, one has to study the Caryāpāda and live as per its rules.

Bhaṭṭa Rāmakaṇṭha in his commentary on the Vidyāpāda of Mataṅgaparāmeśvara (p. 567) states thus: "The *caryā* and *yoga* cannot be practiced without the *vidyā*. It is not possible to contemplate or practice something which is not understood. Knowledge alone will not be able to destroy the bonds. The rituals of initiation alone are able to destroy the bonds and pave the way for the souls to obtain liberation."

The rituals in South Indian temples are practiced traditionally to this day; their sources can be traced to the *Āgamas*. However, the philosophy of the Śaiva school of Śaivasiddhānta which is now followed has had a distinct evolution. This school still claims the Śaiva *Āgamas* for its authority, which are all dualistic. When a soul obtains liberation, all those *pāśas* which bound it in the world cease to function. Hence, he will never come back to the world. He has all the qualities similar to the Supreme (*Śivasāmya*).

But now, in the practice of this living religion, the concept of *mokṣa* has been modified. All three — *Pati* the Supreme, *paśu* the soul and *pāśa* the bondage — are present after liberation. The Supreme is the giver of joy, the soul is the one who enjoys, and the *pāśa* helps the soul to enjoy continuously by arranging new kinds of enjoyments. There is also an evolution in the approach towards liberation. In the basic texts, all the four *pādas* have together (and not separately) one main purpose: to show the way for liberation. Later, each *pāda* was considered to be one kind of approach — *caryāpāda* was *dāsamārga*, *kriyāpāda* was *putramārga*, *yogapāda* was *sakhamārga* and *jñānapāda* was *sanmārga* (*sanmārga* is the path of devotion in which the soul considers one's self as a *nāyikā* and the god as *nāyaka*). Here we can see an evolution of philosophical thought influenced by the Gītā and Upaniṣads which preach *jñāna*, *karma* and *bhakti mārgas*; *dāsamarga* is the evolution of the devotional literature of Śaiva saints called Tevarams. This development, which is visible in the Sanskrit and Tamil texts written after the 13th century, is called *Śuddhādvaita-Śaivasiddhānta*. Here, '*advaita*' does not mean non-dualistic, but rather to appear together as one, like the eye and sunrays are joined to see things. Eyesight and sunrays are mutually different, but they unite to observe objects; this is the specific *advaita*. The *Tattva-prakāśikā* of Bhojadeva has two commentaries, one by Aghoraśiva who follows the dualistic school of Sadyojyoti, Nārāyaṇakaṇṭha and Rāmakaṇṭha, and the other by Kumāradeva which is non-dualistic. Such an evolution is possible in a living religion as is seen in other cases, such as with Śaṅkara, Rāmānuja, Madhva, Vallabha, Nimbārka, Bhāskara etc.

According to Abhinavagupta there are three Śaiva systems of philosophical thought, Dvaita, Dvaitādvaita and Advaita, which according to him are based upon ten, eighteen and sixty-four Śaivāgamas respectively, called Śivabheda, Rudrabheda and Bhairavabheda. The philosophy, metaphysics, epistemology and ethics are dealt in the *jñāna* or *vidyāpāda* of the *Āgamas*. insofar as the 28 Śaiva *Āgamas* are concerned, the *jñānapada* of only a few *Āgamas* are available, namely those of *Mṛgendra*, *Pauṣkara*, *Mataṅgapārameśvara*, *Suprabheda* and *Kiraṇa*. As such we are not in a position to verify from original sources if they are *Dvaita*, *Dvaitādvaita* or *Advaita*, but we have to depend on the commentators and other authors who have seen the original sources and written their views accordingly. The *Vedas* and *Āgamas* constituted a common basis of philosophy. Śaṅkara advocated the worship of Śiva and himself used to wear the characteristic marks of a Śaiva, the *tripuṇḍra* on his forehead and *rudrākṣa* on his neck. He identified the Śaiva philosophy with *Advaita* thought. Rāmānuja and Madhva based their philosophy on Pāñcarātra and *Veda* and advocated Viśiṣṭādvaita and Dvaita.

In Kashmir, Sadyojyoti, a commentator on *Rauravāgama* and *Svāyaṁbhuvāgama*, presented the fundamentals of the Dvaita school of thought. He also wrote *Tattvasaṁgraha*, *Tattvatrayanirṇaya*, *Mokṣakārikā*, *Paramokṣanirāsakārikā*, etc. His teachers were Ugrajyoti and Bṛhaspati. His followers were Śrīkaṇṭha, the author of *Ratnatraya*, Vidyākaṇṭha, Nārāyaṇakaṇṭha, the commentator on *Mṛgendrāgama*, and Rāmakaṇṭha, the commentator on the *Pārameśvarāgama* and *Kiraṇāgama*. All these advocated the Dvaita school of Śaiva philosophy, also followed by Aghoraśivācārya in the south.

Utpalācarya's *Īśvarapratyabhijñā kārikā* (10th cent.) is a recognized authoritative text of the Advaita school of Śaiva philosophy in Kashmir. Abhinavagupta wrote a commentary, the *Vimarśinī*, on this text.

Śrīkaṇṭha, who probably lived in the 11th century, is an advocate of the Viśiṣṭādvaita school of Śaiva philosophy. Appayadīkṣita wrote a commentary on the *Bhāṣya* of Srīkaṇṭha supporting him. Both of them refute the Bhedābheda school.

If we compare the Āgamic dualistic Śaiva Siddhānta with those texts which are known as the Tamil Śaiva Siddhānta, we find that the two are fundamentally identical. Due to the evolution of thought, there may be minor differences in the Sanskrit texts. Despite the great development of ideas, the fundamentals have remained same throughout.

A comparative study of all these texts in Sanskrit and Tamil would be very interesting; such a project could be undertaken by groups of scholars which would surely bring to light the historical development of Indian thought.

Regarding the dates of these *Āgamas*, it is too difficult to discuss this problem. On one hand, we may presume that the Āgamic thoughts are very ancient, existent even before Pāṇini's period, but it is difficult to prove in what form they existed. As per tradition they were handed over by teachers to disciples, and there were always elaborations or abridgements during teaching. It seems from internal evidence that section after section had been interpolated, perhaps to bring them up to date. There is a possibility of interpolation of iconographical and architectural passages, which have been gradually changing over the course of time. However, the main trends of thought seem to have continued throughout the generations. In this context it is interesting to note that all the Śaivites, Siddhānta Śaivites, Vīraśaivites, Pāśupatas and Kashmir Śaivites accept the authority of the Śaiva *Āgamas* and quote from these texts profusely. Kashmir Śaivism claims to be founded on the *Āgamaśāstra*, or the traditional Śaiva doctrines. The home of Kashmir Śaivism is Kashmir, that of Pāśupatas is Gujarat, and that of Vīraśaivism is Karnataka. The pure Āgamic Śaivism seems to continue as per tradition in Tamilnadu. This statement only pertains to philosophical tradition. Regarding temple rituals, Tamilnadu, Kerala, Karnataka and a part of Andhra still follow Āgamic worship, though with slight variations.

The *Āgamas* mainly concentrate on teaching religious practice. These works teach what devotees should know, and especially what they should do in order to attain eternal bliss, union with Śiva. They give instruction about the symbolical meaning, execution and application of those gestures, words and visible forms through which man, while being in this world, can enter into contact with the world of Śiva. They expound the doctrine and ritual application of the mantras, and reveal their potency. They are texts containing descriptions of Śaiva rites, of yoga practices, of right conduct and of meritorious observances. Although they contain philosophical and theological analyses, their philosophical interest is limited. They are a commentary focusing on the ritual; there is little metaphysical speculation. They teach how to attain the highest goal. The later authors, however, developed the teaching of the *Āgamas* into a more philosophical structure with less ritual and religious sense.

The Śaiva *Āgamas* are the main sources of knowledge of the older phases of Śaivite religious practice and the interrelations between the Śaiva systems. They are also helpful to obtain information on the history of Indian religion and philosophy. They serve as a doctrinal basis for Śaivite monasteries and as fundamental manuals for religious practices. They are also important for the study of Hindu art and architecture, iconographical particulars, and various types of sanctuaries. They are mines of information on various aspects of Śaivite religion.

The āgamic literature is also of interest in connection with the spread of Śaivism over South-East Asia; for example, Cambodian Sanskrit inscriptions refer to some Śaiva *Āgamas*.

Works which deal with the philosophy of Śaivism or Śaiva Siddhānta which are presently available are the Vidyā or Jñanapādas of *Suprabheda*, *Kiraṇa*, *Kāmika*, *Mṛgendra*, *Mataṅgapārameśvara*, *Pauṣkara*, *Kālottara* and *Sarvajñānottara*, with abridged versions available from *Raurava* and *Svāyambhuva Āgamas*. Many works have been written based on āgamic literature. The most important among them are *Tattvasaṁgraha*, *Tattvatrayanirṇaya*, *Bhogakārikā*, *Mokṣakārikā*, *Paramokṣanirāsakārikā*, *Rauravavṛtti*, *Svāyaṁbhuvavṛtti* and *Nareśvaraparīkṣā* by Sadyojyoti (9th cent.), *Mṛgendravṛtti* and *Tattvasaṁgrahavṛtti* by Nārāyaṇakaṇṭha (10th cent.) *Mataṅgavṛtti*, *Kiraṇavṛtti*, *Sārdhatriśatī-Kālottaravṛtti*, *Mokṣakārikāvyākhyā*, *Paramokṣanirāsakārikāvyākhyā*, *Vyomavyāpistava*, *Nādakārikā*, and *Nareśvaraparīkṣāvṛtti* by Rāmakaṇṭha (11th cent.), *Tattvaprakāśa* of Bhojadeva (11th cent.), *Ratnatraya* of Śrīkaṇṭha (11th cent.), all from

Kashmir, *Siddhāntaprakāśikā* of Sarvātmaśaṁbhu (12th cent.), commentaries on many of the texts noted above by Aghoraśivācārya, son of Sarvātmaśaṁbhu, *Sarvadarśanasaṁgraha* of Sāyaṇa (13th cent.), *Siddhāntaśekhara* of Viśvanātha (13th cent.), *Pauṣkara-bhāṣya*, and *Śataratnasaṁgraha* by Umāpatiśiva (14th cent.), *Śivajñānabodhabhāṣya* by Śivāgrayogin (16th cent.), *Pauṣkara-vyākhyā*, *Vyomavyāpistavavyākhyā*, *Śaivāgamaparibhāṣāmañjarī*, *Śivajñānasiddhisvapakṣadṛṣṭāntasaṁgraha*, *Śivajñānabodhopanyāsa* by Nigamajñānadeśika (16th cent.), *Śivayogaratna* by Śalivāṭijñana-prākaśa (16th cent.), *Śivapūjāstava* and *Jñānaratnāvalī* by Jñānaśiva, *Siddhāntasārāvalī* by Trilocanaśiva and its commentary by Ananta-śaṁbhu, *Śaivaparibhāṣa* by Sūryabhaṭṭāraka (16th cent.), *Siddhānta-sāra* by Īśānaśivagurudeva, *Rāmanāthasiddhāntadīpikā*, *Madhyārjuna-siddhāntadīpikā*, *Tattvamūrtiprabhavadīpikā*, and so on. Quotations from *Āgamas* are available in *Pāśupatasūtravyākhyā* of Kauṇḍinya (4th cent.), *Prapañcasāra* of Śaṁkara (8th cent.), *Śivadṛṣṭi* of Somānanda (9th cent.). Some authors of the 8th or 9th centuries, like Bṛhaspati and Vyākhyāniguru, are quoted by later Kashmir writers but their works are not available. A small portion of commentary on *Mataṅga* and *Kiraṇa* of Vyākhyāniguru is now available in manu-script. There is a work entitled *Jñānāvaraṇavilakham* by Valliyamba-lavanattampiran (17th cent.), two parts of which have been published by Dharmapuram Adhinam. This work in Tamil has abundant quotations from all the 28 Śaiva *Āgamas*. This is an evidence to prove that all the 28 *Āgamas* with their four *pādas* were available during this period. It is a pity that only portions of many *Āgamas* are available today due to decay and loss of manuscripts, as we are in a handicapped position to make a complete study of this important literature. However, on the basis of whatever is available now, we present here a historical aspect of our most ancient living religion, Śaivism, and about the Sanskrit Āgamic texts which have contributed to its growth.

These Āgamic texts were practically out of reach of the research scholars, and as such a study of them was not possible. A few of them were published as early as 1900, but they were in grantha script and the copies were donated to priests, so they remained practically unknown. The manuscripts were guarded by the priests, who were reluctant to show them to outsiders. They had not many facilities to protect them from decay, and as a result a fairly good portion of manuscript material seems to have been lost. In a private library of a *maṭha* at Tirunelvely in south India, I have seen a catalogue of manuscripts in which names of all the 28 Śaivāgamas were listed. But on verifying the collection in 1956, not a single manuscript of the *mūla Āgama* was found. The catalogue is in the handwriting of the father of the present head of the *maṭha*; thus, within 50 years such a valuable collection of the *mūla Āgamas* was lost. Even now it is very difficult to make these priests understand the value of the manuscripts; often they are not willing even to show their collection. Many of them do not even know what exists in their collection, because now they use printed books for their practical use. The South India Arcaka Association, Madras, has published in grantha script almost all the manuals useful for personal or temple rituals which serve all the needs of the priests. Their manuscripts are put somewhere in a corner and just taken out one day in a year for the Sarasvatī Pūjā. The damaged ones, if any, are secretly thrown into a river. Generally they do not even have a list of their collections.

However for some time we have seen a growing interest in the publication of the available *Āgamas*. Arthur Avalon has made a great effort to make a study of Śakta tantras. His series *Tantrik Texts* is well known, as is Prof. Schrader's introductions to *Pāñcarātra* and the *Ahirbudhnya*.

CHAPTER I

INTRODUCTION

The present work represents an attempt to study the Śaivism of the Āgamiç, Epic and the Purāṇic period, together with its ancillary cults, with special reference to the Śaiva religious practices prevalent in South India.

Few, indeed, are the books which embody a critical and historical survey of Śaivism as a whole. In the religious history of India, no religion has had such a long and continuous tradition as Śaivism. On the basis of archaeological and literary evidence it is possible to show that the religion of Śiva has persisted in India, without a break, since the pre-Vedic times. Few living religions in the world, if any, can boast of such a long and unbroken tradition. The very antiquity of Śaivism implies that that religion must have gone through various vicissitudes in the course of its long history of at least 5000 years. As such, a detailed study of this religion in its entirety can only be made through intensive investigations into the various periods of its history. Insofar as literary sources are concerned, we may in this connection think of three periods, namely the Vedic period, the Epic and Purāṇic period, and the modern period. Scholars have already thrown sufficient light on the Vedic period of the history of this religion. The studies on this subject are either found scattered in the relevant chapters of treatises dealing with Vedic religion and mythology, or are available in the form of independent monographs and papers which concern themselves solely with the problem of Rudra-Śiva in the *Veda*.[1]

[1] Arbmann, *Rudra, Untersuchungen zum altindischen Glauben*, Uppsala, 1922.
Siecke, "Der Gott Rudra im Rig-*Veda*", *Arch. Rel.*, I.113, 209.
Charpentier, "Uber Rudra-Śiva", *WZKM*, XXIII, 151.

Subsequent to this period, as far as the literary history of Śaivism is concerned, we have to take into account the period of the *Āgamas*, the Epics and the *Purāṇas*. It is strange that the Śaivism of the Āgamic, Epic and Purāṇic period has not received adequate attention from scholars interested in religious studies.[2] Incidental references are no doubt made, now and then, to the Epic and Purāṇic characteristics of Śaivism, but a comprehensive (and more or less objective) statement regarding the religion of Śiva and its ancillary cults has long been a desideratum. Without such a statement, the history of Śaivism can by no means be regarded as complete. The present study is undertaken with a view to filling this gap to a certain extent. However, before proceeding, one point needs to be clarified. The term Śaivism is sometimes understood to comprise the Śaiva religion as it is found in the four main periods of the religious history of ancient India, namely, the pre-Vedic proto-Indian period, the Vedic period, the period of heterodox religions, and the period of Hinduism, and at other times it denotes the Śaiva philosophy as represented by the various Śaiva systems, such as the Pāśupata dualism, the Siddhānta dualism, the Dvaitādvaita system of Lakulīśa, Śrīkaṇṭha's Śaiva-visiṣṭādvaita, the Vīraśaiva-Viśiṣṭādvaita, and the monistic Śaivism of Kashmir. It must therefore be pointed out that the scope of the present work is deliberately restricted to the consideration of the Śaiva religion, and that too as reflected in the *Āgamas*, the Epics and the *Purāṇas*. The value

---

Dandekar, "Rudra in the *Veda*", *JUPH*, no. 1, pp. 94-148.
Sitaramiah, "Rudra in the Ṛgveda", *QJMS* 32, Oct, 1941.
Chaudhari, "Rudra-Śiva, an agricultural Deity", *IHQ* 15, June 1939.
Venkataramanayya, *Rudra-Śiva*, Univ. of Madras, 1941.
Fatehsingh, "Rudra", *IHQ* 16, Dec. 1940.
Ray, Panibhushan, "Siva-Mahesvara", *J. Dept. Lett. Univ. Calcutta*, 30.

2 Mention must however be made of *The Religions of India*, vol. 1, Lonvala, 1950, by A.P. Karmarkar, in which the Epics and the *Purāṇas* are cited profusely. But this work is an attempt to study Śaivism from a particular point of view only, namely as an extension of the Mohenjodaro religious cults. The author characterizes all the religious systems discussed in this work as the *vrātya* or the Dravidian systems. With great ingenuity, he connects the Epic and Purāṇic traditions with the Mohenjodaro religious cults. *Karmarkar*'s conclusions are often speculative and far-fetched.

of the *Āgamas*, the Epics and the *Purāṇas* as important literary sources which deal with the various aspects of Śaivism will be discussed elsewhere in this chapter. These valuable sources, however, have not been fully utilized by the few writers who have attempted to present a connected history of Hinduism. All that they have done is to incidentally devote a chapter or two to Śaivism, without any special reference to the Śiva of the Āgamic, Epic and Purāṇic period. A few works of this type may be mentioned here.

Hindu Mythology by Wilkins [3] devotes its first part to the consideration of the Vedic deities. Part II [4] deals with Purāṇic gods like Brahmā, Viṣṇu, Śiva, Umā, Gaṇeśa and Kārttikeya. Wilkins has profusely drawn upon Purāṇic data for the delineation of the various characteristics of these gods, but his general treatment of the subject cannot be said to be either exhaustive or critical and historical.

Monier-Williams has devoted only two chapters of his *Brahmanism and Hinduism* [5] to topics relevant to our studies. One of these chapters (ch. IV) first deals with Śaivism, its definition and modes of worship. This is followed by a statement regarding the god Śiva, the Śaiva sects, and the ceremonies connected to the religion of Śiva. The other chapter (ch. V) describes some Śaiva temples, shrines and sacred places. This work is certainly useful, in that it has collected together quite an amount of material relating to Śiva and Śaivism. In another work entitled *Hinduism*,[6] Monier-Williams devotes one chapter (ch. VII)[7] to the origin and growth of Hinduism and the evolution of the doctrine of triple manifestation, another [8] to the development of Śaivism and Vaiṣṇavism, and the theory of incarnation, and a third [9] to the doctrine of devotion (*bhakti*), as elaborated in the

[3] Wilkins, *Hindu Mythology*, London, 1900.

[4] Pages 89 ff.

[5] Monier-Williams, *Brahmanism and Hinduism*, John Murray, London, 1891, Chapter IV, pp. 73-94 and chapter VII, pp. 180-208.

[6] Monier-Williams, *Hinduism*, London, 1940.

[7] Pp. 83 ff.

[8] Chapter VIII, pp. 97 ff.

[9] Chapter IX, pp. 115 ff.

Purāṇas and the *Tantras*. But in both these books, the Epic and Purāṇic Śaivism as such has failed to receive proper attention. In his *Religions of India*,[10] Barth has sought to make a detailed study of Indian religion. In a chapter on Hindu sects he has dealt at some length with the religion of Śiva. In another chapter, entitled "The sects, their History and Doctrines",[11] he has discussed the religions represented in the *Mahābhārata*, the *Rāmāyaṇa*, and the *Purāṇas*. According to Barth, "the positive history of the sects does not commence till the eleventh or the twelfth century by which time they are capable of re-assertion".[12] Insofar as Śaivism is concerned, Barth seems to be more interested in its various philosophical schools. After a few comments on ancient Śaivism he refers to its importance for Sāṁkhya metaphysics. He then discusses such topics as the systems of the Pāśupatas and the Māheśvaras, the doctrine of grace among the Śaivites, and the Śakti or the feminine principle. He turns his attention to idealistic Śaivism, the sects of the *tridaṇḍins* and the *smārtas*, the Kashmir school of Pratyabhijñā and the great Śaiva religion of the Deccan. He also discusses the sects of the Vīraśaivas and the Liṅgāyats and of the *sittars* and alchemists of South India. In section IV,[13] which is devoted to the study of worship, Barth's discussions centre around the 'diversity of the Hindu worship'. After commenting briefly on the worship of Gaṇeśa, he tries to trace the origin and development of the worship of images. "Liṅga and Yoni", "Private Religious Observances", and "Worship in Temples" are some of the topics relevant to the present study which he has discussed in this chapter. Barth's work can, however, by no means be characterized as an intensive study of Śaivism of the Epic and Purāṇic period. Indeed, it was not intended to be one.

Among non-Indian writers on Indian religions, reference is often made to Farquhar. Three of his works deserve special mention in the

[10] Barth, *Religions of India*, Trubner's Oriental Series, London, 1889.

[11] Pages 186 ff.

[12] Barth, *Religions of India*, p. 186.

[13] Pages 252 ff.

present context, namely, *A Primer of Hinduism*, *The Crown of Hinduism*, and *An Outline of the Religious Literature of India*. However, as far as the topics coming under the purview of this book are concerned, only a few sections of each of these works are relevant. In two chapters of *A Primer of Hinduism*,[14] Farquhar gives a brief account of the *Purāṇas* and the Hindu pantheon. Śiva being just one among the gods discussed here, no intensive study about him was possible. The author discussed the *Śaivasiddhānta* philosophy in passing. Chapter X devoted to *bhakti* cannot be said to be complete, for it deals only with the Vaiṣṇava aspect of it.

The Crown of Hinduism, in the words of Farquhar himself, "is an attempt to discover and state as clearly as possible what relation subsists between Hinduism and Christianity".[15] It is not meant to be an exhaustive treatment of Hinduism, though it deals with most of its prominent features. Later in this book, the author described the Hindu gods as they are represented in early literature, followed by a history of Hindu images and the beliefs about them. In the course of this history of Hindu iconography, the author has tried to indicate "the religious needs which inspire Hindu idolatry".

An Outline of the Religious Literature of India [16] is certainly a valuable book, containing quite a few chapters which are relevant to our present study. For instance, in Chapter III,[17] which deals with the movements towards theism, the discussion is focused on the various aspects of Hinduism, and in the course of that discussion, the Śaiva materials in the Epics are carefully investigated. Chapter IV similarly deals with the Śaiva materials in the *Purāṇas* and also with other Śaiva literature. In Chapter V, the author speaks of various religious and philosophical sects among the Śaivas, such as the Pāśupatas, the Lakulīśas, the Kāpālikas and the Nāthas. Attention is also drawn there to the Āgamic Śaivism of both the Tamil and Kashmiri schools.

---

[14] The Christian Literature Society for India, 1911.

[15] Farquhar, *The Crown of Hinduism*, p. 3.

[16] Oxford University Press, 1920.

[17] Pages 78 ff.

Informative to the general reader is the work of P. Thomas [18] which, being replete with illustrations, gives a detailed account of the gods of the Hindu pantheon. All material for this work is derived from the *Āgamas*, the Epics and the *Purāṇas*, with emphasis generally put on the myths and legends. Reference is occasionally made to a few religious beliefs which differ from place to place. The author, however, devotes only three pages to the description of Śiva,[19] and another three pages in all to that of Gaṇeśa, Kārttikeya and Devī.[20] The illustrations are mostly from North Indian representations, except for one or two taken from the South.

Among more recent works on Indian religions, first of all may be mentioned those of Konnow and Tuxen, and of Renou. In the *Religions of India*,[21] Konnow and Tuxen have undertaken a historical and subject-based treatment of Indian religions, beginning from the pre-Vedic Indus Valley period. Theirs seems to be an attempt to introduce the religious history of India to foreign students. And though in that book there is an independent section about Śaivism, it does not embody any detailed statement on the subject. Renou's *Religions of Ancient India* [22] aims at giving an account of the present state of the main problems concerning the religious history of ancient India. Naturally, many aspects of Indian religions including Śaivism are only briefly treated, while others have received a cursory mention. *The Religion of the Hindus* [23] contains just one chapter which deals with a subject coming under the purview of the present work, entitled "Religious practices of the Hindus". A mention may also be made of J. Filliozat's *La dévotion visnouite en pays tamoul*,[24] which was particularly helpful from the point of view of mythology. The fourth

---

[18] P. Thomas, *Hindu Religion, Customs and Manners*, Bombay.

[19] Pages 28-30.

[20] Pages 30-31.

[21] Copenhagen, 1949.

[22] London, 1953.

[23] Edited by Kenneth W. Morgan, The Renald Press Company, New York, 1953.

[24] Lecture delivered at IsMEO, Rome.

volume of *The Cultural Heritage of India* [25] brings together considerable material which has proved to be of great use for our purpose. It includes an historical sketch of Śaivism (ch. 3) and a discussion regarding Kashmir Śaivism (ch. 4) and Vīraśaivism (ch. 5). But perhaps more relevant to the subject of this work are the chapters dealing with the Śakti cult (ch. 15) and the Skanda cult (ch. 21) in South India. Much useful information is also made available about the Śaiva saints (ch. 24) and the Śākta saints (ch. 29). The third part of the volume of *The Cultural Heritage of India* concerns itself with religion in practice and describes, among other topics, the religious practices of Śaivism.

The monumental work of J. Muir by all means deserves special mention. His *Original Sanskrit Texts*,[26] in five volumes, constitutes a veritable encyclopaedia by themselves, shedding considerable light on the various aspects of Indian culture as portrayed in the early literary works. In the fourth volume of that series, the author has undertaken "a comparison of the Vedic gods with later representations of the principal deities". For the most part, he gives relevant extracts from different literary sources, followed by his own translations, and thereby affords the reader an opportunity to find out for himself in what way the development has taken place. Of special interest is that, along with the extracts from the *Vedas*, he has reproduced ample materials from the Epics and the *Purāṇas* as well.

Coming to the works which deal more specifically with Śaivism and the allied religious cults and which, incidentally, are critically studied and frequently referred to in this thesis, at the very outset one has to mention R.G. Bhandarkar's pioneer work in the field. His treatise on *Vaiṣṇavism, Śaivism and Minor Religious Systems*,[27] which is characteristically scientific in its approach and systematic in its treatment of the subject, makes valuable material available to a

---

25 *The Cultural History of India*, vol. IV, The Religions; published by the Ramakrishna Mission Institute of Culture, Calcutta, 1956.

26 Longmans Green and Co., London, 1902.

27 Verlag von Karl J. Trūbner, Stassburg, 1913.

research scholar and indicates the lines upon which he might proceed in his investigations. Bhandarkar is, however, more concerned with the origin and development of the Śaiva religion from the Vedic times onwards, and consequently, the Āgamic, Epic and Purāṇic Śaivism by itself receives comparatively meager treatment in this work. The author's references to the schools of the Śaiva philosophy and aspects of Southern Śaivism, incidental as they necessarily are, are no doubt most suggestive.

The title of K.R. Subramanian's *The Origin of Śaivism and its History in the Tamil Land* [28] is rather misleading, particularly inasmuch as the latter half of the title is concerned. The author begins by emphasizing the non-Vedic and non-Aryan origin of the religion of Śiva. He then goes on to the discussion of the Buddhist and Jaina remains in Tamil Nadu and of the evolution of the architectural styles in South India. His discussion of the religious rites relating to Śaivism is no doubt useful, but one looks in vain in the book for any history of Śaivism in South India. Rose's study of the various names of Śiva occurring in the *Purāṇas* and of the beliefs and magical ideology underlying those names [29] is a highly suggestive piece of work from the point of view of religious history as well as textual criticism. The author has also taken into account the Vedic *Śatarudrīya* and the *Śivasahasranāma*, and the monograph generally throws considerable light of Śaivism of the Epic and Purāṇic period.

S. Sivapadasundaram's *Śaiva School of Hinduism* treats Śaivism in a general way, while C.V. Narayana Ayyar's book specially refers to Śaivism in South India. Ayyar is of the view that Rudra-Śiva was already a Vedic deity at the dawn of history. Only a few chapters in the earlier part of the book are based on Sanskrit sources and, there too, not much is said about Āgamic, Epic and Purāṇic Śaivism. The author's main contribution is the exploitation of the Tamil sources

---

[28] K.R. Subramaniam, *The Origin of Śaivism and its History in the Tamil Land*, Madras, 1929.

[29] E. Rose, *Beiträge zur Kenntnis des Śivaitischen Namensglaubens nach den Purāṇen*, Bonn. 1934.

for the building of the history of Śaivism, and had he bestowed as much attention on the description of the Śaiva religious practices as represented in the Tamil works as he did to the reconstruction of the history of the religion, his work would have proved of greater use from our point of view. N. Venkataramanayya also believes [30] that there are no valid grounds for presuming a non-Aryan origin for the Purāṇic Śiva. The Vedic Rudra, according to him, was an Aryan deity of solar origin. Venkataramanayya discusses in his work the so-called Dravidic elements in the character of Rudra-Śiva and also traces the evolution of the phallus, but of Āgamic, Epic and Purāṇic Śaivism, or of the Śaiva religious practices, he has very little to say. In the "History and Philosophy of Liṅgāyata Religion", which forms the introduction to his edition of the *Liṅgadhāraṇacandrikā*,[31] M.R. Sakhare deals with Śaivism at length. He traces the history of Śaivism, which he seems to regard as a Dravidian religion, from the Vedic times until the 12th century AD, but his main discussion centers around the Śaiva cult sponsored by Basava in the 12th century. A reference has already been made to A.P. Karmarkar's *The Religions of India*, Vol. I, which treats Śaivism as an extension of the Mohenjodaro ideology. He claims that the *vrātya* (Dravidian?) radiated all culture and civilization from the Deccan to the four corners of the world. *Hinduism in Ceylon* by Cartman,[32] which opens with a brief sketch of the political history of Srilanka, brings together much useful material relating to the Hindu religious beliefs and practices prevalent on that island. Among other things, the author deals with some topics, which are particularly relevant to the subject of this work, such as objects of worship, temples and temple ritual, festivals and pilgrimages, caste, customs, etc. He rightly points out that, for the Srilanka Hindus, the God Śiva is far more important than any other god, and discusses, at some length, the cults and religious practices centering

[30] N. Venkataramanayya, *Rudra-Śiva*, Madras University, 1941.

[31] *Liṅgadhāraṇacandrikā*, edited with an exhaustive introduction dealing with the history and philosophy of Liṅgāyata religion by M.R. Sakhare, Belgaum, 1942.

[32] Cartman, *Hinduism in Ceylon*, Colombo, 1957.

around that god. However, on account of the peculiar nature of his book, Cartman has not been able to go deeply into the subject. Another book which has proved of some help is *Instrument and Purpose: Studies on Rites and Rituals in South India*, by Carl Gustav *Diehl*,[33] but his approach is anthropological rather than purely religio-historical.

It will thus be seen that the present work, which certainly owes a good deal to the works mentioned above (and to many others), differs from them principally in the following respects. It undertakes for the first time a detailed and exhaustive treatment of the religion of Śiva as represented in the *Āgamas*, the Epics and the *Purāṇas*. It also comparatively examines the various cults associated with the religion of Śiva. Also, it critically examines, again for the first time, the Śaivite and allied religious practices prevalent in South India.

This work thus seeks to add a chapter or two to a fuller history of this religion with its long and unbroken tradition.

Although, as indicated above, the scope of the present study of Śaivism is limited to the Āgamic, Epic and Purāṇic sources, with the view that the knowledge of the early history of the religion would provide a suitable background for that study and would aid a proper understanding of the concepts and practices of Śaivism, the origin and development of early Śaivism is studied from the pre-Epic sources of the Mohenjodaro and the Vedic periods. One entire chapter is devoted to this topic. The rise of the trinity of the Hindu gods belongs to the post-Vedic period; the old Vedic gods disappear, yielding place to new deities. The circumstances which led to this phenomenon and the consequent rivalries, inducing the formation of separate sects such as Śaivism and Vaiṣṇavism, form the contents of the third chapter. In this study of Āgamic, Epic and Purāṇic Śaivism, a study of Śiva in the light of this mythological evolution is essential. The fourth chapter presents a complete picture of Śiva as portrayed in the *Purāṇas*. It will be agreed that no study of Śaivism will be complete without a

---

[33] Carl Gustav Diehl, *Instrument and Purpose: Studies on Rites and Rituals in South India*. Pub. C.W.K. Gleerup, Lund, 1956.

study of the related rites and rituals in the *Āgamas*. These religious practices of Āgamic, Epic and Purāṇic Śaivism are best preserved — though in some cases in a developed form — in South India. The Śaiva religious practices of South India have accordingly been exhaustively dealt with in the two subsequent chapters. Though all that concerns Śiva of the Āgamic, Epic and Purāṇic periods has thus been fully treated here, there still remains an important aspect of this religion which deserves special attention: the ancillary cults, which, having their roots in the *Āgamas*, the Epics and the *Purāṇas*, have, over the course of time, become an integral part of Śaivism.

Before proceeding, a word or two may be said here about the significance of the subject of this study. The Epics, or more particularly the *Mahābhārata*, and the *Purāṇas*, bear several common characteristics insofar as the religious material contained in them are concerned. Both these classes of literature present to us a religion in which the Rudra of the Vedic period and the Śiva of the post-Vedic period merge into one. This transition is smooth in the Epics but rapid and marked in the *Purāṇas*. More names are attributed to the god, and the tendency towards sectarian worship becomes prominent. These two types of literary works portray religious faiths which are very close to those prevalent today among the people of India. It is in the *Āgamas*, the Epics and the *Purāṇas*, and not in the Vedic *saṁhitās*, the *Brāhmaṇas* and the *Upaniṣads*, that we have to search for Rāma and Kṛṣṇa, Gaṇeśa and Skanda, or Śiva and Pārvatī. The Hindu religion of today is for the most part constituted of the popular sects which have one or the other of these gods at their head. The great importance of the *Āgamas*, the Epics and the *Purāṇas* as documents for the first time portraying the history of the Indian religion and the popular faiths of the people is thus well established. Compared to the concept of the Vedic period, that of the Śiva of the *Āgamas*, the Epics and the *Purāṇas* is definitely closer to the present day Hindu concept of that god. The forms of worship indicated in the *Āgamas*, the Epics and the *Purāṇas* bear close resemblance to the forms of worship which are prevalent today; and other religious practices also continued to be more or less the same. As such, the study of Āgamic, Epic and Purāṇic Śaivism would be most helpful for a thorough understanding of its modern counterpart. It may also be pointed out that the Āgamic, Epic and Purāṇic Śaivism has been deemed, in more senses than one, a direct continuation of the indigenous Śiva religion of the pre-Vedic times and thus forms the connecting link between the later religion and the religion of the modern Śaivites.

A Study of Śaivism in the present context implies the study of its ancillary cults as well. In South Indian traditions, with which this work mainly concerns itself, Śiva is always represented along with his subordinate divinities. We can trace the gradual evolution of this group of divinities which are associated with Śiva. It is even possible to find some indications of this evolution in the *Veda*. For instance, Rudra of the Ṛgveda is mentioned alone. Over the course of time, he is accompanied by the Maruts, though not exactly like the attendant divinities of later Śiva. In the later Vedic texts, Rudrāṇī and Umā-Haimavatī joined the group. In the *Āgamas* and the Epics, Kārttikeya is added to the group. Later, the *Purāṇas* bring Gaṇeśa. In South Indian Śiva temples of great magnificence, we see a rich display of these subordinate divinities which are installed in the places duly assigned to them. This installation of the subordinate divinities is, indeed, an essential characteristic of the temples in South India. It is on account of these circumstances that an investigation into the ancillary cults of Śaivism is incorporated in the present study.

It might be asked why the Śaiva religious practices of South India should be the specific concern of the present study; the answer is readily available. First of all, it was deemed necessary to limit the scope of this work so that an intensive treatment of the subject would be possible. Secondly, it is in South India that Śaivism has had its full growth and development. It becomes evident that the influences of the Āgamic and the Purāṇic traditions is far more deep-rooted in that region than elsewhere. Instance after instance may be cited in support of this; first to be mentioned in this connection are the temples. Colossal in structure, and long celebrated in history, they stand as grand monuments of the religious traditions which they have preserved intact. These temples have helped to further the growth of several fine arts, such as, architecture, and sculpture, and music and dance.[34] Through many generations, they have preserved for us traditions of worship and ritual which are of great importance. Thanks to the religious generosity of the many South Indian kings of old, who not only established these temples, but who also made endowments [35] for their proper maintenance, the ancient traditions of worship and ritual have been preserved more or less unchanged, through the agency of the continuous line of priests who have been hereditarily attached to the temples.[36] Thus we see that on account of the munificence of the kings of old on the one hand, and the interconnection of music, dance and architecture with religious practices on the other, the old religious traditions have been preserved in South India mostly in their original form up to this day — the contacts with the Āgamic, Epic and Purāṇic ideology having been never lost from sight.

Some indications may be given at this stage regarding the methods adopted in the course of the present investigation. As has been pointed out elsewhere, the present study has two main aspects.

---

[34] The following remark of *Vaiyyapuri Pillai* is significant in this connection: "Big temples with towers of enormous proportions were constructed by them. Temple walls and towers were adorned with beautiful paintings, festivals were instituted with grants of lands for their annual performances, musical entertainments and dances in the temples were arranged for. Thus several of the fine arts received encouragement. More than all, these structures became centers of education also, Itihāsas and *Purāṇas* were expounded here for the benefit of all the masses." *History of Tamil Language and Literature*, pp. 101-102.

[35] P.V. Jagadisa Iyer in his *South Indian Shrines* (p. 35) refers to "the inscriptions recorded in temples which supply us with dates for the several charities made, and occasionally also for the construction of certain *maṇḍapas* or halls, tanks, etc., subsequently set up". This author has further pointed out elsewhere in the same work (p. 58) the fact that "the inscriptions recorded in the walls of the various temples have been copied by the Epigraphical Department during the years 1888, 1890, 1895, 1900, 1906, 1910, 1919 and 1921". He regrets to note that "the great bulk have yet never been published" (p. 25). For an elaborate account of this topic, see "Temple offerings and Temple grants in South India", *Ind. Hist. Cong.*, 4th Session, Lahore, 1940, pp. 156-168.

[36] See Shamsastri, R., "Dravidian Culture", *ABORI*, XI, p. 340.

One is the study of Śaivism and its ancillary cults as represented in the *Āgamas*, the Epics and the *Purāṇas*. The other is an investigation of the Śaivite religious practices described in those literary works with special reference to the form in which these religious practices have been preserved to this day in South India. The basic literary sources of this study have, of course, been the twenty-eight Śaiva *Āgamas*, the Śaiva manuals, two Epics, the *Rāmāyaṇa*, the *Mahābhārata* and the eighteen *Purāṇas*. All material pertaining to Śaivism or its ancillary cults in these works was carefully collected and systematically analysed. Quite an amount of related literature also had to be taken into account. Similarly, most of the modern writings dealing with this subject were examined, with a view to obtaining an idea as to what work had already been done in this field and what still remained to be done.

The material for the other aspect of this study had to be collected in several ways. The best and the most reliable literary sources for an investigation into the Śaiva religious practices are without any doubt the *Āgamas*. Twenty-eight in all [37] and composed entirely in Sanskrit, these extensive works [38] were designed to impart complete information relating to the fourfold path of Śaivism, comprising *caryā*, *kriyā*, *yoga* and *jñāna*. From among the *Āgamas*, special reference must be made to the *Kāraṇa* and the *Kāmika*, which deal entirely with the rites (*kriyā*). The temple worship prevalent in South India is entirely governed by the norms laid down in these authoritative works. These works have laid down the rules pertaining not only to the construction of temples and the fashioning of images, but also to the rites relating to their installation and the daily ceremonies which should be performed, as well as those for special occasions. The *Kāraṇa* and *Kāmika* gave rise to several *Paddhatis* which formed valuable manuals of the

[37] Abhinavagupta, in his *Tantrāloka*, mentions ninety-two Śiva-*Āgamas*. See also Radhakrishnan, *Indian Philosophy*, vol. II, p. 723.

[38] According to the *Śivārcanācandrikā* of Appayya Dīkṣita, the total number of verses in the twenty-eight *Śivāgamas*, which form the basis of the Siddhānta Śaivism, was more than one *parārdha*, one *śaṅkha*, and six *padmas*.

Śaiva rituals. The various *Āgamas*, particularly the *Kāraṇāgama* which contains abundant material on this subject, as well as the *Paddhatis*, have accordingly been often referred to while writing about the Śaiva religious practices. An attempt is made to correlate wherever possible the Purāṇic and Epic Śaivism with the various aspects of the Śaiva rituals represented in the *Āgamas*.

Having already been acquainted with their religious practices, while undertaking the writing of critical editions of Śaiva *Āgamas*, I undertook a study tour of South India, visited several temples, and collected firsthand information about the practices which have been in vogue there. The various religious rites which are performed at these temples throughout the year, both *nitya* as well as *naimittika*, were either actually observed or discussed with the priests who officiated at them. A clear insight was gained into the entire system of worship and ritual in South Indian Śaiva temples. The structure of the temples and the assignment of places in it to the ancillary divinities could also be studied. Similarly, the impressions imprinted on every image, the carvings, the architectural and sculptural representations of the Epic and Purāṇic narratives etc. were personally noted down.

Representative literature in Tamil on this subject, especially the religious works, has also been studied for the purpose of this work. An attempt has been made to ascertain the extent of the influence which the *Āgamas*, the Epics and the *Purāṇas* have had on this Tamil literature. The results of this study are briefly summed up in the Appendix.

Chapter II

A Survey of the Early History of Śaivism

At the onset of the proposed study of the Śaivism of the Āgamic, Epic and Purāṇic periods, it would be desirable to prepare the necessary background by taking a rapid survey of the early history of the religion. This chapter, which is divided into seven sections, aims at such a survey. The investigation begins with a study of the pre-Vedic period. This is based entirely on the materials provided by the finds of the Mohenjodaro and the Harappa excavations. A picture of the Śaivism of the subsequent periods is thereafter presented as portrayed in the various literary sources such as the *Ṛgveda*, the *Yajurveda*, the *Atharvaveda*, the *Brāhmaṇas*, the *Upaniṣads*, and the Sūtras.[1]

1. The Mohenjodaro-Harappa Period

The excavations at Mohenjodaro and Harappa have brought to light quite a wealth of information relating to the early history of India. They have also given rise to — and quite naturally — a series of problems, which deserve the closest attention from scholars working in the field. First of all, we have to tackle the question regarding the date of the Indus Valley civilisation.[2] Thereafter, we have to

---

1 An attempt of a similar character has been made by Narayana Ayyar in his *History of Śaivism in South India*, and also by Bhandarkar in his work entitled *Vaiṣnavism, Śaivism, and Minor Religious Systems*. The present attempt is of a more elaborate nature.

2 Lakshman Sarup has drawn the conclusion that the *Ṛg Veda* represents a period earlier than the Indus Civilisation. See his paper entitled "The Ṛgveda and the Mohenjodaro", *IC*, vol. IV, pp. 158-159. Wheeler holds the opposite view, that "the Indus Civilisation was still living in the early centuries of the second millennium BC." According to him, "It was succeeded by a variety of (materially) inferior cultures, in some cases after a phase of violence". *Vide* "Mohenjodaro", *TC*, vol. II,

determine its character, that is to say, to determine whether it was Aryan or Dravidian.[3] These questions, though they do not directly concern our present study, have nevertheless much bearing upon it. It may be pointed out, at the very outset, that sometimes the religion of the Indus is itself regarded as one of the factors determining the antiquity of that civilisation.[4] It was John Marshall who first advanced a host of arguments with a view to determining the date and authorship of the Indus civilisation.[5] But even after an interval of not less than eighty years following Marshall's work, the whole question still continues to be more or less unsettled. Fully conscious of this, we proceed to investigate the subject at hand, the religion of the Indus Valley. In particular, we have to find the relationship which this religion has with what concerns us most, Early Śaivism.

---

no. 1, pp. 158-159. See also Karmarkar, "The Age of Mohenjodaro Civilisation", *Ind. Hist. Cong.*, (The Proceedings) Sixth Session, 1943, pp. 131-132. Shamshastri seems to be at a loss regarding the fixing of the dates of the two civilizations, for he has begun to suspect whether both the cultures were interrelated. *ABORI*, vol. XI, p. 375.

[3] Srinivasachari is very frank and outspoken when he begins to express his doubts "whether the words Aryan and Dravidian denote two distinct races". "Research in ethnology and philology", he points out, "has not been fruitful in bringing about any decisive result." See: "Pre-Dravidian, Proto-Dravidian and Dravidian", *JBORS*, vol. XXIV, p. 54. Sarup in his article, "The Ṛgveda and the Mohenjodaro", *IC*, vol. IV, expresses views radically different from those of Marshall and Mackay. According to him, "the evidence of anthropology does not support the theory of the Dravidian character of the Indus Valley civilization". (p. 152). Heras refutes Sarup's theory and faces all the arguments one by one; see his article, "Were the Mohenjodarians Aryans?", *JIH*, vol. XXI, pp. 23-33. Chanda in his *Indus Valley in the Vedic Period* (p. 2) observes: "Nothing as yet discovered affords any indication that the builders of the prehistoric cities at Harappa and Mohenjodaro were akin to the Ṛgvedic Aryans. On the other hand the civilization of those holders appears to be of a non-Vedic type." In a paper read at the Indian Historical Congress, 1943 sessions, Pusalkar concludes that "Vedic people were not homogeneous, and were the earliest inhabitants of the Indus Valley". See "Pre-Aryan and Non-Aryan in the Indus Valley", *Ind. Hist. Cong.*, 1943, p. 131. In an article entitled, "Authors of the Indus Culture", Pusalker expresses the opinion that "there is nothing inconsistent in calling the Vedic Aryans the authors of Indus civilization, or styling the civilization as Vedic or Aryan". See also *Vedic Age*, p. 153 by the same author.

[4] Though the date is now generally fixed at circa 3000 BC, schools still differ on the question whether the Indus Civilisation was Vedic, pre-Vedic or post-Vedic.

[5] Marshall, *Mohenjodaro and the Indus Civilisation*, vol. I, pp. 102 ff.

"Religion gives us the most convincing illustration of the explicitly Indian character of the Indus Civilisation."[6] So observes Gordon Childe, while reviewing the early history of the Indus civilization. We shall briefly summarize below the more important views about the religion of the Indus Valley, particularly insofar as they have some relevance for the study of Śaivism. It may be pointed out that no buildings have so far been discovered in the Indus Valley which can definitely be identified as temples.[7] Even those doubtfully classed as such do not seem to contain any religious relics. Religion has always played a prominent part in ancient cultures, and this is all the more so in the case of India.[8] As far as the present aspect of the study is concerned, we have to remain content with the material that has become available and we have to proceed with the reconstruction of the history of the religion relying solely on the testimony of seals and of figurines and stone images.

On the basis of a thorough investigation of the objects that have been discovered in the Indus Valley, Marshall has come to the conclusion that the religion of that period was a composite one and that many cults existed side by side, and continued to flourish without let or hindrance to one another.[9] Of these religious cults, the Mother cult and the Śiva cult must have been most widely prevalent — a fact which is attested by the abundance of relevant materials unearthed in the Indus Valley. In the later religious history, those two cults are seen to have developed into the two parallel religions of Śaivism and Śaktism. The Mother cult is also seen to have been merged into the Śiva cult, so that the Mother or Śakti began to be represented as the consort of Śiva. Other minor cults, like tree worship [10] and the worship of inanimate objects,[11] which had existed separately, were later fused

---

[6] Childe, *New Lights on the Most Ancient East*, p. 184.

[7] Marshall, *ibid.*, p. 48.

[8] Pusalker, *op.cit.*, pp. 63 ff.

[9] Marshall, *op.cit.*, pp. 76 ff.

[10] Marshall, *op.cit.*, pp. 63 ff.

[11] Marshall, *op.cit.*, pp. 66 ff.

into the major cults. For example, the tree worship and the worship of serpents, of which traces are found in the Indus period, have been absorbed by the Śaivism and Vaiṣṇavism of the Epic and Purāṇic periods. The serpent becomes the couch of Viṣṇu; Śiva wears the serpent as *yajñopavīta* and as other ornaments. *Tulasī* and *bilva* are considered to be sacred to Viṣṇu and Śiva respectively.[12] Each temple in South India has its sacred tree under the designation *sthalavṛkṣa*.[13]

A seal from Mohenjodaro depicts a horned deity (Fig. 1). This deity possesses very great significance so far as our study is concerned. A detailed description of it, as given by Marshall, is as follows:[14]

"The god who is three-faced is seated on a low Indian throne, in a typical attitude of yoga, with legs bent double beneath him, heel to heel and toes turned downwards. His arms are outstretched, his hands, with thumbs in front resting on his knees. From wrist to shoulder the arms are covered with bangles, eight smaller and three larger; over his breast is a triangular pectoral or perhaps a series of necklaces ... and round his waist a double band. The lower limbs are bare and the phallus (*ūrdhva-meḍhra*) seemingly exposed, but it is possible that what appears to be the phallus is in reality the end of the waist-band. Crowning his head is a pair of horns meeting in a tall head-dress. To either side of the god are four animals an elephant and tiger on his proper right, a rhinoceros and buffalo on his left. Beneath the throne are two deer standing with head retardant, and horns turned to the centre. At the top of the seal is an inscription of seven letters, the last of which for lack of room, at the right hand top corner had been placed between the elephant and the tiger."

---

[12] Fergusson seems not to have gone deep into the problem. Hurriedly he has made the following observation in his exhaustive work on the tree and serpent worship: "There does not seem to be a trace of Tree worship mixed up with Śaivism, nor any real connection with serpent worship". *Tree and Serpent worship*, p. 75.

[13] Gopinath Rao: "In South India, each Śiva temple has some particular tree which is peculiar to that temple and goes by the name *sthalavṛkṣa*, or the tree of the place ... The *tulasī* plant is held in high esteem and association with Vaiṣṇavism and regular pūja is daily offered to that plant in many Hindu homes today. The leaves of this plant are sacred and pleasing an offering to Viṣṇu as those of bael tree are to Śiva". *Elements of Hindu Iconography*, vol. I, Introduction p. 15.

[14] Marshall, *op.cit.*, p. 52.

Fig. 1: Horned deity on Mohenjodaro seals.

Various attempts have been made to study the seal in detail, and to find out the religious concept represented by it. Marshall,[15] Mackay,[16] and many other scholars [17] are unanimous in interpreting the deity pictured on the seal as the prototype of the later Śiva. That deity is said to display many characteristics of the latter that are prominently assigned to him by Epic and Purāṇic traditions. No attempt, however, is made specifically to impose the name of Śiva upon that deity, though names such as Paśupati are mentioned in that connection.[18]

The pose in which the deity is represented immediately attracts one's attention. He is seated cross-legged in an attitude of meditation. The position of his feet, toes and hands, clearly indicate some yogic *āsana*. It is not difficult to connect Śiva with yoga. This characteristic

---

[15] Marshall, *op.cit.*, pp. 52-55.

[16] Mackay more or less repeats what Marshall has said, and thus endorses the latter's viewpoint. Vide *Early Indus Civilisation*, pp. 56 f.

[17] Law M.N., "Mohenjodaro and Indus Civilisation", *IHQ*, vol. VIII, pp. 121 ff.
Karmarkar A.P. "Fresh and further Light on Mohenjodaro Riddle" *ABORI*, vol. XXI, pp. 115 ff.
The Liṅga-cult in Ancient India, B.C. Law, vol. I, pp. 456 ff.
"Some Nude Gods of the Hindu pantheon", *ABORI*, vol. XXIII, p. 214.
"The Aryo-Dravidian character of the Mohenjodaro Inscriptions", *Prācyavāṇī*, (Calcutta) I, pp. 99-101.
Heras H.S.J. "The Plastic Representation of God Amongst the Proto-Indians", *Sardesai Comm. Vol.*, pp. 223-234.
"The Religion of the Mohenjodaro People according to the Inscriptions", *J. Bom. U.*, V. (1936), pp. 1-29.
"The Worship in Mohenjodaro", *J. Anthrop S. Jubilee Vol.*, 1937, pp. 31-39.
Ghosh A, "Siva, His pre-Aryan Origin", *IC*, vol. II, p. 763.
Diksitar, "Antiquity of Śaivism", *Kalyāṇakalpataru*, vol. VII, 1940, p. 434.
Childe. This author endorses Marshall's viewpoint. He observes: "Mohenjodaro depicts a horned deity..., he is obviously a prototype of Śiva, three-faced lord of beasts, prince of *yogis*, as Marshall has demonstrated in detail", *op.cit.*, p. 185.

[18] The identification of that deity with Śiva is not accepted by T.M.P. Mahadevan, *JGJRI*, vol. IV. (1946), pp. 1-4. See also B.A. Saletore (New Review 10) and K.A. Nilakantha Sastri, *JUPHS*, II (NS), 1954, pp. 1-9). According to Saletore, the deity is to be identified with Agni, while Nilakantha Sastri thinks that "the so-called three-headed Paśupati form of Śiva is in fact a buffalo-headed composite deity whose body is a clever fusion of various deadly animals".

of Śiva is repeatedly emphasized in the *Purāṇas*.[19] The representation of Dakṣiṇāmūrti in a yogic posture, delivering a discourse to his disciples through silence, is still a striking example of the living element of yoga in Śaivism.[20] Several instances may be cited from the *Purāṇas* to prove the closest connections of Śiva with yoga.[21] It is generally assumed that, being pre-Aryan in its origin, yoga was not given its due prominence in the Vedic literature. Though passages infused with yogic ideas are not wanting in the Vedic texts, it is in the Epics and the *Purāṇas* that yoga is frequently mentioned. Again, it is in these latter works that Śiva (and, to a certain extent, Viṣṇu) is constantly described as not only preaching the *yoga-mārga*, but also being himself master-*yogin*.[22] The emphasis on yoga in the Indus

---

[19] This is clearly evident in the following epithets of Śiva:
Yogin: *Kūrma P.*, I.9.58.
Yogapati: *Skanda P.*, I.1.32.150.
Yogināṁ Īśitāram: *Kūrma P.*, I.25.52.
Mahāyogeśvara: *Vāmana P.*, 44.58.
Yogavidāṁ varaḥ: *Kūrma P.*, I.25.33.

[20] "As the teacher of yoga, music and other sciences, he is known by the name Dakṣiṇāmūrti. One account gives an explanation as regards the etymology of the name. It states that because Śiva was seated facing the South when he taught yogajñāna, he came to be known as Dakṣiṇāmūrti." Gopinath Rao, *op.cit.*, vol. II, pt. I, p. 275. In this connection the popular verse relating to this topic may be cited:

Citraṁ vaṭataror mūle vṛddhāḥ śiṣyā gurur yuvā |
Gurostu maunaṁ vyākhānaṁ śiṣyāśca chinnasaṁśayāḥ ||

"Wonder, at the root of a banyan tree are old disciples and a young teacher; the comments of the teacher are silent and the disciples have their doubts cleared!"

[21] The *Kūrma Purāṇa* (II, chapters 1-11) contains a Gītā in imitation of the *Bhagavadgītā*. It must be noted that the colophons of these chapters also are in imitation of those of the *Bhagavadgītā*, and thus this *gītā* too claims to be a *yoga-śāstra*. It is interesting to note that these two gods, Viṣṇu and Śiva, alone continue to wield great influence among their devotees from Upaniṣadic times onwards. This may probably be due to their association with *yoga*. Both of them are teachers of *yoga*, though the implications of the term *yoga* is not the same in the two cases. It may incidentally be noted that Brahmā, the other member of the trinity, reveals no connection with the *yoga-mārga*, and in course of time he withdrew totally from the religious sphere.

[22] Viṣṇu is mentioned as a *mahāyogin*, and he himself speaks of Śiva in similar terms, and points him out as the promulgator of yoga. *Kūrma P.*, I.25.31 ff.

Valley religion is further made clear by other objects unearthed there. The head of a male statue from Mohenjodaro has its eyes focused on the nose.[23] This pose naturally leads to the conclusion that it is a portrayal of an attitude of yoga. Another representation of the deity in yogic posture is depicted on a small faience seal from Mohenjo-daro. On either side of this deity are portrayed two *nāgas*, in a kneeling posture, praying with their hands stretched upwards.[24] All these points may be cited as proof of the prevalence of the yogic ideology which seems to have formed an essential characteristic of the Indus Valley religion.

Besides the yogic posture, there is another characteristic of the Paśupati representation, to which special attention may be drawn. The lower limbs are bare and the phallus is seemingly exposed. This is in sharp contrast to the priest-like figure earlier referred to with a robe thrown over its shoulders, and with eyes fixed on the nose for meditation. In this context, it is suggested that nudity is not necessarily the characteristic of the Indus gods. However, the figure on this seal is shown naked, and it may, in all probability be a prototype of the Purāṇic Śiva, who reveals the same characteristic.[25]

Attention also may be drawn to another characteristic of this figure; three faces are visible in this portrayal. This is explained in various ways. In the later mythology, five heads are ascribed to Śiva,[26] and each denotes a separate function.[27] Sometimes this god is referred to as four-faced.[28] The ascription of three faces to Śiva does not seem to have been common in Hindu mythology. It is, however, not unlikely that the fourth face of the figure in the seal is on the rear, and is left entirely to our imagination to be visualized.[29] Such an assumption would remove any difficulty in relating that figure with Śiva.

---

[23] Mackay, *op.cit.*, pp. 53 ff.

[24] Marshall, *op.cit.*, p. 68.

[25] Cf. *Matsya P.*, 154, 331.

[26] *Skanda P.*, I.1.34.47; *Bhāgavata P.*, VIII.7.29.

[27] *Śiva P.*, *Vāyusaṁhitā*, 8.1-10.

[28] *Kūrma P.*, I.20.63; *Liṅga P.*, II.19.7.

Another noteworthy characteristic of this seal is that a few animals are portrayed as surrounding the central figure. This hints at the lordship of the god over animals. This fact, again, naturally leads one to connect that god with later Rudra-Śiva, who, in a similar capacity, has gained the appellation Paśupati.[30]

However, the horns that are displayed on the head of the figure are indicative of more than what they ordinarily seem to signify in the case of other figures.[31] It has been pointed out that not only in the Indus Valley, but also in all other parallel cultures, the horns have indicated divinity. But in the case of Śiva it has given rise to an elegant headdress.[32] It is exclusively the characteristic of Śiva to arrange his hair in various shapes:[33]*Jaṭāmakuṭa* is the special characteristic of

[29] The explanation given by Stella Kramrisch about the image of Mahādeva may be recalled in this connection:
"The *Viṣṇudharmottara* speaks of the five heads of Śiva. They are Iśāna, Tatpuruṣa, Aghora, Vāmadeva and Sadyojāta. They face four directions. The first, the highest, is not carved as a rule on these images, which are known as *pañcamukhaliṅga*, the five-faced sign or symbol. *Pañcamukhaliṅga* has four faces in the four directions, they are carved against the central *liṅga*-pillar, whose rounded tops surmounts them. Though four faces only are generally carved, they too need not be all visible. Three, two or one face only is required to be shown, if the innermost sanctuary in which stands the liṅga has four, three, two or one doors respectively." "The Image of Mahādeva in the cave of Elephanta Island", *Ancient India*, no. 2 (July 1946), p. 6.

[30] Cf. *Paśūnāṁ pataye namaḥ, TS*, IV.5.1.17. and *Taveme pañca paśavo... AV*, XI.2.9; other names with similar implication occur in the *Purāṇas*.

[31] Marshall, *op.cit.*, p. 67.

[32] That Śiva had an elegant headdress, which invariably happened to be an artistic arrangement of the matted hair, may be seen from the following note:
"The *jaṭāmakuṭa* is as the name indicates made up of twists of matted hair, done into the form of a tall cap. The *Uttarakāmika* gives the following somewhat long and unintelligible description of the *uṣnīṣa* in which the *jaṭāmakuta* is included.
Jaṭābhiḥ pañcabhir granthiṁ trimātreṇa viśeṣataḥ Ekadhā tu tridhā vṛtya śeṣ ābhiḥ pārśvālambanam Jaṭāmakuṭam etad dhi sarvālaṅkāram īritam: "five jaṭās or braids of matted hair are taken and tied into a knot three inches in height by coiling them into one or three loops, the remaining braids being bound and taken through to be left hanging on both sides."
Gopinath Rao, *op.cit.*, vol. I, pt. I, p. 28.

[33] Kapardin is an epithet of Śiva: *YV*, IV.5.1.10; IV.5.1.29 & IV.5.1.49. Śiva is often described as Kapardin in the *Purāṇas*. *Brahmāṇḍa P.*, III.25.12; *Vāmana P.*, 33.24; *Vāyu P.*, I.54.69 and so on.

the anthropomorphic representations of Śiva seen in the temples of the South.[34] Some scholars see in these horns a forerunner of the *triśūla*.[35] It is also suggested that the proto-Indian Śiva was originally represented as a bull (which was his special animal) and that, even after the anthropomorphisation of the god, the horns were preserved as the relic of the original representation. The horns of the Indus Valley Paśupati later came to be regarded as the crescent moon borne on his forehead by the Epic Śiva.[36]

The discovery of stones, varying in size and resembling the phallus, tends to confirm the authenticity of the above identification.[37] The phallic cult has been shown by several scholars to have been closely connected with Śaivism,[38] and this topic is studied in detail elsewhere in this work.[39] It is sometimes suggested that the phallic cult and the Paśupati cult of the Mohenjodaro times, though independent in origin, were amalgamated over the course of time, and that this fusion of these two cults was clearly evident in the *liṅga* worship of later Śaivism.[40]

Among the animals worshipped in the Indus religion was a powerful bull.[41] The bull occupies a prominent place in Śaivism. It is the vehicle of Śiva and at the same time is the crest of his banner. However, it may be incidentally pointed out that no instance can be cited where all these features, individually claimed to characterize

---

[34] See chapter V regarding the various images of Śiva discussed therein.

[35] Marshall, *op.cit.*, p. 54. Regarding the horns of the Mohenjodaro deity, see: Saletore, "The identification of a Mohenjodaro Figure", *N.R.*, vol. X, pp. 31-34. More as G.M. "A Mohenjodaro Figure", *N.R.*, vol. X, p. 443; Ghosh, "Siva — His Pre-Aryan origins", *IC.*, vol. II. p 764 ff.

[36] Dandekar, "Rudra in the *Veda*", *JUPH*, no. 1, pp. 141-142.

[37] Marshall, *op.cit.*, p. 54.

[38] Among these may be mentioned Marshall, Heras, Karmarkar, De, Diksitar, and Sur. Their views are discussed elsewhere in this work. A totally different view is maintained by Mahadevan.

[39] Chapter V of the present work.

[40] However, no positive evidence is advanced in support of this viewpoint.

[41] Marshall, *ibid.*, p. 72.

the Śaiva religion, are portrayed together. In other words, we cannot find a seal in which clear indications are given of the interconnection between the various cult-objects, Paśupati, the Mother goddess, the phallus, and the bull.

From the above study, we may draw the following conclusions about the Indus religion: first of all, there are no religious buildings which can be definitely identified as temples. Secondly, traces are found of several religious cults, such as the Mother cult, the Paśupati cult, the worship of certain cult objects like trees, and the adoration of phallic objects. Thirdly, the male god represented on the famous Paśupati seal, on account of his yogic posture, his three visible faces, and his being surrounded by beasts, is in all probability to be identified as the forerunner of the Epic Śiva. And fourthly, no clear indications are available regarding any interrelation among the various cults mentioned above.

In this connection a passing reference may be made to the attempts made by Father Heras to read the inscriptions of Mohenjo-daro and thereby determine the character of the religion of the Indus Valley. The method adopted by this scholar is not quite scientific and his interpretation of the seals is definitely unconvincing.[42] His interpretations are vitiated by his attempts to read into the Indus Valley inscriptions which belong to the second millennium BC, descriptive phrases and clauses which are modern in character. In some cases they are more modern than even the phrases and clauses which one meets with in the Tamil works of the classical type.[43] Unless a scientific

---

[42] The inefficiency of the method of interpretation of this scholar is thus pointed out: "Father Heras ... laboured with the pictograms discovered from the cities. He assumed that these pictograms were ideograms and tried to weave a consistent annal out of them. He substituted South Indian words for the pictures...How did he know that these pictures did not bear a Sanskrit, Hindi, Bengali or Marathi name? ... His views are influenced by other considerations and consequently the conclusions he draws are one-sided and biased". Samkarananda, *Rgvedic Culture of the Pre-historic Indus*, vol. I, pp. 51ff.

[43] Even a superficial comparison of both the dialects reveals this fact very clearly. There is hardly any phrase in the inscription which is sufficiently archaic to

approach was made to the study of the Indus Valley epigraphy and unless some clues were found as in the case of the hieroglyphics, it might not be possible to arrive at any useful conclusions in the matter.[44] The fact that the interpretations of the inscriptions on the seals by Heras are not quite reliable is even hinted at by his pupil, who seems to be inclined to rely mostly on the data available to him in the Vedic and the other works which he regards as accounts of Dravidian culture recorded in the Sanskrit language.[45]

2. The Ṛgvedic Period

Now we pass on to another period; here we are on firmer grounds insofar as the religious history of ancient India is concerned, for the materials we are able to gather help us to draw conclusions with far greater precision. The importance of the *Ṛgveda* as a cultural-historical sourcebook which has been preserved for posterity, more or less in its original form, is recognized by all.[46]

The position ascribed in the Vedic pantheon to Rudra, in whom we are able to identify the predecessor of the Epic Śiva, is of great significance for our study. This god inspired great awe among the beings, the only other god to have done so being Varuṇa,[47] who was once regarded as the greatest in the Vedic pantheon. Thus it becomes evident that the attitude of the people towards Rudra was, throughout the period, based on feelings of fearful devotion. As against this, the

---

indicate its antiquity. This even leads one to wonder whether this is probably due to the interpreter's lack of acquaintance with the less familiar Śaṅgam dialect, which differs very widely from modern Tamil.

44 Srikantha Sastri, however, holds the view that the language of the Indus inscriptions is not primitive Dravidian, Munda or Burushaski, but primitive Indonesian. Hunter thinks that the Indus signs were borrowed from Austric predecessors. See *QJMS*, vol. XXXII, no. 3, p. 291.

45 Karmarkar, *The Religions of India*, vol. I, pp. 29ff.

46 Winternitz, *A History of Indian Literature*, vol. I, pp. 37ff.

47 "Varuṇa is invoked in far fewer hymns than Indra, Agni or Soma, but he is undoubtedly the greatest of the Vedic gods by the side of Indra." Macdonell, *Vedic Mythology*, p. 54.

minor position of this god in the pantheon is implied by the infrequency of hymns addressed to him. This is a kind of paradox relating to Ṛgvedic Rudra — a paradox, which, indeed, supplies the key to the proper understanding of the personality of the god. As we pass from the Ṛgveda to the later strata of Vedic literature, we begin to feel the gradual growth of the importance and popularity of this god. Of course, the peculiar manner in which Rudra is sought to be isolated from the other gods of the Vedic hierarchy within Vedic ritual continues to be evident even in later Vedic literature.

The Ṛgveda presents a religion which is totally different from that of the Mohenjodaro times. Here, perhaps for the first time, we come across a rich pantheon of divinities, all of which differ from one another in their functions and characteristics. Of these, Indra, being the most often invoked, (*puruhūta*), was certainly the most popular god. This is plainly evident from the number of hymns which celebrate him.[48] Next in importance to him is Agni.[49] In the Ṛgvedic pantheon, a very minor position is assigned to Rudra. He has only three full hymns addressed to him.[50] He is mentioned in the Ṛgveda only seventy times in all.[51] Even on the basis of this meager material it is necessary to reconstruct the personality of Rudra with a view to finding out how and to what extent he is related to the Epic Śiva.

A clear picture of Rudra is given to us in the Ṛgveda, with distinctive representations of his physical features. Explicit references are made to his hands [52] and arms [53] and to his limbs [54] and lips.[55] The

---

48 "His importance is indicated by the fact that about 250 hymns celebrate his greatness more than those devoted to any other god, and very nearly one-fourth of the total number of hymns of the *Ṛgveda.*" Macdonell, *Vedic Mythology*, p. 54.

49 "Next to Indra, he is the most prominent of the Vedic gods. He is celebrated in at least 200 hymns of the *Ṛgveda.*" *ibid.*, p. 83.

50 *ṚV*, II.33; I.114;VII.46.

51 His name occurs about 75 times. Macdonell, *op.cit.*, p. 74.

52 *Rudra mṛḷayākur hastaḥ. ṚV*, II.33.7.

53 *Vajrabāho. ṚV*, II.33.3.

braided hair [56] which he wears is highly significant. His complexion is brown.[57] He has a dazzling appearance, and his brilliance [58] engages the attention of the Vedic poet.

Rudra is armed with weapons of offence. He carries the thunderbolt.[59] He is armed with a bow and arrows,[60] and they are strong and swift.[61] This bow is later retained by Śiva, and he wields it with an attribution of a special name Pināka to it. It is even possible that the thunderbolt mentioned above developed into the *triśūla*.

Rudra has often been described as being constituted of two distinctly opposite personalities. He is fierce [62] and destructive [63] yet at the same time is kind and benign.[64] He is the strongest of the strong [65] and is depicted as the ruddy boar of heaven.[66] Epithets such as 'bull',[67] indicative of immense physical strength, are showered on

---

[54] *Sthirebhir aṅgaiḥ pururūpa ugro*, "with firm limbs, of many forms and terrific" *ṚV*, II.33.9.

[55] *Susipraḥ*. *ṚV*, *II*.33.5.

[56] *Kapardiṇe*. *ṚV*, I.114.1.

[57] *Babhruḥ*. *ṚV*, II.33.5.

[58] *Yaḥ śukra iva sūryo hiraṇyamiva rocate*, "He who shines like Śukra, like Sūrya, like gold". *ṚV*, I.43.5.

[59] *Vajrabāho*. *ṚV*, II.33.3.

[60] *Arhan bibharṣi sāyakāni dhanva*. *ṚV*, II.33.10.

[61] *Imā rudrāya sthiradhanvane ... kṣipreṣave*, "to Rudra whose bow is strong and arrow swift". *ṚV*, VII.46.1.

[62] *Ugraḥ*. *ṚV*, III.33.9. and *ṚV*, X.126.5.

[63] *Upahatnum*. *ṚV*, II.33.11. The *Purāṇas* usually depict him as a calm and peaceful looking god, and to this god of benign qualities the devotees were attracted. But his fury also formed the subject matter of some passages in the *Purāṇas*. This was especially when the gods were oppressed by demons. However, it must be noted that the god is never to be represented in his dreadful form for purpose of worship. The Āgamic texts strictly lay down the rule that the images meant for worship should be devoid of such features. The Śanta aspect, on the other hand, is to be amply displayed.

[64] *Mṛḷayākuḥ*. *ṚV*, 11.33.7.

[65] *Tavastamas tavasām*. *ṚV*, II.33.3.

[66] *Divo varāham aruṣam*. *ṚV*, I.114.5.

[67] *Vṛṣabhaḥ*. *ṚV*, II.33.7.

him. He is the exalted one,[68] always swift and rapid,[69] ever-young [70] and unaging.[71] He is unassailable [72] and unsurpassed in might.[73] Moreover, he is intelligent,[74] wise [75] and beneficient.[76] This self-glorious god [77] rules over the heroes.[78] He is the lord of the world [79] and wins for himself the epithet *īśāna*. Later on, the name *Īśvara*, an appellation derived similarly, is exclusively reserved for Śiva. By his rule and universal sovereignty, he is aware of the doings of men and gods.[80] He is exalted as the father of the world.[81]

Many a time he is called the bountiful god.[82] This easily-invoked god claims for himself the epithet 'auspicious'.[83] This epithet, it is suggested, is used euphemistically, to counteract the natural dreadfulness of the god. It is, however, with this application, that this god gains great prominence in later literature.

As pointed out above, malevolence is a quality frequently assigned to Rudra in the Ṛgveda. He is repeatedly requested not to injure or slay his worshippers, their children, or their cattle. His shafts

---

68 *Bṛhantam*. *ṚV*, VII.10.4.

69 *Prarudreṇa yayinā*. *ṚV*, X.92.5.

70 *Yuvā pitā svapā rudra eṣāṁ*. *ṚV*, V.60.5.

71 *Ajaram*. *ṚV*, VI.49.10.

72 *Aṣāḷhāya*. *ṚV*, VII.46.1.

73 *Ojīyaḥ*. *ṚV*, II.33.10.

74 *Kad rudrāya pracetase*. *ṚV*, I.43.1.

75 *Kavim*. *ṚV*, I.114.4.

76 *Suṣumnam*. *ṚV*, VI.49.10.

77 *Rudrāya svayaśase*. *ṚV*, I.129.3.

78 *Rudrāya ... kṣayadvīrāya*. *ṚV*, I.114.1 and 2.

79 *Īśanād asya bhuvanasya*. *ṚV*, II.33.9.

80 *Sa hi kṣayeṇa kṣamyasya janmanaḥ Sāmrājyena divyasya cetasi*. *ṚV*, VII.46.2.

81 *Bhuvanasya pitaram*. *ṚV*, VI.49.10.
This became a common concept in later times. Kalidāsa refers to Śiva in similar terms: *Jagataḥ pitarau vande Pārvatīparameśvarau* (*Raghuvaṁśa*, I.1.). The Śaiva saints of South India, too, address the god as both father and mother.

82 *Mīḍhvaḥ*. *ṚV*, I.114.3. The liberality of this god is evident in the Epics and the *Purāṇas*, especially in the latter, where he is described as without reserve bestowing on the devotees whatever objects they desire from him.

83 *Śivaḥ*. *ṚV*, X.29.9.

are always dreaded and the appeasement of his wrath is always solicited.[84] In the Ṛgveda itself, Rudra once receives the epithet 'man-slaying'.[85]

But great benevolence is also a characteristic feature this god. He is sought to pacify the anger and the evil that came from the gods.[86] He is prayed to [87] not only for the sake of protection but also for bestowal of blessings.[88] He is invoked to bring about welfare for men and beasts.[89] It may be pointed out that his lordship over man as well as beast ultimately became a prominent characteristic of the god.

Rudra could be beneficient to his worshippers in another way. He was the master of the art of healing [90] and his remedies often cured the sickness of the ailing supplicants. He is said to be possessing a thousand remedies,[91] and his hands too are glorified as restorative and healing.[92] He raises up the heroes with his remedies, and thus

---

[84] *Mā no mahāntam uta mā no arbhakaṁ mā na ukṣantam mā na ukṣitam | Mā no vadhīḥ pitaraṁ mota mātaraṁ mā naḥ priyāstanvo rudra rīriṣaḥ ||*
"Do not kill the great among us, nor the small one, nor our bull, nor the crop grown by us, nor our father, nor our mother, nor our dear selves, o Rudra, in a desire to harm." *ṚV*, I.114.7-8.

[85] *Rudrāya nṛghne*. *ṚV*, IV.3.6. It is significant that this quality attributed to Vedic Rudra disappears almost completely in later times. The idea that he is the lord of beings (*paśupati*) comes to the fore-front, and this idea is emphasized in the subsequent religious texts. In the Epics and the *Purāṇas* his anger is shown to be directed only against the demons, several of whom he is described in these texts to have destroyed.

[86] *Āre asmad daivyaṁ heḷo asyatu*. "Throw away far from us the divine anger." *ṚV*, I.114.4. Cf. Griswold, *The Religion of the Ṛgveda* p. 298.

[87] *Svasti no rudraḥ pātu aṁhasaḥ*. "Hail! May Rudra protect us from evil." *ṚV*, V.51.13.

[88] *Unmā mamanda vṛṣabho marutvān tvakṣīyasā vayasā nādhamānam.*
"He, the bull, beyond measure, rejoiced the one praying him with the most vigorous health." *ṚV*, II.33.6.

[89] *Śaṁ naḥ karatyarvate sugaṁ meṣāya meṣye nṛbhyo nāribhyo gave.*
"May he bring happiness, easy of access, to the horse, the ram, the ewe, the men, the women and the cow." *ṚV*, I.43.6.

[90] *Bheṣajā rāsi*. *ṚV*, II.33.12 and VII.46.3.

[91] *Sahasraṁ te bheṣajā*. *ṚV*, VII.46.3.

[92] *Mṛḷayākur hastaḥ*. *ṚV*, II.33.7.

wins for himself the distinction of being the greatest physician among physicians.[93] Some of the temples of South India maintain this ancient Vedic tradition by ascribing such names as Vaidyeśvara and Vaidyanātha to Śiva enshrined within.

Tryambaka,[94] a common epithet of Śiva in later religion, is already applied to Rudra in the Ṛgveda at least once.[95] This has a different implication altogether; here it merely means that he is a god who has three mothers or sisters.

The significant association of Rudra with the *munis* who are mentioned in the tenth *maṇḍala* has been emphasized. Through that association the Vedic Rudra is sought to be related to later Śiva.[96] This hymn,[97] it has been pointed out, portrays a distinct religious cult, the cult of the *munis*, and provides a graphic description of its adherents. They are called *munis*. They wear long hair and have a tawny complexion. They are described as wearing dirty garments. They follow the course of the wind and are said to have attained divinity. The occult powers which they have acquired are indicated by reference to their wading through the firmament, illumining all objects. Many a time the *munis* are associated with Vāyu in the *muni-sūkta*, and this is a sure indication that they were endowed with superhuman powers attainable through *yoga*. The description of these *munis* wearing coloured garments as wandering through the sky, and as treading the tracts of the Apsarases and the Gandharvas, reminds one of the mysterious achievements of the *yogins*. Rudra is associated with them, sharing a cup of poison with them. This reference naturally suggests an identification of the two gods, Rudra and Śiva.

---

93 *Bheṣajāṁ bhiṣaktamam*. *ṚV*, II.33.4.

94 For a discussion of the appellation *Tryaṁbaka*, see F. Singh, "Rudra", *IHQ*, vol. XVI, p. 788.

95 *ṚV*, VII.59.12. See also Keith, *The Religion and Philosophy of the Veda and the Upaniṣads*, *HOS*, vol. 31, p. 143.

96 Dandekar, "Rudra in the *Veda*", *Journal of the University of Poona*, no. 1, p. 100.

97 *ṚV*, X.136.

3. Rudra in the Atharvaveda

Most of the gods of the *Ṛgveda* appear in the *Atharvaveda*. "But their character has quite faded, and they hardly differ from each other ... and as the magic songs deal mostly with the banishment and destruction of demons — the gods being invoked only for this purpose — they have all become demon killers." [98] It may, however, be pointed out that this observation made by Winternitz does not apply to Rudra, who maintains intact his identity in the *Atharvaveda*, mainly his terror-inspiring personality. He continues to be dreaded and so do his bow and arrows. As a matter of fact, the concept of Rudra becomes more dynamic in the *Atharvaveda*, possibly through its amalgamation with that of Bhava and Śarva, especially the latter, who himself was an eminent archer.

Bhava and Śarva, originally different from Rudra,[99] are mentioned in the *Atharvaveda* and both share the characteristics of Rudra. In the hymns in which these two are addressed, Rudra is substituted either for one or for the other; thus did the identity of Rudra with Bhava and Śarva finally come to be established. Bhava and Śarva are always united and accordant.[100]

Black locks are ascribed to Rudra. He is thousand-eyed [101] and dark in complexion.[102] The devotee pays obeisance to his face, eyes, skin, form, aspect, limbs, belly, tongue, mouth, teeth and nose.[103] Rudra rides in a chariot.[104] Thus, in this *Veda* we come across a rich display of the anthropomorphic features of the god.

---

[98] Winternitz, *History of Indian Literature*, vol. I, p. 124.

[99] Dandekar, *op.cit.*, p. 99.

[100] *Bhavārudrau sayujā saṁvidānau*. *AV*, XI. 2.14.

[101] *Nīlaśikhaṇḍena sahasrākṣeṇa rudreṇa*. *AV*, XI.2.7.

[102] *Śyāvāśvaṁ Kṛṣṇam asitam*. *AV*, XI.2.18.

[103] *Mukhāya te paśupate yāni cakṣūmṣi te bhava |*
Tvace rūpāya sandṛśe pratīcīnāya te namaḥ ||
Aṅgebhyasta udarāya jihvāyā āsyāya te |
Dadbhyo gandhāya te namaḥ || *AV*, XI.2.5-6.

[104] *Mṛṇantaṁ bhīmaṁ ratham*. *AV*, XI.2.18.

Śarva wields a golden bow.[105] Far flies the shaft of Rudra.[106] Bhava and Śarva are implored not to discharge their long arrow.[107] Rudra fires his shafts in the presence of his worshippers.[108] Besides these weapons, Rudra employs various diseases as his weapons, which he directs against his foes. Cough and fever [109] are the most dreaded. He is implored not to overwhelm the worshippers with fever or poison, nor with the fire that comes from Heaven. He is besought to favour those who offer him worship.[110]

Bhava and Śarva are fierce gods.[111] Prayers are offered to them for safe delivery from calamity.[112] Śarva is renowned for his skill in archery,[113] and both he and Bhava are worthy of reverence.[114] This god is repeatedly implored to be gracious, and afford protection, to remove calamity and give life. He is described to be manifoldedly wise. He views the whole world and thus superintends the movements of all beings.[115]

Bhava and Śarva launch their lightning against the wicked and also against those who practise sorcery.[116] They are lords or spirits and birds and beasts.[117] They are besought to not be hostile and also not to discharge their long arrow. "Shoot not the arrow aimed and drawn against us" [118] is the earnest prayer of the devotee. Fear is constantly expressed of harm from the god to bipeds and quadru-

---

105 *Dhanur bibharṣi haritaṁ hiraṇyayam. AV*, XI.2.12.

106 *Rudrasyeṣuh carati. AV*, XI.2.12.

107 *Pratihitām āyatāṁ mā visrāṣṭam. AV*, XI.2.1.

108 *Sahasrākṣam atipaśyaṁ purastād rudram asyantaṁ bahudhā. AV*, XI.2.17.

109 *Yasya takmā kāsikā hetirekam. AV*, XI.2.22.

110 *Bhava rājan yajamānāya mṛḍa. AV*, XI. 2.28.

111 *Ni tasmin dhattaṁ vajram ugrau. AV*, IV.28.6.

112 *Bhavāśarvau ... no muñcatu aṁhasaḥ. AV*, IV.28.1.

113 *Babhruḥ śarvo'stā nīlaśikhaṇḍaḥ. AV*, VI.93.1 and also *Śarvāyāstre, ibid*, verse 2.

114 *Namasyebhyo nama ebhyaḥ. AV*, VI.93.2.

115 *Na te dūraṁ pariṣṭhāsti te bhava sadyaḥ sarvān paripaśyasi bhūmim. AV*, XI.2.25.

116 *Bhavāśarvau asyatāṁ pāpakṛte kṛtyākṛte duṣkṛte vidyutaṁ deva hetim. AV*, X.1.23.

117 *Bhavāśarvau mṛḍataṁ mā bhiyātaṁ bhūtapatī paśupatī namo vāṁ. AV*, XI.2.1.

118 *Pratihitām āyatāṁ mā visrāṣṭam. AV*, XI.2.1.

peds,[119] and anxiety often expressed as to whether he would abandon their bodies to the dogs with mighty mouths. "Covet not thou our kine or men or goats or sheep." [120] Such are prayers usually addressed to Rudra, Bhava and Śarva.

In the *Atharvaveda*, Rudra (Bhava and Śarva) is called Paśupati many a time. Five kinds of animals are within his domain — the kine, horses, men, goat and sheep.[121] He is *ugra*.[122] Whatever breathes on earth is his. He is the ruler of Heaven and the lord of the earth.[123] All the sorcerers act under his behest.[124] He is once mentioned as the slayer of Andhaka.[125] The stars and the moon are under his control.

The fifteenth book of the *Atharvaveda* contains the *vrātya* hymns [126] in which the highest *Brahman* is conceived and exalted as *vrātya*. They seem to speak of the two aspects of the *vrātya*, identified with the great god — Mahādeva, the lord Īśāna, Rudra, and the other, his prototype, the earthly *vrātya*.[127] Strangely enough, some of the qualities attributed to the *vrātyas* bear resemblance to those of Rudra. The *vrātyas* seem to have been beyond the pale of brahminical circles, but they could be accepted within the fold of orthodoxy by virtue of their sacrifices. The achievements of the Ekavrātya are thus recounted: "He became Mahādeva. He gained the lordship of the gods. He became lord. He became the chief *vrātya*. He held a bow. His belly is dark blue and his back is red. At the instigation of the gods, Rudra in his

---

[119] *Mā no hiṁsiṣṭaṁ dvipado mā catuṣpadaḥ*. *AV*, XI.2.1.

[120] *Mā no goṣu puruṣeṣu mā gṛdho no ajāviṣu*. *AV*, XI.2.21.

[121] *Taveme pañca paśavo vibhaktā gāvo aśvāḥ puruṣā ajāvayaḥ*. *AV*, XI.2.9.

[122] *Ugrau*. *AV*, IV.28.3 and also XI.2.21.

[123] *Tava catasraḥ pradiśas tava dyaus tava pṛthivī tavedam ugrorvantarikṣam* |
Tavedaṁ sarvam ātmanvad yat prāṇat pṛthivīm anu ||
"Yours are the four directions, yours the sky, yours the earth, yours this intermediary space, yours all that has a self, yours all that breathes on the earth, you are fierce." *AV*, XI.2.10.

[124] *Tasyeme sarve yātava upa praśiṣamāsate*. *AV*, XIII.4.27.

[125] *Rudreṇāndhakaghātinā*. *AV*, XI.2.7. A variant reading of *andhaka* as *ardhaka* is also found.

[126] *AV*, XV, hymns 1-18.

[127] Winternitz, *op.cit.*, p. 154.

various aspects as Bhava, Śarva, Ugra, Rudra, Mahādeva and Īśāna is ascribed to the various regions as the archer to guard the *vrātya*."[128]

Another hymn which deserves special attention from the point of view of our study is the *Brahmacāri-sūkta*.[129] This has often been explained as extolling the Vedic student.[130] However, a few of the characteristic features of the *brahmacārin* are seen to be against the theory. The hymn also cannot be understood as referring to the concept of *Brahman*. The distinctive features of the *brahmacārin* lead to the assumption of the existence of a *brahmacārī*-cult.[131] Following a life of rigorous discipline, as indicated by the occurrence of such terms as *samidh*, *mekhalā*, *śrama*, *tapas*, *gharma*, *bhikṣā*, the *brahmacārins* are described as "clothing themselves with heat (*gharma*), and standing up with fervour (*tapas*)". The *gandharvas*, also connected with Śiva in later mythology, are associated with the *brahmacārī*, the former being described as following the latter.

4. Rudra in the Yajurveda

The elevation of Rudra to a higher position is clearly evident in the Yajurveda. The simultaneous and steady rise to prominence of Rudra and Prajāpati in that *Veda* seems to proclaim in advance that, over the course of time, these two gods are destined to emerge out of the Vedic pantheon as the most powerful gods. It was towards the end of the Vedic and the beginning of the Epic period that these two gods along with Viṣṇu formed a group by themselves. However, this Trimūrti concept is entirely foreign to Vedic religion.

Great awe for Rudra is the keynote of the relationship that seems to have existed in the *Yajurveda* between the deity and the devotee. Not only the god himself, but also his bow and arrows, and even his choleric temper which constantly roused the sense of awe in the mind of the Vedic worshipper, became the object of reverence.

[128] *AV*, XV 5.1-21.

[129] *AV*, XI 5.

[130] Whitney, *Atharvaveda Saṁhitā*, vol. II, p. 636.

[131] Dandekar, *op.cit.*, p. 100.

The *Śatarudriya*, included in the *Vājasaneyi* [132] and the *Taittirīya*[133] *saṁhitās*, is a collection of verses which is important for two main reasons. First of all, it contains various names of Rudra shared by the Epic Śiva, making the identification of these two gods very easy. Secondly, the series of datives in the texts of the *Śatarudriya*, each followed by *namas*,[134] has helped formation of specific religious formulas, such as *hiraṇyabāhave namaḥ*, *diśāñcapataye namaḥ*, etc. The mode of *arcanā*, employing these formulae with *namas* at the end, is a regular feature of the *arcanā* ritual in the South. Worshipping gods and goddesses by means of the recitation of one thousand names (*sahasranāma*), three hundred names (*triśatī*), or one hundred and eight names (*aṣṭottaraśatanāma*) is a common occurrence in the daily rituals of the temples in South India.

We shall now proceed to form a picture of Rudra in accordance with the description of that god in the *Yajurveda*. We shall particularly note all such characteristics of Rudra that have been inherited by his Epic successor.

Rudra's blessed body is auspicious.[135] It is not terrible, nor does it betoken harm. Red is the distinctive colour of this god, and attributes chosen to describe him imply redness or any other colour approximating it. He is copper-coloured,[136] ruddy or brown. He is golden-haired,[137] golden-armed [138] and thousand-eyed. His neck is blue,[139] and his hair is arranged in a peculiar style which give him the name Kapardin.[140] He wears *yajñopavīta* [141] and is clad in a

[132] *VS*, XVI.7.51.

[133] *TS*, IV.5.1.

[134] *TS*, IV.5.1.17 onwards.

[135] *Śivā tanūḥ*. *TS*, IV.1.2.

[136] *Asau yas tāmro aruṇa uta babhruḥ sumaṅgalaḥ*. *TS*, IV.5.1.6.

[137] *Namo harikeśāya*. *TS*, IV.5.1.17.

[138] *Namo hiraṇyabāhave*. *TS*, IV.5.1.17.

[139] *Nīlagrīvāya sahasrākṣāya*. *TS*, IV.5.1.8.

[140] *Kapardine*. *TS*, IV.5.10, also IV.5.1.20 and IV.5.1.44.

[141] *Upavītine*. *TS*, IV.5.1.IV.

skin.[142] He is even described as wearing a turban.[143] He is of a short stature and is called a dwarf.[144]

Of all the weapons borne by Rudra, it is the bow and arrow that are dreaded most. The poet-devotee with great awe pays obeisance to the god's bow and his arms,[145] which wield deadly weapons. Rudra is implored to loosen the strings from both the ends of his bow,[146] and to discard the arrows which he carries in his hand.[147] It is often desired that his bow should at all times be devoid of a bowstring [148] and his quiver should contain blunt shafts.[149] Besides his bow with which he terrifies people, Rudra also wields a sword [150] which is a source of fear to them. However, it may be noted that the *triśūla*, a prominent weapon of the Epic Śiva, is not mentioned in this *Veda*.

Rudra is described as the dweller of the mountain.[151] He is the

---

[142] *Kṛttiṁ vasānaḥ*. IV.5.1.17.
In the Purāṇic mythology, Śiva is representing as wearing the skin of some animal. This is sometimes described as the skin of the elephant (*Matsya P.*, 154.4301; *Padma P.*, I.43.385.), sometimes the skin of the tiger, (*Kūrma P.*, I.25.51), and at times even the skin of the lion (*Vāmana P.*, 52.6). In one place he is described as wearing the skins of all these animals (*Padma P.*, I.46.21-2).

[143] *Nama uṣṇīṣiṇe*. *TS*, IV.5.1.22.

[144] *Namo hrasvāya ca*. *TS*, IV.5.1.30.

[145] *Ubhābhyām uta te namo bāhubhyāṁ tava dhanvane*. *TS*, IV.5.1.14.

[146] *Pramuñca dhanvanas tvam ubhaya ārtnyor jyām*. *TS*, IV.5.1.9.
The bow of Śiva slowly disappears, and the description of Śiva given in the *Purāṇas* and the representation of the god installed in the temples of South India generally present him with the *paraśu*, *mṛga*, and his other two arms in the *varada* and the *abhaya* poses. However, two representations of Śiva, and the relevant descriptions in the *Purāṇas*, reveal him as wielding a bow. One of them is Kirāta, the bestower of the divine weapon of Arjuna. The other is Tripurāntaka, the destroyer of the three cities. The appellation Pinākin has gained universal recognition in religious circles, and it is a name specially characteristic of Śiva.

[147] *Yāsca te hasta iṣavaḥ parā tā vapa*. *TS*, IV.5.1.9.

[148] *Vijyaṁ dhanuḥ*. *TS*, IV.5.1.10.

[149] *Viśalyo bāṇavan uta*. *TS*, IV.5.1.3.

[150] *Kakubhāya niṣangiṇe*. *TS*, IV.5.1.20.

[151] *Giriśanta*. *TS*, IV.5.1.3. *Girīśa*. *Ibid.*, IV.5.1.4. *Giriśāya*. IV.5.1.29. This tradition of associating Rudra with the mountain became stronger in the later Śaiva religion. The Epic and the Purāṇic literature mention Kailāsa as the abode of Śiva.

lord of the beasts.[152] So fierce and terrible is the god that his gracious favour is repeatedly sought.[153] He is glorified in this *Veda* as a bringer of prosperity and happiness,[154] and also as the most gracious one.[155] He is implored not to slay men and cattle. With auspicious words do the worshippers supplicate him that all their cattle and men be healthy and cheerful.[156] He is auspicious and therefore called Śiva.[157] He is the bringer of prosperity, and is therefore named Śaṅkara.[158] These two appellations mentioned in the *Yajurveda* became more common in later mythology. He is the first divine physician.[159] Rudra is described as being surrounded by attendant spirits. The Rudras, thousands of them, surround him on all sides. In later mythology these came to be known by specific names, *pramatha-gaṇas*, of whom Nandin and sometimes Gaṇeśa are described as leaders.[160]

Names, such as Rudra, Ugra, Bhīma, Bhava, Śarva, Paśupati, Nīlagrīva and Śrīkaṇṭha occur prominently in the *Yajurveda*, and persist to this day as apellations of Śiva frequently employed in the rituals.

---

[152] *Paśūnāṁ pataye namaḥ*. *TS*, IV.5.1.17; also *paśupataye*, *ibid.*, verses 28 and 40.

[153] *Mīḍhuṣṭama śivatama śivo naḥ sumanā bhava*. *TS*, IV.5.1.41.

[154] *Śaṁbhave ca mayobhave ca*. *TS*, IV.5.1.41.

[155] *Mīdḥuṣṭama*. *TS*, IV.5.1.51.

[156] *Āsāṁ prajānāṁ eṣāṁ paśūnaṁ mā bher mā roṅ mo ca naḥ kiñcanāmamat*. *TS*, IV.5.1.47.

[157] *Namaḥ śivāya ca*. *TS*, IV.5.1.41.

[158] *Namaḥ śaṅkarāya*. *TS*, IV.5.1.41.

[159] *Prathamo daivyo bhiṣak*. *TS*, IV.5.1.

[160] "In the post-Vedic literature, Rudra is represented as being followed by various classes of spirits and demoniac beings often referred to as Rudragaṇas, *bhūtas* or the Śiva-*gaṇas* most of whom show an essential affinity with the original Rudras. It would thus seem that the relationship between Rudra and the Rudras was original and organic, that it was temporarily suppressed in the *Ṛgveda*, and the Maruts took the place of the Rudras, that in the later *Vedas* the ancient Rudra-Rudras combination was revived, and that, finally, in the post-Vedic literature the ancient Rudras assumed the form of the Rudra-gaṇas or Śiva-gaṇas." Dandekar, *op.cit.*, p. 104.

5. Rudra in the Brāhmaṇas

The *Brāhmaṇas* are essentially exegetical in character. Indeed, they constitute the earliest commentaries on the Vedic *saṁhitās*. It must be pointed out that the *Brāhmaṇas* seek to interpret the *saṁhitās* mainly — or even exclusively — from the ritualistic point of view. They assume that the verses, formulas, and chants collected in the Vedic *saṁhitās* are intended to be employed within a sacrificial ritual. Thus mythology, which implies the celebration of gods, now falls into the background and sacrifice becomes the central theme. Whatever little mythology there is in the *Brāhmaṇas* is made subservient to the ritual. Insofar as the personality and character of the Vedic gods are concerned, the *Brāhmaṇas* add but little to what has already been said in the *saṁhitās*. Nevertheless, we do come across some references to Rudra in the *Brāhmaṇas*, and on the basis of these it is possible to reconstruct a picture of the *Brāhmaṇic* Rudra.

Generally speaking, in the period of the *Brāhmaṇas*, most of the early Vedic gods begin to lose their importance because, as indicated above, the centre of attraction had shifted from the gods to the sacrifice.[161] Rudra, however, seems to represent an exception to this general rule; the portrayal of Rudra in the *Brāhmaṇas* clearly indicates this god's ascendancy to power. This elevation of Rudra becomes all the more conspicuous on the background of the minor position occupied by him in the *Ṛgveda*. In the *Brāhmaṇas*, Rudra has a strong rival in Prajāpati who also now rises to higher ranks.[162] Rudra is represented to have overpowered Prajāpati.[163] The events relating to this incident are recounted in the *Brāhmaṇas* in detail. We are told of the incest of Prajāpati.[164] The gods were determined to chastise him. Out of their frightful forms they fashioned Bhūtapati.

---

[161] About the Vedic gods as represented in the *Brāhmaṇas*, Winternitz says: "But their significance has faded, and they owe all their power they possess to the sacrifice alone". *History of Indian Literature*, vol. I, p. 196.

[162] *Aitareya Brāhmaṇa*, II.33.

[163] Compare *Śatapatha Brāhmaṇa*, I.7.4.1, II.11.2.8, VI.1.2.8.

[164] *Aitareya Brāhmaṇa*, III.33.

This incident hints at the supremacy which Rudra establishes over Prajāpati.[165]

The *Aitareya-Brāhmaṇa* ascribes a very high place to Rudra. The *Kauśītaki* also adds to the greatness of the god; and this it has done to such an extent that Rudra is definitely raised above the other gods in the *Brāhmaṇas*. This fact is, first of all, reflected in the assignment of a name to Rudra, which hints at his being greater than other gods. He is Mahādeva,[166] the Great God *par excellence*. He is not only great, but also powerful. Īśāna [167] is another name of this god, and this name indicates the power or ruling capacity which he possesses in great measure. Īśāna, Īśa, Īśvara and similar other appellations, such as Maheśa, Maheśvara, Parameśvara, continue even in the later religious literature to be used exclusively for Śiva. Among other names assigned to Rudra by the *Kauśītaki-Brāhmaṇa* are Śarva, Paśupati, Ugra, Rudra, Īśāna and Aśani.

In the *Śatapatha Brāhmaṇa*, Rudra is once mentioned as hundred-headed, thousand-eyed, and hundred-quivered.[168] He is the golden-armed leader of the hosts.[169] He is most kindly yet was originally called *manyu* (angry).[170] Often he is identified with Agni.[171]

There are two passages in the *Brāhmaṇas*, one in the *Śatapatha* and the other in the *Śāṅkhāyana*, which describe the incident which led to the assignment of the various names of Rudra. We are told that this god once began to weep. He was asked why he did so; he replied that he was nameless and requested that he be given a name. Prajāpati responded to his request and gave him a name befitting this action. Because he wept (*arodīt*), he got the name Rudra. Rudra persistently insisted on getting more names, and received eight in all. These are Bhava, Śarva, Paśupati, Ugra, Mahādeva, Rudra, Īśāna, and Aśani.[172]

---

[165] Keith, *Religion and Philosophy of the Veda and the Upanishads*, p. 145.

[166] *HOS*, vol. 25, p. 25.

[167] *Kausītaki Brāhmaṇa*, VI.1.3.10-17. [168] *Śatapatha Brāhmaṇa*, IV.157.

[169] *Ibid.*, IV.160. [170] *Ibid.*, III.157.

[171] *Ibid.*, III.51-64, also III.158 and 159, also I.340.

[172] *Śatapatha Brāhmaṇa*, VI.1.3.10-18, also *Kauśītaki-Brāhmaṇa*, VI.2.ff.

The *Śāṅkhāyana-Brāhmaṇa* associated with these eight names respectively the eight elements, namely water, Agni, Vāyu, the planets, the trees, *āditya*, the moon, food and Indra. We may discern [173] in this eightfold nomenclature a forerunner of the later eight forms of Śiva which were said to constitute his divine body. Of course, the eight elements mentioned in the *Brāhmaṇas* are not wholly identical with those mentioned in the later religious texts.

It is once recounted in the *Brāhmaṇas* that Agni was created as the hundred-headed Rudra.[174] He is the newly-kindled fire.[175] He is Agni in his immortal form.[176] In the process of this identification of Agni with Rudra, the *Brāhmaṇa* mentions the names of Rudra as those of Agni. The following are the names thus mentioned: Śarva, Bhava, Paśūnāṁ-pati, Rudra and Agni.[177] All the names in this list except Agni are said to be ungentle. Therefore, only the gentle appellation, Agni, is retained.

The North is characterized as Rudra's special region.[178] Rudra rules over beasts.[179] He is Paśupati, the lord of beasts.[180] In one of the *Brāhmaṇa* passages, he is described as having been formed of a compound of all terrible substances.[181] He is the ruler of animals.[182] He pursues creatures. Even the gods are afraid of his strung bow and the arrows, for he is powerful enough to destroy them.[183] He is once described as *hotar*.[184] He craves the slaughtered cow,[185] and under the name Mahādeva he is said to slay cattle.[186] He is the *kṣatra*, whereas the Rudras are the *viś*.[187] When the gods rose to heaven, Rudra

---

[173] *Śāṅkhāyana Brāhmaṇa*, VI.1.2-9.

[174] *Śatapatha Brāhmaṇa*, IV.201.

[175] *Ibid.*, I.340. [176] *Ibid.*, III.156. [177] *Ibid.*, I.201.

[178] *Śatapatha Brāhmaṇa*, IV.2.10, also XI.1.1.10; XIV.2.2.38.

[179] *Ibid.*, III.6.2.20; I.7.33.8; VI.3.2.10. [180] *Ibid.*, V.3.37.

[181] *Aitareya-Brāhmaṇa*, III.33.1.

[182] *Śatapatha Brāhmaṇa*, XII.7.3.20.

[183] *Ibid.*, IX.1.1.1-6. [184] *Ibid.*, IV.3.4.25. [185] *Ibid.*, V.3.1.9.

[186] *Tāṇḍyamahā Brāhmaṇa*, VI.9.7.

[187] *Śatapatha Brāhmaṇa*, IX.1.1.15. I.1.1.25.

remained behind.[188] Oblations of wild sesamum and sometimes *gavedhūka* flour on an *arka* leaf are offered to Rudra.[189] He is worshipped with mystic syllables.[190] The *tryaṁbaka* oblations are offered to Rudra.[191] By means of this, the sacrificer is said to deliver from Rudra's power those that are born and those yet to be born; the sacrificer's offspring shall not suffer from disease or blemish. This offering is sometimes made on roads, as these are known to be the favourite haunts of Rudra. At the end of the *tryaṁbaka homa*, Rudra is told: "These are thy portions. Therewith depart beyond Mūjavant".

The *Śatapatha Brāhmaṇa* mentions Ambikā as the sister of Rudra, and not as his consort.[192] She is the dispenser of happiness.

6. Rudra in the Upaniṣads

The religious setting of ancient India undergoes a distinct transformation during the Upaniṣadic period. Curiously enough, Rudra has now the highest attributes ascribed to him, and these attributes are for the most part abstract in nature. In a sense, the god becomes more and more difficult to grasp. His identity with Brahmaṇ is established. It is clearly stressed that, through knowledge of this god, one attains liberation; "only by knowing him does one pass over death. There is no other path going there." [193]

It must be noted that, in the *Upaniṣads*, stress is no longer put upon the anthropomorphic features of the god, nor on the weapons he wields, nor even his terrifying nature. The description of the external features of the god, where it is at all attempted, does in no way help the average devotee to easily visualize his personality. The *Śvetāśvatara Upaniṣad* is the earliest of the Śaiva *Upaniṣads* and belongs to a fairly early period. It is, therefore, this Upaniṣad which has been taken as the main basis for our study of Rudra in the *Upaniṣads*; and all the references are from that *Upaniṣad*.

[188] *Ibid.*, I.7.3.1.

[189] *Ibid.*, IX.1.1.8.

[190] *Ibid.*, IX.1.1.22.

[191] *Ibid.*, I. 438.

[192] *Taittirīya Brāhmaṇa*, I.6.10; *Śatapatha Brāhmaṇa*, II.6.2.9.

[193] *Tameva viditvātimṛtyum eti nānyaḥ panthā vidyate ayanāya*. VI.15.

The *Śvetāśvatara Upaniṣad* characterizes Rudra as *viśvatomukha, viśvataścakṣus, viśvatohasta* and *viśvataḥpāt* "having heads, eyes, arms, feet on all sides".[194] His face is propitious.[195] He is devoid of parts,[196] and free from blemishes.[197] His is the most benign body which is auspicious, unterrifying and revealing no evil.[198] He is to be grasped by the mind.[199] He has many forms,[200] which cannot be seen by mortals with their physical eyes.[201] It is not possible to ascertain his nature even through comparison, for there is nowhere the like of him.[202] The Upaniṣad proclaims that no one has so far grasped him.[203] He is incorporeal.[204] He sheds lustre on all regions — above, beneath, and across — and shines like the sun.[205]

It is in the *Śvetāśvatara Upaniṣad* that we find for the first time a clear allotment of the function of creation, preservation and destruction to Rudra-Śiva. Contrary to later convention, it is to one and the same god that these functions are ascribed here. He is the protector. After creating all the worlds, he absorbs them at the end of time.[206] Rudra creates Brahmā, and gives unto him the *Veda*.[207] He is the author of existence and non-existence.[208] He is the creator of

---

[194] *Viśvataḥcakṣuruta viśvatomukho viśvatohasta uta viśvataḥpāt*. III.3.

[195] *Rudra yat te dakṣiṇaṁ mukham*. IV.21. See Śaṅkara's commentary on this line: *Dakṣiṇaṁ mukham = mukham utsāhajananam.*

[196] *Akalaḥ*. VI.5; and *Niṣkalam*. VI.19.

[197] *Niravadyam*. VI.19.

[198] *Śivā tanūḥ aghorāḥ pāpakāśinī*. III.5.

[199] *Bhāvagrāhyam*.

[200] *Viśvarūpam*. VI.5.

[201] *Na saṁdṛśyate paśyati tiṣṭhati rūpam asya | Na cakṣuṣā paśyati kaścanainam ||* IV.20.

[202] *Na tasya pratimā asti*. IV.19.

[203] *Nainaṁ ūrdhvaṁ na tiryañcaṁ na madhye parijagrabhat*. IV.19.

[204] *Anīḍākhyam*. V.14.

[205] *Sarvā diśa ūrdhva adhaś ca tiryah prakāśayan bhrājate yadvanaḍvān | Evaṁ sa devo...* V.4.

[206] *Sañcukocāntakāle samsṛjya viśvā bhuvanāni gopāḥ*. III.2.

[207] *Yo brahmāṇaṁ vidadhāti pūrvaṁ | Yo vai vedāṁśca prahiṇoti tasmai ||* VI.18.

[208] *Bhāvābhāvakaram*. V.14.

everything.[209] He creates heaven and earth.[210] He is the supreme ultimate cause.[211] Of old he gave rise to the golden germ.[212] He beheld the same when it was born.[213] He is the author of creation and its parts.[214] He is the maker of all.[215] He makes the one seed manifold.[216] He is the maker of all things.[217]

Rudra is described as the protector of the mountain.[218] He is the ruler of nature and spirit.[219] He is the lord of the two-footed and the four-footed beings.[220] He is the cause of the worldly existence, of liberation, of continuance and of bondage.[221] He is the protector of the world in critical time.[222] He is the guardian of the world.[223] He rules this world for ever.[224] He, the great seer, is implored to endow the beings with clear understanding.[225] He is the author of time,[226] the knower,[227] the witness.[228] He is the controller of many.[229] He alone embraces the universe,[230] and by him this whole world is enveloped.[231] He is the knower of all.[232]

209 *Viśvasya sraṣṭāram*. IV.14.

210 *Dyāvābhūmī janayan*. III.3.

211 *Sa kāraṇam*. VI.9.

212 *Hiraṇyagarbhaṁ janayāmāsa pūrvam*. III.4.

213 *Hiraṇyagarbhaṁ paśyata jāyamānam*. IV.12.

214 *Kalāsargakaram*. V.14.

215 *Sa viśvakṛt*. VI.16.

216 *Etaṁ bījaṁ bahudhā yaḥ karoti*. VI.16.

217 *Eṣa devaḥ viśvakarmā*. IV.17.

218 *Giritraḥ*. III.6.

219 *Yonisvabhāvān adhitiṣṭhaty ekaḥ*. V.4.

220 *Ya īśe asya dvipadaḥ catuṣpadaḥ*. IV.13.

221 *Saṁsāramokṣasthitibandhahetuḥ*. VI.16.

222 *Sa eṣa kāle bhuvanasya goptā*. IV.15.

223 *Bhuvanasya goptā*. VI.17.

224 *Ya īśe asya jagataḥ*. VI.17.

225 *Sa no buddhyā śubhayā saṁyunaktu*. III.4.

226 *Kālakāro*. VI.2.

227 *Jñaḥ*. VI.16.

228 *Sākṣī*. VI.11.

229 *Vaśī niṣkriyāṇāṁ bahūnām*. VI.12.

230 *Viśvasyaikaṁ pariveṣṭitāram*. VI.13.

231 *Adhitiṣṭhati eko viśvāni rūpāṇi yonīśca sarvāḥ*. V.2.

232 *Sarvavidyaḥ* VI.2; also cf. *sa vetti vedyaṁ na ca tasyāsti vettā*. III.19.

A special characteristic ascribed to Rudra in the *Śvetāśvatara Upaniṣad* is his ruling power. This function is so frequently ascribed to him that he becomes the ruler *par excellence*. This brings him the appellation such as Īśa, Īśvara and Īśāna. The Upaniṣad describes him as one that rules with his ruling powers.[233] He is the ruler of all.[234] He is the lord of the world,[235] he is the supreme master of masters,[236] and the lord of all. Being the highest deity of deities,[237] he rules over all forms, and all sources.[238] He rules over whatever creatures are born of a womb.[239] He exercises his lordship over all [240] and is the one ruler over the whole world.[241] Of him there is no master in the world, no ruler. Of him there is neither progenitor nor lord.[242]

This ruling power of Rudra, which he wields unrivalled, having no equals or superiors, indicates the monotheistic trend of Śaivism — a trend which is greatly emphasized in the Purāṇic and post-Purāṇic texts. In the *Śvetāśvatara Upaniṣad* this idea is expressed most unequivocally with the words: "He is the ruler over this whole earth. Rudra is one, and there is no place for a second." [243]

Many are the abodes which the *Upaniṣads* ascribe to Rudra. He is, first of all, all-pervading. He is omnipresent.[244] He is hidden in all things,[245] and dwells in all beings.[246] The wise who perceive him as

---

[233] *Sarvān lokān īśata īśanībhiḥ*. III.1.

[234] *Ya īśe asya jagataḥ nityam eva*. VI.17.

[235] *Viśvādhipo*. III.4.

[236] *Patiṁ patīnām*. VI.17.

[237] *Tam īśvarāṇāṁ paramaṁ maheśvaraṁ taṁ devānāṁ paramam*. VI.7.

[238] *Adhitiṣṭhatyeko viśvāni rūpāṇi yonīśca sarvāḥ*. V.2.

[239] *Yonisvabhāvān adhtitiṣṭhaty ekaḥ*. V.4.

[240] *Sarvādhipatyaṁ kurute*. V.3.

[241] *Na īśe asya jagato nityameva nānyo hetur vidyata īśanāya*. VI.17.

[242] *Na tasya kaścit patir asti loke na ceśitā ... Na cāsya kaścid janitā na cādhipaḥ*. VI.9.

[243] *Eko hi rudro na dvitīyāya tasthuḥ Ya imān lokān īśanībhiḥ*. III.2.

[244] *Sarvavyāpī sa bhagavān tasmāt sarvagataḥ śivaḥ*. III.11.

[245] *Śivaṁ sarvabhūteṣu gūḍham*. IV.16; also: *Eko devaḥ sarvabhūteṣu gūḍhaḥ*. IV.11.

[246] *Sarvabhūtāntarātmā*. VI.11.

abiding in their selves, to them belongs happiness.[247] He is in fire and in water. He has entered into the whole world.[248] He is framed in the heart of the thought and by the mind. Those who know him thus become immortal.[249] He dwells in the cave (heart) of all beings. He is a dweller of the mountains.[250] It is perhaps this idea which gained stronger grounds in the Epics and the *Purāṇas*, which speak of the mountain abode of Śiva.

Only a few extracts from the earlier *Saṁhitās* reproduced in the *Śvetāśvatara Upaniṣad* contain a few prayers. Rudra is there implored not to injure man or beast, not to slay the heroes in his anger, not to hurt children, cattle or horses, and not to curtail the life of the worshipper.[251] He is even implored to empart to the suppliant a clear understanding.[252]

Attention may be drawn to the characteristics which are attributed to Rudra for the first time herein. The most noteworthy characteristic ascribed to him is omnipresence.[253] He is the one embracer of everything,[254] the one embracer of the universe.[255] He is hidden in all things like the exceedingly fine oil that comes out of clarified butter.[256] He is the inner self of all beings.[257] He is the firstborn. He is both born and yet to be born.[258] With the thought that he is unborn, he is

---

247 *Hṛdā manīṣā manasābhikḷpto ya etad viduḥ amṛtās te bhavanti.* III.13.

248 *Yo devo agnau yo apsu yo viśvak bhuvanam āviveśa.* III.17.

249 *Sadā janānāṁ hṛdaye sanniviṣṭaḥ ...amṛtāste bhavanti.* III.13.

250 *Giritraḥ.* III.6.; this, though it means the protector of the mountain, indicates his connection with it.

251 *Mā nastoke tanaye mā na āyuṣi mā no goṣu mā no aśveṣu rīriṣaḥ |*
Vīrān mā no rudra bhāmito vadhīḥ || IV.22.

252 *Sa no budhyā saṁyunaktu.* IV.12.

253 *Sarvavyāpi bhagavān ... Sarvagataḥ śivaḥ.* III.11.

254 *Sa bhūmiṁ viśvato vṛtvā.* III.14.

255 *Viśvasyaikaṁ pariveṣṭitāram.* IV.14.

256 *Ghṛtāt paraṁ maṇḍam ivātisūkṣmam.* IV.16.

257 *Sarvabhūtāntarātmā.* VI.11.

258 *Sa eva jāyaḥ sa janiṣyamāṇaḥ.* V.16.

approached in fear.[259] He is the source and origin of the gods.[260] In him all the worlds rest.[261] He is hidden in all beings,[262] and is the origin of all.[263] This auspicious one is without blemish, irreproachable and tranquil.[264] He is adorable,[265] divine [266] and imperishable.[267] He is devoid of beginning and end.[268] He is the possessor of all knowledge,[269] and is to be seen beyond the three kinds of time, the past, the present, and the future.[270] He is eternal among the eternals, and intelligent among the intelligences.[271] He is the beginning.[272] He is the lord of qualities [273] and at the same time devoid of them.[274]

7. Rudra in the Sūtras

The *Śrauta* and *Gṛhya sūtras*, which for the most part form the manuals of scriptural and domestic rituals, present a very particular treatment of Rudra; the *Dharmasūtras* have hardly anything to say about him. While in the *Śrauta-sūtras* the priestly hierarchy isolate Rudra from the generality of the official Vedic gods in a very marked manner, the *Gṛhya-sūtras*, which derive many of their rites from popular practices, assign to him a prominent place, at least in some cases. It is, therefore, mostly on the basis of the *Gṛhya-sūtras* that an attempt is made here to present a picture of Rudra in this part of Vedic literature.

---

[259] *Ajāta ityevaṁ kascid bhīruḥ prapadyate*. IV.21.

[260] *Yo devānāṁ prabhavaḥ*. III.13.

[261] *Asmiṁlloke adhiśritāḥ*. IV.13.

[262] *Eko devaḥ sarvabhūteṣu gūḍhaḥ*. VI.11.

[263] *Viśvayoniḥ*. V.5.

[264] *Śivam*. IV.14 and 16. *Śāntam*. VI.19.

[265] *Īḍyam*. VI.5.

[266] *Devam*. V.14.

[267] *Akṣaram*. IV.18.

[268] *Anādyantam*. V.13.

[269] *Sarvavidyaḥ*. VI.2.

[270] *Paras trikālād akalo pi dṛṣṭaḥ*. VI.5.

[271] *Cetanaścetanānām*. VI.13.

[272] *Ādiḥ saḥ*. VI.5.

[273] *Guṇeśaḥ*. VI.16.

[274] *Nirguṇaḥ*. VI.11.

The Rudra of the Sūtra-period, no doubt, retains many of the features generally associated with him in the pre-Sūtra Vedic times. He continues to be glorified as Mahādeva, Hara, Mṛḍa, Śarva, Śiva, Bhava, Bhīma, Paśupati, Rudra, Śaṅkara, and Īśāna.[275] Curiously enough, Śarva and Bhava are once mentioned as Rudra's sons.[276] Rudra's consort in her various aspects as Rudrāṇī, Bhavānī etc. is mentioned in the *Sūtras*.[277] Rudra's hosts are described as attacking men and beasts with disease and death.[278] Rudra is described in one of the Sūtras as seeking to slay men.[279] He is connected with serpents.[280] Paths, crossroads, waters, forests, mountains, and dung-heaps are mentioned as his usual haunts.[281]

Emphasis must be laid on the fact that the offering of oblations to Rudra, in the *śrauta* ritual, was not performed with much cordiality. Consideration was shown to him merely because it was inevitable. For it was by giving him a share that he was to be gotten rid of. Sometimes, such dismissal of Rudra during the course of the sacrificial performance is indicated by a peculiar movement of the sacrificial ladle.[282] This manner of allotting portions to Rudra is reminiscent of the old *Brāhmaṇa* tradition, and, in this connection, Rudra is told, "these are thy portions; therewith depart to Mūjavat".[283]

Rudra is associated with the cardinal directions. Whenever a sacrifice is offered to him, the quarters are to be worshipped.[284] He is offered oblations specially to remove and prevent diseases etc. When a disease befalls a person, he is to offer boiled rice and grains of

---

275 *Āśvalāyana Gṛhyasūtra*, IV.819.

276 *Ibid.* , IV.20.1.

277 *Hiraṇyagṛhyasūtra*, II.3.7.

278 *Śāṅkhāyana Śrautasūtra*, IV.19.8.

279 Cf. *Āśvalāyana Gṛhyasūtra*, IV.8.30.

280 *Ibid.*, IV.8.28.

281 *Pāraskara Gṛhyasūtra*, III.15.12-15; also *Hiraṇya-Gṛhyasūtra*, I.5.16.10.

282 Twice he holds out the offering ladle to the north. Verily, thus having pleased Rudra in his own quarter he lets (him) go. *Ait.Br.*, II.1.

283 Dandekar, *op.cit.*, p. 97.

284 *Āśvalāyana Gṛhyasūtra*, IV.8.22.7.24.

gavedhukā grass, uttering certain *mantras* to Rudra, the strong one with braided hair.[285] When there is an outbreak of epidemic among men or cattle, a sacrifice is offered to him.[286] If a disease afflicts one's cattle, the owner should offer sacrifice to this god in the middle of the cowshed.[287] When once the cows are driven out, he should repeat the verse: "may the valiant one protect these cows, for me". Rudra is also glorified in the daily *mahāyajñas*.[288]

The fact that Rudra is treated in the ritual differently from other gods is attested by several sacrificial details. First of all, to him are generally prescribed the offering called *balis*,[289] as opposed to *havis*, which is the name given to the oblations made to other gods. It is laid down in one of the *Sūtras* that *arka* leaves filled with blood should be offered to Rudra and his hosts.[290] Blood is, indeed, always associated with this god. If in a sacrifice, blood oozes out of the udder, the cow is to be sacrificed to Rudra. The prescribed formula is repeated for his purification.[291] *Tryambaka-homa* is the only *Śrauta* ritual in which Rudra is given a distinctive place, but even there his character is represented as different from that of other gods.[292]

Another peculiarity of the treatment shown to Rudra in the rituals is the assignment of the *ucchiṣṭa* offerings to him. Rudra is, therefore, characterized as *uccheṣaṇabhāga*.[293] These offerings too are to be offered not in the burning sacred fires, but upon coals.

Offerings to Rudra are always to be confined to areas outside the village. In this connection, the *Āśvalāyana Gṛhyasūtra* lays down the general rule: "One should not take anything associated with the

---

[285] *Śāṅkhāyana Gṛhyasūtra*, V.6.1; also *Āśvalāyana-Gṛhyasūtra*, IV.8.40.

[286] *Ś.Ś.S.* , III.4.8; also IV.8.40; also *Śāṅkhāyana-Gṛhyasūtra*, V.6.1.

[287] *Āśvalāyana Gṛhyasūtra*, IV.8.35.

[288] *Gobhila Gṛhyasūtra*, III.6.1.

[289] *Ibid.*, I.4.31; *Āśvalāyana Gṛhyasūtra*, IV.8.22.

[290] *Pāraskara Gṛhyasūtra*, III.8.6.11.

[291] *Kātyāyana Śrautasūtra*, XXV.2.2.

[292] Dandekar, *op.cit.*, p. 97.

[293] Dandekar, *op.cit.*, p. 87.

worship of Rudra into the village", for this god will do harm to the human creatures.[294] It is further laid down that the sacrificer should keep his people away from the place where he has to perform a sacrifice to Rudra.[295]

However, references are found in the *Sūtras* to the benefits that are derived from the propitiation of this god. Through sacrifices to Rudra, one procures wealth, wide space, purity, sons, cattle, long life and splendour.[296]

Yet another strange detail relating to the offering to Rudra is noteworthy in the present context. When an offering is to be made to Rudra, or when a Vedic verse or formula is to be recited for him, the sacrificer is asked to touch water.[297] Most probably, this touch of water is meant to symbolically wash away all taint which may have adhered as the result of the contact maintained with Rudra during the rituals.

❁ ❁ ❁ ❁ ❁

At the end of this brief survey of the early history of Śaivism, we may observe inclusively these essential characteristics of Śiva which we have noted so far. These characteristics, which have evolved over the course of time, helped to give shape to the present concept of the god. In the Indus Valley religion, we come across certain features, such as the chief god being the lord of animals and the prince of *yogis*, his four (or rather three) faces, the representation of the bull as both an emblem of his banner and as his vehicle, the phallic worship, etc., and these features clearly help us to identify the Indus Valley Paśupati as the prototype of the later Śiva. The Ṛgvedic Rudra also reveals several distinctive features of the later Śiva. Among them are the braided hair, the bow which in later mythology came to be specified as *pināka*, his benevolent and

[294] *Āśvalāyana Gṛhyasūtra*, IV.8.32.
[295] *Āśvalāyana Gṛhyasūtra*, IV.8.33.
[296] *Āśvalāyana Gṛhyasūtra*, IV.8.34.
[297] *Śāṅkhāyana Gṛhyasūtra*, I.10.9; also *Yajñaparibhāṣāsūtra*, 53.

malevolent dispositions, the epithets Śiva and Tryambaka, the association with the *muni* cult, and his character as the divine physician. The Rudra of the *Yajurveda* retains all the above features, and has a few more added as well. These are: a red complexion, golden hair, a blue neck, a peculiar headdress, a skin garment, and an abode in mountains. Names such as Śiva and Śaṅkara came to be generally used, though it should be remembered, they were used rather in their etymological sense and more or less euphemistically. It was much later that these became the special names of the god. The *Atharvaveda* reiterates most of these characteristics of the god, especially his skill in archery and his lordship over the animals. The association of Rudra with the *vrātya* and the *brahmacārī* cults is also very significant inasmuch as his connection with the later Śiva is concerned. The *Brāhmaṇas* hint at the popularity which Rudra was gradually gaining. These texts have also recorded the peculiar treatment which was given to the god in the rituals. The appellations Mahādeva and Īśāna gain prominence during this period. Rudra's ascendancy over the other gods is further indicated by his rivalry with Prajāpati, whom he eventually overpowers. Special reference must be made to the description in the *Brāhmaṇas* of the incident which led to the ascription of eight names to Rudra, for these names may be said to be the forerunners of the later popular concept of the eightfold form of Śiva. In the Upaniṣadic period, no god — neither Brahmā nor Viṣṇu — was elevated to such high position as Rudra. Rudra is seen to have maintained his popularity and to have at times even claimed the abstract attributes of the Brahman, which appealed most to the Upaniṣadic seers. The *Sūtra* texts, naturally enough, reflect the ideas of the *Brāhmaṇas.*

It will thus be seen the basic character and personality of the Epic and Purāṇic Śiva have been derived from a divine prototype which had existed in India, even from the pre-Vedic proto-Indian period and which had been represented differently in different religious complexes: as *yogīśvara-paśupati* of the Indus Valley religion, as the red god (Śivan) of the proto-Dravidian, as the Vedic Rudra, as

Śarva of the Easterners and the Bhava of the Vālhikas,[298] and as the god associated with such cults as the *muni* cult, the *vrātya* cult and the *brahmacārī* cult. No doubt, as will be pointed in the next chapters, several characteristics not seen in the early periods came to be attributed to the Epic and the Purāṇic Śiva; but the essential concept was already there.

[298] Cf. *Śatapatha Brāhmaṇa* I.7.3.8.

Chapter III

The Decline and Fall of the Vedic Gods. The Rise of the Hindu Trinity of Gods

In the foregoing chapter an attempt is made to trace the development of the personality and character of Śiva in both his Paśupati and Rudra aspects. What has so far been considered may be described as the basic structure of Śaivism. It may be incidentally pointed out in this connection that since all orthodox schools of thought in India acknowledge the authority of the *Vedas*, the orthodox adherents of Śaivism also accept the Vedic texts as providing the basis for this religion. Naturally, great importance came to be attached to the Rudra religion of the Vedic period.

The present chapter, coming closely after the one which has dealt with the early history of the Śaiva religion, seeks to follow the further developments in that religion as evidenced in the Epics and the *Purāṇas*. In a sense these developments coincide with the transformation — or rather the extension — of the Vedic (Brāhmaṇic) religion into the Hindu religion. This chapter is divided into three sections. The first section deals with the decline and fall of the Vedic gods, and attempts to discover the reasons for the same. It also discusses the corresponding rise of the Hindu trinity of gods. The next two sections are devoted to the study of this very topic — the first with reference to the Epics and the second with reference to the *Purāṇas*.

1. The Evolution of Ancient Vedic Religion

The supersession of the Vedic gods through the gods of Hinduism must indeed be regarded as a significant landmark in the religious history of ancient India. It is possible to indicate some of the factors which must have been responsible for this important religious phenomenon. To begin with, attention may be drawn to a peculiar tendency which is noticeable in connection with the evolution of Vedic mythology. It may be stated as follows: it has to be assumed that the character of the religion of a community is determined by the kind of life which that community lives. This is particularly true of a people — like the Vedic Indians — for whom religion is a living force. It will be seen that the ideology relating to most of the important gods of the *Veda* arose to meet certain specific conditions of the life of the Vedic people. When these conditions ceased to exist, the particular god who used to be celebrated in connection with those conditions, naturally, fell into the background, and a new god came to the forefront to suit a new set of conditions. As a result of this, generally speaking, no god of the *Veda* could permanently preserve his supremacy. For instance, in the early stages of their life, the Vedic Aryans lived in close proximity with nature. They were deeply impressed by the vastness and brightness of Nature round about them, and they sought to give a religious expression to this fact of life through the mythology of Father Dyauḥ. In course of time, however, these people came to realize that Nature, vast as it is, is by no means chaotic. It functions in a remarkably well-ordered manner. There must be some law which governed all its manifestations — even the minutest ones — and thus transformed into a cosmos what would have otherwise been a chaos. This concept of cosmic law (*ṛta*) and its administrator Varuṇa, consequently superseded the concept of Dyauḥ. Later, when the Vedic Aryans set out from their secondary *Urheimat* in the region of Balkh towards the land of seven rivers, in search of "fresh fields and pastures new", they encountered on their way stout opposition from various antagonistic tribes, whom they collectively referred to as Dāsas or Vṛtras. Warlike activities then constituted the essential feature of their way of life. Naturally, they needed a new god and a new religion to suit the changed conditions of their life. So emerged their national war-god Indra and the religion associated with him. Over the course of time, when the popular tribal religions became prominent, even

Indra was superseded by gods like Viṣṇu and Śiva. Thus corresponding to the changing environments, the important Vedic gods fell into the background, one after another, and made place for newer gods.[1]

Another tendency which must have indirectly helped the decline of Vedic gods is noticeable in the *Ṛgveda Saṁhitā* itself. It is what *Max Müller* has chosen to characterize as kathenotheism or henotheism.[2] Not much need be said about this in the present context. As is well known, as many as thirty gods have found their place in the Vedic pantheon.[3] Among them, gods like Indra and Agni occupy the most prominent position. It is generally assumed that the easiest way of determining the importance of a Vedic god is to consider the number

---

1 The following remarks made by *Pusalker* corroborates the same view: "The theology preached is heterogeneous. In preference to the Vedic deities of whom only Indra and Agni retain their premier positions, popular deities are praised in the *Purāṇas*. The three chief gods are Brahmā, Viṣṇu and Śiva. Varuṇa becomes the lord of the ocean, and his twin Mitra has disappeared. The sun is highly extolled in some *Purāṇas*, details of his worship are given in the *Bhaviṣya*. Yama, the god of the dead, punishes the sinners in his hells. Gandharvas and Āpsarases are celestial musicians and nymphs. Under demons are classed the Asuras, Daityas, Dānavas and Rākṣasas." *Studies in the Epics and Purāṇas*, pp. lx-lxi.

2 Cf. Max Müller, *History of Ancient Sanskrit Literature*, pp. 532 ff. "When these individual gods are invoked, they are not conceived as limited by the powers of others, as superior or inferior in rank. Each god is to the mind of the suppliant as good as all the gods. He is left at a time as a real divinity — as supreme and absolute in spite of the necessary limitations, which to our mind, a plurality of gods must entail on every single god. All the rest disappear for a moment from the vision of the poet; he only who is to fulfil their desires stands in full light before the eyes of the worshippers." For the rationale of henotheism: see Betty Heimann, "Kathenotheism and Dānastutis or Kathenotheism and Iṣṭadevatās", *ABORI* 28, 26-33; "Contrasts in Fundamental Postulates: Monotheism or Henotheism", *Belvalkar Comm. Vol.*, 1957, pp. 219-227.

3 Macdonell in his *Vedic Mythology*, presumably following the *Nirukta* speaks of three groups, the celestial, the terrestrial and the atmospheric, to which these gods belong. 1. Dyauḥ, 2. Varuṇa, 3. Mitra, 4. Sūrya, 5. Savitṛ, 6. Pūṣan, 7. Viṣṇu, 8. Vivasvat, 9. Ādityas, 10. Uṣas and 11. Aśvins belong to the celestial group. 12. Indra, 13. Trita Aptya, 14. Apāṁ Napāt, 15. Mātariśvan, 16. Ahirbudhnya, 17. Aja Ekapāda, 18. Rudra, 19. Maruts, 20. Vāyu, 21. Parjanya and 22. Āpaḥ belong to the atmospheric region. 23. Rivers, 24. Pṛthvī, 25. Agni 26. Bṛhaspati, 27. Soma, 28. Tvaṣṭṛ etc., 29. Prajāpati, 30. Manyu Śraddhā and similar abstract deities belong to the terrestrial group.

of hymns which are addressed to that god. It is further assumed that the various qualities attributed to a god do not necessarily decide the degree of his greatness, for it is often seen that the same set of attributes is ascribed to different deities. For the Vedic seer, the god from whom he seeks favour for the moment is the highest god. This kathenotheistic tendency may be said to have created an atmosphere of scepticism as regards the position of the Vedic gods in general. It may also be said to have, in a sense, adumbrated the later Hindu sectarianism.

Mention may also be made, in the present context, of the rise of ritualism in the period following the *Saṁhitā*-period, namely, the *Brāhmaṇa* period. We are not concerned here with the cultural background of this phenomenon in the history of Vedic religion,[4] but it is certainly relevant to point out that, in the *Brāhmaṇas*, the Vedic gods came to be subordinated to the all-absorbing institution of sacrifice. It would be seen that the *Brāhmaṇas* gave a different twist to the pattern of the earlier Vedic religious faith. Being exhaustive treatises on ritual, they attached great importance to the details of performing them. Ritualism developed to be a science by itself, and elaborate schemes of performing the rites were worked out. Over the course of time the whole system grew more and more complicated. The efficacy of sacrifices depended entirely on the precision with which the aspirant executed the instructions, which the *Brāhmaṇa* texts prescribed in their minute and elaborate versions. A slight error in the process would not only not bring to the sacrificer his desired objects, but would lead him to calamitous consequences.[5] Thus we may note the gradual

---

[4] For a statement of this subject see: *Dandekar*, "Cultural Background of the *Veda*", *Ceylon Univ. R.*, vol. XI, Nos. 3 & 4, (1953), pp. 135-151.

[5] Cf. Eggeling, Translations of *SP.Br.* (*SBE*, vol. XLIV), p. 160: "The prosperity and adversity which may be described to befall the sacrificer depends upon the correct knowledge of all these details. Such, indeed, are the wilds and ravines of sacrifice, and they (take) hundreds upon hundreds of days' carriage drives; and if any venture into them without knowledge, then hunger or thirst, evil-doers and fiends harass them, even as fiends would harass foolish men wandering in a wild forest; but if those who know this do so, they pass from one deity into another, as from one stream into another, and from one safe place to another, and obtain well-being, the world of heaven."

transfer of the potentiality from the gods to the mere mechanical process by which they (the gods) were to be propitiated. Sacrifice was regarded as possessing a mystical potency superior even to the gods, who, it is sometimes stated, attained to their rank by means of sacrifice.

In this connection, it would be interesting to compare Ṛgvedic mythology with the legends in which the *Brāhmaṇas* abound. While the hymns of the *Ṛgveda* were more or less exclusively designed to celebrate the exploits and miraculous deeds of specific gods, the *Brāhmaṇas* invented legends whose main purpose was not so much to glorify Vedic gods as to lay stress on some aspect or other of Vedic ritual. That all attention should be focused on ritual seems to have been the rule, and Brāhmaṇic mythology was not an exception to it.

Moreover, it is not quite unlikely that the elevation of a particular group of mortal beings, namely priests, to the rank of gods (*devas*)[6] contributed, in some small measure, to the undermining of the greatness of the Vedic gods. So far as sacrifice was concerned, the brāhmaṇic priests came to be looked upon as important as — if not more important than — the Vedic gods themselves.

The few characteristic features of the *Brāhmaṇas* which have been mentioned above, no doubt, constituted another blow to the already declining importance of Vedic gods as such.

The attitude of the *Upaniṣads*, again, must be said to have furthered this process of the decline of Vedic gods. For the early Upaniṣadic thinkers, neither the mythology of the *Saṁhitās* nor the ritualism of the *Brāhmaṇas* had any appeal. Search after the highest philosophical truth was their sole aim. They sought to understand the reality underlying the Vedic gods and Vedic ritual, which after all were mere external and temporary manifestations of that reality.

---

6 *Taittirīya Saṁhitā*, 1.7.3.1: "Two kinds of gods are there, indeed, namely the gods are the gods, and the learned and studying brāhmaṇas are the human gods. Between the two the sacrifice is divided. The sacrificial gifts are for the gods, the presents (*dakṣiṇā*) for the human gods ... These *two* kinds of gods transfer him, when they are sacrificed, into the blessedness of heaven" *Sat. Br.*, II.2.2.6.

The plurality of gods, for instance, seems to have caused a severe strain on the mind of these thinkers. We see in the *Bṛhadāraṇyaka Upaniṣad* how Yājñavalkya was repeatedly pressed by Śākalya to state the real number of gods. Reluctantly he went on reducing the number, step by step, from the popularly accepted number of gods, 3306, to one.[7]

There is no doubt that in some of the later Upaniṣadic texts, theistic ideas begin to recur. These *Upaniṣads* may, indeed, be characterized as being sectarian. It should, however, be remembered that they were essentially sectarian only with reference to the Hindu gods like Śiva and Viṣṇu,[8] rather than with regards to the Vedic gods like Indra and Varuṇa. As a matter of fact, they are the result of the Hinduisation of the Upaniṣadic thought. The *Śvetāśvatara Upaniṣad* is a classic example of this trend. Monistic and monotheistic ideas are blended therein into one harmonious concept.[9] The identification of Rudra with Brahman was probably one of the earliest manifestations of this trend, and soon the other sects followed suit.[10] The bold and sudden transfer of the attributes of the Upaniṣadic

---

7 *Bṛh.Up.*, 3.9. 1-9.

8 Cf. "Viṣṇu and Śiva both secured the purpose of the philosophical interpretation. Both were popular gods who became the One god in turn (sectarian differences probably representing geographical distinctions) that One God who even in the *Upaniṣads* is also the All-God. For this reason many passages of the Epic are on the philosophical religious level of the *Śvetāśvatara Upaniṣad.*" *Cambridge History of India*, vol. I, pp. 273-274.

9 Cf. *Tataḥ paraṁ brahmaparaṁ bṛhantaṁ yathānikāyaṁ sarvabhūteṣu gūḍham* | *Viśvasyaikaṁ pariveṣṭitāram īśaṁ taṁ jñātvāmṛtā bhavanti* || *Śv.Up.*, 3.7.
Yasmāt paraṁ nāparam asti kiñcid yasmān nāṇīyo no jyāyo'sti kaścit. Ibid., 3.9.
Udgītam etat paramaṁ tu brahma tasmiṁstrayaṁ supratiṣṭhākṣaraṁ ca |
Atrāntaraṁ brahmavido viditvā līnā brahmaṇi tatparā yonimuktāḥ || *Ibid.*, 1.7.

10 Deussen (*The Philosophy of the Upanisads*, p. 10) speaks of five types of later sectarian *Upaniṣads*. Among these are included: 1. Śiva *Upaniṣads* — These represent the popularly-worshipped Śiva (Iśāna, Maheśvara, Mahādeva etc.) as a personification of the *ātman*. *Atharvaśiras, Atharvaśikhā, Nīlarudriya, Kālāgnirudra, Kaivalya*. 2. Viṣṇu *Upaniṣads* — These represent Viṣṇu as the highest reality *Mahānārāyaṇa, Ātmabodha, Nṛsiṁhapūrvatāpanīya, Nṛsiṁhottaratāpanīya, Rāmapūrvatāpanīya, Rāmottaratāpanīya*.

Brahman to a personal god is a turning point in the history of religious thought in India. It substantially helped the growth of power and popularity of Rudra and Viṣṇu, who had been but minor deities in the Ṛgvedic pantheon. A special place of prominence had already come to be assigned to Prajāpati in the Brāhmaṇic period. We see in the period of the later *Upaniṣads*, most of the Vedic gods, except Rudra, Viṣṇu and Prajāpati, had lost their hold on the minds of the people.

It would be seen that, in the course of its evolution, the religion of the *Veda* had, by and large, become either mythologically and ritualistically hieratic (as in the *Saṁhitās* and the *Brāhmaṇas*) or intellectually abstract (as in the *Upaniṣads*). It was, therefore, natural that it should have failed to take deep roots among the general populace. The exclusiveness of the Brāhmaṇic priests on the one hand, and the high intellectual sophistication and spiritual discipline demanded by the Upaniṣadic thinkers on the other, could have hardly been expected to make the Vedic religion a truly 'popular' religion. This was, then, the time for the so-called heterodox religions to raise their heads. An atmosphere of skepticism regarding the absolute validity of the *Veda* and the efficacy of sacrifice was already created by the *Upaniṣads*, and this was duly taken advantage of by the heterodox systems of thought. The Upaniṣadic period, which in a sense represented the culmination of the Vedic way of life and thought, seems to have been followed by a break in the continuity of Vedic culture and the consequent rise of three main currents of thought. Firstly, the heterodox systems like Jainism and Buddhism forged ahead, taking advantage of this interregnum. Secondly, the orthodox rearguards of Vedism, who loyally continued to adhere to the *Veda* and to all that the *Veda* signified, sought to meet the onslaught of the heterodox systems by resuscitating, reorganizing and systematizing Vedic knowledge and Vedic ritualistic, social, and domestic life. This revival of Vedism is reflected in the *Sūtra-vedāṅga* literature.

But from the cultural-historical point of view, it is the third current of thought which may be said to have ultimately proved far more successful than either of the first two. It is possible to assume that, even while the Vedic religion had been in ascendancy, there co-existed several popular religions. The origin of some of these latter may, indeed, be traced back to a pre-Vedic non-Aryan religious complex. Some of these popular tribal gods must have been so influential that it was found necessary to include them — albeit hesitantly — into the hieratic Vedic pantheon. It is quite understandable that, while being included into the hieratic Vedic pantheon, these popular gods should have been subjected to some kind of deliberate metamorphosis.

During the interregnum following the Upaniṣadic period, these popular tribal religions which over the course of time came to be collectively known as Hinduism, must be said to have followed the way of the golden mean. They were averse to the hieratic pantheon and exclusive ritualism of the *Veda*, but they did not openly revolt against the *Veda*. On the contrary, they claimed allegiance — however weak in actual practice — to the *Veda*. Therefore, in an atmosphere which was still imbued, to a greater or lesser degree, with Vedism, Hinduism did not stand out as something alien. At the same time, Hinduism, which arose essentially as a popular religion, could not acquiesce in the ritual of Vedic religion as such. It, no doubt, accepted Vedic gods, but assigned to them a subordinate position. Vedic gods, like Indra and Varuṇa, gave place to the popular gods like Viṣṇu and Śiva; Vedic ritual was generally superseded by *bhakti*, *tapas*, *yoga*, and *saṁnyāsa*. This is the religious background of the Epics and the *Purāṇas*.

As has been pointed out above, the Epic and the Purāṇic texts register the rise of the three gods, Brahmā, Viṣṇu, and Rudra-Śiva, thereby presenting, in sharp contrast, the decline of the Vedic gods. Some of the Vedic gods had already been forgotten, while the Epics ascribed mere subordinate positions to Indra, Varuṇa and Yama. An indication of their prestige having been undermined may be seen in the fact that only restricted functions now came to be ascribed to them. Indra, for example, was represented as the guardian of the

East, and later became just a figurehead of the gods.[11] He has the *asuras* as his opponents, and they are now represented as having become too powerful for him to tackle easily. Many an *asura*-chief is mentioned in the *Purāṇas* as challenging Indra's position. The helpless and subdued Indra had, in turn, to seek the help of one of the new great gods, Brahmā, Viṣṇu and Rudra.[12] What a contrast between the two personalities — that of Indra, the national war-god of the Vedic Indians, and of Indra, the voluptuous and ever-nervous figurehead of the Epic and Purāṇic texts! Indra's further deterioration is to be seen in the *Rāmāyaṇa*. For his offences of coveting Gautama's wife, he was made to suffer a great ignominy.[13] Over the course of time Indra's character became more and more stereotyped. Though the various names reminiscent of his Vedic exploits were retained, they had completely lost their significance. Even in domestic rituals he seems to have forfeited his importance.[14] Further, it is well known that there are very few temples still dedicated to Indra.

In the Śaiva rituals, the various quarters of the *yāgaśālā* are ceremoniously guarded. The gods in charge of the respective quarters are

---

[11] The setting up of the Epic Indra in an environment totally different from that of the Vedic times, may be seen in the description of his abode. *MBh*, III.164. 42-52; and also the description of his capital. *Ibid.*, III.44.1-32.

[12] Cf. the legend of Andhaka, where Śiva is described as having been approached for help. *Śiva P.*, *Jñānasaṁhitā*, 43; *ibid. Dharmasaṁhitā*, 4; *Kūrma P.*, I.16; *Matsya P.*, 179; *Varāha P.*, 27; *Vāmana P.*, 70. The three worlds were destroyed and the gods with their king Indra were set free by Śiva. *Śiva P.*, *Jñāneśvara Saṁhitā*, 24; *Liṅga P.*, 71 & 72; *Matsya P.*, 140. Jalandhara gave Indra and his followers enough trouble. Śiva came to their rescue *Padma P.*, III.12 and 13; also *Liṅga P.*, I.97.

[13] *Mama rūpaṁ samāsthāya kṛtavānasi durmate* |
Akartavyam idaṁ tasmādviphalatvaṁ bhaviṣyati ||
Gautamenaivamuktasya saroṣeṇa mahātmanā |
Petatur vṛṣaṇau bhūmau sahasrākṣasya tatksaṇāt || *Rāmāyaṇa*, I.48.26-27.
"You have acted assuming my own form, oh evil-minded one. That is a misdeed. Therefore there will be an adverse fruit. Immediately, the testicles of Indra, thus addressed by the great-souled Gautama in anger, fell on the ground."

[14] It may be noted that the main offerings to Vyāhṛti are closely followed by offerings to Prajāpati, Viṣṇu, and Rudra. Offerings to Indra are hardly traceable in such a context.

summoned by the chief priest and an order from Śiva is conveyed to them. The following instruction given to Indra may be cited as an example:

> *Bho bho indra tvayā svasyāṁ diśi vighnapraśāntaye |*
> *Sāvadhānena yāgāntaṁ yāvat stheyaṁ Śivājñayā ||* [15]

"Oh Indra, you must remain in your quarter to check any obstacle and to stay on guard until the end of the ritual, by the command of Śiva."

In a like manner, the other gods in charge of the quarters — Agni, Yama, Varuṇa and others — are instructed to be vigilant and guard their directions until the completion of the *yāga.*

Incidentally, the Epics seem to show that the three gods, Brahmā, Viṣṇu and Śiva, were originally independent of one another. No trace of the concept of *trimūrti* as such is to be found in these works. The three functions of creation, preservation and destruction — possibly the absolute minimum to which all actions may be reduced — are respectively the special functions of these three gods. Brahmā, as Prajāpati, was assigned the function of creation even in the Vedic times.[16] Similarly, the Vedic Viṣṇu and the Vedic Rudra were concerned with preservation and destruction respectively.[17] It may be suggested that these three functions, which in a sense represents a single scheme, brought the gods discharging these complementary functions together to form a group of three.

---

[15] *Śivaliṅga-Pratiṣṭhāvidhi*, II, p. 105.

[16] The god Prajāpati is invoked to bestow abundant offspring. *ṚV*, X.184.1. He is celebrated in another hymn of the same *Veda* as the creator of heaven and earth, of the waters and of all that lives. (X.121).

[17] *Viṣṇurgopāḥ paramaṁ pāti pāthaḥ priyā dhāmānyamṛtā dadhānaḥ |*
Agniṣṭā visvā bhuvanāni veda mahaddevānām asuratvam ekam || *ṚV*, III.55.10.
Also, *Ya u tridhātu pṛthivīm uta dyām eko dādhāra bhuvanāni viśvā*. *ṚV*, I.154.4.
It may be assumed that the malevolent aspect of Rudra was later on exaggerated to such an extent that destruction became, in course of time, his main function.

However, it may be pointed out that the idea of *trimūrti* has never been a dominant feature of the religion of the Hindus.[18] No temples are found in which the three gods have been installed and worshipped simultaneously, with equal importance and status given to each of them. As a matter of fact, Brahmā had altogether lost the privilege of being worshipped in temples.[19] The worship of Dattātreya which persists in Mahārāṣṭra and the adjoining regions may be described as perhaps the only significant representation of the *trimūrti* concept. It must, however, be pointed out that the idea of *trimūrti* has found expression mostly in literary works and in sculpture.[20] The concept of *trimūrti* may, in a sense, be said to be philosophical.[21]

An attempt may now be made to study these three gods one by one with a view to surveying their history up to the end of the Purāṇic times.

---

18 Specially significant is the following extract from Zimmer's *Myths and Symbols in Indian Art and Civilisation*, p. 125 ff. "With the triumph of popular Hinduism (as documented in the art works of the classic, medieval, and modern periods, as well as in the Purāṇic and Tantric texts, the great Epics, and certain passages of the *Upaniṣads*) Brahmā is definitely subordinate to Viṣṇu and Śiva. The modern Hindu is a devotee of either Viṣṇu or Śiva, or the goddess; in serious worship Brahmā now plays no role."

19 *Śiva P.*, *Vidyeśvara-saṁhitā*, 6.1-21.

20 Among all sculptural representations displayed on the towers, and pillars of the temples of the South Brahmā, Viṣṇu and Śiva are portrayed. These portrayals, no doubt, answer to the descriptions of these gods as given in the *Purāṇas*. These are individual representations. It must be noted that the three gods are never presented together on an equal footing. In temples built in Śiva's honour the other two gods are portrayed as subordinate. The following example of the occurrence of a positive reference to the *Trimūrti* may be given from Kālidāsa:

Namastrimūrtaye tubhyaṁ prākṣṛṣṭeḥ kevalātmane | *Kumārasaṁbhava*, II.4.
"Homage to you of triple form, but of single self before creation."

21 *Hopkins* observes as follows: "The relation between the popular and the philosophic trinity is simple. The *Trimūrti* represents three stages or manifestations of the One, as a creative, preservative, and destructive divine Power, that is, as the active God, in distinction from the Absolute (godhead) of the philosopher; but since this Power, despite its active consciousness, is also the universe, it is at once God and godhead." *Origin and Evolution of Religion*, pp. 316-317.

Brahmā

Brahmā appears in the Vedic literature as Prajāpati.[22] He is only mentioned for the first time in the hymns of the tenth maṇḍala of the Ṛgveda.[23] He is one of the few minor Ṛgvedic deities who represented the apotheosis of abstract ideas.[24] Thus, Brahmā's origin and character seem to stem from speculation rather than from a popular cult. In spite of his sublime character, his worship did not appeal much to the religious feeling of the masses. In one of the hymns he is praised as the creator and preserver of the world, and also as the one god.[25] In this hymn there lies hidden the thought that, in reality, there does not exist the plurality of gods, and that the one and only god Prajāpati alone deserves honour. As has been rightly pointed out, in most of the philosophical hymns of the *Ṛgveda*, the idea certainly comes to the foreground of a creator who is now named Prajāpati, now Brahmaṇaspati or Bṛhaspati, or again Viśvakarman, and who is thought of as a personal god.[26] In the *Brāhmaṇas* [27] he is identified with sacrifice,[28] and the function of creation is attributed to him. In the *śrauta* and *gṛhya* rites he is invoked to supervise the rituals.

---

[22] Viśvakarman in the *Brāhmaṇas* is expressly identified with the creator Prajāpati. Prajāpati is distinctly but only once, the name of the supreme god in the ṚV. In the AV and YV and regularly in the *Brāhmaṇas*, he is recognized as the chief god. In the *Sūtras* the identification of Prajāpati with Brahmā is very prominent.

[23] See *ṚV*, X.121.

[24] Macdonell, *Vedic Mythology*, p. 118: "A few other abstract deities originating in compound epithets and all representing the Supreme God who was being evolved at the end of the Ṛgvedic period are found in the Ṛgveda."

[25] *Hiraṇyagarbhaḥ samavartatāgre bhūtasya jātaḥ patireka āsit*. *ṚV*, X.121.1.

[26] Winternitz, *A History of Indian Literature*, vol. I, p. 100.

[27] Zimmer has, in this connection, observed as follows: The mythology of Brahmā seems to have developed during the period of the *Brāhmaṇas* (ca. 1000-700 BC), and to have been a product of orthodox Aryan thinking. Brahmā served for a time as a personification of the supreme Brahman, but even during his greatest period the two rivals, Visṇu and Śiva were rapidly gaining ascendance". Zimmer, *op.cit.*, p. 125 ff.

[28] "The sacrifice is also a power which overwhelms all, indeed, a creative force of nature. Therefore the sacrifice is identical with Prajāpati, the creator. 'Prajāpati is sacrifice' is an oft-repeated sentence in the *Brāhmaṇas*." Winternitz, *op.cit.*, p. 197.

The concept of the god Prajāpati-Brahmā is to a certain extent to be related to that of the Upaniṣadic Brahman, the supreme principle. Brahmā, the personal god, may be regarded as an aspect — of course, on a lower level — of Brahman; on the other hand, he is in a vague way also identified with it.[29] Various factors seem to have contributed towards the deterioration of the greatness and dignity of this god, and led to the ultimate denial of his active worship. For one thing, he has many rivals in the field of creation,[30] a field which originally had been specifically assigned to him. The function of creation is taken away from his charge and placed in the hands of secondary creators who are actually created by Prajāpati-Brahmā and who are themselves styled as Prajāpatis.[31] Brahmā's incest with his daughter may also be regarded as one of the reasons for his losing his popularity.[32] Furthermore, aetiological legends are found in the *Purāṇas* in connection with the absence of temples to Brahmā.[33] And this lack of temples, on its part, may have been one of the reasons for the failure of the continuation of the Brahmā-cult.[34] Besides, it should be noted that Brahmā is almost always represented as subordinate to Viṣṇu and Śiva.[35] Viṣṇu is said to have created Brahmā. And Śiva became a very powerful rival of Brahmā so far as the function of creation was concerned,[36] for Śiva is represented as having created beings of a higher order than Brahmā could.

---

[29] Macdonell, *Vedic Mythology*, p. 119: "In the place of this chief god (i.e. Prajāpati) of the later Vedic theology, the philosophy of the *Upaniṣads* put the impersonal Brahmā the universal soul or the Absolute."

[30] This rivalry is felt even in the Brāhmaṇic period. Rudra is set against Prajāpati as a strong rival.

[31] Brahmā mentally created the five creators. They were Rudra, Dharma, Manas, Ruci and Ākṛti. *Brahmāṇḍa P.*, I.9.1-9.

[32] This myth is of Vedic origin. In the *MS*, 4.2.12, we hear of Prajāpati described as enamoured of his daughter Uṣas. See also *AB*, 3.33; *ŚPB*, 1.7.4.1; *PB*, 8.2.10.

[33] Śiva rebuked Brahmā for uttering a lie and cursed him thus: *Nātaste satkṛtir loke bhūyāt sthānotsavādikam*. "There shall be nothing for you in this world, neither homage nor temple, nor festival or anything else." *Śiva P.*, *Vidyeśvara-saṁhitā*, 6.1-21.

[34] Cf. Moor, *Hindu Pantheon*, pp. 2-3.

[35] Refer to the concluding part of this chapter.

[36] *Vāyu P.*, I.10.52-59.

Brahmā figures in post-Vedic literature as a bestower — perhaps an indiscreet bestower — of boons.[37] Having granted the boons desired by the *asuras*, he later repented for having granted them. It was thus to him that the gods, oppressed by the *asuras* to whom boons had thus been granted, would retreat for remedy and rescue.[38] In such contingencies, he had no other alternative than to lead a deputation of the gods to Viṣṇu and at times to Śiva also.

Viṣṇu

It is interesting to note that Viṣṇu has retained his name throughout the history of religion from the Vedic times onwards. In the *Ṛgveda*, he was not regarded as being a prominent god. However, his two main exploits, namely the help rendered by him to Indra during his encounter with Vṛtra and his having encompassed the whole universe in his three steps, are frequently proclaimed in the Ṛgvedic hymns.[39] In the *Brāhmaṇas*, Viṣṇu is identified with sacrifice.[40] A few later *Upaniṣads* glorify him as the highest godhead.[41] Prominent in many domestic rites are the oblations offered to him.[42]

---

[37] Brahmā was merely compelled to become manifest by the three great demons:

Dahyamāneṣu lokeṣu tais tribhir dānavāgnibhiḥ |
Teṣām agre jagadbandhuḥ prādurbhūtaḥ pitāmahaḥ ||

"When the worlds were being burnt by the three fires (of penance) of these Dānavas, he, parent of the universe, the ancestor, appeared before them." *Matsya P.*, 129. 11-12. Brahmā grants boons to Hiranyakasipu. *Ibid.*, 161. 10-16.

[38] *Matsya P.*, 133, 1-18. Viṣṇu is also among the gods who retreat to Brahmā, seeking remedy. *Ibid.*, 154. 1-49.

[39] *ṚV*, I.154. In the *Brāhmaṇas* Viṣṇu assumes the form of a dwarf, in order by artifice to recover the earth for the gods from the *asuras* by taking his three strides. *SB*, 1.2.5.5; *TS*, 2.1.3.1; *TB*, 1.6.1.5. Viṣṇu's association with Indra is indicated by the fact one whole hymn, VI.69, is dedicated to these two gods conjointly. Such association is referred to in various other hymns of the *RV*, e.g., VI.99.5 & 6; I.155.2; VII.99.4; I.154.6; I.155; VII.12.27; VII.99.4 & 5; I.22.19. For an exhaustive treatment of Viṣṇu in the *Veda* see Dandekar, "Viṣṇu in the *Veda*", *Kane Comm. Vol.*, pp. 95-110; J. Gonda, *Aspects of Early Viṣṇuism.*

[40] *ŚPB*, 14.1.1.

[41] The *Nārāyaṇīya Upaniṣad* deserves special mention in this connection.

[42] The three main offerings in all the *gṛhya* rites are made to Prajāpati, Viṣṇu, the Paramātman, and Rudra Paśupati.

Viṣṇu's association with Indra during the early period probably led to the transfer of some characteristics and exploits from Indra to him. Indra, the subduer of Vṛtra, is in later mythology represented as having a constant struggle with the *asuras*. He thus becomes an avowed enemy of the demons. Yet Viṣṇu claims for himself the title *daityāri*, and, assuming the role of the chief of the enemies of the *asuras*, often fights with the chiefs of the demons in order to afford protection to Indra and his host of followers. Consequently, the function of preservation came to be exclusively assigned to him.

In later history, Vaiṣṇavism could flourish greatly, presumably, on account of the richness derived through its fusion with various other cults. The popular cult of Kṛṣṇa-Vāsudeva and Rāma are seen to have become an integral part of it. Even the Buddha was regarded as an *avatāra* of Viṣṇu. Over the course of time, Nārāyaṇa and Vāsudeva were declared to be identical with the Brahman of the *Upaniṣads*. Both the Vedānta and the Sāṁkhya systems of philosophy came to be pressed into service in order to explain the popular Vaiṣṇavite conceptions of creation and destruction of the world. The ascetic ideal was also duly acknowledged. A new way of life leading to *mokṣa* was worked out. This was the way of devotion, the *bhakti-mārga*, which was celebrated as the shortest and the easiest path leading to this ultimate goal. The *bhakti* cult soon became the most characteristic feature of Vaiṣṇavism. The *Bhagavadgītā*, which is regarded as the most outstanding religio-philosophical text of Vaiṣṇavism, is also one of the earliest works, which preaches the path of *bhakti*.

Rudra

A brief history of the development of the cult of Rudra has already been attempted in the previous chapter. It has been shown how Rudra-Śiva gradually grew in power and prominence through the various periods. Ultimately he became the Great God (Mahādeva). He was often celebrated as the foremost among the *yogins*, and this fact is affirmed several times in the *Purāṇas*.[43] In the early literary works there is no evidence to show that Rudra-Śiva was worshipped in the *liṅga* form. However, the Epics represent the amalgamation of the Rudra and Śiva cults in a very distinct way. Rudra-Śiva is elevated to a very high position in the Epics. He is now the lord of Kailāsa, attended by beings who are known as the *pramathas*. The devotees perform *tapas* to win his favour. He manifests himself before them and grants their desires.

It is, however, strange that in spite of all this, the brāhmaṇical orthodoxy refused to accept Śaivism wholeheartedly within its fold. Even the Epics and the *Purāṇas* betray signs of the struggle which vehemently continued between the older hieratic Vedic religion and the non-Vedic Śaiva faith. Reference has already been made to the peculiar isolation of Rudra from other Vedic gods. An offering to Rudra was closely followed by a rinsing of the palms with water.[44] In this connection, it may be pointed out that, even at the present time, the remnants of an offering made to Śiva, both at home and in temples, are not to be distributed to devotees as *prasāda*.[45]

It seems that Śaivism had to fight very hard to establish itself among the orthodox religions. Victory of Śaivism over the orthodox Vedic tradition may be shown to have been achieved in the Purāṇic period. This is clearly indicated by the Dakṣa episode frequently described in the *Purāṇas*. Dakṣa is said to have once entered the assembly in which his sons-in-law and other juniors were seated. On seeing him, all of them rose in their seats as a mark of respect for

---

43 Reference may be made, in this connection, to the *Īśvaragītā*, a discourse on higher knowledge. This is modeled on the *Bhagavadgītā*. Śiva, in this work, is spoken of as the highest godhead. He is pictured here as a master *yogin*. See *Kūrma P.*, Uttara, chapters 1-11.

44 See chapter 2. This is characteristically a Vedic custom, and offerings to Śiva, or rather Rudra, in the *gṛhya* rites is even at the present time, followed by such a rinsing.

45 An injunction may be cited from one of the *Purāṇas* making such a prohibition: *Abhakṣyaṁ Śivanirmālyaṁ patraṁ puṣpaṁ phalaṁ jalaṁ*. *Varāha P.*, 186.52. "Leaves, flowers, fruits, water, remnants of offerings to Śiva should not be eaten."

him. Śiva deliberately did not do so. Thereupon, in great fury, Dakṣa cursed Śiva that thereafter he would not receive any share in the sacrifices performed in honour of the gods.[46] This is how the *Purāṇas* accounted for Śiva's being denied any share in the Vedic sacrifices. However, the Dakṣa episode itself explains how Śaivism took up the challenge from the orthodox Brahmanism and emerged victorious. We are told that Dakṣa later invited all the gods to a sacrifice performed in their honour, yet purposefully leaving Śiva out. Śiva was denied his share though he appeared on the scene and demanded it. Determined to destroy the sacrifice, Śiva created Vīrabhadra to teach Dakṣa a proper lesson. Dakṣa's sacrifice was upset and the participants were punished; Dakṣa himself was decapitated and his head was thrown into the sacrificial fire. Later on Brahmā intervened and requested Śiva to restore Dakṣa back to life.[47] They all recognized Śiva's greatness and assured him of his share in the future sacrifices.

The Dakṣa episode may be interpreted as marking the suppression of the orthodox Vedic religion by Śaivism and the supremacy it gained over the other religions prevalent at that time. Śiva gets recognition as a god worthy of his share from the sacrifice. He emerges a stronger personality with universal recognition. The eightfold personality of the god comprises Agni and Yajamāna — the two most essential factors in the scheme of sacrifice.[48]

---

[46] Śiva cursed Dakṣa and his associates when they performed a sacrifice without assigning him his due share; Dakṣa retaliated by pronouncing a counter-curse.

> *Yasmāt tvaṁ matkṛte'niṣṭam ṛṣīnāṁ kṛtavān asi* |
> *Tasmāt sārdhaṁ surair yajñe na tvāṁ yakṣyanti vai dvijāḥ* ||
> *Hutvāgniṁ tava krūra hyapaḥ sprakṣyanti karmasu* |

"Because you have committed a wrong to me, an act undesirable to the sages, Brahmins will not offer you a share in sacrifice with other gods. After doing an offering in fire to you, they will rinse palms with water." *Brahmāṇḍa P.*, I.13.72-73.

[47] *Bhāgavata P.*, IV.5-7; *Brahma P.*, I.32; *Brahmāṇḍa P.*, I.13; *Garuḍa P.*, I.5; *Kūrma P.*, I.15; *Liṅga P.*, I.100; *Śiva P.*, *Jñana-saṁhitā*, 7; *Skanda P.*, I.1.1.5; *Vāmana P.*, 5; *Varāha P.*, 21 & 22; *Vāyu P.*, I.30.

[48] In his article, "The Aṣṭamūrti concept of Śiva in India, Indo-China and Indonesia", Kamalesvar Bhattacharya has shown that "in Cambodia, where our information is the most detailed on the subject, the concept of *aṣṭamūrti* had been so thoroughly

2. The Epics and the Rise of Brahmā, Viṣṇu and Śiva

The *Rāmāyaṇa* and the *Mahābhārata* were essentially designed to glorify the heroic deeds of the kṣatriya warriors. One may not, therefore, expect from them any subject matter of a purely religious nature. However, parts are found to have been added to both these Epics from time to time. It was mainly with the view of gaining a wider currency that various religious and philosophical teachings came to be associated with these Epics, which had been rapidly rising in popularity. In this respect, the *Mahābhārata* was affected far more than the *Rāmāyaṇa* — indeed to such an extent that the original bardic-historical poem, *Jaya*, increased in bulk enormously, and it soon acquired its encyclopaedic character. A critical study of the Epics is, therefore, bound to prove useful for reconstructing the religious history of this period. The purpose of this section in the present chapter is to trace the growth of Śaivism in this new environment, which is different from that of the Vedic period which preceded it.

The Epic period, not being very far removed from the Vedic times, retained several religious traditions of the Vedic period. Sacrifices such as the *vājapeya* and the *aśvamedha* were often performed; the *Rāmāyaṇa* mentions these often. It also refers to the gifts, usually of cows, which were lavished in various forms on the brāhmaṇas who were highly venerated and duly respected.

The religion of the *Mahābhārata* is diverse in its character. The *Mahābhārata* prominently depicts the continuation of many Vedic traditions. Frequent references are made to sacrifices, in which liberal gifts were bestowed to brāhmaṇas. A few instances may be cited to illustrate this:

Iṣṭaṁ me bahubhir yajñair dattā vipreṣu dakṣiṇāḥ | [49]

---

and deeply assimilated by the upholders and followers of Brahmanical culture in that country, that far from remaining an abstract concept there (as it appears to have been the case in India itself), it attained a concrete realization, in the form and symbol of worship, in a country far off from its source, as a living ingredient of Śiva's cult". *IHQ* XXIX, p. 241.

[49] *MBh*, IX.5.27.

"I have performed many sacrifices and given daksīṇā to brahmins."

Brāhmaṇebhyo dadau rājā yo'śvamedhe mahāmakhe | [50]

"This king who gave to Brahmins in great horse sacrifice."

Iṣṭvā puṇyair mahāyajñair iṣṭvā lokān avāpsyasi | [51]

"After performing meritorious rites, after performing great sacrifices, you will obtain rewards in the other world."

References are common to the bestowal of different kinds of cows in an *aśvamedha* sacrifice. Moreover, the importance of the sacrifice is duly emphasized, and the fruits it brings are described in great detail:

Yajñair indro vividhair annavadbhir
Devān sarvān abhyayān mahaujāḥ |
Tenendratvaṁ prāpya bibhrājate'sau [52]

"Indra of great power, approached all the gods with diverse offerings of food. He shone having thus obtained lordship."

The following verse refers to the immense power which sacrifice is supposed to bestow even upon gods:

Mahādevaḥ sarvabhūto mahātmā
Hutvātmānaṁ devadevo vibhūtaḥ |
Viśvāṁllokān vyāpya viṣṭabhya kīrtyā
Virocate dyutimān kṛttivāsāḥ || [53]

"Mahādeva, all-pervading, great-souled, who offered his self, god of gods, powerful, who pervaded all the worlds, sustained them with his glory, shines, resplendent, clad in a skin."

The great gods Brahmā, Viṣṇu and Rudra, as well as Indra, are described to have themselves performed sacrifices.[54] Moreover, at the performance of sacrifices by mortals, the gods are said to have regularly appeared to accept the offerings:

---

[50] *MBh*, XIII.29.135.

[51] *Ibid.*, XII.36.6-11.

[52] *Ibid.*, XII.10.11.

[53] *Ibid.*, XII.10.12.

Darśaṁ ca paurṇamāsaṁ ca kurvan vigatamatsaraḥ |
Tasyendraḥ sahito devaiḥ sākṣāt tribhuvaneśvaraḥ ||
Pratyagṛhṇan mahārāja bhāgaṁ parvaṇi parvaṇi | [55]

"[Mudgala performed] new and full moon sacrifices, without selfishness... Indra, the lord of the three worlds, in person, with the other gods took his share, O great king, in each session."

Sacrifices led to an increase in the strength of the gods.[56] The performance of the *rājasūya* by the Pāṇḍavas is mentioned.[57] The king Mahābhiṣa performed a thousand sacrifices and one hundred *vājapeyas*; giving great pleasure to Indra, he thereby attained heaven.[58] It has thus been remarked:

Dṛṣṭvā puṇyairmahāyajñairiṣṭvā lokānavāpsyati | [59]

"After witnessing, after performing great sacrifices, he will obtain rewards."

Great reverence was shown to the brāhmaṇas, whose status, from the religious point of view, seems to have reached the highest.

Brāhmaṇā ... arcanīyāḥ sadā
Ete bhūmicarā devā vāgviṣā saprasādakāḥ | [60]

"Brahmins should be always honoured. They are gods moving on earth. Their speech is poison or grace."

To get the brāhmaṇas pronounce benedictions, which were believed to be bringing immense merits, was a common religious custom:

Brāhmaṇān vācayethāstvamarthasiddhijayāśiṣaḥ | [61]

"You should cause Brahmins to utter wishes of success and victory."

Vācayitvā dvijaśreṣṭhān ...[62]

---

[54] *MBh*, VI. 7.17.
[55] *Ibid.*, III.246.6 & 7.
[56] *Ibid.*, I.202.10.
[57] *Ibid.*, I.84 & also II.49.
[58] *Ibid.*, I.91.2.
[59] *Ibid.*, XII.31.47.
[60] *Ibid.*, XII. 39.38.
[61] *Ibid.*, XII.72.5.
[62] *Ibid.*,VIII.7.11-12 and also III.21.11.

Feeding the brāhmaṇas had become a regular religious practice. Distribution of food to brāhmaṇas in golden vessels is mentioned.[63]

Great importance was attached to the worship of Agni in the *Mahābhārata*. Arjuna, before he set out to obtain the divine weapon, made offerings to Agni.[64] People with religious fervour are described as *kṛtāhnikāḥ sarve* "having, all, performed their daily rites".[65] When the Pāṇḍavas had to spend one year incognito, they could not carry with them the fire which they had always kept lit. As the next best thing, therefore, it was deposited with their *purohita* until their return.[66]

It must, however, be emphasized that in the Epic period various innovations had come to be made in the religious practices, several new elements having been introduced into the older *śrauta* rituals. Many of these new elements are mentioned side by side with the older ones, thereby giving a clear indication of their simultaneous prevalence.

Devān pitṝn manuṣyāṁś ca munīn gṛhyāṁś ca devatāḥ |
Pūjayitvā tataḥ paścād gṛhastho bhoktum arhati ||[67]

"After worshipping gods, Manes, men and sages, home deities, the householder is entitled to eat."

Moreover,

Puṣpopahārair bahubhir balibhir arcayitvā divākaram |
Yogam āsthāya ...[68]

"After worshipping with flower offerings, many oblations to the Sun..."

And also

Gṛhasthaṁ hi sadā devāḥ pitaro ṛṣayastathā |
Bhṛtyāścaivopajīvanti tān bhajasva mahīpate ||[69]

"Gods, Manes, sages and servants always depend on the householder. Honour them, O king."

---

[63] *MBh*, III.28.15. [64] *Ibid.*, III.38.16-27. [65] *Ibid.*, II.52.34. [66] *Ibid.*, IV.4.2.
[67] *Ibid.*, XII.37.27. [68] *Ibid.*, III.3.13. [69] *Ibid.*, XII.23.4.

The same idea is again found in:

Pitṛdevaviprebhyo nirvapanti yathāvidhi [70]

"They do offerings to the Manes, the gods and Brahmins, according to rules."

And,

... tarpayasva yathāvidhi
Devān pitṝn ṛṣīṁścaiva ...[71]

"Offer to gods, Manes and Sages, oblations to their satisfaction, according to rules."

And also,

Tarpayāmāsa devāṁśca pitṝṁścaiva ...[72]

"It offered oblations to satisfy gods and Manes."

Details of the manner in which different offerings were made are sometimes given even in stray references:

Devān vāgbhiḥ pitṝn adbhis tarpayitvā ...[73]

"After satisfying the gods with speech, the Manes with water..."

The *śrauta* sacrifices, in general, may be said to have suffered a little setback, as references were made in the *Mahābhārata* to other religious rites and practices by means of which similar, or even better, results were believed to be attained. To go on pilgrimage (*tīrthayātrā*) and to have a dip in the sacred rivers brought equal merits to the aspirant:

Tatra snātvā divaṁ yānti api pāpakṛto janāḥ | [74]

"After a bath there, sinners go to heaven."

One could also secure the continuity of one's family through such religious tours of sacred places and by bathing in the rivers, whose sacredness is already established.

---

[70] *MBh*, III.37.41.
[71] *Ibid.*, XII.24.22.
[72] *Ibid.*, XII.31.44.
[73] *Ibid.*, I.4.9.
[74] *Ibid.*, III. 81.129.

The change brought about by the Epics in the status of the Vedic gods indicates the vital transformation which religious faith underwent. Indra, Agni and other Vedic gods no doubt continued to receive their shares in the sacrifices. However, it must be remembered that the esteem in which these gods were held in the past definitely began to dwindle. Though one hardly comes across a positive statement to this effect in the Epics, the events portrayed in these works bear ample testimony to this. The *Rāmāyaṇa* clearly indicates the change which had been brought about in the functions of the various Vedic gods. For instance, Varuṇa, Agni, Yama and even Indra had by that point come to assume the mere guardianship of the cardinal directions. The *Mahābhārata* also portrays these gods similarly reduced, posted in different ranks and offices. Indra was installed as the lord of the *devas*, Yama of the Pitṛs, Kubera of the Yakṣas (and also of wealth), and Varuṇa of the waters.[75] Moreover, we find Yama ascribed to the South; Varuṇa to the West; and Soma to the North,[76] with the title of *lokapāla*.[77]

Indra, the foremost god of the Vedic pantheon, is represented in the *Rāmāyaṇa* as a mere king of the gods, one who was morally degenerate and thus subjected to the curse of a sage who had become his superior both spiritually and in power. Moreover, Indra seems to have begun to adopt a new attitude towards sacrificial practices. Constantly in the habit of upsetting *aśvamedha* sacrifices, he would himself appear to steal the sacrificial horse.[78]

The *Mahābhārata* speaks of Indra as one of the *lokapālas*;[79] Indra, Yama, and Kubera introduce themselves to Arjuna as such. Indra has established his kingdom in Svarga.[80] A picturesque description of Indra's capital and the environment with which he is there associated is given.[81] Festivals are described to have been celebrated in his honour.[82] Contrary to the convention that only the three gods

---

[75] *MBh*, XII.122.27-30. [76] *Ibid.*, VIII.30.76-79. [77] *Ibid.*, III. 164.13-15.

[78] *Rām.*, I.39.

[79] *MBh*, III.42.17. and III.6.23. [80] *Ibid.*, III.159.5. [81] *Ibid.*, III.44.1-32.

[82] *Ibid.*, I.52.26.

bestow boons, Indra is only once described to have granted boons to devotees who performed *tapas* in his honour. An aspirant proclaims:

Śakrāc ca labdho hi varo mayā [83]
"I obtained a boon from Indra."

Indra functions as the god of rain [84] and is a great controller of clouds.[85] In his role as the king of gods, he displays in most cases a thorough inefficiency, especially when the *asuras* challenge his power. Vṛtra is still his foe, and in order to kill him he begs of the sage Dadhīci his bones, which the magnanimous sage gives without hesitation.[86] The ignominies which Indra suffers from time to time through such oppression are recounted in the Epics. A passage may be cited as an illustration in this connection:

Devairapi hi duḥkhāni prāptāni jagatīpate |
Indreṇa śrūyate rājan sabhāryeṇa mahātmanā ||
Anubhūtaṁ mahadduḥkhaṁ devarājena ...[87]

"Even the gods incur misfortunes, o king. We hear that Indra, the great-souled lord of the assembly, the king of god, experienced a great misfortune."

Indra's weakness is also shown by his succumbing to the curses of sages. Nahuṣa, while functioning as Indra, was cursed by Agastya.[88] The office of Indra could be secured by any ardent aspirant. The Epics mention at least two ways of attaining Indrahood. It was generally believed that the performance of the necessary sacrifices led to this position. It is stated once in the Epic:

Indratvamarho rājāyam [89]
"This king deserves Indrahood."

Later, even *tapas* was believed to lead to the same result. Nahuṣa considered himself to be the least qualified to become Indra, but the gods entitled him to Indrahood on account of *tapas*.[90]

---

[83] *MBh*, I.87.7. also IV.161.26.
[84] *Ibid.*, I.22.1-5.
[85] *Ibid.*, I.128.
[86] *Ibid.*, III.98 & 99.
[87] *Ibid.*,V.8.36-37.
[88] *Ibid.*, III. 178.33-44.
[89] *Ibid.*, I. 57. 4.
[90] *Ibid.*, V. 16.23-26.

The *Rāmāyaṇa* has many instances in which Vedic gods like Agni and Indra were introduced merely as standards of comparison employed in the description of mortal beings;[91] the same is the case with the *Mahābhārata*.[92] One also finds that, when oppressed by any powerful demon, Indra, Agni and the other gods would go to Brahmā, fall prostrate at his feet, and complain to him of their difficulties. The decline in the power of the gods naturally undermined the great significance of the sacrifices which were performed in honour of them. There are clear indications in the Epics of the *yajña* having lost the important and honourable place which was once assigned to it in the religious sphere.

We discover another factor in the Epics which seems to have contributed to the general decline of the sacrificial cult; this is *tapas*. This religious practice belongs to a totally different religious milieu, and is employed to acquire spiritual power and to propitiate the gods. *Tapas*, as opposed to *homa* (sacrifice), is presumably derived from the pre-Vedic non-Aryan religious ideology.[93] In a sense, it may be regarded as being a complement of *yoga*, which is also derived from that ideology.

Curiously enough, though, *tapas* in the sense of religious self-mortification rarely occurs in the *Ṛgveda*, yet it is frequently referred to in the *Brāhmaṇas*. *Tapas* and sacrifice are both mentioned in these later texts; but with one noteworthy distinction, namely that *tapas* is, broadly speaking, described as being practiced only by gods, while sacrifices are recommended for both gods and men. In the Epics, *tapas* and *yajña* are mentioned side by side, of course, without the distinction implied in the *Brāhmaṇas*. For instance, *tapas* and sacrifice are described in passages like the following as being practiced concurrently:

---

[91] *E.g.* IV.52.4; V.35.9. Some though not comparisons proper, show the mortals as excelling in the qualities concerned. I.6.5; I.7.21; II.2.30; II.68.35; VI.125.16.

[92] *E.g.* I.69.47; III.7.4; III.13.81; III.50.29; III.79.3.

[93] See in this connection: *Dandekar*, "Rudra in the *Veda*", *JUPH* 1, pp. 137.

Devān iṣṭvā tapastaptvā ...[94], and

Tapasā devatejyābhir vandanena ...[95]

At other places, blending of the ideas of *tapas* and sacrifice is implied:

Yaṣṭvemaṁ brahmatapasānveti vidvān
Tena śreṣṭho bhavati hi jīvamānaḥ [96]

But the general tendency is for *tapas* to replace *yajña*.

Tapas originally implied mortification of the body. It meant sacrificing physical comforts and pleasures with a view to gaining spiritual power and elevation. Over the course of time, however, the word came to be used in the very general sense of a religious practice which was closely allied to *bhakti*. It is believed that the *tapas* practiced by a person roused in the god the feelings of gratification and grace. Accordingly, *tapas* is usually represented as being closely followed by the bestowal of boons. In the Epics, Brahmā, Viṣṇu and Śiva are usually mentioned as the gods to be propitiated through *tapas*. This honour is rarely extended to Vedic gods like Indra or Varuṇa, though one or two rare instances may be cited of their having been won over by means of *tapas*. As has been pointed out above, *tapas* eventually superseded the cult of sacrifice. *Tapas* was believed to yield fruits — both spiritual and material — which were far richer than those which sacrifice could yield. Boons of all descriptions are mentioned in the Epics as being obtainable through *tapas*. On many occasions, the boons were such that Brahmā actually repented his having granted them. He could not, however, refrain from granting those boons, for the power of *tapas* is indeed irresistible.

The glorification of *tapas* is a favourite subject of the authors of the Epics. The prowess of *tapas* is celebrated frequently and in a variety of ways. It is said, for instance:

---

94 *MBh*, III.200.12.

95 *Ibid.*, III.196. 16 & 20.

96 *Ibid.*, III.190.66.

Tapasā bhāvita narāḥ [97]

"Men are fostered by *tapas.*"

A person who has attained power through *tapas* boastfully proclaims:

Ahaṁ tapasvī balavān ...

Mayi kruddhe jaganna syād mayi sarvaṁ pratiṣṭhitam | [98]

"I am a powerful ascetic... If I am angry, the world will not exist. Everything rests on me."

The same idea is emphasised elsewhere in the same text:

Lokāḥ paśyantu me vīryaṁ tapasaścabalaṁ mahat | [99]

"Let the worlds see my strength and the great power of *tapas*."

The more severe the *tapas*, the greater was the prowess attained. This idea seems to be implied in:

Tapo'tapyan mahat tīvraṁ suduścaram arindama | [100]

"They conducted a great *tapas*, severe, difficult to do, o chastiser of enemies."

Also in:

Tapasyati tapo ghoram [101]

"He will perform a terrific *tapas*."

And in:

Acaranta tapas tīvram ... bahuvārṣakam [102]

"They conducted a severe *tapas*... for many years."

The efficacy of *tapas* was proclaimed in the Epics to be absolute. Bṛhaspati performed *tapas* to restore Indra to his former position.[103] The curses pronounced at the *asuras* were ineffective; such was the excellence of the *tapobala* they had acquired.[104] Yama is said to have

---

[97] *MBh*, VI.64.8.
[98] *Ibid.*, V.15.16. & 17.
[99] *Ibid.*, V.9.42-
[100] *Ibid.*, V.9.6-8.
[101] *Ibid.*, III.19.26.
[102] *Ibid.*, III.210.2.
[103] *Ibid.*, V.16.26 & 27.
[104] *Ibid.*, I.202.15.

been persuaded to speak to Sāvitrī for two reasons; one was that she was a *pativratā*; the other was that she was endowed with *tapas*.[105] Indra used to feel overpowered by anxiety whenever he heard that some one was engaged in *tapas*.[106] Just as he was in a habit of putting difficulties in the way of the regular performers of sacrifice, lest they usurp his office (*indrapada*)as the result of the successful completion of their sacrifice, he also sought to upset the aspirants who, in a similar spirit of rivalry, practised *tapas*. Viśvāmitra made Indra grow nervous by his severe penance; the latter therefore sent out Menakā to violate the sage's *tapas*.[107] On another occasion, unseated from Indrahood, he was compelled to live in disguise. He is then said to have wondered how and by what kind of *tapas* his rival Nahuṣa had become Indra.[108] The greatness of *tapas* is summed up most effectively in the following passage:

> *Tapaso hi paraṁ nāsti tapasā vindate mahat* |
> *Nāsādhyam tapasaḥ kiñcid iti buddhyasva bhārata* || [109]

"Know, O Bhārata, that nothing is superior to *tapas*. By *tapas* one oblations a great fruit. Nothing is unattainable by *tapas*."

This new method of propitiating the gods is thus coincident with the elevation of Brahmā, Viṣṇu and Śiva to the highest ranks. It is, indeed, with the religion involving these gods that the *tapas* cult, as described above, is predominantly associated.

Now, coming back to the phenomenon of the elevation of Śiva in the Epics, we find that that god is presented in the *Rāmāyaṇa* as a powerful god, second to none in importance. For instance, Viṣṇu, finding himself in a desperate situation, approaches Śiva in all humility, and addressing him as the most senior among the gods, implores him to accept the poison which was otherwise likely to prove fatal to

---

[105] *MBh*, III.281.12.

[106] *Ibid.*, V.9.6-8.

[107] *Ibid.*, I.165.19.

[108] *Ibid.*, V.16.22.

[109] *Ibid.*, III.245.16-25.

all gods and men.[110] The supreme position which Śiva occupies in this Epic is further indicated by the treatment which Rāvaṇa received when he tried to force his way into Śiva's abode. Rāvaṇa arrogantly challenged Śiva as he had earlier done in the case of other gods. He was, however, effortlessly subdued by Śiva who gently pushed the mountain with his toes; Rāvaṇa was almost completely crushed. He then praised Śiva in glorious terms, and consequently won for himself the god's favour. Pleased with Rāvaṇa's valour and devotion, the god presented him with a sword.[111] It was before Śiva alone, among all the gods, that Rāvaṇa is said to have bowed down.

The *Rāmāyaṇa* does not relate in detail all the exploits of Śiva. However, in this Epic, one comes across a very brief account of one or two such exploits. The destruction of the god of love,[112] the receiving of the river Gaṅgā on his matted hair [113] and the birth of Kārttikeya [114] received quite a detailed treatment, yet these episodes cannot be said to be directly relevant to the main theme of the poem. Moreover, the appellations and attributes of Śiva used in the various parts of the *Rāmāyaṇa* seem to suggest that the exploits of the god that they imply, though not actually recounted in this Epic, were quite current among the people. The *Rāmāyaṇa* refers to Śiva as the punisher of the demon Andhaka [115] and the destroyer of the three cities of the demons.[116] He is said to have asserted his superiority by upsetting Dakṣa's sacrifice and by punishing all its participants.[117] The *Mahābhārata* also portrays

---

110 *Uvācainaṁ smitam kṛtvā rudraṁ śūlabhṛtaṁ hariḥ* |
Devatair mathyamāne tu yatpūrvaṁ samupasthitam ||
Tattvadīyaṁ suraśreṣtha surānāṁ agrajo'si yat |
Agrapūjām imām matvā gṛhāṇedaṁ viṣaṁ prabho || *Rāmāyaṇa*, I.45.22.
"Hari smilingly told Rudra, the trident bearer: that which was obtained when the ocean was churned by the gods, let it be yours, O best of the gods, you are their elder. Accept this poison, considering it as the first worship of yourself."

111 *Ram.*, VII. 16.37-47. 112 *Ibid.*, I.23.9-13. 113 *Ibid.*, I.43. 114 *Ibid.*, I.37.

115 *Ityevaṁ tridaśair ukto niśamyāndhakasūdanaḥ*. *Rāmāyaṇa*, VII.6.27.

116 *Hanumatā vegavatā vāṇareṇa mahātmanā Laṅkāpuraṁ pradadghaṁ tad rudreṇa tripuraṁ yathā*. *Ibid.*, V.54.31. "Laṅkā city was burnt by the great-souled Hanumān, quick-moving, like Tripura by Rudra."

117 *Ibid.*, I.45.

Śiva as the great god who is not subordinate to any other. The great Epic recounts many of Śiva's exploits. His giving the Pāśupata weapon to Arjuna [118] must be regarded as one of the more important episodes in the Epic. The favour which he bestowed on Bhagīratha is described in some detail.[119] The destruction of the three cities is also related in detail.[120] Śiva is said to have fought with the demons and eventually destroyed them by means of a sword which he had obtained from a sacrifice.[121] His destruction of Daksa's sacrifice is elaborated at two places in this Epic.[122] It must, however, be pointed out that the accounts of Śiva's glorious deeds are found in larger number in the *Purāṇas* than in the Epics, and that even those few exploits which are described in these latter works have received a less elaborate treatment than in the *Purāṇas*.

Information relating to the Śaiva ritual and religious practices of this period is very scant. The installation and worship of the god in temples is not mentioned at all. Some sacrifices seem to have been performed entirely in Śiva's honour. References are found in the *Rāmāyaṇa* to *Māheśvara-yajña*, which seems to have enjoyed parity with every Vedic sacrifice.[123] Indrajit is said to have performed this sacrifice, invoking the favour of Śiva. Lakṣmaṇa also once mentions such a sacrifice to Rāma.[124] In addition to sacrifice, *tapas* is employed

---

[118] *MBh*, III.41.13-16. [119] *Ibid.*, III.108.

[120] *Ibid.*, VIII.24.3-65. also XIII.160.25-31.

[121] *Ibid.*, XII.160.48-58. [122] *Ibid.*, XII.274.5-56 and XII.330.42-47.

[123] *Ayameko mahābāhur indrajit kṣapayiṣyati |*
Anena hi mahārāja māhesvaram anuttamam ||
Iṣṭvā yajñaṁ varaṁ labdhvā ... Rāmāyaṇa, VI.7.29.
See also *ibid.*, VII.25.6.

[124] *Nānyaṁ paśyāmi bhaisajyam antarā vṛṣabhadvajam |*
Nāśvamedhāt paro yajnaḥ priyaś caiva mahātmanaḥ ||
...
Atha yajñe samāpte ca prītaḥ paramayā mudā |
Umāpatir dvijān sarvān uvāca ... Ibid., VII.90. 8-20.
"I do not see another remedy than Śiva. No sacrifice other than the horse-sacrifice is dear to the great-souled god... When the sacrifice ended, satisfied, with great joy, Śiva told to all the Brahmins..."

to propitiate Śiva.[125] The offerings of flowers, sandalwood, incense, etc. are mentioned very rarely, and such passages are considered to be later interpolations into the Epic. *Liṅga* worship also seems to have not quite been common during this period. Only once, Rāvaṇa is described to have carried a golden *liṅga* wherever he went. He is said to have offered flowers, sandalwood and incense to the *liṅga* after having installed it on the banks of a river.[126] However, it is maintained that such passages are of a later origin. Echoes of the sacrifices of cattle to Rudra are sometimes heard in the *Rāmāyaṇa.* Hanumān grew desperate when he failed to locate Sītā at Rāvaṇa's palace. He got angry with Rāvaṇa for his cruel act, and in this mood remarked:

Athavainaṁ samutkṣipya uparyupari sāgaram |
Rāmāyopahariṣyāmi paśuṁ paśupateriva || [127]

"Or I will throw this Rāvaṇa far over the ocean and offer him as oblation to Rāma, as one offers an animal to Paśupati."

The *Mahābhārata* very rarely refers to sacrifices performed in honour of Rudra. However, expressions like *Rudrāyopajihīrṣati* [128] and *yaṣṭum icchasi śaṅkaram* [129] are not completely absent in the great Epic. At the same time, one comes across references to Śiva being refused a share in the hieratic sacrifice.[130] Practising *tapas* with a view to propitiating Śiva is frequently mentioned. Arjuna performed

---

[125] *Ūrdhvabāhur nirālambo vāyubhakṣo nirāśrayaḥ* |
Acalaḥ sthāṇuvat sthitvā rātriṁ divamarindama ||
Atha saṁvatsare pūrṇe sarvalokanamaskṛtaḥ |
Umāpatiḥ paśupatī rājānam idamabravīt || *Rām.*, I.43. 2-3.

"Arms uplifted, without support, living on wind, without shelter, motionless like a pillar, night and day, he stood erect, o chastiser of enemies, when a year was completed, saluted by all the worlds, Śiva Paśupati spoke thus to the king."

[126] *Yatra yatra ca yāti sma rāvaṇo rākṣaseśvaraḥ* |
Jāmbūnadamayaṁ liṅgaṁ tatra tatra ca nīyate ||
Vālūkāvedimadhye tu tallingaṁ sthāpya rāvaṇaḥ |
Arcayāmāsa gandhādyaiḥ puṣpaiścāmṛtagandhibhiḥ ||
Ibid., VII.31.41-42.

[127] *Ibid.*, V.13.50.

[128] *MBh*, II.20.8. [129] *Ibid.*, II.20.8-10. [130] *Ibid.*, X.18.1-26.

tapas to obtain his divine weapon.[131] Aśvatthāman is also said to have practiced *tapas* to propitiate Śiva and to have finally offered himself into fire.[132] Śiva appeared before Ambā in response to her *tapas* and granted her boons.[133] Śiva himself performed *tapas* for the welfare of the beings.[134] Only those who performed severe *tapas* could behold Śiva.[135] The daily offerings of *tryaṁbakabali* is once mentioned.[136] Jarāsandha worshipped Śiva in a sacrifice.[137] *Pūjā* or the worship of Śiva is fairly frequent, and one often comes across statements like *pūjyate tatra śaṅkaraḥ*.[138] Viṣṇu worshipped Śiva and obtained boons.[139] Brahmā also is represented as having worshipped him.[140] In one passage, most of these ways of worshipping are mentioned together:

> *Pūjopahārabalibhir homamantrapuraskṛtaiḥ* |
> *Ārādhyaḥ* ...[141]

Tīrthas which were held sacred to this god are mentioned in this Epic. Pilgrimages were undertaken to these holy places where the god's immediate presence is emphatically assumed:

> *Mahādevasya sānnidhyaṁ tatraiva bharatarṣabha* | [142]

All beings in the universe, without any distinction, are described to be worshipping Śiva:

> *Brahmādayāḥ piśācāntāḥ yaṁ hi devā upāsate* | [143]

Thus, frequent mention in the Epics of the heroic deeds of Śiva, the strong accent laid on his worship, and the introduction of various new forms of his worship may be regarded as clear indications of the high position which this god had come to assume during the Epic period.

---

131 *MBh*, III.39.20-24.
132 *Ibid.*, X.7.54-68.
133 *Ibid.*, V.188.7 ff.
134 *Ibid.*, V.97.12.
135 *Ibid.*, VI.7.22-25.
136 *Ibid.*, VII.79.4.
137 *Ibid.*, II.13.63.
138 *Ibid.*, VI.12.26.
139 *Ibid.*, III.82.17-21.
140 *Ibid.*, III.83.23-25.
141 *Ibid.*, VIII.25.131-156.
142 *Ibid.*, III.80.89.
143 *Ibid.*, XIII.14.1-4.

In conclusion, it may be pointed out that, inasmuch as the parts of the Epics with specific religious implications are concerned, they elevate and glorify Brahmā, Viṣṇu and Śiva, investing each with an individuality of his own. For instance, an attempt is made to distinguish Brahmā from the Vedic Prajāpati. One of the salient characteristics attributed to him, in contrast to his predecessor, was the capacity to bestow boons. Brahmā is propitiated by *tapas*. His propitiation and gratification by the gods in times of difficulty established him as the god one should approach for boons, as well as one who would suggest remedies for the gods whenever they found themselves faced with a crisis.

Viṣṇu also rose to a similar position in a more or less similar manner. His status is represented as being even superior to that of Brahmā, insofar as he is the Rāma of the *Rāmāyaṇa* and the Kṛṣṇa of the *Mahābhārata.* However, the position achieved by Śiva must be regarded as quite unique in more senses than one. Having no direct connections whatsoever with the main theme of the Epics, he figures in them as an especially important god. This clearly indicates how firmly the Śaiva religion had established itself during this period. Great is his prowess and mighty his achievements which the Epics proclaim with such *gusto*. As has been already pointed out, even Viṣṇu glorifies him as the first among the gods and as one who deserved the foremost rank among them.

3. The Purāṇas and the Individualization of the Three Gods

The *Purāṇas* continued the process which the Epics had initiated. Attention was focused on the consolidation of the power of these three gods. It is possible to trace the various steps which were taken by the authors of these texts to achieve this end. The attainment of their great prowess and high position naturally gave rise to mutual rivalries; each of these three gods claimed supremacy. This becomes particularly conspicuous in the case of Viṣṇu and Śiva, for Brahmā seems to have soon withdrawn himself from this peculiar competition in the religious field. The *Purāṇas* testify to the steady deterioration in the status of Brahmā.

It would be interesting to examine how the *Purāṇas* contributed to the consolidation of the power of the three gods. There are five main factors which need to be considered in this connection. In the matter of bringing about the stability of a religion and of emphasizing the popularity of its god, the religious practices connected with that god play a vital part. New forms of worship were introduced in the *Purāṇas* in a manner more conspicuous than in the Epics. It has already been pointed out that the Vedic religious and ritual tradition granted only a very tenuous status to Rudra. The *Purāṇas* now invented new forms of worship in order to give him new found prestige. Apart from the *yajña* of the Vedic times and the *tapas* of the Epics, the *tīrtha-yātrās*, *pūjā* and *vrata* were given a prominent place among the religious practices of the *Purāṇas*. Images of the gods were installed and their regular worship was encouraged. Connections were, however, maintained with the older Vedic traditions, and sacrifices were not allowed to pass into oblivion entirely. The Vedic ritual was rather adapted to suit the new conditions. One aspect of this revision is represented by Śiva's being assured of a regular share in the sacrifice as the result of the Dakṣa-episode.

In regard to this, it must be noted that the new forms of worship introduced by the *Purāṇas* were surely found preferable to the elaborate Vedic sacrifices as well as to *tapas*, both of which demanded special efforts on the part of the worshipper. The fact that the Purāṇic methods to propitiate a god have continued even to this day will amply testify to their popularity and general adaptability. Such simple and easily obtainable things as water, leaves, flowers and fruits formed the main offerings in this new form of worship. This stands in sharp contrast to the elaborate preparations required for the performance of a Vedic sacrifice. Simple acts characterized by personal devotion now superseded the mechanical sacerdotalism of Vedic ritual. The objects of this new worship were these three gods whose supremacy had become fully established.

Another religious device, initiated in the Epics and greatly popularized in the *Purāṇas*, is the association of these three gods with various localities — rivers, mountains, forests, towns, and so on. The practice of going on pilgrimage to these places gained wide currency. These sacred places were assigned to one or another of these three gods. Images of these gods, often as *liṅgas*, were installed at these sacred spots. Devotees from various parts of the country visited and offered worship at these *tīrthas*; this practice continues to this day. This mode of honouring the god necessarily proved more effective to consolidate his power; for in this way, the names of these gods were connected with something tangible but permanent, and their memory was thus perpetuated. A ceremonial plunge in the rivers at these places would wash off the sins of the sinner; the simple offerings of flowers to the *liṅgas* installed in these places was supposed to secure merit, superior to that acquired by performing numerous sacrifices of the highest order.

Thirdly, it may be mentioned that the greatness of these gods was emphasized in the *Purāṇas* by constant narrations of their glorious deeds. They celebrate the supreme power which each of the three gods wielded in his own individual capacity. It is this supreme power which enabled them to grant boons and destroy the demons who stood in the way of the gods, the role of whose protectors these three had naturally assumed. The great enthusiasm to which the authors of the *Purāṇas* were roused while recounting the exploits of these gods seems to have resulted, in some cases, in their negligence to strictly adhere to the Purāṇic conventions. *Sarga*, *pratisarga*, *vaṁśa*, *manvantara* and *vaṁśānucarita* may be said to have soon ceased to be the main topics of the *Purāṇas*. Narration of the glorious deeds and mutual rivalries of these divinities became their main concern.[144]

The power of the Vedic gods depended on the oblations offered to them. In a like manner, the power of the Purāṇic gods may be said to have depended on the glorifications bestowed on them. And such

[144] See Pusalker, *Studies in the Epics and the Purāṇas*, pp. xlv-xlv.

elegies and hymns abound in these texts. These come in most cases from the mouths of the oppressed gods or the vanquished demons. Many of the verses of this type have played a significant part in the religious life of the people. These verses are employed in worship even today. Among these special mention may be made of the thousand names (*sahasranāmas*) of Śiva, Viṣṇu and Devī. Apart from these, there are also found several minor collections of one hundred and eight names (*aṣṭottaraśatanāmas),* or of eight (*aṣṭakas*) or ten (*daśakas*) names, and they are used in worship in a similar manner.

Deliberate demotion of other gods to a lower rank is the fifth and perhaps the most important factor leading to the firm consolidation of the power of the three gods. The old Vedic god, Indra and others continued to be assigned the subordinate position to which they had been reduced in the Epic period. These gods are represented to be running to one or the other of three gods for help, their position being always insecure. Kārttikeya and Devī, who made their appearance in the Epics, continued to enjoy the same status as that assigned to them in those works. In the *Purāṇas*, new gods like Gaṇeśa, Bhairava and Vīrabhadra appear for the first time. These latter texts were always reluctant to afford them equality with the three gods. Of these subordinate divinities, it is only Devī who is elevated to the highest level. The *Devībhagāvata-Purāṇa* ascribes the highest place to the goddess, brushing aside the three gods and installing Devī as the undisputed godhead in their stead. Viṣṇu is made to confess in this *Purāṇa*:

Nāhaṁ svatantra evātra na Brahmā na Śivastathā |
Nendrāgnir na Yamas tvaṣṭā na sūryo na Varuṇastathā || [145]

"I am not independent all all, nor Brahmā, nor Śiva, nor Indra and Agni, nor Yama, nor Tvaṣṭṛ, nor Sūrya, nor Varuṇa."

For, it is Śakti alone who is the most powerful. Even Śiva is unable to exercise his function without her cooperation. The goddess herself once proclaims:

[145] *Devībhāgavata P.*, IV.18.

Aśaktaḥ śaṅkaro hantuṁ daityān kila mayoñjhitaḥ | [146]
"Without me, Śaṅkara has no power to kill demons."

It has even been pointed out that the incapacity or rather the weakness of a mortal is always expressed with reference to Śakti rather than to other gods:

Śaktihīnaṁ naraṁ brūte lokaścaivātidurbalaṁ |
Rudrahīnaṃ Viṣṇuhīnaṁ na vadanti janāḥ kila || [147]

"The world says of a very week man that he is without Śakti. No one says he is without Rudra or without Viṣṇu."

It may, however, be mentioned in this connection, that this Śakti cult later came to be absorbed, more or less completely, into the cult of Śiva. The glorification of Śakti may therefore be regarded as implying, for all practical purposes, the glorification of Śiva.

As a matter of fact, one of the outstanding achievements of Śaivism in the Purāṇic period was the absorption into itself of all the minor cults. The divinities of each of these cults became, as it were, the members of a common family of which Śiva was the *paterfamilias*. The attempt even to draw in Viṣṇu into this group, as the brother of Umā, is to be seen in the *Purāṇas*. In spite of all such efforts, however, Vaiṣṇavism still maintained its individuality.

An element of rivalry soon crept into the religion during the Purāṇic times. In a sense this was a necessary concomitant of the attempts made by the authors of the *Purāṇas* to emphasise the greatness and the power of one or the other of the three gods. The trend was to glorify one particular god as supreme, and to build up a religious sect round him. The Epics do not reveal any traces of this attitude. In this race for supremacy among the three gods, Brahmā was left behind almost in the very initial stages and was easily superseded by his two rivals. It is, indeed, very rare to see Brahmā represented as the highest god dominating the other two. The chief role which he played in the *Purāṇas* was that of a general bestower

[146] *Devībhāgavata P.*, III.17.18. [147] *Ibid.*, III.17.19.

of boons. He also served as the resort of the gods in times of crisis. On such occasions, he often led the gods in a deputation either to Śiva or to Viṣṇu.

We are here concerned more particularly with the question of how Śiva emerged out of this triangular conflict for supremacy. The following episode narrated in the *Purāṇas* is highly significant in this connection. Brahmā and Viṣṇu are said to have once quarreled among themselves in regard to their superiority. Both the gods were blinded by pride of power. Interference from an external source was imminent. A huge column of flames appeared between the two gods, and it caused consternation to them. They decided to investigate its bottom and top, which had both extended out of sight. Brahmā assumed the form of a swan and flew upwards; Viṣṇu became a boar and dug his way downwards. Both the gods, however, failed in their attempts and returned. The column of fire was the manifestation of Śiva himself, who appeared before them and made them realize that there existed, besides the two, a third power. It was Śiva himself, whose greatness and supremacy the other two gods were asked to recognize without demur.[148]

We may now recount some more Pūraṇic episodes where Brahmā, Viṣṇu and Śiva have been juxtaposed with one another.

The superiority of Brahmā over Viṣṇu is hinted at a few places in the *Purāṇas*. For instance, Viṣṇu requested Brahmā to descend from the lotus of his navel, for he was unable to bear the latter, who was the very accumulation of *tejas*.[149] A kind of subordination is further indicated in the episode where Viṣṇu is enumerated as one of the gods who approached Brahmā to complain to him of the many atrocities which Tāraka had been perpetrating on them.[150] Passages in which Brahmā is glorified in highest terms are, indeed, not rare.[151]

[148] With minor variations, the above narration is given in the following *Purāṇas*: *Śiva P.*, *Vidyeśvara Saṁhitā*, 5.1-32; *Ibid.*, Jñāna-Saṁhitā, Chapters 2-5; *Skanda P.*, I.3.1.1, also 1.3.2.9, also I.6 and III.1.14; *Vāyu P.*, I.35.11 ff; *Kārma P.*, I.26.63-77; *Liṅga P.*, I.17.31-60; *Brahmāṇḍa P.*, I.26.

[149] *Kūrma P.*, I.9.8.

[150] *Matsya P.*, I.154.1-50.

[151] See for instance *Kūrma P.*, I.20.51-55.

The relations between Brahmā and Śiva are more diverse. Brahmā is said to have borne a close physical resemblance to Śiva, for he, too, had five heads. In order to curb the pride which had arisen in the mind of Brahmā on account of this fact, Śiva clipped off Brahmā's fifth head with his finger-nail. At another place we are told that Brahmā, soon after he had caused the coming into being of Rudra, commanded the latter to create.[152] Śiva surpassed Brahmā even in the matter of creation, which was the specific function of the latter. He began to create beings of more excellent type. Brahmā, thereupon protested and made Śiva desist from creating.[153] On still another occasion, Brahmā appeared before Pārvatī and granted her power to change her complexion.[154] Brahmā is described in the *Purāṇas* to have played a prominent part at Śiva's wedding as the officiating priest.[155] In that connection, we are told that when Brahmā appeared at the scene of the wedding, Śiva rose and bowed down to him in great devotion.[156] A very rare instance may be cited from the *Padma Purāṇa*, where Viṣṇu and Śiva are each in turn made to glorify Brahmā at the conclusion of a sacrifice to which all the gods had been invited.[157] It has also to be noted that, in a few cases, many excellent epithets which are otherwise exclusively attributed to Śiva are employed with reference to Brahmā.[158] Śiva once told Brahmā that, in a later *kalpa*, he would be born as his son.[159] The pride which Brahmā felt when he became aware that Śiva was to be born as his son, was, indeed, great.[160] Again, Brahmā had the unique privilege of ascribing names to Rudra, who repeatedly entreated him to do so as soon as he was born.[161]

---

[152] *Vāyu P.*, I.10.42.

[153] *Kūrma P.*, I.7.25 ff; *Brahmāṇḍa P.*, 9.68-81; and also *Vāyu P.*, I.10.42 ff.

[154] *Skanda P.*, I.2.29.

[155] *Liṅga P.*, I.103.45-66; *Matsya P.*, 154.481-94.
The following comment by Martin has relevance to this incident: "Brahma, the act of creation having ceased, becomes less and less worshipped, while the other two rose greatly in honour and importance". *The Gods of India*, p. 83.

[156] *Vāmana P.*, 53.1-37.

[157] *Padma P.*, I.34.

[158] *Vāyu P.*, I.3.25.

[159] *Kūrma P.*, I.26.94-99.

[160] *Vāyu P.*, I.25.58-77.

[161] *Brahma P.*, 10.1-88.

The number of references to Brahmā's relationship with Śiva, particularly inasmuch as these relate to the latter's superiority, is fairly large. Brahmā himself encouraged Śiva's glorification. The thousand names of Śiva occur in the *Liṅga Purāṇa*,[162] and these are declared to have been originally composed by Brahmā. He taught Rāvaṇa the one hundred and eight names of Śiva.[163] Whenever oppressed by the demons, the gods went to Brahmā who offered to lead all of them to Śiva in order to seek his favour.[164] Brahmā once led the gods to Kailāsa and sought Śiva's instructions regarding the installation of a *liṅga*.[165] By worshipping Śiva, Brahmā washed off the sin he had committed by falling in love with his own daughter.[166] It was, as a matter of fact, through Śiva's grace that Brahmā became the creator.[167] We are also told that Brahmā could proceed with the creation only with the strength granted by Śiva.[168] He is said to have worshipped Śiva and obtained several boons.[169] He had realized that Śiva possessed great powers. On one occasion, he prayed to Śiva [170] with folded hands and reminded him that he (Śiva) was once his son. He begged of him to show him consideration and spare him.[171] Brahmā narrated Śiva's glories to Dakṣa at the time when the latter refused a share to that god in his sacrifice.[172]

A mention may now be made of some instances where Viṣṇu is represented to have prevailed over Śiva. Śiva once granted boons to Bāṇa and was very favourably disposed towards him. When there arose an occasion for Bāṇa to fight with Kṛṣṇa, Śiva came forward to his devotee's rescue and battled with Kṛṣṇa. Brahmā intervened and brought about a reconciliation.[173] Elsewhere Śiva is said to have glorified Viṣṇu and himself installed his image at Badarī temple.[174] In one characteristically Śaivite *Purāṇa*, all excellent qualities wor-

[162] *Liṅga P.*, I.65.48-168.
[163] *Ibid.*, I.96.76-94.
[164] *Matsya P.*, 133.18-21.
[165] *Vāmana P.*, 44.1-35.
[166] *Vāyu P.*, I.49.1-51.
[167] *Liṅga P.*, I.41.34-37.
[168] *Vāyu P.*, I.25.80-83.
[169] *Kūrma P.*, I.9.61-69.
[170] *Ibid.*, I.42.73.
[171] *Ibid.*, II. 31.49-85.
[172] *Ibid.*, I.15.81-93.
[173] *Bhaviṣya P.*, X.63.1-53.
[174] *Skanda P.*, II.3.5.

thy of the highest god are ascribed to Viṣṇu.[175] Śiva seeks Viṣṇu's help in his combat with Andhaka.[176] Viṣṇu also came to Śiva's rescue when the latter was getting ready for the destruction of the three cities. On another occasion, Viṣṇu assumed the form of a bull and drank up the water of the lake of immortality to which the *asuras*, overpowered by Śiva's attendants, retreated in order to regain life and energy to continue the combat.[177] The Mātṛ-goddesses, who were created by Śiva to devour the numberless Andhakas issuing out of the drops of blood which the demon shed on the ground, began to torment the world after having fulfilled the purpose for which they had been created. On that occasion, Śiva meditated upon Nārāyaṇa and sought his help with a view to overcoming those evil-minded goddesses.[178] Viṣṇu came to Śiva's rescue on still another occasion in the Bhasmāsura episode, when Śiva had granted to a demon the boon which invested him the power to reduce to ashes the victim over whose head he held his hands. Ironically enough, the demon thought of testing the efficacy of the boon on Śiva himself. Through an ingenious plan, Viṣṇu made the demon hold his hands over his own head, thereby bringing about the demon's end.[179] Viṣṇu's help was sought by Śiva also when the latter struggled with the *kapāla* which stuck fast to his hand.[180] Often Śiva is described as having glorified Viṣṇu. As a matter of fact, the *Viṣṇusahasranāma* is introduced into the *Purāṇas* as having been proclaimed by Śiva to Pārvatī.[181] The greatness of Viṣṇu is seen at its highest when Bhṛgu pronounced a curse on Śiva that he would be worshipped in the *liṅga* form. By means of a similar curse he reduced Brahmā to such a state

---

[175] *Liṅga P.*, I.95.3-4.

[176] *Matsya P.*, 136.63-68; *ibid.*, 179.44 ff.

[177] *Ibid.*, 136.38.

[178] *Kūrma P.*, I.16.220-226; *Garuḍa P.*, I.231.1-25; *Matsya P.*, 129.33-89.

[179] *Bhāgavata P.*, X.88.1-40. An incident is narrated in the *Purāṇas* that Śiva was enticed by Viṣṇu when the latter assumed the Mohinī form. *Ibid.*, VIII.12.1-47.

[180] *Bhaviṣya P.*, 23.1-51; *Nāradīya P.*, II.29.

[181] *Padma P.*, VI.72.

that every kind of worship was denied to him. Viṣṇu alone was recognized by Bhṛgu as the great god.[182] The *Garuḍa Purāṇa* proclaims the superiority of Viṣṇu.[183]

Viṣṇāv eva brahmaśabdo hi mukhyo
Anyeṣv amukhyo brahmarudrādikeṣu
Anantaguṇatvād brahmeti harir
Ucyate ... [184]

"The word *brahman* expresses directly Viṣṇu only, indirectly other gods, Brahmā, Rudra etc. Hari is called *brahman* because of his infinite qualities."

Brahmā and other gods praised Śiva. Śiva in turn instructed them to worship Viṣṇu also.[185] It was Viṣṇu who formed the *piṇḍi* of the *liṇga*.[186] Kāśī was originally a Vaiṣṇavite center. Śiva sought Viṣṇu's permission to establish his permanent abode there. For this, Śiva is constantly engaged in the worship of Viṣṇu.[187] All these and similar references indicate the high position which Viṣṇu maintained in the *Purāṇas* even when he had been associated with Śiva.

Instances may be cited when Viṣṇu sought to vie with Śiva and ultimately suffered ignominy. However, it must be remembered that such instances of rivalry do not concern themselves directly with Viṣṇu as the god of preservation; rather they relate to his *avatāras*. One such legend relates to the *varāhāvatāra*. Viṣṇu had taken this *avatāra* in order to redeem the terrestrial world from the grips of a demon who had carried it away. After restoring the earth to its former position, the *varāha* began to commit intolerable atrocities. In response to the prayers of the suffering, Śiva assumed the form of a *śarabha* and subdued the *varāha*.[188] Śiva, in a spirit of victory, broke the tusks of the *varāha* and wore it as a trophy. The *Liṅga Purāṇa*

---

[182] *Ibid.*, ch. 255.
[183] *Garuḍa P.*, III.2.1-70.
[184] *Ibid.*, III.2.1-2.
[185] *Skanda P.*, I.1.7.
[186] *Ibid.*, I.1.7, and also *ibid.*, I.1.8.
[187] *Nāradīya P.*, II.48.
[188] *Liṅga P.*, I.94.1-32.

also mentions the victory of *śarabha* over Narasiṁha, another *avatāra* of Viṣṇu.[189] Another instance of an encounter of Śiva with Viṣṇu is provided by the legend of Śiva's piercing Viṣṇu's arms with his *śūla* and collecting the blood that flowed out in the *kapāla* which he carried in his hand.[190]

In many other passages, Viṣṇu is portrayed as being subordinate to Śiva. Viṣṇu performed *tapas* and obtained a *cakra* from Śiva.[191] At another place, Śiva is said to have granted to Viṣṇu a *cakra* as well as power equal to his own.[192] Viṣṇu wanted to propitiate Śiva by repeating his one thousand names, offering one flower for each name. To his utter dismay he discovered that there was no flower left for the thousandth name. Therefore, he plucked out his own eye and offered it in the place of the flower.[193] Once, oppressed by the demons, the gods sought Viṣṇu's shelter. The latter propitiated Śiva who gave him a *cakra* to destroy the demons.[194] Hari is shown to have performed *tapas* in order to obtain a son from Śiva.[195] Kṛṣṇa worshipped Śiva by offering the triploid leaves of *bilva*. Consequently, Śiva appeared before him and granted him boons.[196] Rāma is said to have installed a *liṅga* at Rāmeśvaram.[197] Similarly, Bhārgava-Rāma, acting on the advice of Bhṛgu, retired to the Himālaya and there founded aṇ *āśrama* to settle down and propitiate Śiva.[198] Śiva and Viṣṇu are said to have fought with each other at Dakṣa's sacrifice. In the end, Viṣṇu acknowledged defeat and yielded to Śiva, promising him due share in the

---

189 *Liṅga P.*, I.96.37-57.

190 *Kūrma P.*, I.31.86-97. It may, however, be pointed out that, in this case, Śiva acted on a request from Viṣṇu himself.

191 *Skanda P.*, IV.1.26.

192 *Śiva P.*, *Sanatkumāra-Saṁhitā*, 8.1-93.

193 *Liṅga P.*, I.9.8 and I.159.6.

194 *Brahma P.*, II.39; *Kūrma P.*, I.22.51-66; *Śiva P.*, *Jñāna-Saṁhitā*, 70.1-24; *Padma P.*, *Uttarakhaṇḍa*, 100.1-32.

195 *Kūrma P.*, I.24.86.

196 *Harivaṁsa*, 74.1-46.

197 *Skanda P.*, III.1.43-46; *Brahma P.*, II.87; *Kūrma P.*, I.46.22.

198 *Brahmāṇḍa P.*, II.21.71-81.

sacrifice.[199] At another place, Viṣṇu is represented as being incapable of facing Vīrabhadra at the sacrifice performed by Dakṣa.[200] Viṣṇu once glorified himself and challenged Śiva's superiority only to later repent for his rashness.[201] Viṣṇu was once deluded into the belief that he was the highest god. Nandin, however, enlightened him on the point that it was only through Śiva's grace that he had attained Viṣṇu-hood.[202] On one occasion, Brahmā, Viṣṇu and other gods are said to have gone to Kailāsa and worshipped Śiva.[203] Viṣṇu is also said to have glorified Śiva's son Kārttikeya.[204] He also once led the other gods to Kailāsa; there, he asked them whether they could behold Śiva. When the gods answered in the negative, he enlightened them on the true nature of Śiva.[205] Viṣṇu himself went to Śiva seeking higher knowledge. He told Śiva:

Tvaṁ hi vetsi svam ātmānaṁ na hy anyo vidyate śiva |
Vada tvam ātmanātmānaṁ munīndrebhyaḥ pradarśaya || [206]

"You know your own self. No one else knows it, o Śiva. Tell your self by your self. Show it to the chief-sages."

He often proclaimed Śiva's achievements and glorified him.[207] The gods once asked Viṣṇu where Śiva was to be found. "Don't you know where he is? He is in my person, within me". Thus saying, he tore open his own heart and revealed Śiva, who was there in his *liṅga* form.[208] Viṣṇu always found it difficult to destroy the *asuras* so long as they continued to be the devotees of Śiva.[209] He once told king Kṣupa how difficult it was to offend a devotee of Śiva.[210] The king had sought Viṣṇu's help to defeat Dadhīci, an ardent devotee of Śiva. Viṣṇu's *cakra* proved futile against him.[211] Indeed, the highest

---

[199] *Harivaṁśa*, III.32.1-56.
[200] *Skanda P.*, I.1.4.
[201] *Linga P.*, I.86.26-35.
[202] *Skanda P.*, I.3.2.8-9.
[203] *Sūtasaṁhitā*, I.3.1-56.
[204] *Skanda P.*, I.1.29.
[205] *Vāmana P.*, 62.1-14.
[206] *Kūrma P.*, II.1-41.
[207] *Vāyu P.*, I.24.50-88; *Liṅga P.*, I.21 and I.18; also I.96.
[208] *Vāmana P.*, 62.20-28.
[209] *Liṅga P.*, I.71.65-99.
[210] *Ibid.*, I.35.31.
[211] *Ibid.*, I.36.46-50.

status was given to any devotee of Śiva, this being another factor which contributed to Śiva's superiority over the other two gods.

Anyabhaktasahasrebhyo viṣṇubhakto viśiṣyate |
Viṣṇubhaktasahasrebhyo rudrabhakto viśiṣyate ||
Rudrabhaktāt paro nāsti ...[212]

"The devotee of Viṣṇu surpasses thousands of devotees of other gods. The devotee of Rudra surpasses thousands of devotees of Viṣṇu. None surpasses the devotee of Rudra."

Śiva is glorified as the highest of the *trimūrtis* of whom Viṣṇu also is one.

Trimūrtīnāṁ paraḥ śivaḥ[213]

Śiva granted boons to Brahmā and Viṣṇu.[214] These other two gods prayed to Śiva that their devotion to him should always remain firm;[215] Śiva granted the request. He assigned the function of creation to Brahmā and that of preservation to Viṣṇu.[216] Nārada once told Himavat:

Brahmaviṣṇvindramunayo janmamṛtyujarānvitāḥ |
Tasyaite parameśasya sarve krīḍanakā gire ||
Āste brahmā tadicchātaḥ saṁbhūte bhuvanaprabhuḥ |
Viṣṇur yuge yuge jāto nānājātir mahātanuḥ ||
Manyate māyayā jātaṁ viṣṇuṁ cāpi yuge yuge |[217]

"Brahmā, Viṣṇu, Indra, the Sages are subject to birth, old age and death. They are, all, toys for the Supreme Lord, o Himavat Hill. Brahmā, lord of the world, stands and takes birth at his will. Viṣṇu is born in each *yuga*, he of many births and great body. One considers Viṣṇu to be born by his *māyā* in each *yuga*."

---

[212] *Liṅga P.*, II.4.20.
[213] *Ibid.*, I.85.19.
[214] *Ibid.*, I.72.177.
[215] *Ibid.*, I.72.170-175.
[216] *Śiva P.*, *Jñāna-Saṁhitā*, 3.31-50; *ibid.*, 4.41-44.
[217] *Matsya P.*, 154.179-181.

The shortcomings of the gods, according to Pārvatī, were quite evident — especially in the case of Viṣṇu who was known to have had many births (*avatāras*).[218] Maṇikaṅkaṇa praised Śiva and declared that all the gods, including Brahmā, depend on Śiva.[219]

Attempts have been very often made in the *Purāṇas* to bring about an honourable understanding and adjustment among the three gods. In many passages, for instance, the idea of the ultimate identity of the three gods, Brahmā, Viṣṇu and Śiva, has been emphasized. The three gods are referred to as the manifestations of the same Brahman.[220] Over the course of time, however, Brahmā seems to have been more or less completely eliminated from the picture, and only the identity between Śiva and Viṣṇu is frequently spoken of.[221] As for the references in which all the three gods are involved, we may consider the following description which occurs in the *Sūta-saṁhitā*:

Brahmā sṛjati lokān vai viṣṇuḥ pātyakhilaṁ jagat |
Rudraḥ saṁharate kāle traya ete'tra kāraṇam ||
Ekā mūrtistrayo devāḥ brahmaviṣṇumaheśvarāḥ | [222]

"Brahmā creates the worlds, Viṣṇu protects the whole universe, Rudra destroys it at the fixed time. All the three are its cause. The three gods Brahmā, Viṣṇu, Maheśvara are a unique figure."

In another passage, Maṇikaṅkaṇa is told that Brahmā, Viṣṇu and Śiva are the manifestations of the one Brahman.[223] In a more or less similar remark, Śiva takes the place of Brahman, and Brahmā, Viṣṇu and other gods are said to represent different manifestations of Śiva himself:

Brahmaviṣṇvagnivaruṇāḥ sarvedevās tatharṣayaḥ |
Ekasyaivātha rudrasya bhedās te parikīrtitāḥ || [224]

---

[218] *Matsya P.*, 154.339-379.
[219] *Vāmana P.*, 38.7-38.
[220] *Kūrma P.*, I.27.94-99; also *Harivaṁśa*, II.125.1 ff.
[221] E.g. II.11.114-117: also cf. *Liṅga P.*, II.4.20.
[222] *Sūta-saṁhitā*, I.7.3-4.
[223] *Kūrma P.*, II.35.72-73.
[224] *Kūrma P.*, II.46.35-6; see also *ibid.*, I.26.78-93.

The same idea often recurs in the *Purāṇas* in different forms. Such references imply the identity of the three gods, albeit with an unmistakable accent on the superiority of Śiva. Śiva assured Brahmā and Viṣṇu that they had both been produced from his own limbs, Brahmā from those on the right side and Viṣṇu from those on the left side. The important or the central position, namely, of the heart, was represented by Hara himself.[225] In another place, Śiva tells Brahmā that he is divisible into three forms, with reference to these three functions.[226] Instances are, of course, not wanting in which a similar assumption is made with Viṣṇu as the central figure, wherein Viṣṇu is spoken of as the god in whom all the three gods are combined.[227] The same idea is again reflected in another description. Nārāyaṇa appeared at Dakṣa's sacrifice and remarked: "I am Brahmā. I am Śiva, the highest cause. I create; I protect; I destroy. Thus I support the universe. Do not entertain the idea of any distinction between the three gods."[228] The three gods exercise a joint effort in bringing about the destruction of the demon Mahiṣa. Another legend is narrated according to which, while Śiva was engaged with Pārvatī, Brahmā and Viṣṇu appeared before him and appraised him of Andhaka's oppression. The three gods exchanged glances; this led to the birth of a female deity, combining within her the main elements of Brahmā, Viṣṇu and Śiva. She wielded all the weapons which these gods bore. It was this Śakti who later on destroyed the demon Mahiṣāsura.[229]

As mentioned above, the identification of Śiva with Viṣṇu is more frequently expressed in the *Purāṇas*. Brahmā himself is once made to proclaim this identity. During the disturbance at the sacrifice by Dakṣa, Brahmā interfered and tried to maintain order. He remarked:

> *Ubhau hariharau devau loke khyātiṁ gamiṣyatha* |
> *Ayaṁ ca yajño ... saṁpūrṇatvaṁ gamiṣyati* ||[230]

"Both of you, Hari and Hara will obtain fame in the world. This sacrifice... will go to its end."

---

225 *Kūrma P.*, I.26.78-93.
226 *Ibid.*, I.26.94-96.
227 *Ibid.*, I.7.10-20.
228 *Bhāgavata P.*, IV.7.50-54.
229 *Varāha P.*, 90.28-4 and 92-95.
230 *Ibid.*, 21.63.

Brahmā proclaims on another occasion: "One who is keen on victory should by all means worship Viṣṇu. At the same time, one should also bear in mind the identity of that god with Śiva.[231] Similarly, when Śiva, as a defender of Bāṇa, began to fight with Kṛṣṇa, Brahmā interfered and tried to bring about an amicable settlement. He laid stress on the identity of Viṣṇu with Śiva." [232] At Dārukāvana, the sages who were perturbed by the appearance of Śiva were told by Brahmā that Śiva was by no means to be distinguished from Viṣṇu.[233]

Viṣṇu once encouraged the glorification of himself, but emphasized at the same time that *Śiva-nindā* must be avoided at all costs. For, he asserted:

Ahaṁ caiva mahādevo nābhinnaḥ paramārthataḥ | [234]

"I and Mahādeva are not different in reality."

Viṣṇu tells Jyeṣṭhā, the elder sister of the goddess of wealth and an embodiment of poverty and other undesirable qualities, that the wealth of him who censures Śiva and glorifies him (Viṣṇu) alone as the supreme god, will go to her.[235] Kṛṣṇa once proclaimed:

Nāvayor vidyate bhedo vedeṣvetanna saṁśayaḥ | [236]

"There is no difference between us. That is in the Vedas, no doubt."

Those who maintain any difference between Śiva and Viṣṇu go to hell.[237]

Śiva also maintains his identity with Viṣṇu in several passages. At one place he says: "Everything is made of you and made of me; there is no doubt."

Tvanmayaṁ manmayaṁ caiva sarvametan na saṁśayam.[238]

Elsewhere he proclaims to Viṣṇu:

---

[231] *Kūrma P.*, I.22.48-49.

[232] *Harivaṁśa*, II.125.1-65.

[233] *Vāmana P.*, 43. 72-89.

[234] *Kūrma P.*, I.2.95.

[235] *Liṅga P.*, 6.85-88.

[236] *Kūrma P.*, I.26.60.

[237] *Ibid.*, I.16.47-61.

[238] *Ibid.*, I.9.83.66.

Āvayor antaraṁ naiva hy aṇumātraṁ vicārataḥ |
Vastutvecāpyanekatvaṁ carato'pi tathaiva ca ||
Madbhakto yo naro bhūtvā te neḍāṁ yaḥ kariṣyati |
Tasyāhaṁ saphalaṁ puṇyaṁ bhasmikṛtya viśeṣatah ||
Narake pātayiṣyāmi ....[239]

"There is not an atom of difference between us, in well-thought view, and multiplicity in the reality is because of practice. A man who, being my devotee, will not do the praise of you, I will reduce his fruitful merit to ashes and push him to hell."

He again tells Viṣṇu:

Maddarśane phalaṁ yadvai tadeva tava darśane |
Mamaiva hṛdaye viṣṇur viṣṇośca hṛdaye hyaham ||[240]

"The fruit of seeing me is the same as the fruit of seeing you. Viṣṇu is in my heart and I am in the heart of Viṣṇu."

Elsewhere, Śiva observes:

Ye tvevaṁ viṣṇum avyaktaṁ māṁ ca devaṁ maheśvaram |
Ekībhāvena paśyanti na tesāṁ punarudbhavaḥ ||[241]

"Those who see Viṣṇu, the unmanifest and me, the god Maheśvara, as one entity, have no rebirth."

In another striking passage, Śiva remarks:

Yatnāt krakacamādāya chindadhvaṁ mama vigraham |
Tathāpi dṛśyate viṣṇurmama dehe sanātanaḥ ||[242]

"With effort, take a saw and cut my body: the eternal Viṣṇu is seen in it."

Vīrabhadra assumed his terrible form and subdued Viṣṇu at Dakṣa's sacrifice. In the end, the gods glorified Śiva thus:

---

239 *Śiva P.*, *Jñāna-saṁhitā*, 5.19-21.
240 *Ibid.*, *Jñāna-saṁhitā*, 4.63-67.
241 *Kūrma P.*, II.11.114-115.
242 *Vāmana P.*, 67.37.

Eka eva tadā viṣṇuḥ Śivalīno na cānyathā |[243]
"Then one is Viṣṇu, fused in Śiva, and without alterity."

The belief that Viṣṇu is just an embodiment of Śiva is indicated in the *Kūrma Purāṇa*.[244]

The reconciliation between Śiva and Viṣṇu also had practical and demonstrable religious consequences; the yoga of Harihara is one resultant ideology. All the features of Śiva and Viṣṇu are fused together into a single godhead, and this latter is said to be permeated with the features of both the gods in equal proportion.[245] Śiva reveals the *Sadāśiva*-form, in which this idea is well expressed:

Ardhena vaiṣṇavavapur ardhena haravigrahaḥ |
Khagadhvajaṁ vṛṣārūḍhaṁ khagārūḍhaṁ vṛṣadhvajam ||[246]

"In one half the body of Viṣṇu, in one half the body of Hara. That is the god with Bird-banner and Bull-mount, the god with Bird-mount and Bull-banner."

Representations of Śiva-Nārāyaṇa are prescribed, among others, for installation and worship.[247] In one of the chapters of the *Kūrma Purāṇa*, an elaborate form of worship is described, the simultaneous obeisance to Śiva and Viṣṇu being a conspicuous feature.[248]

[243] *Liṅga P.*, I.96.112.
[244] *Kūrma P.*, I.9.82-86.
[245] *Vāmana P.*, 67.44-54.
[246] *Vāmana P.*, 67.48.
[247] *Matsya P.*, 260.27.
[248] *Kūrma P.*, II.5.

CHAPTER IV

ŚIVA IN THE LIGHT OF THE PURĀṆIC MYTHOLOGY

Purāṇic mythology constitutes a very important source of information for the study of the history of Śaivism. The concept of Śiva and the religious practices associated with it, which are at present prevalent all over India, may be said to have been more or less completely dominated by the religious ideology relating to Śiva developed in the Purāṇic texts. An attempt is made in this chapter to critically analyse the various phases of the personality and character of Śiva as reflected in the *Purāṇas*. Various aspects of Śiva such as physical features, dress, ornaments, weapons, vehicles, banner, residence, family, functions, achievements and relationships with mortals, demons and other gods, form the subject of investigation undertaken in this chapter. Significant names attributed to Śiva are also collected and analytically grouped with a view to bringing out their implication for the history of Śaivism.

References to Śiva in the *Purāṇas* are many and diverse. He is usually represented with an emphasis on one of his characteristic physical features such as his five heads, his blue neck, his three eyes or his matter hair. He is sometimes celebrated as the wielder of the *triśūla* and at other times of the *pināka*. He rides the bull, and bears a banner which displays the bull emblem. He wears the skin of an elephant or a tiger. He is praised as the destroyer of several demons. These and several other features of Śiva's character, most of which actually belong to his original pre-Vedic non-Aryan form but which are given a new orientation in the Epics and the *Purāṇas*, have yielded to the god numerous names.[1] A critical study of such details pertaining to this god is essential for a proper understanding of the religious cult and practices which have grown around him.

A study of Śiva in the light of the Epic and Purāṇic mythologies is expected to prove helpful in more ways than one. For one thing, it provides a complete picture of that god even as he is celebrated in modern times. The Epics and the *Purāṇas* not only form the basis of modern Śaivism (as also of Vaiṣṇavism, Śaktism and other minor sects of Hinduism), but it may also be averred that modern Śaivism is not very different from the religion of Śiva that can be reconstructed from these texts. One may even go the extent of making a general observation in this connection, that the religious concepts and practices of orthodox Hinduism have registered but few significant changes in spite of the many vicissitudes since the days of the *Purāṇas*. In this respect, orthodox Hinduism stands in sharp contrast with the Vedic religion which never failed to change with the changing times. The study of the various aspects of Purāṇic Śiva's personality undertaken in this chapter will form an essential background particularly for a subsequent chapter which deals with the many details of Śaivite worship as it is prevalent today. To mention only one point in this connection, it is the Purāṇic conception of Śiva that has governed his formal iconography. Incidentally it may also be pointed out that a study of the Purāṇic Śiva will be useful even for students of Sanskrit literature, for the references to Śiva are, for the most part, drawn from the Epics and the *Purāṇas*.

---

[1] Among such names of Śiva, the more popular ones are the following, mentioned in the *Amarakośa*: Svargavarga, verses 30-35.

Śaṁbhur īśaḥ paśupatiḥ śivaḥ śūlī maheśvaraḥ |
Īśvaraḥ śarva īśānaḥ śaṅkaraḥ candraśekharaḥ ||
Bhūteśaḥ khaṇḍaparaśur girīśo giriśo mṛḍaḥ |
Mṛtyuñjayaḥ kṛttivāsāḥ pinākī pramathādhipaḥ ||
Ugraḥ kapardī śrīkaṇṭhaḥ śitikaṇṭhaḥ kapālabhṛt |
Vāmadevo mahādevo virūpākṣas trilocanaḥ ||
Kṛśānuretāḥ sarvajño dhūrjaṭirnīlalohitaḥ |
Haraḥ smaraharo bhargas tryaṁbakas tripurāntakaḥ ||
Gaṅgādharo 'ndhakaripuḥ kratudhvaṁsī vṛṣadhvajaḥ |
Vyomakeśo bhavo bhīmaḥ sthāṇū rudra umāpatiḥ ||
Aṣṭamūrtir ahirbuddhnyo mahākālo mahānaṭaḥ |
Kṣoṇīratho hariśaro giridhanvāṁbudhīṣudhiḥ ||

Before we proceed with the investigation, it is necessary to make a few remarks on the nature of the treatment of the subject in this chapter. First of all, it must be pointed out that only the *Purāṇas* have been brought within the purview of this study. The Epics have not been taken into consideration, as a masterly presentation of the Epic mythology has already been made by Hopkins.[2] Secondly, the present attempt does by no means claim to be an exhaustive study of Śiva and his religion as reflected in the *Purāṇas*. Indeed, within the limited scope of a single chapter, such a study would be an impossible task. The study of Purāṇic Śiva forms only a part of a wider and more comprehensive topic. Furthermore, it has to be remembered that no critical editions of the *Purāṇas* are still available. This fact puts some obvious limitations on the *Purāṇas* being used for any strict scientific and historical study. All that this chapter seeks to accomplish is to collect together all the essential facts concerning Śiva in his Purāṇic portrayal. References from the *Purāṇas* are given in support of the various observations, and an attempt is generally made to make the treatment as elaborate as the scope of the entire work would permit.

To begin with, it may be pointed out that in the *Purāṇas*, Śiva is represented with two aspects — one benevolent, the other malevolent. This is, indeed, just the continuation of the characterization of Rudra-Śiva as originally conceived.[3] In some places, we come across the

---

[2] Hopkins' *Epic Mythology* is a study from various angles, of the mythology relating to the *Rāmāyaṇa* and the *Mahābhārata*. The entire work is divided into nine sections, the first of which serves as an introduction to the whole work. The second section speaks about the lower mythology; the third and the fourth describe spirits and gods respectively. The fifth section pertains to the eight great *devas*; the sixth discusses the mythology of the hosts of spirits. The seventh section is concerned with the divine seers and the section following that is devoted to a study of the seven ṛṣis. The last section deals with the mythology of the three gods, Brahmā, Viṣṇu and Śiva. The study of Śiva includes that of Umā and Kārttikeya as well.

[3] Cf. "The terrorizing aspect of the god, described as the god of destruction along with Śiva's dance, was derived from the assimilation of the symbolized concept of Maruts described above and also of Rudra." Banerji, "The Evolution of Rudra or Mahesa in Hinduism", *QJMS*, vol. X, p. 238.

god with the most terrible and frightful features, usually in his role as the god of destruction. This form becomes particularly evident when he sets out to destroy a demon or chastise a hostile being who refuses to honour him in a fitting manner. At the time of Andhaka's destruction, for instance, Śiva is said to have assumed a form of the following description:

> *Kṛtvā rūpaṁ mahākāyaṁ viśvarūpaṁ subhairavam* |
> *Sarpair jvaladbhir dhāvadbhir bhīmaṁ bhīmabhujaṅgavat* ||
> *Jaṭāsaṭābhir ākāśaṁ phaṇiratnaśikhārciṣā* |
> *Dahann atīva tejobhiḥ kālāgnir iva saṁkṣaye* ||
> *Mukhair daṁṣṭrānkaiśca dvitīyendukalājvalaiḥ* | [4]

"He assumed a gigantic form, of all shapes, very frightening, with serpents spitting fire and running, terrific, like a frightful serpent, with masses of meshes like the fire of death at the time of dissolution, totally burning the sky with the radiance of the flames from the jewels on the head of dragons, with mouths showing teeths, bright like the digits of a second moon."

At the same time, it is by no means rare to meet the same god with benign features and auspicious qualities.[5] He is shown to make himself readily available to his devotees in response to their propitiation. In this mood of gracious simplicity — for which, as a matter of fact, he is renowned — he favours his devotees almost to the point of indiscretion.

---

[4] *Padma P.*, I.43.17-19.

[5] The examples cited below will clearly indicate the dreadful and the benign qualities by which the god is characterized:
Rudrasya raudravapuṣo jagatsaṁhārabhairavaṁ. *Padma P.*, I.43.241.
Jvalanārkarūpam. *Kūrma P.*, I.16.95.
Kālarūpadharo haraḥ. *Ibid.*, I.16.33.
A few instances below point to the peaceful aspects of Śiva:
Saṁśāntavigraham. *Bhāgavata P.*, IV.6.36.
Saumyamūrtiḥ suśobhanaḥ. *Matsya P.*, 259.8.
Īdṛśaṁ sundaraṁ rūpaṁ jātaṁ varṇanaduṣkaram. *Śiva P.*, *Jñāna-saṁhitā*, 16.8.

Śiva is generally worshipped by his devotees in two forms, the *liṅga* and his anthropomorphic form; the *Purāṇas* refer to both. Today, it is the *liṅga* worship that prevails everywhere in India, from Kashmir to Cape Comorin. A more or less detailed study of this form of worship is attempted in the next chapter. Images of Śiva displaying human features are more commonly installed for worship in South India than elsewhere; this phenomenon also shall be discussed at some length in the next chapter. The present chapter is expected to provide the necessary background for the treatment of the various kinds of images of Śiva subsequently undertaken, for the very descriptions of the god occurring in the *Purāṇas* have been sculpturally translated into these images. A conspicuous point about these images is that the frightful aspect of the god is less commonly represented in sculpture than in the *Purāṇas*. Only a few representations depicted in pillars and towers bear such characteristics. Such features as the *kapālas*, garlands of skulls, teeth prominently protruding about the corners of the mouth etc., are intended to provoke the feeling of awe and submission in the minds of the devotees; a display of these features is found only in a few architectural representations in the South, and can by no means be said to be of general provenance. As a matter of fact, there are some religious texts which forbid the installation of images with horrible features for worship.[6] A representation of Śiva

[6] This is particularly to be observed in the case of images installed for domestic worship. The following observation made by G. Rao speaks of the impending danger that may befall a village in the temple of which *ghora-mūrtis* are installed for worship. "Again the *ugra* and the *śānta-mūrtis* of Viṣṇu and Śiva as looked upon as granting different results according to the position in which their temples are constructed in the village. If the *ugra* form of a god is set up for worship in the east, the village will be soon ruined; if it is set up in the south-east, the women of the place will become immoral; if in the south, ghosts and demons in crowds will cause trouble to the people; if in the south-west, the population will dwindle through sickness; if in the west, mental unhappiness, bad conduct and mournfulness will arise; if in the north-west, bad conduct will become rampant; if in the north, they will be subjected to all sorts of affliction. It is only in the north-east that the *ugra* forms of gods may be enshrined harmlessly so as to grant prosperity and abundance of children. The installation of an *ugra* image in the midst of a village is strictly prohibited. If there

is usually required to be characterized by an expression of calm and peace. A few representations, no doubt, have to bear horrible features, owing to the very nature of things. For example, images like those of Bhikṣāṭana and Bhairava have to be shown with garlands of skulls around their necks and with skulls as begging bowls in their hands. Such images, however, are few. Even the representation of Śiva as Naṭarāja does not reveal any abhorrent features. The general predominance of the peaceful aspects in that image serves effectively to counteract the suggestion of terror given by a few frightful features, such as the fire in his hand symbolizing destruction, the demon upon whom the god plants his foot as he dances, the matted hair which flies about from the vigourousness of his movement, the skull on his head, and the snakes worn all over the body. This corresponds with the general image in the *Purāṇas*, which constantly speak of both aspects of the god, yet to put an emphasis on the peaceful aspect.

We may now attempt a survey of the characteristic features of the god as conceived in his human form. This will be followed by a statement regarding other details of his personality and career.

The representation of Śiva with a single head seems to be the general rule, and most of the images of the god installed for worship in South India maintain this convention. The *Purāṇas* invariably present Śiva in this form, though as many as five heads are sometimes ascribed to the god. The installation of Śiva's image with five heads cannot be found in any religious place of worship. However, when

---

happens to be a *raudramurti* in a village, a *śāntamurti* should be set up before it to counteract the evil effects, or at least a tank must be dug in front of the temple. Gopinath Rao, *op.cit.*, vol. I, pt. 1, Introduction, p. 24-25.

Also Cf.

Bhairavaḥ Śasyate loke pratyāyatane saṁsthitaḥ |
Na mūlāyatane Kāryaḥ bhairavastu bhayaṅkaraḥ || *Matsya P.*, 259.14.

"It is recommended to install a terrific figure in a secondary shrine. A terrific, frightening figure should not be placed in the main shrine."

Possibly falling in line with injunctions of this nature, the temples of the South almost always have the *liṅga* as the central image.

the various offerings are made to the *liṅga*, the five faces are understood to be on all the sides. Moreover, we do come across *liṅgas* with five faces (*pañcamukhaliṅgas*). These are rare in South India.

Pañcavaktra is used as an attribute of Śiva, as for example in:

Pañcavaktro mahādevaḥ.[7]

The five faces of Śiva are once compared with five *Upaniṣads*:

Mukhāni pañcopaniṣadas taveśa [8]

There are a few passages in which only four heads of the god are referred to. Two such passages may be cited by way of example:

Caturvaktraṁ jaṭāmaulim [9]
Caturvaktram [10]

In another passage, further details are given about the faces of Śiva, a different colour being ascribed to each of them:

Tatas trinetrasya samudbhavanti
Vaktrāṇi pañcātha sudurdṛśāni |
Sitaṁ ca raktaṁ kanakāvadātaṁ
Nīlaṁ tathā piñjarakaṁ ca raudram || [11]

"Then for the three-eyed god appear five faces, very difficult to see, white, red, gold-coloured, black, tawny and frightful."

The same details are given elsewhere thus:

Sitapītāsitaśvetajapābhaiḥ pañcabhir mukhaiḥ |
Akṣairyutaṁ glaumakuṭaṁ koṭipūrṇendusaprabham || [12]

"He is endowed with five faces, pale, yellow, black, pure white, of hibiscus colour, with three eyes, the moon as a diadem, the brightness of crores of full moons."

Sometimes the faces are mentioned with special names ascribed to them.

---

[7] *Skanda P.*, I.34.36.
[8] *Bhāgavata P.*, VIII,7.29.
[9] *Kūrma P.*, I.20.63.
[10] *Liṅga P.*, II.19.7.
[11] *Vāmana P.*, 2.35.
[12] *Nāradīya P.*, I.91.88.

Tasya pūrvaṁ mukhaṁ pītaṁ prasannaṁ puruṣātmakam |
Aghoraṁ dakṣinaṁ vaktraṁ nīlāñjanacayopamam ||
Daṁṣṭrākarālam atyugraṁ jvālāmālāsamāvṛtam |
Raktaśmaśruṁ jaṭāyuktaṁ cottare vidrumaprabham ||
Prasannaṁ vāmadevākhyaṁ varadaṁ viśvarūpiṇam |
Paścimaṁ vadanaṁ tasya gokṣīradhavalaṁ śubham ||
Muktāphalamayair hārair bhūṣitaṁ tilakojjvalam |
Sadyojātamukhaṁ divyaṁ bhāskarasya smarāriṇaḥ || [13]

"His east face is yellow, serene, the form of Puruṣa. His south face is Aghora, comparable to a heap of collyrium, terrific with protruding teeth, very fierce, surrounded by garlands of flames. In the north the face has red beard, matted hair, the colour of coral, is serene, called Vāmadeva, bestower of boons, having all forms. His west face has the colour of cow's milk, is beautiful, adorned with pearl necklaces, brightened by a forehead mark; that is the divine Sadyojāta face of the resplendent Śiva."

In one passage cited below which mentions the four faces of Śiva, the functions of the four *dikpālas* Indra, Yama, Varuṇa and Soma are related to the four faces facing the respective quarters:

Pūrveṇa vadanena tvam indratvaṁ prakaroṣi vai |
Dakṣiṇena tu vaktreṇa lokān saṁkṣipase punaḥ ||
Paścimena tu vaktreṇa varuṇastho na saṁśayaḥ |
Uttareṇa tu vaktreṇa somas tvaṁ devasattamaḥ || [14]

"By your east face you assume the form of Indra. By your south face you resorb the worlds. By your west face you stand in the form of Varuṇa, no doubt. By your north face you are the Moon, the best of the gods."

[13] *Liṅga P.*, II.19.9-12.

[14] *Brahmāṇḍa P.*, I.26.40-41; *Vāyu P.*, I.55.38-39 gives a slightly different reading:
Pūrvena vadanena tvam indratvaṁ ca prakāśate |
Daksiṇena ca vaktreṇa lokān saṁkṣipase prabho ||
Paścimena ca vaktreṇa varuṇatvaṁ karoṣi vai |
Uttareṇa tu vaktreṇa saumyatvaṁ ca vyavasthitam ||

Once, Śiva appeared before unmarried Umā in disguise and tried to discourage her from marrying him. This was only to test the sincerity of her devotion. He made a contrast at this time with a reference to his own five faces:

Śaśāṅkavadanā tvaṁ ca pañcavaktraḥ śivaḥ smṛtaḥ | [15]

The ascription of countless faces to Śiva is also not rare in the *Purāṇas*.[16]

Śiva's hair is sometimes pictured as scattered or disheveled, following the description of the god in the *Śatarudriya* (e.g. *vyuptakeśa*). We get various pictures of the arrangement of the hair. Sometimes the hair is tied into a crown-shaped knot. In his dancing pose, the vigorous but rhythmic movement of the body makes his hair wild and dishevelled. When prescribing the construction of Śiva's image with human features, it is said that the hair should be represented as pointing upwards, usually in a knot:

Ūrdhvakeśaśca kartavyaḥ [17]

The loose hair as opposed to that being tied into a knot is also mentioned:

Gaṅgājalāplāvitamuktakeśaḥ [18]

"He has his hair untied, inundated by Gaṅgā water."

More frequent are the references to the matted hair which the god wears with divine poise; he has thereby earned the distinctive appellation, *Jaṭādhara*, the Bearer of Matted Hair. He is also described as *Jaṭājūṭavirājita*,[19] *Jaṭāmaṇḍalamaṇḍita*,[20] and *Jaṭāmaulin*.[21] The arrangement of the matted hair in the shape of a *makuṭa* is a special characteristic of the god:

---

[15] *Śiva P.*, *Jñāna-saṁhitā*, 14.25.

[16] This, however, has an esoteric implication: *Sarvato mukhaḥ*; *Kūrma P.*, II.39.62. *Sahasrapādākṣiśirobhiyuktaṁ*, *ibid.*, I.16.195. The face of the god is sometimes described as possessing the glow of fire: *hutāśavaktraṁ jvalanārkarūpam*, *Kūrma P.*, I.16.95.

[17] *Matsya P.*, 259.5.

[18] *Vāyu P.*, I.54.97.

[19] *Kūrma P.*, II.31.33.

[20] *Ibid.*, I.9.51.

[21] *Ibid.*, I.20.63.

Jaṭāmakuṭadhāriṇam [22]

The weighty lock of the matted hair of Śiva is often described as lifted upwards to a prominent position.

Samunnatajaṭābhāraḥ [23]

In many descriptions of the god, *jaṭā* always finds a conspicuous mention, as in the expression:

Bhasmadaṇḍajaṭājinam [24]
"Having ashes, staff, matted hair and dear skin."

His *jaṭā* [25] is invariably characterized as heavy to bear; this brings to the god the name of *Dhūrjaṭi.* Reference to the *jaṭā* in relation to the river Gaṅgā, who is present within its meshes, adds significance to the concept of Dhūrjaṭi:

... sa dhūrjaṭir
Jaṭām taḍidvahnisaṭograrociṣam
Utkṛtya ... [26]
"This Dhūrjati released his matted hair of fierce shining like the mass of fire of a lightning."

An allegorical exposition is sometimes given of Śiva's *jaṭā*, as in:

Nānāvidhāḥ karmayogā jaṭārūpā bibharti saḥ [27]
"He bears the diverse rituals in the form of his meshes of hair."

Śiva's hair is also not infrequently contrasted with that of Umā:

---

[22] *Liṅga P.*, II.19.7.

[23] *Vāmana P.*, 53.7.

[24] *Bhāgavata P.*, IV.6.36.

[25] For the different styles of arranging the matted hair of Śiva found in iconographic representations see "Geographical and Chronological factors in Indian Iconography" *Ancient India*, no.6, (1950), pp. 53-55.

[26] *Bhāgavata P.*, IV.5.2.

[27] *Skanda P.*, I.2.25.75.

Kabaryāścaiva te rūpaṁ varṇituṁ naiva śakyate |
Jatājūṭaṁ śivasyaiva prasiddhaṁ paricakṣyate || [28]

"The beauty of your braid cannot be described. We speak about the well-known matted hair of Śiva only."

A particularly distinguishing feature of Śiva is his third eye. This feature of Śiva's personality is obviously an afterthought. It is based on the more ancient concept of Śiva as Tryambaka, which, however, originally had little to do with his having three eyes.[29] The third eye of Śiva is said to be located on the forehead:

Cakṣuṣā ca tṛtīyena bhālasthena virājitaḥ | [30]

The third eye is compared with the *tilaka* mark applied onto one's forehead:

Tilakaṁ sundaraṁ hy āsīn nayanaṁ tu tṛtīyakam [31]

Śiva is called the three-eyed god and this epithet exclusively belongs to him. His eyes are long and broad:

Dīrghāyatavilocanaḥ [32]

---

[28] *Śiva P., Jñāna-saṁhitā*, 14.26.

[29] About the concept of Tryambaka, *Dandekar* says as follows:
"Apart from the merging of the Mother Goddess cult and the proto-Śiva cult, which is reflected in the personality of the Vedic Tryambaka-Rudra, there is another and, perhaps, more significant religious phenomenon which is reflected in him. In addition to the Great Mother, and, undoubtedly, as an offshoot of that concept, the primitive people assumed the existence, by the side of a male god, of certain female-divinities, called 'mothers', who were supposed directly to influence their day to day communal life. The number of such 'mothers' varied from community to community. The concept of Tryambaka-Rudra — as developed in the *Veda* — would seem to belong rather to this second type of religious thought. For, like the guardian 'mother' of a village, Ambikā is, sometimes, represented as frightful demoness helping Rudra in his malevolent activity, and other times, being propitiated by the worshippers she is said to turn into a healing, luck-bringing, fertility-giving divinity." "Rudra in the Veda", *JUPH* 1, pp. 145 f.

[30] *Skanda P.*, I.1.34.46.

[31] *Śiva P., Jñāna-saṁhitā*, 16.6.

[32] *Matsya P.*, 259.5.

The number of the eyes of Śiva, however, varies according to the number of faces that are assumed of that god. Each face has, of course, three eyes. The *dvādaśākṣa* [33] of the *Liṅga-Purāna* implies a four-faced Śiva.

The eye on his forehead possesses the properties of fire. It is identified with Agni himself. When Kāma fired his arrow at Śiva, the eye on his forehead began to burn with fire:

Tataḥ Kopānalodbhūtaghorahuṅkārabhīṣaṇe
Babhūva vadane netraṁ tṛtīyam analākulam [34]

"Then on his face, frightening with the terrific sound issuing from the fire of his anger, the third eye was full of flames."

The same description occurs elsewhere thus:

... netravisphuliṅgena krośatāṁ nākavāsinām
Gamito bhasmasāt tūrṇam ... [35]

"By a sparkle from his eye [Kāma] was soon reduced to ashes, while the gods were crying out."

In another context, fire, the sun and the moon are said to be the three eyes of Śiva:

Namo 'gnicandrārkavilocanāya [36]

At the time of Śiva's wedding, these three eyes are said to have added grace to his demeanour:

Virejur nayanāntasthāḥ śambhoḥ sūryānalendavaḥ [37]

The three qualities, *sattva*, *rajas* and *tamas*, are respectively ascribed to the three eyes of Śiva:

Netratrayaṁ sattvarajastamāṁsi.[38]

---

[33] *Liṅga P.*, II.19.7.

[34] *Padma P.*, I.43.240.

[35] *Matsya P.*, 154.250.

[36] *Kūrma P.*, I.16.205.

[37] *Padma P.*, I.43.413.

[38] *Bhāgavata P.*, VIII.7.30.

The three *Vedas* are also associated with them in a similar manner:

Vedatrayī triṇetrāṇi tripuraṁ triguṇaṁ vapuḥ | [39]

A sharp distinction is made between Śiva's eyes and those of Umā, with the intention of praising hers:

Kva tvaṁ kamalapatrākṣī kva cāsau ca trilocanaḥ | [40]

References may be cited to the vision of Śiva's form with a thousand eyes:

Sahasrapādākṣiśirobhiyuktam [41]
"endowed with thousand feet, eyes and heads."

The number of hands ascribed to Śiva is by no means uniform everywhere. The minimum number is four, and most of the representations in the temples of the South conform to this tradition. Eight hands are sometimes ascribed to him, obviously in view of his being represented with four heads:

Aṣṭabāhum [42]

and

Aṣṭahastam [43]

Corresponding to the five heads, sometimes ten arms are ascribed to the god:

Mahādevo bāhubhir daśabhir vṛtaḥ [44]

The ten arms are described as adorned with bracelets:

Daśabhujās tubhyaṁ keyūrāṅgadabhūṣitāḥ [45]

---

[39] *Skanda P.*, I.2.25.75.

[40] *Śiva P.*, *Jñāna-saṁhitā*, 14.25.

[41] *Kūrma P.*, I.16.95.

[42] *Liṅga P.*, II.19.7.

[43] *Kūrma P.*, I.20.63.

[44] *Skanda P.*, I.1.34.47.

[45] *Liṅga P.*, I.21.73.

It is prescribed, in connection with one kind of image of Śiva, that it should be represented with ten arms:

... daśabhujaḥ kāryaḥ [46]

References to five heads and ten arms in the same context are not wanting:

Pañcavaktraṁ daśabhujaṁ karpūragaurakaṁ mune | [47]

Śiva is sometimes spoken of as possessing sixteen or even eighteen arms, though these cannot be satisfactorily related to the number of heads:

Tathā tripuradāhe ca bāhavaḥ ṣoḍaśaiva tu | [48]
"When he burnt Tripura, he had sixteen arms."

and,

Aṣṭādaśabhujo haraḥ [49]
"Hara has eighteen arms."

Though they do not necessarily indicate any specific characteristics of Śiva, a few other passages in the *Purāṇas* describe Śiva's hands. His arms are described as extending as far as his knee.[50] This feature is required to be displayed in the image of the god:

Ājānulaṁbabāhuśca [51]

The arms so portrayed are expected to bear resemblance to the trunk of an elephant. His arms are massive. He, therefore, receives the title *mahābhuja* [52] and *Pīnorobhujaskandha*.[53] He is referred to as golden-armed,[54] in conformity with the description occurring in the

[46] *Matsya P.*, 259.11. Śiva is in some cases sculpturally represented with one head and ten arms.

[47] *Śiva P.*, *Jñāna-saṁhitā*, 3.18.

[48] *Matsya P.*, 259.11.

[49] *Ibid.*, 22,14.

[50] This is a common characteristic of most of the Hindu gods.

[51] *Matsya P.*, 259.8.

[52] *Liṅga P.*, II.19.7.

[53] *Matsya P.*, 259.13.

[54] *Vāyu P.*, I.55.46.

Śatarudriya. As for the representation of the hands in the image, it is laid down that the *abhaya* and the *varada* poses should be depicted.[55] In contrast with Umā's delicate and tender hands, those of Śiva's are fearful, since they are garlanded by serpents:

Kathaṁ karaḥ komalapallavas te
Sameṣyate śārvakaraṁ sasarpam | [56]

"How your arm, a delicate twig will be united to Śarva's arm covered with serpents."

In one extraordinary manifestation, Śiva is said to possess numerous arms and with them to wield a variety of weapons:

Bhujair anekasāhasrair bahuśastrakṛtagrahaḥ |

Śiva's neck also reveals a distinctive feature of the god. It bears a mark caused by the drinking of the poison which was produced when the gods and the demons churned the milky ocean to obtain nectar. The stain became a permanent feature and brought the god the name *Nīlakaṇṭha*.

The blue colour of his neck is often said to contribute to his personality:

Tathā marakataśyāmakandharo 'tīva sundaram | [57]

"His emerald green neck is extremely beautiful."

Viṣaṁ kaṇṭhe virājate [58]

"The poison shines on his neck."

Śobhate deva kaṇṭhaste gātre kundanibhaprabhe |
Bhṛṅgamālānibhaṁ kaṇṭhe 'pyatraivāstu viṣaṁ tava || [59]

"O God, your neck shines in your body which has the colour of jasmin. On your neck let the poison be like a group of bees."

---

[55] *Matsya P.*, 259.10.
[56] *Vāmana P.*, 51.63.
[57] *Skanda P.*, I.1.34.47.
[58] *Śiva P.*, *Jñāna-saṁhitā*, 14.33.
[59] *Matsya P.*, 250.59-60.

The following stanza from the *Agni Purāṇa* explains how Śiva came to be known as *Nīlakaṇṭha.*

Kṣīrābdher mathyamānācca viṣaṁ hālāhalaṁ hyabhūt |
Hareṇa dhāritaṁ kaṇṭhe nīlakaṇṭhas tato 'bhavat || [60]

"From the ocean, when it was churned, came out the hālāhala poison. It was retained by Hara on his neck. Thus he became the Black-necked god."

Śiva himself describes to Umā that poison-drinking episode as follows:

Pibato me mahāghoraṁ viṣaṁ surabhayaṅkaram |
Kaṇṭhaḥ samabhavat tūrṇaṁ krṣno me varavarṇini || [61]

"When I drank the very harsh poison which frightened the gods, my neck quickly became black, O Lady of best complexion."

In another context, the event is described in more or less the same words. On that occasion, Brahmā told the Great God that his black neck added grace to his person:

Pibato me mahāghoraṁ viṣaṁ surabhayapradam |
Kaṇṭhaḥ samabhavat tūrṇaṁ krṣno vai varavarṇini ||
Takṣakaṁ nāgarājānaṁ lelihānam ivotthitam |
Athovāca mahātejā brahmā lokapitāmahaḥ ||
Śobhase tvaṁ mahādeva kaṇṭhenānena suvrata | [62]

"... that poison was like the king of serpents raising its hood, ready to lick out. Then Brahmā, ancestor of the world, of great radiance, told: 'You shine, o Mahādeva of good vows, with such a neck'."

A few of the scant references in the *Purāṇas* to the chest, belly, hips, thighs and feet of Śiva may be reproduced here. Though these cannot be said to imply any special features of the god's personality,

---

[60] *Agni P.*, 3.8-9.

[61] *Vāyu P.*, I.54.90.

[62] *Brahmāṇḍa P.*, I.25.86-89.

they are given here with a view to giving this survey a kind of completeness. The chest, hips and feet of Śiva are mentioned as massive and beautiful:

Uro yasya viśālaṁ ca tatorujaghanaṁ param
Caraṇadvayaṁ ca rudrasya śobhitam ...[63]

"His chest is broad, his thigh and hips are long. The feet of Rudra are resplendent."

Śiva is spoken of as *sujaṭharaḥ*,[64] the one endowed with a beautiful belly.

The feet of Śiva are glorified in glowing terms:

Tad dṛṣṭvā caraṇāravindam atulaṁ tejomayam sundaram
Sandhyārāgasumaṅgalaṁ ca paramaṁ tāpāpanuttiṁkaram |
Tejorāśikaraṁ parātparam idaṁ lāvaṇyalīlāspadam
Sarveṣāṁ sukhavṛttikāraṇaparaṁ śaṁbhoḥ padaṁ pāvanam ||[65]

"... The foot of Śambhu is like a lotus, without equal, full of radiance, beautiful, auspicious like the red sandhyā, supreme means of discarding affliction, a mound of light, superior to the best dwelling of beauty and grace, source of happiness for all. It purifies."

The complexion of the god varies from fair to dark. References have already been cited to the ascription of various colours for each of the five faces of Śiva.[66] The white colour of the god is likened to that of camphor:

Karpūragauraṁ śitikaṇṭhamadbhutaṁ
Vṛṣānvitaṁ devavaraṁ dadarśuḥ [67]

"They saw the excellent god, white like camphor, with cold neck, wonderful, accompanied by the bull."

---

[63] *Skanda P.*, I.1.34.48.
[64] *Brahmāṇḍa P.*, I.26.53.
[65] *Skanda P.*, I.1.34.49.
[66] See above p. 185.
[67] *Skanda P.*, I.1.22.5.

Śiva tells Umā that her dark complexion is visibly reflected by the white colour of his body:

Śarīre me ca tanvaṅgi site bhāsy asitadyutiḥ |[68]

An amusing quarrel is said to have arisen when Śiva mocked Umā in connection with her dark complexion. Umā retaliated very promptly by drawing Śiva's attention to the fact that he himself was known as 'Mahākāla', which means, 'The Great Dark One'.

Yastvaṁ māmāha kṛṣṇeti mahākāleti viśrutaḥ |[69]

We come across another description of the god where he is said to be emanating the lustre of molten gold:

Taptakāñcanasaprabhaḥ [70]

The god is once described as *sindūrābha*,[71] that is, bearing a complexion resembling the colour of the red *sindūra* powder. The resplendence that radiated from Śiva's body is described by such terms as *vidyutkoṭisamaprabha*.[72] It is also likened to the effulgence emanating simultaneously from crores of flames:

Hutabhugjvālākoṭibhānusamaprabhaḥ [73]

In this terrible aspect, Śiva is said to resemble the conflagration marking the end of the world:

Rudraṁ kālāgnisannibham [74]

Śiva's bodily lustre is described in terms of Agni as follows:

... *Agnivarṇam agnikuṇḍanibhekṣaṇam*
Agnyādityasahasrābham agnivarṇavibhūṣitam [75]

"He has the colour of fire; his eye is like a firepit; he is bright like thousands of fires and suns; he is adorned with the colour of fire."

[68] *Matsya P.*, 155.1.
[69] *Matsya P.*, 159.8.
[70] *Ibid.*, 259.3.
[71] *Nāradīya P.*, II.91.103.
[72] *Liṅga P.*, II.19.6.
[73] *Varaha P.*, 21.71.
[74] *Skanda P.*, I.1.32.40.
[75] *Matsya P.*, 132.19-20.

Reference may be made at this stage to two interesting descriptions of the body of Śiva, one where the twenty-seven lunar mansions are identified with the various limbs of Rudra,[76] and the other where the various features of Rudra are described in relation to the letters of the alphabet.[77]

A special note must be taken of one very important concept about Śiva, according to which his person is believed to consist of eight elements. Śiva is thereby called *aṣṭamūrti*. These eight constituents are frequently mentioned to be the five elements, the sun and moon, and the sacrificer:

Tvaṁ bhūjalāgninīranabhorkasoma-
Yajvāṣṭamūrtibhavabhāvano'lam |[78]

The same enumeration in a different form is found elsewhere:

Sūryo jalaṁ mahī vahnir vāyurākāśam evaca |
Dīkṣitobrāhmaṇaścandra ityetā aṣṭamūrtayaḥ ||[79]

Brahmā has provided Rudra with an eightfold body:

Sūryo jalaṁ mahī vāyur vahnir ākaśam evaca |
Dīkṣito brāhmanaś candra ityevam aṣṭadhā tanuḥ ||[80]

The eightfold manifestation of Śiva is mentioned a little more elaborately in the following passage:

Tadāṣṭadhā mahādevaḥ samatiṣṭhat samantataḥ |
Tadā prakāśate bhānuḥ kṛṣṇavartmā niśākaraḥ ||
Kṣitiḥ vāyuḥ pumān ambhaḥ suṣiraṁ sarvagaṁ tathā |
Tadāprabhṛti taṁ prāhur aṣṭamūrtir itīsvaram ||[81]

Brahmā is said to have assigned eight names to Rudra when the latter persistently demanded that he be given eight names. Eight *sthānas* or places were provided for these names. These places ultimately became the eight bodies of the god:

---

[76] *Vāmana P.*, 5.33 ff.
[77] *Liṅga P.*, I.17.73-92.
[78] *Padma P.*, I.46.85.
[79] *Kūrma P.*, I.10.27.
[80] *Brahmāṇḍa P.*, 10.191.
[81] *Liṅga P.*, I.41.35-36.

Cakre nāmānyathaitāni sthānāny eṣāṁ cakāra ha |
Sūryo jalaṁ mahī vahnivāyur ākāśam eva ca ||
Dīkṣito brāhmaṇaḥ soma ity etās tanavaḥ kramāt | [82]

The following verse introduces a series of questions, in which the eight phenomena are mentioned, and the common answer clearly implied that they constitute the body of Śiva:

Kasyaitad gaganaṁ mūrtiḥ kasyāgniḥ kasya mārutaḥ |
Kasya bhūḥ kasya varuṇaḥ kaś candrārkavilocanaḥ || [83]

The twenty-seventh chapter of the *Vāyu Purāṇa* describes at length the eightfold form of Śiva.

Attention may be drawn to another characteristic of Śiva's personality, one which has found greater expression in South Indian iconic and architectural representations. This form of Śiva is composed of two elements, one male and the other female. The features of each sex are evenly distributed. Attempts are often made to show that the *Ardhanārīśvara* concept is exclusively Śaivite and that it bears no connection whatsoever with Śaktism.[84] It may, however, be pointed out that Śiva's connection with Śakti had become an established fact by the Purāṇic times, so much so that the identity of Śiva and Śakti is always emphasized:

Ekā śaktiḥ śivaiko'pi śaktimān ucyate Śivaḥ |
Śaktayaḥ śaktimanto'nye sarvaśaktisamudbhavāḥ ||
Śaktiśaktimator bhedaṁ vadanti paramārthataḥ |
Abhedaṁ cānupaśyanti yoginas tatvacintakāḥ || [85]

"The unique Śakti is called Śivā; though unique, Śiva is called 'Possessor of Śakti'. There are powers and the possessors of powers are different, being born of all powers. We say there is difference

[82] *Markaṇḍeya P.*, 52.8-9.

[83] *Padma P.*, I.43.339.

[84] It may be pointed out, in this connection, that the concept of a hermaphrodite being is not quite unknown to the *Veda*. For a discussion of this subject, see: Dandekar, "Yama in the *Veda*", *B.C. Law Comm. Vol.*, pp. 194-209.

[85] *Kūrma P.*, I.12.27-28.

between Śakti and the possessor of Śakti. Yogins meditating on reality see there is no difference in ultimate reality."

Śiva as Ardhanārīśvara is worshipped in the temples of the South. Clear traces of the Ardhanārīśvara form of Śiva are found in the *Purāṇas*. After recounting the evolution of the world, which is akin to the Sāṅkhyan account of the same, the *Liṅga Purāṇa* [86] continues to narrate how further creation was attempted by Prajāpati with *puruṣa* as the basis. The creator-god thus produced the *mānasa-putras*, and thereafter discovered that he could not progress at all with the creation of beings. In the company of the *mānasaputras* he performed *tapas* in honour of Śiva. Thereafter, piercing through the center of the forehead of Brahmā appeared a form in which the male and the female elements were combined in equal proportions. This was no other than Mahādeva, who for such appearance is named Ardhanārīśvara. The god then destroyed everything including the creator himself. The propagation of the beings was then effected by a yogic process of bringing together the male and the female elements. Hari, Brahmā and the other beings were thereafter created.

Very curt are the references that occur in the *Purāṇas* to the Ardhanārīśvara form of Śiva. Among these the following may be cited with a view to indicate that this appellation of the god is used as if it is one similar to several others which indicate the various characteristics of the god:

> *Aṣṭabāhuṁ caturvaktraṁ dvādaśākṣaṁ mahābhujam |*
> *Ardhanārīśvaraṁ devaṁ jaṭāmukuṭadhāriṇam ||* [87]
>
> *Caturmukhaṁ jaṭāmaulimaṣṭahastaṁ trilocanam |*
> *Candrāvayavalakṣmāṇaṁ naranārītanuṁ haram ||* [88]

The Great God is described in another *Purāṇa* as having assumed the Ardhanārīśvara form characterisecd by dreadful features:

> *Ardhanārīnaravapuḥ pracaṇḍo'tibhayaṅkaraḥ.* [89]

---

[86] *Liṅga P.*, I.41.1 ff.
[87] *Liṅga P.*, II.19.7.
[88] *Kūrma P.*, I.20.63.
[89] *Varāha P.*, 2.49.

When Ardhanārīśvara became manifest, Brahmā is said to have commanded that the form should split into two parts. This division accordingly followed:

Ardhanārīśvaraṁ dṛṣṭvā sargādau kanakāṇḍajaḥ |
Vibhajasveti cāhādau yadā jātā tadābhavat ||[90]

The physical features of the Ardhanārīśvara form are elaborately described in the *Matsya Purāṇa*:

Adhunā saṁpravakṣyāmi ardhanārīśvaraṁ param |
Ardhena devadevasya nārīrūpaṁ suśobhanam ||
Īśārdhe tu jaṭābhāgo bālendukalayā yutaḥ |
Umārdhe cāpi dātavyau sīmantatilakāvubhau ||
Vālikā copariṣṭāttu kapālaṁ dakṣine kare |
Triśūlaṁ vāpi kartavyaṁ devadevasya śūlinaḥ ||
Vāmato darpaṇaṁ dadyādutpalaṁ tu viśeṣataḥ |
Vāmabāhuśca kartavyaḥ keyūravalayānvitaḥ ||
Upavītaṁ tu kartavyaṁ maṇimuktāmayaṁ tathā |
Stanabhāraṁ tathārdhe tu vāme pīnaṁ prakalpayet ||
Parārdhamujjvalaṁ kuryācchroṇyārdhe tu tathaiva ca |
Liṅgārdhamūrdhvagaṁ kuryād vyālājinakṛtāṁbaram ||
Vāme laṁbaparīdhānaṁ kaṭisūtratrayānvitam |
Nānāratnasamopetaṁ dakṣiṇe bhujagānvitam ||
Devasya dakṣinaṁ pādaṁ padmopari susaṁsthitam |
Kiñcidūrdhve tathā vāmam bhūṣitaṁ nūpureṇa tu ||
Ratnair vibhūsitān kuryād aṅgulīṣv aṅgulīyakān |
Sālaktakaṁ tathā pāde pārvatyā darśayet sadā ||
Ardhanārīśvarasyedaṁ rūpam asminn udāhṛtam |[91]

"Now I shall describe the supreme Lord with feminine half. In one half of the god of gods there is a very beautiful feminine half. In the side of the Lord the portion of matted hair has a young moon digit. In the side of Umā one must display the line dividing the hair and the forehead mark and the hair above. In the right hand of the god of

[90] *Liṅga P.*, I.5.28.

[91] *Matsya P.*, 260.1-10.

gods one should place a skull or a trident, but on the left (goddess side) a mirror or a lotus. The left arm should be made with armlets and bracelets. A sacred thread should be made with gems and pearls. On the left half one should make a heavy load of a breast. One should make the other half shining. And in one half at the level of hips one should do half of a male organ erect, a dress made with a skin of tiger or deer. On the left one should put a hanging garment with three hip-chains and diverse jewellery. On the right the right foot of the god is joined to a serpent and firmly resting on a lotus. On the left the left one is decorated with an anklet. One should put rings adorned with precious stones on the fingers. On the foot of Pārvatī one should display red lac."

Another form of Śiva which combines in itself two distinct concepts is that of Hari-Hara, a fusion of the Śaiva and the Vaiṣṇava features within a single representation. The *Matsya Purāṇa* has laid down rules relating to the construction of the image of Hari-Hara.[92] The Hari-Hara form did not, however, gain wide prevalence in the system of worship. Only a few instances of the installation of such images for worship can be cited. One thing, however, needs to be noted in this connection, that even in this form wherein the characteristics of Viṣṇu and Śiva are expected to be evenly represented, the accent on Śaivism seems to be unmistakable.

As has been pointed out elsewhere, in one of his original pre-Vedic non-Aryan forms, Śiva is represented as a *yogin par excellence*. On a Mohenjodaro seal, for instance, the god is seen sitting in a yogic posture. The *Purāṇas* also celebrate this *yogīśvara* aspect of Śiva. At one place he is described as:

Padmāsane copaviṣṭo maheśo yogavittamaḥ |
Kevalaṁ cātmanātmānaṁ dadhyau militalocanaḥ ||
Śuśubhe ca mahādevaḥ samādhau candraśekharaḥ |
Yogapaṭṭaḥ kṛtas tena śeṣasya ca mahātmanaḥ ||
Vāsukiḥ sarparājaś ca kaṭibaddhaḥ kṛto mahān |[93]

[92] *Matsya P.*, 260.21-27.

[93] *Skanda P.*, I.1.34.150-152.

"Sitting in lotus pose, Maheśa, the best knower of yoga, meditated on the self by the self, eyes closed. The great god Candraśekhara shone in samādhi. His yoga belt was made of the great-souled Śeṣa and the great Vāsuki was tied on his waist."

Another description of a similar yogic pose occurs elsewhere:

Dadarśa ca maheśānaṁ nāsāgrakṛtalocanam |
Devadārudrumacchāyāvedikāmadhyagāminam ||
Samakāyaṁ sukhāsīnaṁ samādhisthaṁ maheśvaram |
Nistaraṅgaṁ vinirgṛhya sthitim indriyagocaram ||
Ātmānam ātmanā devaṁ praviṣṭaṁ tapaso nidhim | [94]

"He saw the great Lord, eyes fixed on the tip of the nose, sitted in the centre of a platform under the shade of a *devadāru* tree, body straight, sitting comfortably, established in *samādhi*, experiencing a waveless repose in the field of sense organs, the self by the self, entered in a treasury of penance."

Still another characteristic description is given below to indicate the manner in which Śiva practiced yoga:

Upaviṣṭam darbhamayyāṁ bṛsyām brahma sanātanam |
Nāradāya pravocantaṁ pṛcchate śṛṇvatāṁ satām ||
Kṛtvorau dakṣiṇe savyaṁ pādapadmaṁ ca jānuni |
Bāhuṁ prakoṣṭhe' kṣamālām āsinaṁ tarkamudrayā ||
Taṃ brahmanirvāṇasamādhimāśritam ...[95]

"The gods saw Śiva sitted on a cushion of *darbha* grass, expending the eternal *brahman* to Nārada, his questioner, in presence of a saintly audience, his left lotus like foot placed on the right thigh, an arm on a knee, a rosary on a wrist, with the gesture of deliberation, engaged in the felicity of Brahman, in total psychic repose."

Śiva is conceived by the yogins thus:

Hṛtpuṇḍarīkasuṣire yogināṁ saṁsthitaḥ sadā |
Vadanti sūrayaḥ santaṁ paraṁ brahmasvarūpiṇam ||

---

[94] *Skanda P.*, I.2.24.31-32. [95] *Bhāgavata P.*, IV.6.37-39. [96] *Liṅga P.*, I.71.107-108.

Aṇor alpataraṁ prāhur mahato'pi mahattaram |
Sarvataḥ pāṇipādaṁ tvāṁ sarvato'kṣiśiromukham || [96]

"You are always established in the hollow inside the lotus-like heart of the yogins. Sages say you are the supreme being, whose essence is the *brahman*. They say you are subtler than the atom, greater than the great, with hands and feet on all sides, with faces and eyes in all directions."

An all-embracing portrayal of the god to be visualized at the end of yoga is depicted thus:

Sarvataḥ pāṇipādaṁ sarvato'kṣiśiromukham |
Sarvataḥ śrutimān loke sarvam āvṛtya tiṣṭhati || [97]

At another place, Śiva himself describes his form to Brahmā and Viṣṇu as follows:

Sargarakṣālayaguṇair niṣkalo'yaṁ sadā hare |
Madrūpaṁ paramaṁ brahmann īdṛśaṁ bhavadaṅgataḥ ||
Prakaṭībhavitā loke nāmnā rudraḥ prakīrtitaḥ | [98]

The person of Śiva as reflected in these and other passages must be seen as a whole. His features lose their implication if any of them is singled out and viewed separately. The following description of Śiva reminds us of the *Viśvarūpadarśana* in the *Bhagavadgītā*:

Tato'tikāyastanuvā spṛśan divaṁ
Sahasrabāhur ghanaruk trisūryadṛk |
Karāladaṁṣṭro jvaladagnimūrdhajaḥ
Kapālamālī vividhodyadāyudhaḥ || [99]

"Rudra, touching the sky with his gigantic body, has a thousand arms, the colour of a cloud, three sun-like eyes, fierce protruding teeth, a hair of flames of fire, a garland of skulls, diverse raised weapons."

---

[97] *Ibid.*, I.78.43; also cf. *Bhagavadgītā*, XIII.14.

[98] *Śiva P.*, *Jñāna-saṁhitā*, 4.41-44.

[99] *Bhāgavata P.*, IV.5.2.3; also cf. *Bhagavadgītā*, XI.16-25.

A mention may be made at this stage of a concept of Śiva according to which he is said to be a formless yet all-comprehending god. In this connection, all the highest qualities attributed to the Brahman of the *Upaniṣads* are ascribed to the god. For instance, Śiva is represented in Vedāntic terms as follows:

Paraṁ brahma sa īśānaḥ eko rudraḥ sa eva ca |
Sarvaṁ vyāpnoti yas tasya sarvavyāpī sanātanaḥ ||
Sūkṣmo bhūtvā śarīrāṇi sarvato hy upatiṣṭhati | [100]

"He is the supreme Brahman, the unique lord, Rudra, he who pervades everything, the all-pervader, eternal. Being subtle, he enters bodies from all sides."

Further,

Upāsitavyaṁ yatnena tadetat sadbhir avyayam |
Yato vāco nivartanta aprāpya manasā saha ||
...
Aparaṁ ca paraṁ ceti parāyaṇamiti svayam |
Vadanti vācaḥ sarvajñaṁ śaṅkaraṁ nīlalohitam || [101]

"With effort the sages should worship this imperishable being from whom have returned speech and mind without having reached him... The sacred words say he is the supreme and the second Brahman, the omniscient, Śaṅkara Nīlalohita."

He is described as devoid of characteristic or quality, and possessing a form which cannot be grasped by the senses:

Aliṅginam ālokavihīnarūpaṁ
Svayaṁ prabhuṁ citpratimaikarudram | [102]

"He is without mark, has an invisible body, powerful by himself, the unique Rudra whose body is consciousness."

Śiva's form cannot be indicated or explained. He is devoid of names and functions:

---

[100] *Liṅga P.*, I.18, verses 14, 16 and 17.
[101] *Ibid.*, II.18.27-29.
[102] *Kūrma P.*, I.33.40.

Anirdeśyaṁ ca tadrūpaṁ nāmakarmavivarjitaṁ | [103]

A feeling of surprise is expressed when bodily features are given to him, perhaps out of ignorance of the true nature of his being:

Asyātmano maheśasya dhīmataḥ... |
Adehinas tv aho deham akhilaṁ paramātmanaḥ || [104]

Śiva is also conceived as a god devoid of birth and death, father and mother, kith and kin. He proclaims to Umā about himself:

Na me 'sti mātā na pitā tathaiva
Na jñātayo vāpi na bāndhavāśca |
Nirāśrayo' ham ... [105]

Nārada examined the physical features of Umā and predicted that her husband was devoid of characteristics and of birth:

Na jāto'syāḥ patir bhadre lakṣaṇaiśca vivarjitaḥ | [106]
Sa na jāto mahādevaḥ [107]
Na sa jāto mahādevo bhūtabhavyabhavodbhavaḥ | [108]

Śiva is eternal and beyond death. As he himself once said:

Abravīd bhagavān rudro hyaham ekaḥ purātanaḥ |
Āsaṁ prathama evāhaṁ varttāmi ca surottamāḥ ||
Bhaviṣyāmi ca loke'smin matto nānyaḥ kutaścana | [109]

"The Lord Rudra said: I am unique, ancient; I was the first to exist, I exist, o best gods, I will exist ; in this world, nowhere will there be another than me."

Turning now to the peculiarities of Śiva's dress, it will be seen that some of its characteristic features clearly distinguish that god from others. Śiva wears the skin of an elephant, or sometimes that of a tiger or lion. Clothes made of the hide of the black antelope are also

---

[103] *Śiva P.*, *Jñāna-saṁhitā*, 3.6.
[104] *Liṅga P.*, I.35.50-51.
[105] *Vāmana P.*, 55.44.
[106] *Matsya P.*, 154.146. 17.
[107] *Padma P.*, I.43.174.
[108] *Matsya P.*, 154.178. 124.
[109] *Liṅga P.*, II.17.10-11.

described. The most significant characteristic of the god in respect of his dress is, however, his nakedness; this feature is seen in the Dārukāvana incident, where amidst of the residents of the *aśrama*, he is said to have moved about naked.

Śiva is often described as a wearer of skins. He wears hides and besmears his body with ashes. He is *carmavibhūti-dhārin*.[110] He wears the skin of the antelope as his upper garment. He is accordingly, described as *kṛṣṇājinottarīyaḥ*,[111] and also as *kṛṣṇājinadharaḥ*.[112] He wears nothing other than skin:

Vasanaṁ carma eva ca [113]

Even at the time of his wedding, the hide-garment of Śiva is said to have replaced silken cloth:

Dukūlaṁ carma ucyate.[114]

A garment made of the skin of the elephant is frequently mentioned.[115] At this time of Śiva's wedding, Indra is said to have helped Śiva to put on his elephant's skin.

Śakro gajājinaṁ tasya vasābhyaktāgrapallavam | [116]

In another passage, the god is portrayed as dressed in the skin of the elephant:

Vīrāsanakṛtoddeśaṁ gajacarmaniyāmitam | [117]

In one *Purāṇa*, which is more inclined to glorify Viṣṇu, his hideskin dress is spoken of as inauspicious and unholy:

Gajājinaṁ cāpavitraṁ yato dhārayate haraḥ | [118]

---

[110] *Vāyu P.* I.55.45.

[111] *Liṅga P.*, I.33.17.

[112] *Vāyu P.*, I.55.54.

[113] *Śiva P.*, *Jñāna-Saṁhitā*, 14.32.

[114] *Ibid.*, 16.7.

[115] The incident relating to the adoption of this skin as garment is narrated elsewhere in the chapter.

[116] *Padma P.*, I.43.411.

[117] *Ibid.*, I.43.385.

[118] *Garuḍa P.*, III.18.16.

The following passages mention the god as the wearer of tiger-skin. He is described as *Śārdūlacarmāmbarasaṁvṛtāṅga,*[119] *Śārdūla-carmavasāna,*[120] *Vyāghracarmaparīdhāna*[121] and *Vyāghracarmāṁba-rāvṛta.*[122] In the following passage from the *Padma Purāṇa*, Śiva is described as having put on both tiger skin and elephant skin:

Vyāghracarmaparīdhāno hasticarmaparicchadaḥ |[123]

The skin of the lion is also sometimes mentioned in this connection. For instance, Śiva is referred to as *Mṛgapaticarmavāsas.*[124] Elsewhere he refers to himself as one clad in a lion's skin:

Na me'sti vittaṁ gṛhasañcayārthe
Mṛgāricarmāvṛtadehinaḥ priye |[125]

"I have no fortune to equip the house; my body is covered with a lion-skin, o dear."

Rudra is *Mṛgacarmābhivṛta*[126] and *Siṁhājinin.*[127] We come across one passage in a *Purāṇa* in which the skins of the lion and the tiger are described as being worn as the lower and the upper garments respectively. The elephant skin is also mentioned in the same context:

Siṁhacarma paridhānaṁ vyāghratvaguttarīyakam |
... gajājinakṛtāṭopam[128]

Śiva is once described as wearing the skin of Nṛsiṁha, an *avatāra* of Viṣṇu as a sign of the former's victory over the latter. He is there referred to as *Nṛsiṁhacarmāvṛtabhasmagātra.*[129] The contrast between Śiva's barbarous garments and Umā's soft and beautiful dress is emphasized in one passage:

Kva dukūlaṁ tvadīyaṁ vai gajājinam athāśubham |[130]

---

[119] *Kūrma P.*, I.25.51.
[120] *Ibid.*, II.31.34.
[121] *Matsya P.*, 259.6.
[122] *Nārada P.*, I.125.17.
[123] *Padma P.*, I.5.38.
[124] *Liṅga P.*, I.33.18.
[125] *Vāmana P.*, 1.26.
[126] *Ibid.*, 51.64.
[127] *Ibid.*, 52.6.
[128] *Padma P.*, I.46.21-22.
[129] *Kūrma P.*, I.25.53.
[130] *Śiva P.*, *Jñāna-saṁhitā*, 14.27.

Most frequently, Śiva is represented in the *Purāṇas* as naked. This gives him such names as *Digvāsas* and *Digambara*. This feature of the god is sometimes described as a part of his nature:

Prakṛtyā sa tu digvāsāḥ [131]

Due to this, he is often abused by his opponents:

Nagnatvān na tava trapā.[132]

Śiva is often described as smearing his body with ashes which are supposed to have been collected from the cremation grounds:

Vibhūtyaṅgāni sarvāṇi parimārṣṭī ca nityaśaḥ | [133]

He is referred to as *Bhasmoddhūlana*,[134] *Cārubhasmopalipta*,[135] *Bhasmavibhūṣita* [136] and *Bhasmavibhūṣitāṇga.*[137] Ashes are described as the sandal applied to the body of Śiva:

Bhūtiś candanaṁ hyāsīt [138]

Umā was once told:

Candanaṁ tvadīye'ṅge citābhasma śivasya ca [139]

Śiva is depicted in the *Purāṇas* as wearing ornaments of various description. He wears gems and ornaments of gold. On account of his crest-gem and crown, Śiva is referred to as *Cūḍāmaṇidhara* [140] and *Kirīṭin*.[141] Elsewhere we come across the following description:

Śaurijvalacchiroratnamakuṭaṁ cānalojjvalam | [142]

He wears a golden necklace:

Kaṇṭhas te śobhate śrīmān hemasūtravibhūṣitaḥ | [143]

---

[131] *Matsya P.*, 154.331.
[132] *Padma P.*,I.44.25; also *Matsya P.*, 155.23.
[133] *Padma P.*, I.5.36-37.
[134] *Skanda P.*, I.2.25.60.
[135] *Vāmana P.*, 53.33.
[136] *Ibid.*, 51.64.
[137] *Vāyu P.*, I.55.46.
[138] *Śiva P.*, *Jñāna-saṁhitā*, 16.7.
[139] *Ibid.*, 14.27.
[140] *Liṅga P.*, I.27.70.
[141] *Kūrma P.*, I.25.51.
[142] *Matsya P.*, 154.438.
[143] *Liṅga P.*, I.21.74.

He wears garlands hanging down to his feet:

Mālām atyadbhutākārāṁ dhārayan pādalaṁbinīm | [144]

The ten arms of Śiva are described as being each adorned with *keyūra* and *aṅgada*:

Daśabhujās tubhyaṁ keyūrāṅgadabhūṣitāḥ | [145]

Nānāratnavicitrāṅgo nānāmālyānulepanaḥ | [146]

He is generally said to be *sarvābharaṇasaṁyukta*[147] and *bahvābharaṇabhūṣāḍhya.*[148]

But all this cannot be claimed as any special characteristic of the god. The exclusive peculiarity of Śiva is represented when serpents are said to constitute for the most part his ornaments. They serve as bangles, armlets, girdle, the *yajñopavīta*, etc. Snakes are worn by Śiva as ornaments of all types:

Śaurir vataṁsikāratnaṁ kaṇṭhābharaṇam ujjvalaṁ |

Bhujaṅgābharaṇaṁ gṛhya sajjaḥ śaṁbhoḥ puro'bhavat || [149]

"Viṣṇu, holding a serpent as ornament, jewels, bright necklaces, stood ready before Śambhu."

Śvasadugrabhujaṅgendrakṛtabhūṣaṇabhūṣitam | [150]

Sarpā hyābharaṇāny āsan maṇayo vividhāś ca ye | [151]

He is often described as *nāgabhūṣaṇabhūṣita* [152] and *dvijihvālaṅkṛtāṅga.*[153] Serpents are worn as earrings:

Vāsukiṁ dakṣiṇe karṇe [154]

The serpents which adorn the ears of Śiva are even given names, Padma and Piṅgala:

Karṇe'pi padmaś ca tathaiva piṅgalaḥ [155]

---

[144] *Kūrma P.*, I.9.52.

[145] *Liṅga P.*, I.21.73.

[146] *Brahmāṇḍa P.*, I.26.53.

[147] *Liṅga P.*, II.19.8.

[148] *Padma P.*, I.46.21.

[149] *Padma P.*, I.43.411.

[150] *Matsya P.*, 153.334.

[151] *Śiva P.*, *Jñāna-saṁhitā*, 16.7.

[152] *Nāradīya P.*, I.125.17.

[153] *Skanda P.*, I.2.25.61.

[154] *Matsya P.*, 260.3.

[155] *Vāmana P.*, 1.26.

Referring to the serpents it is said:

Karṇābharaṇāny āsan tāny evābharaṇāni ca [156]

... kaṁbalāśvatarais tathā
karṇadvaye dhārayantam ... [157]

"With Kambala and Aśvatara he wore ear-rings on his two ears."

The following are some other references to serpent ornaments worn by Śiva:

Mahāhiratnavalayahārakeyūranūpuraḥ | [158]

Bhujaṅgahāravalayaṁ [159]

Nāgas tathaivāśvataro hi kaṅkaṇam
... tathā kārkoṭakena hi
Pulahena ca bāhubhyāṁ dhārayantaṁ ca kaṅkaṇe | [160]

"The serpent Aśvatara was his bracelet with Kārkoṭaka and Pulaha he wore bracelets on his arms."

Special mention must be made of the serpents worn as *yajñopavīta*:

Yajñopavītavidhinā urasā bibhrataṁ vratam | [161]

Pannagānāṁ tu rājānam upavītaṁ ca vāsukim | [162]

"He wore Vāsuki, the king of serpents as sacred thread."

The god is often called *Nāga-yajñopavītin* and *Vyāla-yajñopavītin*.[163] Śiva remarks about himself to Umā thus:

Mamopavītaṁ bhujageśvaraḥ phaṇī [164]

An allegorical explanation as to why Śiva wears the serpents is given at one place. The serpents symbolize evils, like anger; Śiva controls all these by wearing them:

---

[156] *Śiva P.*, *Jñāna-saṁhitā*, 16.6.
[157] *Skanda P.*, I.1.22.4.
[158] *Vāmana P.*, 53.7.
[159] *Kūrma P.*, II.31.33.
[160] *Skanda P.*, I.1.22.4.
[161] *Ibid.*, I.1.22.3.
[162] *Padma P.*, I.5.29.
[163] *Liṅga P.*, I.33.7; and *Brahmāṇḍa P.*, I.26.54.
[164] *Vāmana P.*, 1.26.

Sarpāś ca doṣāḥ krodhādyās tān bibharti jaganmayaḥ [165]

At the time of his wedding, Śiva is said to have discarded golden ornaments befitting the occasion and substituted serpents for them:

Nānākāramahāratnabhūṣaṇaṁ dhanadāhṛtam |
Vihāyodagrasarpendrakaṭakena svapāṇinā ||
Karṇottaṁsaṁ cakāreśo vāsukiṁ takṣakaṁ svayam | [166]

"The Lord discarded the ornaments and precious stones brought by Kubera, and with his own hand decorated with great uprising serpents as bracelets made Vāsuki and Takṣaka as his own ear-rings."

The crescent moon is often said to have adorned the matted hair of Śiva:

Candrastu mukuṭasthāne sānnidhyamakarot tathā | [167]
Aṅgena sandhyābhrarucā candralekhāṁ ca bibhratam || [168]

Accordingly, the moon also deserves to be included among his special ornaments; Śiva is described as *somārdhabhūṣaṇa*,[169] *candrāvayavalakṣman*,[170] *candrāṅkitajaṭa*,[171] and *candramaulin*.[172] At the time of Śiva's wedding, Brahmā is said to have fixed the crescent moon upon the head of the bridegroom:

Śarvasyātha jaṭājūṭe candrakhaṇḍaṁ pitāmahaḥ
Babandha ...[173]

Śiva looks graceful with the crescent that bedecks his matted hair.

Ardhacandrāṅkito yasya kapardas tv atisundaraḥ | [174]

He is also known in this connection as *śaśāṅkāṅkitaśekhara*.[175]

In a sense, the waters of the Gaṅgā river contained by Śiva within his matted hair should also be seen as a special ornament of Śiva.[176]

---

165 *Skanda P.*, I.2.25.74.
166 *Matsya P.*, 154.444.
167 *Śiva P.*, *Jñāna-saṁhitā*, 16.5.
168 *Bhāgavata P.*, IV.6.36.
169 *Kūrma P.*, II.31.48.
170 *Matsya P.*, 132.20; and also *Kūrma P.*, I.20.63.
171 *Matsya P.*, 259.4.
172 *Nāradīya P.*, I.91-103.
173 *Padma P.*, I.43.108.
174 *Skanda P.*, I.1.34.46.

In his frightful aspect, Śiva is often described as roaming about in the cemetery with human skulls for his ornaments. He is presented in the *Purāṇas* as:

Kapālamālābharaṇaḥ pretabhasmāvaguṇṭhitaḥ | [177]

"He wears a garland of skulls, and is covered with the ashes of deceased persons"

When adorning Śiva at the time of his wedding, Cāmuṇḍā is said to have hung around his neck a huge garland of skulls:

Kapālamālāṁ vipulāṁ cāmuṇḍā murdhni badhnatī | [178]

Many more references may be cited to the *kapālas* worn as ornaments, along with the bones of human beings:

Citabhasma samādhāya kapāle rajataprabhaṁ |
Manujāsthīmayīmālām ābabandha ca pāṇinā || [179]

"He collected silver coloured ashes from funeral pyres and made a garland of human bones with his hand."

Sravannaravasāsthikapālakṛtabhūṣaṇāt | [180]
Kapālamālām aśivāṁ sadā dhārayate yataḥ |
Ataḥ sadāśivo jñeyaḥ [181]

"Because he always wear an inauspicious garland of skulls, he is known as Sadāśiva (*sadā-aśiva*).

Kapālamālāṁ śirasi [182]

The *kapāla* or the human skull is also mentioned as being carried by Śiva as a begging bowl. This was originally Brahmā's head but, when Śiva severed it, it stuck fast to his hand:

Kapālaśakalaṁ caikam asṛkpūrṇaṁ kare sthitaṁ | [183]

---

[175] *Kūrma P.*, II.1.31. [176] *Brahma P.*, II.4.
[177] *Kūrma P.*, I.16.125. [178] *Padma P.*, I.43.409.
[179] *Matsya P.*, 154.442; also *Padma P.*, IV.3.415.
[180] *Padma P.*, I.43.323. [181] *Garuḍa P.*, III.18.18.
[182] *Padma P.*, I.5.38. [183] *Varāha P.*, 97.13.

His association with the *kapāla* has given the god the name of *Kapālin*. In this aspect, Śiva is often accused of being devoid of pity and compassion:

Nirghṛṇas tvaṁ kapālitvād dayā te vigatā ciram | [184]

In addition to the skulls, Śiva wears tortoise shells and bear tusks as ornaments.[185] These are trophies celebrating his victory over the *kūrma* and the *varāha avatāras* of Viṣṇu.[186]

As the punisher of evil-doers, and especially of demons, Śiva wields weapons. Of these, the *śūla* and the *pināka* deserve special mention. These have brought the god two special names, *Śūlin* and *Pinākin*. *Pināka* is Śiva's bow.

Pinākapāṇaye sāyakacakradhāriṇe [187]

Namo'stu te vajrapinākadhāriṇe [188]

Sometimes, both the *triśūla* and the *pināka* are mentioned together:

Pinākapāṇirbhagavān surapūjyas triśūladhṛk | [189]

Śiva is described as firing his arrow at the three cities of the demons.

Śaraḥ pracoditas tatra rudreṇa tripuraṁ prati | [190]

The axe is also mentioned among his weapons. Indeed, this is the weapon which is invariably shown in most of the images of Śiva installed in the temples of South India. Śiva is called *Paraśvadhā-saktakara*.[191] The *triśūla*, however, seems to be Śiva's most prominent

---

[184] *Padma P.*, I.44.25.

[185] For the significance of the *kaparda* worn by Rudra-Śiva, see: Dandekar, "Rudra in the *Veda*", *JUPH* 1, p. 97.

[186] *Liṅga P.*, I.96.37-57.

[187] *Vāyu P.*, I. 55.45.

[188] *Brahmāṇḍa P.*, I.26.46.

[189] *Ibid.*, I.26.54.

[190] *Padma P.*, III.15.9.

[191] *Kūrma P.*, I.25.53.

weapon.[192] The *triśūla* is prescribed as a necessary adjunct of Śiva's image for installation:

Triśūlaṁ cāpi kartavyaṁ devadevasya śūlinaḥ | [193]

Tvaṣṭar, the divine architect, is said to have pulverised the radiance of the sun and, from such particles, to have fashioned the weapons of the gods. Among these was the *triśūla*, which was given to Śiva[194]. When Śiva prepared for a battle with demons, the Vasus informed him that the *śūla* was ready for him to wield:

Tataś ca vāsavo devaḥ śūlaṁ tasmai nyavedayat [195]

Śiva is said to have fixed Andhaka's body crosswise on the *śūla*:

Śūlena ca tato daityaṁ bibheda tripurāntakaḥ | [196]

and

Triśūlāgreṣu vinyasya prananarta satāṁ patiḥ | [197]

"The lord of sages placed him at the tips of his trident and danced."

The employment of *śūla* in the fight with the demons is often mentioned:

Yuyudhe bhairavo devo śūlam ādāya [198]

Triśūlam ādāya kṛśānukalpaṁ [199]

Gṛhītvā śūlam ātiṣṭhed daṁṣṭrāravadharo ruṣā | [200]

Tatas triśūlam atyugraṁ mumoca girijāpatiḥ | [201]

---

[192] Sivaramamurti has pointed out the fact that "with the exception of a few Pallava sculptures where Śiva is represented as carrying the *śūla* (trident), this weapon is absent from his hand in all South Indian representations of the deity, and the axe and the deer are invariably held in his upper hands." "Geographical and Chronological factors in Indian Iconography", *Ancient India*, Number 6, pp. 51-52. See p. 228 for his comments on the *ḍamaru* being replaced by the *śūla*.

[193] *Matsya P.*, 260.3.

[194] *Matsya P.*, 11.29.

[195] *Skanda P.*, I.2.26.26.

[196] *Padma P.*, I.46.82.

[197] *Kūrma P.*, I.16.190.

[198] *Ibid.*, I.16.140.

[199] *Ibid.*, I.16.177.

[200] *Padma P.*, I.46.27.

[201] *Ibid.*, VI.18.65.

Among other weapons which Śiva is described to have wielded from time to time, the following may be mentioned: *gadā*, *ṭaṅkā*, *kṛpāṇa*, *khaḍga*, *daṇḍa*, *asi*, *vajra*, *kheṭa*, and *śakti*. One interesting reference is to Śiva's arrow being called *Viṣṇumaya*.

Gadinaṁ pinākinaṁ śūlinaṁ.[202]

Śūlaṁ taṅkaṁ kṛpānaṁ ca vajrākhyāhipatīn karaiḥ |
Dadhānaṁ bhūṣaṇoddīpaṁ ghaṇṭāpāśavarābhayān || [203]

Kapālapātradhṛk śūlī khaṭvāṅgaṁ ca kare sthitaṁ | [204]

Kheṭakaṁ vāmahaste tu khaḍgaṁ caiva tu dakṣiṇe |
Śaktiṁ daṇḍaṁ triśūlaṁ ca dakṣiṇe tu niveśayet ||
Kapālaṁ vāmapārśve tu nāgaṁ khaṭvāṅgameva ca |
Śaṅkhaṁ cakraṁ gadā śārṅgaṁ ghaṇṭā tatrādhiko bhavet ||
Tathā dhanuḥ pinākaśca śaroviṣṇumayastathā |[205]

"One should place a shield in his left hand and a sword in a right one, a dagger, a staff and a trident in right hands, a skull, a serpent and a *khaṭvāṅga* mace in left hands. There may conch and discus, mace, bow and bell in addition, then the bow Pināka and the arrow made of Viṣṇu."

Nevertheless, none of these weapons are indispensable for Śiva. His mere glance can replace them all:

Puratrayaṁ virūpākṣa tatkṣaṇāt bhasmasātkṛtam |
Dagdhum apy atha deveśa vīkṣaṇena jagat trayam ||
Asmadyaśo vivṛddhyarthaṁ śaraṁ moktum ihārhasi | [206]

"O Virūpākṣa, the three cities have reduced to ashes in an instant. By your eye you are able to burn the three worlds; you may release an arrow to increase our fame."

Vṛṣabha, the bull, is the chief vehicle of Śiva, and the function of the bull as the *vāhana* is often mentioned. This vehicle was used

[202] *Kūrma P.*, I.25.51.
[203] *Nāradīya P.*, I.91.89.
[204] *Padma P.*, I.5.37-38.
[205] *Matsya P.*, 259.8-12.
[206] *Śiva P.*, *Jñāna-saṁhitā*, 24.40.

by the god when routing hostile demons, and at other times when he travelled from place to place:

Bāṇārthe bhagavān rudraḥ sasutaiḥ pramathair vṛtaḥ |
Āruhya nandivṛṣabhaṁ yuyodha rāmakṛṣṇayoḥ || [207]

"For the sake of Bāṇa, the Lord Rudra, surrounded by *pramathas* and their sons, mounted the Bull Nandin and fought with Rāma and Kṛṣṇa."

Vṛṣa is specifically mentioned at several places as Śiva's vehicle:

Vṛṣaṁ vibhūṣayāmāsuḥ harayānaṁ manojavam | [208]
Vṛṣam āruhya giriśaḥ sarvabhūtagaṇair vṛtaḥ |
Saha devyā yayau draṣṭuṁ yatrāste madhusūdanaḥ || [209]

"Mounting the Bull Giriśa, surrounded by all ghosts and *gaṇas*, with the goddess went to see where Madhusūdana resides."

It was the bull who carried Śiva in his wedding procession to his bride's residence. The vehicle is described as being prepared for the occasion thus:

Vāyuśca vipulaṁ tīkṣṇaśṛṅgaṁ himagiriprabham |
Vṛṣaṁ vibhūṣayāmāsa harayānaṁ mahaujasam || [210]

"Vāyu decorated the Bull, mount of Hara, big, of sharp horns, bright like Himagiri, of great strength."

Karamālaṁbya viṣṇośca vṛṣabhaṁ ruroha śanaiḥ | [211]

"And taking the help of Viṣṇu's arm, slowly, he mounted on the Bull."

When the god manifests himself before his devotees, he is invariably mounted on the bull:

Vṛṣānvitaṁ devavaraṁ dadarśuḥ [212]

Kailāsa is Śiva's principal abode. Several other places are also mentioned as the home of the god, such as a few mountains, temples,

---

[207] *Bhāgavata P.*, X.63.6.
[208] *Padma P.*, I.43.414.
[209] *Bhāgavata P.*, VIII.12.2.
[210] *Matsya P.*, 154.440.
[211] *Skanda P.*, I.2.26.26.
[212] *Ibid.*, I.1.22.5.

and even cremation grounds, where he revels in the company of the *bhūtas*. At Kailāsa, his oft-mentioned abode, all beings assemble to worship Śiva. The temple is sometimes described as located on the hill to the north of the river. The gods often assemble there; they admire the structure of Śiva's abode. After their marriage, Śiva brought Umā to Kailāsa:

Kailāsamāsādya śivāṁ sametya
Śobhāṁ prapede'titarāṁ śivo'pi |[213]

The gods marvel at Kailāsa's many wonderful features:

Vilokya bhūteśagiriṁ vibudhā vismayaṁ yayuḥ | [214]

Śiva describes himself as a mountain dweller. He proclaims to Umā:

Nirāśrayo'haṁ giriśṛṅgavāsī [215]

Śiva is once described to have abandoned Himavat at the request of Umā, who was insulted by Menā her mother. They made their home on Meru:

Śrutvā devyā vacanaṁ sureśaḥ
Tasya priyārthaṁ śvasuraṁ vihāya |
Jagāma meruṁ surasiddhasevitaṁ
Bhāryāsahāyaḥ svagaṇaiśca yuktaḥ || [216]

Bhūtavaṭa is mentioned as one of the special abodes of Śiva:

Tatra bhūtavaṭaṁ nāma nanābhūtagaṇālayam |
Mahādevasya prathitaṁ tryaṁbakasya mahātmanaḥ ||
Dīptam āyatanam ...[217]

The *vaṭa* often serves as a home of Śiva, especially when engaged in the practice of yoga.

---

[213] *Śiva P.*, *Jñāna-saṁhitā*, 19.3.

[214] *Bhāgavata P.*, IV.6.22.

[215] *Vāmana P.*, 53.44.

[216] *Brahmā P.*, I.36.40.

[217] *Vāyu P.*, I.40.20.

Vaṭaṁ kālābhrasadṛśaṁ dadarśa daśayojanam |
Tasyādhastāt samāsīnaṁ yogimaṇḍalamadhyagam || [218]

"He saw a banyan looking like a dark cloud, ten yojanas large, and below Śiva sitting in the center of a circle of yogins."

Vārāṇasī also is mentioned as having been sanctified by Śiva by making it his special abode; Śiva is said to be permanently residing there. The god has never abandoned it. Śiva himself has expressed this idea thus:

Vimuktaṁ na mayā

For this reason, the place came to be known as Avimukta, and the god as Avimukteśvara.[219]

The North-east is the direction assigned to Śiva; accordingly, it is called the *Aiśānya-dik*, the quarter of Īśāna, namely Śiva.

Īśānakoṇe saṁsthito yastu rudraḥ [220]

The hearts of the living beings are also described as the abode of this god:

Sarvam eva bhūtānāṁ hṛdy eṣa parameśvaraḥ [221]

His wanderings in the cemetery brought him the epithet *Śmaśānavāsin*. He is also called *Śmaśānanilaya*.[222] Of him it is said:

Śmaśāne ramate sadā [223]

So'yaṁ śmaśānavasatiṁ kartum aicchad yato haraḥ |
Ataḥ sadāśivo jñeyaḥ [224]

"Because Hara desired to make his residence in cemeteries, he is known as Sadāśiva (sadā-aśiva)."

Śmaśānavāsān nirbhīstvam [225]

---

[218] *Bhāgavata P.*, IV.6.22.

[219] *Matsya P.*, 22.7; also *ibid.*, 181.

[220] *Garuḍa P.*, III.18.24.

[221] *Kurma P.*, I.15.82.

[222] *Skanda P.*, I.2.25.60.

[223] *Padma P.*, I.2.25.60.

[224] *Garuḍa P.*, III.18.19.

[225] *Matsya P.*, 155.23.

Dakṣa abuses Śiva on account of his inauspicious habit of roaming about in cremation grounds:

Kiṁ vā śivākhyam aśivaṁ na vidus tvadanye
Brahmādayas tvām avakīrya jaṭāḥ śmaśāne |[226]

"Do other than you, Brahmā etc., not know you, called Śiva (Pure), as aśiva (impure), spreading your disheveled meshes, in a cemetery (you made your residence...)?"

The banner of Śiva bears the sign of the bull. No event can be traced in the *Purāṇas* relating either to this choice of symbol or to its being raised on any significant occasion. Only the occurrences of Śiva's names such as Vṛṣāṅka and Vṛṣabhadhvaja give us any details about Śiva's banner. However, it seems to have been the practice to choose the *vāhana* of a god as the symbol on his banner. Viṣṇu's *garuḍadhvaja* is suggestive in this connection.

The functions of creation, preservation, and destruction are ascribed to Brahmā, Viṣṇu and Śiva respectively. The *Purāṇas* often speak of this specific assignment of functions to the three gods; however, deviations from this convention are not infrequent. Śiva, for instance, is sometimes spoken as discharging all these functions alone. Brahmā, the creator, is said to have instructed Rudra to create. The latter readily consented to do so, but the difficulty was that Rudra created beings only of the highest order. Brahmā, therefore, grew impatient and asked Rudra to desist from creating. Rudra adamantly persisted, refusing to create beings affected by death and decay:

Taṁ prāha bhagavān brahmā janmamṛtyuyutāḥ prajāḥ |
Sṛjeti so 'bravīdīśo nāhaṁ mṛtyujarānvitāḥ ||
Prajāḥ srakṣya iti ...[227]

The same episode is mentioned in the *Purāṇas* in various versions. For instance, it is said:

---

[226] *Bhāgavata P.*, IV.4.16.

[227] *Kūrma P.*, I.10.33-38; also *ibid.*, I.70.30-31.

Ityādiṣṭaḥ sa guruṇā bhagavān nīlalohitaḥ |
Satvākṛtisvabhāvena sasarjātmasamāḥ prajāḥ || [228]

and

Prajāḥ sṛjeti vyādiṣṭo brahmaṇā nīlalohitaḥ | [229]

In this connection, it may be pointed out that Śiva is once mentioned as the creator of the creator Nārayaṇa himself:

Nārāyaṇaḥ sarvam idaṁ viśvaṁ vyāpya pravartate |
Tasyāpi jagataḥ sraṣṭuḥ sraṣṭā devo maheśvaraḥ || [230]

"Nārāyaṇa put this world in motion, pervading it. Maheśvara created this creator of the universe."

Even in the scheme of the evolution of the universe, Śiva has a function of primary importance. The Sāṁkhya principles are enumerated with Śiva as the highest of them.[231] On him rests the responsibility of giving the initial impulse for the process of evolution. He is said to be the cause of both the *sāmya* and the *laya* of the *guṇas*:

Sāmye laye guṇānāṁ tu tayorhetur maheśvaraḥ [232]

"Maheśvara is the cause of both, the equipoise and inhibition of the *guṇas* (*sattva*, *rajas*, *tamas*)."

To Maheśvara is ascribed this function of disturbing the equipoise of the *guṇas*, which sets the process of evolution in motion.[233] Further, every happening in the universe is the result of the will of this Great God. He controls all actions. Śiva himself once proclaims:

Mayaiva preryate kṛtsnaṁ cetanācetanātmakam |
So 'ntaryāmī sa puruṣo ...[234]

Thus, though Śiva is generally regarded as the god of destruction, he is sometimes represented in the *Purāṇas* as discharging the other

---

[228] *Bhāgavata P.*, III.12.15.

[229] *Vāyu P.*, I.10.43.

[230] *Ibid.*, I.1.184.

[231] *Liṅga P.*, I.41.1-5; also *ibid.*, II, chapters 15 and 16.

[232] *Ibid.*, I.4.53.

[233] *Vāyu P.*, I.5.11-12.

[234] *Kūrma P.*, II.35.63-64.

two functions as well. A few passages may be quoted here which show the god as being responsible for all the three functions:

Sargasya pratisargasya sthiteḥ kartā maheśvaraḥ | [235]

"Maheśvara is the agent of creation, secondary creation, and maintenance."

Sargarakṣālayaguṇaiḥ niṣkalaḥ parameśvaraḥ | [236]

"I (Śiva, divided in three parts with the names of Brahmā, Viṣṇu, Hara) and by the properties of creating, maintaining and destroying, am the Supreme Lord without parts."

Sṛjatyeṣa jagat kṛtsnaṁ pāti saṁharate tathā |
Kālo bhūtvā mahādevaḥ kevalo niṣkalaḥ śivaḥ || [237]

"Śiva, the great god, liberated, without parts, creates the whole world, protects it, and, being death, dissolves it."

Guṇamayyā svaśaktyāsya sargasthityatyayān vibho | [238]

"By his Power made of the properties (of *sattva*, *rajas* and *tamas*), he does creation, maintenance and destruction."

Śaṅkaro lokakartā ca hartā pālayitā svayam | [239]

"Śaṅkara is the creator of the world, the protector and destroyer by himself."

Śiva is characterized as *jagajjanmatrāṇasaṁhārakāraka* [240] and *sṛṣṭisthitisaṁhārakāraka*.[241] In the following passages, only creation and destruction are mentioned as the functions of Śiva:

Ataśca saṁkṣepam imaṁ śṛṇudhvam
Maheśvarah sarvam idaṁ purāṇam |
Sa sargakāle ca karoti sarvān
Saṁhārakāle punar ādadīta || [242]

---

[235] *Liṅga P.*, I.3.35.
[236] *Kūrma P.*, I.10.78.
[237] *Ibid.*, I.9.60.
[238] *Bhāgavata P.*, VIII.7.23.
[239] *Śiva P.*, *Jñāna-saṁhitā*, 17.23.
[240] *Kūrma P.*, II.1.34.
[241] *Liṅga P.*, II.19.8.
[242] *Vāyu P.*, I.1.185.

"Therefore, hear this summary. Maheśvara is this whole Purāṇa. At the time of creation, he creates all beings. At the time of dissolution, he will take them back."

Eṣa devo mahādevo vijñeyastu maheśvaraḥ |
Na tasya paramaṁ kiñcit padaṁ samabhigamyate ||
Devatānām ṛṣīṇāṁ vā pitṝṇāṁ cāpi śāśvataḥ |
Sahasrayugaparyante pralaye sarvadehinām ||
Samharatyeṣa bhagavān kālo bhūtvā maheśvaraḥ |
Eṣa caiva prajāḥ sarvāḥ sṛjatyeva svatejasā ||[243]

"This god should be known as the great god, the great Lord. Nothing is superior to him. His foot is approached by the gods, the sages and the Manes. He is eternal. At the time of dissolution of all beings at the end of a thousand yugas, the Lord Maheśvara, being death, resorbs all. He himself creates all beings with his own power."

The following descriptions depict the god only as the destroyer of the universe:

Sarvalokaikasaṁhartā kālātmā parameśvaraḥ |[244]

Tvām ṛte bhagavān śaktaḥ hantā nānyasya vidyate |
Tvaṁ hartā sarvalokānām ...[245]

"Parameśvara, whose essence is death, is the unique destroyer of all the worlds."

Elsewhere it is said of Śiva:

Kalau saṁhārakartā tvaṁ mahākālaḥ smṛto hyasi |[246]

"In Kali age you are the agent of dissolution; you are remembered as Mahākāla."

Rudraḥ saṁhāramūrtiśca nirmito brahmaṇā tataḥ |[247]

"Rudra, dissolution embodied, was created by Brahman."

Brahmā and Viṣṇu themselves glorify Śiva as the god of destruction:

---

[243] *Kūrma P.*, I.38.65-67.
[244] *Ibid.*, I.15.13.
[245] *Ibid.*, I.16.183-184.
[246] *Padma P.*, I.14.116.
[247] *Garuḍa P.*, III.17.7.

Saṁhartā sarvalokānāṁ kālo mṛtyumayo'ntakaḥ | [248]

"He is the destroyer of all the worlds, Kāla made of death, Antaka."

Kiṁ na jānāsi viśveśaṁ saṁhartāraṁ pinākinam |
Tena saṁhāradakṣeṇa kṣaṇāt saṁksayam eṣyati || [249]

"Do not you know the Lord of the world, the destroyer, Pinākin? Powerful in destruction in an instant he will bring everything to destruction."

One Vaiṣṇava *Purāṇa* states that Śiva is the god of destruction, but it is interesting to note that the *Purāṇa* asserts that Viṣṇu assumes the form of Rudra and discharges this function:

Sraṣṭā sṛjati cātmānaṃ viṣṇuḥ pālyaṃ ca pāti ca |
Upasaṁhriyate cānte saṁhartā ca svayaṁ hara ||
Brahmā bhūtvāsṛjad viṣṇuḥ jagatpatir hariḥ svayam |
Rudrarūpī ca kalpānte jagatsaṁharate 'khilam || [250]

"Viṣṇu, creator, creates the self and protects that which is to be projected and at the end, destroyer, destroys by himself, o Hara. Being Brahmā Viṣṇu created the world, he protects it in his own form. Assuming the form of Rudra, at the end of a kalpa, he destroys the whole world."

In another *Purāṇa*, Śiva is said to have ordained that the functions of creation and preservation would be discharged by Brahmā and Viṣṇu respectively and that the function of destruction would be reserved for himself:

Sṛṣṭikartā bhaved brahmā sṛṣṭeś ca pālako hariḥ |
Madīyaś ca tathāpy aṁśo bhaviṣyati tadantakṛt || [251]

"Brahmā will be the agent of creation; Hari the protector of the creation; a part of myself will be the destroyer."

Destruction, the characteristic function of the god discharged by him at the end of the world, is described in detail as follows:

---

[248] *Brahmāṇḍa P.*, I.26.39.
[249] *Liṅga P.*, I.96.37 & 39.
[250] *Garuḍa P.*, I.4.11-12.
[251] *Śiva P.*, *Jñāna-saṁhitā*, 3.34-35.

Gate parārdhadvitaye kāle lokaprakālanaḥ |
Kālāgnir bhasmasātkartuṁ carate cākhilaṁ jagat ||
Svātmany ātmānam āveśya bhūtvā devo maheśvaraḥ |
Dahed aśeṣaṁ brahmāṇḍaṁ sadevāsuramānuṣam ||
Tam āviśya mahādevo bhagavān nīlalohitaḥ |
Karoti lokasaṁhāraṁ bhīṣaṇaṁ rūpam āśritaḥ || [252]

"When the two halves of Brahmā's life are gone, Kālāgni, destroyer of worlds, proceeds to reduce the whole universe to ashes. Bringing his self into his self, being the god Maheśvara, he may burn the whole Brahmāṇḍa with gods, demons and men. The great god, the Lord of black neck and red hair, assuming a terrific form destroys the worlds."

Śiva is often featured as the god of dance. The *Purāṇas* provide the basis for this concept of Śiva as the Dancer,[253] though references to this form of his are not as numerous as one would expect them to be. A characteristic description of the *tāṇḍava* dance performed by Śiva at the hour of destruction may be given here:

Yas tv antakāle vyuptajaṭākalāpaḥ
Svaśūlasūcyarpitadiggajendraḥ |
Vitatya nṛtyaty uditāstradordhvajān
Uccāṭṭahāsastanayitnubhinnadik || [254]

"At the time of dissolution, Śiva, spreading his disheveled meshes, offers the elephants of directions to the pikes of his trident, uplifts his banner-like arms and his weapons, dances, breaking the cardinal points by the thunder of his loud laugh."

It is often mentioned in the *Purāṇas* that all these functions are discharged by Śiva in a spirit of *līlā* (play):

Viśvaṁ sṛjati paśyasi krīḍann ūrṇapaṭo yathā | [255]

"See, He creates everything, playing, like a spider."

[252] *Kūrma P.*, II.46.2-4

[253] *Nṛtyaty anantamahimā tasmai rudrātmane namaḥ. Kūrma P.*, I.10.67.

[254] *Bhāgavata P.*, IV.5.10.

[255] *Bhāgavata P.*, IV.6.43.

Līlayā devadeveśaḥ kāryaṁ sarvaṁ kariṣyati | [256]

Līlayā devadevena sargās tv īdṛgvidhāḥ kṛtāḥ | [257]

The number of universal functions is sometimes increased from three to five. It is significant that where these five functions are mentioned it is always Śiva to whom they are ascribed. The details concerning these functions and the manner in which the god discharges them are elaborately described in one *Purāṇa* as follows:

Sṛṣṭiḥ sthitiś ca saṁhāras tirobhāvo'py anugrahaḥ |
Pañceme jagatkṛtyaṁ nityasiddham ajācyutau ||
Sargaḥ saṁsārasaṁrambhas tatpratiṣṭhā sthitir matā |
Saṁhāro mardanaṁ tasya tirobhāvas tadutkramaḥ ||
Tanmokṣo'nugrahastan me kṛtyam evaṁ hi pañcakam |
Sargādi yaccatuṣkṛtyaṁ saṁsāraparijṛmbhaṇam ||
Pañcamaṁ muktihetur vai nityaṁ mayi ca susthiram |
Tadidaṁ pañcabhūteṣu dṛśyate māmakair janaiḥ ||
Sṛṣtir bhūmau sthitis toye saṁhāraḥ pāvake tathā |
Tirobhāvo'nile tāvadanugraha ivāṁbare |
Sṛjyate dharayā sarvam adbhiḥ sarvaṁ pravarddhate ||
Ardyate tejasā sarvaṁ vāyunā cāpanīyate |
Vyomnā tu gṛhyate sarvaṁ jñeyam evaṁ hi sūribhiḥ ||
Pañcavaktram imaṁ voḍhuṁ mamāsti mukhapañcakam |
Caturdikṣu caturvaktraṁ tanmadhye pañcamaṁ mukham ||
Yuvābhyāṁ tapasā labdham eva kṛtyadvayaṁ sutau |
Sṛṣṭisthityabhidhaṁ bhāgyaṁ mattaḥ prītād atipriyam ||
Tayo rudramaheśābhyām anyatkṛtyadvayaṁ param |
Anugrahākhyaṁ kenāpi labdhuṁ naiva hi śakyate || [258]

"Creation, maintenance, destruction, concealment, grace, these five are my actions regarding the world, which are eternally accomplished, o Brahman and Viṣṇu. Creation is the beginning of the world of

[256] *Śiva P., Jñāna-saṁhitā*, 20.23.

[257] *Liṅga P.*, I.4.53.

[258] *Śiva P., Jñāna-saṁhitā*, 8.1-10.

rebirths, maintenance is its stabilization, destruction is the crushing of it, concealment is its passing forward, grace is the final release of it. That is the five actions. Four of them, starting with creation, manifest the world of rebirths, the fifth is the cause of release and is eternally well stable in me. My followers see all that in the five elements: creation in earth, maintenance in water, destruction in fire, concealment in wind, and grace in space. Everything is created with earth, everything grows with water, is burnt with fire, is spread away with wind, is brought together with space. Sages know everything of that. To carry on these actions I have five faces, four in the four directions, the fifth in the center. By your penance, o my sons, from me who is satisfied you have detained two of those actions, your share is called creation and maintenance, the most agreeable. Other two have been obtained by Rudra and Maheśa. The action called grace cannot be entrusted to any one."

The various gods and goddesses who are connected with Śaivism form, as it were, a homogeneous household of which Śiva is the *paterfamilias*. Umā is represented as the mother of the family, and Gaṇeśa and Kārttikeya as the two sons. A host of attendants known as *pramathas* are always at Śiva's service. These are led by Nandin, who also functions as the doorkeeper. The leadership of the *gaṇas* is sometimes ascribed to Gaṇeśa, and this is implied in his very name. Curiously enough, Viṣṇu also is brought into the family as the brother of Umā. This tradition must be said to be stronger in the South, where Vaiṣṇavism and Śaivism flourish side by side. Śiva and Umā are said to manifest themselves in various forms, and the family grows through the incorporation of each of these forms as independent members. Similarly, many religious cults which had originated independently of Śaivism over the course of time were fused into the latter as its integral parts. The gods and goddesses of these cults had to be also given their place in the growing family of Śiva. As will be discussed later, a definite place is assigned to each of these divinities in a Śaivite temple.

The *Purāṇas* devote quite large parts to the narration of the great deeds of Śiva. Eight of these deeds are particularly significant: the clipping of Brahmā's fifth head; the overpowering of Andhaka; the annihilation of the three cities; the destruction of Dakṣa's sacrifice; the overthrowing of Jalandhara and Gajāsura; slaying Kāma, the god of love; and the punishment of Yama for harassing his devotees. The traditions of the South claim that all these events took place in that particular region, and eight places in South India are identified as the sites of these events.[259] Other important exploits of Śiva that may be mentioned are: drinking the world poison; containing the river Gaṅgā in the meshes of his matted hair; the humiliation of the sages of Dāruvana; sheltering the moon on his head; punishing Narasiṁha and Varāha; and giving the *cakra* to Viṣṇu. Each of these exploits has left its enduring impression on the system of worship of this god, and therefore shall be treated at some length in the following chapter.

A few general observations may be made here about the attitude of Śiva towards the demons, the gods and the mortals. Śiva is always represented as the punisher of the demons and the defender of the gods, and most Purāṇic episodes reflect this. As a champion of the gods, he detects some flaw or the other in the behaviour of the demons to whom he has already granted boons, and then, in quite a justifiable manner, he brings about their destruction. His relationships with the greater gods have been discussed at length in an earlier chapter. All the gods are described as his subordinates, and often they are shown to have sought his favour for the removal of calamities. As for mortals, sections of the *Purāṇas* that deal with the performances of rituals, the observance of *vratas*, the installation of images for worship, and the glorification of *tīrthas* or holy places worthy of being visited on pilgrimage directly relate to them. The various aspects of the relationship between Śiva and the mortals are clearly brought out in

[259] Cf. *Madras Lexicon*, p. 45. Under *Aṭṭavīraṭṭam* the following comments are given: "Eight places celebrated as the scene of Śiva's exploits viz: Kaṇḍiyūr, Kaḍavūr, Atikai, Vaḷuvūr, Pariyalūr, Kovalūr, Kurukkai, Virkuḍi".

these sections. At one place, for instance, it is expressly said that the god can be attained by men through *dhyāna* alone:

> *Tapasā naiva vṛttena dānadharmaphalena ca* |
> *Na śakyaṁ mānavair draṣṭum ṛte dhyānād ahaṁ tv idam* || [260]

"Except by meditation, I cannot be seen by men, neither by penance, nor by conduct, nor by the result of donation or meritorious duty."

Purāṇic Names of Śiva

A study of the various names by which Śiva is celebrated in the *Purāṇas* would now prove highly instructive. Of course, only those names with some significant implication can be considered here. Among these names, a few had become current in the Vedic texts themselves; others indicate overlordship which Śiva assumes over the course of time. Some relate to the places in which he is supposed to dwell; others pertain to his vehicle, or to his banner, or to his functions and deeds, or to the ornaments and dress he wears. Names which he shares with other gods are not helpful in his characterization, and shall not be taken into consideration. However, a few attributes of the absolute *Brahman* are assigned to Śiva as names. Some of them are mentioned so as to indicate how the god is conceived of in philosophical terms.

In one of the *Purāṇas* we are told that Rudra cried incessantly and persisted that Brahmā should give him names; he was not satisfied until he received eight of them:

> *Bhavaṁ bhīmaṁ tatheśānaṁ tathā paśupatiṁ prabhuḥ* |
> *Bhīmam ugraṁ mahādevam uvāca sa pitāmahaḥ* || [261]

The wide popularity and endurance which these Vedic names had gained in the Purāṇic times may be judged from the frequency of their occurrence as shown below:

---

[260] *Liṅga P.*, I.24.8.

[261] *Mārkaṇḍeya P.*, 52.7.

I. RUDRA *Bhāgavata P.*, IV.5.2; *Bhaviṣya P.*, II.4.14.53; *Garuḍa P.*, III.8.71; *Kūrma P.*, I.10.46; I.16.176; I.25.61; I.10.39; II.31.52; II.39.25; *Matsya P.*,133.22; *Padma P.*, I.5.1; I.5.60; I.5.82; *Skanda P.*, I.1.21.175; I.1.10.8; I.1.22.7; I.1.32.40; *Vāmana P.*, 51.23. 70.63. *Varāha P.*, 2.3; 21.77; 97.5.

BHAVA *Bhāgavata P.*, IV.2.1; IV.6.5; *Bhaviṣya P.*, III.4.14.86; *Liṅga P.*, I.7.54; I.72.121; I.72.176; *Matsya P.*, 133.22; *Padma P.*, III.15.56; *Vāmana P.*, 33.24; 47.77; *Varāha P.*, 21.77; *Vāyu P.*, I.10.29.

ŚARVA *Brahma P.*, I.35.17; *Brahmāṇḍa P.*, III.25.17; *Liṅga P.*, I.41.30; *Matsya P.*, 47.35; *Padma P.*, I.43.65; I.44.6; *Vāmana P.*, 6.78; 69.30; 47.77; *Varāha P.*, 21.77; *Vāyu P.*, I.54.75; I.55.30.

ĪŚĀNA *Kūrma P.*, I.9.53; I.9.58; I.21.46; I.30.39; I.30.47; II.34.117; *Matsya P.*, 133.23; *Vāmana P.*, 6.79; 44.38.

PAŚUPATI (= Paśūnāṁ pati) *Bhāgavata P.*, IV.3.12; *Brahma P.*, I.35.18; *Kūrma P.*, I.25.71; *Liṅga P.*, I.41.31; *Matsya P.*, 133.22; *Vāmana P.*, 47.77; 70.63; *Varāha P.*, 21.81; 21.84.

BHĪMA *Brahma P.*, I.35.17; *Matsya P.*, 47.134; 133.24; *Skanda P.*, I.1.22.8.

UGRA *Brahma P.*, I.35.17; *Liṅga P.*, I.41.34; *Matsya P.*, 47.134; 133.22 *Vāmana P.*, 47.83.

MAHĀDEVA *Bhāgavata P.*, VIII.7.21; *Bhaviṣya P.*, III.4.14.17; *Brahma P.*, I.35.19; *Brahmāṇḍa P.*, III.25.14; *Kūrma P.*, I.1.46; I.9.57; I.9.71; I.10.44; I.10.55; I.25.66; I.26.64; I.30.44; I.30.45; I.30.47; II.1.33; II.39.21; II.39.30; II.39.33; *Liṅga P.*, I.41.32; *Matsya P.*, 47.135; 133.23; *Padma P.*, I.43.78; I.44.124; *Skanda P.*, I.1.21.173; I.1.34.152; I.1.10.8; I.2.26.24; *Vāmana P.*, 33.25; 44.5; 44.38; 47.62; 69.30; *Vāyu P.*, I.10.61; I.5.38; *Varāha P.*, 21.77; 22.24.

II. A few of the names mentioned in the *Śatarudriya* also occur in the *Purāṇas*, but less frequently. They seem to have lost their significance and so fell out of use gradually. Some of these are:

VARŪTHIN	*Matsya P.*, 47.155.
UṢNĪṢIN	*Matsya P.*, 47.130.
KAVACIN	*Matsya P.*, 47.155.
NĪLALOHITA	*Brahmāṇḍa P.*, III.25.7.
BABHRU	*Varāha P.*, 97.5. *Matsya P.*, 47.138.
TĀMRA	*Matsya P.*, 47.134.
BUDDHNYA	*Nārada P.*, II.73.101.
HRASVA	*Matsya P.*, 47.131.
JAGHANYA	*Nārada P.*, II.73.101.

III. Among the most popular names of Śiva are the following:

HARA *Agni P.*, 18.43; *Bhāgavata P.*, IV.4.22; IV.5.23; *Bhaviṣya P.*, III.4.14.44; *Brahmāṇḍa P.*, III.25.22; *Kūrma P.*, I.9.50; I-10.55; I.55.15; I.25.70; II.39.24; *Padma P.*, I.43.399; I.43.413; *Vāmana P.*, 70.52.

ŚAṄKARA *Bhāgavata P.*, IV.4.1; *Bhaviṣya P.*, III.4.14.8; III.4.14.53; *Brahmāṇḍa P.*, III.25.16; *Kūrma P.*, I.9.58; I.9.70; I.10.42; I.15.10; I.16.32; I.21.47; *Liṅga P.*, I.31.40; I.72.171; *Padma P.*, I.5.61; I.11.17; I.14.117; I.43.380; I.43.396; I.44.68; III.15.56.

ŚIVA *Bhāgavata P.*, IV.2.15; VIII.7.19; *Bhaviṣya P.*, III.4.18.15; III.4.14.53; *Brahma P.*, I.37.17; *Garuḍa P.*, III.18.13 & 14; *Kūrma P.*, I.9.58; I.10.45; I.26.64; II.1.33; *Matsya P.*, 47.134; *Nārada P.*, II.73.101; II.73.122; *Padma P.*, I.5.60; I.5.82; III.15.56; *Vāmana P.*, 33.24; 47.89; 70.63.

SADĀŚIVA *Skanda P.*, I.1.21.178; *Vāmana P.*, 44.38.

ŚAṀBHU *Bhāgavata P.*, X.88.23; *Bhaviṣya P.*, III.4.14.15; *Kūrma P.*, I.9.58; I.26.77; I.10.34; II.39.27; *Matsya P.*, 133.21; *Padma P.*, I.43.413; *Skanda P.*, I.1.21.180; I.1.22.2; I.1.32.11; I.1.32.58; I.1.32.62.

DEVA *Kūrma P.*, I.24.59; *Liṅga P.*, I.72.121.

DEVADEVA *Bhāgavata P.*, IV.5.5; *Padma P.*, I.5.69; *Kūrma P.*, I.9.70; I.16.152; I.25.35; I.30.45; *Skanda P.*, I.1.21.174; I.2.26.24; *Varāha P.*, 21.76 33.16; *Vāyu P.*, I.54.58.

STHĀṆU *Matsya P.*, 47.136; *Skanda P.*, I.1.10.8.11; *Vāmana P.*, 70.52; *Varāha* P., 33.20.

IV. The following names are associated with the physical features of the god:

DHŪRJAṬI *Bhāgavata P.*, IV.5.2; X.88.19; *Matsya P.*, 155.6; 133.27; 250.29; *Nārada P.*, II.29.37; *Padma P.*, I.44.6.

KAPARDIN *Brahmaṇḍa P.*, III.25.12; *Kūrma P.*, I.25.39; I.25.49; I.25.67; *Matsya P.*, 47.128; *Nārada P.*, I.125.17; *Padma P.*, I.14.114; I.17.32; *Skanda P.*, I.1.32.84; I.1.10.11; *Vāmana P.*, 33.34; *Varāha P.*, 33.20.

JAṬĀDHARA *Vāmana P.*, 44.38.

VYOMAKEŚA *Bhaviṣya P.*, I.23.15.

MUKTAKEŚA *Matsya P.*, 47.131.

MUÑCAKEŚA *Vāmana P.*, 47.98.

GAṄGĀLULITAKEŚA *Vāmana P.*, 47.98.

GAṄGĀSALILADHARA *Kūrma P.*, II.39.27; *Liṅga P.*, I.31.38.

JAṬĀMAKUṬADHĀRIN *Varāha P.*, 33.17.

PAÑCĀSYA *Padma P.*, I.5.85.

BHĪMĀṬṬAHĀSAVAKTRA *Varāha P.*, 33.67.

TRIṆETRA *Kūrma P.*, I.10.47; I.25.53; I.25.66; I.30.44; II.1.32; *Linga P.*, I.31.9; *Matsya P.*, 47.137; *Padma P.*, I.5.87; *Skanda P.*, I.1.22.7; *Vāmana P.*, 47.72; *Varāha P.*, 33.16; 70.50.

TRILOCANA *Kūrma P.*, I.9.54; I.10.42; I.16.152; II.39.31; *Liṅga P.*, I.22.2; *Padma P.*, I.5.44; I.43.380; I.46.26; *Vāmana P.*, 44.22; 44.38.

TRYAṀBAKA *Bhāgavata P.*, IV.5.22; *Kūrma P.*, I.10.51; I.25.71; I.10.44; II.39.21; *Liṅga P.*, I.31.39; *Matsya P.*, 47.137; 133.23; *Vāmana P.*, 6.78; 44.38; 47.72; *Varāha P.*, 21.69. *Vāyu P.*, I.31.46.

VIRŪPĀKṢA *Kūrma P.*, I.54.65; I.30.39; I.30.42; I.30.46; II.34.12; *Liṅga P.*, I.22.2; 1.71.108; *Matsya P.*, 154.331; 250.28; *Nārada P.*, I.125.17; *Padma P.*, I.43. 321; *Skanda P.*, I.21.176; I.2.25.61; *Vāmana P.*, 47.64.

TRYAKṢA *Vāmana P.*, 47.64.

TṚTĪYANAYANA *Brahma P.*, II.35.10.

SAHASRĀKṢA *Vāmana P.*, 47.64.

SAHASRANETRA *Varāha P.*, 21. 70.

PIṄGĀKṢA *Varāha P.*, 97.2.

VIṢAMANETRA *Varāha P.*, 21.69.

LALĀṬANAYANA *Brahma P.*, I.35.12; *Kūrma P.*, 1.9.51.

ARKĀGNĪNDUCAKṢUS *Brahmāṇḍa P.*, III.25.12.

ŚAŚĀṄKĀDITYANETRA *Brahma P.*, I.35.12.

SOMĀGNYARKĀGRACAKṢUS *Matsya P.*, 250.30.

NĪLAKAṆṬHA *Kūrma P.*, I.20.66; I.25.66; *Padma P.*, V.1.17; *Vāmana P.*, 21.75; 35.22; 44.38.

NĪLAGRĪVA *Kūrma P.*, I.15.15; *Matsya P.*, 133.24.

ŚRĪKAṆṬHA *Brahmāṇḍa P.*, III. 25.19; *Kūrma P.*, II.39.25; *Nāradīya P.*, II.73.119.

ŚITIKAṆṬHA *Bhāgavata P.*, IV.3.12; IV.4.18; *Matsya P.*, 47.128; *Skanda P.*, I.1.32.64.

DAŚABĀHU *Vāmana P.*, 47.83.

NARANĀRIŚARĪRA *Kūrma P.*, I.25.72; II.39.24.

ARDHANĀRĪŚARĪRA *Liṅga P.*, I.33.26.

UMĀŚARĪRĀRDDHADHARA *Vāmana P.*, 44.38.

NĪLALOHITA *Bhāgavata P.*, IV.6.41; *Kūrma P.*, I.15.15; I.21.20; *Matsya P.*, 133.21; *Skanda P.*, I.1.10.11; *Varāha P.*, 97.2.

KARĀLA *Vāmana P.*, 33.24.

AṢṬAMŪRTI *Liṅga P.*, I.41.34.

AMŪRTI *Kūrma P.*, I.25.49.

UNMATTAKĀKĀRA *Padma P.*, I.43.321.

UGRARŪPIN *Vāmana P.*, 47.77.

ŚĀNTA *Skanda P.*, I.1.32.11.

ŚĀNTIVIGRAHA *Bhāgavata P.*, IV.2.2.

V. The following names relate to his dress and ornaments:

KṚTTIVĀSAS *Brahmāṇḍa P.*, III.25.14; *Kūrma P.*, I.21.46; I.25.32; I.25.71; I.30.39; II.34.118; II.39.25; *Matsya P.*, 47.157.

MṚGENDRACARMADHARA *Vāmana P.*, 53.32.

GAJENDRACARMADHARA *Vāmana P.*, 44.38.

DIKCARMADHARA *Padma P.*, I.5.80.

HIRAṆYAVĀSAS *Brahmāṇḍa P.*, II.26.47.

DIGVĀSAS *Kūrma P.*, I.10.51; I.25.67; II.39.22; *Matsya P.*, 250.40; *Nārada P.*, II.73.101; *Skanda P.*, I.2.2.25; *Vāmana P.*, 2.33; *Vāyu P.*, I.54.71.

NAGNA *Kūrma P.*, I.15.11; *Matsya P.*, 154.331.

ŚAŚĀṄKACIHNA *Matsya P.*, 154.266; *Padma P.*, I.43.256.

ŚAŚIMAULIKṚT *Varāha P.*, 35.21.

CANDRĀVAYAVABHŪṢAṆA *Kūrma P.*, I.30.51.

ŚAŚĀṄKAŚEKHARA *Bhāgavata P.*, IV.6.41.

CANDRABHŪṢAṆA *Kūrma P.*, II.1.32; *Vāmana P.*, 47.62.

CANDRAVIBHŪṢAṆA *Kūrma P.*, I.16.153.

INDUMAULIN *Padma P.*, L.43.259.

CANDRĀRDDHADHARA *Vāmana P.*, 44.38.

CANDRAŚEKHARA *Skanda P.*, I. 1.34.152.

KIRĪṬIN *Kūrma P.*, II.39.32.

MAHĀHIHĀRĀṄKITAKUṆḌALA *Vāmana P.*, 53.32.
KUṆḌALIN *Kūrma P.*, II.39.32.
BHUJAṄGAHĀRA *Kūrma P.*, II.39.32.
BHUJAGEŚAHĀRA *Vāmana P.*, 70.50.
NĀGAYAJÑOPAVĪTA *Kūrma P.*, I.25.68.
KṚTAKAṄKAṆABHOGĪNDRA *Vāmana P.*, 33.22.

VI. The following names of Śiva are derived from the weapons specifically ascribed to him:

PINĀKIN *Kūrma P.*, I.16.154; I.25.48; I.25.48; I.25.67; II.39.22; *Liṅga P.*, I.22.2; *Nārada P.*, II.73.126; *Padma P.*, I.43.65; I.43.391; I.44.42; I.5.69; *Skanda P.*, I.1.10.9; I.1.22.1; *Vāmana P.*, 44.5; 53.31; *Varāha P.*, 21.77.

PINĀKADHṚK *Padma P.*, I.46.28; *Skanda P.*, I.1.21.174.

PINĀKADHARA *Vāmana P.*, 44.38.

PINĀKAPĀṆI *Skanda P.*, I.1.32.58.

PINĀKAHASTA *Kūrma P.*, I.10.47; *Matsya P.*, 250.28.

ŚŪLAPĀṆI *Bhāgavata P.*, VIII.12.14; *Kūrma P.*, I.9.54; *Matsya P.*, 133.18; *Padma P.*, I.43.391; *Vāmana P.*, 6.78.44.2; 44.8; 51.23; *Varāha P.*, 21.70.

ŚŪLIN *Brahma P.*, I.35.19. *Kūrma P.*, I.10.46; I.26.66; I.30.44. *Matsya P.*, 133.25; *Skanda P.*, I.1.32.71; I.2.25.60; I.2.25.72; *Vāyu P.*, I.55.30.

ŚŪLADHṚK *Vāmana P.*, 38.17.

ŚŪLABHṚT *Matsya P.*, 6.13.

ŚŪLADHARA *Vāmana P.*, 44.38; 55.31.

TIGMAŚŪLIN *Varāha P.*, 33.22.

TRIŚŪLADHĀRIN *Kūrma P.*, II.39.21; *Liṅga P.*, I.31.39.

TRIŚŪLAPĀṆIN *Kūrma P.*, II.31.34.

TRIŚŪLAHASTA *Matsya P.*, 250.29.

TRIŚŪLĀSAKTAPĀṆI *Vāmana P.*, 47.72.

KHAṬVĀṄGAHASTA *Varāha P.*, 21.70.

KHAṬVĀṄGADHĀRIN *Padma P.*, I.5.83

KHAṆḌAPARAŚU *Liṅga P.*, I.22.2.

DṚḌHADHANVIN *Matsya P.*, 47.153.

NIṢAṄGIN *Kūrma P.*, I.25.70.

PINĀKAŚŪLĀSIKHAḌGAMUDGARADHĀRIN *Brahma P.*, II.35.10.

VII. The following names are derived from Śiva's abode:

KAILĀSAVĀSIN *Brahmāṇḍa P.*, II.25.9.

GIRĪŚA *Bhāgavata P.*, IV.2.17; IV.6.39; VIII.12.2. & 14; X.88.15; *Kūrma P.*, I.25.32; I.25.69; I.30.51; *Matsya P.*, 47.133; 133.18; *Nārada P.*, II.73.118; II.73.120; *Padma P.*, I.43.375; I.43.390; I.43.392; I.43.409.

GIRITRA *Bhāgavata P.*, IV.3.15; VIII.7.31.

PARVATAVĀSIN *Bhāgavata P.*, II.35.11.

ŚMAŚĀNAVASIN *Brahma P.*, I.35.13; *Brahmāṇda P.*, III.25.9; *Matsya P.*, 154.335; *Padma P.*, I.43.324; *Skanda P.*, I.1.23.23.

VIII. Names indicating his relationship with Pārvatī are very common:

UMĀPRIYA *Matsya P.*, 250.38; *Vāyu P.*, I.54.75.

PĀRVATĪPRIYA *Matsya P.*, 133.21.

GIRIJĀPATI *Bhaviṣya P.*, III.4.14.31.

UMĀPATI *Kūrma P.*, I.25.34; *Liṅga P.*, I.22.2; *Vāmana P.*, 21.75.

AMBIKĀPATI *Brahma P.*, I.35.3; *Kūrma P.*, I.9.71; I.25.71; I.30.47.

IX. A few names of Śiva are connected with the bull, either as his vehicle or as the emblem on his banner:

VṚṢABHAVĀHANA	*Skanda P.*, I.2.25.60.
VṚṢABHĀRŪḌHA	*Vāmana P.*, 2.33.
VṚṢENDRAYĀNA	*Padma P.*, I.43.257; I.154. 267.
VṚṢENDRAVARAVĀHANA	*Kūrma P.*, I.16.157.
VṚṢĀSANA	*Padma P.*, I.5.80.
VṚṢIN	*Skanda P.*, I.2.25.74.

VṚṢA(BHA)DHVAJA *Bhāgavata P.*, IV.4.23; VIII.12.1; *Brahmāṇḍa P.*, IV.25.6; *Kūrma P.*, I.15.19; I.16.113; I.25.36; *Liṅga P.*, I.31.40; *Padma P.*, I.14.114; *Matsya P.*, 133.27; *Vāmana P.*, 6.78; 70.51; *Vāyu P.*, I.54.44; I.24.59; *Skanda P.*, I.1.10.9; I.1.10.19.

X. Names relating to the functions which the god is supposed to discharge are numerous:

VIŚVAKARTṚ	*Kūrma P.*, I.25.61.
AKHILALOKAPĀLA	*Bhāgavata P.*, VIII.7.31.
VARADA	*Vāmana P.*, 47.77.
PRAPANNĀRTIHARA	*Bhāgavata P.*, VIII. 7.22.
KĀMADA	*Kūrma P.*, I.30.51.
BHAVAMOCANA	*Kūrma P.*, I.16.91.
SAṀSĀRATĀRAṆA	*Kūrma P.*, I.25.48.
ĀCĀRYA	*Kūrma P.*, I. 25.48.
KĀLA	*Kūrma P.*, I.10.46; I.10.56; II.31.52; *Padma P.*, I.43.258.
MAHĀKĀLA	*Padma P.*, I.14.116; I.44.8.
KĀLARŪPA	*Kūrma P.*, I.25.68; I.20.66; *Vāmana P.*, 6.79.

KĀLARŪPIN *Kūrma P.*, II.34.117; II.39.29.

KĀLAMŪRTI *Kūrma P.*, I.25.49.

SAṀHĀRAKARTṚ *Kūrma P.*, I.25.61; *Liṅga P.*, I.31.38.

KALPĀNTERUDRARŪPA *Brahmāṇḍa P.*, III.25.22.

KALPĀGNI *Kūrma P.*, I.30.51.

KĀLĀGNISANNIBHA *Bhaviṣya P.*, III.4.14.53.

JAGATSAṀHĀRAKARTṚ *Brahmāṇḍa P.*, III.25.22.

SARVASAṀHARAṆA *Kūrma P.*, II.39.23.

DĀHAKA *Kūrma P.*, II.24.117.

KALPASANDHYĀVICĀRIN *Vāmana P.*, 47.102.

MAHĀGRĀSA *Kūrma P.*, I.10.46; I.30.46; II.34.120.

LOKAKṢAYAKĀRIN *Vāmana P.*, 2.33.

XI. Names relating to the various incidents in the career of Śiva may be now mentioned:

KAPĀLIN *Bhaviṣya P.*, III.4.14.12; *Brahmāṇḍa P.*, III.25.8; *Kūrma P.*, I.15.11; *Matsya P.*, 47.137; 154.331; *Padma P.*, I.14.15; I.14.131; I.43.321; *Varāha P.*, 97.5; *Vāyu P.*, I.54.69.

KAPĀLAPĀṆI *Kūrma P.*, II.39.31; *Vāmana P.*, 70.50.

KAPĀLAHASTA *Vāyu P.*, I.54.76.

KAPĀLĀSAKTAPĀṆI *Vāmana P.*, 47.84.

KAPĀLADHĀRIN *Vāmana P.*, 21.75.

KAPĀLAPĀTRADHṚK *Padma P.*, I.5.36.

TRIPURĀNTAKA *Brahmāṇḍa P.*, III.25.5; *Liṅga P.*, I.72.171; *Nārada P.*, II.73.101; *Padma P.*, III.15.46; *Skanda P.*, I.1.32.60; I.2.26.24.

PURĀNTAKA *Matsya P.*, 154.267.

TRIPURAGHNA *Matsya P.*, 47.148; *Padma P.*, I.5.87; *Vāmana P.*, 21.75.

TRIPURĀRI	*Padma P.*, I.5.2.
TRIPURĀRĀTI	*Liṅga P.*, I.72.121.
TRIPURANĀŚANA	*Kūrma P.*, I.24.59.
TRIPURADHVAṀSIN	*Brahmāṇḍa P.*, III.25.13.
DAKṢAYAJÑAVIDHVAṀSIN	*Brahmāṇḍa P.*, III.25.13.
DAKṢAVINĀŚAKARTṚ	*Vāmana P.*, 53.31.
DAKṢAYAJÑAVINĀŚANA	*Liṅga P.*, I.22.2.
DAKṢAYAJÑAVINĀŚA	*Varāha P.*, 33.24.
BHAGĀKṢIHAN	*Padma P.*, I.43.431; *Vāmana P.*, 53.31.
BHAGĀKṢISAṀSPHOṬANA	*Vāmana P.*, 21.74
BHAGANETRANIPĀTANA	*Brahma P.*, II.35.9.
PŪṢADANTAHARA	*Brahma P.*, II.35.9
KĀMANĀŚA	*Kūrma P.*, I.25.70.
KĀMANĀŚANA	*Kūrma P.*, I.30.51.
MANMATHĀṄGAVINĀŚANA	*Vāyu P.*, I.54.68.
MANMATHADEHANĀŚANA	*Brahmāṇḍa P.*, 26.94.
KUSUMĀYUDHADEHAVINĀŚAKARA	*Padma P.*, III.15.56.
KĀMAGHNA	*Vāmana P.*, 47.102.
KĀMAŚARĪRANĀŚANA	*Brahmāṇḍa P.*, II.26.47.
MAḌANĀNTAKARA	*Skanda P.*, I.1.22.7.
ANDHAKĀSURAHANTṚ	*Vāmana P.*, 47.77.
ANDHAKĀSURAMARDIN	*Brahmāṇḍa P.*, III.25.12.
KĀLĀNTAKA	*Skanda P.*, I.1.32.60.
KĀLADAHANA	*Kūrma P.*, I.30.51.
ANDHAKAGHĀTIN	*Matsya P.*, 133.23.
ANTAKĀNTAKṚT	*Brahma P.*, III.35.11.

Sometimes a single name reflects two or more exploits:

KRATUKĀLĀNTAKA *Padma P.*, I.5.80.

YAJÑATRIPURAGHĀTIN *Matsya P.*, 250.33.

KĀMĀDHVARATRIPURAKĀLĀDYANEKABHŪTADRUH *Bhāgavata P.*, VIII.7.32.

XII. Some names occurring in the *Purāṇas* show Śiva as the divine dancer *par excellence*. He is also the lord of drama and music. The tradition claims that the syllables in grammar arose out of the *ḍhakkā* played upon by Śiva.

NARTANAŚĪLA *Vāmana P.*, 47.81.23.

NṚTYAŚĪLA *Kūrma P.*, II.39.23

NĀṬYOPAHĀRALUBDHA *Vāmana P.*, 47.81.

XIII. Śiva's connection with *yoga* is evident. The following names are significant in this connection.

YOGIN *Kūrma P.*, I.9.58; I.25.75.

YOGAPATI *Skanda P.*, I. 1.34.150.

YOGĀDHIPATI *Kūrma P.*, I.10.46. II.39.27

YOGAGAMYA *Kūrma P.*, I.10.51; I.25.48; I.25.75.

YOGINĀṀGURU *Kūrma P.*, I.25.48

MAHĀYOGA *Kūrma P.*, I.30.47; II.34.117.

MAHĀYOGIN *Kūrma P.*, I.16.158; *Vāmana P.*, 44.38.

MAHĀYOGEŚVARA *Vāmana P.*, 44.38.

YOGADĀTṚ *Kūrma P.*, I.30.47.

YOGINĀṀVARA *Kūrma P.*, I.25.33.

XIV. The following names point to Śiva as the Great Lord:

ĪŚVARA *Bhāgavata P.*, VIII.7.22; *Kūrma P.*, I.9.57; I.16.191; I.16.199; I.25.35; II.1.35; *Liṅga P.*, I.72.121; *Matsya P.*, 47.137; *Padma P.*, 1.17.38; *Skanda P.*, I.1.22.9; *Vāyu P.*, I.5.38; I.54.77.

ĪŚA *Bhāgavata P.*, IV.6.42; *Kūrma P.*, I.10.44; I.21.20; I.25.33; *Padma P.*, I.43.417; *Liṅga P.*, 41.30.

BHŪTABHAVYEŚA *Kūrma P.*, I.9.71.

MAHEŚA *Kūrma P.*, I.9.58; I.10.45; *Nārada P.*, II.73.118; *Padma P.*, III.15.56; *Skanda P.*, I.32.58; I.34.151; *Vāmana P.*, 69.29.

MAHEŚVARA *Bhāgavata P.*, VIII.7.35; *Bhaviṣya P.*, III.4.14.63; *Kūrma P.*, I.10.55; I.30.42; *Padma P.*, I.5.2; I.5.87; I.14.113; I.17.35; *Skanda P.*, I.1.22.9; *Vāmana P.*, 6.79; 70.52; *Varāha P.*, 22.24; *Vāyu P.*, I.9.114.

PARAMEŚVARA *Kūrma P.*, I.9.58; I.10.42; I.10.44; I.15.10; I.25.34; I.25.49; II.1.132; *Liṅga P.*, I.72.176; *Padma P.*, I.17.39; *Skanda P.*, I.32.12; *Vāmana P.*, 44.38; *Varāha P.*, 21.77; 22.45.

VIŚVEŚVARA *Kūrma P.*, II.39.30.

TRILOKEŚA *Varāha P.*, 22.24.

TRIVIṢṬAPEŚA *Skanda P.*, I.22.7.

PAREŚA *Skanda P.*, I.1.32.11.

DEVEŚA *Padma P.*, I.44.124.

BHŪTAPATI *Kūrma P.*, II.1.33; *Vāyu P.*, I.55.31.

BHŪTĀDHIPATI *Kūrma P.*, I.16.158; II.39.27.

BHŪTEŚA *Kūrma P.*, II.34.118.

SARVABHŪTEŚA *Brahmāṇḍa P.*, III.25.

GOPATI *Matsya P.*, 133.21.

PRAMATHANĀTHA *Kūrma P.*, II.39.30.

XV. The following names may be said to be of philosophical import. They represent the god in his highest aspect:

BRAHMAN	*Kūrma P.*, I.16.199
AKṢARA	*Kūrma P.*, I.16.199.
ĀNANDARŪPA	*Kūrma P.*, I.16.199.
NIḤSPṚHA	*Kūrma P.*, I.16.160.
VIBHU	*Bhāgavata P.*, IV. 5.5.
NIṢPARIGRAHA	*Kūrma P.*, I.16.160.
PARĀTPARATARA	*Skanda P.*, I.31.32.11.
KEVALA	*Kūrma P.*, I.16.160.
PARAṀJYOTIS	*Kūrma P.*, I.10.56.

In imitation of the tradition of the *avatāras* of Viṣṇu, *avatāras* of Rudra also are mentioned in the *Purāṇas*. As many as twenty-seven of them are enumerated. Śiva explained the purpose of his *avatāras* as follows:

Na tīrthaphalabhogena kratubhir vāptadakṣiṇaiḥ |
Na vedādhyayanair vāpi na vittena na vedanaiḥ ||
Na śakyaṁ mānavair draṣṭum ṛte dhyānād ahaṁ tv iha |

"Except by meditation, I cannot be seen by men, not by experiencing the fruit of pilgrimage, nor by sacrifices with proper dakṣiṇā, nor by recitation of Veda, nor by riches, nor by knowledge."

... ...
Anugrahārthaṁ lokānāṁ brāhmaṇānāṁ hitāya ca |
Utpatsyāmi tadā Brahman punar asmin yugāntike || [262]

"To bestow grace on the worlds and for the welfare of brahmins, I will be born again, o Brahmā, at the end of this *yuga*."

---

[262] *Liṅga P.*, I.24.7-11.

One of the *Purāṇas* recounting the twenty-eight *avatāras* of Śiva lists them in the following order: Śveta, Sutara, Damana, Suhotra, Kaṅka, Lokākṣi, Vibhu, Dadhivāhana, Ṛṣabha, Tripāt, Ugra, Atri, Balin, Gautama, Vedaśiras, Gokarṇa, Guhāvāsin, Śikhaṇḍin, Jaṭamālin, Aṭṭahāsa, Dāruka, Lāṅgulin, Śveta, Śūlin, Daṇḍin, Sahiṣṇu, Somaśarman, and Lakulin. This concept of the *avatāras* of Śiva, however, never gained any popularity.

This mythological account of Śiva may be concluded with a quotation from one of the *Purāṇas* which seeks to define his position among the Hindu gods.

Gīyate sarvamāyātmā śūlapāṇir maheśvaraḥ |
Enam eke vadaty agniṁ nārāyaṇam athāpare ||
Indram eke'pare prāṇaṁ Brahmāṇam apare jaguḥ |
Brahmaviṣṇvagnivaruṇāḥ sarvadevās tatharṣayaḥ ||
Ekasyaivātha rudrasya bhedās te parikīrtitāḥ |
Yaṁ yaṁ rūpaṁ samāsthāya yajanti parameśvaram ||
Tat tat rūpaṁ samāsthāya pradadāti phalaṁ śivaḥ | [263]

"The great Lord, holding the trident is celebrated as the essence of the whole māyā. Some call him Agni, others Nārāyaṇa, some Indra, others call him Prāṇa, others Brahmā. Brahmā, Viṣṇu, Agni, Varuṇa, all the gods and the sages are well-known as differentiations of the unique Rudra. The supreme Lord Śiva bestows the fruit of worship, assuming the form in which one worships him."

These stanzas are, in a sense, reminiscent of the famous Vedic saying: *"Ekaṁ sad viprā bahudhā vadanti"*: "Sages call the unique Being in many ways".[264]

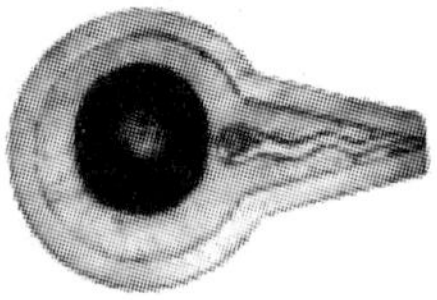

[263] *Kūrma P.*, II.46.34-37.

[264] *ṚV*, I. 164.46.

CHAPTER V

THE LIṄGA AND THE IMAGES OF ŚIVA

Śaivism is unique in that it has prescribed the worship of its supreme deity, Śiva, in two main visual forms: through the anthropomorphic images,[1] such as those of Naṭarāja and Somāskanda, and the *liṅga*, which is not characterized by any human features (Fig. 2). The worship of Śiva through the *liṅga* form has been prevalent all over India. The worship of this god in his anthropomorphic image is, on the other hand, found to be mostly restricted to south India. It is evident that both forms are mentioned in the Epics and the *Purāṇas*, especially in the latter.[2] However, in view of the conspicuous prevalence of the worship of Śiva images in south India, special attention is here paid to that aspect of Śiva worship.

The present chapter is devoted, among other things, to the study of the technique of image making and other associated topics. Incidentally, it also aims at an evaluation of the contribution made by the Epics and the *Purāṇas* to the subject of image making, with reference to the relevant Āgamic [3] traditions prevalent in south India. Actually, only a few chapters in the *Purāṇas* deal with this subject, and even those references are quite brief. Consequently, the information to be

[1] It must, however, be pointed out, in this connection, that the earliest known anthropomorphic representation of Śiva belongs to North India. It is the Paśupati-seal discovered at Mohenjodaro.

[2] *Agni P.*, chapters 50-62; *Bhaviṣya P.*, I.132; also II.12; *Matsya P.*, chapters 257-263.

[3] The following comments made by P.K. Acharya on the *Āgamas* and the *Purāṇas* give a general idea of what these texts say about architecture and sculpture. "The *Āgamas* of Southern India are the prototypes of the *Purāṇas* of Northern India, both being huge compendations, dealing with heterogeneous subjects covering practically all matters known to the compilers. Out of the seventy-five chapters comprising the *Kāmikāgama*, sixty chapters are devoted to architecture and sculpture.

derived from these texts is scant. It would seem that these portions in the *Purāṇas* had been designed mainly to satisfy the needs of the individual worshippers, instructing them in the matter of the type of image which should be installed for worship.[4] They do not appear to concern themselves at all with the artists who are expected to make these images, as they do not describe the process of making the images. However, these works are, in their own way, important for the study of Hindu iconography. The present chapter seeks to show how the iconographic art owes much to the *Purāṇas*, which may even be said to have given it its entire shape. Unfortunately, no writer in this subject[5] has so far laid due stress on the indispensability of the Purāṇic texts for a proper understanding of Hindu iconography. As a matter of fact, it is the Purāṇic ideology in its multifarious aspects which may be said to have inspired the iconographic art. This becomes overwhelmingly evident in the temples of south India.[6] As has been pointed

---

It has been discussed in detail and shown elsewhere that the *Purāṇas*, the *Āgamas*, and some two or three hundred small architectural texts are both directly and indirectly indebted for the architectural and sculptural matters to the standard work, Mānasāra." See "Aspect and Orientation in Hindu Architecture", IV, vol. I, p. 398.

4 The *Bhaviṣya Purāṇa*, for example, proclaims in the beginning of the chapter entitled *Pratimālaksaṇa*:

Pratimālakṣaṇaṁ vakṣye yathāśāstram atah śrṇu |

Pratimāṁ lakṣaṇahīnāṁ gṛhītāṁ naiva pūjayet || *Bhaviṣya P.*, II.12.1.

"I will tell the characteristics of icons, according to scriptures, therefore, listen. One should not worship an icon taken without its characteristic features."

5 Among the most worthy writers on Hindu iconography, the names of Gopinath Rao and Benarjea must be specially mentioned. In the course of his work, the former, no doubt, refers to Purāṇic events (e.g. *Elements of Hindu Iconography*, vol. II, Part I, p. 105. Here the Pūraṇas are merely mentioned, but no specific references are given citing chapters etc.) But he has nowhere tried to evaluate the debt which the iconographic art in India owes to the *Purāṇas*. Even in the *Development of Hindu Iconography* of the latter, the *Purāṇas* have not been assigned their due place.

6 In this connection, the following few lines will be found quite pertinent: "But great forces (grouped under the designation of the Puranic renaissance) had long been at work preparing the way for the emergence of the old cults of Shiva and Vishnu in forms which gave renewed inspiration to art — sculpture and poetry in the South, and poetry and painting in the North." Ananda K. Coomaraswamy, *The Dance of Shiva*, p. 50.

Fig. 2: Liṅga at Elephanta.

out, the Purāṇic traditions are better preserved in southern India than in any other part of the country.[7] The entire religious atmosphere which prevails in the south Indian temple is, so to say, permeated with Purāṇic ideology.

Image worship has long been an essential characteristic of Hinduism. The large variety of words denoting an image, such as *bimba*, *vigraha*, *mūrti*, and *pratimā*, would point to the importance and the wide prevalence of image worship as reflected in ancient literary works. It may, however, not be out of place to attempt a brief historical survey of the practice of image worship. We may as well begin this survey with the Mohenjodaro period. The so-called cultic objects discovered at Mohenjodaro have given rise to many questions.[8] These objects could have been made use of in a variety of ways, though the religious character of some of them has been established as a definite fact. Of these objects, some might have been used as amulets;[9] some others could have been symbols with religious implications, but need not necessarily have been intended for worship.[10] The complete absence of worship structures such as could be identified as temples is itself a fairly valid challenge to the religious character of these objects. The same arguments may be advanced against the so-called phallic objects, some of which are shown to be representations of the male and the female sex-organs. The use for which they were actually meant still remains a mystery.[11] As a matter of

[7] It must, however, be added that Śaivism as practiced in South Indian temples conforms to the tradition initiated by the *Āgamas*; frequent references are, therefore, made to these works in the present work. The *Āgamas*, as will be shown in the subsequent pages, give descriptions of the various images, which resemble the Purāṇic descriptions.

[8] See in this connection also chapter II, pp. 30 ff.

[9] Mackay: *Early Indus Civilisation*, pages 59-63, also 65, 70 and 71.

[10] It may be pointed out, in this connection, that the images carved on the pillars, domes and *gopurams* of the temples in South India are not intended for worship.

[11] Many scholars working in this field assume that they are not cult objects used for worship. Some others assert that they were used as amulets. There does not seem to be any unanimity of views in this respect.

fact, the entire interpretation of the Mohenjodaro civilization is based on conjecture. Scholars are prone to attribute a religious character [12] to the objects unearthed at this site. However, in this connection, it needs to be remembered that until their script is deciphered, whatever conclusions one may draw in this field will have to be regarded as speculative and therefore only tentative.

The Vedic hymns include picturesque descriptions of the physical features of various gods. This fact may give rise to the suspicion that the Vedic people were in the habit of worshipping images. But, the Vedic traditions in general do not favour at all such a view. It may be pointed out that, according to the magico-cosmic ideology of the early Vedic period, gods and men were regarded as but aspects of a common cosmic potence, and not as being 'apart' from each other. The Vedic people could not, therefore, have ever thought of concretely representing gods as separate entities. It must also be noted that no positive clues are traceable in the Vedic hymns to prove the existence of image worship, or even places of worship such as temples. The picturesque descriptions referred to above must therefore be regarded as essays in poetic imagery.

The *Brāhmaṇas* also reveal a complete absence of references to images or temples. This was a period when all religion was concentrated in ritual, and the very fact that oblations intended for the various gods were offered to the fire conclusively proves that the gods were not at that time represented in the form of images. A critical study of the Brāhmaṇic ritual would indeed show that the gods actually played but a subsidiary role in sacrifices. Sacrifice *per se* was all that mattered, and gods, like other accessories of sacrifice, were subservient to the sacrificial ritual as a whole. It is, however, not unlikely that the details regarding the construction of the various types of *cayanas*, given in the ritualistic literature [13] may have influenced the art of temple-building of later times, at least to a certain extent.

[12] It is true that there are a few scholars who have challenged the religious character of these objects. But most of them seem to endorse the views expressed by Marshall.

The Upaniṣadic period, which followed the period of the *Brāhmaṇas*, was noted for its philosophical attitude. The higher knowledge (*parā vidyā*) which the *Upaniṣads* represent was by no means conducive to image worship. Even the theistic portions of the *Upaniṣads* speak of a supreme god who is incapable of being grasped and understood by means of our sense organs.[14] Abstract terms and negative statements are often preferred to positive descriptions in the matter of the characterization of the god.[15] It is very rare for physical features to be attributed to him. The term *pratīka* that is found in the *Upaniṣads* does not mean an image as such. It refers to some kind of symbol which served the practical purpose of facilitating meditation on the highest reality. In this connection, Deussen very aptly observes: "The Indian word for symbol, *pratīkam*, depends upon a similar conception. It denotes originally (from *prati-añc*) the side 'turned towards' us, and therefore visible, of an object in other respects invisible ... they understand by the term definite representations of Brahman under some form perceptible by the senses, e.g. as name, speech, etc., as *manas* and *ākāśa*, as *āditya*, as the fire of digestion, or even of *oṁ*, which for the worship are regarded as Brahman, and are related to the latter as the images of the gods (*pratimā*, *arcā*) to the gods that they represent." [16]

---

[13] "The *Vājasaneyi-Saṁhitā* (XI-XVIII) contains numerous prayers and sacrificial formulae for the *agnicayana* or the building of the fire altar, a ceremony which extends over a whole year... It is built of 10,800 bricks, in the form of a large bird, with spread wings." Winternitz, *HIL*, vol. I, p. 172 f. Reference may also be made to *ŚPBr.*, X.

[14] *Śvetāśvatara Upaniṣad*, IV.20.

[15] *Bṛhadāraṇyaka Upaniṣad*, 4.2.4, 4.4.22, 4.5.15, 3.9.26 and also 2.3.6.

[16] *The Philosophy of the Upaniṣads*, pp. 99 ff.
As for the Vedic period, scholars for the most part are unanimous that the Vedic religion was characterized by a total absence of idol-worship. The following observation made by Farquhar iterates the same view-point: "The actual practice of image-worship is reflected in fragmentary fashion in most of the great books from the fourth century onwards; but no Vedic work describes the ritual or prescribes the liturgy; and there is not a hint given as to the history of the introduction of the cult." "Temple and Image Worship in Hinduism", *JRAS*, 1928, p. 16.

Very few are the references to temples and image worship to be found in the *sūtra* texts. Naturally enough, the *Śrauta-Sūtras*, which pertain solely to the sacrificial cult, do not contain any such references. The *Gṛhya-Sūtras*, which prescribe rites for the householders, contain stray passages which can be shown to be related, in some way or other, to temple worship.[17] For instance, a *snātaka*, while riding in a chariot, is directed to alight when he approaches *daivatāni*,[18] which may refer either to images being carried in procession or to temples in which they are enshrined. The occurrence in them of such words as *devagṛha*, *devāyatana*, and *devakula* is also indicative of the acquaintance of these texts with image worship.[19]

The earliest direct reference to images is to be found in the *Aṣṭādhyāyī* of Pāṇini. The *sūtra* "*Jīvikārthe cāpaṇye*" clearly suggests that the images were in vogue in the fifth century BC. Pāṇini has another *sūtra*, "*bhaktiḥ*",[20] which implies that the cult of *bhakti* which promoted image-worship had by then become widely prevalent. It is possible to infer from these two *sūtras* that there were two types of images, one for sale and the other for worship. Patañjali's comment on the former *sūtra* [21] is also very significant. There, he specifically mentions a few gods like Śiva, Skanda and Viśākha; this shows that the images of these gods were definitely in vogue in Patañjali's time. Another significant point in this connection is that no Vedic gods are mentioned by Patañjali.

As can be easily imagined, the doctrine of *bhakti* gave great impetus to the cult of image worship.[22] Though clear traces of *bhakti*

---

17 Cf. *ĀpGs.*, VII.20.

18 Cf. Banerjea: *The Development of Hindu Iconography*, p. 69.

19 *Aṣṭādhyāyi*, V.3.99.

20 *Ibid.*, IV.3.95.

21 *Apaṇya ity ucyate. Tatredaṁ na sidhyati. Śivaḥ Skandah Viśākha iti? Kiṁ kāraṇam? Mauryair hiraṇyārthibhir arcāḥ prakalpitāḥ Bhavet tāsu na syād yās tv etāḥ saṁprati pūjārthās tāsu bhaviṣyati. Mahābhāṣya*, commentary on V.3.99.

22 "The Hindu *śāstras* prescribe image worship to weak unevolved persons in particular". Gopinath Rao: *op.cit.*, vol. I, pt. I, p. 26.

are to be found even in early Vedic literature,[23] it came to the forefront as an independent form of religious practice only with the rise of Hinduism.[24] This coincides with the age of Pāṇini, in whose work we find a direct reference to images.[25]

It will be shown in the following pages how the Epic and Purāṇic ideas have influenced the iconic representations of the minor gods in a very marked manner, though references to the aniconic form of worship are not wanting in these texts. As a matter of fact, it is in the Epics and the *Purāṇas* that the information relating to this topic is seen to have been recorded for the first time. So far as the present work is concerned, we shall first of all study the aniconic form of the worship of Śiva, the *liṅga* form of worship, at some length. Thereafter, we shall try to examine how the *Purāṇas* gave rise to the various types of anthropomorphic images of that god.

The problem relating to the origin, development and nature of the *liṅga* cult is highly controversial. The early history of this cult has to be reconstructed from the materials furnished by literary sources, archaeological excavations, and information provided by traditional accounts. To begin with, it may be pointed out that no feature of Hinduism has spread out so uniformly in all parts of India as did the *liṅga* worship.[26] From Kashmir in the farthest north down to Comorin in the extreme south, the worship of the *liṅga* as a column

---

[23] Attention may be drawn in this connection particularly to the hymns addressed to Varuṇa by Vaśiṣṭha (*RV*, Seventh Maṇḍala).

[24] See Dandekar, "Hinduism and Bhagavadgītā", Proceedings IX, *ICHR*, 1958.

[25] The following remark made by Farquhar, though it does not mention Pāṇini's reference to images in his *sūtras*, is significant and informative: "All that we can make out from this literature is established and recognized within Hinduism round about 400 BC. References to images, temples and temple priests make their appearance first in the literature of the fourth century BC. They are found in the *Adbhuta Brāhmaṇa*, *Gṛhyasūtras*, the *Dharmasūtras* and in the early sections of both the epics; while such references are not to be found in earlier literature." See "Temple and Image Worship in Hinduism", *JRAS*, 1928, p. 16.

[26] Hinduism may be shown to possess features which are peculiarly associated with a particular place only, and are absent elsewhere. The *liṅga* cult, on the contrary, enjoys almost universal prevalence in India.

of stone with or without a base is very common. Devotees of Śiva worship the *liṅga* as his symbol alone.[27] Literary references show that this tradition has been prevalent for a long time. The *Mahābhārata* and the *Rāmāyaṇa* are the earliest literary works which make a specific mention of *liṅga* worship.[28] The *Purāṇas*, of course, mention it very frequently.[29]

What does the *liṅga* imply? Considering the faith with which this object is worshipped even today, one may say that Śiva is believed to be immediately present in the *liṅga* as he is invoked to be. Thus, so far as the faith of the Śaivites is concerned, the *liṅga* is conceived of as a *pratīka*, an image or a form of the very god who is supposed to be present in it. Such presence of the god in the *liṅga* is brought about by means of various rituals which will be briefly described later. As against this religious belief of the worshippers of Śiva, it is often suggested that the *liṅga* cult in its origin was a phallic cult. Such a view seems to be plausible on two grounds — one, the references which one comes across in old religious and philosophical texts,[30] and two, the structural resemblance of the *liṅga* to the phallus and its female counterpart.[31] It would be necessary to examine these grounds in some detail, and to see if they unequivocally establish the phallic nature of *liṅga* worship. Such an examination may as well be preceded by a brief study of phallism itself.

---

[27] Cf. Kramrisch. "The Image of Mahādeva in the cave on Elephanta Island", *Ancient India*, no. 2, p. 6.

[28] *Mahābhārata*, XIII, chapters 13 & 17; *MBh*, VII, ch. 201; *MBh*, X, ch. 7; *Rāmāyaṇa*, VII.31.41. In this connection, Banerjea observes: "It is only in the Epic literature, that we find for the first time unmistakable evidence of the worship of Śiva, in his phallic form, and that too, in sections adjudged as late ones by Indologists". *Op.cit.*, p. 456.

[29] Out of the numerous references, a few may be cited here: *Skanda P.*, 1.3.1.2; *Kūrma P.*, I.26.94-99; *Matsya P.*,263; *Agni P.*, chapters 53 & 54; *Brahmāṇḍa P.*, I.26; *Śiva P.*, *Jñānasaṁhitā*, chap. 1-4.

[30] Some portions of even the Epics and the *Purāṇas* contain allusions to this effect.

[31] Regarding the structure of the *liṅga*, it may be pointed out, that the base, which bears a mere coincidental resemblance to *yoni*, was intended mainly for conducting out the water with which the *liṅga* is bathed. Śiva is constantly bathed with water

One authority on this subject observes: "Phallism may be defined as the worship of the reproductive powers of nature symbolized by the organs of sex. ... The exaggerated organs are intended to represent, for cultural purposes, the power of reproduction, paternity, fertility, the powers that multiply the peoples and provide abundance of cattle and crops and all other things necessary for prosperity. In these cases the object worshipped seems not to be regarded as a symbol, or as the outward and visible form of an indwelling divinity, but to be honoured for its own sake." [32] Speaking of the nature of the phallic cult as it is seen around the world, the author continues: "Certain of the Shinto gods of Japan are ithyphallic. They are represented in wood and stone and are the objects of offerings and worship. Whether similar deities were honoured by ancient Gauls we do not know. It is certain that in the middle ages, and since, in various parts of France and Belgium ithyphallic saints have been worshipped for the purpose of obtaining offsprings or curing impotence and sexual disease. ... East and west of Dahomy, along the Slave Coast, the phallus is seen everywhere in front of the house, in the streets and the public places, sometimes alone, but more frequently in connection with the images of Legba, to whom the organ is held sacred, and whose principal attribute is the exciting of sexual desires. Both the Ewhe and the Yonuha attribute sexual desires to possession of the god and he removes the barrenness." [33] It would thus seem that two main factors determine the phallic character of a cult. First of all, the object of worship should be shown to bear a realistic resemblance to the phallus,

---

(*abhiṣekapriyaḥ Śivaḥ*). At the foot of the columnal structure a base was provided in course of time to allow the water out. Such provision is made in all the *garbhagṛhas* in the temples of the South, and it has nowhere been associated with phallism. This outlet of the water with which the image is bathed is not peculiar to the temples of Śiva alone. It is generally known as the *gomukha*. Its non-phallic character is further confirmed by the fact that even square-shaped bases are found in the case of some *liṅgas*. This latter shape certainly cannot be supposed to bear any resemblance to the *yoni*.

32 Hartland, "Phallism" *ERE*, vol. 9, pp. 815-816.

33 *Ibid.*, *ERE*, vol. 9, pp. 817, 819.

even though it be exaggerated in size. Secondly, the beliefs and practices relating to the object should emphasise the concepts of fertility, procreation, reproduction, etc. In identifying phallic symbols other than with regards to purely realistic representations, however, the greatest caution must be exercised. Such caution is all the more necessary in the respect of objects which are believed to have been conventionalized so as to hide its obscene appearance.[34] All sorts of objects have, indeed, been claimed to be phallic by writers whose imagination outpaces their circumspection.[35] Similarly, mere semblance — actual or fancied — of the object to a sexual organ cannot by itself be regarded as adequate evidence, unless there is the confirming evidence of the beliefs attached to the object or of the rites performed in relation to it. The excavations at Mohenjodaro have brought to light many artefacts which have been easily identified as phallic objects. Some of them are undoubtedly realistic representations of the phallus. It is, therefore, highly probable that phallic worship was prevalent during the Indus Valley period. It has been already shown that Mohenjodaro presents a civilization in which various religious cults existed side by side.[36] Of these, the Paśupati cult attracts our attention the most. There is, however, hardly any evidence to show that the religious cults were fused with the Paśupati cult at that period. For instance, one fails to see any connection between the Paśupati cult and the phallic cult. The seal which portrays Paśupati does not reflect any traces of the phallism which was evidently prevalent during that period. The only clue which may be regarded as suggestive of phallism is unfortunately vague and therefore

[34] Hartland, "Phallism", vol. 9, p. 819.

[35] The following remark of Hartland is particularly significant in this connection "He who is preoccupied with the subject will see phallic emblems everywhere". *Ibid.*, p. 820: Attention may also be drawn to the following observation: "The Buddhist origin of the *liṅga* comes as an amusing explanation. No doubt the Buddhist *stūpa* is as old as the fifth century BC. It is of the shape of the *liṅga*, and today two such *stūpas* at Gundapalli and Sankaram are worshipped by the people who have mistaken them for the *liṅga*". Subramaniam, *Madras Univ. Journ*al, I, Part 2.

[36] See above chapter I, p. 34.

unreliable. Sir John Marshall, while describing that seal, draws pointed attention to the figure of Paśupati "with his phallus seemingly exposed". Yet he does not fail to record some degree of doubt in this connection by introducing a parenthetical comment which suggests the probability of that portion of the figure representing the waist-band. It is, indeed, strange that no serious attention has so far been taken of this comment.[37] The Śaiva religion, or rather its ancestor of the Mohenjodaro times, is more a Paśupati cult than a phallic cult. The prevalence of the phallic cult as evidenced by the phallic objects excavated on the site may certainly not be denied; only the connection between the phallic cult and the Paśupati cult of those times is disputed. No less an authority than Mackay observes in this connection: "Certain large smooth cone-like stones unearthed at Mohenjodaro and Harappa, were undoubtedly the *liṅga* of those days but it is impossible to say whether they were associated with the worship of Śiva at that very early date." [38] He obviously hesitates to rush to any conclusion and associate objects discovered at the site of the excavations with the full-fledged latter-day Śaivite *liṅgas*. He further writes: "In thc same way certain large stone rings which are considered by some authorities to be the *yonis* or the female counterpart of the phallic emblem may have been employed to build up columns. Until a *liṅga* and one of the ring stones are found in close association, the matter cannot be definitely settled." [39]

Coming to literary sources, it is suggested that even as early as a text as the *Ṛgveda* mentions phallism. The seventh and the tenth *maṇḍalas* of the *Ṛgveda* [40] are said to contain references to the worshippers of *śiśna* or the phallus.[41] The prevalence of phallism in

---

[37] T.M.P. Mahadevan ("Saivism and the Indus Civilisation", *JGJRI*, IV, p. 1ff) has, however, emphasized this point.

[38] Mackay, *"Early Indus Civilisation*", p. 61.

[39] Mackay, *op.cit.* p. 62.

[40] *ṚV*, VII.21.5, and X.99.3.

[41] See for example: Chandorkar G.K., "A note on Śiva and Phallic Worship", p. xxxvii: "Śiva means 'Śiśna' — phallus. Hence Śivāḥ, were the people who had phallus as

the earlier Indus Valley period has led some scholars to assert the phallic implication of the references. These scholars point out that the Ṛgvedic authors are only referring to the phallic worshippers who perpetuated the already-existing religious cult. Sāyaṇa and other orthodox scholars, however, do not accept the phallic interpretation of the word *śiśna-deva* in these contexts. At any rate, it must be admitted that the reference is rather curt and cannot be used as unambiguous evidence for the prevalence and the consequent condemnation of this worship. The Rudra cult of the Ṛgvedic period is amalgamated with the Śiva cult of the Epic period. Such a fusion of the two cults is indisputably accepted by all scholars, traditional and modern. But the Rudra of the Vedic period cannot be said to reveal any traces of a phallic cult. That god is associated with Soma,[42] who himself is associated with Indra in two full hymns.[43] Indra, for his part, is implored to feel hostility towards the *Śiśnadevas*.[44] Under such circumstances, can Rudra be associated with the *Śiśnadevas*, the phallic worshippers, as is done by some scholars?

An elaborate picture of Rudra is given in the *Śatarudriya* of the *Vājasaneyi Saṁhitā*.[45] Numerous names and attributes of this god have been listed in this hymn of adoration of the god. It is to be noted that none of these epithets can be shown to have any phallic im-

their totem ... Śivaḥ and the śiśnadevāḥ must therefore be the same — meaning the people with a totem of phallus". *Proceedings and Transactions of First Oriental Conference*, Poona 1919. Vidusekhara Bhattacarya holds a totally different view, for he sees no reference to phallism in these Vedic lines. He therefore asserts that he differs from "both European and their Indian followers, who have tried to prove the practice of phallus worship in the *Veda*". See "Phallus worship in the *Veda*", *IHQ*, vol. IX, p. 103. See also *IHQ*, vol. X, p. 156 for further comments on the topic by the same author.

42 *ṚV*, VI.74. Rudra is associated with Marut and Viṣṇu (V.3.3.). He is also associated with Mitra and Varuṇa, all of whom are accorded a definitely high place in the Vedic pantheon (I.43.3.).

43 *ṚV*, II.30, and VI.72. Regarding the association of Rudra with Soma and of Soma with Indra, see Keith, *Religion and Philosophy of the Veda*, *HOS*, vol. 31, p. 220 ff.

44 *ṚV*, VII.21.5.

45 *Vājasaneyi Saṁhitā*, 16.7.51.

plications. The *Atharvaveda* also provides no evidence in favour of the phallic character of Rudra. The contents of this *Veda* are shown to belong, to some extent, to a period earlier than that of the *Ṛgveda*; it is therefore strange that even the slight traces of phallism which are alleged to be found in the *Ṛgveda* are not discovered in this *Veda*. Exorcistic hymns and practices relating to fertility and procreation abound in the *Artharvaveda* and its ancillary literature. Had Rudra been a god of fertility and procreation, he would have by all means found a fitting place in all such hymns and practices. This does not, however, seem to be the case.

Neither do the *Brāhmaṇas* ascribe any phallic character to Rudra. On the contrary, the original non-phallic character of Rudra may be said to have been clearly suggested in the Rudra-Prajāpati conflict.[46] There, Bhūtapati is represented to have chastised Prajāpati for committing incest. The peculiar treatment indicative of isolation from other gods which Rudra received during this period has already been discussed in an earlier chapter.[47] This kind of treatment was solely due to other characteristics of his personality, such as his frightful and awe-inspiring features and actions.[48] As is well known, certain sections of the *Brāhmaṇas* discuss rituals with obscene implications.[49] This being so, they would not have hesitated to exploit the phallic features of Rudra, if there had actually been any, especially in connection with such rituals.

The words *liṅga* and *yoni* occur in the *Śvetāśvatara Upaniṣad*.[50] Similarly, the word *liṅga* occurs in some other *Upaniṣads*.[51] An

---

[46] *Aitareya Brāhmaṇa*, III.33.

[47] See above Chapter II.

[48] In this connection Keith (*RPVU*, p. 331) observes: "The exclusion of Rudra, which seems, however, to be post-Vedic, though it is marked in the ritual, is the obvious result of his hostile nature".

[49] Cf. *ŚB*, II.5.2.20; also compare similar characteristics of obscene nature, belonging to the *Sūtra* literature (Keith, *RPVU*, pp. 345, 346 and 351).

[50] *Śvetāśvatara Upaniṣad*, IV.11; V.2,4,5,16.

[51] The word *liṅga* occurs at *Kaṭha Up.*, VI.8; *Śvet.Up.*, VI.9.

attempt [52] has been made to interpret these words in the *Upaniṣads* as being indicative of the existence of the phallic cult. It may be pointed out that in the *Upaniṣads*, generally, the word *liṅga* is merely used in the sense of 'mark' or 'characteristic'. In a few places,[53] it is also used in the sense of the 'subtle body'. The *Śvetāśvatara Upaniṣad* characterizes Rudra as the lord of *yonis*. But the suggestion [54] that this reference implies that god's association with the phallic cult is obviously farfetched. As a matter of fact, the general trend of the teaching of the *Upaniṣads* is such that no traces of the phallic cult in general and of Rudra's association with that cult in particular could be discovered in them.

Attention may be drawn in this connection to another significant point: those who suggest that Vedic texts such as the *Ṛgveda* and the *Śvetāśvatara Upaniṣad* were acquainted with the phallic cult will find it difficult to account for the total disappearance of that cult in the subsequent period. It will be seen that the Buddhist texts are generally silent about the *liṅga* cult. Had such a cult been widely prevalent during that period, naturally they would have condemned it. The absence of any such references would lead us to the conclusion that the cult was unknown in the Buddhist and pre-Buddhist periods. The *Kalpa-sūtras* also are silent about phallic worship as such. It may, therefore, be concluded that neither the *liṅga*-worship nor the association of Rudra with it is evidenced for the Vedic period.

It may be further pointed out that, as against the presumed wide prevalence of *liṅga* worship, the information provided by archaeological data is scant. Available are only a few early instances of the *liṅga* worship which can be dated with some precision. In this connection may be mentioned the *liṅga* discovered at Gudimallam, near Reniguntha in Andhra Pradesh.[55] This is ascribed to the third century BC, and is accordingly perhaps the earliest datable *liṅga*.[56]

52 Karmarkar, *The Religions of India*, vol. I, p. 83.

53 *Śvet. Up.*, I.13; *Maitri Up.*, VI.10,19.

54 Karmarkar, *op.cit.*, p. 83.

The *liṅga* cult has often been shown to be of a non-Aryan origin. For instance, Farquhar observes: "The question of its origin has often been discussed. Archaeologists tell us that *liṅgas* belonging to pre-Christian dates are in existence; so that they must be earlier than the first mentioned in literature. The explanation probably is that the *liṅga* is of aboriginal origin, as the *śiśnadeva* of the *Ṛgveda* implies, that it passed into popular Hinduism and into sculpture at an early date, but did not receive Brahmanical recognition until after the Christian era."[57] Attempts have also been made to establish the purely Dravidian character of the original Śiva worship and, consequently, of the *liṅga* cult.[58] Evidence in support of this theory is said to have been sup-

---

[55] *IHQ*, vol. VII, p. 830. Hopkins in his *Religions of India* (p. 470) refers in clear terms to the non-existence of phallic worship in the third century BC. He says: "Śiva is on all sides opposed to Viṣṇu. The Greek account of the third century BC says that he taught the Hindus to dance the Kordax, but at this time there appears to have been no such phallic worship in his honour as is recorded in the pseudoepic."

[56] Another *liṅga* is found in the collection of the Lucknow museum. This is said to be a realistic type of this emblem from the North. The sculpture is said to come from the Mathura region. Another is a huge stone *Śivalinga* in the Mathura museum collection. Also may be mentioned the *liṅgas* of the Gupta age. It is then that the conventionalisation is believed to have begun. Reference may be made to a symbol displayed on a coin hailing from Ujjain ascribed to the second or the third century. This symbol is described as "a Śivaliṅga on the pedestal, placed between two different trees. Attention has been drawn also to the extremely realistic phallic emblems of Śiva beside a hill ... and inscribed in Brāhmi characters". Banerjea, *op.cit*, p. 114.

[57] *Outlines of the Religious Literature of India*, p. 102.

[58] The following footnote found in Barth's *Religions of India*, (p. 261) is highly significant: "Kittel, *Ueber den Ursprung des Lingacultus in Indien*, p. 46: The author of this little piece, full of valuable information on the religions of Southern India, has completely refuted the hypothesis of the Dravidian origin of the worship of the *liṅga*".

The following remarks made by A.C. Das are significant in this connection "It is customary both with European and Indian scholars to father the inauguration of these symbols on the Dravidians and to trace their source to Non-Aryan agency. But I have come across the word *śiśna-devāh* in the *Ṛgveda* (VII.21.5), which referred to those Aryan tribes who worshipped the symbol of the male organ of generation. Of course these Aryan tribes were hated by the Vedic Aryans for their mode of worship, and classed with the *rākṣasas* or demons. It is very likely that this worship was carried by these tribes to Southern India where it was freely adopted by those who came in contact with them". *Ṛgvedic India*, p. 278.

plied by the classical Tamil texts called the *Saṅgam* works. Here the chief gods mentioned are Śiva, Śubrahmaṇya and Kṛṣṇa. The frequent references to Śiva and his son Murugan in Tamil literature have made scholars theorize that Śiva was a Dravidian god or at least a non-Aryan god who was later on identified with the Aryan god Rudra.[59] G.U. Pope points out, in this connection, that "Śaivism is the old prehistoric religion of south India, essentially existing from pre-Aryan times, and holds away over the hearts of the Tamil people." [60] Emphasis, however, needs to be laid on the fact — which unfortunately has not received adequate attention from scholars — that the literature in ancient Tamil does not at all speak of phallism; nor does it refer to Śiva as frequently as is generally presumed by scholars. It is

---

[59] Sur, in an article entitled "Pre-Aryan elements in Indian Culture" (*IHQ* vol. X, p. 19), observes thus: "Now it seems possible that Rudra in the *Ṛgveda* was an Aryanised form of pre-Aryan proto-Śiva. This supposition to a certain extent finds support in the fact that the word Rudra in Sanskrit meaning 'red' is identified with the Dravidian word for 'red' Śiva".

[60] *Tiruvācakam* (Translated) p. lxxiv.
Similar views are expressed by a few others also:
Elmore in his *Dravidian Gods in Modern Hinduism* (p. 81) remarks: "The Dravidian gods are more commonly connected with Śiva. There is more in the nature of Śiva worship that is Dravidian than in Viṣṇu worship. It is quite probable that Śiva himself is an aboriginal god". Slater is compelled to share the same view, for he observes (*The Dravidian Element in Indian Culture*, p. 51): "If Kālī and Śiva and Viṣṇu are not Vedic deities, and certainly they are not, they can hardly be Aryan, and there seems no other possible alternative than to suppose they are Dravidian." Kanagasabai in his *Tamils Eighteen Hundred Years Ago* (p. 231) asserts that Śiva and Kālī were the most popular deities of the non-Aryans and they were first admitted into the Brahmin pantheon ... Similarly Muruga, the patron deity of the hunting tribes was adopted as the son of Śiva." See Sesha Iyengar, *The Ancient Dravidians*, pp. 52, 53, 156 and 167. Fergusson records the same views in his *Tree and Serpent Worship* (p. 75) in very emphatic terms as follows: "It has been attempted to identify Śiva with the Rudra of the *Vedas* and it may be so, but it is certainly a local not an Aryan form of faith, and seems originally to belong rather to the South than to the North of India". Besides these foregoing observations associating Śiva with the Tamils, or rather the non-Aryans, views of a contrary nature also have been expressed; See for example the following comments made by Sarup, in his paper entitled, "Ṛgveda and Mohenjodaro", *IC*, vol. IV, p. 166. He observes: "I should like to submit that Śiva is an Aryan deity. Although Śiva occupies a subordinate place in the Ṛgveda, he, nevertheless, is a member of the Vedic pantheon."

the Vedic gods like Varuṇa and Indra who figure prominently in the oldest of the ancient *Saṅgam* works. The more frequent mention of Śiva is found only in comparatively later works. It is also to be remembered that the few references to Śiva in ancient Tamil works actually represent that god as possessing human features.

The *Tolkāppiyam* does not mention Śiva, nor does it refer even indirectly to his features. In other classical works of fairly ancient date, such as *Narriṇai*, *Aiṁkurunūru*, *Patirruppattu*, *Paripāṭal*, *Akanānūru*, *Puranānūru*, *Kalittokai*, and *Tirumurukārruppaṭai*, many references are found to Śiva, but it is significant that the name Śiva does not occur at all in any of these works. Only the description of this god is given — and this always with reference to his physical features, such as the matted hair, black neck, etc. The god is described as having Umā by his side. He is three-eyed, a bearer of the Gaṅgā and a rider of the bull. He is seated under the banyan tree. He wears the crescent. He is eight-armed. He wears the skin of the tiger. One half of his body is assigned to Umā. He is the destroyer of the three worlds. He besmears his body with ashes. He is a dancer, particularly noted for the dance which he performs at the hour of destruction. He carries a skull on his hand. The Himālaya is his abode. Such is the characterization of Śiva found in the early literary works in the Tamil language. There is conspicuous absence in them of references either to *liṅga* or to phallism.

Even the *Cilappatikāram* and *Maṇimekhalai* of comparatively later date are silent about the *liṅga*. Some Tamil works of a still later date alone refer to *liṅga* worship in clear terms.[61] Among these, some assume phallism [62] whereas others do not associate *liṅga* worship with it. At any rate, references to *liṅga* worship in later Tamil literature need not be taken into consideration at this stage, because they are

---

[61] The *Tevarams* sung by the Śaiva saints of the post-Saṅgam period and *Tirumantiram* of *Tirumūlar* of the same period are the works which need special mention in this connection.

[62] The assumption is only in a limited sense. It is the higher philosophical meaning that is implied here. See *Tirumantiram*, VII.5, verses 1753-1762.

merely the result of the influence of the Purāṇic and other allied concepts, which shall be discussed at a later part of this chapter.

Ingenious etymological explanations are given of the word *liṅga*,[63] and an attempt is thereby made to emphasise the phallic character of the *liṅga*-worship. A correct understanding of the word *liṅga* is necessary to decide the nature of this concept. As has been pointed out above, *liṅga* originally meant 'sign', 'symbol' or 'mark', and it often stood for something more than what it actually denoted. It is this sense of the word which is prominent in the more ancient texts — be they religious, philosophical or secular. Reference has already been made to the meaning of the word *liṅga* as it occurs in the *Upaniṣads*. In the grammatical texts, the word *liṅga* denotes gender alone. It is in this sense that the word is used by Pāṇini. The use of the word *liṅga* is not restricted to denote the male only (as in *pulliṅga*). The forms *strīliṅga* and *napuṁsakaliṅga* are also there. This is a sufficient indication that even in the grammatical use of the term, whereby it denoted the sex, the word *liṅga* maintains its original meaning. It is thus only secondarily that the meaning 'sex' came to be assigned to this word.

Przyluski has made a special linguistic study of the word '*liṅga*'. He has suggested that both the words *lāṅgala* (plough) and *liṅga* (penis) are of austro-asiatic origin, and that etymologically they mean one and the same thing. He has pointed out that *liṅga*, in the sense of penis, has equivalents in the non-Aryan languages of the East, whereas, it has no equivalent in the Indo-European languages of the

---

[63] Cf. *Bhaṁ vṛddhiṁ gacchatītyarthād bhagaḥ prakṛtir ucyate*
… … …
Mukhyo bhagastu prakṛtih bhagavān śiva ucyate |
Bhagavān bhogadātā hi nānyo bhogapradāyakaḥ ||
Bhagasvāmī ca bhagavān bharga ity ucyate budhaiḥ |
Bhagena sahitaṁ liṅgaṁ bhagaṁ liṅgena saṁyutam ||
Ihāmutra ca bhogārthaṁ nityabhogārtham eva ca |
Bhagavantaṁ mahādevaṁ śivaliṅgaṁ prapūjayet ||
… … …
Śivaśaktyos ca cihnasya melanaṁ liṅgam ucyate |
Śiva P., *Vidyeśvara-saṁhitā*, 14.101-107.

West. It has further been shown that *lāṅgalam*, when introduced in the Sanskrit vocabulary, came to imply both the plough and the penis. The author further points out that in the *sūtras* and the *Mahābhārata* one form *lagula* is found to mean both the penis and the tail (of an animal). If the same could be said for *lāṅgula*, the semantic evolution of the word would be easily understood. In support of this theory, Przyluski has drawn attention to the evident analogy between the act of copulation and the act of ploughing, by which one digs the earth for depositing the seed.[64] Following Prkzyluski, A.K. Sur says: The Aryans of India have borrowed from the aborigines not only the cult of the *liṅga* but also the name of the symbol.[65]

Even in the face of what Przyluski has tried to prove, it may be averred that the explanation of the word *liṅga* as 'symbol' or 'sign' is by no means based on flimsy grounds. It seems that the teachings of the *Upaniṣads*,[66] especially those relating to the *upāsanāmārga*,[67] as well as the *yoga* school of thought with which Śaivism had always maintained close connections,[68] suggested to the worshippers of Śiva the idea of meditating on some external symbols suggestive of the god, for the god himself was believed to be beyond the direct grasp of the sense organs.[69] It is very difficult to determine what this symbol to be meditated upon was actually intended to be, because we do not possess any direct evidence in this connection. It is, however, not

---

[64] Przyluski, *Pre-Aryan, Pre-Dravidian, and Proto-Dravidian India*, p. 10.

[65] "Beginnings of Linga cult in India", *ABORI*, vol. 13, p. 152.

[66] The *Upaniṣads* concern themselves mainly with the higher knowledge. They do not sponsor the rituals, which by themselves cannot lead to the ultimate goal.

[67] This becomes essential when the lower aspect of Brahman, as opposed to the higher one, is thought of. The following passages from the *Upaniṣads* indicate the evolution of such an idea: *Bṛh.Up.*, 2.1.20; *Kaṭha Up.*, 4.9; *Ait.Up.*, 1.1.3. Also compare *Bṛh.Up.*, 1.4.10; 4.3.33; 5.2.1; *Tait.Up.*, 2.8; *Kauṣīt.Up.*, 4.20; *Kaṭha Up.* 1.21; *Bṛh.Up.*, I.4.10. See also *Ch.Up.*, 8.12.6; *Bṛh.Up.*, 1.4.10. The *Śvetāśvatara Upaniṣad* contains, through out the text, this idea of the god. The *upāsanā*, the worship of the god, becomes indispensable under such circumstances.

[68] Numerous passages may be cited from the *Purāṇas* which witness to the connections of Śaivism with yoga. *Liṅga P.*, I.88; *Vāyu P.*, I, ch. 10 & 19.

[69] Cf. *Nainaṁ ūrdhvaṁ na tiryañcaṁ na madhye parijagrabhat*. *Śvet.Up.*, IV.19.

improbable that to the minds of the ancient Indians accustomed to the sacrificial systems some symbol vitally associated with that system, such as the tapering flame of Agni, or the *yūpastaṁbha*,[70] appealed as the most suitable symbol to be meditated upon. Over the course of time, a conventionalized representation came to be fixed upon as the symbol for meditation and adoration; this symbol came to be referred to as the *liṅga*. As the symbol of the *liṅga* was employed with particular conspicuousness in connection with meditation on Śiva, the concepts of Śiva and the *liṅga* came to be very closely associated with each other. This naturally resulted in the term *liṅga* being always coupled with Śiva. In other words, *liṅga*, which originally meant a 'symbol' employed for meditating on any god, was eventually restricted in its connotation and consequently came to denote only the symbol to be meditated upon in the worship of Śiva. Thus both *liṅga* and *Śiva-liṅga* became almost synonymous and actually came to refer to one and the same symbol which greatly facilitated meditation on Śiva. However, over time, the word *liṅga* ('symbol' or more particularly the symbol of Śiva) came to be confused with the word *liṅga* ('phallus').

It may be incidentally pointed out here that the idea for the original *liṅga* (symbol of Śiva) was presumably derived from the *yūpa*. It took the form of a column or a pillar-like object. Since it was conceived of as erect, it came to be known as *sthāṇu*. Later on, this *sthāṇu* also was mistaken for the erect phallus. The phallic theorists have similarly misinterpreted another epithet of Śiva, namely, *ūrdhvaliṅga*. This latter merely meant one whose *liṅga* or symbol stood erect.

A few other points may be mentioned here to show that *liṅga* originally denoted not a 'phallus' but 'a symbol for meditation, employed more particularly in the worship of Śiva'. It should be noted that one who meditates on the *liṅga* and worships it with devotion always sees in it the god Śiva himself and never recognizes in it —

[70] The similarity of the *liṅga* and the *yūpa* is quite apparent. Allan has offered two suggestions for the symbol — a *liṅga* or a *yūpa*, the latter of which is acceptable. See Banerjea, *op.cit.*, p. 109.

even remotely — the concept of a phallus. This attitude characterizes the *liṅga* worship from the earliest known times. All ancient texts would clearly testify to this. Even in such texts that give phallic nature to the *liṅga*, an attitude contrary to this is not seen. The Epics and the *Purāṇas*, especially the latter, deal at some length with the ways in which the *liṅga* is to be propitiated. Many of these texts no doubt understand the *liṅga* as phallus, but they do not mention any rites with phallic implications.[71] For instance, nowhere do these texts describe fertility rites in connection with the *liṅga* worship. If the *liṅga* had really possessed any phallic character, there would have been in existence several such rites and reference to them would have been unavoidable. Actually, the ascription of phallic character to the *liṅga* worship in these texts stops at merely equating the *liṅga* with a phallus. As will be shown later in this chapter, this was also done out of error. It should be remembered that the *Mahābhārata* and the *Purāṇas* unanimously assert the presence of Śiva in the *liṅga*.[72] For instance, Chapter 70 of the *Agni Purāṇa* describes the rituals for bringing the presence (*sānniddhya*) of Śiva into the *liṅga*. Whenever the ritual relating to the *liṅga* is prescribed, the fruits derived from that ritual are also listed; it is to be noted that none of such fruits has any phallic character about it. The presence of Śiva in the *liṅga* and his acknowledging the rites performed are always assumed. Ritualistically, these texts never think of any phallus, not even of that of Śiva. Moreover, the fact that, sometimes the *liṅga* has the anthropomorphic features of the god inscribed or carved on it is distinctly suggestive of the *liṅga* meaning 'symbol' and not '*phallus*'.[73]

---

[71] George Scott, in his *Phallic Worship* (p. 209), quotes an authority who has in one of his works pointed out the fact that "nothing whatever belongs to its worship, or to the terms in which this is mentioned, which has the slightest tendency to lead the thoughts from the contemplation of the god, to an undue consideration of the object by which he is typified".

[72] Śiva proclaims to Umā: *Tasmiṁlliṅge ca sānniddhyaṁ mama devi suresvari... Matsya P.*, 183.9.

[73] George Scott, contrary to his phallic interpretation of *liṅga*, is compelled at one stage to confess as follows: "The essence of phallic worship in India, it has been

In the light of what has been said above, we may trace three distinct phases in the evolution of the iconography relating to Śiva. One of them, possibly the earliest, is the aniconic symbol, the *liṅga*. Probably on account of its antiquity, the *liṅga* is assigned the greatest importance all over the country, and is installed as the central object of worship in many temples dedicated to Śiva. The second phase is represented by the *liṅga* with the features of the god Śiva partially displayed on it. This is the *liṅgodbhava* form of Śiva, and is described later in this very chapter.[74] The various kinds of images with an elaborate display of the physical features constitute the third phase.

As far as the first phase is concerned, it would by no means be farfetched to suppose the original symbol, which resembled the *yūpa* or the tapering flame of Agni, was gradually replaced by forms which, on account of their shape, could be easily mistaken for a phallus. It is thus confusion between the *liṅga* symbol and the *liṅga* phallus which presumably misled some Purāṇic writers who had frequent occasions to speak of the Śiva *liṅga* to accept the phallic idea. For the first time in these works we come across cleverly invented stories,[75] purely aetiological in character. These stories contain impressive treatments of this topic accompanied by many legendary narrations. The *Purāṇas* may thus be said to have concocted new legends to explain the concept of the *liṅga* as newly understood — or misunderstood — by them; the fanciful etymologies given in this connection remind one of similar etymologies found in the *Brāhmaṇas*. In such etymologies, one proceeds to new meaning on the basis of the already-accepted sense of a given word. Etymology does not procede and govern the sense, as it normally should do. The fact that the authors of the *Purāṇas* worked out their explanation to a set plan is evident; they argued that if the *liṅga* worship was to be explained as the worship of the phallus,

stated, is its characteristic symbolism. The lingam is considered to be merely a means of bringing the invisible god into the presence of the worshipper" (*Phallic Worship*, p. 208).

[74] See pages 349 ff.

[75] E.G. *Skanda P.*, VI.1; *Vāmana P.*, 44.1-45; *Padma P.*, *Uttara Khaṇḍa*, ch. 255.

and that too of the phallus of Śiva, it must inevitably follow that the phallus was detached from the person of Śiva. How otherwise could the *liṅga* be worshipped separately? This gave rise to the accounts in the *Purāṇas* relating to the detached phallus.[76] It is also to be noted that the *Purāṇas* give manifold explanations — often contradictory — regarding the coming into existence of the practice of *liṅga* worship; this would create some doubt about the genuineness of those explanations.

A usual argument in support of the original phallic character of the *liṅga* cult is its supposed remote antiquity. It is argued that such a form of worship, because of its primitiveness, could have been only of phallic nature. The *liṅga* worship originally flourished, according to some scholars, as an independent cult.[77] Over the course of time, it was amalgamated into the worship of Śiva.[78] As civilization progressed and a sense of decency developed, obscene elements in the worship gradually disappeared. This is the explanation given by these scholars for the complete absence of phallic traits in *liṅga* worship as it prevails today. As regards this argument, it may be first asked why

---

[76] Cf. *Brāhmāṇḍa P.*, I.27; *Śiva P.*, *Jñāna-saṁhitā*, 42; *Skanda P.*, I.5; *Vāmana P.*, 6.57-73.

[77] A.P. Karmarkar, "The Liṅga-cult in ancient India", *B.C. Law Volume*, p. 456.
The same view is upheld by A.K. Sur, in a paper entitled "The Beginnings of *Liṅga*-Cult in India". He observes, "Phallus worship in India is of non-Aryan origin and dates from the Neolithic times. It was a flourishing cult in the Indus Valley in the period of the *Ṛgveda*. It became fused with the cult of Śiva in the Epic period. The earlier archaeological specimens date from about the Christian Era. The early specimens show definitely that *Śiva-liṅga* in its origin is of phallic origin." *ABORI*, XIII, p. 153.

[78] A.P. Karmarkar, *The Religions of India*, vol. I, pp. 81 ff.
Moreas G.M. (*NR*, vol. X, p. 448) subscribes to the same view. He says: "Later on as the contact with the Dravidian tribes grew, some Aryan tribes adapted the worship of Āṇ = Śiva. In all probability, the *liṅga*-cult was not yet adopted. As time passed the now sufficiently Dravidianised Aryans ceased to fight shy of Śiva and admitted him into their pantheon by identifying him with Rudra, one of their own gods. From this, to the adoption of the *liṅga*-cult was only a step; the evolution of Śaivism was thus completed. In this manner the historic Śiva was evolved from Āṇ, the supreme God of the proto-Indian period".

the *Purāṇas* and similar other texts, which have accepted the phallic character of the symbol, should have hesitated to assimilate the phallic elements in the ritual traditions of the *liṅga* worship as well. The *Purāṇas*, which in some chapters speak of Śiva in rather indecent and obscene terms, cannot be supposed to have suddenly developed a sense of decency while describing the details of the *liṅga* worship and to have therefore avoided or rather eliminated the indecent elements in the rites associated with it. There also does not exist any adequate reason to suppose that the phallic elements in the rituals connected with the *liṅga* cult were replaced by other decent ones. The religious tradition of India is noted for the unbroken continuity of its practices.[79]

Hinduism, over the course of its history, has no doubt assimilated new elements, but the total eradication of one set of practices and a substitution with another has never been seen. If, therefore, phallism had been originally associated with the *liṅga* cult, it could never have been so very completely eliminated from that cult in later times. Phallism is too vital an ideology to be set aside easily. Reference may be made in this connection to Śaktism. The association of phallic rites with this cult in its very early stages is beyond dispute. Over the course of time, many phallic elements in Śaktism gradually came to be eliminated. Nevertheless, it must be pointed out that the Śākta texts are by no means silent about the so-called *vāmamārga*. Paiyne remarks: "According to Śākta apologists, the *dakṣiṇācara* and the *vāmācara* are both recognized forms of worship, presented by tantras for different grades of worshippers." [80]

[79] The following observation of Tylor (*Anthropology*, vol. I, p. 12: Thinker's Library) is very significant in this connection: "To what yet more distant periods of civilization such survivals may reach back is well seen in an example from India. There, though people have for ages kindled fire for practical use with the flint and steel, yet the Brahmans, to make the sacred fire for the daily sacrifice, still use the barbaric art of violently boring a pointed stick into another piece of wood till a spark comes ... But to us it is plain that they are really keeping up by unchanging custom a remnant of the ruder life once led by their remote ancestors".

[80] *The Śāktas*, p. 24.

On the same analogy, one would have expected the presumedly original phallic character of *liṅga* worship to be reflected in the literary and ritual traditions of the Śaivites. That Śaktism was subordinated and assimilated by Śaivism is an undisputed fact.[81] Naturally enough, this amalgamation of the two cults (which must have occurred in pre-epic times, since the Epics refer in clear terms to Śakti being Śiva's consort)[82] may be held responsible for the supposed association of phallism with *liṅga* worship.[83]

Nilakantha Sastri seems to have put the whole situation in its proper perspective when he says: "And the preponderance, real or supposed, of orgiastic rites in some forms of Śaktism has doubtless sometimes influenced modern students of Śaivism into accepting exclusively phallic interpretations of the *Śiva-liṅga*. But the *liṅga* may have been in origin no more than just a symbol as the *sālagrāma* is for Viṣṇu." [84]

If phallism in one form or another was assumed to have been associated with Śiva, quite a series of questions would crop up and

---

[81] This is evident from the fact that almost all the temples of Śiva in the South have a separate shrine for the Śakti. The *Ardhanārīśvara* concept points to the fact that Śiva and Śakti are accorded equal importance. Indicating the influence Śaktism is said to have on Śaivism, Sur remarks: "The development of Śaktism gave a great fillip to the propagation of the cult. Throughout the tāntric literature we have the injunction that all religious merit will go in vain if one does not worship the *liṅga*." "Pre-Aryan Elements in Indian Culture", *IHQ*, vol. X, p. 22.

[82] *Mahābhārata*, III.40.4.

[83] Even in the Epic and Purāṇic accounts of the *liṅga* cult, Śakti is prominently mentioned. Is this not suggestive?

[84] "A Historical sketch of Śaivism", *The Cultural Heritage of India*, vol. II, p. 23. In his Foreword to C.V. Narayana Aiyar's *Origin and Early History of Śaivism in South India*, Nilakantha Sastri supports the former viewpoint by citing P. Mus who also holds the view that *liṅga* has no connections with phallism. Nilakantha Sastri says, "It may, however, be noted that recent research into the symbolism of the *liṅga* from this standpoint tends to support Mr. Narayana Aiyar's conclusion which denies exclusively phallic origin and nature of the *liṅga*. Thus Professor Mus has said: "Que le liṅga soit un phallus, il n'y a pas à en douter. Mais il n'est pas qu'un phallus, anatomiquement, si j'ose dire; il n'est même pas peut-être surtout cela". ("There is no doubt that the *liṅga* is a phallus. But it is not only a phallus, anathomically, if I may say so; may be even it is not mainly this.")

challenge the authenticity of such an assumption.[85] Is Śiva a god of fertility? [86] Is he ever invoked at the time of marriage or impregnation? As a matter of fact Śiva is Kāmāri, the destroyer of the god of love.[87] That god is nowhere specifically invoked for granting progeny.[88] On the contrary, among three functions of creation, preservation and destruction, it is the last one that is usually ascribed to him.[89]

The Epics, especially the *Mahābhārata*, took a long time to crystalise into their final forms. Portions of religious and philosophical import were being added on to their bulk from time to time. The portions relating to Śaivism, it may be maintained, were added in a period much later than when those pertaining to Vaiṣṇavism were added.[90] It may be further presumed that among the Śaivite sections, the references to rituals and forms of Śiva worship, particularly the *liṅga* worship, belonged to a still later period. There are very few

---

[85] Before associating the *liṅga* with phallism, it is necessary that the following questions about Śiva are satisfactorily answered: Why is Śiva worshipped? How is he worshipped? By whom is he worshipped? What are his connections with fertility? What led to the standardization of the *liṅga*? When did it happen?

[86] Rudra, the Ṛgvedic predecessor of Śiva, has no doubt been associated with phallic rites, and only implicitly. He has been only shown as having connections with the *munis* and the *brahmacāris*. The *Atharvaveda* does not so much as hint at this phallic connections. The *Brāhmaṇas* too do not connect Rudra directly with phallism, and certainly not the *Upaniṣads*. In the Epics and the *Purāṇas* there are no indications of the phallic cult, except in the interpolations consisting of stories which refer to the dropping by Śiva of his phallus. No fertility rites connected with Śiva are recorded in the Epics and the *Purāṇas*.

[87] *Liṅga P.*, I.101; *Padma P.*, I.43; *Vāmana P.*, 6; *Rām.*, I.23.10-15.

[88] In the Epics and the *Purāṇas*, Śiva has received a large number of names and epithets. But he is nowhere called a giver of progeny. In only a few almost negligible passages, Śiva is said to have granted progeny to a worshipper. But this is obviously a mere conventionalized boon.

[89] About the function of Śiva, Heras ("A proto-Indian representation of the fertility god", *D.R. Bhandarkar Vol.*, p. 121) observes: "A serpent in the hands of Śiva is a symbol of destruction, but according to Indian ideology, destruction is necessary for creation; death is required for generation. Hence a symbol of destruction was to be as well a symbol of creation".

[90] Cf. "Myths in which the god Śiva occupied a position far above all gods indicate a much later stratum of Brahmanical poetry in the *Mahābhārata*". Winternitz, *HIL*, vol. I, p. 396.

references to *liṅga* worship found in the *Mahābhārata*; the *Rāmāyaṇa* mentions it only in one context,[91] where Rāvaṇa is said to have carried a golden *liṅga* for worship wherever he went. The most important role played by Śiva in the *Mahābhārata* is in connection with his giving the *Pāśupata* weapon to Arjuna. There, Śiva is featured in his human form.[92] It is also significant that Arjuna propitiates the god by performing *tapas*,[93] and that the *liṅga* worship is nowhere mentioned in that context.

It is also to be noted that wherever the *liṅga* concept is presented in the *Mahābhārata* it is presented in a dignified form.[94] It adds immensely to the greatness of Śiva and ascribes to him a unique position hitherto unknown to any other.[95] Brahmā, Viṣṇu, and other gods are said to have worshipped the *liṅga*.[96] The sage Upamanyu is represented

---

[91] *Rām.*, VII.31.41.

[92] *MBh*, III.39 and 40.

[93] *Ibid.*, III.39.20-24.

[94] There are, no doubt, a few passages in the Epic where the phallic character of the *liṅga* is clearly indicated. Cf., for instance,

Na padmāṅkā na cakrāṅkā na vajrāṅkā yataḥ prajāḥ |
Liṅgāṅkā ca bhagāṅkā ca tasmān māheśvaraprajāḥ || *MBh*, XIII.14.229.

"Since the creatures are not marked by a lotus, nor a discus, nor a thunderbolt, but are marked by a *liṅga* (male organ) or a *bhaga* (female organ), therefore they are creatures of Maheśvarī."

The *liṅga* cult as portrayed in such verses of the *Mahābhārata* may be explained as an expression of a biological fact that the creation of the world is governed by the two principles of the male and the female. Cf.

Puṁlliṅgaṁ śarvam īśānaṁ strīliṅgaṁ viddhi cāpy umām |
Dvābhyāṁ tanubhyāṁ vyāptaṁ hi carācaram idaṁ jagat ||

"Know the Lord Śarva as having male marks, Umā female marks. This world, moving and motionless is pervaded by their two bodies..."

Devyāḥ kāraṇarūpabhāvajanitāḥ sarvā bhagāṅkāḥ striyaḥ |
Liṅgenāpi harasya sarvapuruṣāh pratyakṣacihnīkṛtāḥ || *MBh*, XIII.14.230-231.

[95] *Hetubhir vā kimanyaistair īśaḥ kāraṇakāraṇaṁ* |
Na śuśruma yadanyasya liṅgam abhyarcanaṁ suraiḥ || *MBh*, XIII.14.226.

"Why other reasons? The Lord is the cause of causes. We do not hear the *liṅga* of any other is an object of worship by gods."

[96] *Tasya brahmā ca viṣṇuśca tvaṁ cāpi saha daivataiḥ* |
Arcayethāḥ sadā liṅgaṁ tasmāc ceṣtatamo hi saḥ || *Ibid.*, XIII.14.229.

as a prominent promulgator of the *liṅga* cult in the *Mahābhārata*.[97] He speaks of that form of worship as if it had been a long-established tradition.[98] The detailed account of *liṅga* worship occurring in this context is considered to be the earliest literary record relating to that cult.[99]

Coming to the *Purāṇas*, one finds that these texts afford a variety of interesting explanations of the *liṅga* concept. In their own characteristic manner, they narrate the events leading to the origin of this cult. So diverse are the narrations, and so contradictory the observations made on the subject, that it becomes impossible to desire any coherent theory from them. For the sake of the convenience of discussion, the Purāṇic materials relating to the *liṅga* cult may be classified into two major groups, corresponding to the two main trends of thought which had been in vogue in this connection. It must be remembered that each of these two groups contains several versions and that the descriptions in the same version are by no means completely identical in their details. However, it may be generally stated that, according to one major group, Śiva becomes manifest to Brahmā and Viṣṇu as a column of fire. This account is elaborately related at several places in the *Purāṇas*.[100] The other group of accounts refers to the detached phallus of Śiva.

---

97 *MBh*, XIII.14.63.

98 *MBh*, XIII.14.134-135.

99 On this subject, Nanimadhab Chaudhuri (*IHQ*, vol. XXIV, no. 4, p. 292) observes as follows: "From Alexander's invasion to the days of the later Kushans is a long period and literary, archaeological and numismatic evidences testify to the prevalence of the worship of Rudra-Śiva in the Northern provinces of ancient India. Buddhistic influence was predominant in these areas and was also the channel through which wave after wave of new ethnic elements poured into the plains of India. Constantly exposed to outside influences these areas were also the place where indigenous ideas and things were liable to undergo involuntary transformations. In the absence of reliable data no definite conclusion is possible but the Kamboja affinities of the sage Upamanyu the propagator of a new synthetic cult of the *liṅga* and his admission that he was initiated into the new religion by his mother should be given due weight in enquiries regarding the origin of the Epic *liṅga* worship."

100 *Kūrma P.*, I.26; *Vāyu P.*, I.1 and I.55; *Liṅga P.*, I.17; *Śiva P.*, *Jñāna-saṁhitā*, 2; *Brahma P.*, II.65; *Skanda P.*, III.1.14 and so on.

The accounts constituting the first major group evidently understand the *liṅga* in its earlier implication, namely, as 'sign' or 'symbol'. The *liṅga* mentioned in these narrations stands for Śiva, and the god manifests himself through this symbol whenever the need arises.[101] In one of the chapters of the *Liṅga Purāṇa*, a few questions about the *liṅga* have been posed.[102] "How did the *liṅga* come into existence?" "Why is Śiva worshipped in it?" "What is *liṅga* and who is *liṅgin*?" The answers to these questions are embodied in the narration of the various events which led to the genesis of the *liṅga* concept. The story may be briefly reproduced here (Fig. 3): Brahmā and Viṣṇu quarreled between themselves, each claiming superiority over the other. When the quarrel exceeded the limits of decorum, Śiva deemed it necessary to interfere. A huge column of fire blazed forth between Brahmā and Viṣṇu. It extended both upwards and downwards without end. Anxious to face its limits, Brahmā assumed the form of a swan and flew upwards, and Viṣṇu became a boar and dug his way downwards. Defeated in their pursuit, they returned to the starting point and humbly acknowledged defeat. It was thus that Brahmā and Viṣṇu had the occasion to realize that there existed an entity which was superior to them both, and that it was Śiva. Thereupon they submitted themselves to the supremacy of Śiva and worshipped the *liṅga*, through which he had become manifest to them and eventually granted them their requests. This legend is brought to a close with the observation: "Thenceforward the worship of the *liṅga* came into vogue in the world".[103] It must be emphasized that the *liṅga* which thus became manifest to Brahmā and Viṣṇu had no phallic implication whatsoever and is everywhere described in glorious terms.[104] Similar is the account

[101] Cf. the legend of Śveta, who prayed to Śiva to save him from the snares of Yama. *Liṅga P.*, I.30.

[102] *Ibid.*, I.17.

[103] *Tatah prabhṛti lokeṣu liṅgārcā supratiṣṭhitā*. *Liṅga P.*, I.19.15.

[104] ... *Śivātmakaṁ*
Kālānalasamaprakhyaṁ jvālamālāsamākulam |
Kṣayavṛddhivinirmuktam ādimadhyāntavarjitam || *Kūrma P.*, I.26.72-73.

Fig. 3: Liṅgodbhava, Bṛhadīśvara Temple at Tanjavur.

of the origin of *liṅga* worship given in the *Brahmāṇḍa Purāṇa*.[105] The *Śiva Purāṇa* relates the story in more or less the same manner.[106] The origin of the *jyotirliṅga* has been discussed in two full chapters of the same text.[107] The *Skanda Purāṇa* refers to the liṅga as *vahnistambha*.[108] The *liṅga* at Aruṇācala later receives the epithet *sthāvaraliṅga*.[109] According to the *Kūrma Purāṇa*, when Brahmā and Viṣṇu failed to find the top or bottom of the *liṅga* of Śiva, they worshipped the *liṅga*, and thus initiated the cult which has since been adopted by all living beings.[110]

There is one more point which should be mentioned at this stage. All the accounts referred to above describe the *liṅga* as a column of fire — a 'symbol' which stands for Śiva, a 'medium' through which that god manifests himself. How was it that this symbol — the *tejoliṅga* or pillar of fire — lost its properties of heat? This question was once raised by Umā and was answered by the sage Gautama. The sage explained that the *tejoliṅga* was cooled down by the request of the gods.[111] The *Skanda Purāṇa* mentions this incident more than once.[112] The same version is elaborated in the *Śiva Purāṇa* [113] and also in the *Brahma Purāṇa*.[114]

We shall now pass on to other explanations given of the *liṅga* concept, clearly ascribing phallic qualities to the *liṅga*. It must, however, be noted that no two descriptions belonging to this type can be shown to agree. The Purāṇic accounts in this connection differ widely among themselves,[115] the only common point among them is that they seek to connect the *liṅga* with the phallus in any way possible,

---

105 *Brahmāṇḍa P.*, I.26.

106 *Śiva P.*, *Jñāna-saṁhitā*, chapters 1-4.

107 *Ibid.*, chapters 46 and 47.

108 *Skanda P.*, I.3.1.2.

109 *Ibid.*, I.3.1.2.

110 *Tataḥ prabhṛti lokeṣu liṅgārcā supratiṣṭhitā* |
Liṅgaṁ tattu yato Brahman brahmaṇaḥ paramaṁ vapuḥ || *Kūrma P.*, I.26.99-100.

111 *Skanda P.*, I.3.1.7.

112 *Ibid.*, I. 3.2. and III. 1.4.

113 *Śiva P.*, *Sanatkumārasaṁhitā*, 19; and *Śiva P.*, *Vidyeśvara-saṁhitā*, 5.

114 *Brahma P.*, II,65.

115 On the contrary, the accounts representing the non-phallic character of the *liṅga* are uniform, except for minor variations.

seemingly. The legendary account relating to this subject may be outlined thus: while Śiva was moving about nude in the vicinity of the *āśramas* at Dāruvana, his *liṅga* (phallus) is said to have fallen down, This falling of Śiva's phallus has been explained in different ways in different *Purāṇas*. One of them, for instance, describes it as being voluntary.[116] Another narrates that the *liṅga* dropped down as the result of curses uttered by the sages of Dāruvana;[117] still another declares that Śiva uprooted his own *liṅga* in protest and hurled it at the sages before he disappeared.[118] In all these narrations, the sages are in the end made to realize their folly;[119] the consequences of Śiva's *liṅga* falling to earth were disastrous.[120] The sages, therefore rushed to Brahmā for protection and sought his help in the face of Śiva's displeasure.[121] Brahmā blamed the Sages for their shortsightedness,[122] for it was none other than Śiva who was moving about in their midst. They had failed to realize this and had consequently committed a great offence by having disparaged the Great God.[123] By way of expiation, Brahmā directed the sages to make a replica of the *liṅga* that had fallen, to install it and to worship it.[124] According to one Purāṇic version, an attempt was made to install the original fallen *liṅga* itself. The gods, including Brahmā, are said to have had a

---

[116] *Brahmāṇḍa P.*, I.27.

[117] *Vāmana P.*, 43.46-72.

[118] *Kūrma P.*, II.38.2-57.

[119] *Atha tān duḥkhitān dṛṣṭvā brahmā vacanam abravīt |*
Aho mugdhā yathā yūyaṁ krodhena kaluṣīkṛtāḥ ||
Na dharmaṁ ca kriyāṁ kāñcijjānate mūḍhabuddhayaḥ | *Vāmana P.*, 43.77-78.

[120] *Tataḥ papāta devasya liṅgaṁ prthvīṁ vidārayan |*
Antardhānaṁ jagāmātha trīśūlī nīlalohitaḥ ||
Tatas tat patitaṁ liṅgaṁ vibhedya vasudhātālam |
Rasātalaṁ viveśātha brahmāṇḍe cordhvato'bhinat ||
Tataś cacāla pṛthvī girayaḥ sarito nagāḥ |
Pātālabhuvanāḥ sarve jaṅgamājaṅgamaśritāḥ || *Vāmana P.*, 6.66-68.

[121] *Vāmana P.*, 43.72-89.

[122] *Upekṣito vratacaraiḥ bhavadbhiriha mohitaiḥ |*
Kāṅkṣante yogino nityaṁ yatanto yatayo nidhim || *Kūrma P.*, II.38.60-61.

[123] *Kūrma P.*, II.38.59-82.

[124] *Ibid.*, II.39.1-12.

difficult task in moving that *liṅga* to the place chosen for the installation.[125] Thereupon, having been implored by the gods, Śiva himself intervened and helped them to shift the *liṅga* to Hāṭakeśvara, where it remains.[126] Incidentally, it may be pointed out that most of these accounts refer to the *liṅga* without any base. A few versions, no doubt, speak of it.

For the sake of easy reference, the various Purāṇic versions which represent the *liṅga* in its phallic associations are briefly recounted below:

1. A naked Śiva wandered among the *āśramas* at Dāruvana. The sages recognized him and worshipped him. The details of the *liṅga* worship were laid down.[127]

2. The sages, who noticed Śiva moving about naked, protested to Brahmā about this strange behaviour. Brahmā told them that it was Śiva himself and asked them to worship him in a befitting manner.[128]

3. Śiva roamed about naked in the vicinity of the *āśramas*. The sages pelted him with stones and got ready to cudgel him. The god suddenly disappeared, and, as he did so, he dropped his *liṅga* of his own accord.[129]

4. The sages were enraged at the strange behaviour of Śiva. Therefore, they pronounced a curse which caused the dropping of the *liṅga*. Later, Brahmā directed the sages to install the *liṅga* and worship it.[130]

5. After the *liṅga* of Śiva had fallen, it began to bounce from place to place, causing great confusion in the world. The earth trembled from the violence of its movement; thereupon the sages and the gods (with Brahmā as their leader) prayed to Umā for rescue and remedy. The goddess granted this request and provided her *yoni*

---

[125] *Vāmana P.*, 44.1-35.

[126] *Skanda P.*, VI.1; *Vāmana P.*, 44.1-35.

[127] *Liṅga P.*, I.31.

[128] *Ibid.*, I.29.

[129] *Brahmāṇḍa P.*, I.27.

[130] *Śiva P.*, *Jñāna-saṁhitā*, 42.

as the receptacle for the *liṅga*.[131] It will be seen that, in this Purāṇic account, the male organ and its female counterpart are clearly mentioned together. The account goes on to say that, in the end, Śiva became manifest to the sages at Dāruvana at their request, and explained to them the true significance of the concept of the *liṅga*.[132]

6. The gods assembled at Vaikuṇṭha and implored Viṣṇu to offer himself as the base for the *liṅga* of Śiva, which had dropped down and which was without a support.[133]

7. Dākṣāyaṇī abandoned her original body to be reborn as Pārvatī, the daughter of the king of mountains. Śiva was unable to bear the pangs of separation from her. Unable to suppress his passions, he moved about naked in the presence of the sages, who then subjected him to the aforementioned curse.[134]

8. Viṣṇu seduced Śiva, who was deeply enamoured of the former in his Mohinī form. Naked, he followed the protector-god to Dāruvana, where the sages cursed Śiva and his *liṅga* fell down.[135]

9. Śiva's strange behaviour aroused the anger of the sages, by whose curse the *liṅga* fell. The moment it fell to the ground, it extended upwards and downwards. Brahmā and Viṣṇu appeared on the scene and began their search for the top and the bottom of the *liṅga*.[136]

10. The sage Bhṛgu once went to Kailāsa to visit Śiva. At that moment, Śiva, who was enjoying sexual intercourse with Umā, did not see him. The sage grew angry at this and pronounced a curse that henceforth Śiva and Umā would be worshipped in the *liṅga* and the *yoni* forms respectively.[137]

---

31 *Ibid.*, *Jñāna-saṁhitā*, 42.

132 *Brahmāṇḍa P.*, I.27.106 ff. In this connection also cf.
Strīliṅgam akhilaṁ devi prakṛtir mama dehajā |
Puṁlliṅgaṁ puruṣo viprā mama dehasamudbhavaḥ ||
Ubhābhyāmeva vai sṛṣṭir mama viprā na saṁśayaḥ | Liṅga P., I.33.3-4.
Sā bhagākhyā jagaddhātrī liṅgamūrtes trivedikā |
Liṅgas tu bhagavān dvābhyāṁ jagatsṛṣṭir dvijottamāḥ || Ibid., I.99.6-7.
Umā ca bhagarūpeṇa harapārśvaṁ na muñcati | Vāmana P., 46.3.

133 *Skanda P.*, I.1.7 and I.1.8.

134 *Ibid.*, VI.1.

135 *Kūrma P.*, II.38.2-57.

136 *Vāmana P.*, 6.57-73.

137 *Padma P.*, *Uttara Khaṇda*, 255.

Apart from the two main types of accounts regarding the genesis of the *liṅga* which have been detailed above, the *Purāṇas* discuss several other aspects of the concept of the *liṅga*. For instance, some *Purāṇas*, like the *Agni Purāṇa* and the *Matsya Purāṇa*, explain the structure of the *liṅga* and its significance.[138] Others discuss the etymology of the term,[139] while still others speak purely about its philosophical implication.[140] Various types of *liṅgas* are mentioned,[141] and all the gods are described to have worshipped them.[142] The *liṅga* is said to pertain to Śiva alone. It is described as being devoid of *gandha* (odour), *rasa* (taste), *śabda* (sound) and *sparśa* (touch).[143] The *Purāṇas* generally speak of two kinds of *liṅgas*, one *sūkṣma* and

---

[138] *Agni P.*, 53; *Matsya P.*, 263.

[139] *Līyante tatra liṅge ca īśvarasya mahātmanaḥ* |
Lingād utpādayāmāsa trilokān sacarācarān || *Śiva P.*, *Sanatkumāra-saṁhitā*, 14.27.

[140] *Avyaktaṁ liṅgam ityāhur ānandaṁ jyotir akṣayam* |
Veda maheśvaraṁ devam āhur liṅginam avyayam ||
... *śivātmakam*
Kālānalasamaprakhyaṁ jvālamālāsamākulam |
Kṣayavṛddhivinirmuktam ādimadhyāntavarjitam ||
Kūrma P., I.26.63-73.

Tadeva vimalaṁ liṅgam oṁkāraṁ samavasthitam |
Śāntyatītā parā śāntir vidyācaiva yathākramam ||
Pratiṣṭhā ca nivṛttiś ca pañcārthaṁ liṅgam aīśvaram |
Pañcānām api devānāṁ brahmādīnāṁ yadāśrayam ||
Oṁkārabodhitaṁ liṅgaṁ pañcāyatanam ucyate |
Dehānte tatparaṁ jyotir ānandaṁ viśate punaḥ ||
Kūrma P., I.32.6-9.

"This pure *liṅga* is established as Oṁkāra. The *liṅga* of the Lord has five aims: the supreme beyond *śānti*, *śānti* (repose), *vidyā* (knowledge), *pratiṣṭhā* (stabilisation), *nivṛtti* (restraint). The *liṅga* taught as Oṁkāra, which is the resort of the five gods, Brahmā etc., is called 'Pañcāyatana'. One who meditates on it enters in that supreme light and happiness, at the demise of the body."

Tatkṣaṇāt paramaṁ liṅgaṁ prādurbhūtaṁ śivātmakam |
Jñānam ānandam advaitaṁ koṭikālāgnisannibham ||
Ibid., I.34.47.

[141] *Agni P.*, 54.

[142] *Yasya brahmādayo devāḥ ṛṣayo brahmavādinaḥ* |
Arcayanti sadā liṅgaṁ sa śivaḥ khalu dṛśyate ||
Kūrma P., II.31.39.

[143] *Liṅga P.*, I.3.2-27.

the other *sthūla*. One is *niṣkala*, and the other *sakala*. One is *ābhyantara*, and the other *bāhya*. The authority to worship one or the other kind of the *liṅga* is determined on the basis of the capacity of the individual worshipper.[144] The identity between the *liṅga* and the *praṇava* is suggested in the *Śiva Purāṇa*.[145] Śiva himself characterizes the *liṅga* as both tangible and intangible.[146] In one *Purāṇa*, Viṣṇu instructs the gods to worship the *liṅga*, as the *liṅga* comprehends all the gods.[147] Such references to the *liṅga* would seem to confirm the assumption that, even in the major portion of the *Purāṇas*, the *liṅga* was generally regarded as but a symbol that stood for Śiva; how otherwise might one understand such legends as when Śiva emerged from the *liṅga* to save Śveta from the snares of Kāla, the god of death? [148] At Avimukta, Śiva is said to be ever-present in the *liṅga*.[149]

Among other details of the *liṅga* that can be gleaned from the *Purāṇas*, the following may be mentioned: Brahmā and the other gods made *liṅgas* out of gems and worshipped them. Prahlāda, Bali and other demons are also described to have engaged themselves in the *liṅga* worship.[150] Various divine and human personalities are described as having installed different types of *liṅgas*;[151] for instance, a *saikata-liṅga* was installed by Umā at Ekāmra.[152] The goddess installed another *liṅga* at Aruṇācala in order that it should be wor-

---

[144] *Karmayajñaratā ye ca sthūlaliṅgārcane ratāḥ |*
Asatāṁ bhāvanārthāya sūkṣme tu sthūlavigraham ||
Śiva P., Jñāna-saṁhitā, 26.

"There is a gross image in place of the subtle (mental) one for meditation by the lower devotees who are fond of ritualistic worship and are pleased by worshipping a gross liṅga."

[145] *Śiva P., Vidyeśvara-saṁhitā*, 6.

[146] *Amūrtaṁ caiva mūrtaṁ ca jyotīrūpaṁ hi tatsmṛtaṁ | Matsya P.*, 183.58.

[147] *Sarvaliṅgamayo devaḥ sarvaliṅge pratiṣṭhitaḥ |*
Śiva P., Jñāna-saṁhitā, 25.

[148] *Liṅga P.*, I.30.2-29; *Kūrma P.*, I.32.15-25.

[149] *Tasmiṁlliṅge ca sānnidhyaṁ mama devi ... Matsya P.*, 183-9.

[150] *Skanda P.*, I.1.8.

[151] *Śiva P., Jñāneśvara-saṁhitā*, 25.38-47.

[152] *Skanda P.*, I.3.1.4.

shipped by the gods.[153] Viṣṇu worshipped the *liṅgas* installed along the banks of a river before he came to the sage Abhimanyu to be initiated by him in the worship of Śiva.[154] There are also references to Viṣṇu revealing the *liṅga* in his heart [155] and manifesting himself in a *liṅga* form.[156] At another place Viṣṇu is said to have realized the greatness of Śiva through his *liṅga*.[157] Three *liṅgas* were installed by Skanda to ward off the sins incurred by him in killing the demon Tāraka, who himself was a great devotee of Śiva.[158] Rāma installed a *liṅga* at Rāmeśvaram.[159] The greatness of this *liṅga* is indicated by an incident narrated in connection with it: when Rāma decided to worship the *liṅga* with a view to freeing himself from the sins incurred by him by killing Rāvaṇa, Hanumān set out to fetch a *liṅga* for installation. The hour deemed as most auspicious for the worship was fast approaching, and Rāma grew anxious about the delay. Sītā, therefore, heaped sand available there and fashioned a *liṅga* out of it. The ceremonial installation was performed. When Hanumān returned with the *liṅga*, he saw that another *liṅga* had been already installed by Rāma. What he had brought with him was the *bāṇa-liṅga* in which the immediate presence of the god was assured even without the *pratiṣṭhā*. With the permission of Rāma, Hanumān attempted to root out the *liṅga* which the former had installed in order that he might substitute for it the *bāṇaliṅga* which he had brought with him. However, in this attempt he met with disastrous failure, for he lost his tail in his attempt to pull out the *Rāma-liṅga* with it.[160]

The *Purāṇas* often were eloquent in their glorification of *liṅga* worship. One *Purāṇa*, for instance, insists that the very sight of the *liṅga* bestows on the beholder the fruit of the performance of *Agniṣṭoma*.[161] Another *Purāṇa* tells us that the very thought of a *liṅga*

---

153 *Skanda P.*, I. 3.1.4.

154 *Kūrma P.*, I.25.2-26.

155 *Vāmana P.*, 62.20-28.

156 *Garuḍa P.*, I.82.1-6; *Liṅga P.*, II.11.1-4.

157 *Liṅga P.*, I.18.

158 *Skanda P.*, I.2.33.

159 *Ibid.*, III.1.1.; III.1.43; also *Liṅga P.*, II.11.1-41.

160 *Skanda P.*, III.1.44.

161 *Darśanādeva agniṣṭomaphalaṁ labhet. Vāmana P.*, 46.33.

purifies sins.[162] Varied, indeed, are the merits that are derived through the worship of the *liṅga*.[163] The sin which had accrued to Brahmā as the result of his having fallen in love with his own daughter was washed off when he installed and worshipped Śiva in the *liṅga* form.[164] It is claimed that the *liṅga* worship is superior to all other ways of propitiation.[165] Numerous *liṅgas* are mentioned in connection with the *tīrthas* scattered all over the country. The *Skanda Purāṇa* devotes a large section to the enumeration, description and glorification of many of them.[166]

With reference to the Śaivite religious practices that are prevalent today all over the country, it may be pointed out that the *liṅga* still occupies the central position in this system of worship. Even where idols of Śiva with human features are installed, attention is still focused on the central object of worship in the temple, which is invariably the *liṅga*. In all the temples of Śiva in south India, the *liṅga* is installed

---

[162] *Kūrma P.*, I. 22. 46-52.

[163] *Na ca liṅgārcanāt puṇyaṁ loke durgatināśanam |*
Tathā liṅge hitāyaiṣāṁ lokānāṁ pūjayecchivam ||
... ...
Yājyaḥ pūjyaḥ ca vandyaśca jñeyo liṅge maheśvaraḥ |
Kūrma P., I.26.58-61.
Liṅgasya darśanān muktiḥ sparśanāc ca varasya ca |
Tatsannidhau jale snātvā prāpnoty abhimataṁ phalam ||
Vāmana P., 45.25.
Pade pade yajñaphalaṁ sa prāpnoti na saṁśayaḥ | Ibid., 46.17.
Liṅgasya darśanādeva agniṣṭomaphalaṁ labhet | Ibid., 46.33.
Saṁsmared aiśvaraṁ liṅgaṁ pañcāyatanam avyayam |
Dehānte tatparaṁ jyotir ānandaṁ viśate punaḥ ||
Kūrma P., I.32.9.
Vājapeyaśatairiṣṭvā yallabheta dvijottama |
Viprā liṅgatrirātreṣu rudrabhaktyā tad aśnute ||
Aśvamedhasahasrasya saṁyag iṣṭasya yatphalam |
Māsena tad avāpnoti rudraliṅgārcane ratāḥ ||
Śiva P., Sanatkumāra saṁhitā, 14.48 ff.

[164] *Vāmana P.*, 49.1-51.

[165] *Śivaliṅgapraṇāmasya kalāṁ nārhanti ṣoḍaśīm*. *Śiva P.*, *Sanatkumāra saṁhitā*, 14.1-20.

[166] The whole of *Avantīkhaṇḍa* of the *Skanda Purāṇa* and the first two sections of the *Nāgarakhaṇḍa* are entirely devoted to the recounting of the glories of these *liṅgas*.

in the *garbhagṛha*, the innermost shrine of the temple. The other forms of Śiva along with the ancillary deities are set up at various points in the temple assigned to them.[167] In the temples of the North, it is generally the *liṅga* alone that is worshipped, for no images with physical features are installed therein. Thus, the *liṅga* as the central object of worship in Śaivism receives universal recognition. Indeed, Śaivism without the *liṅga* is quite inconceivable.

The popular rituals relating to the *liṅga* cult are mainly composed of offerings of water, flowers and fruits.[168] Tradition ascribes to Śiva a special fondness for *abhiṣeka*. The custom is consequently prevalent all over the country of anointing the *liṅga* with water which is made to trickle down in an unbroken stream through a hole in a copper vessel hung above the *liṅga*. Similarly, flowers and the leaves of the bilva tree are offered to the *liṅga*. A perusal of the various portions in the *Purāṇas* which deal with Śaiva rituals would disclose the conspicuous absence of any 'obscene' associations. Such associations could have been traced if there had been any genuine phallic elements in the *liṅga* cult.[169]

---

[167] See chapter VII.

[168] *Śiva P.*, *Jñāna-saṁhitā*, 27-29.

[169] Brahmā has laid down the procedure of worshipping the *liṅga* as follows:
Vaidikaireva niyamair vividhair brahmacāriṇaḥ |
Saṁsthāpya śāṅkarair mantrair ṛgyajuḥsāmasaṁbhavaiḥ ||
Tapaḥ paraṁ samāsthāya gṛṇantaḥ śatarudriyam |
Samāhitāḥ pūjayadhvaṁ saputrāḥ sahabandhubhiḥ ||
Sarvaiḥ prāñjalayo bhūtvā śūlapāṇiṁ prapadyatha |
Kūrma P., II.39.3-5.

Chapter 95 of the *Agni Purāṇa* is fully devoted to the *pratiṣṭhā* of the *liṅga*, and the 'obscene' element is not at all traceable there. See also chapters 79 and 35 of the *Liṅga Purāṇa* (pt. I).

The following extract from Scott's *Phallic Worship* (p. 209) may be noted in this connection: "Now it is largely in view of the alleged innocuous and somewhat metaphysical nature of the worship that it has been again and again reiterated and emphasized that the *liṅgam* and *yoni* worship of India cannot in any way be compared with the priapic worship of Greece, Rome, Egypt and many other parts of the globe. Many even of those who deplore the phallicism inherent in every form of Hinduism are of opinion there is no consciously obscene or depraved meaning associated with the rites peculiar to this worship."

We may now examine the iconic forms of the god Śiva. As has been already indicated, the worship of Śiva images is a distinctive feature of the Śaivism of the South. The first thing that strikes one in this regard is the remarkable manner in which the Purāṇic literature has influenced the Southern traditions. The entire religious life of the South may indeed be said to have been moulded by the Purāṇic ideals.[170] The great importance attached to the *Purāṇas* in the South may be realized from the fact that numerous *Purāṇas* have been produced in Tamil,[171] which also embodies a rich collection of religious Śaiva literature from the Pallava and subsequent periods.[172] Some of these Tamil *Purāṇas* are translations; others are free-verse translations of the originals.[173] There are also some independent compositions,[174] but they mostly follow the model set by the great Sanskrit *Purāṇas*.[175]

---

170 It may be pointed out that Southerners imagine Śiva as he is represented in the Epics and the *Purāṇas*; the portrayal of this god in the religious literature of the local languages also conform strictly to the Purāṇic tradition. Of course, such of the features of the Vedic Rudra as are endorsed by the *Purāṇas* are permitted.

171 It may be incidentally pointed out that so far no attempt has been made to collect and critically study all these Tamil *Purāṇas*. The histories of literature do not give any proper account of them. Among the *Purāṇas* belonging to this category, the more important ones are enumerated in the appendix 4.

172 These periods, especially the Chola period, are noted for the numerous colossal temples built in the South. Among the works produced during these periods, the following are of great importance:

PALLAVA PERIOD: (corca 6th-9th centuries AD): The *Tevāram* hymns of Appar and Suntarar are said to have been written during this period.

CHOLA PERIOD: saw the compilation of all the religious hymns. The *Periya Purāṇam*, a biographical account of the saints of the South, belongs to this period. Even the *Kantapurāṇam* is assigned to this period.

173 The *Kantapurāṇm* belongs to this category.

174 The *Periyapurāṇam* may be said to be a composition of this type.

175 It has already been pointed out that the *Purāṇas* in Sanskrit eventually began to disregard the original convention which expected their contents to deal with the famous five topics. The *Purāṇas* thus have been shown to violate the norm and only devote themselves to the glorification of one god or another. It is interesting to note that the Tamil *Purāṇas* also deviated in such a manner. Thus even the independent *Purāṇas* in Tamil are seen to be sincerely following the footprints of the Sanskrit models.

However, the most remarkable evidence of the great influence which the *Purāṇas* have wielded on the traditions of south India is to be seen in the claim that almost all the main events which are described in the eighteen *Purāṇas* occurred in that region.[176] Each locus of these events has a temple of Śiva, and the god enshrined in that temple is given a special name that describes the great deed which the god is believed to have performed there. Moreover, these Purāṇic events are annually commemorated in the respective places.[177] Over the course of time, local *Purāṇas* were produced, mainly connected with the god enshrined in the temple at a particular place (*sthala*) to which they were related. They speak only of such events that are associated with the temple. For example, the *Hālāsyamāhātmya* speaks only of the great deeds of Śiva which he is believed to have performed at Madura for the benefit of his devotees.[178]

Inasmuch as the fashioning of the various types of the images of Śiva is concerned, it must be pointed out at the very outset that this fabrication is almost invariably done in accordance with the picture of that god presented in the *Purāṇas*.[179] Broadly speaking, these

---

[176]

At Tirukkaṇḍiyūr:	Brahmā's head was clipped.
At Tirukkovalūr:	Andhaka was destroyed.
At Tiruvatikai:	The destruction of the three cities.
At Tiruppariyalūr:	The destruction of of Dakṣa's sacrifice.
At Tiruvirkuḍi:	Jalandhara was destroyed.
At Valuvūr:	The skin of the elephant was torn.
At Tirukkorukkai:	The reduction of Kāma to ashes.
At Tirukkaḍavūr:	Yama was kicked.
At Tiruvaṇṇāmalai:	Brahmā Viṣṇu searched the top and bottom of the *liṅga*.
At Katavūr:	Brahmā was authorized by Śiva to create.
At Tirumārperu:	Viṣṇu worshipped Śiva and got a *cakra*.

[177] These annual celebrations consist, for the most part, of a ritual dramatization of the respective Purāṇic episodes. For example, at Tirukkorukkai, an effigy of Kāma is made of combustible material and ultimately set on fire.

[178] This *Purāṇa* is generally supposed to have been originally composed in Tamil and later translated into Sanskrit in metrical form, probably because Sanskrit continued to be the religious language of India. It is this Sanskrit rendering that is now presented as the original work.

[179] A complete picture of Śiva according to the Purāṇic descriptions is given in the previous chapter.

images fall into two categories; one set of images are used by way of illustration and embellishment;[180] those belonging to the other category are intended exclusively for worship. Of course, the latter have greater sanctity because of the presence of the deity in them. The images and representations which are exhibited on the pillars, walls, towers, and domes are so designed as to associate Śiva with one of his glorious deeds and thereby impress the god's greatness on the minds of the devotees. In this regard, it must be noted that all the episodes from the career of Śiva thus portrayed are derived from the *Purāṇas*.

The images intended for worship are to be clearly differentiated from the decorative images described above. The images for worship are ceremoniously installed inside the temples. Through the performance of special rites like the *pratiṣṭhā*, they are infused with the god's very essence. After the necessary rites of this nature have been duly performed, the immediate presence of the god within it is always assumed.[181] Of course, as it will be pointed out in the next chapter, the various features of these images are also mostly determined by the descriptions of Śiva from the *Purāṇas*.

Before we proceed to study the various kinds of images of Śiva installed for worship, we may present a few verses from the *Śivaparākramam* [182] which succinctly enumerate the various repre-

---

[180] Cf. "A special feature of temple architecture is the carving of figures representing the stories of the *Rāmāyaṇa* and the *Mahābhārata* on the towers and walls of temples and on the body of temple cars". Shamasastry, "Significance of Temple Architecture" *AIOC* (Baroda), 1933, p. 781.

[181] Cf. "The image in the temple is not a mere symbol of something that is intangible, accepted as a means for people of a lower stage in spiritual evolution to grasp the absolute. A symbol has a value only as having a significance attached to it through the subjective activity of a person. But the Divine Nature in the Temple Image is absolutely independent of the subjective activity of the worshipper; it is an objective reality in the image, as much as life in our body is a reality". Kunhan Raja, "The Hindu Temples and their role in the Future life of the Country", *ALB*, vol. XI, pt. 1, p. 30.

[182] The *Śivaparākramam* (Ratnavelu Mudaliyar, Madras, 1895) is a treatise in Tamil proclaiming the various aspects of Śiva and his exploits. The book deals exhaustively with the sixty-four manifestations of Śiva. The *līlās* (sportive feats) connected

sentations of Śiva, other than the *liṅga*, which are prescribed for worship:

Lingaṁ lingodhavaṁ mukhaliṅgaṁ sadāśivam |
Mahāsadāsivaṁ comāmaheśvaramataḥ param ||
Sukhāsanam umeśaṁ tu Somāskandaṁ tathaiva ca |
Candraśekharamūrtiṁ ca vṛṣārūdhaṁ vṛṣāntikam ||
Bhujaṅgalalitaṁ caiva Bhujaṅgatrāsam eva ca |
Sandhyānṛttaṁ sadānṛttaṁ tāṇḍavaṁ jāhnavīdharam ||
Gaṅgāvisarjanaṁ caiva tripurāntakam eva ca |
Kalyāṇasundaraṁ caiva ardhanārīśvaraṁ tathā ||
Gajayuddḥaṁ jvarāpaghnaṁ sārdūlaharavigraham |
Tathā pāśupataṁ caiva kaṅkālaṁ keśavārdhakam ||
Bhikṣāṭanaṁ tu siṁhaghnaṁ caṇḍeśvaraprasādakam |
Dakṣiṇāmūrtitadbhedaṁ yogavīṇādharaṁ tathā ||
Kālāntakaṁ tu kāmāriṁ lakuleśvarabhairavam |
Āpaduddhāraṇaṁ caiva vatukaṁ kṣetrapālakam ||
Vīrabhadram aghorāstraṁ dakṣayajñaharaṁ tathā |
Kirātaṁ gurumūrtiṁ ca aśvārūḍhaṁ gajāntikam ||
Jalandharavadhaṁ caivam ekapādaṁ trimūrtakam |
Trimūrtir ekapādaṁ caiva tathā gaurīvarapradam ||
Cakradānasvarūpaṁ ca gaurīlīlāsamanvitam |
Viṣāpaharaṇaṁ caiva garuḍāntikam eva ca ||
Tathā brahmaśiraśchedaṁ kūrmasaṁhārameva ca |
Matsyāriṁ tu varāhāriṁ prārthanāmūrtam eva ca ||
Raktabhikṣāpradānaṁ ca siṣyabhāvaṁ tathaiva ca |
Ṣaḍānana tathāṣṭāṣṭavigrahaṁ bhāvayet sadā || [183]

---

with each of these manifestations are said to have been performed by the god for the welfare of the beings of the world. Dealing with these topics, the book has been aptly named *Śivaparākramam*. The book is full of Purāṇic citations, which it quotes as authorities on issues relating to the various aspects of the descriptions occurring in it. The *Vedas* and *Āgamas* are also profusely quoted therein. The illustrations given of each manifestation enhance the value of the book.

[183] *Śivaparākamam*, p. 22. The above extract, like every other extract quoted in this text, is transcribed from the Tamil script. Also Cf. *Pratiṣṭhāvidhi* II, p. 3. 270-272.

For the sake of convenience, the various images of Śiva may be divided into two main types;[184] to the first belong such images as reveal the direct connection of Śiva with some prominent episodes described in the *Purāṇas*. The following are some such episodes which are so reflected: Śiva as punisher of the demons Andhaka,[185] Jalandhara[186] and Gajāsura;[187] he upsets the sacrifice performed by Dakṣa;[188] he destroys the three cities;[189] he reduces the god of love to ashes;[190] he drinks poison;[191] he bestows the *cakra* on Viṣṇu.[192] Thus, Śiva is portrayed differently in accordance with each of the various Purāṇic episodes. He is conceived as Andhakāri, Jalandharāri, Gajāri, Vīrabhadra, Tripurāntaka, Kamāri, Viṣāpaharaṇa, and Cakradāyaka.

The images belonging to the second type cannot be said to be as directly connected with any Purāṇic episodes as the former. Nevertheless, these images also are fashioned in accordance with the various descriptions of the god given in the *Purāṇas*. For example, Śiva is represented as the rider of the bull.[193] The *Purāṇas* may not have

---

[184] Zimmer suggests another way of division: "He is described also under twenty-five 'playful manifestations' (*līlāmūrti*), or according to another tradition sixteen. Occasionally we find the multitude of expressive aspects reduced to five. (1) The Beneficient Manifestation (*Anugrahamūrti*). (2) The Destructive Manifestation (*Saṁhāramūrti*). (3) Vagrant Mendicant (*Bhikṣāṭamamūrti*). (4) The Lord of Dances (*Nṛttamūrti*). (5) The Great Lord (*Maheśamūrti*)." *Myths and Symbols in Indian Art and Civilisation*, p. 126.

[185] *Harivaṁśa*, 87; *Padma P.*, I.46; *Śiva P.*, *Jñāna-saṁhitā*, 43; *ibid.*, *Dharmasaṁhitā*, 4.

[186] *Padma P.*, *Uttarakhaṇḍa*, 12-18; *Liṅga P.*, I.97; *Skanda P.*, II.4.14-22.

[187] *Kūrma P.*, I.32.15-25.

[188] *Brahmāṇḍa P.*, I.13; *Kūrma P.*, I.14 and 15; *Liṅga P.*, I.96; *Vāmana P.*, 5; *Varāha P.*, 21.

[189] *Bhāgavata P.*, VII.10.53-71; *Harivaṁśa*, III.133; *Kūrma P.*, I.18; *Liṅga P.*, I.72; *Matsya P.*, 129-140; also 187; *Padma P.*, III.15.

[190] *Brahma P.*, I.36; *Kālikā P.*, 44; *Liṅga P.*, I.101; *Padma P.*, 43; *Śiva P.*, *Jñāna-saṁhitā*, 11.1-38; *Vāmana P.*, 6.

[191] *Agni P.*, 3; *Bhāgavata P.*, VI.7; *Brahmāṇḍa P.*, I.25; *Matsya P.*, 250; *Rām.*, I.45; *Vāyu P.*, I.1.95.

[192] *Brahma P.*, II.33; *Kūrma P.*, I.22.51-56; *Liṅga P.*, I.98.14-17.

[193] *Skanda P.*, I.2.25.60; *Kūrma P.*, I.16.157.

prominently narrated any events leading to Śiva's adoption of the bull as his vehicle, yet Vṛsabhārūḍha is a name of Śiva which occurs frequently in these texts.[194] References may be made to other similar portrayals. Śiva is often featured as accompanied by Umā and Skanda.[195] He is represented in the meditative pose as Dakṣiṇāmūrti.[196]

We now proceed to describe in some detail the more important images of Śiva belonging to both these types.

1. Sadāśivamūrti

This form possesses great philosophical significance, and the adherents of Śaivism hold it in very high esteem. The philosophy of the *Śuddha-śaiva* school is at the basis of the concept of Sadāśiva. According to this school of philosophy, Sadāśiva is the supreme Being, formless, incomprehensible, subtle, effulgent and omnipresent.[197] From this supreme Being everything in the world takes its origin, and it is into this Being that everything is finally absorbed. This rather abstruse concept underlying the *Sadāśivamūrti*, which even the *Āgamas* have not been able to expound fully, is not easily grasped by

---

194 *Kūrma P.*, I.16.157; *Padma P.*, I.43.257; *Vāmana P.*, 2.33; *Skanda P.*, I.2.25.60.

195 See pp. 387 ff.

196 See pp. 398 ff.

197 In this representation, the idealistic conception of Śiva is given expression to. The *Purāṇas* are by no means unfamiliar with this concept as will be clear from the following passage in the *Śiva Purāṇa* (*Vidyeśvarasaṁhitā*, 7.28-37), in which Śiva himself proclaims to Brahmā and Viṣṇu as follows:

Sakalaṁ niṣkalaṁ ceti svarūpadvayam asti me |
Nānyasya kasyacit tasmād anyaḥ sarvopy anīśvaraḥ ||
Purastāt staṁbharūpeṇa paścādrūpeṇa cārbhakau |
Brahmatvaṁ niṣkalaṁ proktam Īśatvaṁ sakalaṁ tathā |
Dvayaṁ mayaiva saṁsiddhaṁ na madanyasya kasyacit ||
… … …
Ahameva paraṁ brahma matsvarūpaṁ kalākalam
Brahmatvād īśvaratvācca brahmāhaṁ brahmakeśavau
Samatvād vyāpakatvāc ca tathaivātmāham arbhakau.

"I and no other have two proper forms, manifest and unmanifest. Therefore all others are not lords. I am in the form of a pillar in front, and in a form behind it. My nature of brahman is called unmanifest, my nature of Īśa manifest. Both are established by me only, not any others than me..."

people, so it is prescribed to be expressed through representations for the benefit of devotees.[198] The *Mahāsadāśivamūrti* is conceived as having twenty-five heads and fifty arms wielding as many weapons in them.[199] It should be noted in this connection that, in practice, *Sadaśiva* images are not generally installed. This is presumably due to the difficulty which one meets with while trying to give a tangible shape to such sublime and subtle concepts which are usually beyond one's grasp.[200]

2. Liṅgodbhavamūrti (Fig. 4)

Brahmā and Viṣṇu were blinded by pride; they began to quarrel between themselves about which of them was the supreme god. They had both forgotten that there was a third entity besides them who was superior to both of them, the greatest being in the universe. While Brahmā and Viṣṇu were thus quarrelling, there suddenly appeared between them a huge and effulgent pillar. Its top and bottom were beyond the reach of sight, as it extended limitlessly upwards and downwards. This roused the curiosity of the two gods, and they set out to find its top and bottom. Brahmā assumed the form of a swan and flew upwards; Viṣṇu became a boar and burrowed downwards. When they realized that their attempts had failed, they came back humiliated. Thereupon, Śiva became manifest in this pillar. Later, pleased with their devotion, Śiva also bestowed boons on them.

Liṅgodbhavamūrti is based on the Purāṇic episode recounted above.[201] The importance of this image may be realized from the fact that almost all the temples of Śiva, particularly in south India, have it installed in the southern niche of the central shrine (*garbhagṛha*). In a few temples, Brahmā and Viṣṇu are separately represented on

---

[198] Cf. Gopinath Rao, *op.cit.*, vol. II, pt. 2, p. 371.

[199] *Śivaparākramam*, pp. 45-54.

[200] Gopinath Rao, *op.cit.*, vol. II, pt. 2, p. 361 ff. See also Zimmer, *Myths and Symbols in Indian Art and Civilisation*, p. 135.

[201] *Brahmā P.*, II.65; *Kūrma P.*, I.26; *Liṅga P.*, I.17; *Śiva P.*, *Jñāna-saṁhitā*, 2; *ibid.*, 46 & 47; *Sanatkumāra-saṁhitā*, 19; *Skanda P.*, I.3.1.1; *ibid.*, I.3.2.9-16; *ibid.*, III.1.14.

Fig. 4: Liṅgodbhavamūrti, Kailāsanātha Temple at Kanchipuram.

Fig. 5: Gaṅgādharamūrti, Kailāsanātha Temple at Kanchipuram.

either side of the *Liṅgodbhavamūrti*. The *Āgamas* have laid down the rules which regulate the construction of this kind of image.[202]

A *liṅga*, measuring four units, is constructed. Two units in the middle are reserved for carving the figure. This space is given an oval shape, the extremities of which are made to resemble a crescent. At the center, the figure of Śiva is carved with four arms. Only the portion of the body extending from his forehead to his knee should be represented. Two of his hands are shown in the *abhaya* and the *varada* poses. Ornaments such as *kuṇḍala*, *hāra*, *keyūra* and garlands of gems adorn the image. On the top right is shown a swan, and at the bottom on the left side, a boar. On the sides of the *liṅga*, two full images of Brahmā and Viṣṇu with folded hands are also added.

3. Gaṅgādharamūrti (Fig. 5)

Bhagīratha was a king of the solar dynasty. It fell to his lot to redeem his forefathers, who had been reduced to ashes by the anger of the sage Kapila in the netherworld, where they had gone in search of a sacrificial horse. Bhagīratha practiced severe *tapas* in order to bring the celestial river, Gaṅgā, down from the heaven to the earth, for it was the waters of Gaṅgā which were destined to raise the sixty thousand sons of Sagara from their ashen state. Pleased with Bhagīratha's penance, the celestial river agreed to come to earth. Śiva foresaw the danger that might follow if the mighty Gaṅgā was allowed to flow as she willed. He also wanted to humiliate her pride. He, therefore, checked her progress by receiving her as she descended within his matted hair, where she almost disappeared. Later, on Bhagīratha's request, the god let her flow down.

This Puranic episode [203] gave rise to the portrayal of Śiva with Gaṅgā on his head. As a matter of fact, in all iconic forms, Śiva is depicted with Gaṅgā. But the foregoing Purāṇic episode has given

---

[202] *Kāraṇāgama*, II.69.1-5; *Kāmika*, II.50.

[203] *Brahma P.*, I.4; *ibid.*, I.18; *Brahmāṇḍa P.*, I.18.27-37; *Kūrma P.*, I.21.7-8; *Rām.*, I.43.1-10; *Vāyu P.*, 42.36-40; *ibid.*, I.47.29-37.

rise to a separate image, and this is *Gaṅgādharamūrti*. Gaṅgā is usually featured in all representations of Śiva as borne on his matted hair; with a view to commemorate the Purāṇic episode, the *Āgamas* provided for this separate *mūrti* of Śiva, depicting the event with strong accent on the relevant features.[204] The *Āgamas*, however, prescribe only the details relating to the installation of this *mūrti*.[205] From these details one can gather that Śiva, Bhagīratha, Gaṅgā and Gaurī are presented as a group in this representation.[206]

4. Tripurāntakamūrti

A demon named Maya practiced *tapas* and obtained boons from Brahmā. On the strength of these boons he harassed the gods severely. He came in possession of three mobile cities — one of gold, another of silver, and the third of iron. The demon himself is represented in the *Purāṇas* as a great devotee of Śiva. Greatly distressed on account of Maya's harassment, the gods prayed to Śiva to save them. Śiva, finding some excuse to justify his action, reduced Maya's three cities to ashes, and thus gave protection to the gods. Because Śiva brought about the destruction of the three cities,[207] he came to be known as Tripurāntaka.

The ritual texts prescribe the method of producing the image of Tripurāntaka,[208] and also give details relating to its installation.[209] In

---

[204] The Tanjore Art Gallery has a fine specimen of the image. See *Souvenir*, *The Tanjore Art Exhibition*, 1955, p. 15. See also Śivaramamūrti, "Geographical and Chronological factors in Indian iconography", *Ancient India*, no. 6, p. 61.

[205] *Kāranāgama* I.81.2-91; *Kāmika*, II.63.

[206] *Kāraṇa I*, verses 76-87.

[207] The most detailed account of this episode occurs in the *Matsya Purāṇa* (chapters 129-140). The other places of occurrence are: *Mahābhārata*, XIII.160.25 ff; *Bhāgavata P.*, VII.10.53-71; *Harivaṁśa*, III.133; *Kūrma P.*, I.18; *Liṅga P.*, I.72; *Matsya P.*, 187; *Padma P.*, III.15; *Śiva P.*, *Jñāneśvarasaṁhitā*, 19; *ibid.*, *Sanatkumāra saṁhita*, 51 and 52; *ibid.*, *Dharmasaṁhitā*, 3. For a detailed discussion on these accounts see Kumari Bhaktisudha Mukhopadhyaya, "Tripura Episode in Sanskrit Literature", *JGJRI*, vol. VIII, pt. IV, p. 391-392.

[208] *Kāraṇāgama*, I.85.1-86 and *ibid.*, II.60.1-5.
See also *Kāmika* II.49.1-10. Sivaramamūrti, *op.cit.*, p. 58.

[209] *Kāraṇāgama* II.60.6-13.

this representation, a gentle smile is to be shown on the face of Śiva, who is featured as having three eyes and four arms and as wielding in his hands *kṛṣṇamṛga*, his bow and arrows. *Kuṇḍalas* and *hāra keyūra* are worn as ornaments, and a serpent is to be shown as the *yajñopavīta*. The *śiraścakra* is also mentioned in this context. Gaurī is figured besides this image. Among her features are especially mentioned her hand hanging down and her head adorned with the *karaṇḍamakuṭa*.

Like the other *saṁhāramūrtis*, the image of Tripurāntaka is only installed very rarely. The Tanjore Art Gallery has a beautiful specimen of this image. At Tiruvatikai, in a temple located towards the south-east of Panrutti Railway Station, the god enshrined is connected with this Purāṇic episode.

5. Kalyāṇasundaramūrti

Umā was reborn as the daughter of Himavat. She practiced severe *tapas* with a view to winning Śiva as her husband. Śiva appeared before her in disguise and discouraged her from marrying Śiva, who, he told her, was endowed with all undesirable qualities. Umā still persisted in her resolve. Pleased by her sincerity and devotion, Śiva revealed himself and granted her request. The seven sages were deputed to Himavat formally to arrange the marriage. Preparations were made for the celebration of the marriage with *éclat*. Brahmā officiated as the priest, and Viṣṇu played an important role at the wedding ceremony. This event in the career of Śiva, which is narrated several times in the *Purāṇas*,[210] gave rise to the conception of Śiva as Kalyāṇasundara.

The *Āgamas* prescribe the rules relating to both the construction[211] and the installation (*pratiṣṭhā*) of this *mūrti*.[212] In this representation, Śiva is to be portrayed as a youth of sixteen, with a majestic

---

[210] *Bhaviṣya P.*, III.14.67 ff; *Brahma P.*, I.34 & 35, also II.3; *Matsya P.*, 154.423-494; *Padma P.*, I.46; *Śiva P.*, *Jñāna-saṁhitā*, chapters 15-18; *Vāmana P.*, 53; *Varāha P.*, 22.

[211] *Kāraṇāgama*, II.56.2-8; *Kāmika*, II.58.

[212] *Ibid.*, I.78.2-17; II.56.9-47. See also Sivaramamūrti, *op.cit.*, p. 57.

bearing, four arms, three eyes, and the *jaṭā* with the crescent within it. His face should wear a beaming smile, and his eyes should express peace and tranquility. The figure is to be decked with *kuṇḍalas* and *karṇapatra*, and shown wielding *ṭaṅka* and *kṛṣṇamṛga*. One hand of Śiva is placed on that of Gaurī, and the other is in the *varada* pose. The feet are shown with sandals. Viṣṇu waits on the left. Brahmā, the priest, is presented in the *vīrāsana* pose by the side of the sacred fire.

6. Ardhanārīśvaramūrti (Fig. 6)

In the beginning, when Brahmā wanted to create, there was produced a being marked by a combination of the male and the female features. The creator god was frightened at the sight of this hermaphroditic being. He implored that being to split into two, which it did. This bisexual being was none other than Rudra. The form thus assumed by Śiva is called the '*Ardhanārīśvara-vapuḥ*' by the Purāṇic authors. This Purāṇic episode gave rise to the worship of Śiva as Ardhanārīśvara in whom the features of Śiva and Umā are combined. The *Āgamas* prescribe the procedure of the installation of such an image, and also give the details relating to its construction.[213] The image reflects in an amplified manner the Purāṇic descriptions of Ardhanārīśvara.[214]

The image is conceived as being divided into two equal parts, the left portraying the features of Umā and the right those of Śiva. Śiva's half bears the lustre of coral. It is shown with a *jaṭāmakuṭa*, an additional eye on the forehead, which is only half visible, and two arms, one wielding the axe and the other placed on the back of the bull. This half is clad in the skin of an elephant. The left half of the image, portraying Umā, is presented as dark-complexioned. The head is crowned with *karaṇḍamakuṭa*; there is no eye on the forehead. There is only one hand which is shown as carrying a lotus. A single breast characterizes Umā's half, which is clad in a silken garment.

---

213 *Kāraṇāgama* II.63.2-5.

214 *Liṅga P.*, I.41, verses 10 and verses 42-47; *Kūrma P.*, I.8.4-5; *ibid.*, I.11.1 ff. See also Sivaramamurti, *op.cit.*, pp. 56-57.

Fig. 6: Ardhanārīśvaramūrti, Nāgeśvara Temple at Kumbhakonam.

The image is set on a lotus pedestal, with a bull standing behind. The relevant rituals connected with the worship of this image are also related in the *Kāraṇāgama*.[215]

The Ardhanārīśvara form is mostly found displayed for illustrative purposes, though instances of the installation of the image are not rare. The Nāgeśvarasvāmi temple in Kumbhakoṇam has a remarkable image of Ardhanārīśvara.

7. Gajāri (Fig. 7)

A demon assumed the form of an elephant and attacked devotees engaged in the worship of Śiva. The god manifested himself before them out of the *liṅga* and attacked the demon with his trident. Eventually he destroyed the demon, tore off his skin, and wore it as his garment.[216]

Another version of the episode of the elephant-demon is found in the *Varāha Purāṇa*, which relates how the demon Andhaka assumed the form of an elephant and attempted to carry Umā away. Śiva attacked the demon, tore off his skin, and wore it as his garment.[217]

These are the two specific references which are found in the *Purāṇas* portraying Śiva as Gajāri. However, one comes across other names of the god which point to this feat. The Purāṇic concept of Śiva as Gajāri has found much expression in the religious practices of the Śaivites,[218] and the ritual texts provide for the installation and worship of Śiva in this form.[219]

A red complexion, teeth jutting out of the corners of his mouth, and three eyes are prescribed as the special features of the Gajāri representation. The feet are planted on both sides of the elephant, whose tail is raised as far as its head. The right hands of the god

---

215 *Kāraṇāgama*, II.63.6-16.

216 *Kūrma P.*, I.32.15-25. This feat of Śiva is very popular and has become the theme for a verse in Kālidāsa's *Meghadūta* (I.39).

217 *Varāha P.*, 27.1-45.

218 *Kāraṇa*, II.77.2-7.

219 *Ibid.*, I.83.3-70; II.77.8-13; see also Sivarāmamurti, *op.cit.*, p. 59.

Fig. 7: Gajāri, Hoysaleśvara Temple at Halebid.

shown in a bent posture are lifted up and tilted backwards. *Śūla*, *ḍamaru*, *pāśa*, *kapāla*, *khaḍga*, *kheṭa* are the weapons wielded by the image. The *prabhāmaṇḍala* also is prescribed.

8. Keśavārdhamūrti or Hariharamūrti

In an earlier chapter, a reference has been made to the fact that, to a certain extent, the *Purāṇas* reflect a spirit of rivalry between Śaivism and Vaiṣṇavism. At the same time there are clear indications in these texts of a tendency towards bringing about a harmony between the two sects. Attempts were made to amalgamate into a common ideology the essential elements of both the sects. Those who emphasized upon and profited from the supposed difference between Śiva and Viṣṇu were condemned as being fit for hell. This amalgamation of Śaivism and Vaiṣṇavism led to the evolution of a new divine concept, the concept of Harihara. The origin of the Harihara image, in which the features of Śiva and Viṣṇu are combined, is to be traced back to this movement.[220]

The Purāṇic idea of Harihara [221] is thus seen to have given rise to the worship of Śiva in this form. The ritual texts prescribe the rules relating to the construction,[222] installation, and worship of the image.[223] The right half should bear the characteristics of Viṣṇu and the left half those of Śiva. The *jaṭāmakuṭa*, the ear hanging down, the half-revealed third eye, two hands, one bearing *ṭaṅka* and the other in the *abhaya* pose, and the dark neck are the features on Śiva's side. Viṣṇu's side is characterized by the *kirīṭa*, the ear decked with earrings, the hands wielding the *kurava* flowers, and dark complexion. Śiva's half is clad in the elephant's skin, while a *pītāmbara* adorns Viṣṇu's half. The *padmapīṭha* is prescribed in connection with this image. Gaurī is shown on the left. She is featured with two arms and two eyes. One of her arms hangs down, and she maintains a *tribhaṅga* pose.

---

[220] This combination of Śiva and Viṣṇu would remind one of another combination namely, that of Śiva and Umā.

[221] *Harivaṁśa* II.125; *ibid.*, III.86-90; *Vāmana P.*, 67.27-31; *ibid.*, 67.44-54.

[222] *Kāraṇāgama*, II.62.1-6.

[223] *Ibid.*, II.62.7-20.

9. Bhikṣāṭana (Fig. 8)

Disguised as a beggar, Śiva roamed naked around the *āśrama* in Dāruvana. The sages did not recognize the god and consequently showed no veneration to the beggar. Later on, however, realizing the true divine nature of the beggar, they worshipped him in the *liṅga* form. Since Śiva roamed in Dāruvana in the guise of a beggar, he came to be known as Bhikṣāṭana. This event is narrated in the *Purāṇas* in diverse versions.[224]

The *Suprabhedāgama*,[225] prescribing the procedure of the installation and worship of the *Bhikṣāṭanamūrti*, narrates the following legend. The sages at Dāruvana performed an *abhicāra-homa*. Out of the sacrificial fires were produced an axe, a deer, snakes, and a trident — all of which were directed against Śiva. Śiva adopted all these — some as weapons, and some as ornaments. An *apasmāra* (a demon) was also produced in the similar manner, and the god subjugated him too. The sages at last recognized Śiva's greatness and worshipped him as the great god.

In conformity with the narration in the *Āgama*, the figure of Śiva in the Bhikṣāṭana-form is presented [226] as wearing serpents and carrying a trident and an axe. A deer and the *apasmāra* are presented beside him. According to the *Kāraṇāgama*, three eyes, four arms, a peaceful expression, a dark complexion, tawny hair, and well-shaped limbs are the physical features of the Bhikṣāṭana image. The image is shown wearing *kuṇḍalas* and having a snake as *yajñopavīta*, another snake as *kaṭisūtra*, and a pair of sandals. He carries in his hands a *ḍamaru*, fresh grass, *śūla* and a *kapāla*. By the god's side, a deer is represented as being fed by the grass he carries. The deer is depicted with its head lifted up. The figure of Śiva is naked and is set up on a lotus pedestal.

---

224 *Brahmāṇḍa P.*, I.27.1-30; *Kūrma P.*, I.16.125 ff; *ibid.*, II.38.2-58; II.39.19-20; *Padma P.*, 17.1 ff; *Śiva P.*, *Jñāna-saṁhitā*, 42.1-19; *Vāmana P.*, 6.46-73.

225 See Gopinath Rao, *op.cit.*, vol. II, pt. I, p. 113 ff.

226 *Kāraṇāgama*, II.57.2-10. The rituals relating to the installation etc. are given in verses 10-18. *Kāmika*, II.52.

Fig. 8: Bhikśāṭana, Kailāsanātha Temple, Kanchipuram.

10. Siṁhaghnamūrti or Śarabhamūrti

Viṣṇu assumed the Nārasiṁha *avatāra* and killed the demon Hiraṇya, but became blinded by his pride for this achievement. He considered himself to be the highest god. Forgetting completely that it was for the welfare of living beings that he had taken *avatāra*, he did wicked deeds in the world. The oppressed beings sought the intervention of Śiva, who assumed the form of a *śarabha* and subdued Narasiṁha.[227] This is one episode which is clearly indicative of the Purāṇic rivalry between Śiva and Viṣṇu, and also of the supremacy which Śaivism had established over Vaiṣṇavism. This episode, naturally gave rise to the installation and worship of Śiva as *Śarabhamūrti*.

The *Āgama* prescribes in this connection as follows:[228] The image of Śarabha is to be given a crystal-like complexion. Various features are to be combined in this representation. The sun, the moon, and fire are his three eyes. The *bāḍavāgni* is his tongue. Kālī and Durgā are his two wings. Indra is his talon, *kalāgni* his belly, and *kālamṛtyu* his thigh. Two out of his four legs rest on the floor. The image is clad in a garment of skin; *ḍamaru*, *paraśu*, *triśūla*, *khaḍga*, *kheṭa*, *śara*, *śārṅga*, and *bhiṇḍipāla* are the weapons wielded by the *Śarabhamūrti*. His tail is lifted upwards. Narasiṁha is depicted at the foot of the Śarabha who is glorified as the king of birds. The pose in which the image is presented is called the *saṁhāra-tāṇḍava*.

The image of Śiva as Śarabha is found to be installed very rarely. Among such rare occurrences may be mentioned the image installed for worship at Tirupuvanam. Probably on account of its horror-inspiring features, the image is not commonly installed in temples.

11. Kālāntakamūrti

The Epics and the *Purāṇas* speak of Yama, the god of Death; Śiva is often conceived as the destroyer of Yama. In the *Ṛgveda* one comes across references in which Rudra is sought by his worshippers

---

[227] *Liṅga P.*, I. 95; *Kālikā P.*, 31.

[228] *Kāraṇāgama*, II.73.3-9. Rituals prescribed in 16-26. See also *Kāmika*, II.54.

to save them from death.[229] According to a popular legend still current among adherents of Śaivism, a sage by the name of Mārkaṇḍeya was freed from the god of death because he was a great devotee of Śiva.[230] This legend has not found place in the principal *Purāṇas*.[231] However, Śiva is frequently called Kālāntaka,[232] Kāladahana,[233] Antakaghātin,[234] Antakāntakṛt.[235] These names clearly point to the traditional belief that he is the destroyer of the god of death. The *Skanda Purāṇa* mentions a sage called Mārkaṇḍeya,[236] who is said to have obtained longevity by practicing *tapas* to propitiate Śiva. However, unlike the other episodes, the Mārkaṇḍeya episode does not occur very frequently in the *Purāṇas*. Mārkaṇḍeya is believed to have installed a *liṅga* at Hāṭakeśvara. Another great devotee of Śiva who was saved from falling a victim to Yama was king Śveta.[237]

As regards the Kālārimūrti, Banerjea observes [238] that it is easy to find in south India this form in which Śiva chastised Kāla or Yama for his attempt to take away the life of Mārkaṇḍeya while he was engaged in worship. In this connection that scholar also refers to the striking Ellora sculpture depicting the theme. The *Āgamas* describe only the rituals connected with the installation of the *Kālāntaka-mūrti*.[239]

---

[229] *Tryaṁbakaṁ yajāmahe ... mṛtyormukṣīya māmṛtāt*. *ṚV*, VII.59.12. "We worship Tryambaka... May he free us from death, not of immortality."

[230] *Skanda P.*, VI.21, however, mentions Mārkaṇḍeya, the son of Mrkaṇdu. He is said to have worshipped at Hāṭakeśvara and obtained longevity.

[231] On the contrary, a Mārkaṇḍeya is mentioned as having been saved from the god of death by Viṣṇu. *Garuḍa P.*, I.283.1-11.

[232] *Skanda P.*, I.1.32.60.

[233] *Kūrma P.*, I.30.51.

[234] *Matsya P.*, 133.23.

[235] *Brahma P.*, III.35.11.

[236] *Skanda P.*, I.1.32.
This narration is identical with the one found in the Tamil version of the *Skanda Purāna*. In the Sanskrit text the name Mārkaṇḍeya, is, however, missing, and the name Śveta is given instead.

[237] *Liṅga P.*, I.30.2-29; *Kūrma P.*, II.36.1-38.

[238] *The Age of the Imperial Kanauj*, p. 308.

[239] Cf. *Kāraṇa*, II.84.72; *Kāmika*, II.57.

12. Kāmāri

The gods, unable to bear the harassment of the demon Tāraka, were told by Brahmā that they should bring about the union of Śiva with Umā, for the son born to them was destined to kill the demon. The gods, therefore, commissioned Kāma, the god of love, with the task of bringing about such a union. Kāma went to the Himālayas where Śiva was engaged in meditation, and fired his flowery arrows at Śiva. The latter, enraged, cast a glance at Kāma and thereby reduced him to ashes.[240] Thus Śiva came to be known as Kāmāri, the enemy of Kāma. The *Kāmārimūrti* of Śiva is installed for the purpose of worship;[241] for instance, near Māyavaram in Tiruvādi, is a temple of Śiva commemorating this Purāṇic episode of the destruction of the god of love.

13. Bhairavamūrti or Andhakāri, Brahmaśiraśchedakamūrti (Fig. 9)

The *Purāṇas* often refer to the terrible aspect of god Śiva. Śiva's terrible (*bhairava*) form is connected with several episodes in the *Purāṇas*. The demon Andhaka harassed the gods on the strength of boons obtained from Brahmā. He even threatened to carry away Umā; thereupon Śiva assumed the Bhairava form, killed the demon, placed him across his *śūla*, and performed a ferocious dance.[242] There is another Purāṇic episode in which Śiva is said to have assumed the *bhairava* form, when Brahmā became extremely haughty and regarded himself as an equal of Śiva, as he too had five heads. In order to teach him a lesson, Śiva assumed the Bhairava form and clipped off Brahmā's fifth head.[243]

---

[240] *Brahma P.*, I.36, also II.2; *Kālikā P.*, 44; *Liṅga P.*, I.101; *Padma P.*, I.43 and 58. *Rām.*, I.23.10-15; VII.6.6; *Śiva P.*, *Jñāna-saṁhitā*, 11.1-38; *Skanda P.*, I.1.21; *ibid.*, I.2.24. Kālidāsa has described the episode in his *Kumārasaṁbhava*, ch. III.

[241] *Kāraṇa*, I.83.2.

[242] *Harivaṁśa*, 87; *Matsya P.*, 179; *Padma P.*, 46; *Śiva P.*, *Jñāna-saṁhitā*, 43; *ibid.*, *Dharma-saṁhitā*, 4; *Vāmana P.*, 70; also *MBh*, VII.49.10-11; VII.59.1-6.

[243] See No. XX in this series.

Fig. 9: Bhairava, Hoysaleśvara Temple at Halebid.

On the basis of such episodes, Śiva is conceived, installed, and worshipped as a dreadful god. The *Āgamas* have laid down the rules relating to the worship of Bhairava.[244] However, in practice, we find that this image is assigned only a subordinate place in the system of worship. Bhairava is otherwise known as Kṣetrapāla,[245] the guardian of the temple.[246] He has a dog as his vehicle, and is always represented naked. He is armed with a *kapāla*.[247] At times, he is no doubt identified with Śiva. The place assigned to him in the temple is the area adjoining the outer gate, where he is posted as a sentinel.

14. Vīrabhadramūrti

Dakṣa performed a sacrifice to which he invited all the gods except Śiva. Despite her husband's exhortations, Umā went to the place of sacrifice, where both Śiva and Umā were denounced. The goddess discarded her body through *yoga* and was later reborn as the daughter of the mountain. Śiva's rage knew no bounds when he came to know about what had happened. He created Vīrabhadra [248] (according to some versions, he himself assumed the form of Vīrabhadra) in order to teach Dakṣa a lesson. Vīrabhadra appeared on the sacrificial ground and demanded Śiva's share. On being refused this by Dakṣa, he upset the sacrifice and punished the participants. At last, Śiva's supremacy over other gods was recognized and his share of the sacrifice was assured.[249]

---

[244] *Kāraṇa*, II.70.1-18.

[245] See Chakravarti's remarks in this connection ("Śaivite Deity Kṣetrapāla", *IHQ* IX, p. 238): Kṣetrapāla appears to be a Śaivite deity from the descriptions that are found in various works. In one place he is definitely called a son of Śiva (Śaṁbhutanaya)".

[246] *Kāraṇa*, I.103.

[247] *Ibid.*, 103.15-17.

[248] "Vīrabhadra is sometimes called a son, sometimes an *avatāra* of Śiva". Moor, *Hindu Pantheon*, p. 177. For a statement that Vīrabhadra and Bhairava are sons of Śiva, see *ibid.*, p. 61.

[249] *MBh*, X.18.1-26; XIII.160.24; *Rām.*, I.66 (casual reference only); *Brahma P.*, I.32, also 37; *Brahmāṇḍa P.*, I.13; *Garuḍa P.*, I.5.35-38; *Kūrma P.*, I.14 and 15; *Liṅga P.*, I.96 and 100; *Skanda P.*, I.1.3 and 4; *Śiva P.*, *Jñāna-saṁhitā*, 7; *ibid.*, *Vāyu-saṁhitā*, 15-20; *Vāmana P.*, 5; *Varāha P.*, 21; *Vāyu P.*, I.30.

Upon this oft-repeated Purāṇic episode is based the concept of Vīrabhadra. Following the rules laid down in the *Āgamas*, the image of Vīrabhadra is fashioned and installed [250] With four arms, three eyes, bright flame-like hair and shining teeth. These physical features are intended to express his valour and dreadful character, and the general fearful effect so created is further enhanced by a display of bells, skulls, crab-shaped ornaments, *nāgayajñopavītas*, and anklets. The dress prescribed is *ūrukañcuka*. The god wields as his weapons *khaḍga*, *kheṭa*, bow and arrow, *bhiṇḍi* and *kapāla*.

The god enshrined in the temple at Pariyalūr (also known as Parasalūr), close to Māyavaram, is associated with the destruction of the sacrifice performed by Dakṣa. This Purāṇic event is annually celebrated at this temple. At Tiruveṇkāṭu, the *Vīrabhadramūrti* is specially installed for worship.

15. Kirātamūrti

Arjuna went to Kailāsa to propitiate Śiva and to obtain from him the Pāśupata weapon. On the summit of the mountain he practiced severe *tapas*. Śiva was greatly pleased at his devotion, but, with a view to testing Arjuna's capability, appeared before the hero in disguise. He showed himself as a *kirāta*, and Umā followed him as a female hunter. Śiva forced Arjuna to a combat. In the struggle which ensued, Arjuna hit the *kirāta* hard on his head with his bow. Śiva finally revealed his identity, and, impressed with Arjuna's skill in archery as well as with his devotion, offered to grant him whatever he chose. Arjuna expressed his desire to get the *pāśupata* weapon, and Śiva readily granted him his request.[251]

This story, originally recounted in the *Mahābhārata*, forms the basis for the installation and worship of Śiva as *Kirātamūrti*.[252] Śiva is represented as a *kirāta*. His hair is tied up into a knot with bird

[250] *Kāraṇa*, II.61.2-6. Rituals prescribed at 7-17.

[251] *Mahābhārata*, III.40 and 41; *ibid.*, VIII.80.19-21; *Śiva P.*, *Jñāna-saṁhitā*, 64-67. In *Brahmāṇḍa P.*, I.24, a description occurs in which Śiva disguised as *kirāta* bestows on Bhārgava-Rāma the *Śivāstra* and the axe.

feathers. His dress is made of skin, and he is shown as dark-complexioned. Jvāla and Kuṇḍodara stand by his side as his attendants. The *Kirātamūrti* wields a bow in one hand and an arrow in the other. Arjuna, with his head bent down, is presented opposite the image of Śiva. On the left is depicted *pāśupata*, the divine weapon. Umā stands on one side and carries a *kamaṇḍalu* in her hand.

This image is fairly common in the temples of the South. In the Kumbheśvarasvāmi temple at Kumbhakonam, the *Kirātamūrti* is especially installed for worship. The *vigraha* is represented as granting the weapon to Arjuna.

16. Jalandharāri

Jalandhara was a powerful demon. He opposed the gods, eventually subduing all of them. Śiva was the only exception. The demon was on his way to Kailāsa to meet Śiva and try his prowess on him. Śiva, disguised as a traveler, met the demon on the way. He drew a *cakra* on the floor, and asked the demon whether he could lift it from the ground. With an overbearing attitude, the demon scoffed at Śiva, gathered all his strength, and lifted the *cakra* above his head. Unable to bear the burden of the *cakra* which grew heavier and heavier, he rested it upon his head, but the *cakra* finally cleft his body in two.[253]

With this Purāṇic episode, the image of Jalandharāri is introduced in the system of Śiva worship.[254] Śiva is presented with two eyes and two arms. His complexion is red. He is depicted as wearing long hair. He is armed with an umbrella and a staff, clad in a white garment and besmeared with ashes. He also wears the sacred thread and *mālā*. The demon is portrayed beside the image with a bow and arrow. He is depicted as lifting a *cakra* above his head.

---

[252] *Kāraṇa*, II.79.1-5. Rituals prescribed at 6-14.

[253] *Padma P.*, VI. Chapters 12-18, also 102 ff; *Liṅga P.*, I.97.1-43; *Skanda P.*, II.4.14-22.

[254] *Kāraṇa*, II. 80. 1-4.

According to the tradition prevalent in the South, Tiruvirkkuṭi near Tiruvārūr is identified as the place where Jalandhara was destroyed.

17. Ekapādatrimūrti

The *Purāṇas* generally glorify the Hindu triad of gods, Brahmā, Viṣṇu and Rudra. In this context, one of these three gods is shown as supreme, dominating the other two. It is, however, very rare that Brahmā assumes the highest role.[255] In one *Purāṇa*, Śiva is described as the highest being. He becomes manifest to Kṛṣṇa and tells them: "You are both produced from my limbs — Brahmā from my right side and Viṣṇu from the left. And I myself represent the heart." In this concept the three gods are viewed as parts of a single whole — Śiva forming the very core of that whole.[256]

The foregoing episode from the *Purāṇas* is the basis for the *Ekapādatrimūrti*. In one single representation, Brahmā, Viṣṇu and Śiva are combined in such a way that Śiva forms the central figure. According to the *Āgamas*,[257] Śiva is to be shown with three eyes, four arms, a serene appearance and *jaṭāmakuṭa*. The god wields *ṭaṅka* and *śūla* as his weapons, and wears a *kuṇḍala* of pearls. The image stands on a single leg and thereby receives its appellation *ekapāda*. Brahmā and Viṣṇu are shown as shooting out from the hips of their common trunk. Two of the four hands of each of these two subordinate gods are folded. The other two hands of Brahmā hold a *kamaṇḍalu* and a ladle; those of Viṣṇu bear the conch and the disc. The legs of

---

[255] See: Chapter III.

[256] *Kūrma P.*, I.25.11-59 provides the background for this *trimūrti* concept. Remote echoes of the idea of this type of *trimūrti* may be seen in *Kūrma P.*, I.26.94-99; *Śiva P., Jñana-saṁhitā*, 4.1-30; *Skanda P.*, I.3.2.8. Incidentally it may be added that actually two kinds of *trimūrti* images are found in the temples of South India. In one of them Viṣṇu is the central figure. In the other, Śiva is at the center. It is this latter form which is installed in Śiva temples. Also Cf. *Raghuvaṁśa*, III.23.

[257] *Kāraṇa*, II.66.2-7; *Kāmika*, II.61. Sivaramamurti (*op.cit.*, p. 58) points out the fact that this representation is totally absent in north India.

these two gods, other than those fixed to the trunk of the image, are each a little bent. The *prabhā* encircles the entire figure.[258]

18. Cakradānamūrti

Viṣṇu was once engaged in the worship of Śiva. He was repeating the thousand names of Śiva, and wanted to offer thousand lotus flowers, one flower for each name. As he came to the thousandth name, he discovered that all his flowers had been exhausted and there was no flower left to be offered for that name. Viṣṇu desired that his worship of Śiva be done perfectly at any cost, so he plucked out his own eye and offered it as a flower. Śiva was highly pleased with this devotion of Viṣṇu, and granted him the *cakra* which became his special weapon.[259]

In accordance with the above-mentioned Purāṇic episode, Śiva is sometimes propitiated in his *Cakradānamūrti*.[260] As usual, four arms are prescribed. The *jaṭāmakuṭa* adorns his head. His left leg is bent and laid flat on the seat; his right leg hangs down. In the right hands the god wields the axe and the *cakra*, and in one of the left hands he carries the *kṛṣṇamṛga*. The other left hand is in the *varada* pose. On the left, Viṣṇu is depicted with folded hands. Gaurī and Brahmā are also shown in the group. Viṣṇu is portrayed as offering his eye. The *prabhā-maṇḍala* encircles the image. The *Cakradāna-mūrti* is found installed for worship at Tirumālpeṛu in Tiruvīlimilalai.

19. Viṣāpaharaṇamūrti

The *devas* and the *asuras* made a joint effort to churn out the milky ocean with a view to obtaining nectar. However, at the first

---

[258] "The Ekapādatrimūrti and Śarabha, are mainly South Indian in character, as are those of the sixty-three *nāyanmars* or *Śiva-bhaktas* of the Tamil land which were sometimes placed in particular sections of important Śiva temples of Southern India". Banerjea, *The Age of the Imperial Kanauj*, p. 310. Also see Zimmer, *Myths and Symbols in Indian Art and Civilisation*, p. 134-135.

[259] *Brahma P.*, II.33; *Kūrma P.*, I.22.51-66; *Liṅga P.*, I.98.14-17, 159-162; *Padma P.*, VI.100.1-32; *Śiva P.*, *Jñāna-saṁhitā*, 70.1-24; *ibid.*, *Sanatkumāra saṁhitā*, 8 ff.

[260] *Kāraṇa*, II.81.2-5.

attempt, only poison was produced. Thereupon, all the gods rushed to Śiva for protection, for if the poison was allowed to persist it would certainly destroy the whole world. Śiva, therefore, took the poison in his hands and swallowed it. As it passed through the neck, it became stuck there. His neck turned blue, and this became a permanent feature of the god. Śiva thenceforth came to be called Nīlakaṇṭha.[261]

The *Viṣāpaharaṇamūrti* is designed to correspond with the details of the Purāṇic episode mentioned above, the *Āgama* texts have authorized the installation of such an image and have given details about its construction.[262] In the *Viṣāpaharaṇamūrti*, Śiva is represented with four arms, three eyes and *jaṭāmakuṭa*, and the god's canine teeth are shown to be protruding a little. The trident and the *khaṇḍikā*, shaped like the *gokarṇa* (the ears of the cow), are borne in his right hands, and the *kapāla* in his left. Gaurī is presented on the right. Her left leg is folded and laid flat on the seat, and her right leg hangs down. The god is featured as seated on his bull. He is shown as devouring poison.

20. Brahmaśiraśchedakamūrti

As has been already related before, Brahmā grew very haughty because he bore a close resemblance to Śiva in that he too had five heads. In order to curb his pride, Śiva assumed the Bhairava form and clipped off his fifth head. Following this, the skull of Brahmā is said to have fastened itself to Śiva's hand.[263]

The image portraying this episode can be installed for worship.[264] Knitted eyebrows, frightful eyes, hair resembling flames, and three eyes are the special physical features of the representation. The god

---

[261] *Agni P.*, 3.8-9; *Bhāgavata P.*, VIII.7.1-46; *Brahmāṇḍa P.*, I.25.45-117; *Matsya P.*, 250.10-61; *Rām.*, I.45; *Skanda P.*, I.1.9-10; *Vāyu P.*, I.1-95; I.54.30-103.

[262] *Kāraṇa*, II. 65.1-4.

[263] *Bhaviṣya P.*, III.13.1-19; *Brahma P.*, II.43; *Brahmāṇḍa P.*, III.23.75-81; *Kūrma P.*, II.31.23-58; *Matsya P.*, 183.80-100; *Nāradīya P.*, II.29; *Śiva P.*, *Jñāna-saṁhitā*, 49.65-96; *ibid.*, *Vidyeśvara-saṁhitā*, 6.1-21; *Skanda P.*, II.3.2; *ibid.*, III.1.24; IV.1.1.31.

[264] *Kāraṇa*, II.1.70.

holds his *ḍamaru*, *pāśa* and *kapāla*. A garland of skulls and *kiṅkiṇī* are among the ornaments.

Tirukkaṇḍiyūr, near Tanjore, is traditionally identified as the place where Brahmā's head was clipped off by Śiva. The *Brahmaśiraśchedakamūrti* is installed for worship in the temple at this place.

21. Rāvaṇānugrahamūrti

Rāvaṇa travelled over the Kailāsa mountain in his *puṣpakavimāna*. As he neared the abode of Śiva, Nandin stopped him. The demon-king was enraged at this unexpected treatment which he had received, for no one had ever before dared to block his way. He therefore came down from his airborne car and pressed his shoulders against the mountain with a view to rooting it out. Śiva gently pressed the mountain down with his toe, and thus pinned Rāvaṇa beneath it. The demon then sang the praises of Śiva. The latter, moved by Rāvaṇa's devotion, granted him boons.[265]

The *Kāraṇa-Āgama* does not mention this *mūrti* at all. This has, however, found prevalence in sculpture and painting.[266] It may incidentally be pointed out that a vehicle (*vāhana*) known as the *Kailāsavāhana* is used in the temples of Śiva to carry the image of the god in procession on festival days. This *vāhana* depicts the above Rāvaṇānugraha episode.

22. Caṇḍeśvarānugrahamūrti (Fig. 10)

The *Periyapurāṇam* is a Tamil language *Purāṇa*. It recounts the lives of the Śaiva devotees who hailed from the South.[267] Among others, the *Periyapurāṇam* contains the biography of a Śaiva saint called Caṇḍeśvara. This devotee was ultimately raised to the ranks of a god and is accorded worship in the temples. All the temples of Śiva in the South install the image of this devotee-god; it is traditionally

---

[265] *Rām.*, VII.16.32-36.

[266] Cf. Banerjea, *Development of Hindu Iconography*, p. 484 ff.

[267] See Appendix 4, p. 517.

Fig. 10: Caṇḍeśvarānugrahamūrti, Rājendracōḷeśvara Temple at Gangaikondacolapuram.

believed that the propitiation of Śiva is incomplete without the worship of this devotee.[268]

Vicāraśarman was, from his very childhood, noted for his wisdom and devotion. He once saw a cowherd of his village treating his cows with cruelty, and therefore took charge of the cows himself. The cows thereafter received very kind treatment and consequently yielded more milk. The abundant quantity of milk which spontaneously poured from the udders of the cows was used by the new cowherd to bathe the *liṅgas* which he used to fashion every day for worship during the time when the cows went about grazing. The villagers, who came to know about this, complained to his father of the misappropriation of their milk despite the fact that the milk he used was not drawn out, but flowed forth by itself. Thereupon, his father appeared on the scene and handled his son roughly, though he was enwrapped in meditation and worship. Enraged at this disturbance, Vicāraśarman took up a stick which lay nearby, which immediately was transformed into an axe, and cut off the leg of his father, because the latter had kicked the materials of worship with it. Śiva then made himself manifest to him and, pleased with his devotion, elevated him to the high rank of a saint. The god further laid down that thereafter no worship of his would fructify without obeisance being paid to this new god. Śiva is represented as *Caṇḍeśvarānugrahamūrti* [269] in the pose of bestowing blessings on the saint. It is rightly pointed out that this image is essentially south Indian in character.[270]

23. Umāmaheśvaramūrti (Fig. 11)

In the *Purāṇas* there are many passages where Umā and Maheśvara are presented together.[271] This Umāmaheśvara combination can, therefore, be said to have no special connection with any

[268] Reference to this tradition is also found in the *Śiva Purāṇa*, *Kailāsa-saṁhitā*, 7.12; *Agni P.*, 76 is fully devoted to the description of the *Caṇḍeśvara-pūjā*.

[269] *Kāraṇa*, II.64. 3-9. Rites prescribed at 10-21. *Kāmika*, II.55.

[270] Banerjea, *op.cit.*, p. 306.

[271] Even the *Mahābhārata*, III.40.4 presents Śiva and Umā together.

Fig. 11: Umā-Maheśvara (Vṛṣabhāntika) at Pallaveshvaram

particular episode. In this representation, both Śiva and Umā are seen to have been assigned such features as are commonly ascribed to them in the *Purāṇas*. In this image,[272] the figure of Śiva bears crystal-like lustre. His left leg is bent and laid flat on the seat, and his right leg hangs down. His right and left hands are in the *abhaya* and the *varada* poses respectively. His other two hands wield *ṭaṅka* and *kṛṣṇamṛga*. The goddess is shown to have a dark complexion. She has two arms, of which the left one hangs down. In her right hand she holds an *utpala* flower. She wears a *karaṇḍamakuṭa* and is clad in a variety of garments. Gems, garlands and jewels adorn the image. The *śiraścakra* also is properly depicted. Engirt by the *prabhā-maṇḍala*, the god and the goddess are seated in the *sukhāsana*.

24. Somāskandamūrti

This representation of Śiva has no specific Purāṇic episode as its basis either. In it, Śiva, Umā and Skanda are presented together in a group. Śiva in such a combination is called *Somāskandamūrti*. Of course, the Purāṇic background is always there. The *Purāṇas* have narrated at several places how Śiva and Pārvatī went to Śaravaṇa, where their son Kārttikeya was born. Śiva and Umā took the child and embraced him.[273] The *Somāskandamūrti* presumably portrays this happy moment which Śiva and Umā enjoyed in the company of Skanda.

Śiva is featured [274] in this image with a single face, four arms, his right leg hanging down, and the left one folded and laid on the seat. The *śikhā-cakra* is represented. *Dhuttura* flowers and the crescent moon adorn his matted hair. *Nakrakuṇḍala*, *karṇapatra*, *siṁhakarṇa* and *kaṭaka* are among the ornaments prescribed. The figure is clad in a garment of skin and wears an *upavīta*. His upper garment hangs down like a tail on either side. The god is represented as holding the

[272] *Kāraṇa*, II.2-6. Rites prescribed at 7-19.

[273] *Skanda P.*, I.1.27; I.2.29.

[274] *Kāraṇa*, II.33.5-19; *Kāmika*, II.47.

mṛga and his axe in two hands, the other two hands being in the *abhaya* and the *varada* poses. Skanda is shown in the middle. The height of Skanda's image comes up to Umā's ear, *tālu*, or breast. Featured with two eyes and two arms, Skanda wears a *makuṭa* studded with gems and holds lotuses in both the hands. He bears a childlike appearance, and is depicted naked; his legs are bent a little sideways in a dancing pose. Umā is represented with two arms, two eyes, two breasts, a *kirīṭamakuṭa* and *yajñopavīta*. Her right leg is laid on the seat and the left one hangs down. She holds an *utpala* in the right hand, while the other hand is in the *varada* pose.

This image is always made of bronze and is regarded as an *utsavavigraha*, meant to be taken in procession. In all temples of Śiva, this *mūrti* holds a position second in importance to the *mūla-vigraha*, the *liṅga*. In all important festivals, such as the *rathotsava*, it is this *vigraha* that is taken in the *ratha* in procession. However, the *Somāskandamūrti* installed at Tirumālapāḍi is made of stone.

25. Candraśekharamūrti

This image of Śiva presents the god with the crescent moon displayed in his matted hair. The episode relating to the wearing of the crescent moon by Śiva does not occur very frequently in the *Purāṇas*. Nevertheless, the *Purāṇas* quite often refer to the god as the wearer of the crescent. Dakṣa, it is told, once cursed the moon for showing partiality to Rohiṇī, who was one of the twenty-seven daughters of Dakṣa who were given to the moon. As the result of that curse, the moon began to waste away. Fearing total extinction, he ran to Śiva for protection. Śiva afforded him shelter by wearing him in the crescent form to which he had been already reduced by that time. He also modified Dakṣa's curse to the effect that the moon would wax and wane periodically.[275]

In the *Candraśekharamūrti* [276] the god is shown with three eyes. On the right side of the *jaṭāmakuṭa* is fitted the crescent moon. The

[275] *Śiva P.*, *Jñāna-saṁhitā*, 45.1-55.

[276] *Kāraṇa*, II.54.2-10. Rites prescribed at 11-35. See also *Kāmika*, II.48.

right ear is decked with *patra* and *nakrakuṇḍala*. The *śikhācakra* is prescribed. The figure is depicted as standing erect. The right leg below the knee is decked with a bell tied round it. The god wears a lion's skin and the *yajñopavīta*. *Hāra*, *keyūra*, *kaṭaka*, *valaya* and anklets are among the ornaments that are prescribed.

The height of the image of Umā which also is shown by the side of Śiva comes up to the ear, shoulder or chest of the figure of Śiva. The goddess may be optionally assigned a separate *pīṭha*. Two arms, two eyes, hanging ears, her body a little bent to the left, and her left hand hanging down are the main physical features of the goddess. As usual, the *prabhā* and the *padma-pīṭha* are prescribed.

It will be thus seen that the *Candraśekharamūrti* is more or less similar to the *Umāmaheśvaramūrti* (23). However, the former is designed to emphasize the fact that Śiva is the wearer of the crescent. This type of *mūrti* is installed in almost all the temples of the South. The *Candraśekharamūrti* installed at the temple in Tiruppukalūr is a great attraction.

26. Vṛṣārūḍhamūrti (Fig. 12)

In this representation, Śiva is portrayed as the rider of the bull. In several places in the *Purāṇas* this aspect of Śiva is presented, but nowhere does one come across the events leading to the adoption of this animal as his vehicle. There are, however, frequent references in the *Purāṇas* to the god's becoming manifest to his devotees in this form; in all such instances he is accompanied by Umā.

The *Vṛṣārūḍhamūrṭi*[277] depicts Śiva with four arms and wielding *ṭaṅka* and *kṛṣṇamṛga*. His right foot is fixed to the *padmapīṭha* and his left one is lifted up and rests against the right in such a way that its toes touch the ground. The hand is placed on the bull's hump. Gaurī may be presented on the *pīṭha*, or on a separate one. One of her hands hangs down. The crown she wears is studded with gems.

Another version of the image is also found. In it, Śiva is represented with two arms. He is depicted as bearing a tranquil appearance.

[277] *Kāraṇa*, II.59.2-11. Rites prescribed at 11-35. See also *Kāmika*, II.62.

Fig. 12: Vṛṣabhārūḍhamūrti, Lokeśvara Temple at Pattadakkal.

One of his hands is placed on the bull, and the other on his thigh. Gaurī, bedecked with the *jaṭāmakuṭa*, is shown on his left.

27. Naṭarājamūrti or Nṛttamūrti (Fig. 13)

In the temple [278] of Chidambaram [279] in south India, Śiva is represented as the dancing god. He is Naṭarāja and his consort is celebrated as Śivakāmasundarī. The main characteristics of both the god and the goddess as represented in these images generally conform to the Purāṇic descriptions. For instance, Śiva wears matted hair, is three-eyed, has four arms, wears a skin, carries Gaṅgā, and has serpents for his ornaments. However, there are some features which are peculiar to these representations. First of all, Śiva is portrayed as a dancing god. In no other representation of Śiva is this idea of the dancer even slightly reflected, although the *Purāṇas* refer now and again to the dances of Śiva.[280] Names of Śiva hinting at the same idea are also not wanting in the *Purāṇas*.[281] Those texts, however, cannot be said to show even faint traces of the concept of Naṭarāja as it later developed. In other words, nowhere in the *Purāṇas* does one come across a god

[278] For the legendary and historical accounts relating to the temple see: Narayanasami Nayudu, "The temples of Śiva-Natarāja at Chidambaram", *Krishnaswamy Aiyyangar Commomoration Volume*, p. 381-382. Also Somasundaram, J.M., *University Environs*, p. 59.

[279] An etymological study of this place name has led Raghavan to draw the following conclusions: "Among the Śiva shrines mentioned in the S.S. Chidambaram occupies a vital place. Now, in all the places where Chidambaram is spoken of, it is found as Vyāghrapuram, or Puṇḍarīkapuram (Puliyūr in Tamil), and Dabhrasabhā (Siṟṟambalam — the Small Hall). There are older names, *Dabhra sabhā*, subsequently fashionably changed into *Abhrasabhā* (the Ether Hall), and the Tamil Siṟṟambalam fashionably changed into Chidambaram (The Small Hall became the Hall of Consciousness)." "The Sūta-saṁhitā", *ABORI*, XXII, p. 2.

[280] The following are the references to the dances performed by Śiva on various occasions: *Kūrma P.*, II.35.45-61. The dance performed at *pralaya*, the hour of destruction, is described as the *ghora-tāṇḍava*. *Ibid.*, II.46.1-25. Śiva fixed Andhaka to the trident and danced. *Ibid.*, I.16.74.190. Śiva performed the *tāndava* dance. *Liṅga P.*, I.106.1-28; *ibid.*, I.71.121-134; *Nāradīya P.*, II.73. Śiva's *ugra-tāṇḍava*. *Vāmana P.*, 69.40-96. Śiva fixed Andhaka to the trident and danced. *Varāha P.*, 27.1-43. Śiva danced to entertain Umā. *Skanda P.*, VI.254; *Sūtasaṁhitā*, I.6.

[281] Cf. Nartanaśīla. *Vāmana P.*, 47.81. Nṛtyaśīla, *Kūrma P.*, II.39.23 etc.

Fig. 13: Naṭarāja, Ūrdhvatāṇḍaveśvara Temple at Tiruvalankadu.

in a dancing pose, encircled by a halo, and trampling *apasmāra* beneath his feet. No reference can be found in the *Purāṇas* to the god performing a dance which signified the five great acts; no *Purāṇas* speak of the god who in his dancing pose reveals himself as the five sacred letters which constitute the *mantra par excellence* of the Śaivites.[282]

The representation of Śiva as Naṭarāja is believed to have had its origin at Chidambaram.[283] However, it may be pointed out that over time it gained a wide popularity all over the South. Indeed, there is hardly any temple in the South which does not have the *Naṭarāja-mūrti* displayed prominently among the other representations of Śiva.[284] It is however, highly interesting to note that, irrespective of

---

[282] Cf. "In a much more arbitrary way the dance of Śiva is identified with the *pañcākṣara*, or five syllables of the prayer *shi-vā-ya-na-maḥ*, Hail to Śiva ... Another verse in *Unmaivilakkam* explains the fiery arch: The *pañcākṣara* and the Dance are identified with the mystic syllable *Oṁ*, the arch being the *kombu* or hook of the ideograph of the written symbol. The arch over Śrī Naṭarāja is *Oṁkāra*; and the *akṣara* which is never separate from the *oṁkāra* is the contained splendour. This is the Dance of the Lord of Chidambaram". Ananda Coomaraswamy, *The Dance of Shiva*, p. 92.

[283] Among all the sacred placed held in reverence by the Śaivites, there is none that can vie with Cidambaram. Its legends are recounted in a work entitled *The Koyil Purānam*, where *koyil* (meaning temple in Tamil), is used *par excellence* of Cidambaram. The dance performed by Naṭarāja at Cidambaraṃ is considered by this *Purāṇa* as a repetition of the performance given by the god earlier at Dāruvana. The following extract, from G.U. Pope from the introduction to his translation of *Tiruvācakam*, refers to the dance as follows: "Of this dance the sacred *Vedas* know the excellence, but are not cognizant of its cause, its time, its place, its full intention. In the forest at Tāruvanam (Dāruvana), in the midst of the *ṛṣis*, the gods beheld it; but because that is not the world's center, it trembled beneath His foot. In sacred Tillai, which is the center of the universe, shall this dance be finally revealed and there the God promises Ādiśeṣan that he shall again behold it ... The next book of the *Purāṇa*m expatiates at great length upon the first institution, as it would seem, of the great festival still observed when Sivan is supposed to dance in the Golden Hall". Pope, G.U., *Tiruvācakam*, p. lxvi-lxvii.

[284] Among the temples in the South besides Cidambaram, the following are the most celebrated for the Naṭarāja images installed in them: Tiruvālaku, Tiruvālavāy, Tirukkaḷar, Kurrālam, Tiruṇaḷḷam, and Tirunelveli. All these images are made of metal, usually bronze. A rare exception is the Naṭarāja installed in stone at Tiruppuvaṇam, Kañcanūr, Tiruppattūr and Tirunelveli.

the place where the temple in which the Naṭarāja is installed may be located, that form of the god is always identified as the lord of Cidambara (Cidambareśa). Among all the representations of Śiva mentioned in this chapter, the *Somāskandamūrti* and the *Naṭarāja-mūrti* have been assigned the greatest prominence.[285]

The *Āgamas* mention various details relating to the construction, installation and worship of the image.[286] Three eyes, four arms, a serene look, the *jaṭāmakuṭa*, the right leg shaped like a *svastika*, and the left lifted up a little and planted on the *apasmāra* are the principal physical features. Among the ornaments prescribed are the *karṇapatra*, *nakrakuṇḍala*, *dhuttura* flower, the *arka*, the crescent moon and the Gaṅgā; *nāgayajñopavīta*, *kaṭaka*, *hāra*, *keyūra* and anklets are also mentioned. The skin of a lion is to be the lower garment, and that of a tiger the upper one. In one of his right hands, the god holds a *ḍamaru* and in the left he carries fire. The other hand, which is shown in the *abhaya pose*, is to be girt by a serpent. The deity is portrayed as encircled by the *prabhāmaṇḍala*.

As for the *pañcakṛtya*, the fivefold activity of the god, it consists of *sṛṣṭi*, creation, which is represented by the drum that Naṭarāja bears in his hand; *sthiti*, preservation, indicated by the hand in the *abhaya* pose; *saṁhāra*, destruction, denoted by the fire that the god carries;

---

[285] On rare occasions only are these images taken out of the shrines.

[286] *Kāraṇa*, II.55.2-12. Rites prescribed at 13-26. *Kāmika* II.171. See also Sivaramamurti, *op.cit.*, p. 60. In this connection the following extract from a descriptive discussion made by V. Raghavan, is given below to show the wide difference which prevails between the accounts found in the literary and religious works on the one hand, and the sculptural and iconographic representation on the other: "The dances of Śiva as described in works of dance, (*Nāṭyaśāstra*) and as dealt with in religious works of Śaivism (*Āgamas* and *sthalamāhātmyas* pertaining to different Śiva shrines) show differences. There is no doubt that the latter grew out of the former, and even in the form in which they are spoken of in the latter, they keep some tell-tale names in a few cases which show their links with the *Nāṭyaśāstra*. Bharata describes one hundred and eight poses of *tāṇḍava* dance in his *Nāṭyaśāstra*; in Śaiva literature, Śiva is said to have danced in 64 shrines, but the exact forms of these latter 64 dances are not given, and we cannot therefore trace in full detail the interrelation of the dances of Śiva in *Nāṭya Śāstra*, Śaiva literature and sculpture and iconography". Trouvailles de Nedoungadou, *Tāṇḍavas de Śiva*, p. 20-21.

tirobhava or veiling, hinted by the leg planted on the dwarf-demon beneath; and *anugraha*, indicated by his raised leg.[287]

28. Dakṣiṇāmūrti (Fig. 14)

In various contexts in the *Purāṇas*,[288] Śiva is described as a *yogin* engaged in meditation. Such descriptions form the basis for the concept of *Dakṣiṇāmūrti*. In the temples of Śiva, this image is always assigned the southern niche of the central shrines and it is made to face towards the south. In Dakṣiṇāmūrti, Śiva is represented as the great teacher imparting higher knowledge to his disciples. The concept of Śiva as Dakṣināmūrti was later expanded with the result that different expositions of the same representation came into vogue.

Three eyes, four arms, a serene appearance and a crystal-like splendour characterize the image. The *jaṭāmakuṭa*, a pair of *kuṇḍalas* of the *nakra*-design, and *karṇapatra* are among the ornaments worn by the god. The limbs are shown to be beautiful and perfectly shaped, his navel is given the appearance of the glowing fire. His right hand indicates the *jñānamudrā*. His right leg hangs down; his left one is bent and laid on the seat. The *yoga* belt is worn around his left knee. The right leg treads on the *apasmāra*. A banyan tree and a bull are depicted behind him.[289]

In the vicinity of Kanchipuram, about a mile and a half away from Paḷḷūr Station in the village Kovintavati (Akaram), on the southern border of a stream called Pālāru, is located a temple dedicated to Dakṣiṇāmūrti. In the temple at Tiruneittānaṁ near Tiruvāñjam Dakṣiṇāmūrti is depicted in a standing posture.

---

[287] Cf. Ananda Coomaraswamy, *The Dance of Shiva*, p. 87.

[288] *Matsya P.*, 154.380-382. Śiva and the *guru* are identified: *Śiva P.*, *Kailāsa-saṁhitā*, 8.43-90; *ibid Sanatkumārasaṁhitā*, 14.1-20; *Skanda P.*, I.1.22.

[289] *Kāraṇa*, II.2-7. Rites prescribed at 8-16. *Kāmika*, II.51. See also Sivaramamurti, *op.cit.*, p. 58, and Balasubramaniyam, "Daksinamurti in the Subramaniya temple at Kaṇṇanur", *IHQ*, vol. XV, p. 287.

Fig. 14: Dakṣiṇāmūrti, Kailāsanātha Temple at Kanchipuram.

Generally, the *Purāṇas* do not provide us with any systematic information relating to the technique of image-making as such. As may be seen from the foregoing pages, the main contribution of these texts lies in the light they throw upon the genesis of particular images. High technique is involved in the construction of these images, which are made out of stone, metal or are carved in wood,[290] but the *Purāṇas* do not deal with it as an independent topic. Of course, incidental references to this and allied topics do occur in the *Purāṇas*,[291] and these make it possible for one to formulate a statement about what these texts have to say regarding the construction of images.

To begin with, the *Purāṇas* emphatically enjoin that one should not worship images which do not show the necessary characteristic marks or which are defective and deformed.[292] This injunction then gave rise to various commentaries which, naturally enough, attempt to expound the process of making the right kind of images. The main concern of the *Purāṇas* was to acquaint the devotees with such details as would help them to choose the proper images for installation. A note of warning is always sounded against the disastrous results which might follow if the wrong kind of images were installed.[293] The limbs

[290] The tradition of making images is still preserved intact to the present time.

[291] Though the following remark on the Purāṇic contribution to iconography has not been properly assessed, Shamasastry seems to have succeeded in assigning the *Āgamas* and the *Tantras* their due shares. He observes, "While the *Purāṇas* were devoted to the praise of idolatry, the *Āgamas* and the *Tantras* were written to explain the forms of worship". See "Dravidian Culture", *ABORI*, vol. XI, p. 340.

[292] *Pratimāṁ lakṣaṇair hīnāṁ gṛhītāṁ naiva pūjayet. Bhaviṣya P.*, II.12.1.

[293] *Nādhikāṅgā na hīnāṅgāḥ kartavyāḥ devatāḥ kvacit* |
Svāminaṁ ghātayen nūnāṁ karālavadanā tathā ||
Adhikā śilpinaṁ hanyāt kṛśā caivārthanāśinī |
Kṛṣodarī tu durbhikṣaṁ nirmāṁsā dhananāśinī ||
Vakranāsā tu duḥkhāya saṁkṣiptāṅgī bhayaṅkarī |
Cipiṭā duḥkhaśokāya anetrā netranāśinī ||
Duḥkhadā hīnavaktrā tu pāṇipādakṛśā tathā |
Hīnāṅgā hīnajaṅghā ca bhramonmadakarī ṇṛṇām |
Śuṣkavaktrā tu rājānaṁ kaṭihīnā ca yā bhavet ||
Pāṇīpādavihīno yo jāyate mārako mahān |
Matsya P., 259.15-20.

of the image should neither be exaggerated nor minimized to a disproportionate size. Deficiency in any detail would prove detrimental to the owner's life. Exaggeration of features would destroy the sculptor. An emaciated depiction would result in the destruction of wealth. A contracted belly brings famine. A lack of plumpness causes poverty. A contraction of the limbs rouses fear. An absence of an eye affects the eye itself. A deficient mouth causes misery, and a deformity in the knee leads to insanity. The *Matsya Purāṇa* goes on enumerating many such defects of commission and omission and the evils following from them. These evils, unless otherwise specified, affect the *yajamāna* who is responsible for the installation. Conversely, the worship of the images which are perfect in all their features prolongs life and adds to prosperity. The *Purāṇas* enumerate the materials which are to be used for making an image. Stone, wood, copper and clay are frequently mentioned in this regard. In one passage, wood is said to be the best material for constructing an image in the *kali* age. *Candana*, *agaru*, *bilva*, *śrīparṇa* and *padmakāṣṭhā* are among the trees prescribed in this context.[294] The *Matsya Purāṇa* recommends gold, silver, copper, gems, stone, wood, iron, *rītikā*, minerals and bronze as materials with which to construct images.[295] The *Agni Purāṇa* speaks of various types of the *liṅgas*, such as *lavaṇaja* (made of salt), *ghṛtaja* (made of ghee), *vastraja* (cloth), *mṛṇmaya* (fashioned out of clay), *dārumaya* (constructed from wood), and *śailaja* (sculptured from chiseled stone). *Liṅgas* made of pearls (*muktāmaya*), gold (*svarṇamaya*), silver (*rajatamaya*), copper (*tāmramaya*), brass (*paittala*) and mercury (*rasaja*) are also mentio-

---

294 *Kalau dārumayaḥ aśaktau mṛṇmayo 'thavā* |
Candanāgarubhiḥ kuryād bilvaśrīparṇakasya ca ||
Padmakāṣṭhāmayaś caiva vāmamasya tathaiva ca |
Bhaviṣya P., II.12.

295 *Sauvarṇī rājatī vāpi tāmri ratnamayī tathā* |
Śailī dārumayī cāpi lohasaṁghamayī tathā ||
rītikā dhātuyuktā va tāmrakāṁsyamayī tathā |
Śubhadārumayī vāpi devatārcā praśasyate ||
Matsya P., 258.20-21.

ned in that *Purāṇa*.[296] Clay is to be used only when other recommended materials are not obtainable. The *pīṭhikā* is to be constructed with the same materials as the image; any change of material is strictly forbidden.[297] *Ratna*, *sphaṭika*, clay and wood are prescribed as suitable materials for making a *liṅga*.[298]

The various detailed measurements given in connection with the construction of images [299] go to show how the entire technique had assumed a fairly developed level. The construction of a *liṅga* also implies quite an elaborate process.[300] It has been said that the size of the *liṅga* should be in proportion to the temple or the *garbhagṛha* in which it is to be installed.[301] While speaking of the structure of the *liṅga*, its three sections are clearly demarcated. The nethermost portion of the *liṅga* is called the *Brahma-bhāga*. It is just above the *kūrma-śilā*, and forms the basis of the entire structure. Above the *Brahma-bhāga* is the *Viṣṇu-bhāga*. This is also known as the *piṇḍikā*. The *piṇḍikā* itself is divided into such sections as the *kaṇṭha* and the *paṭṭikā*.[302] Above these is set the *ūrdhva-paṭṭikā*. The *liṅga* proper is represented by the *Śiva-bhāga*.[303] Also, in connection with anthropo-

---

[296] *Agni P.*,54. 1-5.

[297] *Devasya yajanārthaṁ tu pīṭhikā daśa kīrtitāḥ* |
Śaile sailamayīṁ dadyāt pārthive pārthivīṁ tathā ||
Dāruje dārujāṁ kuryād miśre miśrāṁ tathaiva ca |
Nānyayonistu kartavyā sadā śubhaphalepsubhiḥ ||
Matsya P., 262.19-20.

[298] *Evaṁ ratnamayaṁ kuryāt sphaṭikaṁ pārthivaṁ tathā* |
Śubhaṁ dārumayaṁ cāpi yadvā manasi rocate ||
Ibid., 263.25.

[299] See Appendix. P. 892 ff.

[300] *Matsya P.*, 263.

[301] *Prāsadasya pramāṇena liṅgamānaṁ vidhīyate. Matsya P.*, 263.2.

[302] Gopinath Rao refers to these terms and comments on them as follows: "The *pīṭhas* are made of one, two or three slabs of stones placed one over another and they are shaped with various kinds of ornamental mouldings which are arranged in tiers one over another ... the various items of the mouldings are known as *upāna*, *padma*, *kampa*, *kaṇṭha*, *paṭṭikā*, *nimna and ghṛtāvarī*". Gopinath Rao, o*p.cit*., vol. II, pt. I, p. 101.

[303] *Matsya P.*, 263.15-17.

morphic images of Śiva, the *Purāṇas* refer to these three sections. From the foot to the knee is the *Brahmā-sthāna*; from the knee to the navel is the *Viṣṇu-sthāna*; and the remaining figure above the navel is the *Śiva-sthāna*.

The *liṅga*, broad at the bottom and tapering towards the top, looks beautiful and is, therefore, desirable for worship; such a *liṅga* brings prosperity to the worshipper. The *liṅga* which does not answer to the prescribed specifications is condemned as unfit for worship.[304] The *piṇḍikā* should be so sufficiently deep and should extend towards the outlet, which itself should always point towards the north.[305]

Several designs are mentioned while referring to the shape of the top of the *liṅga*. For instance, when the *pañca-liṅga* is constructed, the top assumes a circular shape. Normally, the *Purāṇas* speak of three designs for the top of the *liṅga*: the umbrella, the egg, and the crescent.[306] In the description of the *liṅga*, even physical features such as a face, forehead, chin, neck, arms and eyes are sometimes ascribed to it.[307] The *Purāṇas* refer to three faces, and sometimes to four. The details of the measurements in this connection are elaborately worked out and systematically laid down.

---

[304] *Evaṁvidhaṁ tu yalliṅgaṁ bhavet tat sarvakāmikam |*
Anyathā yadbhavelliṅgaṁ tatastat saṁpracakṣate ||
Matsya P., 263.24-25.

[305] *Agni P.*, 55. 2-3.

[306] *Pañcaliṅgavyavasthāyāṁ śiro vartulaṁ ucyate |*
Chatrābhaṁ kukkuṭābhaṁ vā bālendupratimākṛtiḥ ||
Agni P., 54.34-35.

[307] *Śironnatiḥ prakartavyā lalāṭaṁ nāsikā tataḥ |*
Vadanaṁ cibukaṁ grīvā yugabhāgair bhujākṣibhiḥ ||
Karābhyāṁ mukulīkṛtya pratimāyāḥ pramāṇataḥ |
Mukhaṁ prati samaḥ kāryo vistarād aṣṭamāṁśataḥ ||
Caturmukhaṁ mayā proktaṁ trimukhaṁ cocyate śṛṇu |
Karṇapādādikaṁ nyasya lalāṭādīni nirdiśet ||
Bhujau caturbhir bhāgaistu kartavyau paścimorjitau |
Vistarād aṣṭamāṁśena mukhānāṁ prati nirgamaḥ ||
Ekavaktraṁ tathā kāryaṁ pūrvasyāṁ saumyalocanam |
Lalāṭanāsikāvaktragrīvāyāṁ ca vivartayet ||
Agni P., 54.42-46.

The *Purāṇas* refer to the various categories of *liṅgas*. The *Agni Purāṇa*, for instance, prescribes the worship of the *liṅgas* installed by great *siddhas*.[308] The *svayaṁbhu-liṅgas*, which spring into existence by themselves and are thus not given shape by human hands, the *bāṇa-liṅgas*, and the reflection of the sun in a mirror are mentioned in this category.[309] No human agency being responsible for their construction, they are not required to conform to the rules relating to the structure and measurements of the *liṅga*. The *liṅgas* installed in houses for domestic worship are distinguished from those installed in public places of worship.[310] The height of the former category of *liṅgas* varies from one to fifteen *aṅgulas*. The *sthira-liṅgas* are differentiated from the *cala-liṅgas*. The *liṅgas* varying in measurement from one to five *aṅgulas* belong to the lowest of the *cala* type; those measuring from eleven to fifteen *aṅgulas* are the best of this type. In the description of the *ghana-(sthira)-liṅga*, greater emphasis is put on their structure than on their measurements.

Among the Purāṇic texts, the *Matsya* and the *Bhaviṣya Purāṇas* prescribe the rules relating to the construction of the images.[311] The *Matsya Purāṇa* insists on a strict adherence to the measurements laid down in this connection.[312] This *Purāṇa* mentions the limbs of the image one by one, and thereby regulates their construction. Technical terms such as *navatāla* and *pañcatāla* are employed to denote the height of the image.[313] Different measurements are prescribed in reference to the images of female divinities.[314] The *Matsya Purāṇa* also gives individual descriptions for the images of Śiva in his various

---

[308] *Agni P.*, 54.5.

[309] *Ibid.*, 54.6.

[310] *Aṅgulād gṛhaliṅgaṁ syād yāvat pañcadaśāṅgulam. Agni P.*, 54.8.

[311] *Matsya P.*, 257 ff; *Bhaviṣya P.*, II.12.

[312] *Matsya P.*, 258.

[313] *Ibid.*, 258.16 ff. Regarding the details of *tāla* measure for separate gods, see P.K. Acharya, *Jha Com. Vol.*, p. 6.

[314] *Stryaḥ kāryās tu tanvyaṅgyaḥ stanorujaghanāntikāḥ*
Caturdaśāṅgulāyāmaṁ udaraṁ nāma nirdiśet.
Matsya P., 258.71-72.

aspects.[315] It is interesting to note that as many as ten, and in some cases, even twelve, arms are prescribed in one of the representations of Śiva. The *Matsya Purāṇa* lays down a far more elaborate process for the preparation of the Ardhanārīśvara image.[316] It describes in detail every limb of the figure from head to foot. Umāmaheśvara is another representation of Śiva which is discussed in a similar manner.[317] Contrary to what has been said elsewhere, this *Purāṇa* prescribes that Śiva and Umā be shown separately in the Umāmaheśvara representation.[318] Among other related images described in detail in the *Matsya Purāṇa* are those of Harihara,[319] Kārttikeya,[320] Gaṇeśa,[321] Kātyāyanī and Mahiṣāsuramardanī.[322] The measurements of the *piṇḍikā* form the sole topic of a whole chapter in the *Agni Purāṇa*. This *Purāṇa* also gives rules governing the construction of the images of Caṇḍikā [323] and Vīrabhadra.[324]

One of the distinctive features of the temples in south India which must be addressed at this stage is the *dhvajastaṁbha*,[325] which are installed at various points in the temple. The one located opposite to the central image of the temple is of the highest importance, its location is fixed close to the Nandin and the *Balipīṭha*. The *Āgamas* have prescribed the ceremonial installation of the *dhvajastaṁbha*.[326] The annual festival of the temple (*brahmotsava*) is inaugurated with the hoisting of the flag on this staff. The *dhvajārohaṇa* marks the beginning and its *avarohaṇa*, the conclusion of the *brahmotsava*, which incidentally is the greatest event in connection with the temple during the year. In this festival, the images are taken in procession round the temple on vehicles as prescribed, and the *ratha* and the *tīrtha-utsavas*

---

315 *Matsya P.*, 259.

316 *Ibid.*, 260.1-10.

317 *Ibid.*, 260.11-21.

318 *Ibid.*, 260.14.

319 *Ibid.*, 260.21-27.

320 *Ibid.*, 260.45-49.

321 *Ibid.*, 260.52-54.

322 *Ibid.*, 260. 55-65.

323 *Agni P.*, 50.

324 *Ibid.*, 62.

325 Cf. "When one enters by the *gopuram* on the East of the temple of Śiva, one finds successively before him the *balipītham* (the seat of sacrifice) the *dhvajastaṁbha* and the Nandi". Dubreuil, *Dravidian Architecture*, p. 19.

326 *Kārana*, II.102.

are celebrated at the end of the festival. The three topics of the *dhvajastaṁbha*, the *ratha* and the *vāhana* are interrelated and a brief reference to what the *Purāṇas* have to say about them would not be out of place here.

To begin with, it may be pointed out that the *dhvajastaṁbha*, the *ratha* and the *vāhanas* are usually to be constructed from wood, but, according to the capacity of the worshippers, they should be covered with either silver or golden plates. Brass and copper coverings are also sometimes found. References are found in the *Agni Purāṇa* to the installation of the *dhvajastaṁbha*, and the rituals relating to it are also described in another chapter.[327] These rituals generally reveal Vaiṣṇava traditions, but in the concluding part of their descriptions it has been remarked that the same procedure is applicable to other deities as well,[328] the only variation being the insertion of the special symbol of the particular god in whose honour the *dhvajārohaṇa* is performed. For instance, *vṛṣabha* is the crest of Śiva's banner. This explains his name *Vṛṣabha-dhvaja*.[329] The *Agni Purāṇa* gives a philosophical interpretation of the *dhvajastaṁbha* on the *sāṁkhya* lines. Here, the *patāka* is identical with *prakṛti*, and the *daṇḍa* with *puruṣa*. The importance of the *dhvajastaṁbha* is also emphasized in another way. First of all, the *prāsāda*, the temple, is identified with the god enshrined within it. The temple, for its part, is declared to be symbolically represented by the *dhvaja-daṇḍa*. A more or less close symbolical relationship between the *dhvajadaṇḍa* and the deity is thus established.[330]

From among the other details of the *dhvajastaṁbha* mentioned in the *Agni Purāṇa*, the following may be specifically referred to. The *dhvaja* is erected on a *kalaśa*, which itself is set on an egg-like

---

[327] *Agni-P.*, 61 and 102.

[328] *Eṣa sādhāraṇaḥ prokto dhvajasyārohaṇe vidhiḥ* |
Yasya devasya yaccihnaṁ tanmantreṇa sthiraṁ caret ||
Agni P., 61. 49-50.

[329] Kārttikeya has *mayūra* and Gaṇeśa has *ākhu* as their crests.

[330] *Agni P.*, 61.28.

structure.[331] The *daṇḍa* should be of the measure of half the height of the image. The likeness of the god is also inscribed on the *daṇḍa*. An alternative is also suggested that the *daṇḍa* should be of the measure of half the height of the temple, measured from the base to the *śikhara*.[332] The north-eastern or the north-western corner of the temple is the site chosen for the erection of the *daṇḍa*.[333] The banner is made of silk, and is decked with *ghaṇṭā*, *cāmara* and *kiṅkiṇī*. Bamboo and *śālā* are prescribed as suitable for the construction of the *daṇḍa*.[334] If the *daṇḍa* gives way during the hoisting, it brings disaster to both the king and the *yajamāna*.

The *Purāṇas* may be said to be the earliest texts to specifically refer to the vehicles (*vāhanas*) of the various gods. The *Āgamas* have further elaborated this allocation.[335] Vṛṣabha is the vehicle of Śiva, as is clearly indicated by the names Vṛṣabhārūḍha and Vṛṣavāhana of frequent occurrence in the *Purāṇas*.[336] The lion is the vehicle of Umā,[337] the peacock that of Kārttikeya,[338] and the *mūṣaka* that of Gaṇeśa. Sometimes during a festival, the same god is assigned different *vāhanas*, one for each day.[339]

---

331 *Aṇḍordhvaṁ kalaśaṁ nyasya tadūrdhvaṁ vinyased dhvajam |*
Biṁbārdhamānaṁ daṇḍasya tribhāgenātha kārayet ||
Aṣṭāraṁ dvādaśāraṁ vā madhye mūrtimatānvitam |
Agni P., 61.29-30.

332 *Prāsādasya tu vistāre mānaṁ daṇḍasya kīrtitaṁ |*
Śikharārdhena vā kuryāt tṛtīyārddhena vā punaḥ ||
Ibid., 61.31.

333 *Dhvajayaṣṭiṁ devagṛhe aisānyāṁ vāyave' tha vā. Ibid.*, 61.32.

334 *Agni P.*, 102.

335 *Kāraṇa*, *I.*140.78-80.

336 *Vāmana P.*, 2.33; *Skanda P.*, I.2.25-60.

337 *Matsya P.*, 157.1-19.

338 A direct reference to the granting of a vehicle to this god is as follows: *Dadau hutāśanas tejo dadau vāyuś ca vāhanam. Matsya P.*, 159. 10.

339 *Prathame śibikāṁ caiva dvitīye kalpapādapam |*
Bhūtarūpaṁ tṛtīyaṁ tu caturthe gajavāhanam ||
Pañcame vṛṣabhaṁ proktaṁ Kailāsaṁ caiva ṣāṣṭake |
Saptame rathamāropya aṣṭame turagaṁ bhavet ||
Navame tu vimānaṁ ca daśame tīrtham ācaret |
Kāraṇa, I.140.78-80.

"On the first day one should assign a palanquin, on the second a wish granting tree, on the third a *bhūta* spirit, on the fourth an elephant, on the fifth a bull, on the sixth

The *ratha* or the chariot is perhaps the most majestic available conveyance in the temple, and the day on which the deity's chariot procession takes place is of great significance. The *Kāraṇa-Āgama* [340] prescribes the rituals for the consecration of the chariot designed for the *rathotsava*. The *rathas* are designed in various patterns. The same amount of skill required for constructing the images is also required for the construction of the *ratha*.[341] The chariot is for the most part built of wood. Various Purāṇic episodes are portrayed around the circular base of the chariot, which extends from the axle to which the wheels are fixed to the *pīṭha* which is provided for the occupation of the deity. Wooden horses are shown dragging the car. Brahmā is presented immediately behind these horses as the charioteer. A strong rope is fastened round the base of the chariot, and holding the ends of the rope hundreds of devotees drag the chariot around the temple. This chariot procession may remind one of the Purāṇic times, for in

the Kailāsa, on the seventh a temple car, on the eighth a horse, on the ninth a celestial car, on the tenth one should perform the ceremonial bath."

[340] *Kāraṇa*, I.142.

[341] The following extract from Kandasamy Mudaliyar's "Tamil Architecture — Its Development" speaks of the skill displayed by the workmen of ancient times in temple architecture and sculpture: "The ancient temples were the repositories of the different arts that flourished at the times. Besides the builder and the sculptor who embellished the temples, there were also painters ... the metal caster made bronze deities and statue lamps; the wood-carver fashioned the mounts (*vāhanams*) and richly carved the temple car; the jeweler did the jewellery and the embroiderer did the colourfully appliqued saddle cloths and face-masks of the temple bull and elephant, and the banner, flags and festoons. Even culinary artists prepared delicious food offerings". *TC*, vol. II, nos. 3 and 4, p. 323. The scheme of allocation of depictions on walls of temples and temple cars is thus explained: "The space on the walls of temples and on the body of temple cars is divided into four parts; the lowest part is allotted to the figures representing *dharmapuruṣārtha* or mortal law. The second is assigned to the delineation of *arthapuruṣārtha* or wealth-producing activities. The third part is taken up for the representation of *kāmapuruṣārtha* or pursuits of humanity in the field of enjoyment of animal passion. The topmost part is allotted to delineation of *mokṣapuruṣārtha* or religious pursuits to attain emancipation. This seems to be the order followed in the artistic carvings made on the walls of temples and temple cars." Shamasastry, *Proceedings and Transactions of the 7th All India Oriental Conference*, Baroda, 1933. p. 781.

the *Purāṇas* one comes across descriptions of how the gods prepared a chariot for Śiva, and of how Śiva riding in that chariot set out to destroy the three cities.[342] An elaborate description of that *ratha* is given. The universe itself was the *ratha*, the sun and the moon were the wheels, the four *Vedas* were the four horses, and Brahmā was the charioteer. It is not unlikely that the idea of the procession in *ratha* was derived from this Purāṇic description.

It would be quite appropriate to briefly consider at this stage a vital question related to the subject of Śiva-worship regarding the temple cult. Today, the temple cult prevails all over the country, but it is very difficult to determine with any degree of precision the date when temples as we know them today began to be built.[343] The Śaiva religion is perhaps the earliest known iconic religious cult, but there is evidence to show that the icon representing Śiva was usually worshipped in the open rather than within any built structure. The remains of a structure excavated at Mohenjodaro may suggest the existence of halls for congregation or worship in that period, but there are no indications that the idols of Paśupati or any other god were installed in connection with these congregation halls. The Vedic religion is conspicuous by the absence of any references to images of gods or temples. Sacrifice was evidently the essence of the religious practices in the Vedic period. At the end of the Vedic period, however, the sacrificial cult began to recede into the background, presumably making way for the temple cult. This had been perhaps the most outstanding feature of the transition from Brahmanism to popular Hinduism. All the same, it must be remembered that no specific references to temples are found in the older *Purāṇas*.[344] At the same time, there can be hardly any doubt that the

[342] *Matsya P.*, 133. 16-48; *Liṅga P.*, 1.72.3-24; *Śiva P.*, *Jñāneśvara-saṁhitā*, 24. *Rathotsavādi kalyāṇaṁ jānavāsaṁ tu sarvataḥ*. *Śiva P.*, *Vidyeśvara-saṁhitā*, 7.22.

[343] See Appendix 5, pp. 804 ff.

[344] The *tīrthas* are mentioned quite often. Similarly, one comes across references to special apartments in the houses where images of gods were installed for domestic worship.

temple cult of the Hindus has a definite Epic and Purāṇic basis. This statement possesses special reference in respect of the temples of south India. Of course, the few references to temples occurring in some *Purāṇas* do not by any means reflect the colossal structures of the South. Incidentally, it may be pointed out that some Purāṇic passages such as *Liṅga Purāṇa* I.76; 92.120-162 are full of materials which may be said to have provided the background for the temple cult.

A hypothesis may be hazarded here, that the temple of Śiva is merely an elaboration and an artificial depiction of Kailāsa, the original mountain abode of that god. Kailāsa is mentioned in the Epics as well as the *Purāṇas* as the permanent abode of Śiva.[345] There he lives in the company of Umā, Skanda and Gaṇeśa, who are the members of his family. He is also surrounded by his various attendants; this presumably gave rise to the development of the concept of the god's dwelling in a gorgeous palace with his family and attendants duly stationed within it. The *Purāṇas* actually describe Śiva's abode as equipped with halls and pillars.[346] Apart from Kailāsa, a few other mountain summits are also mentioned as the dwelling places of Śiva.[347] Among those are the Devakūṭa and the summit of the Mandara mountain.

Another factor which must have helped the development of the temple cult was the assumption of Śiva's immediate presence in the *liṅgas* installed for worship. After the performance of the *pratiṣṭhā* ritual, he is believed to be permanently dwelling within the *liṅga*. This being so, it was but inevitable that the environments in which the *liṅga* is installed should also be befitting the god's presence. Thus it must have occurred to the devotees to create around the *liṅga* an atmosphere similar to that of Kailāsa. A structure was accordingly built for Śiva in which places were specifically assigned to the ancillary gods and other attendant deities.

---

[345] *Vāyu P.*, I.30.82-93.

[346] *Liṅga P.*, I.80.5 ff; I.51.20-30.

[347] *Ibid.*, I.77. 7 ff.

As pointed out above, the *Mahābhārata* and the *Purāṇas* must be said to indicate the earliest stage of temple worship. Though the terms *devāyatana* and *devālaya* do not occur in these early descriptions, they mention various *tīrthas* which continue to be centers of attraction for pilgrims up to this day.[348] *Liṅgas* are said to have been installed in all such sacred places, which were also known as *kṣetras*. The *liṅgas* installed along the river banks under trees were worshipped by pilgrims. Śiva himself asserts that the offerings made to him in such places are most acceptable to him.[349] Most of the Śaivite temples of the later times presumably grew out of these original places of worship, surrounded by natural scenery, in forest areas (Kaṭampavanam, Punnaivanam, Nellikkā, Ālaṅkāṭu, Tillaivanam), on mountain tops, and on the banks of rivers or tanks or on the seashore. As Dorai Rangaswamy rightly observes,[350] "In every Śiva temple, there is a special tree or plant connected with the temple, probably because there was no other temple except the tree, to start with." A few temples have actually come to be named after the names of such trees or plants. Indeed, every temple of Śiva which was subsequently constructed had a *sthalavṛkṣa* and a sacred river or *tīrtha* attached to it.[351] The *sthalavṛkṣas* in all south Indian temples are in the close vicinity of the central shrines. It may also be noted

[348] The *Mahābhārata*, III.80-154 constitutes the 'Tīrtha-yātra-parvan'. Of this chapters 80-83 speak of *tīrthas* associated with Śiva. A greater bulk of the Purāṇic material on this subject relates to Śiva and to the gods subordinate to him. The following are some references to important *tīrthas* occurring in the *Purāṇas*: Avimukta: *Agni P.*, 109.18; *Matsya P.*, 22.7; *Skanda P.*, IV.1.26. Brahmatīrtha: *Agni P.*, 115.36; *Nārada P.*, II.55; *Skanda P.*, V.3.129. Dhanuṣkoṭi: *Skanda P.*, III.1.31. Dharmāraṇya: *Skanda P.*, III.2.1. Gokarṇeśvara: *Varāha P.*, I.213. Hāṭakeśvara: *Skanda P.*, VI.1. Kāñci: *Brahmāṇḍa P.*, IV.35. Kedāra: *Skanda P.*, VI.122. Rāmeśvara: *Skanda P.*, VI. 101. Vārāṇasi: *Matsya P.*, 22.7. A fairly detailed list of the *tīrthas* is given in the Appendix.

[349] *Atra dattaṁ hutaṁ japtaṁ sarvaṁ koṭigunaṁ bhavet*
Matkṣetrādapi sarvasmāt kṣetrametan mahattaraṁ.
Śiva P., *Vidyeśvara saṁhitā*, 7.23.

[350] "Rise of temple cult in Śaivism with special reference to Tevaram", *Annals of The Oriental Research University of Madras*, XII, Parts I & II.

[351] Gopinath Rao, *op.cit.*, vol. I, Introduction, p. 15.

that each of these temples has a *Purāṇa* which proclaims the greatness of the temple, its *vṛkṣa*, and the *tīrtha* associated with it.[352]

As pointed out above, the *Liṅga Purāṇa* mentions a few features of the temple built for Śiva by Viśvakarman on the mountain.[353] The halls were made of gold and the *vimānas* were set in various designs. The four entrances were decorated with bells and *cāmaras*. The *gopuras* and the *prākāras* are distinctly mentioned. The following description gives us the idea of the temple as conceived by the Purāṇic author:

Sūryamaṇḍalasaṅkāśair vimānaiśca vibhūṣitam |
Sphaṭikairmaṇḍapaiḥ śubhrair jāmbūnadamayais tathā ||
Nānāratnamayaiś caiva digvidikṣu vibhūṣitam |
Gopurair gopateḥ śambhoḥ nānābhūṣaṇabhūṣitaiḥ ||
Anekaiḥ sarvato bhadraiḥ sarvaratnamayais tathā |
Prākārair vividhākārair aṣṭaviṁśatibhir vṛtam ||
Upadvārair mahādvārair vidikṣu vividhair dṛḍham |[354]

"(Śiva's residence on Kailāsa) is adorned with towers looking like the orb of the sun, halls of crystal, bright, full of gold and diverse precious stones, decorated in cardinal and intermediary directions with gopuras ornamented with varied decorations, numerous, auspicious, full of precious stones, surrounded by twenty-eight compounds of diverse shapes, with main and secondary gates, diversified in intermediary directions."

In this connection, attention may be drawn to the fact that Nandin was posted as the guardian at the entrance of the temple. This practice continues even to this day, as Nandin is installed at the entrance of every temple of Śiva. Wood and bricks are mentioned as the materials

---

[352] See Appendix 6, pp. 806 ff.

[353] At the end of the description of Kailāsa, the temple of Śiva is mentioned. *Liṅga P.*, I.51.

[354] *Liṅga P.*, I.80.23-26.

commonly used for the construction of the temples.[355] The *Liṅga Purāṇa* also speaks of various styles of temple structures, such as *drāviḍa, nāgara* and *Vesāra*.[356] Reference to *kūṭa* and *maṇḍapa* is significant. The building of temples is encouraged by the assurances of merits accruing therefrom. The builder of a temple is accorded a very high place in the next world.[357] Even children who make *liṅgas* of Śiva and worship them are said to attain Rudraloka. The *Liṅga Purāṇa* further enumerates the various mountain abodes of Śiva, which, in all probability, served as models for various types of temples of Śiva in later times. Among those mountain-abodes are mentioned Kailāsa, Mandara, Meru, Niṣada, Nīlādri, Śikhara and Mahendra-Śaila.

The proper maintenance of a temple is said to bring greater merit than its very erection. The fact that the repairer of the temple excels the builder is duly emphasized. It has been suggested that if one cannot afford to build a temple oneself, one should at least seek employment where the construction of a temple is in progress. Similarly, immense merit is said to accrue even from the mere keeping of a temple clean. The *Purāṇas* speak of the merit derived by people performing various services for the temples. The highest place among these, of course, is assigned to worship in temples, which is proclaimed as being superior to the sacrifices like the *aśvamedha*.[358]

---

[355] See K.V. Vaze, "Construction of Hindu Temples", *ABORI*, vol. VIII, p. 206 for an account of Hindu writers on temple architecture: "It is significant to point out nowhere in the *Āgamas* and the allied texts the episodes relating to the separate *mūrtis* are described. The *Purāṇas* alone seem to have done this."

[356] *Liṅga Purāṇa*, I.77. P.K. Acharya explains the three styles as follows: "A building must belong to one of the three main styles called *nāgara* or northern, *Vesara* or Eastern, and *Drāvida* or Southern. The northern style is distinguished by its quadrangular shape. The Eastern style of temple is marked by its round shape from the neck upwards. In the Southern style the upper portion of buildings from the neck is octagonal". P.K. Acharya, "The Origin of Hindu Temple", *IC*, vol. I, p. 93. For further information about the Southern style of the Hindu Temple, see Zimmer, *Art of India and Asia*, pp. 278-287.

[357] *Tasmāt sarvaprayatnena bhaktyā bhaktaiḥ śivālayam |*
Kartavyaṁ sarvayatnena dharmakāmārthasiddhaye ||
Liṅga P., I.77.6.

[358] *Liṅga P.*, I.77.55.

However, the paucity of references to images and temples in the Epics and the *Purāṇas* cannot be gainsaid. All that can be said about these texts with some amount of certainty is that they prepared the way for such worship which became an established fact soon after.

Chapter VI

Forms of Śaiva Worship and Ritual in the South

It has been shown in the previous chapter that the *Purāṇas* constitute, to a large extent, the basis of the iconolatry which is widely prevalent as an essential characteristic of the Āgamic Śaivism of the South. The present chapter, which forms a continuation of the study of the same characteristics of Āgamic Śaivism, seeks to investigate another important aspect, the rites and religious practices associated with these images. This investigation will reveal the fact that this new form of Śiva worship did not by any means emerge suddenly, but that it was the outcome of a long and gradual development. It would become evident that it had been influenced in no small measure by the old Vedic traditions which had continued to be held in high veneration. Of course, the introduction into a new context of the image cult — which, incidentally, was foreign to Vedic religion — did imply the need for the invention of new rites which would be more suitable for the worship of these images. Most of these rites can, accordingly, be shown to not belong to the Vedic ritual traditions,[1] yet the influence

---

[1] By comparisons and contrasts, in his *History of the Tamils* P.T.S. Aiyangar has revealed the special characteristics of the *Āgamas* (pp. 104-106). In this connection he points out that "the essence of the Vaidika rites is the pouring of oblations, but of the Āgamika one is *upacāra*, washing, decking and feeding the god, in fact, showing him all the attentions due to a human guest, or a human king. Hence in the Vaidika rite no physical representation or representative of the deity worshipped was necessary, visible fire representing all the gods; in the Āgamika rites the only deity worshipped had to be represented by some visible emblem, the emblem being ... a *liṅga*, a *sālagrāma*, or above all a picture or statue of the deity in brick or mortar, stone or metal made in shape assigned to him by his worshippers." P. 106.

While commenting on the relative importance of the *Vedas* and the *Āgamas*,

of the latter on the system of the Śaiva rituals (with which we are immediately concerned) becomes manifest in several ways. A brief survey of Vedic ritualism is therefore expected to provide a suitable background for the present investigation. This survey may be followed by a study of the forms of worship which had evolved in the Epics and the *Purāṇas*, as these texts form a connecting link between the earlier and the later system of Śiva worship. It is significant that such features of the Purāṇic religious practices as *tapas*, *tīrtha*, *dhyāna*, *vrata*, and *stotra*, which were unknown to the Vedic system of worship, played an intrinsic rule in the later system of worship. However, as pointed out above, one can ill-afford to ignore the tremendous influence which Vedic religion has exercised on almost all the Hindu religious cults of the later period.

To begin with, attention may be drawn to the fact that the Vedic literature has served as a veritable repository of religious materials from which the new religious systems of the Epic and the Purāṇic period drew liberally. Vedic *mantras* are usually employed for repetition during the performance of Āgamic rituals.[2] In this regard, a

---

Radhakrishnan says, "The only real books are the *Vedas* and the *Śaiva Āgamas* ... Of them, the *Vedas* are general and given out for all. The *Āgamas* are special and revealed for the benefit of the blessed, and they contain the essential truth of the Vedānta. Both are said to be given out by god." Radhakrishnan, *Indian Philosophy*, vol. II, p. 723.

[2] Cf. *Atha vā brāhmaṇān viprān śivakumbhasamanvitān* |
Rudrasaṅkhyān samāhūya ardhamaṇḍapasaṁsthitān ||
Japet saṁkalpapūjāṁ ca ekādaśaparāyaṇam |
...
Rudrapārāyaṇānte ca punaḥ punar nivedayet |
Kāraṇa, I.42.8-11.

"Or after calling learned brāhmaṇas..., eleven in number, standing in the *ardhamaṇḍapa*, one should do the recitation of announcement of the worship and the recitation by the eleven reciters... At the end of recitation of the Rudra hymns, one should again perform offerings."

And: *Vyāhṛtyāhutikaṁ kāryam pratidravyaṁ punaḥ punaḥ* |
...
Brahmajajñānamantreṇa hutvā brahmaśilāṁ spṛśet |
Ibid., I.59.150-2.

"An offering should be done of each substance again and again with a *vyāhṛti*... After offerings with *mantras* from the *Veda* one should touch the *brahmaśilā*."

special reference may be made to chapter 65 of the *Pūrva-kāraṇa*, entitled *Mantradravyahomavidhi-paṭala*,[3] which contains Āgamic injunctions prescribing the employment of various Vedic *mantras* at the offering of the *homadravyas*. Similarly, many of the elements of Vedic sacrifice can be shown to have become essential constituents of later Śaiva ritualism. Among these may be mentioned the use of the *vedi* and the *agni-kuṇḍas* and the employment of the three *agnis* *āhavanīya*, *gārhapatya* and *dakṣiṇāgni*, to which a few more can be added. The production of *agni* from the *araṇis* and the several types of officiating priests (*ṛtviks*) are other important features of the Vedic sacrificial tradition which are retained in Āgamic ritual. In almost all these cases, the *ācārya* or the *guru* performs the rituals on behalf of the *yajamāna*, as does the *adhvaryu* in the case of the Vedic *yajña*.

A reference may be made at this stage to the view that the origin of the Epic and Purāṇic religion, especially of the Śaivism of these texts, was to be traced to the pre-Vedic period. This view, though highly plausible, may not be given serious consideration here because no positive evidence can be adduced in support of it. For one thing, enough material has not been forthcoming which might throw light on the ritualism of the Mohenjodaro period.[4] As has been pointed out

---

And: *Śaṅkhadundubhinādaiśca gītanṛttasamāyutam |*
Brahmaghoṣasamāyuktaṁ nānābhaktisamanvitam |
Ibid., I. 59.196.

"To the accompaniment of songs and dance with the sound of the conch and large drum, joined to the recitation of *Veda*, full of devotion...."

For the employment of Vedic *mantras* in non-Vedic rituals, see *Agni P.*, 56.18-31, and also *ibid.*, 96.37-41.

3 *Kāraṇa*, I, p. 373.
Cf. "The *Āgamas* and the *Tantras* amplify the teaching of the *Vedas* by giving us new *mantras* and rituals and by clarifying and amplifying and systematizing the philosophic thought containted in the *Vedas*." Ramaswamy Sastri, "The Āgamic Advance on Vedic Thought", *Kunhan Rajah Presentation Volume*, p. 75.

4 Attempts have, however, been made to expound upon the ritual system of Mohenjodaro, but these are not at all convincing. They are characterized by a lack of factual and direct evidence from the Mohenjodaro finds. Among such attempts, those made by A.P. Karmarkar in his *The Religions of India* are noteworthy. The author discusses in this work the main offshoots of the religion which he calls the

elsewhere, even the religious character of the various objects unearthed in the Indus Valley is under dispute. Under such circumstances, how could one speak of the rituals of the period? Most of the views expressed so far about the religion of the Indus Valley are at best speculative. Karmarkar, who follows on the foot-steps of Father Heras, asserts that the new elements in the Epic and Purāṇic rituals which are completely absent in the Vedic counterpart can only be explained away as being foreign to the Aryan tradition, and therefore Dravidian in character. The civilization of Mohenjodaro is, according to Karmarkar, essentially Dravidian. He therefore argues that the Mohenjodaro religion must be assumed to have been the source of the religion of the Epics and the *Purāṇas*, which are therefore also Dravidian in character.[5] Otherwise, he asks, how is one to explain the sudden appearance of these elements in the Epic and the Purāṇic periods? According to Karmarkar, the religion of the Epics and the *Purāṇas* is therefore nothing but the continuation of the religion of Mohenjodaro. He further asserts that the Epics and the *Purāṇas* must be regarded as essentially containing the statement of the Dravidian religion recorded in the Sanskrit language.[6] It is, indeed, difficult to persuade oneself either to accept or to reject these views completely. All that one can say about them is that the materials so far made

---

Vrātya religion (Dravidian?), and he even speaks of a philosophy propounded in the Indus Valley period. The author claims to have done, in this work, a detailed survey of the Mohenjodaro inscriptions and other finds, the original of some twenty *Purāṇas*, *Upa-Purāṇas*, the Vedic, Brāhmaṇic, Upaniṣadic, Epic, Tantric and other allied literature. The author is of opinion that the *Purāṇas* contain the history of man from the early beginnings of history down to about the 14th century AD. With a view to establishing this, he fabricates an ingenious theory that the Epics and the *Purāṇas* reflect a tradition which is merely a continuation of that of the Mohenjodaro period.

5 "But the relics found on the proto-Indian site have really thrown a wonderful light on the history of the pre-Aryan gods, temples and ritual. In fact, it can be emphatically stated that the Mohenjodarians had an independent religious cult of their own, which was generally called *anyavrata* by the Vedic bards. It is really from this that the later systems of rituals must have drawn inspiration". Karmarkar, *The Religions of India*, vol. I, p. 195.

6 Karmarkar, *op.cit.*, pp. 29 f; also p. 35.

available in connection with the Mohenjodaro civilization do not warrant any definite statement regarding the religious practices of that period. One cannot be sure of any hypothesis in that regard until the Mohenjodaro seals are satisfactorily deciphered. On the other hand, the *Veda* can definitely be shown to have chronologically preceded the Epics and the *Purāṇas*. What may therefore be assumed to follow logically from this circumstance is that the Vedic religion must have influenced the religion of the Epics and the *Purāṇas*. Accordingly, in the present chapter, a large part of which is devoted to the study of the rituals of Āgamic Śaivism, an attempt is made to present a connected picture of the ritual traditions, particularly of the Epic and Purāṇic rites and their continuation in the Āgamic Śaiva religion, taking into account the Vedic influences incidentally.

Inasmuch as the ritualism in the Vedic period is concerned, we may begin by pointing out that, contrary to the usual assumption, even the *Ṛgveda* reflects a fairly well-developed ritual tradition which varies between the simplest offerings of oblations like ghee and honey and its advanced forms like the sacrifices. Sacrificial accessories like the *vedi*, ladles, pressing stones, ox-hides, and *yūpa* are mentioned at various places in the *Veda*.[7] Instances may also be cited of the occurrences of the names of such officiating priests as *potṛ*, *praśastṛ*, *neṣṭṛ*, and even *brahman*, though the functions ascribed to these priests are not quite distinct.[8] However, it may be safely asserted that the religion of the *Ṛgveda* was for the most part a religion of prayer and invocation which was on its way in its development into a religion of sacrifice. This latter religion attained further elaboration only in the *Yajurveda* and the *Brāhmaṇas*. The *Ṛgveda* mostly reveals a simple form of worship which may be characterized as a precursor of all subsequent forms of complex rituals. The poet-priest of the *Ṛgveda* composed songs and devoutly offered them as his humble offering.[9]

---

7 See Potdar, *Sacrifice in the Ṛgveda*, pp. 63-94.

8 *Ibid.*, pp. 163-168.

9 *ṚV*, I.31.6; I.154.3; II.29.8; II.41.18; IV.3.3; IV.6.1; IV.16.2; V.11.3; VI.5.6; VI.38.4.

The poet is even said to have taken the care to shape his songs in such a way as would make these songs worthy of being offered to the divinity.[10] Incidentally, it may be pointed out that references are also not wanting to bowing down before the gods while paying obeisance to them.[11]

As indicated above, the *Yajurveda* represents the next stage in the development of ritual. This *Veda* mainly contains a detailed description of the sacrificial rites which had grown highly complex in the meantime, interspersed with endless discussions. One sees in this *Veda* a forerunner of the *Brāhmaṇas*. The Ṛgvedic *mantras* repeated in this *Saṁhitā* are adapted to some or another aspect of the sacrificial ritual. These sacrificial ceremonies, as well as the *yajus* formulas employed in connection with them, were designed not so much to serve the purpose of worshipping the gods in the sense in which we understand the word 'worship' today, but rather to magically influence the gods and to induce them to grant the desires of the performer of the sacrifice. However, the *Yajurveda* may be also said to have initiated a religious practice which has a special relevance to the subject matter of this chapter and which has continued to exercise its influence up to the present times. This practice consists of enumerating within a single homogeneous text the various names and epithets of the same god. The *Śatarudriya* [12] in this manner enumerates the many epithets of Rudra. In this regard it may be mentioned that in the temples of the South where Āgamic traditions prevail the god is propitiated with a religious rite (*arcanā*) in which flowers are offered accompanied by a recital of the various names of the god. As has been already pointed out, this practice is already referred to in the *Purāṇas*. In one *Purāṇa*,[13] for instance, Viṣṇu is said to have performed an *arcanā* of Śiva with an offering of one thousand flowers, each flower being offered accompanying the utterance of one separate

---

[10] *ṚV*, VII.86.8; also I.143.7 and VII.28.1-2.

[11] Cf. *ṚV*, I.67.3; II.23.13; III.1.2; IV.5.11; V.1.12; VII.2.4; VIII.19.5; IX.11.6; X.31.12.

[12] *TS*, IV.5.1.

[13] *Liṅga P.*, I.98.

name. The origin of the *arcanā* can be definitely traced back to the *Śatarudriya* in which, as in the *arcanā* formulas, the names of the god are enumerated in the dative case, each name being followed by the word *namas*. Several such collections of names and epithets attributed to Śiva, such as the *Śivasahasranāma* and the *Śivāṣṭotta-raśatanāma*, have come down to us. Some of them have originally formed parts of the *Purāṇas* and the *Mahābhārata*.[14] Also written are similar collections of names of all the ancillary deities of Śaivism, such as Gaṇeśa, Kārttikeya and Devī.[15] It may be pointed out that the repetitions of these names in the dative case with the word *namas* affixed to each of them, as in the *Śatarudriya*, may be spoken of as a ritual tradition which had been more particularly developed in the South. Another significant contribution to the Śaiva ritual tradition made by the *Yajurveda* consists of the various *mantras* and the mystic syllables which, along with several others modeled on them, were often employed in the rituals of Śaivism. Among such terms of mystic import may be mentioned *svāhā* and *svadhā* which also occur in the *Ṛgveda*, and *vaṣat*, *veṭ*, *vaṭ* and, above all, the most important *Oṁ*.[16] The *vyāhṛtis bhūḥ*, *bhuvaḥ*, and *suvaḥ* also belong to the same category. Modelled on these are the syllables *haṁ*, *hāṁ* and *hauṁ*

---

14 *Mahābhārata*, XIII.17.1-182; *Śiva P.*, *Jñāna-saṁhitā*, 1-132; *Brahmāṇḍa P.*, I.38; *Liṅga P.*, I.65.48 ff; *Vāyu P.*, I.30.180-284. One thousand names of Umā are enumerated in *Kūrma P.*, I.12.61-199.

15 The following are some of the most important post-Purānic *sahasranāmas*. (These are contained in the *Bṛhatstotraratnākaraṁ* edited in two volumes by the Nirnaya Sagar press, Bombay, 1952) *Gaṇeśasahasranāmastotraṁ* (p. 34), *Śivāṣṭottaranāma-stotram* (p. 189), *Subrahmaṇyāṣṭottaraśatanāmastotram* (p. 351), *Lalitāsahasra-nāmastotram* (p. 351) and so on. The latter, according to the popular version, forms part of the *Brahmāṇḍa Purāṇa*. The colophon of the *sahasranāma* as given in the popular version (e.g. *Bṛhatstotraratnākara*, p. 372) reads: *Itī śrībrahmāṇḍapurāṇe Lalitopākhyāne Hayagrīvāgastyasaṁvāde lalitāsahasranāmastotraṁ saṁpūrṇam*. The Bombay edition of the *Brahmāṇḍa Purāṇa*, however, does not give this *sahasranāma*.

16 Winternitz, *HIL*, vol. I, p. 185.

17 Most probably this '*hrīṁ*' is taken from the *pañcadaśākṣarī*, consisting of fifteen syllables (in some cases sixteen) held sacred to the goddess.

relating to Śiva, *gaṁ* to *Gaṇeśa*, *śaṁ* to *Śaravaṇabhava* or *Kārttikeya* and *hrīṁ* to Devī.[17] Every time the divinities are invoked, their respective mystic syllables, the *bījākṣaras*, are prefixed to the *mantras*.

An analysis of the contents of the *Atharvaveda* would indicate the close connections this *Saṁhitā* has with the ritual cult. The hymns and the *mantras* of the *Atharvaveda* are related to one rite or another, though not necessarily sacrificial in character. As a matter of fact, most of these rites are outside the pale of orthodoxy.[18] In them, one sees a kind of blending of magic and ritual — a mix which has an important bearing on the Śaiva ritual practices in the later times.

The contribution of the *Brāhmaṇas* to the ritual cult is immense, and naturally so, for these texts have ritual as their sole concern. The term *Brāhmaṇa* itself implies a collection of pronouncements and discussions by the priests regarding the theory and practice of sacrifice. The various sacrifices, big and small, mentioned in the *Saṁhitās* of the *Kṛṣṇa* and the *Śukla Yajurveda* are again dealt with in this literature in a more elaborate manner. The change in the religious outlook and practices registered in the *Brāhmaṇas* becomes soon evident. For instance, the importance of the gods of the *Ṛgveda*, who had continued to wield power for a long time, now began to definitely dwindle. In the *Brāhmaṇas*, these gods became merely subservient to sacrifice. Indeed, it was to sacrifice itself that they are indebted for their very existence and power.[19] The repercussions of this Brāhmaṇic phenomenon of the act of worship dominating and superseding the very divinity to be worshipped on the later forms of worship cannot be said to have been inconsequential.

The *Āraṇyakas* mark the transition from the ritual cult of the *Brāhmaṇas* to the spiritual tendencies which reached their climax in

---

[18] Winternitz, *HIL*, vol. I, p. 126. The invocations and incantations found in this *Veda* are used both to bring prosperity to the performer *(śānta*, *pauṣṭika*, *bhaiṣaja*) as also to cause calamity to his enemy (*abhicāra*, *ghora*, *yātu*). At the same time this *Saṁhitā* contains hymns and *mantras* intended for sacrificial purposes as well. These were included in this *Saṁhitā* presumably with a view to secure for it a connection with orthodoxy and recognition as the fourth *Veda*.

[19] Cf. Winternitz, *HIL*, vol. I, p. 196.

the Upaniṣadic and the Buddhist periods.[20] It is true that the *Āraṇyakas* do not dilate as the *Brāhmaṇas* do upon the rules relating to the performance of the sacrifice, nor do they undertake to expound the various details of the sacrificial procedure. Neither have they repudiated sacrifice altogether; they speak of it in mystic and philosophical terms. In other words, they preach a new doctrine of the symbolism of sacrifice.[21] In the *Āraṇyakas*, one sees the transition from the physical to the psychological plane in the matter of performing sacrifices. The *Upaniṣads* go still further. They advocate a higher path, the path of pure knowledge. Ritualism now begins to recede to the background. Passages discouraging or, in some cases, even denouncing sacrificial practices are not rare in the *Upaniṣads*.[22] These texts neither indulge in the mythological glorification of the gods of the *Ṛgveda*, nor occupy themselves with the elaboration of the sacrificial ritual which is represented in all its complex details in the *Brāhmaṇas*.[23]

On the whole, sacrificial ritual in one form or another may be said to have been the center of Vedic religion. In most of its forms, the offerings made to the gods were assigned the greatest importance.

---

[20] While the *Muṅḍaka-Upaniṣad* says, *plavāhyete adṛḍhāḥ yajñarūpāḥ* (I.2.7), the Buddhist texts totally denounce the sacrificial systems: for instance, according to *Dhammapada*, Vagga 8, verses 7-9, the worship of an Arhat is better than sacrifice.

[21] Reference may be made to the sacrifice performed by the king of Kosala and the Buddha's discourse on it. Purification by water is meaningless. This idea is emphasized in the *Saṁyuttanikāya*, 9th sutta. The Puṇyatīrthas are condemned in the *Majjhimanikāya*, 1.7.

The Buddhist attitude towards sacrifice is expressed in the *Dīghanikāya* also (I.st.Vagga Kūṭadanta sutta).

[22] Cf. Deussen, *The Philosophy of the Upaniṣads*, p. 2 ff and also 120. "The older *Upaniṣads* were so deeply conscious of the hostile character of the entire ritualistic systems of the *Brāhmaṇas* that they could concede to it only a relative recognition. It is true that direct attacks are rarely found in the extant texts. Antagonistic explanations, however, of the sacrificial rites are all the more frequently offered by way either of allegorical interpretation or the substitution of other and usually psychological ideas in their place." Deussen, *The Philosophy of the Upaniṣads*, p. 62.

[23] It must, however, be pointed out that a few *Upaniṣads* share the characteristics of the *Brāhmaṇas*.

Even within the *gṛhya* rites this peculiarity was evident, though on a smaller scale. Quite a rich variety of *śrauta* and *gṛhya* rituals had evolved during the Vedic period, and for a time they more or less completely eclipsed the other forms of worship. As indicated elsewhere, in these rituals the form of worship dominated over the spirit of worship. The religion of the Epics and the *Purāṇas*, on the other hand, was essentially composite in form and eclectic in spirit. While not discouraging the *yajñas* of the Vedic model, it adopted and actively sponsored various other forms of worship, some of which had formerly been in vogue in the pre-Vedic non-Aryan period, while some others had been developed by the popular tribal religious cults. Among these may be prominently mentioned *tapas*, the cult of the *tīrthas*, the *stotras* or the worship of the gods by means of the utterances of praise hymns, *dhyāna* or meditation on the gods, the observance of *vratas* in honour of the gods, and the *pūjā*, which soon became the most popular mode of propitiation. These non-Vedic ways of propitiation and worship were presumably adopted and sponsored on account of the pressure of circumstances. The center of religious interest now shifted from the Vedic gods and the sacrifices offered to them to the trinity of the Hindu gods and the various new modes of worshipping them.

It would be before this background and on the basis of the materials derived from the Epics and the *Purāṇas* that we might now undertake a brief study of these new modes of worship, namely *yajña*, *tapas*, *tīrthas*, *stotras*, *dhyāna*, *vrata* and *pūjā*, particularly inasmuch as they relate to Śaivism.

1. Yajña

Throughout the history of Hindu religion, the *Vedas* have always been held in high veneration, and their ultimate authority has been unanimously recognised by all the orthodox schools of thought.[24] The high regard for the *Vedas* and the respect that was generally shown

[24] Excepting the Buddhists, the Jains and the Cārvākas, all the other schools of thought, both religious and philosophical, regard the *Vedas* with high veneration. In later religious sects, in an enthusiasm to glorify *bhakti*, the *Vedas* are much belittled.

to the *śrotriyas* who were proficient in them was reflected in the Epics and the *Purāṇas*,[25] though in the latter works such regard and respect become less marked. As a matter of fact, this Epic tendency to afford a high place to the brāhmaṇas (who were characterized as the veritable gods on earth),[26] especially those well-versed in the *Vedas*, may be said to have continued even to this day. There is therefore no wonder that the *yajñas* continued to be performed even in the Epic and Purāṇic periods.[27] Nevertheless there are clear indications in the Epics and the *Purāṇas*, particularly in the latter, that conditions were then becoming less propitious for sacrifice and that the Vedic ritual traditions were steadily losing their hold on the minds of the people.[28]

As for the continuation of the sacrificial tradition in the Epics and the *Purāṇas*, two distinct places of that tradition may be indicated. One of these relates to the performance of sacrifices prescribed by the *Veda* and systematized by the *śrauta* texts. Prominent among the *śrauta-yajñas* mentioned in the Epics and the *Purāṇas* are the *vājapeya*, the *rājasūya*, the *aśvamedha* and the *sautrāmaṇi*.[29] The

---

[25] Cf. *Vācayitvā dvijaśreṣṭhān dadhipātraghṛtākṣaṭaiḥ* |
Niṣkair gobhir hiraṇyena vacobhiś ca mahādhanaiḥ ||
Vardhamānā jayāśīrbhiḥ sūtamāgadha vandibhiḥ |
MBh, VIII.1.11-12.
Iṣṭaṁ me bahubhir yajñaiḥ dattā vipreṣu dakṣiṇāḥ | *Ibid., IX.5.27.*
Brāhmaṇās tāta loke'sminn arcanīyāḥ sadā mama |
Ete bhūmicarā devā vāgviṣā saprasādakāḥ ||
Ibid., XII.39.38.

"I have offered many sacrifices and given *dakṣinās* to brahmins. Brahmins should always be honoured by me in this world. They are gods moving on earth; they have a speech harsh like poison or a favourable mind."

[26] *Brāhmaṇān vācayethās tvaṁ arthasiddhijayāśiṣaḥ* | *MBh*, XII.72.5.

[27] It was, of course, not to be expected that the faith in such a deep-rooted religious institution like sacrifice would be demolished all of a sudden.

[28] The *trimūrti* cult, for instance, presumes the subordination of Indra, Agni and all other Vedic gods, who are afforded high place in the sacrifice.

[29] The *Mahābhārata* contains more specific references to actual performance of sacrifices. King Mahābhiṣa is said to have performed one thousand sacrifices and one hundred *vājapeya* sacrifices and thereby incurred the pleasure of Indra and thus attained *svarga*: *MBh*, I.91.2. The Pāṇḍavas performed the *rajasūya* sacrifice:

importance of sacrifice in general is indicated in the *Mahābhārata* by the mention of the gods having themselves performed sacrifice. In one passage, Brahmā, Rudra and Śakra are described as having been engaged in performing sacrifices in which *dakṣiṇā* was liberally distributed.[30] Indra is said to have attained Indrahood and excelled all other gods by performing various sacrifices. Similarly, Mahādeva, who had offered himself as an oblation in a *sarvamedha*, had his glory spread out in all the worlds.[31] In the Epics and the *Purāṇas*, sacrifices are described to have been performed by kings as well as,

---

Ibid., I.1.84-85. Bharata performed many sacrifices, and in this respect he is said to have resembled Indra: *Ibid.*, 1.69.7. Other references to sacrifices are: *ibid.*, I.48.4-10; III.187.8-9; III.121.1-8; III.27.14 and so on.

Frequent are the references that are found to the (Vedic) sacrifice performed by Dakṣa, and in it Śiva was refused his share. For references see Chapter V under Vīrabhadra. Among the many references to the Aśvamedha, the following may be cited: *Padma P., Pātāla khaṇḍa*, 44; *Brahma P.*, II.57; *Liṅga P.*, II.1.6-7. The following quotations indicate how the sacrifices in vogue during the Purāṇic period had a strong rival in the *liṅga*-form of worship:

Pade pade yajñaphalaṁ sa prāpnoti na saṁśayah | Vāmana P., 46.17.
Liṅgasya darśanādeva agniṣṭomaphalaṁ labhet | Ibid.,46.33.
Smaraṇaṁ pūjanaṁ caiva praṇāmo bhaktipūrvakam |
Pratyekam aśvamedhasya yajñasya samam ucyate ||
Liṅga P., II.1.6-7.
Sautrāmaṇeśca yajñasya phalaṁ prapnoti mānavah | Matsya P., 183.75.
Vājapeyaśatair iṣṭvā yallabheta dvijottamaḥ |
Vipro liṅgatrirātreṣu madbhaktyā tadaśnute ||
Aśvamedhasahasraiś ca samyag iṣṭvā ca yat phalam |
Māsena tad avāpnoti ...
Śiva P., Sanatkumāra-saṁhitā, 14.48-62.

[30] *Tatra brahmā ca rudraś ca sakraś cāpi sureśvaraḥ |*
Sametya vividhaiḥ yajñaiḥ yajante'nekadakṣinaiḥ ||
MBh, VI.7.17.

[31] *Yajñair indro vividhair annavadbhir*
Devān sarvān abhyayān mahaujāḥ |
Tenendratvaṁ prāpya vibhrājate'sau
Tasmād yajñe sarvamevopayojyam ||
Mahādevaḥ sarvamedhe mahātmā
Hutvātmānaṁ devadevo vibhūtaḥ |
Viśvān lokān vyāpya viṣṭabhya kīrtyā
Virocate dyutimān kṛttivāsāḥ ||
MBh, XII.20.11-2.

rarely, by sages.[32] Such sacrifices, however, soon receded into the background, because the new religious atmosphere created by the Epics and the *Purāṇas* was not conducive to their further continuation.

The other phase represents a tradition of the Vedic sacrifice itself, which was considerably altered and adapted to suit the new conditions.[33] This modified sacrificial system has a special relevance to our study. The *Purāṇas* often refer to the sacrifice performed by Dakṣa.[34] In the normal Vedic sacrifices, Rudra was given a rather odd treatment. The god, who was regarded as not belonging to the hierarchical Vedic pantheon, did not receive any share in the regular sacrificial oblations.[35] Even later, all that he got was the remnants of the oblations. In the post-Vedic period, however, the conditions had changed drastically and Rudra, or rather Śiva, had become a powerful member of the trinity and could no longer be denied his due share of

---

[32] *Tena yajñair bahuvidhair iṣṭaṁ paryāptadakṣiṇaiḥ |*
Sa rājā vīryavān dhīmān avāpya vasu puṣkalam ||
MBh, VII.58.3.

Śibi, a regular performer of sacrifice, was favoured by Rudra. *MBh*, VII.58.12-15.

[33] Ramaswamy Sastri, in his paper entitled "The Āgamic advance on Vedic Thought", draws our attention to the fact that "Very few of the Vedic sacrifices have survived, though abundant lip homage is paid to them. They have been sublimated and transcended by Āgamic rituals, and sacrifices and other *sādhanās*". See *Kunhan Raja Presentation Volume*, p. 77.

[34] *MBh*, X.18.1-26, also XIII.160; *Brahma P.*, I.32, also 37; *Brahmāṇḍa P.*, I.13; *Bhāgavata P.*, IV.5; *Garuḍa P.*, I.5.35-38; *Harivaṁśa* III.32; *Kālikā P.*, 17; *Kūrma P.*, I.14 and 15; *Liṅga P.*, I.96 and 100; *Śiva P.*, *Jñāna-saṁhitā*, 7; *ibid.*, *Vāyu-Saṁhitā*, 15-20; *Skanda P.*, I.3 and 4; *Vāmana P.*, 5; *Varāha P.*, 21; *Vāyu P.*, I.30.

[35] Cf. Dandekar, "Rudra in the *Veda*", *JUPH*, 1, pp. 97. This treatment which is reflected in the references given in the previous footnote, is clearly recorded in the following verses:

Yasmāt tvaṁ matkṛte'niṣṭam ṛṣīṇāṁ kṛtavānasi |
Tasmāt sārdhaṁ surair yajñe na tvāṁ yakṣyanti vai dvijāḥ ||
Hutvāhutiṁ tava krūra hyāpaḥ sprakṣyanti karmasu |
Brahmāṇḍa P., II.3.73.

"Because you have committed an undesired gesture to me and the sages, the Brahmins will not offer you an oblation with other gods in sacrifices. After doing an oblation to you, they will touch water in rituals."

In this connection also see chapter II. Pp. 93-94.

the sacrifice. In the *Purāṇas* one reads detailed accounts of the punishments meted out to Dakṣa for having refused Śiva his share.[36] Actually, Dakṣa had invited to his sacrifice all the gods except Śiva, and even these participants were punished by Śiva.[37] Matters were set right only after Brahmā proclaimed that, from that day onwards, Śiva was to be given a prominent share in the sacrifices.[38] Thus we may note the coming into existence of a new sacrificial tradition which differed from the regular Vedic tradition, particularly in respect of the allotment of a share to Rudra-Śiva. The *Mahābhārata* refers to the *yajñas* which were performed in honour of Śiva.[39] King Jarāsandha propitiated Śiva by performing a *yāga* in his honour.[40] One also comes across casual references in the *Rāmāyaṇa* and the *Mahābhārata* to the animals offered to Śiva in sacrifice.[41]

At the same time, passages are not wanting in the *Purāṇas* which seek to minimize the importance of sacrifices by means of such statements saying the propitiation of Śiva by the various methods

---

36 He cursed that Dakṣa be born a mortal. *Garuḍa P.*, I.5.35-38.

37 *Kūrma P.*, I.15.49-80; *Varāha P.*, 21.39-77.

38 *Evam uktvā hariharau tadā lokapitāmahaḥ* |
Brahmā lokān uvācedaṁ rudrabhāgo'sya dīyatām ||
Rudrabhāgo jyeṣṭhabhāga itīyaṁ vaidikī śrutiḥ |
Stutiṁ ca devāḥ kuruta rudrasya parameṣṭhinaḥ ||
Varāha P., 21.66-67.

39 *Sa kathaṁ mānuṣair devaṁ yaṣṭum icchasi śaṅkaram* | *MBh*, II.20. 8-10.

40 *MBh*, II.13.63.

41 While searching for Sītā, Hanumat is said to have grown desperate and to have remarked:
Rāvaṇaṁ vā vadhiṣyāmi daśagrīvaṁ mahābalam |
Kāmam astu hṛtā sītā pratyācīrṇaṁ bhaviṣyati ||
Athavainaṁ samutkṣipya uparyupari sāgarām |
Rāmāyopahariṣyāmi pasuṁ paśupateriva ||
Rām., V.13.49-50.

The *Mahābhārata* refers to the offering of animal-offerings to Rudra:
Atraiva rudro rājendra paśum ādattavān makhe |
Rudraḥ paśuṁ mānavendra bhāgo'yam iti cābravīt ||
Hṛte paśau tadā devās tam ūcur bharatarṣabha |
Mā parasvam abhidrogdhā mā dharmān sakalān naśīḥ ||
MBh, III.114. 7-8.

taught in the *Purāṇas* is far superior to the performance of the Vedic *yajñas*.[42] This may be said to represent the third phase.

It was natural that the *yajña*-tradition should become generally unpopular in the *Purāṇas*, for these texts essentially reflect a religion of the people at large. A Vedic sacrifice was usually unwieldy and was often beyond the reach of the common man. The *Purāṇas*, therefore, sought to cater to his needs by providing alternative modes of worship which would be easily accessible to even the average devotee. It may also be pointed out that, while a Vedic sacrifice held forth the promise of the fruits to be enjoyed only in the life hereafter, most Purāṇic forms of worship were believed to yield results during the course of this life itself. In this regard, a comparison between Vedic *yajña* and Purāṇic *tapas* would prove quite revealing. The *asuras* who practiced *tapas* by subjecting their bodies to severe mortification are described to have derived the relevant benefits and to have lived long to enjoy the superiority which they gained over the *devas*.[43] In the *Purāṇas* one often reads of the *asuras*, who through their *tapas* secured boons from the gods and who, on the strength of these boons, often had those very gods at their mercy. It has to be noted that wherever the practicing of *tapas* is mentioned in the *Purāṇas*, the almost immediate securing of its benefits is also invariably mentioned. This cannot be said to be the case with sacrifice. And if *tapas* was found difficult to practice, there were also other easier but equally efficacious ways of winning the favour of the god. Reference may be made to another significant point, that while *yajña* concerned itself with several gods at a time, the new modes of worship such as *tapas*, *dhyāna* and *pūjā* usually centred around one single god who usually happened to be one of the trinity.[44] As may be easily imagined, this feature of the new worship considerably enhanced its 'effectivity'.

---

[42] *Vārāṇasījāhnavībhyāṁ saṁgame lokaviśrute |*
Upavāsaṁ tu yaḥ kṛtvā viprān santarpayennaraḥ ||
Sautrāmaṇesca yajṅasya phalaṁ prāpnoti mānavaḥ | *Matsya P.*, 183.73-75.

[43] The *asuras* became the rulers of the three cities which were given to them by the god, and they lived long to enjoy the results of their achievements.

[44] The ultimate withdrawal of Brahmā from the sphere left only Śiva and Viṣṇu to share this high honour.

2. Tapas

The word *tapas* is of very early occurrence. Even in the *Ṛgveda*, for instance, the seven *ṛṣis* are referred to as together betaking themselves to the practice of *tapas*.[45] Again, in one of the later hymns of the *Ṛgveda*, Truth, Righteousness, and with them the entire universe are said to be born of *tapas*.[46] In the well-known *Nāsadīyasūkta*,[47] *tapas* is also shown to be playing an important role in the matter of the creation of the universe. According to the *Atharvaveda*, the first born *skambha* arose out of *śrama* and *tapas* and permeated the universe.[48] We are further told in that *Veda* that it is through the *tapas* with which he discharges his duties that the *brahmacārin* satisfies his teacher, the gods, and the realms of space, he ascends as high as the sun, he protects both the worlds, ands so on.[49]

Two significant facts seem to emerge out of these references to *tapas* in the *Ṛgveda* and the *Atharvaveda*. Firstly, the very small number of references to *tapas* (particularly in comparison with those to sacrifice) occurring in the Vedic *Saṁhitās* would show that the practice of *tapas* was not widespread in the Vedic period. At the same time, the connection with the cults of *munis* and *brahmacārins* clearly suggests the very important role which *tapas* must have played in the pre-Vedic non-Aryan religious ideology.[50] It may be presumed that the pre-Vedic non-Aryan practice of *tapas* was temporarily suppressed in the Vedic period but that it again assumed great importance when the Brāhmanism of the *Veda* was superseded by the popular Hinduism of the Epics and the *Purāṇas*. Indeed, the traces of this revival of *tapas* can be seen even in some *Brāhmaṇas* and *Upaniṣads*. It is, however, in the Epics and subsequently in the *Purāṇas* that *tapas* may be understood to clearly denote a mode of propitiating a god with a view to winning his favour. One endowed with qualities derived from austerities is called a *tapasvin* and the

45 *ṚV*, X.109.4. 46 *Ibid.*, X.109.1. 47 *Ibid.*, X.129.

48 *AV*, X.7.38. 49 *Ibid.*, XI.5.

50 Cf. Dandekar, "Rudra in the *Veda*", *JUPH*, no. 1, pp. 99-100.

power acquired by him is *tapobala*. Similarly the excellence of *tapas* is indicated by its being dreadful or by its being practiced with untiring perseverance.

The word *tapas* [51] literally means heat, and the semantic development from heat to ascetic fervour and then to asceticism itself is quite understandable. Indeed, it would appear that despite the term *tapas* representing in later times manifold forms of mortification, heat must have been the most prominent instrument of mortification originally. Another characteristic of *tapas* is its close connection with *yoga*. The discipline of the mind aimed at by *yoga* necessarily presupposes the great austerity on the physical plane implied by *tapas*. Like some schools of yoga, the *tapas* cult of the *Purāṇas* is necessarily centred around a god, usually one of the three. The mortification of the physical body and the subjugation of the senses prevent an undesirable dissipation of energies and thereby provide one's undivided concentration to the god. Self-mortification and concentrated meditation on the deity are the most salient features of *tapas*.[52]

---

[51] For further explanations of the term *tapas* see Bhattacarya's note on *tapas*, *IHQ*, vol. IX., p. 104.

[52] *Brahmacaryaṁ japo maunaṁ nirāhāratvam eva ca* |
Ityetat tapaso mūlaṁ sughoraṁ tad durāsadam ||
Vāyu P., I.59.41.

"Chastity, recitation, vow of silence, fast, that is the base of *tapas*, very harsh and difficult to achieve."

Svastikopaviniṣṭaśca namaskṛtvā maheśvaram |
Samakāyaśirogrīvaṁ dhārayen nāvalokayet ||
Ibid., I.19.35.

"Sitting in *svastika* pose, after paying homage to Maheśvara, one should fix one's mind on one point, keeping straight the body, head and neck; one should not look around."

See also verses 36-40.

Dharmamantrātmako yajñas tapaścānaśanātmakam |
Yajñena devān āpnoti vairāgyaṁ tapasā punaḥ ||
Ibid., I.57.117.

"Sacrifice consists in righteous rites and *mantras*, *tapas* in fast. By sacrifice one reaches the gods, but by *tapas* one achieves dispassionateness."

Tapas is represented in the Epics and the *Purāṇas* as a powerful rival of *yajña*. While in the Epics one still comes across references to *yajña*, the *Purāṇas* do not seem to give any prominence to it. In these latter works, *tapas* is definitely assigned a place higher than that of *yajña*. A statement made by Śiva himself strongly recommends *tapas* as the most efficacious means of propitiating gods in the Kali age:

Tasmāt sarvaprayatnena kalau kuryāt tapo dvijaḥ | [53]

"Therefore, in Kali age, a Brahmin should perform penance by all efforts."

Indra, who as Śatakratu is credited with the accomplishment of a hundred sacrifices, is described in the *Mahābhārata* as having performed his various exploits be means of *tapas*. In another part in the Epic,[54] Bṛhaspati is said to have practiced *tapas* to restore Indra to his former status. The *Mahābhārata* also presents to us the king Nahuṣa, who usurped the office of Indra not through the performance of sacrifices but through *tapas*.[55]

At the same time one reads of a *tapas* which is sometimes mixed up with *yajña*. In the *Mahābhārata*, for instance, we are told that a sage practiced *tapas* for a long time, but that the god did not favour him by manifesting himself. The sage then offered himself as an oblation on the sacrificial fire. When the sage had almost put an end to his life, the god became manifest and granted him his desires.[56] Through their severe *tapas*, the *asuras* propitiated the gods to such an extent that they could obtain from them whatever they wanted, with the exception of immortality. Brahmā refused the demon Tāraka the boon of immortality when the latter asked for it after the god had manifested himself before him at the end of his *tapas*. Brahmā said to the demon:

---

[53] *Vāyu P.*, I.32.36.

[54] *MBh*, V.16.26-27.

[55] *Ibid.*, V.16.22.

[56] *Ibid.*, X.7.54-68.
Rāvaṇa also offers himself on the fire in a similar manner. *Śiva P.*, *Jñāna-saṁhitā*, 55.1-38.

Na yujyate vinā mṛtyuṁ dehino daityasattama |
Yatas tato'pi varaya mṛtyuṁ yasmān na śaṅkase || [57]

"O excellect Daitya, no one who has a body escapes death. Therefore choose a death from a source you do not fear."

Svarga may be generally regarded as the principal goal aimed at by the various kinds of sacrifices, but the goals attainable by *tapas* are almost unlimited. The gods seem to feel compelled to fulfill all the desires of the practitioner of *tapas*, whatever these may be. In a sense, the fructification of both *tapas* and *yajña* is mechanical, for if properly practiced they do not fail to bring the desired fruits. In both these modes of worship, the gods became subservient to the actual procedure of performance as well as to the compelling desires of the performer. In other words, these modes of worship are by no means rooted in devotion, which necessarily implies complete self-surrender of the devotee before the god. Incidentally it may be added that often a god like Brahmā who had been compelled to grant boons later repented for having done so.

It may be presumed that the practice of *tapas* originally developed among the forest-dwellers; subsequently, all those who wanted to practise penance betook themselves to the forest, which was evidently best suited for *tapas*. The Epics and the *Purāṇas* show that it was not only the mortals and the lower generation of gods who would revert to *tapas*, but even the three great gods — Brahmā,[58] Viṣṇu [59]

[57] *Matsya P.*, 148. 22.

[58] Brahmā practiced *tapas* for a long time. This ultimately resulted in the appearance of Rudra to whom Brahmā gave several names (*Kūrma P.*, I.10.20-24). In another passage (*Padma P.*,I.17) we are told that, while Brahmā was practicing penance, Śiva went to him. According to *Kūrma P.*, I.11.1-13, Rudra issued forth in the Ardhanārīśvara form from the mouth of Brahmā, who was living a life of penance. But the more frequent references are found to the *tapas* which Brahmā practiced on the eve of the creation of the universe. Cf. *Liṅga P.*, I.22.18-24.

[59] Viṣṇu practiced *tapas* on the banks of Cakrapuṣkariṇī (*Skanda P.*, IV.1.1.26). Nārāyaṇa, soon after he was born, practiced *tapas*. At the end, Śiva appeared before him and granted him boons. *MBh*, VII.201. *Kūrma P.*, I.24.86. refers to the *tapas* which Hari practiced in honour of Śiva: Cf. *Dṛṣṭvā lebhe sutaṁ rudraṁ taptvā tīvraṁ mahat tapaḥ.*

and Śiva [60] — had occasions to do so. Such references to the three great gods practicing penance are highly significant, for they clearly show that *tapas* was not merely a mode of propitiating some god, but that it possessed an essentially cosmic character. *Tapas* constituted the most prominent force in all cosmic functions like creation and sustenance of the universe. Most of the Vedic references to *tapas*, given alone, would corroborate such a view.

However, usually the three members of the post-Vedic trinity — particularly Śiva and Viṣṇu — were the gods with reference to whom *tapas* was practiced by the aspirants of the Epics and the *Purāṇas*. Among such aspirants are mentioned Indra,[61] Umā,[62] the *asuras* [63]

---

[60] The *svarūpasamādhi* and *tapas* of Śiva are described in *Skanda P.*, I.1.22. Elsewhere we are told that, when Śiva was defeated in a game of dice by Umā, he abandoned Kailāsa and retired to a lonely spot to practise *tapas* (*ibid.*, I.1.34). Similarly according to *Padma P.*, I.5, Śiva, after granting a boon to Dakṣa when the latter prayed to him and repented for his mistakes, retired to the bank of the Gaṅgā and began to practise severe *tapas*. The *Bhāgavata Purāṇa* narrates the following legend: On instructions from Brahmā, Rudra began to create. The former was, however, not satisfied because of the high quality maintained by the latter. He, therefore, asked Rudra to stop creating and exhorted him to perform *tapas* (III.12.4-20). Śiva was for a long time plunged into *mahāmoha*, and enjoyed union with Umā. Consequently he lost his *tejas*. He had to practise *tapas* to regain it (*Vāmana P.*, chapters 59 and 60). *MBh*, XII.278.22-23 speaks of Śiva's feat of practicing *tapas* under water, which Brahmā greatly commended. The following passage from the *MBh* (V.97.12) is particularly significant:

Atha bhūtapatir nāma sarvabhūtamaheśvaraḥ |
Bhūtaye sarvabhūtānām acarat tapa uttamaṁ ||

"Then the Lord of beings, indeed, Great Lord of all beings, performed the extreme *tapas* for the prosperity of all beings."

[61] Indra thrown out of power by Nahuṣa, wondered as to what kind of *tapas* the latter had practiced to attain Indrahood. *MBh*, V.16.22.

[62] After Madana had been burnt to ashes, Pārvatī began to practise *tapas* with a view to winning Śiva as her husband. Brahmā and the other gods were awed at the vehemence of that penance (*Skanda P.*, I.1.21). In another passage in the same *Purāṇa*, one reads that Nārada visited Himavat and advised Pārvatī to practise *tapas* (II.2.25). Elsewhere, Pārvatī is said to have practiced *tapas* in honour of Brahmā so that her complexion would be changed (*ibid.*, I.2.29. 3.2.18). Pārvatī is further said to have retired to Kāñci to practise *tapas* in order to wipe off the sin incurred by covering the sight of Śiva for a moment and thereby plunging the

and the *ṛṣis*,[64] as well as several other persons.[65]

---

universe into darkness, which was crores of years for the beings of the world. (*ibid.*, I.3.1.3). Ākāśavāṇī advised Pārvatī to go to Aruṇācala and there practice *tapas* under the guidance of the sage Gautama. Accordingly, Umā set up a hermitage at Aruṇācala and settled down there to practise *tapas* (*ibid.*, I.3.1.4-9). The *Purāṇa* further narrates that Umā practiced *tapas*, and at that moment, the gods oppressed by the demons Mahiṣa came to solicit her help (*ibid.*, I.3.1.10). According to the *Kālikā Purāṇa*, 45, Kālī practiced *tapas* to win Śiva as her husband. The legend that Pārvatī practiced *tapas* to have her complexion changed because she was mocked by Śiva for being dark-complexioned is also narrated in the *Padma Purāṇa*, I.46. References to the *tapas* practiced by Umā or Pārvatī for one reason or other are: to win Śiva as her husband (*Vāmana P.*, 51); to change her complexion (*Vāmana P.*, 54); to free herself from the stains caused by her being the daughter of Dakṣa (*Varāha P.*, 22); to acquire strength to kill Mahiṣa she retired to Nīlādri and began to practise *tapas* (*Varāha P.*, 90). Umā realized that *tapas* was the only means by which she could win Śiva as her husband (*Matsya P.*, 154.273-300). Umā practiced *tapas* and had her complexion changed (*ibid.*, 155.1-34).

63 Mayāsura oppressed the gods through his *tapobala* (*Garuḍa P.*, I.82.1-6). The three sons of Tāraka practiced *tapas*; as the result of it Brahmā appeared before them and granted them boons (*MBh*, VIII.24). The demon Vṛka is said to have practiced severe *tapas* and to have even gone to the extent of offering his own head into the fire (*Bhāgavata P.*, X.88). According to *Varāha P.*, 27, Andhaka practiced *tapas*, and obtained boons from Brahmā. Rāvaṇa practiced *tapas* and won the favour of Śiva (*Śiva P.*, *Jñāna-saṁhitā*, 55.1-38). The *Liṅga P.* tells us that Jalandhara had obtained power through *tapas*. Śiva would not kill him because he did not like to falsify Brahmā's boons. According to *Matsya Purāṇa*, 129, Maya, Tāraka and Vidyunmāli practiced *tapas*. The *Matsya Purāṇa* (148.4-14) also narrates the legend of Tāraka having practiced *tapas* and obtained the boons.

64 Harikeśa, the only child of his parents, was deeply devoted to Śiva. He, therefore, performed *tapas* in honour of that god (*Skanda P.*, IV.1.1.52). Similarly, Mārkaṇḍeya practised *tapas* and secured longevity (*ibid.*, VI.21). According to *Brahmaṇḍa P.*, 21 and 22.1..1-46), Bhārgava Rāma practiced *tapas* in honour of Śiva and won the god's favour. Atri went to Gokarṇa and practiced *tapas* (*Śiva P.*, *Dharma-saṁhitā*, 2.77-111). Sanatkumāra is also said to have practiced *tapas* (*Kūrma P.*, II.1.16-41).

65 At Vṛddhācala a brāhmaṇa performed *tapas*; Śiva appeared before him and granted him boons (*Skanda P.*, IV.1.1.26). Nārāyaṇa went to Bharadvāja's *āśrama* and practiced *tapas* at Kāśī in honour of Śiva (*Skanda P.*, IV.1.1.16). Śiva appeared before Ambā in response to the *tapas* practiced by her (*MBh*, V.188.7-15). Siddhanātha practiced *tapas* and thereafter he was accepted by Śiva and Umā as their own son. (*Nāradīya P.*, II.69). Śukra practiced *tapas* and obtained from Śiva the *mṛtasañjīvinī mantra* (*Vāmana P.*, 62.39-44). Arundhatī practiced *tapas*, which was highly commended (*MBh*, IX.48.1-68). Asvatthāman practiced *tapas* and obtained a sword from Śiva (*ibid.*, X.7.64-68). Arjuna also is said to have practiced *tapas* and obtained the divine weapon from Śiva (*Śiva P.*, *Jñāna-saṁhitā*, 64). Śilāda practiced *tapas* in honour of Śiva (*Kūrma P.*, II.43.19-42).

The purposes for which *tapas* was practiced were many and varied. The *Purāṇas* often narrate legends of the *asuras* who practiced *tapas*, exhibiting immense physical courage to withstand its severe strains,[66] and in the end acquired sufficient power to suppress the gods and to enjoy supreme sovereignty. Umā is said to have practiced *tapas* in order to propitiate Brahmā so that he might change her complexion.[67] Elsewhere she is said to have practiced penance in order to win Śiva for her husband.[68] Kṛṣṇa practiced *tapas* in honour of Śiva with a view to obtaining a son. Brahmā practiced *tapas* immediately before creation, while Viṣṇu did so in honour of Śiva [69] in order to obtain the *sudarśana cakra*. Śiva himself is described as having practiced *tapas* for the benefit of all beings.[70] The sages are described to have practiced *tapas* for various definite reasons.[71]

The practice of *tapas* is often shown in the Epics and the *Purāṇas* as concluding with the propitiated god manifesting himself before the *tapas* practitioner. Such manifestation depended on the degree of

---

[66] The *tapas* practiced by the three *asuras* Maya, Vidyunmāli, and Tāraka, is described as follows:

Lokatrayaṁ tāpayantas te tepur dānavās tapaḥ |
Hemante jalaśayyāsu grīṣme pañcatape tathā ||
Varṣāsu ca tathākāśe kṣapayantas tanūḥpriyāḥ |
Sevānāḥ phalamūlāni puṣpāṇi ca jalāni ca ||
Anyadācaritāhārāḥ paṅkenācitavalkalāḥ |
Magnāḥ śaivālapaṅkeṣu vimalā vimaleṣu ca ||
Nirmāṁsāśca tato jātāḥ kṛśā dhamanisantatāḥ |
Matsya P., 129.6-10.

"Burning the three worlds, those Dānavas practiced penance, in water during winter, in the midst of five sources of heat in summer, in open space during the rains, wasting their dear bodies, worshipping with fruits, roots, flowers and water, taking food on alternate days, wearing bark garments covered with mud, immersed in the mud of quatic plants, and pure in pure places, they became devoid of flesh, lean with rows of visible veins."

[67] *Matsya P.*, 156.1-39.

[68] *Ibid.*, 154.

[69] *Skanda P.*, IV.1.1.26.

[70] *MBh*, V.97.12. Cf. *Kumārasaṁbhava*, I.57, in which, himself having no desires to be fulfilled, Śiva is said to have commenced *tapas*.

[71] See Supra.

the austerity of the *tapas*. Through *tapas* one could even achieve the *sākṣātkāra* of Śiva.[72] The *siddhas* were noted for their immense capacity for *tapas*. They practiced *ugra tapas*, as a result of which they enjoyed a vision of their god.[73] The *Purāṇas* also often describe that when *tapas* was practiced the fire produced therefrom began to glow and spread its scorching heat everywhere. Indeed, the fire of *tapas* is often described as scorching the beings of the world.[74] The god who was sought by means of *tapas* was, as it were, compelled to appear before the aspirant and fulfil his desires. It is said that the *tapas* which was practiced according to the set rules brought great pleasure to the god. Śiva, for instance, was greatly gratified by the austerities of Kṛṣṇadvaipāyana and so granted him the fulfilment of his desires.[75] As a matter of fact, when Śiva was thus pleased, he unhesitatingly granted boons to the devotees.[76] As for the traditional rules relating to the practice of *tapas* mentioned above, it may be pointed out that apart from the special austerities, certain general conditions have been laid down in different contexts in the Epics and the *Purāṇas*. First of all, such times and environments are to be chosen for the practice of *tapas* that are in no way conducive to the comforts of the practitioner.[77] For instance, during the hot season, *tapas* was practiced with roaring fires all around; during the cold season, it was practiced with the body immersed in ice-cold water up to the knee or the neck. Rough garments made from such materials as tree bark were worn, and food was strictly restricted or was forsaken

---

[72] *MBh*, VI.7.22-25.

[73] *Tam ugratapasaḥ siddhāḥ ... paśyanti*. *MBh*, VI.7.25.

[74] *Lokatraye tāpayantaḥ te tepur dānavās tapaḥ* | *Matsya P.*, 129.7.
Tata udvejitāḥ sarve prāṇinas tattapogninā | *Ibid.*, 154.310.

[75] *MBh*, XII.310.1-29.

[76] *Ibid.*, III.163.45. Also Cf.
Ugreṇa tapasā tena praṇipātena śaṅkaraḥ |
Īśvaraḥ toṣitaḥ ... Ibid., I.207.18.

[77] *Hemante jalaśayyāsu grīṣme pañcatape tathā* |
Varṣāsu ca tathākāśe kṣapayantaḥ tanūḥ priyāḥ ||
Matsya P., 129.8.

entirely.[78] The essential characteristics of *tapas* are summarised in a *Purāṇa* as follows:

Brahmacaryaṁ japo maunaṁ nirāhāratvam eva ca |
Ityetat tapaso mūlaṁ sughoraṁ tad durāsadam || [79]

"Chastity, recitation, vow of silence, fast, that is the base of *tapas*, very harsh and difficult to achieve."

The two passages reproduced below — one from the *Mahābhārata*, and the other from the *Matsya Purāṇa* — may be regarded as representing, in broad outline, the concept of *tapas* of the respective periods:

Tapasy ugre vartamānaḥ ugratejo mahāmanāḥ |
Darbhacīraṁ vivasyātha daṇḍājinavibhūṣitaḥ ||
Pūrṇe pūrṇe trirātreṣu māsamekaṁ phalāśanaḥ |
Dviguṇenaiva kālena dvitīyaṁ māsam atyagāt ||
Tṛtīyam api māsaṁ sa pakṣeṇāhāram ācaran |
Śīrṇaṁ ca patitaṁ bhūmau parṇaṁ samupayuktavān ||
Caturthe tvatha saṁprāpte māsi pūrṇe tataḥ param |
Vāyubhakṣo mahābāhur abhavat pāṇḍunandanaḥ ||
Ūrdhvabāhur nirālambaḥ pādāṅguṣṭhāgraviṣṭhitaḥ |
Sadopasparśanāc cāsya babhūvur amitaujasaḥ ||
Vidyudambhoruhanibhā jaṭās tasya mahātmanaḥ | [80]

"Engaged in a terrific penance, the son of Pāṇḍu, of fierce ardour and great spirits, put on a rag of *darbha* grass, adorned with a staff and a

---

[78] *Tatrāmbarāṇi saṁtyajya bhūṣaṇāni ca śailajā* |
Saṁvītā valkalair divyair darbhanirmitamekhalā ||
Triḥ snātā pāṭalāhārā babhūva śaradāṁ śatam |
...
Nirāhārā śataṁ sābhūt samānāṁ tapasāṁ nidhiḥ |
Matsya P., 154.308-310.

"Discarding her dress and ornaments, covered with bark, wearing a belt made of *darbha* grass, three times bathing, she lived on leaves of trees for a hundred years ... without food for another hundred years; she was a treasury of penance."

[79] *Vāyu P.*, I.59.41.

[80] *MBh*, III.39.20-24.

deer skin, lived on fruits, once in three days, for a month. He spent a second month, doubling the time of fast, a third month taking food once in a fortnight. He lived on dry fallen leaves, for a fourth month. And when it was passed, he was feeding on wind, arms uplifted, without support standing on the tip of the toe of one foot. Because of constant bath, the hair of this great-souled here, of unlimited strength, took the aspect of the lotus or the lightning."

> *Sthāṇubhūto hy animiṣaḥ śuṣkakāṣṭhopalopamaḥ* |
> *Sa niyamyendriyagrāmam avatiṣṭhad aniścalaḥ* ||
> *Atha tasyaivam aniśaṁ tatparasya tadāśiṣaḥ* |
> *Sahasram ekaṁ varṣāṇāṁ divyam apy abhyavartata* ||
> *Valmīkena samākrānto bhakṣyamāṇaḥ pipīlikaiḥ* |
> *Vajrasūcimukhais tīkṣṇaiḥ vidhyamānas tathaiva ca* ||
> *Nirmāṁsarudhiratvak ca kundaśaṅkhendusaprabhaḥ* |
> *Asthiśeṣo 'bhavat sarvaṁ dehaṁ vai cintayann api* ||[81]

"He was like a pillar, never winking, comparable to a stone or a dry trunk of a tree. Controlling all his sense organs, he stood, motionless. While he was engaged always in his meditations, with his wish, are thousand divine years passed on. He was covered by an ant-hill, being eaten by ants, pierced with their sharp stings hard like thunderbolt. Being devoid of flesh, blood and skin, only bones were left, with the colour of jasmine, conch or moon. Still he was meditating."

Now to speak more specifically about *tapas* as a mode of worshipping Śiva, one finds quite a large number of allusions to it in the Epics and the *Purāṇas*. The *Mahābhārata* tells us that *tapas* had to be practiced in order to propitiate Śiva and thus win his favour.[82] Arjuna, for instance, practiced *tīvra-tapas* and won Śiva's favour.[83] Similarly, Śiva appeared before Ambā in response to her *tapas*.[84] Drupada is

---

[81] *Matsya P.*, 180. 15-19.

[82] *Ugreṇa tapasā tena praṇipātena śaṅkaraḥ*
Īśvarastoṣitah ... MBh, I.207.18.
Also *Ibid.*, I.157.8.

[83] *Ibid.*, III.41.13-15.

[84] *Ibid.*, V.188.7-15.

also said to have propitiated Śaṅkara by means of his *tapas* and achieved his goal.[85] As soon as Nārāyaṇa was born, he practiced *tapas* and gratified Śiva.[86] Aśvatthāman also is represented as having himself practiced penance in order to propitiate Śiva. Kṛṣṇadvaipāyana practiced *tapas* and Śiva granted him a son. It is said that during his severe austerities, the sage showed no signs of fatigue at all.[87] Special mention may be made of the *tapas* practiced by Arundhatī. As the result of her *tapas*, Śiva manifested himself before her and proclaimed that her *puṇya* was far greater than what the sages had acquired during the preceding twelve years.[88] As mentioned already, Śiva, when pleased through *tapas*, is described as bestowing boons unhesitatingly on any and every devotee.[89]

From among the Purāṇic references to Śiva having been propitiated by means of *tapas*, the following may be regarded as typical: on the advice of Bhṛgu, Rāma retired to Himavat, established an *āśrama* there, and practiced *tapas* to win Śiva's favour.[90] Yama, the god of death also practiced *tapas* in honour of Śiva.[91] Kālī practiced *tapas* to obtain Śiva as her husband.[92] The intensity of the *tapas* practised by the goddess is said to be indicated by her name Umā.[93] Her mother feared that the austerities would greatly oppress her tender body. She therefore constantly accosted her and advised her to desist from them, but Umā refused to do so. The *yogis* and the *tāpasas* are often described in the *Purāṇas* as meditating on Śiva and worshipping him to have their desires fulfilled.[94] According to the *Śiva Purāṇa*, the sage Upamanyu categorically told Kṛṣṇa that *tapas* alone could bring him a boon from Śiva.[95]

---

85 *Matsya P.*, V.189.3-8. 86 *Ibid.*, VII.201.57-97. 87 *Ibid.*, XII.310.1-29.

88 *MBh*, IX.48.1-68. 89 *Ibid.*, III.39.

90 *Brahmāṇḍa P.*, I.21.71-80; also I.22.69-81.

91 *Matsya P.*, 11.21.

92 *Kālikā P.*, 45.

93 *Matsya P.*, 154.298-299.

94 *Kūrma P.*, I.25.29-46.

95 *Śiva P.*, *Dharma-saṁhitā*, 2.35-55.

It has to be noted that the cult of *tapas* had begun to grow unpopular in the Purāṇic period itself, for the references to *tapas* in these texts gradually tend to become more sparse. After all, *tapas* demanded an austere life and physical mortification, and could only be practised by a select few. It could not ever have become the common general religious practice of people. Other popular and easily accessible modes of the propitiation of god, therefore, came into vogue. Of course, as will be shown in the next section, a few characteristics of *tapas* did find their way into these popular forms of worship.[96]

3. Tīrthas

The word *tīrtha* literally means a passage, way, road or ford. It also denotes the stairs for landing from or descending into a river, and so it then came to mean a bathing place as well. Ultimately, a *tīrtha* acquired the sense of a place of pilgrimage situated on the banks of sacred streams. The Epics and the *Purāṇas* speak of several *tīrthas*, devoting several chapters to the enumeration and description of these holy places.[97] All such accounts usually conclude with a proclamation that pilgrimage to these places would bring immense merit.[98] These *tīrthas* are normally associated with certain specific

---

96 In the scheme of *vrata*, for example, certain characteristic features of *tapas* such as restraint of the body and senses, and renunciation of food and other comforts are fairly predominant.

97 The *Mahābhārata* has one full sub-*parvan* entitled *tīrthayātrā-parvan*. This occurs in the third book of the Great Epic (80-154). The *Śānti* and the *Anusāśana parvans* also contain references to a few *tīrthas*. Among the *Purāṇas*, the *Padma* and the *Skanda Purāṇas* have devoted greater portions of their texts to the description of the *tīrthas*. The *Skanda Purāṇa* should be specially mentioned in this connection. Only a very few chapters are devoted to the description of Skanda after whom the *Purāṇa* is named. One full section is devoted to *Veṅkaṭācalamāhātmya*; this speaks of the sacred *tīrtha* or rather *kṣetra* in which Viṣṇu is enshrined. Jagannātha, Ayodhyā, Setu, Dharmāraṇya, Kāśī, Avantī, Prabhāsa, Vastrapatha are the places proclaimed in this *Purāṇa* as sacred and many *tīrthas* found in them are described in this single *Purāṇa* of not less than 1500 chapters. The other *Purāṇas*, of course only to a lesser extent, have devoted a fairly large number of their chapters to the description of the *tīrthas*.

98 E.g. see *Nārada P.*, 49.

gods whose immediate presence there is believed to add to the sanctity of those places.[99] Among these gods, Brahmā Viṣṇu, and Śiva — particularly the last two — are by far the most prominent. They have quite a number of *tīrthas* connected with them. The other gods more or less gradually disappeared. These *tīrthas* are scattered all over the country, and pilgrims from all parts visit these places. It is interesting to note in this connection that just as the association with a particular god enhances the sanctity of a *tīrtha*, the pilgrimages to that *tīrtha* tend in return to enhance the god's popularity. As has been pointed out elsewhere, the advent of the *tīrtha* cult contributed much to the high position at which the Purāṇic trinity of Brahmā, Viṣṇu and Śiva has been established. This simple yet exciting method of the propitiation of the gods by periodically visiting the various sacred places was practised by a large number of pilgrims throughout the year, and every year it resulted in the continuity and the consequent perpetuation of the memory of these gods. For so long as the gods continued to have connection with these places, they were not likely to pass into oblivion.

In our context, the *tīrthas* are regarded as constituting a type of ritual. Such a characterization of the *tīrthas* may not be said to be quite unwarranted, for visits to the *tīrthas* imply certain ceremonial observances and also the worship of the gods with whom those places are associated. From this point of view, they can be included among the religious practices of the Hindus; indeed, they occupy a prominent place among such practices. Simple to perform but by their very nature constituting an exciting experience, the pilgrimages to the *tīrthas* were always preferred to the elaborate complexities of the *yajña* or the severe austerities of the *tapas*. Merit gained through visits to the *tīrthas* was immense and was often proclaimed to be superior to that brought about by the *yajñas*.[100]

---

[99] Cf. *Prayāge brahmaviṣṇvādyāḥ devā munivarāḥ sthitāḥ* |
Saritaḥ sāgarāḥ siddhāḥ gandharvāpsarasaḥ tathā ||
Agni. P., 111.1-2.

[100] *Śiva P.*, *Sanatkumāra-saṁhitā*, 14. 1-12.

The number of *tīrthas* that are regarded to be sacred on account of the association with Śiva or other ancillary divinities of Śaivism is great.[101] They are to be found scattered all over the country. The *Mahābhārata* mentions various *tīrthas* with which Śiva [102] or Kārttikeya [103] are connected. To those who propitiated him at these places Śiva granted *gāṇapatya*, the highest rank to which a devotee of Śiva was entitled.[104] The immediate presence of the god at such places is repeatedly emphasised.[105] Even Brahmā propitiated Śiva at these places.[106] Vārāṇasī is by far the most important of the *Śaiva-tīrthas*. With reference to Vārāṇasī, it is claimed that the sin incurred elsewhere is wiped off by undertaking a pilgrimage to that place.[107]

We may now briefly describe the typical form of ritual — particularly insofar as it concerns Śiva — which is implied in the *tīrtha-yātrā*. To begin with, it may be pointed out that, like *tapas*, *tīrtha-yātrā* also precludes the enjoyment of all comforts.[108] A fully disciplined life is enjoined on the person who goes on *tīrtha-yātrā*. Keeping under restraint one's hands, feet, and mind, as well as one's knowledge, *tapas* and fame, is proclaimed as being necessary for

---

[101] A more or less comprehensive list of the *tīrthas* is given in Appendix 8.

[102] The third book of the *Mahābhārata* mentions the *tīrthas* connected with Śiva. These are found scattered in chapters 80, 81, 82, 83, 93 and 118, of this book. Some of these *tīrthas* are merely mentioned and no details are given about them. As these are interspersed with *tīrthas* associated with other deities, it is necessary to single out the *tīrthas* which pertain to Śiva and indicate their occurrence as follows:
Chapter 80, verses 12, 55, 68, 69, 73, 76, 77, 80, 82, 87-89, 108, 111, 113, 118, 124.
Chapter 81, verses 18, 46, 59, 70, 71, 85, 114, 141, 142, 149, 153, 155.
Chapter 82, verses 10, 16-19, 24, 35, 69, 79, 87, 103, 116.
Chapter 83, verses 11, 16-18, 22, 46, 59, 63.
Chapter 93, verses 4, 10.
Chapter 118, verses 3, 4, 16.

[103] *Mahābhārata*, III.81.116-7; III.81.143; III.82.68.

[104] *Ibid.*, III.82.10; III.81.18.

[105] *Mahābhārata*, III.80.84.

[106] *Ibid.*, III.83.23-25.

[107] *Anyatra tu kṛtaṁ pāpaṁ vārānasyāṁ vyapohati* | *Liṅga P.*, I.103.75. Also see *Kūrma P.*, I.31.

[108] *Pratigrahād upāvṛttaḥ laghvāhāro jitendriyaḥ* | *Agni P.*, 108.2.

gaining the fruits of *tīrtha-yātrā*.[109] It has also been laid down that a true pilgrim should show complete aversion to *pratigraha*, to keep his sense organs under control, and to take only light food. It is only when a *tīrtha-yātrā* is thus carried out in a more or less austere manner that a person obtains the fruits otherwise achieved by performing all kinds of sacrifices. A pilgrim is, indeed, said to possess all kinds of virtues.[110]

As has been mentioned elsewhere, the *tīrthas* are generally located in the vicinity of waters — on the sea shore, on the bank of a river or a stream, or by the side of a lake. A bath in these holy waters constitutes an essential feature of the ritual of the *tīrtha-yātrā*.[111] Such a bath is supposed to wash off even the most dire of sins. Along the banks of these waters are often installed the *liṅgas* of Śiva. The bath in the holy rivers is, therefore, closely followed by the worship of these *liṅgas*,[112] in which the immediate presence of Śiva is definitely assumed. In this, perhaps, one may see the earliest traces of the temple cult of the Hindus, which later developed rich and varied traditions and which rapidly expanded all over the country. These *liṅgas* installed at water banks were probably sheltered only by the trees which grew

---

[109] *Yasya hastau ca pādau ca manaś caiva susaṁyatam* |
Vidyā tapaśca kīrtiśca sa tīrthaphalam aśnute ||
Agni P., 109.1.

[110] *Akrodhanaśca rājendra satyaśīlo dṛḍhavrataḥ* |
ātmopamaśca bhūteṣu sa tīrthaphalaṁ aśnute ||
MBh, III.80.33.

[111] Cf. *Pañcanadyaśca rudreṇa kṛtā dānavabhīṣanāḥ* |
Tena sarveṣu lokeṣu tīrthaṁ pañcanadaṁ smṛtam ||
...
Tasmin tīrthe naraḥ snātvā dṛṣṭvā koṭīśvaraṁ haram |
Pañcayajñān avāpnoti nityaṁ śraddhāsamanvitaḥ ||
Vāmana P., 34.27-29.

"Five rivers were created there by Rudra; they were frightening Dānavas. Thus in all the worlds this *tīrtha* is known as Pañcanada... The man who bathes in this *tīrtha* and sees Hara, lord of crores of beings, always full of faith, obtains the fruit of five sacrifices."

[112] While indicating the great merit derived by engaging oneself in the *liṅga*-worship, it is said: *Śivaliṅga-praṇāmasya kalāṁ nārhanti sodaśīm. Śiva P., Sanatkumāra-saṁhitā*, 14.

there, but when the peculiar form of worship associated with the *liṅgas* was gradually consolidated and became more and more popular, some kind of permanent structures began to be built for the installation and worship of the god. It must be noted that even these structures sought to retain, in some form or other, these original features of the river and the tree to which great sanctity had been ascribed. The temple worship of Śiva in the South is always focused around the *liṅga*. A temple dedicated to this god is significantly designated as *tīrtha*.[113] Any temple in the South invariably has some river associated with it, as well as a tree specifically assigned to it.[114] This tree stands, in most cases, immediately behind the *garbhagṛha* or the central shrine. The *Purāṇas* which specifically belong to these various temples elaborately proclaim the glories of the *sthala*, the *tīrtha*, the *sthala-vṛkṣa* and the *mūrti* of those temples.

The merits acquired by the visits to and the observances and worship at the *tīrthas* are often described in great detail.[115] Even merely remembering these sacred places is said to constitute a meritorious act. The sight of them destroys all sin, while bathing there brings immense merit, even to those who have committed highly despicable deeds.[116]

Those who remember the gods in these places give special pleasure to the gods, and we are also told that those who bathe at these places have all their desires fulfilled. Among these desires are

---

[113] Also cf. *Bhūteśvaraṁ ca tatraiva jvālāmāleśvaraṁ tathā* |
Tacca liṅgaṁ samabhyarcya na bhūyo janma cāpnuyāt || *Vāmana P.*, 34.36.

[114] Cf. Gopinath Rao: *op.cit.*, vol. I, Introd., p. 15.

[115] Cf. *MBh*, XIII.26.

[116] *Darśanāt sparśanāt pānāt tathā gaṅgeti kīrtanāt* |
Punāti puṇyapuruṣāñ chataso'tha sahasraśah ||
Agni P., 110.6.

"By seeing, touching, drinking, calling 'Gaṅgā' the water of a tīrtha, it purifies meritorious people, hundred and thousand times."

Tatra brahmādayo devāḥ ṛṣayaḥ siddhacāraṇāḥ |
Gandharvāś cāpsaroyakṣāḥ sevante sthānakāṅkṣiṇaḥ ||
Vāmana P., 33.17.

Gamanaṁ smaraṇaṁ caiva sarvakalmaṣanāśanaṁ | *Ibid.*, 34.10.
See also *Nārada P.*, II.51.

mentioned progeny, *mokṣa* or *svarga*, destruction of sin — in short, all pleasure in this world and in the hereafter. As mentioned in an earlier context, the merits acquired by performing various *yajñas* are easily attained by visiting the *tīrthas*.[117]

4. Stotra

Stotras are verses of praise, which glorify in various terms the greatness of the gods. The formal enumeration of the many exploits of the gods as narrated in the Epics and the *Purāṇas* also share characteristics with the *stotras*. Several saints of both the North and the South have composed *stotras* in praise of the great gods and their ancillary divinities. These *stotras* are composed for the most part in the languages prevalent in the respective parts of the country. In the South, the saints known as the Nāyanmārs composed verses of praise called *tevārams*. These are remarkably permeated with Purāṇic ideas.[118] Recitation of *stotras* has found a distinct place among the Hindu forms of worship. This mode of worship could easily be practised, and the householders to whom the *tīrthas*, *tapas* and *yajña* were not ordinarily accessible found this method of propitiating the gods most suitable. Even today, many householders are seen to engage themselves, after their daily ablutions, in reciting *stotras* — particularly those which relate to their own particular family god or goddess. The *pārāyaṇa* of the *Sahasranāmastotras* of Viṣṇu, Śiva,[119] and Lalitā (Śakti), most of which have found some place in the *Purāṇas*,[120] is a regular feature of the daily worship by a devout Hindu.[121]

---

[117] *Na dānaiḥ na tapobhiśca na yajñair nāpi vidyayā |*
Prāpyate gatir utkṛṣṭā yā vimukteṣu labhyate || *Kūrma P.*, I.3.44-45.

[118] See Appendix 3 for details.
Among such composers of *stotras*, the name of Śaṅkara may be regarded as perhaps the most prominent. His compositions are even today recited devoutly by way of *pārāyaṇa* by all Śaivas, Vaiṣṇavas and Śāktas, by both householders and by others.

[119] *Brahma P.*, I.38; *Śiva P.*, *Dharma-saṁhitā*, 28; *Liṅga P.*, I.65.

[120] Also *Gaṇapatisahasranāma* in the *Gaṇeśa Purāṇa* I.46.1-22. The *Lalitā-sahasranāmastotra* has a colophon, which declares that the *stotra* is derived from the *Brahmāṇḍa Purāṇa*, *Uttarakhaṇḍa*. See *Bṛhatstotraratnākara*, pt. I, p. 372.

The origins of the *stotra* may be traced back to the *Ṛgveda*. The *stotras*, like several hymns of the *Ṛgveda*, sing of the glorious deeds of the god concerned. However, apart from this their essential nature, both the Purāṇic *stotras* and the Vedic hymns also implores the god on the part of the devotee — the only difference perhaps being that while in the Purāṇic *stotras* there is an emphasis on favours in this world as well as in the next, the Vedic hymns mostly pertain to favours in this world alone. The *stotras* are also generally characterized by a sense of sinfulness, an attitude of complete self-surrender and an earnest longing for personal communion with god on the part of the devotee. In other words, *bhakti* is the keynote of these *stotras*.[122] We are told in the *Liṅga Purāṇa* [123] how Brahmā and Viṣṇu sang in praise of Śiva, how the latter manifested himself before them, and how when Śiva had offered them boons, both of them asked for nothing but devotion to Śiva. Brahmā is said to have then said:

Tvayi bhaktiṁ parāṁ me'dya prasīda parameśvara.

In another context in the same *Purāṇa*,[124] Umā raises the question by what means Śiva's favour can be obtained by a devotee. Neither *tapas* nor *vidyā* nor even *yoga* is recommended as the way to win the god's favour; *bhakti* alone is mentioned as the most efficacious means in this regard. In the *Purāṇas*, these songs of praise, which are usually preceded by the bowing down of the head,[125] are put into the mouth of the oppressed ones, sometimes the *devas* and sometimes the *asuras*.

---

[121] The significance of the repetitions of the names of the various gods has been explained by Raghavan as follows: "Hymns on the names of the Lord are recited as a means of salvation, being the easiest means and the best suited for the present age, when higher spiritual qualifications are difficult for attainment. The repetition of the names helps to recall to mind the presence of the Lord, his infinite excellences and exploits, and enables one to become wholly absorbed in him." *The Religion of the Hindus*, p. 396.

[122] This fact may be regarded as constituting another point of difference between the *stotras* and the Vedic hymns in general. Of course, the doctrine and practice of *bhakti* are clearly reflected in the Varuṇa hymns, particularly those in the seventh *maṇḍala* of the *Ṛgveda*.

[123] *Liṅga P.*, I.72.170-175.

[124] *Ibid.*, I.10.39 ff.

[125] *Praṇamya śirasā rudraṁ vacaḥ prāha sukhāvaham* | *Kūrma P.*, II.1.14.

For instance, at their final hour of destruction, the *asuras* are said to have repented for their many misdeeds and to have glorified Śiva with various verses of praise. Pleased with their devotion, the god ultimately elevated them to the rank of *gaṇa*.[126] From among the most significant *stotras* found in the Epics and the *Purāṇas*, the following may be especially mentioned:

Contents	**Reference**
Kṛṣṇa and Arjuna praise Śiva	*MBh*, VII.80.55-65.
Nārayana glorifies Śiva	*Ibid.*, VII.201.72-78
A glorification of Śiva	*Ibid.*, VII.1.50.
Taṇḍin glorifies Śiva	*Ibid.*, XIII.16.13-66.
Śivasahasranāmastotra	*Ibid.*, X.17.1-182.
Kṛṣṇa glorifies Śiva	*Harivaṁśa*, 74.22-34.
The gods glorify Śiva	*Ibid.*, 1. 34.
Viṣṇu praises Śiva	*Ibid.*, 16.38.
The *devas* pray to Śiva and request him to free them from bondage of the *asuras*	*Ibid.*, III.13.1-83.
Sahasranāmastotra	*Brahma* P., 38.
Paraśurāma glorifies Śiva	*Brahmāṇḍa P.*, 25.5-32.
Andhaka glorifies Śiva	*Kūrma P.*, I.16.194-206.
Brahmā and Viṣṇu glorify Śiva	*Ibid.*, I.26.78-93.
Śakuntalā praises Śiva	*Ibid.*, I.34.36-45.
Brahma praises Śiva	*Ibid.*, II.31.49-53.

[126] *Kūrma P.*, I.16.194-206.

The sages praise Śiva	*Ibid.*, II.39.21-32.
Brahmā praises Śiva	*Liṅga P.*, I.10.44-73.
Viṣṇu glorifies Śiva in verses which contain one hundred names of the god	*Liṅga P.*, I.96.
A *stava* in which Śiva, Umā and Nandin are glorified; this is called the *vyapohastava*	*Ibid.*, I.82.
The gods glorify Śiva and attribute to him the qualities of Brahman	*Liṅga P.*, I.71.100-114.
The sages at Dāruvana sought Śiva's pardon by repeating the names of the god	*Ibid.*, I.32.
The *devas* and the *asuras* jointly praise and seek the god's protection from the poison which was produced as a result of the churning of the milky ocean	*Matsya P.*, 250.28-40.
Bāṇa prayed to Śiva and sang verses composed in the *troṭaka* metre noted for its pleasant rhythm	*Ibid.*, 188.63-67
The thousands names of Śiva	*Śiva P.*, *Jñāna-saṁhitā*, 71.1-166
Kāvya, the preceptor of the *asuras*, falls prostrate before Śiva and praises him	*Vāyu P.*, II.35.160-203.
Brahmā and Viṣṇu glorify Śiva	*Ibid.*, I.24.84-164.
Viṣṇu proclaims the achievements of Śiva	*Ibid.*, I.24.50-88.
Śiva is glorified by Brahmā	*Ibid.*, I.27.
Dakṣa praises Śiva and recites verses containing one hundred and eight names of Śiva	*Ibid*.I.30.180-284.
The gods praise Śiva	*Sūta-saṁhitā* I.1-56.

Even as literary productions, the *stotras* must be assigned a special place of their own in the history of Sanskrit literature. They are often characterized by great poetic merit and musical quality. Such excellent religio-literary compositions are by no means rare in the *Purāṇas* themselves. For instance, the verses sung by Bāṇa in praise of Śiva [127] may be cited as a striking example of religious lyrics. They are replete with both *śabda* and the *artha-alaṁkāras*. Similarly, the *Viṣṇu-sahasranāma-stotra* and the *Lalitā-sahasranāma-stotra* are both noted for a remarkable blending of poetry, music and philosophy. It is also worth noting that the authors of these *stotras* sought to enhance the dignity, sanctity and authority of the *stotras* by incorporating within them several Vedic and other *mantras*. Over the course of time, the *stotras* themselves attained the character and status of the *mantras*. A devout repetition of the *stotras*, like that of *mantras*, was believed to bring immense merit which could otherwise be acquired only by means of far more difficult modes of worship. The *phalaśruti* [128] appended to the *stotras* — especially the *sahasranāma-stotras* — proclaims the merit resulting from their recital.[129]

5. Dhyāna

Dhyāna is usually regarded as an essential accessory of other religious practices such as *tapas*,[130] *yoga* and *pūjā*.[131] Nevertheless, it

---

[127] *Matsya P.*, 188.63-67.

[128] At the end of the *Mantra-mātṛkāpuṣpamālāstava*, Śaṅkara speaks of the merits which one may gather through this *stava*:
Śrīmantrākṣaramālayā girisutāṁ yaḥ pūjayet cetasā
Sandhyāsu prativāsaraṁ suniyatas tasyāmalaṁ syān manaḥ |
Cittāmbhoruhamaṇḍape girisutā nṛttaṁ vidhatte sadā
Vāṇī vaktrasaroruhe jaladhijā gehe jaganmaṅgalā ||
Bṛhatstotraratnākara, pt. II, p. 425.

[129] *Lalitāsahasranāmastotra* pp. 24-32 (at the end of the book) and *Viṣṇusahasranāmastotra*, pp. 12-13 (at the end of the book).

[130] The connection between *dhyāna* and *tapas*, though not explicitly mentioned anywhere in the *Purāṇas*, is implied by the fact that meditation on the god who is to be propitiated by the worshipper, is a necessary condition of *tapas*.

[131] It is significant that the *ślokas* employed in connection with *pūjā* are designated as *dhyāna-ślokas*. These verses help the worshipper to meditate upon the god, as they are recited in the course of the *pūjā*.

deserves to be classed as a separate form of worship, for the *Purāṇas* often speak of *dhyāna* as an independent method of propitiating a god and winning his favour. In the *Kūrma Purāṇa*, for instance, the *dhyāna* of Śiva is especially prescribed.[132] *Dhyāna* is actually referred to as the highest religious practice,[133] and is, indeed, especially mentioned in connection with the Kṛta age.[134] The *Mahābhārata* mentions *dhyāna* as a religious practice, along with *japa*.[135]

The importance of *dhyāna* as an independent religious practice is clearly pointed out in the *Mahābhārata*, where it is mentioned side by side with *yajña*, *saṁnyāsa*, *dāna* and *pratigraha*.[136] Actually, the manner in which *dhyāna* is mentioned in this context would seem to suggest that the author of the *Mahābhārata* regarded it as superior to the other religious practices mentioned there. This is confirmed in unequivocal terms by a Purāṇic passage where various types of *yajñas* are enumerated, and *dhyāna* is exalted as the best among them.

> *Yāvajjñānasya saṁprāptis tāvat karma samācaret* |
> *Karmayajñasahasrebhyas tapoyajño viśiṣyate* |
> *Tapoyajñasahasrebhyo japayajño viśiṣyate* ||
> *Japayajñasahasrebhyo dhyānayajño viśiṣyate* |
> *Dhyānayajñāt paraṁ nāsti dhyānaṁ jñānasya sādhanam* ||[137]

---

[132] Cf. *Dhyānaṁ samādhāya japanti rudram* | *Kūrma*, *P.*, I.32.27. Also: *Dhyāyitvā devam īśānaṁ vyomamadhyagataṁ śivam* | *Ibid.*, II.19.98.

[133] *Dhyānaṁ hi paramaṁ dharmaṁ kathitaṁ paramaṁ padam* | *Śiva P.*, *Sanatkumāra saṁhitā*, 9.

[134] Cf. *Dhyānaṁ paraṁ kṛtayuge tretāyāṁ yajña ucyate* |
Bhajanaṁ dvāpare śuddhaṁ dānameva kalau yuge ||
Liṅga P., I.39.7.

"Meditation is told to be the best in Kṛta age, sacrifice in Tretā, devotional service in Dvāpara, donation in Kali."

[135] *Anudhyānena japena vidhāsyati śivaṁ tava* | *MBh*, III.2.11.

[136] *Yajñam eke praśaṁsanti saṁnyāsam apare janāḥ* |
Dānam eke praśaṁsanti kecid eva pratigraham ||
Kecit sarvaṁ parityajya tūṣṇīṁ dhyāyanta āsate |
MBh, XIII.21.8.

[137] *Śiva P.*, *Jñāna-saṁhitā*, 26.1-10.

"One should perform rites upto the attainment of knowledge. Worship by *tapas* is superior to a thousand worships by rites. Worship by recitations is superior to a thousand worships by *tapas*. Worship by meditation is superior to a thousand worships by recitation. There is nothing superior to worship by meditation. Meditation is the means to achieve knowledge."

The *yatis* are, accordingly, advised to take recourse to *dhyāna*.[138] It is further claimed in that very context that *dhyāna* is the highest form of worship and it destroys sins of all kinds.

Dhyāna plays a particularly important role in the religion of Śiva. The *Vāyu Purāṇa* expressly states that meditation on Maheśvara and *yoga* are the only ways of warding off the evil effects of *ariṣṭas*.[139] In the same *Purāṇa*, Śiva is shown exhorting Brahmā that *dhyāna* is the only way which can lead the devotee to a vision of him.[140] Elsewhere, Śiva proclaims to Brahmā that the only way of perceiving him is by *dhyāna*. This is especially prescribed for the mortals:

Tapasā naiva vṛttena dānadharmaphalena ca
Na tīrthaphalabhogena kratubhir vā pradakṣiṇaiḥ
Na vedādhyayanair vāpi na vittena ca vedanaiḥ
Na śakyaṁ mānavair draṣṭum ṛte dhyānād ahaṁ tvidam.[141]

A very subtle meditation is described in the *Liṅga Purāṇa*.[142] Elsewhere in that *Purāṇa*, the *japa* murmuring of Śiva's names is also prescribed during the course of meditation.[143] Indeed, great emphasis is laid on the indispensability of *dhyāna* in all modes of worshipping Śiva. The following account of *dhyāna*, which speaks of the identity of the self with Śiva, is significant in this connection:

---

[138] *Kṛtvā hṛtpadmanilaye viśvākhye viśvatomukhaṁ* |
Ātmānaṁ sarvabhūtānāṁ parastāt tapasaḥ sthitam ||
Kūrma P., II.29.11-24.

[139] *Vāyu P.*, I.19.35-40.

[140] *Ibid.*, I.23.93-94.

[141] *Liṅga P.*, I.24.68. See translation p. 209.

[142] *Ibid.*, I.28.

Dhyānaniṣṭhasya satataṁ naśyeta sarvapātakam |
Tasmān maheśvaraṁ dhyātvā taddhyānaparamo bhava ||
... ...
Nānyaṁ devaṁ mahādevād vyatiriktaṁ prapaśyati |
Tam evam ātmanātmeti yaḥ sa yāti paraṁ padam ||
Manyante ye svam ātmānaṁ vibhinnaṁ parameśvarāt |
Na te paśyanti taṁ devaṁ vṛthā teṣāṁ pariśramaḥ || [144]

"All sin will be destroyed for one who is always engaged in meditation. Therefore, fix your mind on Maheśvara, be engaged in the highest meditation on him ... He, who does not see any other god than Mahādeva, who sees him as his self by himself, goes to the supreme goal. Those who think their own self different from the Supreme Lord, do not see him. Their effort is useless."

6. Vratas [145]

The observance of *vratas* became a particularly popular religious practice in the Epic and the Purāṇic periods. Accordingly, there have been prescribed in the *Purāṇas* various kinds of *vratas* which are intended for the propitiation of the great gods and the other ancillary divinities. The present context does not call for any discussion about the origin of the concept of *vrata.* Suffice it to say that *vrata* is *tapas* in a miniature form, for the underlying idea of *vrata*, like that of *tapas*, is a rigorously disciplined religious life. Of course, the austerities implied in *vrata* are by no means as severe as those demanded by *tapas. Vrata* is, indeed, a kind of *tapas* which may be practiced even by ordinary men and women. Unlike *tapas*, it does not involve continuous rigorous practice. It is a periodical observance, and its main features may be said to be a code of restrictions in respect to the normal amenities of life and a particular mode of worship. Specific *vratas* are prescribed in connection with specific times of the year; they thus constitute an annual religious calendar.

---

[143] *Ibid.*, II.19.1-43.

[144] *Kūrma P.*, II.29.37-44.

[145] A note on the important Śaiva *vratas* is given as an addendum to this chapter.

7. Pūjā

The Epics and the *Purāṇas* speak for the first time of *pūjā* as a form of worshipping the gods.[146] Generally speaking, this form of worship seems to have been originally restricted only to the great gods, with the exception of Brahmā.[147] However, the ancillary deities of the Śiva cult, Gaṇeśa, Kārttikeya and Śakti, are also represented in the *Purāṇas* as having received the honour of being worshipped in this form. The Sun god is sometimes identified with Śiva and sometimes with Viṣṇu; probably on account of this identification this god also is offered *pūjā*. Thus the *pañcāyatanapūjā*, that is to say, the worship of the five gods Gaṇeśa, Sūrya, Viṣṇu, Śiva and Śakti has been widely prevalent all along. This *pañcāyatana-pūjā* must be dated back to fairly early times, for the god Śiva himself is said to have

[146] Though literary references to *pūjā* occur at a rather late stage, the concept of *pūjā* undoubtedly dates from very early times. Indeed, it can be shown to belong to the pre-Aryan period. However, the *pūjā* form of worship was for a long time superseded by the Vedic form of worship, *homa*. When, however, the popular Hinduism established itself, the ancient practice of *pūjā*, which was obviously simpler than *homa*, came to be revived. For further discussion on the subject, see: Dandekar, "Rudra in the *Veda*", *JUPHS*, no. 1, p. 129 ff. In his elaborate paper "Dravidian Origins and the Beginnings of Indian Civilisation", S.K. Chatterji has found an occasion to discuss the term *pūjā*. According to him '*pūjā*' is unknown to the Aryan world of the *Veda*; *homa* has taken only a secondary place in the Hindu ritual, and *pūjā*, together with the great gods to whom it is now offered in India, namely Śiva and Umā and Viṣṇu (in his new form), is in all likelihood a pre-Aryan, Dravidian ritual; the word certainly is non-Aryan in origin, as there is no cognate of this root in other Indo-European languages, but it once recalls the Dravidian *pū*, 'flower' and it reappears in Sanskrit words like *puṣkara*, lotus, *puṣpa*, flower". *Modern Review*, 1924, p. 668.

[147] Cf. *Śiva P.*, *Vidyeśvara-saṁhitā*, 61.21. Banerjee, however, feels that the introduction of this new form of worship in Hinduism was chiefly due to the advent of Maheśa or Śiva as a prominent figure in the Hindu pantheon. He observes, "The advent of Maheśa or Īśvara as a prominent figure or conception of divinity marks an epoch in ancient Hindu Civilisation. A new method of worship and a new mythology were inaugurated and developed into *tantras* and the tantric system. Music, art, literature, *yoga* were all getting a new life and form." The author ascribes about eight reasons for the orientation of this new epoch. See "The Evolution of Rudra or Maheśa in Hinduism". *QJMS*, vol. X, no.1, pp. 221-222.

started it.[148] Inasmuch as the *Śiva-pūjā* itself is concerned, its popularity becomes quite evident from the many references to it occurring in the Epics and the *Purāṇas*.[149]

By and large, *pūjā* as reflected in the Epics and the *Purāṇas* may be equated with *upāsanā*,[150] *saparyā*, *ārādhanā*,[151] or *arcanā*.[152] This form of worship involves the employment of a variety of *pujopakaraṇas* and *pūjāsaṁbhāras*. These include many kinds of utensils, flowers, sandalwood,[153] *dhūpa*, *dīpa*,[154] and various articles

---

[148] *Devī-Bhāgavata* P., XI.17. The *Śiva Purāṇa* describes the *pañcāyatana* as follows:
Sivasya pratimā vāpi śivāyāḥ pratimā tathā |
Viṣṇoścaiva prayatnena sūryasyaivāthavā punaḥ ||
Gaṇapater vā punas tatra pañcāyatanaṁ uttamam |
Jñāna-Saṁhitā, 26.46-47.

[149] The topic of *Śiva-pūjā* receives repeated attention in the *Purāṇas*. Cf. *Śiva P.*, *Jñāna-saṁhitā*, 7 & 8; *Skanda P.*, I.2.41. In this latter reference is made to the Āgamic traditions. *Skanda P.*, I.3.1.8; *Liṅga P.*, I.79. The *liṅga-pūjā* is elaborately described in *Agni P.*, 27 & 28. Kṛṣṇa performs *liṅga-pūjā*. *Kūrma P.*, I.26.47-61. The same topic again in discussed in *Skanda P.*, I.2.12; *Sūta-saṁhitā*, I.4; *Liṅga P.*, I.25 & 27; *ibid.*, I.74.

[150] Cf. *Brahmādayaḥ piśācāntāḥ yaṁ hi devam upāsate*. *MBh*, XIII.14.4.

[151] See the occurrence of *ārādhanā* in the following:
Jñānayogaratair nityam ārādhyaḥ kathitas tvayā | Kūrma P., II.1.2.
Āradhayen mahādevam. Kūrma P., II.19.94.
Sarve prāñjalayo bhūtvā śūlapāṇiṁ prapadyata |
Ārādhayitum ārabdhāḥ brahmaṇā kathitaṁ yathā ||
Ibid., II.39.7-8.
See also *Liṅga P.*, I.35.31.

[152] *Arcanā* is described in the *Śiva Purāṇa* as exceedingly superior to sacrifices of various types:
Vājapeyaśatair iṣṭvā yal labheta dvijottama |
Vipro liṅgatrirātreṣu rudrabhaktyā tad aśnute ||
Aśvamedhasahasrasya samyag iṣṭvāsya yat phalam |
Māsena tad avāpnoti rudraliṅgārcane rataḥ ||
Śiva P., *Sanatkumāra-saṁhitā*, 14.48-49.
The *Garuḍa Purāṇa*, though Vaiṣṇavite in character, has devoted five chapters to the description of Śivārcanā (chapters 22-26).

[153] *Puṣpaiḥ patrair athādbhir vā candanādyair maheśvaram*. *Kūrma P.*, III.19.96.

[154] In the *Śiva Purāṇa Jñāna-saṁhitā*, 29, *dhūpa* and *dīpa* are mentioned as the *upacāras* offered in the *pūjā*. See also *Agni P.*, 74.75-76.

of *upacāra* [155] like *darpaṇa*, *chatra*, *cāmara*, *vyajana*, *patāka* and *tālavṛnta*. *Śaṅkha* and *ghaṇṭā* are also mentioned as accessories of the *pūjā*.[156] Over time, the *pūjā* rituals came to be further elaborated. The idol of the divinity constitutes the essential basis of all *pūjā* rites. Vedic *mantras* were often recited to accompany these rites. For instance, Vedic *mantras* were recited when the idol was bathed or when the *naivedya* was made and *upacāras* were offered to it. Thus, the same kind of connection was attempted to be maintained between the *pūjā* and the *Veda*.[157]

The *pūjā* form of worship which in its initial stages was presumably more or less simple [158] became more and more elaborate, particularly in the case of Śaivism. The *Āgamas* [159] seemed to have

---

[155] Sixteen *upacāras* are offered in the *pūjā*. Cf. *Ṣodaśair upacaraiśca śivaliṅgaṁ prapūjayet*. *Śiva P.*, *Vidyeśvara-saṁhitā*, 14.109.

[156] Cf. *Skanda P.*, II.5.5-6. See also Moore, *Hindu Pantheon*, p. 69.

[157] It may, however, be pointed out in this connection that, so far as the meaning of the Vedic *mantras* was concerned, they could hardly be said to be related, in any intrinsic manner, to the various rites in the *pūja* which they were expected to accompany. Their use was often determined in a very strange manner. For instance, a Vedic *mantra*, which actually referred to the horse, *dadhikrāvan*, was employed at the time of the bathing of the idol with *dadhi* or curds. It may be recalled that, even in Vedic ritual itself, the Vedic *mantras* were employed without any regard to their original meaning. The following comment of K.S. Srinivasapatracharya also speaks of this peculiar usage of the Vedic *mantras*. "Various passages from the *Vedas* are very often taken away from their context and used on occasions not contemplated by the *Vedas* themselves. One instance is the passage *gaṇānāṁ tvā gaṇapatim* etc. This hymn is used nowadays by persons who worship Vināyaka because the passage contains the word gaṇapati, a popular appellation of that god". *Gopalakrishnamacharya Commemoration Volume*, 4.48.

[158] As the word, *pūjā*, suggests, this form of worship must have originally consisted of besmearing the idol of the divinity with some unguent. To this were perhaps added the offerings of water, leaves and flowers.

Ananda Coomaraswamy in his *History of Indian and Indonesian Art* (p. 5) shows how "the popular Dravidian element has played the major part in all that concerns the development and office of image worship, that is *pūjā*, as distinct from *yajña*".

[159] The *Āgamas* which deal with the rituals are mainly three. Though the number of the *Āgamas* is said to be twenty-eight, only a few of them are available to us. Of these, *Kāraṇāgama*, *Kāmikāgama*, *Ajitāgama*, *Rauravāgama*, *Mṛgendrāgama*, *Mataṅgapārameśvarāgama*, *Kiraṇāgama* and *Suprabheda* deal at some length with the rituals. The *Skanda Purāṇa* refers to the Āgamic traditions of worship (I.3.1.8.).

paved the way for such an elaborated system of worship, stating that Śiva could be conceived and worshipped in various ways. The main *Āgamas*, namely, *Kāraṇa*, *Kāmika*, *Suprabheda*, *Raurava* and *Ajita*, have described in detail the various images of Śiva.[160] They also describe the rituals relating to the installation (*pratiṣṭhā*) of these images. These *Āgamas* concern themselves for the most part with the rituals relating to these images. Such rituals are of two kinds, those which are to be performed daily (*nitya*) and those which are to be performed on special occasions (*naimittika*). The process of elaborating upon the Śaiva *pūjā* ritual which seems to have been started in the *Purāṇas* may be said to have reached its culmination in the Āgamic Śaiva rituals. These will be examined under the four divisions into which the Āgamic ritualism is divided, namely *karṣaṇa*, *pratiṣṭhā*, *utsava* and *prāyaścitta*.

As indicated above, in the Epics and the *Purāṇas* we do not come across the full-fledged elaboration of *pūjā* of the *Āgamas*. In these works we only see the *pūjā* ritual in its early development and growth. As a matter of fact, the Epics make but very curt references to this form of worship. In some passages of the *Mahābhārata*, mere *pūjā* is mentioned, for instance:

Bhagavān pūjyate cātra hāsyarūpeṇa śaṅkaraḥ [161]

Also

Pūjyate tatra śaṅkaraḥ [162]

Elsewhere, it is said that when Kṛṣṇa entered the apartments after consoling Subhadrā who was mourning the death of her son,

---

[160] As pointed out in an earlier chapter, the descriptions of all these representations of Śiva, given in the *Āgamas*, are based on the Purāṇic accounts. The *Āgamas* refer to the representations, but do not relate the details of the events which gave rise to the conception of the representations. They, therefore, seem to assume that the accounts are already made known by the *Purāṇas* and the Epics, which should, on this account, be assigned an earlier date.

[161] *MBh*, I.57.21. For a critical discussion of this passage, see *Sukthankar Memorial Volume I*, "Critical Studies in the Mahābhārata", pp. 416-422.

[162] *MBh*, VI.12.26.

the *paricārakas* offered the *tryambaka bali* to Śiva.[163] This is one of the very few instances where Śiva is described to have been offered *bali*.[164]

On the other hand, the importance of *pūjā* is fully realized and frequently proclaimed in the *Purāṇas*. In the following statement from the *Liṅga Purāṇa*, the *pūjā* cult is represented as being far superior to the sacrificial cult:

Smaraṇaṁ pūjanaṁ caiva praṇāmo bhaktipūrvakam |
Pratyekam aśvamedhasya yajñasya samam ucyate || [165]

"Thinking of the Lord, worshipping him, prostrating, each, performed with devotion is told to be equal to an aśvamedha sacrifice."

Elsewhere, Viṣṇu is described to have worshipped Śiva with flowers to the accompaniment of the recital of the one thousand names of Śiva.[166]

The importance of *upāsanā* in general is pointed out in the *Liṅga Purāṇa*, but special emphasis has been placed there on the Śiva *pūjā*.[167] The *Skanda Purāṇa* gives a detailed description of the Śiva *pūjā*.[168] The advantages of worshipping Śiva and the disadvantage of not worshipping him are often recounted.[169] Various details of the Purāṇic Śiva-*pūjā* would become clear from the following passages:

Sampūjya śivasūktena tryaṁbakena śubhena ca |
Japtvā tvaritarudraṁ ca śivasaṁkalpam eva ca ||
Nīlarudraṁ ca śākteyaḥ tathā rudraṁ ...[170]

---

[163] *MBh*,VII.79.4.

[164] This kind of reference is rarely found in the *Purāṇas*, and the practice of *bali* has almost disappeared in modern times. The *MBh*, however, mentions *bali* along with other rites: *Pūjopahārabalibhir homamantrapuraskṛtaiḥ*. (VIII.25.131-56).

[165] *Liṅga P.*, II.1.6-7.

[166] *Ibid.*, I.98.159-62; also *Śiva P.*, *Jñāna-saṁhitā*, 70.1-24; also 71.

[167] *Liṅga P.*, II.18.26; also II.11.1-41.

[168] *Skanda P.*, I.2.12; I.2.41.

[169] Cf. *Liṅga P.*, I.75.20-29.

[170] *Liṅga P.*, I.64.75 ff.

Ārādhayen mahādevaṁ bhavabhūto maheśvaram |
Mantreṇa rudragāyatryā praṇavenātha vā punaḥ ||
Iśānenāthavā rudraiḥ tryaṁbakeṇa samāhitaḥ |
Puṣpaiḥ patraih tathādbhir vā candanādyair maheśvaram ||
Uktvā namaḥśivāyeti mantreṇānena vā japet |
Pradakṣiṇaṁ tataḥ kuryāt ...
Dhyāyīta ...[171]

"One should worship the great god Maheśvara, with concentrated mind, having became Bhava, with *mantras*, *Rudragāyatrī*, Oṁ, Īśana, Rudra, Tryambaka with flowers, leaves, water, sandal etc. After saying 'namaḥ Śivāya', with this mantra one should do a recitation. Then one should do a circumambulation ... One should meditate ..."

Devatābhyarcanaṁ kuryāt puṣpaiḥ patreṇa cāmbunā | [172]

"One should perform the worship of a deity with flowers, leaves and water."

Svamantrair arcayed devān puṣpaiḥ patraiḥ tathāṁbubhiḥ |
Brahmāṇaṁ śaṅkaram ...[173]

"One should worship gods with his own *mantras*, with flowers, leaves and water, Brahmā, Śaṅkara ..."

Flowers, *dhūpa*, *dīpa*, and *naivedya* are often specifically mentioned as the requisites of the *pūjā*.[174] *Pūjā* with *gandha*, *puṣpa* and *akṣata* is found in the *Śiva Purāṇa*.[175] Various other aspects of the *pūjā* such as *namaskāra*, *pradakṣiṇa* and *nyāsa* are found in the *Purāṇas*.[176] *Bhūtaśuddhi* and *nāḍīśodhanā* are among the rites mentioned in the *Devībhāgavata-Purāṇa*.[177] In the *Skanda Purāṇa*, *pañcāmṛta* and *śaṅkhodaka* are referred to in connection with the bathing of the image.[178] Two chapters in the *Śiva Purāṇa* contain a

[171] *Kūrma P.*, II.19.88-98.
[172] *Ibid.*, II.12.18.
[173] *Ibid.*, II.19.
[174] *Śiva P.*, *Jñāna-saṁhitā*, 29.1-86.
[175] *Ibid.*, 20.26-29.
[176] Cf. *Matsya P.*, 54.8-23.
[177] *Devībhāgavata P.*, XI.2.
[178] *Skanda P.*, II.5 and 6.

detailed description of the bathing (*snapana*) of the idol of Śiva.[179] Bathing the image with *pañcagavya* is mentioned in the *Liṅga Purāṇa*.[180] A description of bathing of image with the waters of the *kumbha* or the *kalaśa* is given in the *Matsya Purāṇa*.[181] The *Skanda Purāṇa* has laid down that all the *upacāras* be offered in connection with the Śiva *pūjā*,[182] and this practice is still followed in the temples of the South.

Pūjā seems to have been the main — or perhaps the only — form of worship in respect of the *liṅga*. It may be mentioned in this connection that the *pūjā* of the *liṅga* did not differ from other types of *pūjā*. The following passage would give an idea of the *pūjā* offered to the *liṅga*:

> *Vaidikair eva niyamair vividhair brahmacāriṇaḥ* |
> *Saṁsnāpya śāṅkarair mantrair ṛgyajuḥsāmasaṁbhavaiḥ* ||
> *Tataḥ paraṁ samāsthāya gṛṇantaḥ śatarudriyam* |
> *Samāhitāḥ pūjayadhvaṁ saputrāḥ sahabandhubhiḥ* || [183]

"Being chaste, take bath, according to the diverse rules told in the Veda, with *mantras* from Ṛk, Yaju and Sāmaveda, then be engaged in reciting Śatarudriya, attentively worship, with sons and relatives."

It may be pointed out that the various rites and religious practices of the Epics and the *Purāṇas* which have been described earlier in this chapter, such as *yajña*, *tapas*, *tīrthas*, *stotras*, *dhyāna* and *vrata*, are harmoniously blended into the *pūjā* ritual, as we find a reflection of all them within the fully developed form of that ritual best recorded in the *Āgamas*. It is this fully developed form of *pūjā* which is prevalent in the temples of the South. As mentioned elsewhere, the *Āgamas*, regarded as the principal authoritative texts dealing with the *pūjā*

---

179 *Śiva P.*, *Jñāna-saṁhitā*, 27 and 28.

180 *Liṅga P.*, I.15.18 ff.

181 *Matsya P.*, 68.15-39.

182 *Skanda P.*, I. 3.1-9.

183 *Kūrma P.*, II.39.3-5.

ritual, are twenty-eight in number.[184] However, of these twenty-eight *Āgamas*, only a few are still available; and out of these which are available in print, *Kāraṇāgama*, *Kāmikāgama*, *Rauravāgama*, *Ajitāgama*, *Mṛgendrāgama*, *Mataṅgapārameśvarārāgama*, *Kiraṇāgama* and *Suprabhedāgama* are particularly important for the study of ritual.[185] The *Āgamas* have given rise to several manuals or *Paddhatis* which help the worshippers with many practical details in connection with these rituals.[186]

It will be seen that many essential constituents and accessories of Āgamic Śaiva ritualism occur in the *Purāṇas* in connection with the worship of Śiva; an indication of some of these has already been given elsewhere in this chapter. A few more may be referred to at this stage. The *bilva* tree, for instance, is represented in the *Purāṇas* as being sacred to Śiva;[187] the triploid leaves of the trees are therefore

---

[184] The following verses from the *Siddhāntasārāvalī* (*Caryāpāda*) contain a list of the twenty-eight *Āgamas*:
Śaivaḥ kāmika-yogajājitamadho cintyaṁ ca dīptāhvayam
Sūkṣmaḥ kāraṇam aṁśumāṁśca daśadhā sāhasrakaṁ suprabham |
Raudraste vijayaṁ ca rauravam adho niśvāsam āgneyakam
Santānaṁ kiraṇākhyasiddhavimalaṁ śrīcandrahāsaṁ param ||
Udgītaṁ lalitaṁ ca mākuṭam adho śrīnārasiṁhaṁ tathā
Śrīsvāyambhuvapārameśamukhayugbiṁbānibhadrāhvayam |
Tenāṣṭādaśasaṅkhyavordhvamukhatas sākṣāt sadeśena te
Proktaḥ so'pi parāpta eva nikhilo tīrṇo'khilajñānavān ||

[185] These *Āgamas* occupy themselves mainly with the rituals, and the system of worship that prevails in the temples of South India is based on these texts.

[186] The eighteen authors after whom the different *Paddhatis* are named are enumerated in the following verses:
Durvāsāḥ piṅgalaścaiva, ugrajyotiḥ subodhakaḥ |
Śrīkaṇṭho viṣṇukaṇṭhasca vidyākaṇṭhastathaiva ca ||
Rāmakaṇṭho jñānaśiva jñānasaṅkara eva ca |
Somaśaṁbhur brahmaśaṁbhus trilocanaśivas tathā ||
Aghoraśiva evātha prasādaśiva eva ca |
Rāmanāthaśivaścaivam īśānaśiva eva ca ||
Vāruṇākhyaśivaścaivatadāsācāryapuṅgavaḥ |
Etair divyaiḥ śivācāryaiḥ paddhatiḥ paribhāṣitā ||
Aghoraśivācāryapaddhati, *Kriyākramajotikā* (*Upodghāta*), p. 10.

[187] *Skanda P.*, I.1.33; I.2.8; III.3.2; VI.250; *Harivaṁśa*, 74; *Bhaviṣya P.*, III.10.1-20; *Vāmana P.*, 62.27-31.

offered to the god in *pūjā*. Similarly, *bhasma* (holy ash) is mentioned in the *Purāṇas* as being of high significance to Śaivites.[188] Great importance is attached to *rudrākṣa* beads;[189] these are worn with great reverence by the devotees of Śiva, especially during the performance of *pūjā*. The *pañcākṣaras* are the five sacred syllables which express obeisance to Śiva, and in the *Purāṇas* they are regarded as superior even to the *Veda*.[190] It is the *mūla-mantra*, the most fundamental of all the *mantras* associated with Śiva. The *Purāṇas* also describe the *dīkṣā* rites, only after going through which a person is admitted into the fold of Śaivism.[191] It is only on becoming properly initiated by means of these rites that a devotee can engage himself in the *pūjā* of Śiva. Some other accessories of the Āgamic Śaiva rituals such as *āsana*, *pādya*, *arghya* and *ācamanīya* are also mentioned in the *Purāṇas*.[192]

However, perhaps more vital elements of the Āgamic Śaiva ritualism are *mantras*, *yantras*, *maṇḍalas*, *kuṇḍas* and *mudrās*, faint traces of which are found in the *Purāṇas*.

8. Mantra

The term *mantra* was originally applied to a Ṛgvedic prayer, an Atharvaṇic incantation or a ritualistic formula.[193] In Śaivism, it denotes all utterances which possess the characteristics of one or more of these three: prayer, incantation or ritualistic formula. Generally speaking, the Śaivites regard as *mantras* all utterances — whether Vedic or non-Vedic [194] — which relate to the god and the vocalization

[188] *Skanda P.*, I.1.5; III.3; I.1.13.15-16; *Brahmāṇḍa P.*, 27.106-15; *Sūta-saṁhitā*, IV.30; *Devībhāgavata P.*, XI.10-15; *Kūrma P.*, I.14.32-33; *Śiva P.*, *Vidyeśvara-saṁhitā*, 16.58-64.

[189] *Padma P.*, I.61; *Śiva P.*, *Jñāna-saṁhitā*, 37.20-76; *Skanda P.*, I.1.5; III.31; III.3.20; *Agni P.*, 325; *Devībhāgavata P.*, XI.5 and 5.

[190] *Skanda P.*, III.3.1; *Āgni P.*, 304.

[191] *Agni P.*, chapters 81-90.

[192] Cf. *Suta-saṁhitā*, I. 4.

[193] Dandekar, "Cultural Background of the *Veda*", *CUR*, vol. XI, Nos. 3 & 4, p. 143; see also Winternitz, *HIL*, vol. I, p. 276.

[194] In this regard, reference may be made to chapter 317 of the *Agni Purāṇa* which serves as a ready proponent of the important *mantras* relating to various gods.

of which helps the worshipper to meditate upon the god over the course of worship.

Among the Vedic *mantras*, first place is assigned to the *Śatarudriya.*[195] In the *Purāṇas*, the repetition of this hymn is often recommended to the worshipper for the propitiation of Śiva.[196] Sometimes a few verses from the *Ṛgveda*, the *Yajurveda* and the *Sāmaveda* are selected and a composite *sūkta* is formed out of them as a prayer to Śiva.[197] Verses from the *Atharvaveda* are sometimes mentioned in this regard.[198] The Vedic *mantras* are no doubt given great prominence, and they generally gain precedence over other kinds of *mantras*, except the *pañcākṣara-mantra*, which according to the Śaiva viewpoint actually represents the very quintessence of the *Vedas*. The five *mantras* relating to the five aspects of Śiva,[199] being Vedic in origin, are also assigned a prominent place in the worship of Śiva.

---

[195] "It is a sacred hymn in constant use, recited during worship in the home and temple when the image is bathed, used as an expiation for sins, and for attaining material and spiritual rewards. It is the source of the greatest *mantra* of the Śaivas, the famous five syllable *mantra, namaḥśivāya* to which Śaivas attach the highest sanctity." Raghavan, *Religion of the Hindus*, p. 285.

[196] *Kūrma P.*, I.14.28-31; I.32.15-25; II.31.50-58; II.35.52-61; *Vāmana P.*, 62.14.

[197] *Vaidikair eva niyamair vividhair brahmacāriṇaḥ |*
Saṁsthāpya śāṅkaraiḥ mantraih ṛgyajuḥsāmasaṁbhavaiḥ ||
Tapaḥ paraṁ samāsthāya gṛṇantaḥ śatarudriyam |
Kūrma P., II.39.3-4.

[198] *Vaidikair vividhair mantraiḥ stotraiḥ māheśvaraiḥ śubhaiḥ |*
Atharvaśirasā cānye rudrādhyair arcayan bhavam ||
Kūrma P., II.39.20.

Idaṁ devasya talliṅgaṁ kapardīśvaram uttamam |
Pūjitavyaṁ prayatnena stotavyaṁ vaidikaiḥ stavaiḥ ||
Kūrma P., I.33.12.

See also *Liṅga P.*, I.64.75-78 and *Vāyu P.*, I.54.5-6.

[199] *Sadyojātaṁ prapadyāmi sadyojātāya vai namo namaḥ. Bhave bhave nāti bhave bhavasva māṁ bhavodbhavāya namaḥ Vāmadevāya namo jyeṣṭhāya namaḥ śreṣṭhāya namo rudrāya namaḥ kālāya namaḥ kalavikaraṇāya namo balavikaraṇāya namo balāya namo balapramathanāya namaḥ sarvabhūtadamanāya namo manonmanāya namaḥ.*

Aghorebhyo'tha ghorebhyo ghoraghoratarebhyaḥ sarvebhyaḥ sarvasarvebhyo namaste'stu rudrarūpebhyaḥ

Tatpuruṣāya vidmahe mahādevāya dhīmahi. Tanno rudraḥ pracodayāt.

Īśānaḥ sarvavidyānām Īśvaraḥ sarvabhūtānāṁ brahmādhipatiḥ brahmaṇo'dhipatiḥ brahmā śivo me'stu sadāsivom. Taittirīya Āraṇyaka, X.43-47.

But as indicated above, the five syllables *Śi-vā-ya-na-maḥ* form the *mantra par excellence* of the Śaivites. This mantra is often called *pañcākṣara*.[200] This is the *mūla-mantra* of the god, and is invariably employed when rites of high significance such as *āvāhana* or *prāṇapratiṣṭhā* are performed. The *mūla-mantra* is repeated by way of *japa* [201] several times according to the capacity of the individual devotee. The *Kūrma Purāṇa* narrates how Nandin once became overpowered with a strong longing to recite the *japa* of the *pañcākṣara*. When he repeated the *pañcākṣara-mantra* a lakh of times, Śiva is said to have manifested himself before him and to have asked him what he wanted. Nandin prayed to him to grant him the necessary energy for a second round of the *japa* of the *mantra*. The desire was granted. In this manner Nandin accomplished five rounds of *japa*, after which Śiva stopped him from the continuation of his strenuous penance and elevated him to higher ranks.[202]

The sacred syllable *oṁ* may be ranked next to the Vedic *mantras* and the *pañcākṣara*. The *Upaniṣads* identify *oṁ* with the higher self.[203] The ritual texts and the *smṛtis* refer to it as the sacred syllable which is always to precede the recital of the *Vedas* and the repetition of the *gāyatrī*.[204] On the same analogy, *praṇava*, as this syllable is generally

---

[200] The efficacy of the *pañcākṣara* is proclaimed in the following words:
Tasmān mantrāntaraṁ tyaktvā pañcākṣaraparo bhava |
Tasmin jihvāntaragate na kiñcid durlabhaṁ bhavet ||
Śiva P., *Vāyu-saṁhitā*, I.30.
Chapter 304 of the *Agni Purāṇa* deals with the *upadeśa* of the *pañcākṣara-mantra* by the teacher to his disciple.

[201] *Uktvā namaḥ śivāyeti mantreṇānena vā japet* | *Kūrma P.*, II.19.96.
The method of repeating the *pañcākṣara-mantra* is laid down in *Śiva P.*, *Vāyu-saṁhitā*, II.12, chapters 128-131. See also *Śiva P.*, *Vidyeśvara-saṁhitā*, 15; *Jñāna-saṁhitā*, 3.50; *Agni P.*, 52; *Liṅga P.*, I.71.141; II.8.1-8. Several ways of repeating the *mantra* by way of *japa* are given. The *japa* may be *vācika*, that is, uttered in an audible manner, *mānasika*, that is articulated mentally in such a way that it is not heard by others. *Liṅga P.*, I.15.6 ff. The three-fold way of performing *japa* forms the topic of discussion in *ibid.*, I.8.39-40.

[202] *Kūrma P.*, II.43.19-42.

[203] *Taittiriya Up.*, I.8; *Kaṭha Up.*, II.16; *Praśna Up.*, 5.2; *Māṇḍūkya Up.*, I; *Maitri Up.*, 6.22.

[204] *Manusmṛti*, II.78.

known, is prefixed to all *mantra* utterances made in the course of Śaivite rites. Akin to the *praṇava* are other syllables, such as *gaṁ* for Gaṇeśa, *śaṁ* for Śaravaṇabhava or Kārttikeya, *haṁ* and even *hāṁ* for Śiva and *hrīṁ* for Śakti. These syllables are known as *bījākṣaras*.

Different kinds of *gāyatrīs* arose over time to be employed as *mantras* during rituals. All of these were modeled on the original *gāyatrī* verse.[205] Perhaps the earliest of such imitations may be seen in the *śivagāyatrī*[206] or the *rudragāyatrī*.[207] Similar *gāyatrīs* relating to Gaṇeśa, Kārttikeya, Devī and other subordinate divinities are also mentioned.

Besides the *mantras* already referred to the five names of Sadyojāta, Vāmadeva, Aghora, Tatpuruṣa and Īśāna were themselves regarded as possessing the character and authority of *mantras*.[208] In the ritual texts they are designated as *pañcabrahma-mantras*[209] or *saṁhitā-mantras*. The *mantras* which constitute a complement to these five and which refer to the six parts of the body, namely the *hṛdaya*, *śiras*, *śikhā*, *kavaca*, *netra* and *astra*, are called the *ṣaḍaṅgamantras*.[210]

---

205 *ṚV*, III.61.10.

206 The Śivagāyatrī is proclaimed in the *Agni Purāṇa* (319.7) as follows:
Tanmaheśāya vidmahe mahādevāya dhīmahi |
Tannaḥ śivaḥ pracodayāt ||

207 The *Kūrma Purāṇa* refers to the *Rudragāyatrī* as follows:
Mantreṇa rudragāyatryā praṇavenāthavā punaḥ | *(II.19.95).*
Rudragāyatrī: Tatpuruṣāya vidmahe mahādevāya dhīmahi |
Tanno rudraḥ pracodayāt || See p. 512, Fn. 1.

208 *Liṅga P.*, I.16.6-35; I.11-14 and also 23; *Śiva P.*, *Vāyu-saṁhitā*, II.4; *Kailāsa-saṁhitā*, 10; *Vāyu P.*, I.23; *Garuḍa P.*, 21.

209 *Śiva P.*, *Kailāsa-saṁhitā*, 11.

210 *Ibid.*, *Dharma-saṁhitā*, 37. The following extract from the *Agni Purāṇa* throws light on the *pañca-brahma* and the *ṣaḍaṅga-mantras*:
Īśānaṁ ojasākrāntaṁ prathamaṁ tu samuddharet |
Tṛtīyaṁ puruṣaṁ viddhi dakṣinaṁ pañcamaṁ tathā ||
Saptamaṁ vāmadevaṁ tu sadyojātaṁ tataḥ param |
Rasayuktantu navamaṁ brahmapañcakam īritam ||
Oṁkārādyāścaturthyantāḥ namo'ntāḥ sarvamantrakāḥ |
Sadyo devā dvitīyaṁ tu hṛdayañcāṅgasaṁyutam ||
Caturthaṁ tu śiro viddhi īśvaranāma nāmataḥ |
Ūhakaṁ tu śikhā jñeyā viśvarūpasamanvitā ||
Tanmantram aṣṭamaṁ khyātaṁ netraṁ tu daśamaṁ matam |
Astraṁ śaśī samākhyātaṁ śivasaṁjñam śikhidhvajaḥ ||
Namaḥ svāhā svadhā vauṣaṭ hūṁ ca phaṭ krameṇa tu |
Agni P., 317.9-14.

At the time of *āvāhana*, which implies a special invocation to the god to make himself immediately present in the image, certain verses are recited. These verses contain a more or less detailed description of the god, and thereby enable the *upāsaka* or the worshipper to meditate on the god in some specific form.[211] They may, therefore, be included in the category of *mantras*. Such verses are also known as *dhyāna-ślokas*. In the *Paddhatis* where these *dhyāna-ślokas* are given, they are almost always followed by the instruction that the god is to be invoked into the idol with this *mantra* (*iti mantreṇa āvāhya*) — in other words, they are referred to as *mantras*. Even in the present *pūjā* ritual, *mantras* of various types play the same role as before, and it is impossible to think of rituals without them.

9. Yantras and Maṇḍalas

Yantras may be generally described as mystic diagrams drawn according to various set patterns which are often used in worship as substitutes for the image of the gods.[212] Usually they are flat plates made from various metals, such as copper, silver or gold, or from a mixture of the chief metals. Each god has a *yantra* specifically assigned to him, the diagram of the *yantra* and the syllables (*bījākṣaras*)[213] inscribed upon it varying from god to god. The presence of the god is assumed in a *yantra* exactly in the same way as for an image.

The *yantras* are employed in rituals in two ways. One is that the *yantra* or the diagram of the god is inscribed on a flat plate. After the *āvāhana* and the other ceremonies have been performed, the *yantra* is placed on the *āsana-śilā* (the stone-seat) upon which the stone

---

211 For the *dhyāna-ślokas* see *Śivaliṅgapratiṣṭhāvidhi*, pt. II, p. 72 ff; also cf. *Agni P.*, 74.50-54.

212 Gopinath Rao, *op.cit.*, vol. I, pt. I, Introduction p. 12; also see *ibid.*, p. 325. The *yantroddhāraṇavidhipaṭala* (ch. 12) of *Kiraṇāgama* deals with the details relating to the structure and construction of the various *yantras*.

213 For an elaborate discussion on the *bījamantra*, and for the *bījamantras* of the various *devatās* see Woodroffe's *The Garland of Letters*, pp. 241-249.

image of the god is set up and to which it is permanently fixed.[214] This is only possible before the *pratiṣṭhā* rite. The other way involves the employment of the *yantra* for installation and external worship; there are three main types of the *yantra* intended for this.[215] The *bhūprastāra* is the *yantra* where the diagram is inscribed on a metal plate. The *kailāsaprastāra* and the *meruprastāra* are the two other types of *yantras*, distinguished by their various dimensions.

The *yantra* cult is closely connected with Śaktism, and its introduction into the Śaiva ritual system is perhaps due to the amalgamation of Śaktism with Śaivism. Incidentally it may be pointed out that the *śrīcakra*, which is held sacred to Devī, is found installed in various temples in south India.

The *maṇḍala* [216] is, in many respects, similar to a *yantra*. The difference between the *yantra* and the *maṇḍala* may, however, be easily seen. The latter is of a more or less temporary nature, for, it is designed so as to last only for one occasion. Each god has a *maṇḍala* specifically designed for him, and the god is invoked to be present in that *maṇḍala* till the end of the ritual. Powders of different colours are used for the drawing of these *maṇḍalas*, different symbols and different colours being specified for different gods. The *navagraha-maṇḍala*, for example, is constructed by first drawing a large square and then dividing it into nine equal squares. The appropriate symbols are thereafter inscribed in these squares. The lotus is the symbol of the Sun, a square of the Moon, a triangle of Mars, an arrow of Mercury, and so on. The *āvāhana* of the *grahas* is made on the *maṇḍalas*. *Vāstu-śānti* is a special rite performed in connection with the house-

[214] Cf. "Each deity has its armourial bearing or distinguishing mark that is to be buried below the seat of the deity and to be carved on the lintel of the door of the main room". K.V. Vaze, "Construction of Hindu Temples", *ABORI*, vol. VIII, p. 206. For an elaborate discussion of the etymology implication, and employment of *yantras* for ritual purposes see Zimmer, *Myths and Symbols in Indian Art and Civilisation*, pp. 140-141.

[215] Cf: "*Cakrarājasya trayaḥ prastārāḥ bhūmikailāsamerubhedāt*". Bhāskararāya's commentary on '*merunilayā*' *Lalitāsahasranāma*, Nirnaya Sāgar ed., p. 153.

[216] *Bhaviṣya P.*, II.21; *Śiva P.*, *Kailāsa-saṁhitā*, 4. See also *Kiraṇāgama*, 18.

warming ceremony.[217] For that rite, the *vāstu-maṇḍala* is constructed very elaborately, and the relevant deities are invoked into it.[218]

The ritual texts also prescribe the decoration of the site of the rituals with similar designs. *Raṅgavallī*, as it is popularly known, is purely for decorative purposes, but reminds one of the *maṇḍalas*.

10. Kuṇḍas

As has been already pointed out, in post-Vedic times Agni was not accorded the great prominence which he enjoyed in Vedic times. However, the worship of Agni is seen to have continued in the Purāṇic and the post-Purāṇic periods, albeit with certain modifications. In this connection it is interesting to note that the ritual involved with the worship of Agni is given a Śaivite colouring. Further, the worship of Agni is regarded as indispensable in Śaiva rituals.[219] The *Suprabheda* lays down that the kindling of Agni should take place in all daily and special rites such as *pratiṣṭhā*, *utsava*, *dīkṣā*, *garbhādāna* and *dahana*.[220] It is averred that Agni is the essence of all the gods and all the *mantras*. He is therefore required to be propitiated in all rituals in the prescribed manner.[221]

---

[217] For the ritual see the sequel.

[218] For two basic *vāstu-maṇḍalas* see pp. 379-380.

[219] *Agni P.*, 75-76.

[220] *Nitye naimittike caiva pratiṣṭhāyām athotsave |*
Grahaṇe viṣusaṅkrāntyāṁ śatrūṇāṁ ca pradarśane ||
Śāntike pauṣṭike caiva dīkṣāyāṁca pavitrake |
Garbhādānādike teṣāṁ śaivānāṁ dahanādiṣu ||
Prāyaścittādikāleṣu vahnikarma samācaret |
Śivaliṅgapratiṣṭhāvidhi, II, p. 125.

[221] *Sarvadevamayo vahniḥ sarvamantramayas tathā |*
Tasmāt sarveṣu kāryeṣu dhyātavyo vidhimārgataḥ ||
Agnipūjāṁ vinā yatra tatraiva niṣphalaṁ bhavet |
Agnivaktre ħuneccaiva sarvadevapriyaṁ bhavet ||
Ibid., p. 129.

"Fire is made of all the gods and made of all *mantras*. Therefore, in all rituals, one must meditate on him according to rules. A performance without worship of Fire will have no fruit. That which is offered in the mouth of Fire will please all the gods."

A regular kindling of Agni implied the preparation of *agnikuṇḍas* of various shapes. Usually nine *kuṇḍas* are prescribed. When this is not possible, their number is reduced to five or, in some cases, even to one. From among the more common *agnikuṇḍas*, the *caturasra-kuṇḍa* is square-shaped; the *yoni-kuṇḍa* resembles the womb; the *ardha-candra-kuṇḍa* is like the crescent moon. The *trikoṇa* and the *vṛtta kuṇḍas* are respectively triangular and circular in shape, while the *pañcakoṇa* and the *aṣṭakoṇa kuṇḍas* are a pentagon and octagon respectively. The *padmakuṇḍa* is designed like a lotus. A few passages are found in the *Purāṇas* giving details about the *kuṇḍas*. The *ardha-candra*, the *caturasra* and the *vartula kuṇḍas* are specifically mentioned and the rules relating to their construction are prescribed.[222]

As is to be expected, the *Āgamas* [223] deal with the subject of the various *kuṇḍas* in greater detail. The *Kāmikāgama*, for instance, describes the eight important types of *kuṇḍas* as follows:[224]

222 *Agni P.*, 24; *Bhaviṣya P.*, II.13-14.

223 *Suprabheda*, 11; *Kiraṇāgama*, 17; *Rauravāgama*, 14.

224 In the present context, the method of producing the *kuṇḍas* is given in modern geometrical terminology.

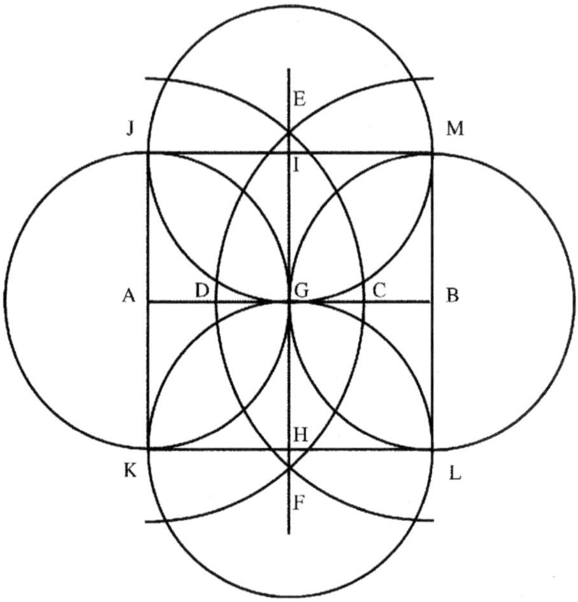

Caturasrakuṇḍa [225]

This *kuṇḍa* is square and forms the basis for all the other *kuṇḍas*. Twenty-four *aṅgulas* are prescribed as the standard measurement for its construction. A line AB is drawn measuring 24 *aṅgulas*. This line is drawn as *prācī-sūtra*. G is the center of this *prācī-sūtra*. Points D and C are then marked on it so that AD = DG = GC = CB. With A and B as centers and AC and BD as radii, two arcs are drawn to cut each other at points E and F. EF is then joined. EF is called the *soma-sūtra.* On EF, points H and I are marked so that GH = GA = GI. With the points A, H, B, and I as centers and AG as the radius, four arcs are described intersecting one another at J, K, L, and M. JKLM is the square required. The construction of the *kuṇḍa* attains perfection when the other features, such as *mekhalā*, *kuṇḍanābhi* and *padma*, are added to it.[226]

[225] *Sūtraṁ pūrvāparaṁ pūrvaṁ nyased diksādhanakramāt* |
Tenaiva sādhayet sūtraṁ dakṣinottaragaṁ kramāt ||
Tajjñaḥ kṣetrārdhamānānāṁ vṛttaṁ vā hastanirmitam |
Kāmikāgama, I.7.3.; see also *AŚP*, p. 534. and *Kuṇḍaratnāvalī*, 94.

[226] These are described below.

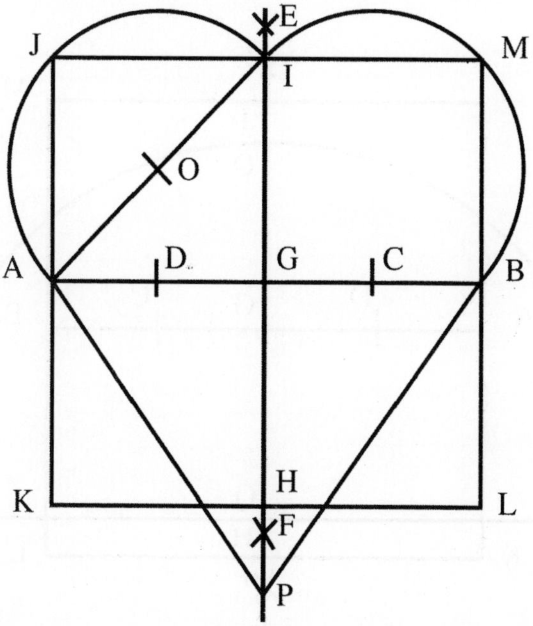

Yoniku ṇḍa [227]

The design of the *caturasrakuṇḍa* is taken as its basis. The *prācī-sūtra* AB and the *soma-sūtra*, EF and the four corners of the square are first fixed. AB and HI intersect at G. HI is produced to P so that PH is equal to one-fifth of HI. AP and BP are joined. AI and GL intersect at O. With O as center and OA as the radius, a semicircle is drawn on AI. Similarly another semicircle is drawn on BI. The *kuṇḍa* is given its full shape with the addition of the usual features.

---

[227] *Hastamātraṁ bhavet kuṇḍaṁ liṅge kanyasyakaṁ bhavet |*
Dvyaṅgulordhvaṁ tayor vṛddhiḥ dvitryaṁśataḥ kramāt ||
Pañcamāṁśaṁ puro nyastvā koṇavedāṁśamānataḥ |
Bhramād aśvatthapatrābhaṁ kuṇḍam āgneyam ucyate ||
Kāmika, I.7.13-14. See also *Kuṇḍaratnāvalī*, 97 and *AŚP*, p. 539.

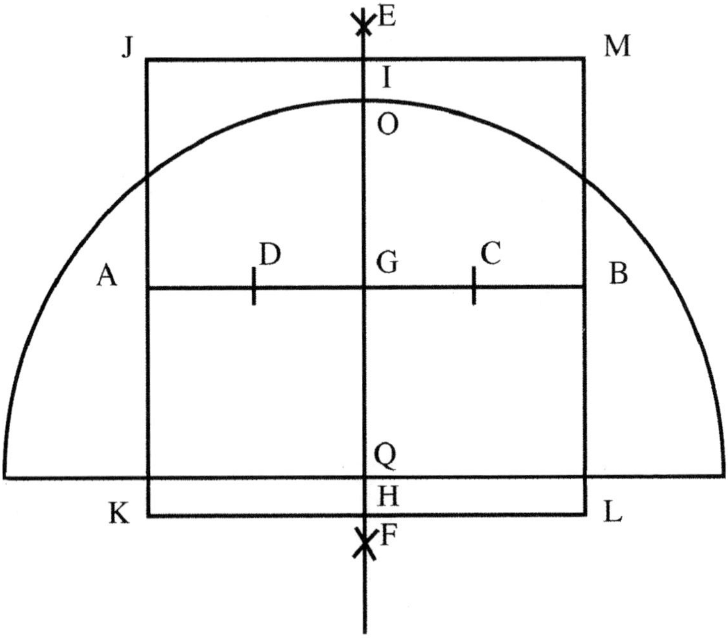

Ardhacandrakuṇḍa [228]

On the *soma-sūtra* HI, the points O and Q are marked. IO = QH = 1/9 th of IH. With Q as center and OQ as a radius, a semicircle is described. With the provision of the other features, the *kuṇḍa* is given its final shape.

[228] *Caturasre gṛhe bhakte tyaktvādyante tadaṁśake |*
Madhyasaptāṁśamānena kuṇḍaṁ khaṇḍenduvad bhramāt ||
Kāmika, I.7.15-16; *Kuṇḍaratnāvalī*, 99 and *ASP*, p. 287.

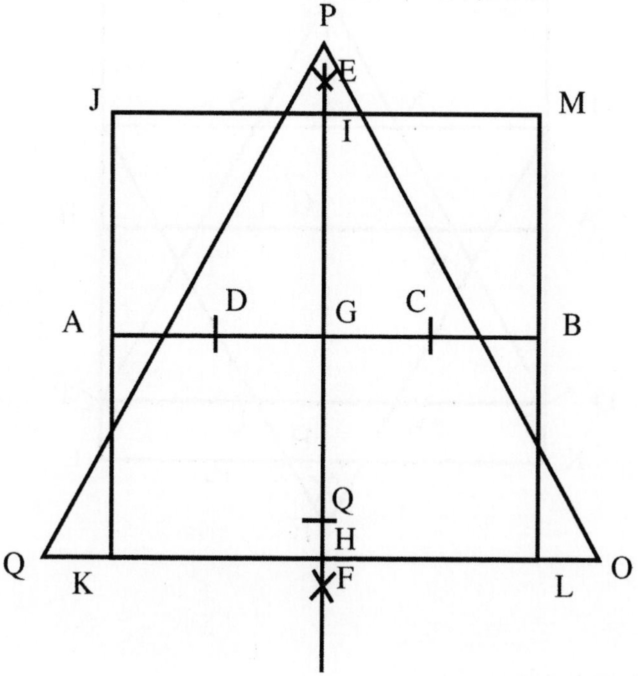

Trikoṇakuṇḍa [229]

On LK extended both ways, points O and Q are marked so that OL = KQ = 1/6 th of LK. HI is extended to P so that IP = OL. POQ is the required triangle. The *kuṇḍa* is then given its final shape.

[229] *Iṣṭadikṣu nyaset paścād uttare sūtrapātanam* |
Tribhāgavṛddhito matsyais tribhir naiśācaraṁ bhavet ||
Kāmika, I.7.16-17; *Kuṇḍaratnāvalī* 100-101 and *AŚP*, p. 540.

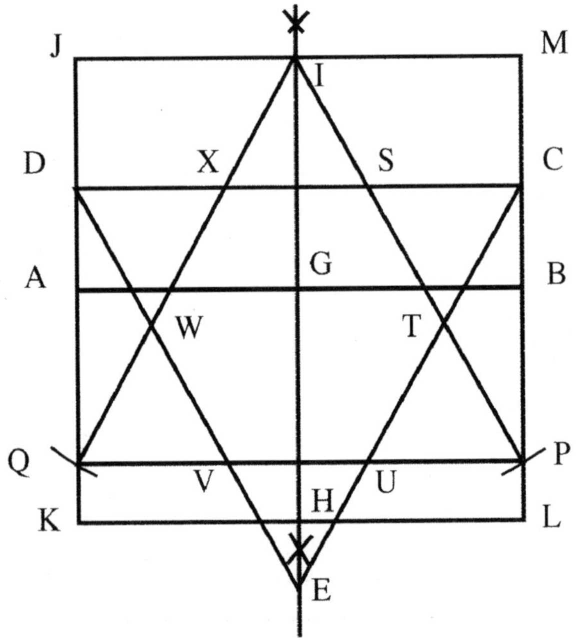

Saṭkoṇakuṇḍa [230]

I is the mid-point of MJ. With I as center and MJ as a radius, an arc is described cutting ML and JK at points P and Q respectively. IP, IQ and PQ are joined. Points S and T are fixed on IP so that PT = TS = SI. Similarly, U and V are fixed on PQ so that PU = UV = VQ. W and X are fixed on IQ, so that QW = WX = XI. A line is drawn through S and X to cut ML and JK at C and D. With C as a center and CD as a radius, an arc is described to cut IH extended to E. DE is joined. The lines SX, XW, WV, VU, UT, TS are erased. The *kuṇḍa* is then given its final shape with the necessary additions.

[230] *Ṣaḍbhāgaviddhito matsyaiś caturbhiḥ syāt ṣaḍasrakam* | *Kāmika*, I.7.17; see *AŚP*, 540.

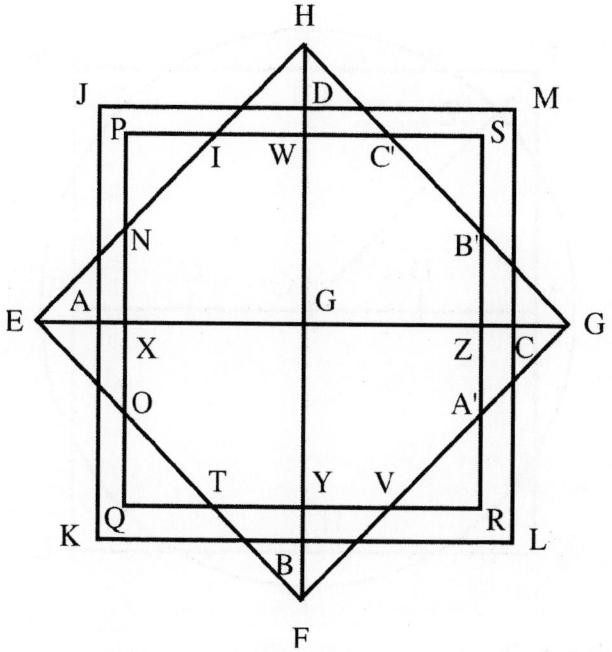

Aṣṭakoṇakuṇḍa [231]

JKLM is the basic square. A, B, C, and D are the midpoints of JK, KL, LM and MJ respectively. A square PQRS is described within JKLM. PQ and SR meet AC at X and Z respectively. QR and PS meet BD at Y and W respectively. DW = 1/16 th of JM. BD is extended to H so that DH = 1/8 th of JM. Similarly, CA is extended to E so that AE = 1/8 th of JM. DB is extended to F so that BF = 1/8 th of JM. AC is extended to G. GC = 1/8 th of JM. The squares PQRS and EFHG intersect each other as follows: EF cuts PQ at O, and QR at T. FG cuts QR at V and RS at A'. Similarly, other points of intersection are B′, C′, I and N respectively. Thus the *Aṣṭakoṇakuṇḍa* is given its structure with the angles thus formed at the eight points E, Q, F, R, G, S, H, and P.

[231] *Kuṇḍaratnāvalī*, 3; see also *ASP*, p. 540.

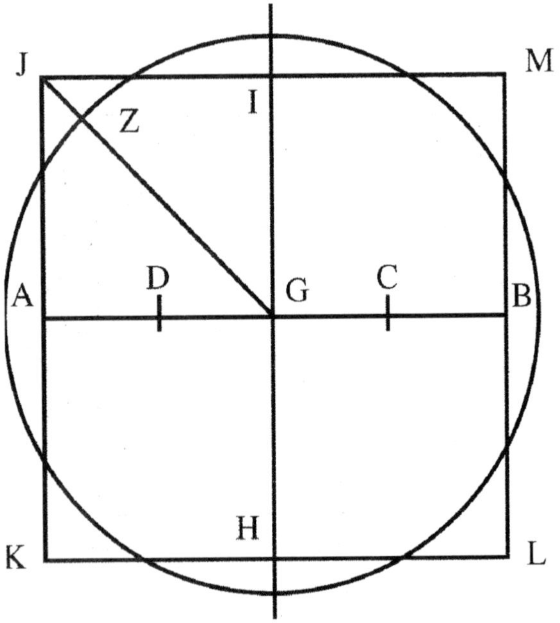

Vṛttakuṇḍa [232]

Point Z is marked on GJ so that ZJ is 1/8th of GJ. With G as center and GZ as radius, a circle is described. With the provision of the *mekhalā* and the other features the *kuṇḍa* is given perfection.

Padmakuṇḍa [233]

This is merely an elaboration of the *vṛttakuṇḍa* with an additional display of eight petals resembling those of the lotus.

As suggested above, each type of *kuṇḍa*, after its basic construction, is sought to be given a kind of perfection by the addition of certain special features. For instance, a lotus design is displayed at

---

232 *Kaṇṭhārdhāṣṭāṁśasantyāgaṁ vṛttakuṇḍam ihoditam* | *Kāmika*, I.7.18.

233 *Caturasreṣṭabhāgeṣu karṇikā syād dvibhāgataḥ* |
Tadbahistvekabhāgena kesarāṇi prakalpayet ||
Tṛtīyadalamadhyāni turīyadalakoṭayaḥ |
Bhramaṇāt padmakuṇḍaṁ syād dalāgraṁ darśayed budhaḥ ||
Kāmika, I.7.18-20.

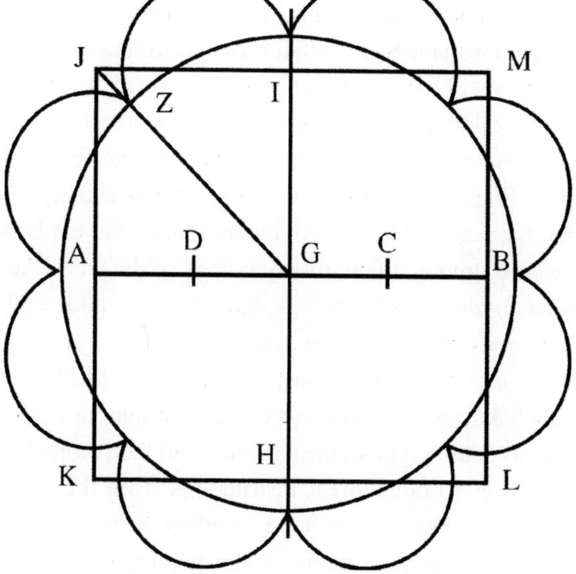

the center of the *kuṇḍa*. Then there is the *mekhalā*, the bordering wall, running around the *kuṇḍa*, which thus has the same shape as that of the *kuṇḍa*. Three *mekhalās* are prescribed for each *kuṇḍa* — the height of the outer *mekhalā* being less than that of the interior one. The innermost *mekhalā* is four *aṅgulas* in width and four *aṅgulas* in height. The middle one is three *aṅgulas* in width as well as in height and the outermost is two *aṅgulas* in width and height. Each *kuṇḍa* is provided with a *kuṇḍayoni*. It is located on the highest *mekhalā* at its center, and is eight *aṅgulas* wide and twelve *aṅgulas* long. Its pointed edge touches the *kaṇṭha* or the space adjacent to the inner *mekhalā*. It is designed like the leaf of the *pippala* tree (as in the case of the *yonikuṇḍa*). The *kuṇḍas* constructed in the east and the south should have the *kuṇḍayonis* [234] pointing towards the north; otherwise, they should point towards the east.

[234] *Kuṇḍaratnāvalī*, 140; *Kiraṇāgama*, 15.

11. Mudrās [235]

Mudrās are commonly employed in the Śaivite rituals. They seem to have evolved with the Śakti cult, for the *mudrās* are included among the five *makāras* of the celebrated *vāma* school of Śaktism. One of the names of the goddess refers to her as one adored with ten *mudrās*.[236] *Mudrās* may be generally described as the outward expressions of the inner feelings — the medium of expression usually being the hand. The *Āgamas*, however, provide an interesting explanation of the term *mudrā*, giving a fanciful etymology of the word. According to the *Kāraṇāgama*, *mudrā* brings delight to the gods and chases away the demons; therefore, it is called *mudrā*.[237]

The *Āgama* texts mention thirty-two *mudrās*, while those mentioned in the Śākta texts number only ten. The definitions of the various *mudrās* are no doubt given in the *Āgamas*, and their *modus operandi* explained.[238] Yet without direct instructions from the teacher and constant practice, one cannot hope to adequately learn the art of *mudrās*. By holding the fingers in the prescribed positions, the desirable shapes are obtained. For instance, the *triśūla-mudrā* resembles a trident, the *dhenu-mudrā* is like the udder of a cow, and so on.

A list of the various *mudrās* is given in the following passage from the *Kāraṇāgama*:[239]

---

[235] The *Agni Purāṇa* describes a few *mudrās* in chapter 26. An instance, for example, may be cited in *Agni P.*, 74.55-57, of occurrences of *mudrās*, in the course of a rite.
The following remarks made by Przyluski in his article "Mudra" (*IC*, vol. II, p. 716) explain the term *mudrā* and speak of its use. "*Mudrā* means also, mode of holding the fingers (in religious worship or magic rites). These practices hold an important place in Tantric Buddhism ... Mr. Finot has shown that 'notwithstanding the diversity of the Tantric ceremonies the following four elements remain always unchanged; the *maṇḍala*, the *mantra*, the *pūjā*, the *mudrā*. The gods are put on the *maṇḍala*, *mantras* are recited *pūjās* offered to them, with the accompaniment of *mudrās*, or ritual gestures'."

[236] *Daśamudrāsamārādhyā*, *Lalitāsahasranāma*, p. 348.

[237] *Mudaṁ karoti devānāṁ drāvayaty asurāṁs tathā |*
Modanād drāvaṇāccaiva mudreyaṁ saṁprakīrtitā ||
Kāraṇa, I.28.1-2.

[238] *Ibid.*, I.28.7-47; *Suprabheda*, pp. 46-48.

[239] *Kāraṇa*, I.28.2-7.

Liṅgamudrā namaskārā tālākhyā śaṅkhamudrikā |
Surabhī mukulī caiva vārāhī caiva niṣṭhurā ||
Bījākhyā pañcavaktrī ca dravyamudrā śikhākhyakā |
Saṁhāramudrikā caiva sadākhyā caiva mudrikā ||
Asanī ca maheśākhyā vajrākhyā śaktimudrikā |
Daṇḍamudrā tathā khaḍgā pāśamudrāṅkuśākhyakā ||
Gadāmudrā ca śūlākhyā padmamudrā tathaiva ca |
Cakramudrā tathā ṭaṅkā mahāmudrā tathaiva ca ||
Ghaṇṭāmudrāstramudrā ca śaramudrā dhanus tathā |
Mudrāṇām ucyate caiva dvātriṁśallakṣaṇaṁ param ||

It has been pointed out above that several features of the full-fledged Śaiva ritual are already more or less clearly adumbrated in the *Purāṇas*. However, a critical study of the *Āgamas* would show that, in more senses than one, they must be said to have evolved a form of Śaiva worship of their own.[240] As has been indicated, out of the few *Āgamas* which are available, only three or four are specifically concerned and described under four main heads, namely, *karṣaṇa*, *pratiṣṭhā*, *utsava* and *prāyaścitta* [241] — each of these heads comprehending various rites. To the *karṣaṇa* group belong all the preliminary rites. The *pratiṣṭhā* group includes the rites relating to installation. The *utsava* pertains to the rites relating to festivals. The last group is made up of expiatory rites. Most of these rites certainly have a Purāṇic basis, but they have attained fuller and more elaborate forms in the *Āgamas*.

[240] In this connection Das Gupta observes, "The *Āgamas* contain some elements of philosophical thought, but their interest is more on religious details of the cult of Śaivism. We find therefore a good deal of ritualism, discussion of the architectural techniques for the foundation of temples, and *mantras* and details of worship connected with the setting up of the phallic symbol of Śiva." *History of Indian Philosophy*, vol. V, p. 20.

[241] The contents of the *Kāraṇa Āgama* given on pages 60-64 of the printed edition of the text, indicate this four-fold division. These pages contain the ritual topics which form the titles of the chapters, and these are arranged under the heads, *karṣaṇa*, *pratisthā*, *utsava* and *prāyascitta*. Of the one hundred and forty-seven chapters, chapters 1-53 occur in the *karṣaṇa* section, chapters 54-137 in the *pratiṣṭhā*, 138-143 in the *utsava*, and the remaining chapters in the section entitled *prāyaścitta*.

The *karṣaṇa*, as pointed out above, deals with the rites preliminary to the *pratiṣṭhā*. This section, accordingly, includes all rites beginning from the ploughing of the site chosen for the construction of the temple.[242] Another rite discussed under this heading relates to the selection of the stones for sculpting the image. However, as far as the arrangement of the *Āgamas* is concerned, one can hardly draw any line of demarcation between the *karṣaṇa* and the *pratiṣṭhā*.

The piece of the land chosen for the construction of the temple is first ploughed, then the various parts of the temple are properly measured out. It may be mentioned in this regard that the topic of *vāstu-vinyāsa* receives considerable elaboration in the *Purāṇas*. The *garbhagṛha* is the central apartment in a temple, and the entire procedure of its construction is described in detail, though this topic cannot be said to have any direct connection with the form of worship as such. It is, however, necessary because even slight deficiencies in this respect are likely to lead to disastrous results. Other topics dealt with in this section include the choice of stone for making the image, the construction of the *prākāras*, and such rites as *mṛtsaṁgrahaṇa*, *aṅkurārpaṇa* and *rakṣābandhana*. The structural plan of the *yāgaśālā*, the preparation of the *kuṇḍas* and other allied preparations for the *pratiṣṭhā* also fall within the purview of the *karṣaṇādi* group of rituals.

Some of the more important rites falling under the heading *karṣaṇa* are briefly described below:

12. Karṣaṇa

This consists of the ceremonial ploughing of the site chosen for the construction of the temple.[243] The site is first chosen, and then grains such as *māṣa*, *mudga*, *tila*, *yava* and *siddhārtha* are sown there. Cows are made to stay on that site for a few days, presumably with a view to fertilizing and enriching the soil. Moreover, the presence of the cow is believed to ward off all evils that are associated with the site. A pair of bulls is yoked to the plough, and, after giving *dakṣiṇā* to the brāhmaṇas, the site is ploughed.[244]

---

[242] It is for this reason that this has received the name *karṣaṇa*.

[243] *Suprabheda*, 25.

[244] *Kāraṇa*, II.3.299-306.

Anujñā

This rite authorizes the performer of a ritual to function in that capacity. Being the chief person connected with the ritual and assisted by a host of others, he is called *pradhānācārya*. As a performer of the *pratiṣṭhā*, he is also called *pratiṣṭhācārya*. Through *anujñā* he obtains the ceremonial sanction from the brāhmaṇas who are gathered for this purpose. After the distribution of the *dakṣiṇā*, the brāhmaṇas are implored to grant the sanction;[245] they respond readily and express their approval. This *anujñā* is similar to the *anujñā* performed in all *gṛhya* rites in the South. A similar sanction is obtained from the god Gaṇeśa, and for this reason this rite is known as *gaṇeśānujñā*,[246] as against the former one which is called *brāhmaṇānujñā*.

Mṛtsaṅgrahaṇa

This rite consists of a ceremonial collection of soil for sowing seeds. After an invocation of Gaṇeśa and Varuṇa, the *puṇyāhavācana* is performed for the sanctification of the spot from which the soil is to be collected. First, a square is drawn on the floor of the site, and it is divided into nine equal squares. Sandalwood, flowers and *akṣata* are offered. The goddess Earth is invoked and worshipped to grace the *maṇḍala* already constructed by her presence. The *gāyatrī* assigned to her is recited. A soil cutter (*kundālī*) is procured; it is bathed in water and decked with sandalwood and flowers. The performer of the ritual faces north, and with the *kundālī* collects the soil from within the square-shaped *maṇḍala* which was sanctified by the foregoing rites. The hole made thereby is covered with earth, and seeds are scattered over it. The soil is taken to the *yāgaśālā* [247] in procession to the accompaniment of music, and is stored there.

---

244 *Kāraṇa*, II.3.299-306.

245 *Śivaliṅgapratiṣṭhāvidhi*, pt. I, p. 10.

246 *Ibid.*, p. 8. Similarly performed are the *anujñās* in respect of Dakṣiṇāmūrti, Subrahmanya, Śiva, Devī, Nandikeśvara, and Caṇḍeśvara. *ASP*, p. 104-263.

Aṅkurārpaṇa

The *aṅkurārpaṇa* is a *gṛhya* rite regularly performed in the South. The *Āgama* texts have adopted it, duly emphasizing its importance.[248] The vessels chosen for the rite of *aṅkurārpaṇa* are known as *pālikās*. These are filled with the soil already collected. Five such *pālikās* are employed in this rite, but sometimes twenty-five *pālikās* are also used. The *pālikās* should be made of any of the prescribed materials, namely gold, silver, copper or earth. Dark-coloured vessels and those that are broken or emitting putrid smell are precluded. The vessels are decorated with the leaves of *udumbara*, *aśvattha* and *pāṭali*. Nine kinds of grain are prescribed for sowing in connection with this rite. Soma, the Moon-god, is especially invoked to be present on this occasion, together with his consorts Kṛttikā and Rohiṇī. The grains soaked in milk are first sanctified by the recital of the *oṣadhisūkta*.[249] This is followed by the sowing, which is done to the accompaniment of the proper *mantras*.

Rakṣābandhana

This consists of tying a cord around the wrist of the performer and his assistants. The cord is also known as *pratisara*.[250] The *pratisarabandha* is prescribed at the commencement of the *pratiṣṭhā* rite. The cord is usually made of cotton fibre, but silver and gold threads are also sometimes used. The *rakṣabāndhana* starts with the Ganeśa-*pūjā* and the *puṇyāhavācana*. From one end to the other the cord is besmeared with *bhasma* (holy ash); it is then tied around the wrist of each of the participants in the rites.[251]

---

[247] *Kāraṇa* I, p. 148-153. See also *AŚP*, pp. 96-111.

[248] *Suprabheda*, 35; *Śivaliṅgapratiṣṭhāvidhi*, pt. I, pp. 152-9; *AŚP*, pp. 114-127.

[249] *Yājuṣa-mantra-ratnākara*, p. 95.

[250] For the special significance of the word '*pratisara*' see Gonda. Altind. *Pratisara*, sraj, und Verwandtes". *AO*, 15.

[251] *Śivaliṅgapratiṣṭhāvidhi*, I, pp. 169-71. *AŚP*, pp. 131-135.

Grāmaśānti

Grāmaśānti is performed before the *pratiṣṭhā* and the *utsava* rites in order to placate the evil spirits of a village; it is also believed to add to the welfare and prosperity of the inhabitants. The normal procedure of this rite is as follows: a *maṇḍapa* is erected and the required materials are gathered. A *sthaṇḍila* is then prepared in the *maṇḍapa* and a *yantra* is inscribed upon it. The *asuras*, *rākṣasas*, *piśācas* and *brahmarākṣasas* who are supposed to be frequenting the village are duly invoked. The *kṣetrapāla* is also invoked, and *balis* are also offered to all of them. The *bali* consists of *māṣāpūpa* and balls of rice. The offerings are made to them on the fire kindled on the *sthaṇḍila*.[252]

The *grāmaśānti* is followed by *rakṣoghna-homa* which is intended to drive away the evil spirits. With the *grāmaśānti* is also associated the *praveśa-bali*, in which balls of rice and prescribed materials are offered at the various points of the *maṇḍala*, which is drawn with *iṣṭaka* and *rajanī* powders.[253]

Navagrahamakha

For this rite, the *navagrahamaṇḍala* is first drawn with coloured powders. The symbols of the *grahas* are then duly added to it. The nine planets are invoked to present themselves in the *maṇḍalas* with their *adhidevatās* and *pratyadhidevatās*. This is followed by the *navagraha-homa*, wherein offerings are made to the planets through fire. Ghee, *samidh* and *dhānyas* constitute the main offerings. The prescribed Vedic *mantras* are recited as various offerings are poured out on the fire.[254] This propitiation of the planets is expected to remove the evil influences which they might otherwise exercise. It may be incidentally pointed out that, over the course of time, the *navagrahas* became somewhat like a group of ancillary deities connected with Śiva, and they even came to be included among the *parivāradevatās* in a temple dedicated to Śiva.

---

[252] *Śivaliṅgapratiṣṭhāvidhi*, pp. 28-38. [253] *Ibid.*, pp. 60-64.

[254] *Yājuṣamantra-ratnākara*, p. 154.

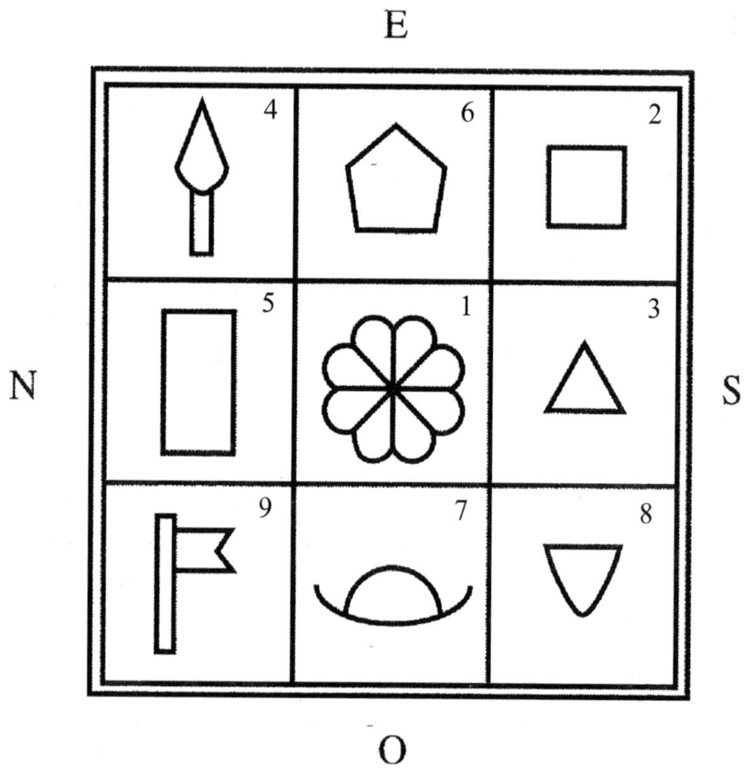

Navagrahamaṇḍala

1	Sūrya	Sun	Centre	Red	*Padma*
2	Candra	Moon	South-East	White	Square
3	Aṅgāraka	Mars	South	Red	*Trikoṇa*
4	Budha	Mercury	North-East	Green	Arrow
5	Bṛhaspati	Jupiter	North	Yellow	Rectangle
6	Śukra	Venus	East	White	*Pañcakoṇa*
7	Śani	Saturn	West	Black	*Dhanus*
8	Rāhu		South-West	Grey	*Śūrpa*
9	Ketu		North-West	Variegated	*Dhvaja*

Vāstuśānti

As has been already indicated, the *vāstuvinyāsa*, the *vāstu-maṇḍala* and the ascription of the *maṇḍalas* to the various *devatās* are some of the topics which have received not inconsiderable attention in the *Purāṇas*.[255] Two types of *maṇḍalas* are used in connection with the *vāstuśānti*; one is known as *maṇḍūkapada* and the other as *paramaśāyipada*.[256] Sixty-four deities [257] are invoked at the various points of the *maṇḍala*. Brahmā and his consort Sāvitrī are invoked at the center. *Balis* are offered to them and the relevant *homas* performed.[258] The *vāstuśānti* is a rite which must be performed; otherwise, the various deities would withdraw themselves from their respective places of guardianship, and a disaster might befall the site.[259]

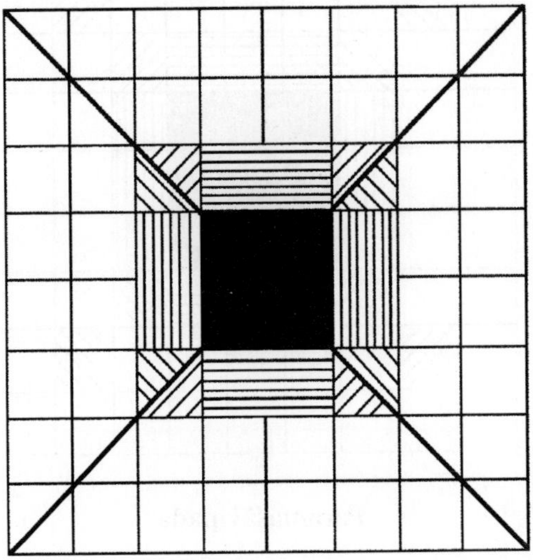

Maṇḍūkapada

[255] Cf. *Agni P.*, 92 and 93.

[256] See the position of deities in slightly varying charts in Mayamata, vol. I, fig. 5-8, IGNCA, Delhi, 1994.

[257] *Matsya P.*, 253. 23-36.

[258] For the details of the rite see *AŚP*, pp. 1-82.

[259] *Śivaliṅgapratiṣṭhāvidhi*, I, p. 104.

Under the heading of *pratiṣṭhā* [260] are mentioned all the rites which pertain to the installation of the images for worship. These images are of two types, either made of stone or of bronze. One finds both types of images installed in the temples of the South. A more or less fixed convention seems to have already evolved in this connection, that the images to be installed in the central shrine as the *mūlamūrti* are made of stone, while the images meant to be taken out in procession are made of bronze. In the Śiva temples the *mūlamūrti* is always the *liṅga* and this is invariably made of stone.[261]

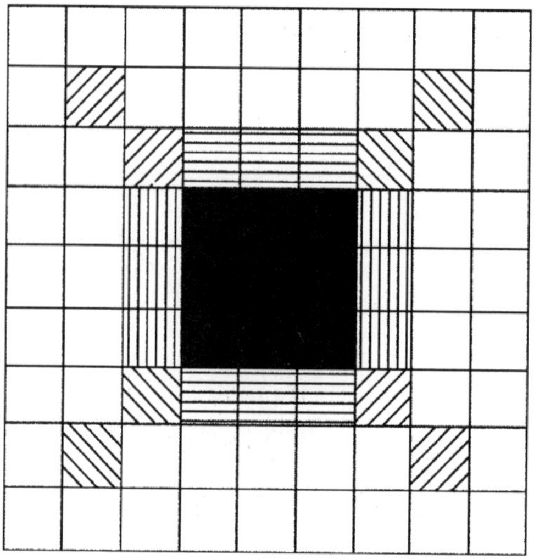

Paramaśāyipada

[260] Cf. *Agni P.*, 68, and also 95-97; *Bhaviṣya P.*, II.17; *Śiva P.*, *Vāyu-saṁhitā*, II.28; *Śiva P.*, *Vidyeśvara-saṁhitā*, 9-11.

[261] Cf. Zimmer, *The Art of Indian Asia*, p. 111: "For, South Indian bronze belong to the category of 'moving images' (*calamūrti*) or 'ceremonial images' (*utsavamūrti*, *bhogamūrti*), which are carried around in processions and festivals in contradistinction to the 'fixed image' (*acalamurti*, *dhruvamūrti*), i.e. the *liṅgam*, or the main stone image in the innermost cellar, in the so-called 'womb chamber' (*garbhagṛha*), which is the holy of holies, and life center of the sanctuary".

The idea underlying the *pratiṣṭhā* ritual is somewhat like this: the image chiseled out according to the prescribed measurements is ready for installation, but it still remains stone or metal until the god penetrates it. Such penetration of the god into the image is brought about by means of the various *saṁskāras* which are duly performed in respect of that image.[262] These *saṁskāras* are briefly described in the following pages. For all practical purposes, *pratiṣṭhā*, *kuṁbhābhiṣeka* and *sthāpana* are synonymous terms, and they all imply the same ritual of installation.

When the temple is to undergo repairs, the process of penetration is reversed. A *kalaśa* is prepared, and the god who is believed to have penetrated into the image is transferred from the image to the *kalaśa*. The *kalaśa* [263] is then installed in the *yāgaśālā* and the daily worship is offered to the *kalaśa*, the god having now made his abode in it. This state of things continues till the temple is ready for reoccupation by the god. If the repairs are likely to take a longer period, sometimes other symbols such as a portrait or an image carved out of wood are used in place of the *kalaśa*. However, the *kalaśa* is essential for the final transfer of the god to the *vigraha* at the *garbhagṛha*. Therefore, the god, whose presence is assumed in the portrait or the wooden image, has to be first transferred to a *kalaśa*. After the due performance of the *yāgapūjā*, which is described below in detail, the *kumbhābhiṣeka* is proceeded with as usual. The reinstallation after repairs is known as *jīrṇoddhāraṇa-kuṁbhābhiṣeka*.

After this brief statement regarding the essential significance of the *pratiṣṭhā*, the entire ritual may now be studied in its various details, each of which is important in its own way. To begin with something needs be said about the structure of the *yāgaśālā*.

---

262 See Kunhan Rajah, "The Hindu temples and their role in the future life of the country", *Adyar Literary Bulletin*, vol. XI, pt. I, p. 30.

263 The *Bhaviṣya Purāṇa* (II.5) gives a description of the *kalaśa*. The introduction into the *kalaśa* of the various substances and finally water to the accompaniment of the *mantras* is also mentioned.

Yāgaśāla

Great attention has to be paid to the construction of the *yāgaśālā*.[264] Each item in this respect must be characterized by utmost precision, for every part of the *śālā* possesses its own special significance. The pillars, flag and doors are all regarded to be sacred, and they are assumed to be presided over by their respective attendant divinities, to whom obeisance is to be paid during the rite. Stone is usually recommended as the most suitable material to be used for the construction of the *yāgaśālā*, though clay also is mentioned as its substitute. It is specifically prescribed that the western side of the temple is never to be chosen for the erection of the *yāgaśālā*.[265]

The model type of the *yāgaśālā* should measure thirty-two *hastas*. It is provided with sixty-four pillars, each being sixteen spans in height. Wood of mango, coconut, *jambu*, *plakṣa*, *yajñavṛkṣa*, *nimba*, *pāṭalī* and *campaka* trees is recommended for the pillars. At the center of the *śālā*, four pillars are erected. The *maṇḍapa* signifies the union of the five elements. Four entrances are provided to the *yāgaśālā*. The eastern one is the main entrance. In the event of some disaster, when the temple falls into a dilapidated condition, or even in some cases at the time of a festival, the western entrance gains importance. However, during the *pratiṣṭhā* ritual or when the *aṣṭabandhana* [266] gives way, the eastern door is used as the main entrance. The door measures nine or sometimes seven *hastas*. The main *vedikā* is set up at the center of the *śālā* and is cubic in shape.[267] The *upavedis* [268] are set at the extremities of the *śālā*, and on these *upavedis* are arranged the *kalaśas* in which the attendant divinities are invoked. Thirty-two

---

[264] *AŚP*, pp. 516-528.

[265] *Pūrve vā dakṣiṇe vāpi uttare iṣṭadeśake |*
Yāgaśālottamaṁ vidyāt paścime naiva kārayet ||
Śivaliṅga Pratiṣṭhāvidhi, p. 81 (quoted from the *Kāraṇa*).

[266] The *aṣṭabandhana* is fully explained later.

[267] *AŚP*, p. 528.

[268] *Ibid*, p. 530.

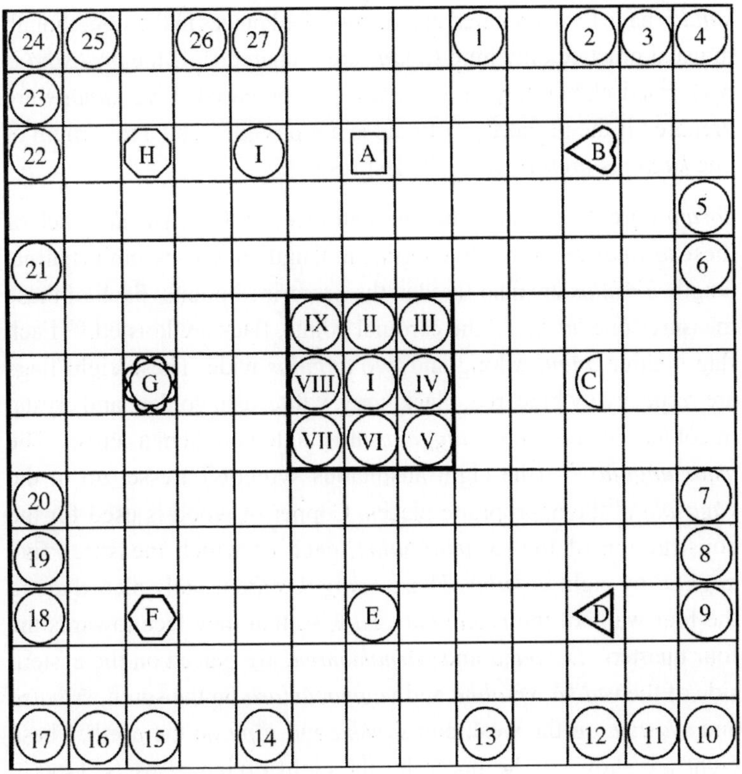

Yāgaśālā

Gods for whom a *kalaśa* is placed on the central *vedikā*:

I. Śiva, II. Ananta, III. Sūkṣma, IV. Śivottama, V. Ekanetra, VI. Ekarudra, VII. Trimūrti, VIII. Śrīkaṇṭha, IX. Śikhaṇḍin.

Kalaśa of the surrounding gods: 1. Mahākāla, 2. Indra, 3. Sūrya, 4. Agni, 5. Vidyākalā, 6. Bhṛṅgin, 7. Vināyaka, 8. Yama, 9. Brahmā (Vāstvadhipati), 10. Nirṛti, 11. Viṣṇu, 12. Nivṛttikalā, 13. Vṛṣabha, 14. Skanda, 15. Varuṇa, 16. Mahālakṣmī, 17. Vāyu, 18. Vighneśvara, 19. Pratiṣṭhākalā, 20. Devī, 21. Caṇḍeśa, 22. Kubera, 23. Guru, 24. Īśāna, 25. Brahmā, 26. Śāntikalā, 27. Nandin.

Kuṇḍa: A. *Caturasra-kuṇḍa*, B. *Yoni-kuṇḍa*, C. *Ardhacandra-kuṇḍa*, D. *Trikoṇa-kuṇḍa*, E. *Vṛtta-kuṇḍa*, F. *Ṣaḍasra-kuṇḍa*, G. *Padma-kuṇḍa*, H. *Aṣṭakoṇa-kuṇḍa*, I. *Pradhāna-kuṇḍa*, (left to individual choice; invariably *vṛtta*).

kuṇḍas have to be prepared at the prescribed places in the *śālā*, though in usual practice only nine *kuṇḍas* are prepared.[269] If the *pratiṣṭhā* is performed elaborately, nine *kuṇḍas* are prepared. Five *kuṇḍas* are prepared if the proportion of nine is not possible, and a minimum of one *kuṇḍa* is prescribed as the last resort.

Toraṇas are displayed at the four entrances of the *yāgaśālā*. Each of these *toraṇas* measures five *hastas* in length, and its width is half its length. *Triśūlas* are also fixed at the prescribed points. Each of these measures one *hasta*. At the cardinal points, flags are hoisted.[270] Each flag is three *aṅgulas* long and two *aṅgulas* wide. These eight flags are respectively blue, red, black, grey, white, ash, golden, and crystal in colour. The respective *diggajas* are painted on them as crests. The *aṣṭamaṅgalas* [271] (the eight auspicious symbols) are set up in the *yāgaśālā* at the appropriate places. Copper or wood is used for the construction of the *aṣṭamaṅgalas*, each of which measures five *aṅgulas* by eight *aṅgulas*. These *maṅgalas* are usually placed along the four walls of the *pradhānavedikā*, so that they face towards the four quarters. *Darpaṇa* and *pūrṇakumbha* are placed on the eastern side of the *vedikā*, *vṛṣabha* and *yugmacāmara* on the south, *śrīvatsa* and *svastika* on the west, and *śaṅkha* and *dīpa* on the north. These eight are shown to be borne by the eight divine damsels, Ūrvaśī, Menakā, Kāmukī, Kāmavardhamī, Sumukhī, Rambhā, and Tilottamā respectively. The ten weapons [272] (*daśāyudhas*) are also displayed in a similar manner. They are the *vajra*, *śakti*, *daṇḍa*, *khadga*, *pāśa*, *dhvaja*, *gadā*, *padma*, *śūla* and *cakra*. Among the articles used for decoration [273] are *darbhamālās* which are woven out of seven, five or

[269] The rules relating to the preparation of the *kuṇḍas* have already been described earlier in this chapter.

[270] Cf. *Matsya P.*, 264. 20-21.

[271] *AŚP*, p. 616.

[272] *AŚP*, p. 624.

[273] It may be pointed out in this connection that though in later times these *maṅgalas*, symbols and *āyudhas* together with other articles of decorations mentioned here were regarded as having been used for purely decorative purposes, each of them originally possessed an essentially magical significance. This is clearly indicated by their being associated with divinities who are said to be presiding over them.

three blades of *darbha*, a white canopy, *kadalī*, *pūga*, *punnāga*, *hintāla*, *ikṣu*, *veṇu*, *puṣpa*, and the tender leaves of the *nālikera*. However, the most essential appartenance of the *yāga-śālā* is the *kalaśa* or the *kumbha*. It is into this *kalaśa* that the presence of the god is first invoked. After a *kalaśa* answering to the prescribed specifications has been chosen, it is covered on all sides except the mouth with a fine net-like texture fabricated out of cotton thread, accomplished by passing the thread around the *kalaśa* several times to a set order. This process is known as *tantuveṣṭana*. Various patterns are prescribed in connection with this net-like covering. Among the many *kalaśas* in the *yāgaśālā*, the central *kalaśa* is easily distinguishable from the others, being made of a better material and being bigger in size. The smaller *kalaśas* are meant for the *parivāra-devatās*. The *kalaśas* are filled with water and their tops are spread over with tender sprouts of the mango tree. Coconuts are placed upon these mango sprouts — one for each *kalaśa*. The three eye-like spots on the coconut should be prominently visible [274] and a small tuft of its fibres should be dressed up and arranged on the top to point upwards. The *kalaśas* are finally clad in garments and blades of *kuśa* grass, tied into knots, are spread over them.

Nayanonmīlana

Coming now to the actual *pratiṣṭhā* ritual, mention must first of all be made of the *nayanonmīlana*, an important rite relating to the *pratiṣṭhā* of a deity. It consists of the ceremonial inscribing of the inner circular line on the eye of a scupture, called the *jyotirmaṇḍala*. This rite is performed in collaboration with the *śilpin*, the sculptor. Usually, a golden needle is used for the inscription in this ceremony. The entire procedure of the *nayanomīlana* rite is described in detail

[274] It may be incidentally pointed out in this connection, that, on account of its three eyes, the coconut is called *tryambaka* (= three eyed) and, therefore, regarded as the special symbol of god Śiva. Cf. "Coconut is the origin of Śiva cult", 14 *AIOC* (summaries), 7-9.

in the *pratiṣṭhāvidhi*.[275] The *guru* or the *pradhānācārya* first draws the line of the right eye; this is followed by a similar marking on the left eye and then on the third eye on the forehead. The line marking the eyebrows is drawn first, and the circular line at the center of the eye is drawn next. The *śilpin* retires at this stage, and a few more rites are then performed. Various objects enumerated [276] in the *Pratiṣṭhāvidhi* are brought in before the image immediately after the opening of the eye to encourage the viewing of these auspicious items.

Jalādhivāsa

Jalādhivāsa is a rite in which the image is kept immersed into water. A river is recommended as the best place for such an immersion. The rite commences with the *puṇyāhavācana*, whereby the river is purified from all pollutions caused by the presence of aquatic beings. Waters collected from sacred rivers are added to the water into which the image is to be immersed. The head of the image is kept above the water level and is made to face towards the east. This immersion may last through a single *yāma*, one day or even three days according to the availability of time.[277]

Yāga-pūjā

On the central *vedi* of the *yāgaśālā*, a lotus design with eight petals is displayed. On it the plantain leaves are then spread out with their ends pointing towards the east. Eight *droṇas* of paddy are first heaped upon them before being spread out in layers. Other kinds of grains are also spread out in separate layers. The grains prescribed

---

[275] *Śivaliṅgapratiṣṭhāvidhi*, I, 128-133. Cf. *Matsya P.*, 264.28.34; also *Agni P.*, 96.50-60.

[276] *Prathamaṁ dhenuvatsaṁ ca dvitīyaṁ kanyādarśanam |*
Tṛtīyam kṣīragavyādi caturthaṁ navadhānyakam ||
Pañcamaṁ sarvadhānyaṁ ca ṣaṣṭham darpaṇadarśanam |
Saṁnyāsaṁ saptamaṁ caiva aṣṭamaṁ vedaghoṣakam ||
Navamaṁ śivabhaktānāṁ sevitaṁ bhaktimārgataḥ |
Śivaliṅgapratiṣṭhāvidhi, I, p. 131.

[277] *Trirātram ekarātraṁ vā yāmamātrādhivāsanam* | *Śivaliṅgapratiṣṭhāvidhi*, II, p. 137.

are *taṇḍula*, *māṣa*, *mudga*, *tila*, *godhuma*, and *niṣpāva*. *Kalaśas* are chosen as indicated earlier.[278] Burning incense is first made to pass through these *kalaśas* for the sake of purification. They are then filled with water to the accompaniment of the Vedic *mantra* which begins with *āpo vā idaṁ sarvam*. Various substances such as *ela*, *lavaṅga*, *karpūra* and *keśara* are put into the *kalaśas*. The nine gems are also placed into them. The *kalaśas* become ritualistically perfect after the mango sprouts are placed on the top and a *nālikera*, with its tuft pointing upwards is placed upon these sprouts.[279] The various features of the *kalaśa* are identified with different parts of the human body. Foor instance, the *ghaṭa* itself is seen as flesh, and the waters poured into it as blood. The nine gems are as bones, the net-like cover with the threads running round are the veins, the Vedic *mantra* is *prāṇa*, the coconut is the head, and so on.[280] As already seen, the *pradhāna-kumbha* is the largest in size, and is assigned a prominent place on the central *vedikā*. Around it are arranged the eight *vidyeśvara-kumbhas*. The *vardhanī-kalaśa* is placed close to the *pradhāna-kalaśa*. On the *upavedis* are arranged the twenty-seven *parivāra-kumbhas*, which are supposed to be the abodes of the guardian and other attendant deities.[281]

The *yāgaśālā* is thus made ready for the *maṇḍapapūjā*, which begins with the worship of Sūrya, the Sun god.[282] The *dvāras*, *toraṇas*, *dhvajas* and *triśūlas* are worshipped with their presiding deities. *Dhyānas* are recited for each of them. These *dhyānas* are made up of *mantras* with which these deities are invoked. The *dvārapālas* [283]

---

[278] *Bhaviṣya P.*, II.5; *Matsya P.*, 68.15-34; also 93.21; *Agni P.*, 57.

[279] *Śivaliṅgapratiṣṭhāvidhi*, II, pp. 45-50; also *Matsya P.*, 18-20.

[280] *Ghaṭo māṁsam iti proktaṁ toyaṁ raktam iti smṛtam |*
Ratnam asthi nyased dhīmān sūtraṁ nāḍī tathaiva ca ||
Vastreṇa tvak, samākhyātaṁ mantraṁ prāṇāḥ prakīrtitam |
Kūrcaṁ tu keśasaṁyuktaṁ cūtapatraṁ jaṭāsmṛtaṁ ||
Dāḍimīphaladantaṁ ca nālikeraṁ śiras tathā |
Gandhapuṣpair alaṅkuryād ityete kumbhalakṣanam ||
Śivaliṅgapratiṣṭhāvidhi, II, p. 47.

[281] *Ibid.*, II, p. 65.

[282] *Matsya P.*, 58.1-49.

[283] *Ibid.*, 234.22-28.

and the other attendant deities are then invoked with the relevant *dhyānaślokas* into the *kalaśas* ready on the *upavedis*. This is followed by two significant rites which deserve special attention. The *bhūta-śuddhi* is performed with a view to bringing about the purification of the physical body constituted of the five *bhūtas* (elements); the *antaryajana* is the other rite, and it is performed internally or rather mentally.

The rite of *bhūtaśuddhi* [284] seems to have close connections with *yoga* practices. Regular control of breath, inhalation and exhalation through the *iḍā*, *piṅgalā*, and *suṣumnā nāḍīs*, and the various *bhāvanas* assumed at the various stages of the rite indicate its yogic character. The purification of the gross body is effected by means of the process called *śodhana*, which is practised in stages. The attainment of purification is marked by assuming a new body obtained after the former physical body is destroyed by the fire which originates in the big left toe. The impurities of the gross physical body consequent upon the contact with the five elements (*bhūtas*) are cleansed. The ensuing flow of *amṛta* from the *sahasrāra* flows about and annoints the newly assumed body.[285] The *bhūtaśuddhi* [286] is followed by the *nyāsa*.[287] This is the act of touching the limbs of the body with the prescribed fingers. Each limb is believed to be presided over by a deity, and the name of that deity is recited while touching the particular limb.[288]

Antaryajana [289] is worship which is performed internally as a mental performance of the rituals.[290] All the materials of worship are mentally conceived, the rites are mentally performed and the offerings

[284] *AŚP*, pp. 627-636; *Somaśaṁbhupaddhati*, pp. 25-29. Cf. *Agni P.*, 74.8-27.

[285] *Śivaliṅgapratiṣṭhāvidhi*, II, pp. 90-94.

[286] *Devībhāgavata P.*, XI.8.

[287] *Nyāsa* is mentioned in the *Purāṇas* also, e.g. *Nārada P.*, 91; *Matsya P.*,5 4.8-23; *Śiva P.*, *Kailāsa-saṁhitā*, 5 & 6; *Agni P.*, 145.

[288] *Śivaliṅgapratiṣṭhāvidhi*, II, pp. 94-96; *AŚP*, pp. 648-678. See also *Agni P.*, 145.5-30.

[289] *ASP*, pp. 636-642; *Somaśaṁbhupaddhati*, p. 30; also *Agni P.*, 74.28-37.

[290] Mental or internal form of worshipping Śiva is also described in the *Purāṇas*. Cf. *Liṅga P.*, I.28.

are made to the god enshrined in the lotus of the heart of the performer. The *homa* is performed in the *nābhikuṇḍa* and *pūrṇāhuti* is offered. This *yajana* terminates with the *samādhi*. At the end of the *antar-yajana*, permission is sought from the god enshrined in the heart to begin the external *pūjā* — which, if it is not preceded by the *antar-yajana*, is declared to be futile.[291]

The *maṇḍaṇa-saṁskāras* are performed for the purpose of refining and cleansing the *maṇḍapa*. They are eighteen in number. Though actually performed earlier, they are supposed to be ritualistically performed at the commencement of the *yāgapūjā*. These *saṁskāras* are *nirīkṣaṇa*, *prokṣaṇa*, *tāḍana*, *abhyukṣaṇa*, *avakīraṇa*, *pūraṇa*, *samīkaraṇa*, *secana*, *kuṭṭana*, *saṁmārjana*, *samālepana*, *abhyarcana*, *sūtraveṣṭana*, *rekhātrayanyāsa*, *vajrīkaraṇa* and *catuṣpathanyāsa*.[292]

Attention may be drawn at this stage to another significant rite. Immediately after the scattering of *vikira* and the worship of *yāgeśvara* and *yāgeśvarī* in the north-eastern corner of the *upavedi*, to Indra, Agni, Yama and other guardians of the quarters are delivered the orders from Śiva that they remain alert and guard their respective quarters till the *yāga* is over.[293]

An important stage in the *maṇḍapa-pūjā* is reached with the commencement of the worship of Śiva in the *pradhānakalaśa*.[294] The five *āsanas*, namely *anantāsana*, *siṁhāsana*, *yogāsana*, *padmāsana* and *vimalāsana*, are ritualistically arranged — one *āsana* placed above the other — with *ādhāraśakti* as the nethermost basis. Śiva is then invoked. *Nyāsa*, *dhyāna*, *āvāhana* and *prāṇapratiṣṭhā* infuse the *kalaśa* with the essence of the god. With the *prāṇapratiṣṭhā*, the assumption of the *sānnidhya* or the immediate presence of the god is definitely confirmed. The five *āvaraṇārcanās* bring the *pradhāna-kalaśa-pūjā* to its close.

---

291 *Antaryāgaṁ vinā yatra bāhya-pujā na siddhyati*. AŚP, p. 636.

292 *Śivaliṅgapratiṣṭhāvidhi*, II, p. 100.

293 *Śivaliṅgapratiṣṭhāvidhi*, II, p. 105.

294 *AŚP*, 678 ff.

With the permission obtained from Śiva who is now present in the *kalaśa*, the *pradhānācārya* then proceeds to perform the *agnikārya*.[295] The Vedic practice of kindling the fire is adopted in the Śaiva rituals with certain modifications. The fire used in the Śiva-*yāga* receives oblations for Śiva alone. The kindling of the fire over the course of the rituals is indeed regarded as an event of great significance. Many purificatory rites are passed through before the fire is actually deposited into the *kuṇḍa*. First of all, the eighteen *saṁskāras* mentioned above [296] are performed. The *kuṇḍa* is made fit for the occupation by the fire after it has been produced. In the middle of the *kuṇḍa*, Vāgīśvarī and Vāgīśvara, the parents of the fire yet to be born, are invoked to grace the occasion with their presence. The ritual begins with the impregnation ceremony; Vāgīsvarī is meditated upon as being worthy of such an event.[297] At this stage, fire is procured; three sources are suggested in this connection. The first, and therefore of primary importance, is the fire from the *araṇis*.[298] Next preference is the fire produced from the *sūryakānta*. The third is the fire produced from the house of a *dvija*.[299] This fire is called *bhūtāgni*, and is considered to be the *retas* of Vāgīśvara. The fire is collected in a copper vessel, and placed in the south-east or the north-east of the *kuṇḍa*. A piece of

---

[295] *AŚP*, p. 722 ff.

[296] See page 555 of this chapter; also *Somaśaṁbhupaddhati*, p. 42, and *Bhaviṣya P.*, II.15.

[297] The following is the description of Vāgīśvarī as she is meditated upon by the performer:

Devīm āvāhayed vidvān vidhivad viśvamātaram |
Śyāmām ṛtumatīṁ dhyātvā sadvāsomālyabhūsaṇām ||
Śivaliṅgapratiṣṭhāvidhi, II, p. 140.

"One should invoke the goddess meditating on her as mother of the world, of dark complexion, in the period favourable to procreation, adorned with a beautiful dress and ornaments."

[298] For *Araṇilakṣaṇa* see *AŚP*, p. 252; also *Agni P.*, 75.

[299] In this connection, however, cf.

Sūryakānte bhavaḥ śreṣṭhaḥ kāṣṭhajo madhyamo bhavet
Śrotriyāgrajo vahniḥ kanyāsas tv iti kīrtitaḥ.
Śivaliṅgapratiṣṭhāvidhi, II, p. 140 Fn.

burning charcoal is picked up and thrown towards the quarter of Nirṛti as the share of *kravyadas*.[300] The deposited fire is then sanctified by means of *mudrās* such as *nirīkṣaṇa*. *prokṣaṇa*, *tāḍana*, *abhyukṣaṇa* and *avaguṇṭhana*. By means of the *mudrā* called the *saṁhāra*, the *bhūtāgni* is collected through a mental process and brought up to the navel. After mixing it with the *nābhyagni* and the *bindavagni* located in the forehead, the fire is brought out through *recaka* (exhalation) and placed back into the fire contained in the vessel. The vessel is waved around the *kuṇḍa* three times. The fire is then deposited into the *kuṇḍa*, thereby assuming that Vāgīśvara is depositing the *retas* into the womb of Vāgīśvarī.[301] This marks the *garbhādāna* rite.

All the other *gṛhya* rites follow in succession. Each of these is marked by a special *āhuti* or offering. For instance, *puṁsavana*, which is normally performed in a fetus's third month, is performed, and three *āhutis* are offered.[302] Symbolising the *sīmantonnayana* to be performed in the sixth month, the prescribed offerings are then made.[303] On the completion of ten months the birth of the child is celebrated. Scattering the *lājas* (fried rice), Śiva is besought with the formula *bālakaṁ pālayiṣyatha*.[304] The *saṁskāras* in respect of the ladle and the spoon are then performed.[305] The *ājya-saṁskāra*

---

[300] *Agniśakalaṁ kravyādārthaṁ nairṛte niḥsārya* | *Ibid.*, p. 140.

[301] *Śivabījam iti dhyātvā pitarau īśadiggataśirasau*
dhyāyan vāgīśvarī-garbhanāḍyāṁ vāgīśvareṇa
kṣipyamāṇaṁ tejorūpaṁ vibhāvya.
Śivaliṅgapratiṣṭhāvidhi, II, p. 141.

"After meditation over the fire as Śiva's semen, meditating on the parents, as facing north-east, imagining the fire as thrown by Vāgīśvara in the womb-vessel of Vāgīśvarī ..."

See also *Agni P.*, 75. 10-11.

[302] *Puṁsavanārthaṁ tṛtīye māsi vāmadevena abhyarcya* ... *Śivaliṅgapratiṣṭhāvidhi*, p. 142; also see *Agni P.*, 75.15.

[303] *Sīmantonnayananimittaṁ ṣaṣṭhe māsi aghoreṇābhyarcya*. *Śivaliṅgapratiṣṭhāvidhi*, II, p. 142; also see *Agni P.*, 75.16.

[304] *Lājapuṣpair alaṅkṛtya, bālakaṁ pālayiṣyatheti śivājñāṁ śrāvayet* ... *Śivaliṅgapratiṣṭhāvidhi*, II, p. 143.
Agni P., 75.24.

[305] *Śivaliṅgapratiṣṭhāvidhi*, II, pp. 143-144; *ASP*, p. 293; *Agni P.*, 75.25-28; *Bhaviṣya P.*, II.19.

performed thereafter renders the clarified butter pure and fit for offerings.[306] Then follows the *nāmakaraṇa*.[307] The fire is given the name of *Śivāgni*,[308] uttering the formula *Śivāgnisvaṁ hutāśana*. The *nāmakaraṇa* is followed by *upaniṣkramaṇa*,[309] *annaprāśaṇa*,[310] *caula*,[311] *upanayana*[312] and *vratakrama*.[313] Fire is then meditated upon as a youth.[314] Over time, the *vaivāhya* stage is reached. Ultimately, the fire is worshipped as *Vṛddhāgni*.[315] A *pūrṇāhuti*[316] is offered to mark the culmination of these long series of rites. The fire is apportioned and transferred to the other *kuṇḍas*, each of which is placed in charge of a separate assistant known as *mūrtipa*.[317] The prescribed materials such as *samidh*, grains, *oṣadhis* and various drugs and cooked articles are offered to the fire in the accompaniment of the relevant Vedic *mantras*.[318]

Śayanāropaṇa[319]

For this rite, a bed is prepared to the east of the *yāgaśālā*. The bed is made of five materials arranged in five layers. The wooden

---

[306] *Śivaliṅgapratiṣṭhāvidhi*, II, p. 145 f. *ASP*, p. 266; *Agni P.*, 75.29-41.

[307] *Tato nāmakaraṇārtham īśānena saṁpūjyārghyaṁ datvā astreṇāhutipañcakaṁ hutvā ... Śivaliṅgapratiṣṭhāvidhi*, p. 148.

[308] *Śivāgnis tvam iti nāma kṛtvā. Ibid.*, p. 148; *Agni P.*, 75.43.

[309] *Upaniṣkramaṇāya hṛdābhyarcya. Śivaliṅgapratiṣṭhāvidhi*, II p. 148.

[310] *Annaprāśanakarmārthaṁ sadyojātenāhutipancakaṁ hutvā. Ibid.*, p. 148.

[311] *Caulakarmārthaṁ sadyojātena pancāhutīr hutvā. Ibid*, p. 148.

[312] *Upanayanārthaṁ vāmadevenāhutipañcakaṁ hunet. Ibid.*, p. 148.

[313] *Vratakramārtham aghoreṇāhutipañcakaṁ hutvā. Ibid.*, p. 148.

[314] *Yauvanāgniṁ dhyātvā ... Śivaliṅgapratiṣṭhāvidhi*, II, p. 148.

[315] *Vṛddhāgniṁ dhyātvā ... Ibid.*, p. 148.

[316] *Sarpiṣā srucam āpūrya puṣkaroparyadhomukhaṁ sruvaṁ*
kṛtvā tadagre puṣpaṁ datvā vāmadakṣiṇahastābhyāṁ śaṅkhavat
saṁsaktābhyāṁ punaḥ savyena saṁlagnau tāv ubhāv ādāya
srugagradattadṛṣṭir vauṣaḍantamūlam uccārayan vāmastanāntaṁ
sruṅmūlam ānīya anudvigno yavapramāṇadhārayā samastam ājyaṁ
vahnau kṣipet — iti pūrṇāṁ vidhāya.
Ibid., p. 149. See also *Agni P.*, 75.44-56; also *Bhaviṣya P.*, II.20.

[317] AŚP, pp. 534-540 deal with *navāgnivibhajana* — the division of Agni into nine parts, one part for each *kuṇḍa*.

[318] *Bhaviṣya P.*, II. 15, 16 and 18.

bedstead forms the first layer. The fur of the *śabarī* deer, a goat or even a white or red *kambala* is spread over it. This is covered with a layer of cloth, on which feathers of *haṁsa* are strewn. Grains are scattered over these, and above them are spread skins of tiger and antelope. Pillows also are arranged on the bed. The image of the god to be installed is then laid upon it face up and with the head pointing towards the east. The image is covered in full with a red cloth.[320] The usual *nyāsa-vidhi* is then performed.[321]

Then follows the rite of preparing the pinnacle (*stūpi*) atop of the dome (*stūpa*) of the central shrine. The *stūpi* is also referred to as *sthūlaliṅga*. This terminates with the *abhiṣeka* of the *kumbha*, which was already set up and in which had been invoked the presence of the deity presiding over the *stūpi*.[322] The *stūpi* is widely known as *kalaśa*.[323] This is made of gold or of copper or of bronze. The *darśana* and worship of the *stūpi*, which symbolically represents the god installed within the shrine, is not at all unknown; by worshipping it even from outside, far away from the temple, one attains the merit which one would have gathered by worshipping the god himself as enshrined in the *garbhagṛha*.

In the meantime, the *śilpin* sets the *ādhāraśilā* in the correct position at the center of the *garbhagṛha*, where the image which has gone through the ceremonies aforementioned (*nayanonmīlana*,

---

319 This rite is hinted at in *Agni P.*, 96.49.

320 The significance of the various materials used in connection with the *śayanāropaṇa*, particularly *kambala*, feathers of *haṁsa*, tiger and antelope skins, and red cloth, from the point of view of the personality and original character of God Śiva, is quite obvious.

321 *Śivaliṅgapratiṣṭhāvidhi*, II, pp. 206-244.

322 AŚP, p. 880.

323 Venkataramanayya, in his book entitled *An Essay on the Origin of the South India Temple* speaks of the *stūpi* as follows: "*Stūpi*, as the *vimāna* is called, is the corrupted form of Sanskrit *stūpa* which signifies 'A Buddhist shrine'. It has a striking resemblance to the developed *stūpa*, and is also called by the name '*stūpi*'. Therefore, it is nothing more or less than a conventionalized model of a medieval Buddhist *stūpa*, erected purely as an architectural ornament, denoting the position of the image enshrined within the building." Pp. 37-38.

jalādhivāsa and *śayanāropaṇa*) is to be installed. At the center of this *śilā*, a square hole is dug, and gems (*navaratnas*) are deposited into it.[324] The *yantra* of the god is also placed therein. The hole is covered, and the image of the god is properly set atop the *āsanaśilā*. The image is glued to the *śilā* with a thick sticky substance specially prepared for this purpose.[325] This substance, which may be said to possess the properties of cement, is called *aṣṭabandhana* because it is made of eight ingredients, and is generally used for joining two objects made of stone. The process of preparing the *aṣṭabandhana* consists of heating and boiling together the eight prescribed adhesive substances, which solidify when cooled. It is made into small balls which are pounded with a pestle before use. When repeatedly struck with a pestle, the friction makes it soft and clay-like. It is then applied to the joints of the base of the image and the top part of the *āsanaśilā*. This gluing must be done in an aesthetically appropriate manner. On the whole, the *śilpin* plays an important role in this ceremony.[326]

The *aṣṭabandhana* is followed by the *abhyañjana* rite, when all the devotees participate by anointing the image with oil. This is possibly the last chance given to the lay devotees to touch the image. Thereafter, the image is consecrated by means of several purificatory rites, after which only an initiate who has undergone the special *dikṣā* rites can touch it. Among these purificatory rites, the *bimbaśuddhi* [327] is then performed. After the commencement of this rite, even the *śilpin* is not allowed to come near the image. The *bimbaśuddhi*, as the name suggests, is intended for removing any stains which may have appeared on the image from the various handlings. In connection with this rite, the image is bathed in sanctified water in which the bark and sprouts from the five prescribed trees are soaked. A *nyāsa* marks the culmination of this rite.[328]

---

[324] AŚP, p. 776.

[325] For the description of the *aṣṭabandhana* rite see *AŚP*, pp. 800-805.

[326] *Śivaliṅgapratiṣṭhāvidhi*, II, pp. 275-278.

[327] *AŚP*, pp. 805-824. See also *Agni P.*, 96.65-71.

[328] *Śivaliṅgapratiṣṭhāvidhi*, II, pp. 290-313.

The purification of the three *bhāgas* or sections of the image is brought about by means of a rite called *sparśāhuti*.[329] This oblation consisting of *ājya* is offered in two places — first on the fire deposited in the *kuṇḍas* at the *yāgaśālā*, and then on the image which is already fixed up on the *āsanaśilā*. At the end of the recital of the formula which ends with the sacred word *svāhā*, this utterance is only partially articulated. That is to say, the offering of clarified butter to the fire is made with *svā*, and the pouring of the remaining clarified butter stored in the *sruk* onto the image is done with the remaining *hā*. During this ceremony, fire, the *pradhānakumbha* and the image, however mutually distant they may be, are all connected by cords of cotton, *darbha* and metals like silver and gold.[330]

The worship of the fire in the *kuṇḍas* is brought to an end with the *pūrṇāhuti*. In each *kuṇḍa*, the respective *mūrtipas* [331] (*ṛtviks*) who were appointed and entrusted with the kindling and offering of the *āhutis* at the eight *kuṇḍas* [332] offer the *pūrṇāhutis* separately. The aspects of the god invoked in these separate *kuṇḍas* are transferred in the reverse order in which they were earlier distributed, from one *kuṇḍa* to the other,[333] until all the aspects (*aṣṭamūrtis*) are gathered in the *pradhānakuṇḍa*, the ninth one, which is in the sole charge of the *pradhānācārya*. Then the *mahāpūrṇāhuti* is offered.[334] This *pūrṇāhuti* is followed by the transfer of the god from the fire to the *pradhānakalaśa*.

Finally, the *dīpārādhana* [335] or the final *pūjā* is elaborately performed and the distribution of *dakṣiṇās* to the brāhmaṇas is performed as a preliminary to the removal of the *kumbha* (*kumbha-utthāpana*). The *kumbha* is removed from the *vedi*, taken around the temple in

---

329 *AŚP*, pp. 824-877. See also *Agni P.*, 96.108-119.

330 *Śivaliṅgapratiṣṭhāvidhi*, II, pp. 316-341.

331 Cf. *Matsya P.*, 265. 36-42.

332 *AŚP*, pp. 832-854.

333 *Ibid.*, pp. 855-878.

334 *Śivaliṅgapratiṣṭhāvidhi*, II, p. 348.

335 The details of the *dipārādhana* are given in the *Kāraṇāgama*, I.32.32-37.

procession, brought into the *garbhagṛha* and deposited near the image. At the advent of the auspicious moment, the deity is ritualistically transferred from the *kalaśa* to the *bimba* or *vigraha*.[336] This is the most significant event in the *pratiṣṭhā* ritual. The climax of the ritual is reached when the contents of the *kalaśa* are poured on the image.[337] This is marked by music, bells, conches and the shouts raised by the devotees witnessing the *pratiṣṭhā* expressive of the obeisance paid to the god, such as *"Namaḥ pārvatīpataye"*, and "*Hara Hara Mahādeva*".

The *kumbhābhiṣekas* of the subordinate deities also take place accordingly, and these are concluded with the *abhiṣeka* of Caṇḍeśvara.

Nitya Rites

The daily obligatory rites or *pūjās* begin to be performed in the temple immediately after the *pratiṣṭhā*. In most cases these *pūjās* are performed six times a day. Each *pūjā* is preceded by *abhiṣeka*, that is, the bathing of the images with the prescribed materials.[338] After bathing, the image is dressed in new garments and decked with ornaments and garlands. *Abhiṣeka*, *alaṁkāra* and *dīpārādhana* constitute the characteristic features of each *pūjā*.[339] The *dīpārādhana* consists of waving in front of the image various kinds of lit lamps to the accompaniment of Vedic *mantras*. The *dīpārādhana* is followed by the offering of the *upacāras* [340] such as *darpaṇa*, *chatra*, *cāmara*, *vyajana*, *patāka* and *tālavṛnta*. Then comes the *arcanā* or the offering of flowers, usually one hundred and eight in number, and the *pūjā* is

---

[336] *AŚP*, pp. 920-924.

[337] It is on account of this that the entire ritual is also designated *kumbhābhiṣeka*.

[338] Cf. *Skanda P.*, I.3.2.7; also *Matsya P.*, 267 and *Agni P.*, 74.65-68; *ibid.*, 267. 1-15.

[339] Cf. *Śiva P.*, *Dharma-saṁhitā*, 40. For the reference of Śiva image with honey, curd, *pañcagavya*, and the offering to it of *gorocana*, *kuṅkuma*, *candana*, *bilva*, lotus, camphor etc., see *Vāmana P.*, 62.1-14. *Śiva P.*, *Dharma-saṁhitā* mention in chapters 15 and 16 *nitya* and *naimittika* rites. *Liṅga* worship and the merits accruing therefrom are also recounted in that connection. See also *Śiva P.*, *Sanatkumāra-saṁhitā*, 19.

[340] See *Kāraṇa*, I. 65.1-16 for details of the *upacāras*.

brought to a close with the *ārātrikā* or the waving of burning camphor before the image. At the end of the *pūjā*, representative passages from each *Veda* are recited.[341] Benedictory formulas are also repeated, invoking the favour and blessings of the god.[342] Thereafter follows the singing of devotional songs composed not in Sanskrit, but in the local language of the Śaiva saints.

Besides what may be called the official *nitya pūjās*, there are also *arcanās*, which are often performed on behalf of the devotees by the official priests of the temple. The *arcanā* usually consists of an offering of flowers to the accompaniment of the recital of the names of the gods.[343] The names number sixteen, one hundred and eight, three hundred, or even one thousand.[344] Plantains, betel, arecanut and coconuts are offered as *naivedya*, and after the *arcanā*, portions of these together with flowers and the like are returned as *prasāda* to the devotee on behalf of whom that particular *arcanā* is performed.

On special occasions, the *abhiṣeka* is very elaborately performed.[345] It begins with anointing the image with *taila*, and the other materials used for the bathing are taken up in the following order: *piṣṭa*, *āmalaka*, *rajanī*, *pañcagavya*, *kṣīra*, *dadhi*, *madhu*, *ghṛta*, *ikṣusāra*, *phalasāra*, *nāḷikerodaka*, *anna*, *uṣṇodaka*, *vibhūti*, *kuṅkuma*, *candana*, *gandhodaka* and sacred Gaṅgā waters (*Gaṅgājala*). The *abhiṣeka* is followed by wiping the image with a soft cloth.

Silken garments, golden *kavacas*, precious ornaments studded with diamonds and other stones, and garlands of flowers are used to decorate the image.

---

[341] This is *caturvedaghoṣa*.

[342] The *āśirvāda* consists of a series of benedictory utterances intended to invoke the blessings of the god. Each utterance is followed by the iteration of the same by the priests, who are assembled on the spot to assist the performer of the rituals.

[343] The *Purāṇas* also speak of similar traditions. Śiva is said to have told Kratu that he should worship him with those names which are held in secret. *Kūrma P.*, I.20.67-70.

[344] Numerous names of Śiva are repeated by the *ṛṣis* at Dāruvana. *Liṅga P.*, I.32.

[345] See the detailed description of the *abhiṣeka* given towards the end of the present chapter.

Cooked food of various kinds, like *citrānna*, *māṣāpūpa*, *laḍḍuka*, fruits, arecanuts, betel and *nālikera*, form the main offerings at the *naivedya*, both for daily rituals and on special occasions.[346]

13. Utsavas [347]

Apart from the *nitya-pūjā*, each Śaiva temple celebrates what are called *utsavas*. The most characteristic features of such an *utsava* in the South where the Āgamic tradition prevails is the *pradakṣiṇa*, or the circumambulatory procession of the image, which is usually made of bronze and decorated with ornaments and garlands. It is given a pose and vehicle befitting the occasion. The *utsavas* also are of two types, *nitya* and *naimittika*. The *nitya* festival is of daily occurrence, while the *mahotsava*, also called the *brahmotsava*, takes place on some fixed day or days in the course of the year. Different temples celebrate *mahotsavas* on different days.

For the daily festivals, a special image is to be prepared.[348] Gold, silver or copper is prescribed for the preparation of this image.[349] The procession or the *pradakṣiṇa* of the image is characterized by the use of a canopy, umbrella, chowrie and *dīpas* (torches) and by singing, dancing and playing various instruments.[350] The *tālas* to be played in the course of the procession are prescribed. Among these are men-

---

[346] Cf. *Kāraṇa*, I.35. The details of the offerings to be made are given in 184 verses.

[347] Gonda has emphasized the magical significance of *utsava*.

[348] *Nityotsavāya bimbaṁ tu kārayet lakṣaṇānvitam |*
Sauvarṇam uttamaṁ proktaṁ madhyamaṁ rājataṁ bhavet ||
Adhamaṁ tāmram ityuktaṁ kalpayet kalpavittamaḥ |
Kāraṇa, I.140.2-3.

[349] Cf. "The principal image had, therefore, to be supplemented by images in human shape that could be moved about. The device of the peripatetic image was thus adopted not only in those temples in which the image in the *sanctum sanctorum* was in human shape, but also in those in which it was a symbolic representation, and the peripatetic images were made to receive all the honours appropriate to royalty." Aravamuthan, *Survivals of Harappa Culture*, p. 36.

[350] *Vitānaṁ chatrasaṁyuktaṁ piñcacāmarasaṁyutam |*
Sarvatodyasamāyuktaṁ gītanṛttasamākulam ||
Nānādīpasamāyuktaṁ nānābhaktajanair yutam |
Kāraṇa, I.140.20-21.

tioned *paṅgaṇi*, *vṛṣatāla*, *bhṛṅgitāla*, and so on. The devotees also join the procession.

The celebration of the *mahotsava* is much more elaborate. It commences with the *vṛṣayāga* which is followed by the *dhvajāroha* [351] or the hoisting of the flag, *aṅkurārpaṇa*, *yāgapūjā*, *astrayāga, balidāna*, *yānakrama*, *nīrājana*, *cūrṇotsava* and *tīrtha*. These various rites are described in detail in the treatises on the Śaiva rituals.[352] The duration of the special festival can extend up to eighteen or even twenty-seven days;[353] the normal duration, however, is ten days. The *brahmotsava* is timed so that the *tīrtha-utsava* celebrated on the last day falls on the new moon or full moon day, or under a special *nakṣatra*. The festival begins with worship offered in honour of *Gaṇeśa*. The rites of *mṛtsaṅgrahaṇa*, *rakṣābandhana*, *aṅkurārpaṇa*, *vāstuśānti* and *grāma-śānti* are duly performed. The *vṛṣa-yāga* in honour of the *vṛṣabha* is performed on the night preceding the day of the hoisting of the flag.[354] For this rite, the *dhvaja-paṭa* is prepared as prescribed, and the symbol of the god and other auspicious signs are drawn upon it. The *pratiṣṭhā* rite infuses the banner with vital force. The *dhvajapaṭa* is then taken out in procession and brought to the flagstaff. With an invocation for the various gods to be present, the flag is hoisted. The rite of invoking the gods is called *samastadevatāvāhanam*.[355] The *yāgaśālā* is established in the north-eastern corner of the temple. Preceding the *avarohaṇa* of the flag, the *yāgapūjā* must be performed daily. *Balis* in the form of balls of rice are offered daily at the *dhvajadaṇḍa* and at the cardinal points of the quarters. After these rites, the image is taken out in

---

351 Cf. *Bhaviṣya P.*, I.138.1-84.

352 *Aghoraśivācārya-paddhati*, *Mahotsavavidhi*, p. 1 ff.

353 See: *Kāraṇa*, I.141 (Under *aṣṭādaśadinotsava-vidhi* and *saptaviṁśadinotsavavidhi*).

354 The *dhvajārohaṇa* is a topic discussed in the *Agni P.*, (chapters 61 and 102).

355 See appendix to the *Mahotsavavidhi* in *Aghoraśivācāryapaddhati*. By way of specimen, one of such invocations is given below. Viṣṇu, one of the gods thus invoked, is invited in the following manner:

Dharaṇī-salila-dahana-pavana-gagana-gandha-rasa-rūpa-sparśa-śabdādi-bhava-bhedādibheda-bhinna-vividha-prapañcātmaka-maheśa-kṛpā-nirdiṣṭa-sakala-

procession in the morning and again at night. Different vehicles are prescribed for this purpose on different days.[356]

The procession in the *ratha* must be regarded as the grandest event in the *brahmotsava*. The *ratha* or chariot is normally used for the procession on the penultimate day. It must be pointed out that this practice varies from place to place.[357] The *Kāraṇāgama* devotes one full chapter to the *pratiṣṭhā* or the formal installation of the *ratha*.[358] The *guru*, the performer of the rite, accompanied by his assistants, follows the *ratha* while silently repeating the *mūlamantra*. The devotees follow closely; some of them go ahead, dragging the chariot by the ropes fastened to it. The procession of the image of the god from the temple to the chariot and back is always formal and is performed with pomp.

The *cūrṇotsava* marks the end of the festival. The ceremony begins with the usual preliminary rites. *Sahadevī*, *koṣṭha*, *rajanī*, *tāṁbula*, *gandha*, and *puṣpa* are among the materials required for it. Turmeric is put into the *ulūkhala*, which symbolizes this mundane world. It is powdered and then, mixed with *taila*, *ghṛta*, *gandha* and

---

bhuvana-rakṣaṇa-vicakṣaṇaḥ, śaṅkha-cakra-gadā-khaḍgādi-divyāyudhālaṅkṛta-kara-kamala-virājamānaḥ, trivikramākrānta-sakala-bhuvanatalaḥ, nijodara-puṭa-vidhṛta-nikhilāṇḍa-bhārabhuvanatalaḥ, nijodara-puṭa-vidhṛta-nikhilāṇḍaṭaṇḍa-bhāra-niyamita-kharvīkṛta-darvīkara-garva-sarvaṁkaṣa-parākrama-parikrānta-sudṛḍha-garuḍa-vāhanaḥ, manoharāravinda-sundara-nābhimandira-janita-pitāmahaḥ, sakala-jalanidhi-nimagna-kāśyapī-samuddharaṇa-parigrhīta-varāha-rūpaḥ, sakala-jagadādhāra-bhūta-vikaṭa-kamaṭha-rūpaḥ, matsyāvatāra-vihāra-sādhana-mahāmbudhi-viśālollola-kallolamālā-jāla-kalita-vicitra-caritaḥ, asahya-nārasiṁha-vikrama-vikāsita-nakhara-śikhara-vidalita-hiraṇya-vakṣaḥ-sthala-galita-bahula-rudhira-dhārā-saṁpādita-sandhyā-rāga-rūkṣita-marakata-śaila-bandhura-kandhara-manohara-vigrahaḥ, aravinda-mandirendirā-kaṭhina-kuca-taṭa-pāṭīra-paṅkila-vakṣaḥsthalaḥ, jagadādhāra-daṇḍa-prakāṇḍa-caṇḍatara-caturbhuja-daṇḍakāṇḍaḥ, parameśvarājñā-paripālita-sakalalokaḥ, Śivadhyānayogāmṛta-pāraṇa-parāyano, nārāyaṇamūrtiḥ, śivāstra-divya-śūla-vāma-patre sānnidhyaṁ karotu.

356 *Kāraṇa*, I.141: *Daśadinotsavavidhipaṭala*, 78-80.

357 Cf. *Kāraṇa*, I.141. Verse 79 of the *Daśadinotsavavidhipaṭala*, for instance, prescribes the *rathotsava* for the seventh day. *Ratha* is mentioned in the *Purāṇas*, also Cf. *Śiva P.*, *Vidyeśvara-saṃhitā*, 7.22.

358 *Kāraṇa*, I.142.

other substances; the mixture is then collected in a vessel, and the image is anointed with it. Subsequently, the devotees also besmear themselves with it.[359] The image is then taken to the *tīrthasthāna* or a river. The *astrarāja*, who serves as the substitute for the principal deity, is first bathed with the *abhiṣeka-dravyas* and is then immersed into the waters of the river, which have already been sanctified through purificatory rites. The *avarohaṇa* of the flag marks the end of the *brahmotsava*. The deities invoked to be present on the *dhvaja-daṇḍa* on the first day are now implored to retire to their respective abodes.[360]

One of the most important festivals in the Śaiva temples of the South is the *vaivāhya-utsava*, which represents the celebration of the wedding of Śiva with Umā. This *utsava* is invariably celebrated immediately after the *brahmotsava*, that is, on the day following the *dhvaja-avarohaṇa*. In some temples, the *vaivāhya-utsava* is celebrated before the *avarohaṇa* itself. *Gaṇeśa-pūjā* and *puṇyāhavācana* mark the commencement of the *vaivāhya* ritual. These are followed by the usual rites of *aṅkurārpaṇa*, *rakṣābandhana*, *kanyādāna*, *pāṇigrahaṇa*. *sūtradhāraṇa*. *agnipradakṣiṇa*, *lājahoma* and finally *āśirvacana*. Vedic *mantras* are employed in the appropriate places.

The *śāntihoma* and *prāyaścitta* are performed at the end of elaborate rites like *pratiṣṭhā* and *utsava*. They are expected to bring about a peaceful atmosphere and to rectify any shortcoming or discrepancy which may have (quite likely) crept in over the course of the performance of such lengthy and elaborate rites.

A reference must be made at this stage to other special festivals which have some bearing on the subject under discussion. The eight great episodes in the career of Śiva which have been described in various places in the *Purāṇas* are reenacted by way of festivals.[361]

---

359 *Aghoraśivācāryapaddhati*, *Mahotsavavidhi*, p. 34.

360 *Aghoraśivācāryapaddhati*, *Mahotsavavidhi*, pp. 35-39.

361 Provision is made for such festivals in the *Āgamas*. See *Kāraṇa*, I.141, under *aṣṭādaśadinotsavavidhipaṭala*, verses 81-94. Even the destruction of the demon Tāraka by Kārttikeya, an episode repeatedly recounted in the Epics and the *Purāṇas*, is ritually staged every year in some temples of the South dedicated to Kārttikeya.

A few Śaiva temples of the South celebrate special festivals of this nature, portraying exploits of the god which do not find any place in the great *Purāṇas*. The temple at Madura, for instance, celebrates sixty-four exploits, all of which proclaim the greatness of god Śiva enshrined in that temple. These exploits are recorded in the *sthala-Purāṇas*, which are works specifically associated with those temples alone. The *Hālāsya-māhātmya*, which glorifies the god in the temple of Madura, contains detailed descriptions of all these exploits.

14. Prāyaścitta

The *prāyaścitta* is the rite performed to rectify any defects and shortcomings which may have crept in, knowingly or unknowingly, during the performance of any other rites and which thus may have adversely affected the perfection of the ritual as a whole. Whenever any discrepancies are suspected, the *prāyaścitta* or the expiatory rite must be performed.[362] An expiatory rite is, indeed, essential for the welfare and prosperity of the performer, as worship which is even slightly deficient not only does not serve the desired purpose but leads to positively calamitous results. Various *prāyaścittas* are therefore prescribed in the ritual texts [363] in respect of the various kinds of violations that may have occurred. They sometimes take the form of *abhiṣeka*, or other times of *homa*, in which *prāyaṣcitta-āhutis* are offered to the fire. It may be pointed out that, besides the expiatory rites, *śānti-homa* and *diśā-homa* are also prescribed to be performed at the end of *naimittika* ritual.[364]

---

[362] It may be incidentally mentioned in this connection that the detailed *prāyaścitta* rites are prescribed in the *Śrauta-Sutras* for every conceivable defect or deficiency in the performance of the *Śrauta* ritual.

[363] *Sarveṣāṁ eva kāryāṇāṁ kriyāvaikalyasaṁbhave* |
Prāyaścittaṁ purā kuryād ātmanaḥ kṣamahetave ||
Kāraṇa, I.144.2-3.

"Since there is a possibility of deficiency of actions in all the rituals, one should perform an expiation rite before, for oneself's welfare."

[364] *Kāraṇa*, I.144.71-242; *Suprabheda*, 55.

General

Before concluding this section, a few words must be said about the performers of the rites described above. The officiant is known by various designations such as *deśika*, *guru*, *ācārya* and *arcaka*.[365] The chief performer is called the *pradhānācārya*. Those who assist him in the *agnikārya* are called *ṛtviks* or even *mūrtipas*. Another priest who assists the *pradhānācārya* in various ways is the *sādhakācārya*. It is his duty to refer to the *Paddhati* (the practical manual of ritual) during the performance and thereby to draw the attention of the officiant to the proper order of the various rites and their details.[366] The chief *ācārya* performs the *naimittika* rites, while the *arcakācārya* performs the *arcanā* or the daily *pūjās*.[367] The *alaṅkaraṇācārya* is in charge of the decoration of the image. In addition to the duties mentioned above, the *sādhakācārya* collects the various materials required for the rites and presents them when needed.[368]

The *ācārya* should have been born in a Śaiva family. He should be a householder, and his age should be between sixteen and seventy years. He should be endowed with perfect limbs. He should wear a *śikhā*, but should be devoid of facial hair. He should have already gone through the *dīkṣā* rite. He should be eloquent and of amiable personality. He should be an adept in all the various branches of

---

[365] Cf. *Śiva P.*, *Vāyusaṁhitā*, II.113: *Yo guruḥ sa śivaḥ proktaḥ yaḥ śivaḥ sa guruḥ smṛtaḥ* | Also see *Śiva P.*, *Vidyeśvara-saṁhitā*,16.82-97.
"He, who is the officiant is told to be Śiva; he, who is Śiva, is evoked as being the officiant."

[366] *Śivaliṅgapratiṣṭhāvidhi*, I, p. 20-26.

[367] E.G. Minaksi refers in her work, *Administration and Social Life under the Pallavas*, to several inscriptions of the Pallava period which speak about the employment of *arcakas* in the temples built during that period. See pp. 174-177.

[368] *Ācāryaś cārcakaś caiva sādhako'laṅkṛtas tathā* |
Vācakaśca kulodbhūtāḥ pañcācāryāḥ prakīrtitāḥ ||
Ācāryaś cāgamālokād yajen naimittikakriyāḥ |
Evam ācāryakṛtyaṁ syād arcakenārcanaṁ kuru ||
Alaṅkṛtenālaṇkṛtya sādhako dravyasādhakaḥ |
Vācakas tu śruteḥ kartā pañcācāryakramaṁ viduḥ ||
Śivaliṅgapratiṣṭhāvidhi, I,p. 23.

learning, and should be a regular worshipper of Śiva, Agni and *guru*. He should be skilled in all *mantras*, *mudrās* and rituals, and must be acquainted with other branches of Śaivism, namely *caryā*, *yoga*, and *jñāna*. He should also be well-versed in the *Śaivasiddhānta* philosophy. Among the functions assigned to him are *sthāpana*, *yajana*, *yājana*, *adhyayana*, *adhyāpana*, *dāna* and *pratigraha*.[369] The *dīkṣā* rite is performed to properly initiate the devotee into the folds of Śaiva orthodoxy.[370] It is designed to bring about the spiritual purification of the *upāsaka* and thereby qualify him for participation in the rituals of both daily and special occurrence. The *guru* plays a prominent part in the *dīkṣā* rite. He himself performs the rite and formally effects the initiation of the *śiṣya*, or disciple. The *śiva-dīkṣā*, *samaya-dīkṣā*,[371] *viśeṣa-dīkṣā* and *nirvāṇa-dikṣā* [372] are performed sequentially after intervals, whenever the *guru* feels satisfied about the spiritual maturity of the *śiṣya*. *Śiva-dīkṣā* is prescribed for anyone irrespective of caste.[373] The *viśeṣa-dīkṣā* and the *nirvāṇa-dīkṣā* are very elaborate affairs, and only *śiṣya* accomplished in the matter of Śaiva ritual and philosophy is fit to receive them.

Each kind of *dīkṣā* mentioned above presupposes the use of the regular requisites of ritual, such as *yāgaśālā*, *kumbha*, *kuṇḍa*, and *maṇḍala*. The *maṇḍapa-pūjā*, *kalāśodhana* or *homa* are all performed by the *guru* himself. The *maṇḍapa-pūjā* and the *homa* have been already referred to above. The *kalāśodhana* [374] is an elaborate ritual whereby the purification of the *kalās* like *śānti*,[375] *pratiṣṭhā*,[376] *vidyā*

---

369 *Kāraṇa*, I.26. See also verses 14,17,19, and 23.

370 *Suprabheda*, *Caryā*, 4; See also *Kiraṇāgama*, 6 and 11.

371 See *Śiva P.*, *Vāyu-saṁhitā*, 16 and 17, and *ibid.*, *Kailāsa-saṁhitā*, 11; also *Agni P.*, 81.

372 *Agni P.*, 81-88. See also *Somaśaṁbhupaddhati* pp. 131-166.

373 *Agni P.*, 83.

374 The *Sivappirakācam* (verse 8) mentions the six *adhvās* (*mantra*, *pada*, *varṇa*, *bhuvana*, *tattva*, *kalā*), of which *Kalā* is the last mentioned. Once the purification of each of these is effected, the individual attains a high state; it is then he becomes the initiated (*dīkṣita*) in the real sense of the term.

375 *Agni P.*, 87.

376 *Ibid.*, 85.

and *nivṛtti* are effected through various *bhāvanās* or mental processes, as well as by means of *nyāsas* performed with the appropriate *mantras*. The impurities of the physical body are thus removed and the *śiṣya* becomes endowed with a new body called *śivamaya-śarīra* or *śāṁbhava-śarīra*. For these rites, a highly developed personality and a strong will power are expected from the *guru*, for he must assume a subtle form and enter into the body of the *śiṣya* in order to effect the necessary changes to bring him to a spiritually advanced state.[377] After these rites are performed, the *guru* instructs the *śiṣya* about his duties.[378]

A reference may also be made to the close connection that exists between the Śaiva rituals and the fine arts like music, dance and architecture. It should be remembered that the association of the *bharata-nāṭya* with ritual is to no small degree responsible for the preservation of that art form today. The *gaṇikās* [379] were formally attached to the temples and they had to perform duly-prescribed dances, both daily and on special occasions.[380] Similarly, the *maṅgala-vādya*, accompaniment from the drum and the *nādasvara*, provides music during the performance of rites. Eighteen *vādyas* [381] are often mentioned in the ritual texts. The tunes which are to be played at particular moments over the course of the ritual are also specified in those texts.

The devotional songs associated with the *pūjā* almost enjoy the high status and prestige of the *Vedas*. These songs were composed by the saints of the South, and are arranged into twelve sections. They are recited at appropriate moments over the course of the ritual to the

---

377 *Aghoraśivācāryapaddhati*, *Dikṣāvidhi*, pp. 334-6. See also *Kāmikāgama*, II.20.83-91.

378 *Agni P.*, 92.

379 See Minaksi, *op.cit.*, pp. 177-178; 239 ff; 276 ff. In these pages, the author refers to the inscriptions which have recorded the endowments made to the *gaṇikās* for the service they were enjoined to perform on daily and special occasions.

380 It is unfortunate that this tradition is now fast dying out.

381 Diksitar, V.R.R., in his *Studies in Tamil Literature and History*, mentions the musical instruments in use in ancient Tamil Nad. See p. 299.

prescribed *rāga* and *tāla*. This practice has undoubtedly helped the preservation of some rare compositions which would have otherwise been lost. These religious melodies play a prominent role in the musical system of the South. In the performance of these devotional songs,[382] the *paṇ* and the *tāla* are given special consideration.[383] Indeed, they are to the songs what *svara* is in relation to the Vedic *mantras*. At the *dhvajārohaṇa* or the hoisting of the flag, the rite known as *sandhyāvāhana* is performed; in connection with this rite, the *rāga*, *tāla*, *paṇ* and *nṛtta* are prescribed by the texts.[384]

[382] Cf. Poornalingam Pillai, *Tamil Literature*, p. 156: "The hymns of the Śaiva and Vaiṣṇava devotees form two huge collections known as *Tirumurai* and *Nālāyirappirapantam* respectively. Both the encyclopaedic compilations contain like the *Vedas* praises and prayers offered to the deity".

[383] Vaiyapuri Pillai, in his *History of Tamil Language and Literature* traces the origin and development of the *paṇ*. He observes (pp. 102-103): "In front of the deity, they poured out their hearts, in fervent recitation of songs, composed by their leaders and such joint recitations necessitated a kind of simple chorus music in which any one could join. Thus developed the *paṇ* system of music, so peculiar to the Tamils. It must not be supposed that the *paṇs* were invented by the religious leaders. The oldest of them were presumably popular melodies to which in very early times semi-religious songs were sung at communal celebrations and national festivals, and we may compare their origin and development with those of the ancient music of the *Sāmaveda*."

[384] Separate *rāga*, *tāla*, etc. For each quarter, one set for the east, another for the south-east, still another for the west, and so on, are prescribed in the ritual texts.

An excursus on the Śaiva Rituals as practised at present

The religious practices prevalent around the entire country do not differ widely from those that are in vogue in south India. The general resemblance which the temples bear to those in south India is due to the fact that this religion was known throughout the whole of India. Since then, as time passed, Śaivites have always looked to south India for guidance in all religious matters. Indeed, such guidance can be shown to have been indispensable in several ways. It is from the South that experts are invited to assume the responsibilities of raising new temples and of renovating older ones. Again, it is from south India that learned priests, proficient in the theory and practice of rituals, are invited to officiate at special rites such as *pratiṣṭhā*, a rite of very rare occurrence. It is also from this center of Āgamic Śaivism that *śilpins* skilled in the art of carving images have often been commissioned to produce *mūrtis* meant for installation in newly built temples. Some of these *śilpins* have made their permanent home there, though they still maintain contact with their native land. The same is the case with the musicians who play during *pūjā*, on such instruments as the *nādasvaram* or the drum. Experts in this field are still invited from south India to provide music during *utsava* rites. Religious discourses, popularly known as *kathākālakṣepa*, are given in the temples on various special occasions. These discourses do not necessarily bear any ritualistic stamp on them, yet they have their special place in the scheme of temple worship, which is mainly meant for the average devotees who is far from the path of *jñāna*. They are helpful for disseminating religious knowledge among the masses. These discourses are mainly based on the Epics and the *Purāṇas*, from which passages are liberally quoted. The Puranic events themselves may sometimes form the theme of the *kathā-kālakṣepas*.[385]

---

[385] These discourses center around such episodes as *Pārvatipariṇaya* (the wedding of Pārvatī), *Kumārasaṁbhava* (the birth of Kārttikeya), *Yamasaṁhāra* (the destruction of Yama).

Experts of such events might not be locally available, so they are invited from south India to give performances. It may be pointed out that the religious practices in some temples of the north are guided entirely by authorities in south Indian temples. For instance, when there is any controversy regarding the dates of the rituals or relating to their actual performance, the priests officiating at the temples appeal for guidance to the authorities in charge of the temples in south India. Even today, Śiva temples across India constantly refer to temples in south India for the clarification of doubts relating to the rites.

Temples may be divided into eight categories, with a view to studying the traditions relating to them from various angles. (1) The temples with particularly great religious significance form the first of these categories. (2) Next to these may be mentioned those temples which can be chronologically assigned to a fairly ancient date. (3) Temples with an elaborate layout form a small group by themselves. (4) Those with a rich variety of attendant gods and goddesses may again be grouped together. (5) There are a few temples which are noted for regular and detailed performance of the rituals — both the daily and the special ones. (6) There are some temples which do not conform to the rigid rules of the *Āgamas* and are thus outside the pale of orthodoxy. The structure of the temples in this group and the ritual traditions connected with them do not conform to the orthodox pattern laid down in the *Āgamas*. (7) There are a few temples which, like those in Benares and Ramesvaram, attract huge crowds of devotees from various parts of the land to pay their obeisance and acquire the consequent merits. As such, these temples may be said to form a category by themselves. Some of such temples attract devotees even from other parts of India. (8) The last group is constituted of those insignificant temples which are scattered all over the country — particularly in the areas with predominantly Hindu population.

The existence of these temples can be accounted for in several ways. To begin with, building new temples and renovating and maintaining older ones are acts which are highly commended in religious texts. The immense merits that are said to accrue from such acts are a sufficient inducement for religious-minded people to take up this kind of work. It is in this way that the coming into existence of the innumerable temples that are scattered througout the villages is to be explained. There is also a Tamil proverb, current among the people, which expressly discourages people from residing in villages without temples.[386] Efforts seem to have been made to build at least one temple in every village.

There is a category of Śaiva temples which do not rigidly conform to the orthodox ritual practices as laid down in the *Āgama* texts. Even the structure of these temples does not follow the conventional style of the Śaiva temples of south India. In some temples the rites are performed by brāhmaṇa priests, and in others by people of other castes, and this has been going on for generations. No elaborate rites are performed in these temples.

There are also Śaiva temples of a miscellaneous character. They are dedicated to various deities — some to Śiva, some to the Mother Goddess, some to Kārttikeya, and some to Gaṇeśa.

A few remarks of a general nature on the structural layout of the temples may not be out of place at this stage. Even the smallest temple with limited resources has a *garbhagṛha*, or inner shrine, in which the central deity is installed. This shrine has a single door which leads to the *ardha-maṇḍapa* situated immediately in front of the *garbha-gṛha*. The *ardha-maṇḍapa* itself leads to the *mahā-maṇḍapa*. Temples consisting of these *maṇḍapas* are surrounded by *prākāras* running around the temple. Wherever possible, such *prākāra* walls are erected to indicate the boundaries of the temple. The *prākāra* in front of the temple includes the *gopura*, which forms the main entrance to the temple. Actually, only a few temples have *gopuras*, while none of them has four *gopuras* like the great temples of south India. Each of the two *maṇḍapas* mentioned above is fitted with a *dvāra*, and these *dvāras* are arranged in such a manner as to make it possible for the

[386] *Koyililla uril kutiyirukka Ventam*. See: *Ten Tamil Ethics*, ed. South India Śaiva Siddhānta Works Publishing Society, Madras, p. 30. The translation appears on p. 31, which reads: "Live not in any place which is without a temple".

devotees to have the *darśana* of the deity through these doors even while standing outside the temple.[387] The walls of the temples are usually built of brick, with perhaps the sole exception of granite stone. Similarly, in some places the temples are provided with tiled roofs. The *garbhagṛha*, however, must be regarded as a significant exception to these two general rules. The walls of the *garbhagṛha* are built of well-chiselled stones, either white or black. The temples invariably face towards the east. The *garbhagṛha* has a *gomukha* which is designed as an outlet for the water with which the image is bathed.[388] The *gomukha* is set in the northern wall of the *garbhagṛha*. The type of construction of the dome atop the *garbhagṛha* varies according to the financial resources of the temple. Some temples have five storeys, some three, and some only one. On the top of the dome is placed the *kalaśa*. This pinnacle is invariably made of some metal such as copper, brass or bronze.

At the center of the *garbhagṛha* is placed the principal deity. If the temple is dedicated to Śiva, the *liṅga* is installed there. The image installed in the *garbhagṛha* is always carved out of stone. A typical Śiva temple may be described as follows: the *garbhagṛha* has the *liṅga* at its center, the *pūjābhāga* of which points towards the north. The *ardhamaṇḍapa* is, for all practical purposes, the place from where the priests perform the *ārādhana*. The waving of *dīpas* round the image, the offering of *upacāras* and similar other items of worship are all accomplished from this *maṇḍapa*. Only at the time when *arcanā* has to be performed and *naivedya* is to be offered do the priests enter

---

387 It may be pointed out that, in contrast to this, the temples of South India, on account of their colossal structures, do not provide the facility for those who stand outside the main entrance to have the *darśana* of the deity installed in the innermost shrine. The untouchable devotees, who were denied entry in some temples, could otherwise even while standing beyond the main entrance see the image and offer worship to it from there.

388 Cf. "The divinity is always placed in the middle of the *garbhagṛha*, upon which a pedestal called *āvuḍaiyār* which serves to receive the liquid matter with which the god is bathed, and to throw it out of the sanctum by means of a channel called *gomukha*." Jouveau Dubreuil, *Dravidian Architecture*, p. 23.

the *garbhagṛha*, and they perform these rites maintaining a close proximity with the image. In the *mahāmaṇḍapa* immediately opposite to the *liṅga* is assigned the place for Nandin, facing the *liṅga* installed in the *garbhagṛha*. The images of Gaṇeśa and Kārttikeya are installed respectively on the right and the left sides of the *garbhagṛha* in small shrines separately constructed for them. The bronze images of Naṭarāja, Somāskanda and Candraśekhara are installed on their respective *pīṭhas* or in shrines provided for them. Even other images which cannot be provided with separate shrine rooms elsewhere are installed in this *maṇḍapa*, but this is purely a matter of convenience.[389] Most Śiva temples have separate shrines provided for the Mother goddess. This is always situated close to the main *garbhagṛha* and to the left of the central deity. The shrine assigned to Śakti is smaller than the one assigned to the *liṅga*. This faces towards the south. In a few temples, the *garbhagṛha* of the goddess faces towards the same direction as the main *garbhagṛha* of the temple. The goddess installed in this shrine adjoining the one in which Śiva is represented in the *liṅga* form is endowed with anthropomorphic characteristics. A Nandin is installed separately against the image of the Śakti as well. The *garbhagṛha* of Śakti also is provided with a *gomukha*. The *pāka-śālā*, in which the cooked offerings to the deities are prepared, is located in the *agni-dik*, or the south-eastern corner of the temple, usually on the outskirts of the inner *prākāra* of the temple. Close to the *gomukha* of the central shrine is located the well which supplies water for all ritual purposes. The temples which can afford it have a separate well in the *pākaśālā* for supplying the water needed to cook the *naivedya* offerings. Those temples which celebrate the *brahmo-tsava* have *dhvajastaṁbhas* installed immediately behind the Nandin. These temples are also provided with *vasanta-maṇḍapas* in which

[389] The rules relating to the setting up of images of subordinate deities at suitable points in a temple can be strictly enforced only in temples which are properly laid out. In most of the temples where this is not possible, the images are set up according to convenience. For the correct positions of the attendant deities in the temple of Śiva, see chapter VII.

bronze images of the deities are installed. These images are decorated with garments, ornaments and garlands, and a detailed *dīpārādhana* is performed for them. They are then mounted on their respective *vāhanas*, one each day, and they are taken out in procession around the temple along the *prākāras*. The *vasantamaṇḍapa* has its door facing towards the south, and is located between the north and the north-east.

The temples are provided with *vāhana-śālās* in which the *vāhanas* used on festival occasions are kept. *Vṛṣabha-vāhana*, *gaja-vāhana*, *bhūta-vāhana*, *sarpa-vāhana*, *siṁha-vāhana*, *kāmadhenu-vāhana* and *kailāsa-vāhana* are the commonest *vāhanas* found in the temples of Śiva. The temples of Gaṇeśa have the *mūṣaka-vāhana* and those of Kārttikeya the *mayūra-vāhana*. *Śibikā* and *vimāna* are among the other *vāhanas* found in these temples. The *vāhanas* found in the temples are for the most part made of wood; in some temples, they have been plated with silver. However, the *vāhanas* in small temples can hardly equal those in the great temples of south India, some of which are even decorated with gold plates.

Close to the *gopura* is erected a tower in which a huge bell is hung. This bell is rung during the *pūjā* and on other special occasions.[390] Also next to the *gopura* a shrine is dedicated to the *kṣetra-pāla*.[391] The image of this attendant deity is placed in this shrine to face towards the west.

The *garbhagṛha* can be entered only by the initiated priests who are authorized to perform the rituals. The *ardhamaṇḍapa* is specifically intended for the performance of rites, and only brāhmaṇa

---

[390] According to the following injunction, two types of bells are to be used, one small and the other large.

Āvāhane ca pūjānte pūjāraṁbhe visarjane
Arghye vilepane snāne dīpe gandhābhiṣecane
Abhiṣeke ca dhūpe ca naivedye balikarmaṇi
Anyeṣu sarvakāryeṣu mahāghaṇṭāṁ pratāḍayet.
Kāraṇa, I.30.189-191.

[391] The *kṣetra-pāla* is identified with Bhairava, one of the aspects of Śiva. For details see pp. 272-274.

devotees can enter this *maṇḍapa*. Other devotees gather in the *mahā-maṇḍapa*, but they are not allowed to go beyond that point.[392]

Before proceeding to the description of the various rites performed in these temples, a brief account may be given of the temple employees and their duties. Even the smallest temples in the South with very limited financial resources have the following minimum employees. The first to be mentioned is the temple manager, who is in charge of the administration of the temple. He is called the *dharma-kartā*, and this title is indicative of his functions. He is the highest authority of the temple and decides upon all matters relating to the temple rites, both daily and special. Of course, he always does this in consultation with the officiating priests. The *arcaka* in charge of the actual rituals is known by various designations, such as *bhaṭṭa*, *ācārya* and *guru*.[393] He has to qualify himself for the various functions which he performs by going through the prescribed *dīkṣās* such as *samaya-dīkṣā*, *viśeṣa-dīkṣā*, and *nirvāṇa-dīkṣā*.[394] Before engaging himself in the *pūjā* which he performs for the benefit of others (*parārtha-pūjā*), he has to perform some *pūjā* for his own sake (*ātmārtha-pūjā*).[395] It is to be noted that the priest, possessing the necessary qualifications, can discharge his functions only so long as his wife is alive. During the period of his wife's pregnancy, as well as when he is polluted by *jananāśauca* and *maraṇāśauca*,[396] he cannot even enter the temple

[392] The untouchables were not allowed entry into most of the Hindu temples. They have been now granted such permission by the Constitution of India.

[393] Cf. *Kāraṇa*, I.30.

[394] See chapter VI, pp. 584 ff. number to adjust after final pagination

[395] *Vakṣye nityārcanaṁ puṇyaṁ śubhadaṁ pāpanāśanam |*
Mahāpātakadoṣaghnaṁ sarvayajñaphalapradam ||
Ātmārthaṁ ca parārthaṁ ca pūjā dviṁdham ucyate |
Datte ca guruṇā liṅge sthaṇḍile svayam ātmani ||
Kṣaṇike maṇḍale toye'py ātmārthaṁ yajanaṁ smṛtam |
Kāraṇa, I.30.1-3.

[396] *Āśauca* is the pollution caused by the birth of a child or the death of a person within the closest circles of the family. Until the end of the period of *āśauca*, which is usually of ten days' duration, the persons affected are forbidden from participation in all religious rites of an auspicious character.

premises. The temple *arcaka* performs the daily *pūjās*, which consist of *abhiṣeka*, *alaṅkāra*, the offerings of the *naivedya*, and the waving of the *dīpas* (*dīpārādhana*). He also performs the *arcanā* rites whenever he is requested to do so by devotees. On special occasions he has other functions to perform. Of course, on all such occasions he is assisted by the *paricāraka*, the *pācaka* and the *adhyayana-bhaṭṭa*, to all of whom are assigned their respective functions. In small temples, the functions of the *pācaka* and the *paricāraka* are combined into one and are discharged by the same assistant. He has to cook the *naivedya* offerings, provide water for bathing the image, place the various materials of worship like *puṣpa*, *candana* and *akṣata* where needed, and always stand beside the *arcaka* to help him in the performance of the *pūjā*. He lights the *dīpas* when the *ārādhana* requires them. He looks after the lamps in the *garbhagṛha* and sees that they are constantly supplied with oil and wicks until the end of the day's programme. He accompanies the chief priest on his rounds to make the *pūjā* offerings to the *parivāra-devatās* installed at various points in the temple. It is also his responsibility to sweep, clean and wash the inner shrines like the *garbhagṛha* and *ardha-maṇḍapa* at the appropriate moments set apart for such functions.

The *adhyayana-bhaṭṭa* has an important function to perform. He recites the appropriate Āgamic and Vedic *mantras* [397] over the course of the performance of the rites. The *Śatarudriya*, *Puruṣa-sūkta*, *camaka*, *pañca-śānti*, *ghoṣa-śānti*, and other important *sūktas* are recited during the *abhiṣeka* hours. The waving of each *dīpa* [398] is

---

[397] *Vedādhyayanaṁ kuryāt agramaṇḍapamadhyame |*
Camakaṁ caiva puṁsūktaṁ pavamānakam ||
Śrīsūktaṁ pañcaśāntiṁ ca kalāsūktaṁ hiraṇyakam |
Vipro vātha caturvedī mahāśaivo 'tha deśikaḥ ||
Vedādhyayanayuktaḥ san gandhavāri prapūjayet |
Kāraṇa, I.42.72-74.

[398] *Dīpaṁ saṁpūjya vidhivat agnibījena buddhimān |*
Śaṅkhadundubhinirghoṣais tato maṅgalavācakaiḥ ||
Stotradhvanisamāyuktaṁ vedadhvanisamanvitam |
Kāraṇa, I.32.14-15.

done to the accompaniment of a separate Vedic formula. The *adhyayana-bhaṭṭa* also repeats the names of the god during the *arcanā* ceremony. At the end of the *dīpārādhana*, he recites aloud representative extracts from the four *Vedas*. The *adhyayanabhaṭṭa* should possess a thorough knowledge of the *Vedas*, and he is expected to have received adequate instruction in the art of their recitation. In connection with the performance of special rites he also must recite the relevant Vedic *mantras*. Wherever possible, assisted by other priests possessing similar training and experience, he accompanies the procession of the image on festival days and recites extracts from the *Vedas*. Such *Vedapārāyaṇa* is done quite elaborately in the temples of south India. Experts in Vedic recitation form themselves into separate groups — one for each *Veda* — and then recite the *Vedas* in a chorus. The *Vedādhyāyins* always first study texts of the Vedic *śākhā* to which they belong. This always takes a good deal of time; consequently, they have little time at their disposal to study the texts of the other *śākhās*. It therefore often becomes necessary to appoint different experts to represent different Vedic *śākhās*. The *Atharvaveda*, it may be mentioned, has no place in this scheme of Vedic recitation.

The *sādhakācārya* employed in the temples assists the chief priest in various ways, mainly by reading out from time to time the relevant parts of the *Paddhati* [399] during the performance of the rituals. The *Paddhatis* recited indicate the proper sequence of rites for their performer. The *Paddhati* also gives the Āgamic *mantras* to be recited. If these *mantras* are of Vedic origin, the *adhyayana-bhaṭṭa* recites them. The services of the *sādhaka* are of course not required for the daily rites, but his assistance on special occasions is quite essential, for the rites to be performed on such occasions are lengthy and complicated, and since they are only performed occasionally, the chief priest cannot be expected to remember their every minute detail.

[399] The *Paddhatis* are practical manuals relating to the actual performance of the rituals. For detailed information about them see Appendix 1, p. 507.

The musicians who play on the *maṅgalavādyas* are permanent and daily employees of the temple.[400] However, wherever possible, expert artists are invited on special occasions or festivals. There is also the garland maker who supplies garlands (*mālās*) for daily worship. He also collects those flowers,[401] leaves, *samidh*, *darbha*-blades, and *bilva* needed for the daily *pūjā*. A regular employee in charge of the storeroom maintains a stock of all the *pūjā-dravyas*. He also attends to various other functions, like ringing the bell during *pūjā* hours, sweeping the temple premises, decorating the floors with *raṅgavallī*, lighting the lamps set in places other than the *garbhagṛha* and *ardha-maṇḍapa*, and so on. In certain temples, if resources permit, these functions are assigned to different employees.

A reference may be made at this stage to the *pūjā* utensils. These utensils are normally made of metals, varying from temple to temple according to their financial resources. Some temples use copper, some brass, others silver or even gold. In some temples, all these metals are used for making the utensils. The *kalaśa*, the *dīpa*, the *nīrājana-dīpa* and the handle of the bell are made of silver. The *upacāras*, such as the *darpaṇa*, *chatra*, *cāmara* (the handle only), *vyajana* and *tālabṛnda*, are also made of silver. There are a few temples in which most of the *dīpas* in the *dīpārādhana* are made of silver. The *bhasma-pātra*, in which the holy ash is kept, is invariably made of silver. The *saṅkha* used for the *abhiṣeka* and the *pūjā*-rites is covered with golden plates. The rhinoceros or bull *śṛṅga* used in the *abhiṣeka* rite is covered with ornamental work in silver. In the shrines are brass lamps.

---

400 Among these instruments are found *śaṅkha*, *dundubhi*, *ḍhakkā* and *jhallarī*, *Nṛtta* and *gīta* are also mentioned in this connection. See *Kāraṇa*, I.19.62.

401 From the list of flowers given in ritual texts the following may be mentioned as those which are mostly commonly used: Lotus, *punnāga*, *śaṅkhapuṣpa*, *mallikā*, *nandyāvarta*, *śriyāvarta*, *mandāra*, *bahukarṇikā*, *dvikarṇi*, *kurava*, *jāti*, *lakṣmī*, *vakula* and *mālatī* (among white flowers). Lotus (red), *palāsa*, *raktotpala*, *pāṭali*, *dhuttūra*, *karavīraka* and *raktamandāra* (among red flowers). *Karṇikāra*, *campaka*, *hemadhurdhura*, *āragvadha*, *karaṇḍa* (among the mixed variety). Leaves of, among others, *bilva*, *tapasvī*, *sahapatrī*, *apāmārga*, *kuśa*, *dūrvā*, and *pañca-bilva* are offered to Śiva. An exhaustive list is given in the chapter entitled *arcanāṅga-vidhi*. *Kāraṇa*, I.31.55-89.

The small *ghaṇṭā* [402] used for the *pūjā* rites is made of an appropriate alloy so that it can produce a pleasant resonant sound. The vessels used for the water required for the *abhiṣeka* are made of copper.

The articles needed daily for the *abhiṣeka* are oil, rice flour, turmeric powder, *pañcagavya*, *pañcāmṛta*, milk, curd, fruits and coconut water. The *udvartana* or the towel for drying the image after the *snapana* is also made available. The articles required for the daily *alaṁkāra* are garments and ornaments; *kavacas* or coverings made of silver or gold are also sometimes used. These *kavacas*, studded with precious gems, are fitted onto the images in such a manner that the original shape of the image is in no way affected. They bear the features of the original, and are skillfully made by the *śilpin* to fit exactly. In certain places, *kavacas* are provided only for certain parts of the body, such as hands, feet, chest, etc. *Naivedya* [403] consists of offering the cooked food to the god during the *pūjā* rites. *Śuddhodana* or plain cooked rice is the most common article of food offered in daily rites. The offering made at noon consists of rice, curry, dhal, curds, and so on — which constitute the normal noon meal for most south Indians. *Apūpa*, *lāja,* milk, plantains, *nālikera*, betel and arecanut are among other *naivedya* articles offered at the various *pūjās*. On special occasions, a rich variety of *citrānna*, such as *dadhyodana*, *tintriṇyodana*, etc., is offered as *naivedya.*

The *dīpāradhana* consists of waving the *dīpas* in front of the image. The wicks fitted on these lamps are lit by the *paricāraka* and

---

[402] The following verse, recited when the bell is rung during the rites, indicates the significance of the ringing of the bell:
Āgāmārthaṁ ca devānāṁ gamanārthaṁ tu rakṣasām |
Kurve ghaṇṭāravaṁ tatra devatāhvānalānchanam ||
"For the coming in of gods and the going out of demons, I sound the bell, sign of calling the gods."

[403] Rules have been laid down relating to the *naivedya*; the types of vessels to be used, the dress to be worn by the *pācaka* and his conduct are the topics first discussed. The various possible shortcomings of the cooking are indicated. Among the cooked offerings prescribed are found *kṛsarānna*, *pāyasānna*, *marīcyanna*, *mudgānna*, *kṣīrānna*, *gulānna* and *ghṛtānna.* Vegetables used for the cooking are also enumerated. The cooking of rice etc. for the *bali* offerings is also prescribed. *Kāraṇa*, I.33.

given to the *arcaka*. The *dīpas* are displayed in the prescribed order. *Dhūpa* is first offered, then follows the *dīpa* with a single wick. The *naivedya* is offered with the appropriate *mantras*, Vedic and non-Vedic, and with the display of the *mudrās* prescribed for the *pañca-prāṇahuti*. The *alaṁkāradīpa* is the first to be displayed, lifted with the bottom handle. The *dīpa* has three to nine levels, each with several wicks. The circular levels are of decreasing diameters up the *dīpa*, with proportionally fewer wicks as well. The number of levels of the *dīpa* is always odd, so that there are three, five, seven or nine levels in all. The wicks used are very small and are fed with sufficient oil so that they burn as long as needed. *Nāgadīpa*, *vṛṣabhadīpa*, *bilvadīpa* and *kumbhadīpa* are among the *dīpas* used daily for waving.[404] The wicks in these lamps are so arranged that, when they are lit, the various figures after which the *dīpas* are named become clearly manifest through the lit wicks. Each *dīpa* has its specific Agamic and Vedic *mantra* which is to be recited when waving that *dīpa*. The mode of waving the lamps is prescribed in the ritual texts.[405] The *dīpa* is first held high up against the forehead of the image, then at the level of the eyes, then of the mouth, the neck, the hands, and the feet. The final waving, which should describe a *praṇava* in front of the images, marks the end of the *ārādhana* performed with that *dīpa*. The other *dīpas* also are then displayed in the same manner.

The *dīpārādhana* is followed by the offerings of the *upacāras* like *darpaṇa*, *chatra*, *cāmara*, *vyajana* and *tālavṛnta*. These *upacāras*

---

[404] *Nāgadīpaṁ samārabhya ghaṭadīpāvasānakam |*
Dīpārcārādhanaṁ kuryāt namaḥ sarpādimantrataḥ ||
Kāraṇa, I.32.32.

[405] *Prathamaṁ dakṣiṇe netre dvitīyam apasavyake |*
Tṛtīyaṁ phāladeśe tu gale caiva caturthakam ||
Pādādimastakāntaṁ vā trivāraṁ bhrāmayed budhaḥ |
Mastake ca lalāṭe ca kaṇṭhe vakṣasi pādayoḥ ||
Pratyekaṁ praṇavākāraṁ dīpaṁ saṁvedayed budhaḥ |
Kāraṇa, I.32.35-37.

"The wise should wave the lamp, first to the right eye, in the second place to the left eye, in the third place to the forehead, in the fourth place to the neck, or, three times, from the feet to the head. The wise should offer to the head, forehead, neck, chest and feet, in each offer light describing the form of *praṇava*."

also are displayed in more or less the same manner as the *dīpas*. This is then followed by *arcanā*, the offering of flowers with the recital of the names of the god. Each name is put in the dative case and is followed by the word *namaḥ* (e.g. *Śivāya namaḥ*, *Maheśvarāya namaḥ*, *Śaṁbhave namaḥ*, and so on). Usually, the one hundred and eight names are thus recited. *Puṣpāñjali* is offered to the accompaniment of a Vedic *mantra*. This is followed by the *pañcārātrika*, which marks the end of the *pūjā*. Then follows the symbolical recital first of the four *Vedas* [406] and then of the *Śrauta-sūtras*.[407] Then come benedictions and the singing of Tamil devotional songs composed by the saints of south India.[408] Except for this occasional singing of devotional songs in Tamil, the proceedings of the rituals are entirely conducted in Sanskrit, and the *mantras* employed are taken either from the *Vedas* or from the *Āgamas*. When the recitals mentioned above are over, *vibhūti*, *candana*, and *tīrtha* are distributed among the devotees as *prasāda* of the god.

A more or less detailed statement may now be made regarding the daily programme of the rituals normally performed in the leading Śaiva temples.

The *uṣaḥkāla-pūjā* marks the beginning of the day's programme. The doors of the *garbhagṛha* are opened to the accompaniment of the blowing of a conch, the ringing of a bell and playing auspicious musical instruments. The priest and his assistants enter the temple after bathing and performing the *sandhyopāsanā*. Worship is first offered to Bhairava, and the keys of the inner shrine are obtained. The *pūjā* in this connection is performed with simple *dīpārādhana* and *naivedya*. The doors of the *garbhagṛha* are opened as indicated

---

406 The opening *mantras* from the four *Vedas*, *Agnim īle* of the *Ṛgveda*, *ise tvorje tvā* of the Yajurveda, *Agna āyāhi* of the *Sāmavedā* and *Śanno devīrabhiṣṭaye* of the *Atharvaveda* are recited. The recital commences and ends with the sacred word *oṁ*.

407 This consists of: *Athādau darśapūrṇamāsau vyākhyāsyāmaḥ*.

408 The collection of devotional songs in Tamil is divided into 12 sections. Five representative songs are sung on every such occasion. They are songs from *Tēvāram*, *Tiruvācakam*, *Tiruvicaippā*, *Tiruppallāṇḍu* and *Tiruppurāṇam*.

earlier. The *uṣaḥkāla-pūjā* begins with the *dīpārādhana* and the *naivedya* offering made to Śakti, then is performed the *ārādhana* of Śiva. This sequence is the reverse of that which had been followed for the *pūjā* the previous night.

Many temples are provided with the *śayana-gṛha*. The god and the goddess are roused from sleep by soft music and by devotional songs imploring to the divinities to awaken. The images of the god and the goddess are then mounted on a *śibikā* and, to the accompaniment of music, are taken from the *śayanagṛha* to their respective places.

The *prātaḥkāla-pūjā* is performed at about 8 a.m. All the *parivāra* deities installed in the temple are offered *pūjā*. The stone images are all bathed with water and dressed with garments, *candana* and garlands. The chief deities, Śiva and Śakti, are elaborately bathed. In a few temples *Rudrakumbha* [409] is installed, and after the *abhiṣeka* is over but before the *udvartana*, the contents of the *kumbha* are poured on the *liṅga*. The *abhiṣeka* is followed by *alaṁkāra*. The *pūjā* proceeds with the offering of *naivedya*, *dhūpa*, *dīpa* and *karpūrārtika* to Gaṇeśa. The *pūjā* offered to Śiva is elaborate, as the one performed in honour of Śakti. It is also characterized by offerings of *naivedya*, *dīpas* and *karpūrārtika*.

The noontime *madhyāhna-pūjā* is characterized by *abhiṣeka*, *alaṁkāra*, *naivedya*, and *dīpāradhana*. The *pūjās* are only offered to the main deities. A curtain is then dropped and the doors are closed, to be opened again in the evening for the *sāyaṅkāla-pūjā*.

The *sāyaṅkāla-pūjā* is offered to Gaṇeśa, Śiva and Śakti. The *abhiṣeka*, *alaṁkāra*, *naivedya*, and elaborate *dīpārādhana* are the main characteristics of this *pūjā*. It is usually attended by a large number of devotees, who find the hour quite suitable to gather and offer worship in a leisurely manner. The interval between this *pūjā*

---

[409] *Athavā brāhmaṇān viprān śivakumbhasamanvitān |*
Rudrasaṁkhyān samāhūya ardhamaṇḍapasaṁsthitān ||
Japet saṁkalpapūjāṁ ca ekādaśaparāyaṇam |
Kāraṇa, I.42.8-9.

and the next, which is performed about three hours later, is mostly filled by the priest performing *arcanās* for the devotees. The *arcanās* performed in the temples sometimes consist of the repetition of one hundred and eight or one thousand names. In certain temples, *arcanās* are performed by offering one *lakh* of flowers as one *lakh* names of the god are recited. This great number of names can be spoken by the repetition of the *sahasranāma* one hundred times.

The *pūjā* performed next is similar to the one performed in the morning. The *parivāradevatas* are offered *abhiṣeka*, *alaṁkāra*, *naivedya* and *dīpārādhana*. The *pūjās* offered to Śiva and Śakti are elaborate and exhibit their usual characteristics.

The *ardhayāmapūjā* is the last *pūjā* of the day. This is also characterized by *abhiṣeka*, *alaṁkāra*, *naivedya* and *dīpārādhana*. The *naivedya* offered at this *pūjā* consists of *pāyasa* and *māṣāpūpa*. The *pūjā* is confined to Śiva, Śakti and Kṣetrapāla. It is to this last divinity that the keys of the *garbhagṛha* are ritualistically entrusted overnight. The temples provided with a *śayana-maṇḍapa* celebrate the daily *utsava* of the procession of the image to the accompaniment of the *maṅgalavādya* and other honours. After the images of Śiva and Śakti are finally taken to the *śayana-maṇḍapa*, they are left reclining on couches arranged with mattresses and pillows. The couch is sometimes set on a swing (*dolā*), which is rocked as music is played. The doors of the *śayana-maṇḍapa* remain closed until the following morning.

The details of the daily rituals as outlined above vary from temple to temple. Most temples, lacking in adequate funds, cannot afford any elaborate performance of rituals. As far as the regular performance of the rituals even in their bare outlines is concerned, only the big rich temples can properly afford it.

The special or *naimittika* rites, which are distinct from the daily ones, are for the most part each performed once every year. A few of such rites which are commonly celebrated have been mentioned below. The month of *Caitra* is noted for the *vasanta-utsava*.[410] As is proper

[410] Some temples celebrate the festival called *uḍupotsava*. This festival, which usually takes place during the *vasanta* season, is characterized by the image of the deity

for the hot season, this festival is characterised by particularly elaborate *abhiṣeka* rites. In the month of *Vaiśākha*, the temples of Kārttikeya celebrate the festival of his birth. A reference has already been made to the *brahmotsava*; this is generally celebrated in the temples dedicated to Kārttikeya in such a way as to have the *tīrtha-utsava* fall on that day. On the *caturthī* of the bright half of *Śrāvaṇa* is celebrated the *Vināyaka-caturthī*. The temples of Gaṇeśa are decorated on that day, and elaborate *abhiṣeka*, *alaṁkāra* and *utsava* ceremonies are performed. In the month of *Āśvina* occurs the *Navarātri* festival,[411] which is celebrated in almost every temple. Mondays in the month of *Kārttika* are held to be sacred to Śiva. On these days the devotees undertake fasts and also observe other vows. In every Śiva temple, the *somavāra* festivals are characterized by *abhiṣeka*, *alaṁkāra*, *naivedya* and *dīpārādhana*. The highlight of these festivals occurs when Śiva and Umā, decked in ornaments and garlands, are mounted on the *vṛṣabha-vāhana* and taken about in procession. In some temples, the *śaṅkhābhiṣeka* is performed by bathing the *liṅga* with water and other *abhiṣeka-dravyas* contained in a thousand conches. On the full moon day of *Kārttika* is celebrated the *Kṛttikādīpa-utsava*.[412] This is celebrated in every home by lighting several rows of lamps. This festival is celebrated in temples by setting fire to a large circular structure made of a combustible material such as palm leaves. The mighty flames which thereby reach high into the sky are presumably reminiscent of the well-known Purāṇic episode when a column of fire appeared between Brahmā and Viṣṇu.[413] In the month of *Mārgaśīrṣa* occurs the *ārdrā* festival.[414]

being taken in procession and led to a boat specially prepared for the occasion. The site chosen for the celebration of this festival is invariably a tank in the vicinity of the temple.

411 *Kāraṇa*, I.127.

412 *Ibid.*, I.112.

413 *Kūrma P.*, I.26; *Vāyu P.*, I.1; *Liṅga P.*, I.17. A similar fire is produced on the hills at Aṇṇāmalai in South India. There large pieces of new cloth profusely dipped in ghee are lit and the flame so produced on the full moon day of *Kārtika* persists for days until it burns itself out.

414 *Kāraṇa*, I.114.

This is celebrated everywhere with special offerings to Naṭarāja. Special *abhiṣeka* rites are performed six times a year, but this one is the most important of them all.[415] In connection with the *ārdrā* festival, in all temples in which the Naṭarāja image is installed, the *abhiṣeka* is performed early in the morning at about 2 a.m. At sunrise, the *darśana* of the god is made possible.[416] The festival of *Dīpāvalī* has no Śaivite features in it, therefore its celebration is mainly confined to home. However, in some temples, the images are bathed with oil and are clad in new clothes on that day, in imitation of the practice prevalent in south Indian families. The day which is held most sacred to Śiva, falls in the month of *Māgha*. It is the fourteenth day in the dark half of the month and is popularly known as *Śivarātri*. Special *abhiṣeka* and *pūjā* are performed throughout the whole day and night. The devotees observe fast on that day and keep awake through the whole night, devoting the entire time to the worship of Śiva.

In addition to these special rites which are commonly performed throughout the year, there are a few rites which some temples celebrate as being exclusively their own. The *brahmotsava* belongs to this variety. Different temples have different days assigned for their *brahmotsava*; they may fall in any part of the year. The *brahmotsava* is characterized by the *dhvajārohaṇa* or the hoisting of the flag on the opening day of the festival, the *rathotsava* performed on the penultimate day, and the *tīrthotsava* and *dhvajāvarohaṇa* both performed on the last day. This last day is always so chosen that it coincides with the new moon, full moon, or the *saṅkrānti* day. On each day of the festival, the *utsava-vigraha* is decked with costly ornaments and garlands and is honoured with an elaborate *dīpārādhana*, followed

---

415 The *abhiṣeka* is performed in the Naṭarāja temple at Chidambaram as also in other temples of Śiva in South India and Srilanka six times a year, namely, in the months of *Caitra*, *Jyeṣṭha*, *Śrāvaṇa*, *Bhādrapada*, *Mārgaśīrṣa* and *Māgha*. The *abhiṣeka* performed in *Mārgasīrṣa* is the most elaborate of all.

416 This festival is celebrated on a large scale at Chidambaram in South India. See also *Kāraṇa*, I.118.

by *Veda-ghosa*, *āśīrvacana*, the singing of devotional songs and being taken in procession.[417]

In some temples are performed special festivals which clearly reflect well-known Purāṇic episodes. For instance, there are the *saṁhāra-utsavas* which depict the destruction wrought by Śiva for the benefit of his devotees or by Kārttikeya for the benefit of the gods. Of these *saṁhāra-utsavas*, the *sūra-saṁhāra* festival depicting the destruction of Tāraka and his allies is performed in almost all the important temples of Kārttikeya. During the *saṁhāra* festivals, one sees the dramatization of such well-known Purāṇic episodes as the destruction of Kāma, the burning of the three cities, the annihilation of the *yāga* performed by Dakṣa, the *vadha* of the demons Andhaka and Jalandhara and the clipping of the fifth head of Brahmā.

There are not many differences among the *mantras* employed during the various Śaiva rites performed in the temples of south India. In both ritual systems, due place is assigned to the *mantras* of Āgamic and Vedic origin. Great importance is attached to the hymns addressed to Rudra in the *Ṛgveda*, the *Śatarudriya* from the *Yajurveda*, to those parts relating to Rudra-Śiva from the *Brāhmaṇas* and the *Śvetāśvatara* and the *Atharvaśiras Upaniṣads*. However, the *mantra* which is most significant from the point of view of the Śaivites is the *pañcākṣara*, and this is employed along with the *praṅava* and the *bījākṣaras* [418] for all important rites, especially at the time of *āvāhana*, *prāṇa-*

[417] *Pratiṣṭhā*, *utsava* and *prāyaścitta* are some of the special rites prescribed in the *Āgamas*. The *pratiṣṭhā* is to be performed only when the temple is faced with any calamities or when it requires renovation. A few temples perform *pratiṣṭhā* once every twelve years. *Utsavas* of various types have been already described. The *prāyascitta* is performed as expiation against the evils which may have been caused by the deficiencies of various kinds.

[418] The second chapter of *Kāraṇa*, I, entitled *Mantravidhipaṭala*, deals with the various details in this connection, such as *mantrasvarūpa*. It also gives the *bījākṣaras* of Gaṇeśa, Ṣanmukha, Dakṣiṇamūrti and other gods. The *pañcabrahmamantra* and the *ṣaḍaṅgamantra*, and more particularly the *pancākṣara* are the *mantras* which are enlisted with specific comments, wherever necessary. The *bījākṣaras* assigned to the various subordinate deities, such as *dikpālakas*, are also given in this chapter.

pratiṣṭhā etc. These sacred letters occur for the first time in the *Śaṭatarudriya*. The religious-mystic significance of these five letters has been repeatedly emphasized in the *Purāṇas*. As has been pointed out in an earlier section, the *Āgamas* and the Tamil literature dealing with Śaiva religion also speak about the *pañcākṣara*.[419] The five *saṁhitā-mantras* and the six *aṅga-mantras* are repeatedly employed during rituals. By and large, the *mantras* used in the Śaiva rituals performed in the temples are identical, as they are prescribed in the *Paddhatis* and their source texts, the *Āgamas*, which are accepted as authoritative.

The foregoing description of the rituals prevalent in Śaiva temples would make it clear that the ritual tradition mainly comprises *abhiṣeka, alaṁkāra, naivedya, dīpārādhana, arcanā* and *utsava*. These constituents of the *pūjā* ritual receive wider elaboration when performed on special occasions in connection with the usual *naimittika* rites, namely *karṣaṇa, pratiṣṭhā, utsava* and *prāyaścitta*.[420]

The *Navarātri* festival celebrated in the temple is distinguished by the *abhiṣeka* performed in the morning, by the *alaṁkāra* and *naivedya* performed thereafter, and by the elaborate *Śrīcakra-pūjā, arcanā, naivedya, dīpārādhana* and *caturvedaghoṣa* at night. In the *maṇḍapa*, the goddess in whose honour the *Navarātri* is celebrated is enthroned on a *siṁhāsana* [421] which is only used for this ritual. To the accompaniment of the *maṅgalavādya*, the goddess is led in all pomp and grandeur, and with stately honours of *chatra, cāmara* and *tālavṛnta*, to the *snānamaṇḍapa* where a seat on an elevated platform (*snānavedi*) has been prepared for the occasion. The procession is further characterized by the blowing of conches and trumpets announcing the movements of the goddess, and by *Veda-ghoṣa*. The goddess is then duly installed on the *snānavedi*.

---

[419] See earlier pp. 512 ff.

[420] These four have already been dealt with in Chapter VI.

[421] The *Lalitāsahasranāma* mentions the *simhāsana*:
Śrīmātā śrīmahārājñī śrimatsiṁhāsaneśvarī |
Lalitāsahasranāma, opening verse.

The preliminary preparations, as indicated below, are made long in advance of the arrival of the deity to the *snānamaṇḍapa* and her installation on the *snānavedi*. First, one hundred and eight *śaṅkhas* are arranged and filled with water, and various kinds of herbs and other *abhiṣekadravyas* are added.[422] Each *śaṅkha* is decked with *candana*, *kuṅkuma*, *akṣata* and *puṣpa* and is covered with blades of *kuśa* grass. The central *śaṅkha* is kept on an elevated *pīṭha* and is duly adorned with *darbha*, garlands, mango sprouts, silken clothes etc. This *śaṅkha* is filled with water and mixed with such *abhiṣeka-dravyas* as camphor, *gorocanā*, saffron and *kastūri*. The elaborate *śaṅkha-pūjā* begins with the invocation of the goddess into the *pradhāna-śaṅkha*. The attendant deities are then invoked into their places in the other *śaṅkhas*. The *pūjā* is followed by *agnikārya*. The sacred fire is kindled and the goddess is invoked into the *agni* to receive her oblations. All the prescribed *homadravyas* [423] are offered on the fire and the *homa* is brought to a close with the *pūrṇāhuti*.[424] This *śaṅkha-pūjā*, which takes more than three hours to complete, is performed some time before the ceremonial entry of the goddess into the *snāna-maṇḍapa*. Another preparation which has to be made in advance is the orderly arrangement of the *abhiṣekadravyas* before the *snānavedī*. These articles have to be placed in the order in which they are to be used during the *abhiṣeka*. The various *abhiṣekadravyas* [425] contained in silver pots are placed on a long, slightly elevated platform opposite to the *snānavedi* in the following order: oil for the *abhyañjana*, *piṣṭa* (rice flour), *āmalaka*, *rajanī*, *pañcagavya*, *pañcāmṛta*, milk, curd, honey, ghee, sugarcane juice, fruit juices (mango, *jak*, orange, woodapple, lime, plantain and pomegranate are commonly used; the juice of each fruit is kept in a separate vessel), the liquid contents of tender coconuts, cooked rice, hot water, *bhasma*, *kuṅkuma*, *candana*, *himatoya*, and water from sacred Gaṅgā (Ganges).

---

422 *Kāraṇa*, I.38.38-46.

423 *Kāraṇa*, I.63. enumerates at length the various oblation materials used on the occasion and the Vedic *mantras* to be recited to accompany the offerings.

424 For the full description of the *pūrṇāhuti*, see p. 392.

Besides these is placed a clean and dry towel to wipe the image (*udvartana*) after the bathing ceremony.

The assistants with specific functions assigned to them are stationed in the *abhiṣeka-maṇḍapa* in their proper places. On either side of the goddess now installed on the pedestal two attendants fan her with *vyajanas*. This fanning begins when the goddess is installed on her pedestal, and continues until the *abhyañjana* or the application of the oil over her body. A *paricāraka* is in charge of the fruits and *tāmbūla* which are to be offered with a separate *dravya* to the goddess as *naivedya* when the bathing is performed. Another *paricāraka* is appointed to light the *karpūrārātrika* to be waved before the goddess each time a new *abhiṣeka-dravya* is used to bathe her. Before the use of each *dravya*, the goddess is washed with fresh water kept ready in a large silver tub. The *ghanapāṭhins* recite the *Veda* in groups. Some officiants perform the *pārāyaṇa* of the *Saptaśatī* [426] (also known as *Devīmahātmya*), others the *pārāyaṇa* of the *Lalitopākhyāna*,[427] which sings of the glories of the goddess. It is significant that these two texts which are chosen for the occasion are derived from the *Mārkaṇḍeya Purāṇa* and *Brahmāṇḍa Purāṇa* respectively.

---

[425] *Prasthatailapramāṇasya kadalīpañcaviṁsatiḥ* |
Piṣṭaṁ prasthārdhakaṁ caiva tathācāmalakaṁ bhavet ||
Rajanīṁ rasadravyañca tatpramāṇaṁ vidhīyate |
Kuḍupam ghṛtasaṁyuktaṁ tadardhaṁ kṣaudram ucyate ||
Dugdhaṁ tu śivasaṅkhyā ca dadhi cāḍhakameva ca |
Daśaphalaṁ tu śarkarā āḍhakam ikṣuśārakam ||
Likucaṁ daśa saṅkhyā ca nāraṅgaṁ dvayam eva ca |
Cūtaṁ pañcadaśaṁ jñeyaṁ dāḍimītrayameva ca ||
Mātulaṅgāni ca trīṇi kulañcirasasaṅkhyayā |
Tamaraṁ trayam evoktam ekaṁ panasam eva ca ||
Devatāmraphalaṁ trīṇi dasakaṁ nālikerakam |
Annābhiṣekamantrānnaṁ dvitriprasthaṁ ca kārayet ||
Gandhatoyaṁ cārdhaphalaṁ gandham ekaphalaṁ bhavet |
Tato kumbhābhisekaṁ ca nadyāṁ snānaḥ tataḥ param ||
Tato sahasradhārā ca ... ...

Kāraṇa, I.50.3-10.

[426] This is contained in the *Mārkaṇḍeya-Purāṇa*, chapters 81-93.

[427] *Lalitopākhyāna* forms the last section of the *Brahmāṇḍa Purāṇa*.

Then there is a group recitation of the *Lalitāsahasranāma* [428] and the *Lalitatriśatī*.

The *abhiṣeka* begins with a special *dhyāna* and the *āvāhana* of the goddess to grace the occasion with her presence in the image, performed during the *abhiṣeka* ceremony. Such *āvāhana* would seem somewhat superfluous, because after the *pratiṣṭhā* rite has been performed, the presence of the goddess in the image is felt as a matter of course both by the priests who perform the daily worship as well as by the devotees who gather every day to pay their obeisance. The *āvāhana* at the commencement of the *abhiṣeka* is purely ceremonial and by convention, and should not lead one to any misinterpretation.

The offerings of *pādya*,[429] *arghya*,[430] and *ācamanīya* [431] are the first rites to be performed during the *abhiṣeka*, immediately after the entry into the *snānamaṇḍapa*, the provision of the seat for the goddess, the *dhyāna* and the conventional *āvāhana* as mentioned above. The *pādya* is prepared long before the arrival of the goddess in the *snānamaṇḍapa*, by pouring water mixed with ingredients like *kuṅkuma* and sandal into the *pādya-pātra*, which is purified by washing and *abhimantraṇa*. The feet of the goddess are washed with the *pādya* water, *candana* and *akṣata* and flowers are offered to her feet, and *nīrājana* is performed. The bath water, which is regarded as

---

[428] The colophon at the end of the *Sahasranāma* reads: *Iti śrī brahmāṇḍapurāṇa uttarakhaṇḍe śrīhayagrīvāgastyasaṁvāde śrīlalitāsahasranāmastotraṁ nāma dvitīyo'dhyāyah*. See *Bṛhatstotraratnākara* I, p. 372. This would indicate that the text is included in the *Brahmāṇḍa Purāṇa*. But the edition of the *Purāṇa* used for the present study, namely that published by Venkaṭesvara Steam Press, Bombay, does not contain it.

[429] *Kuṅkumaṁ candanaṁ dūrvā siddhārthośīrakaṁ tathā* |
Jalenaiva samāyuktaṁ pādyam uttamam ucyate ||
Kāraṇa, I.31.38.

[430] *Āpakṣīrakuśāgraiś capy akṣatair yavataṇdulaiḥ* |
Tilaiḥ siddhārthakaiś caiva arghyam uttamam ucyate ||
Kāraṇa, I.31.46-47.

[431] *Uśīraṁ jātikarpūraṁ truṭitaṁ tu lavaṅgakam* |
Mureṇa salilopetaṁ śreṣṭham ācamanīyakam ||
Kāraṇa, I.31.43.

particularly sacred, is collected and sprinkled by the performer of the *abhiṣeka* upon his own head. A curtain (*tiraskaraṇī*) is then dropped, and the image of the goddess is prepared for her bath by removing all her ornaments, garlands and clothes. The curtain is then removed, and the *abhiṣeka* ceremony is witnessed by the hundreds of devotees gathered in the *maṇḍapa* for that purpose. *Dantadhāvana* [432] or the cleaning of her teeth is performed with a small twig of mango shaped like a painting brush. This teeth cleaning is followed by the offering of *gandūṣa* or water for washing her mouth. Then follows a thorough application of oil to her whole body. This *tailābhyaṅga* in the *abhiṣeka* is performed along the same lines as the normal bathing practice of the south Indians.[433] Oil is applied all over her body and her limbs are lathered and gently caressed. Such application of oil is marked by offering *phala* and *tāmbūla*, and waving the *nīrājana*. The image is then bathed with cold water, and *piṣṭa* is applied all over her body.[434] The application of *piṣṭa* also is marked by the offering of betel and the *nīrājana*. The *abhiṣeka* ceremony then proceeds in a like manner. The various *abhiṣeka* materials are duly poured over the image in succession, and after bathing the image with each material, *tāmbūla*, *phala* and *nīrājana* are offered. The *abhiṣeka* of *candana*, one of the materials to be taken up towards the end of the *abhiṣeka*, is followed by bathing the image with the contents of a hundred *kalaśas* filled with cold water. Then there is the bathing with water poured

---

[432] *Vastrāṇi santyajed eva tatpuruṣeṇa pūjayet |*
Dhūpadīpaṁ hṛdā datvā dantakaṣṭhaṁ daded budhaḥ ||
Kāraṇa, I.42.5.

[433] Such *tailābhyaṅga* is a characteristic of the south Indians. Once a week, most South Indians and the Srilankan Tamils, who follow the same tradition, take this *tailābhyaṅga-snāna*, which consists of applying oil all over the body and its subsequent washing away with various powders which are capable of removing the oil. The rich employ attendants who are adepts in the art to massage the limbs by soft caresses. A reference may be made in this connection to Gode: "Massage in Ancient and Mediaeval India", *ABORI*, vol. XXXVI, parts I & II, pp. 111-112.

[434] The chapter entitled "*Tailābhyaṅgavidhipaṭala*" (*Kāraṇa*, I.43) lays down the rules relating to the anointing of the *Śivaliṅga*. The powders to be applied thereafter are also specified in that connection.

through the *śṛṅga*. This *śṛṅga* or horn, which is specially designed to receive water at one end and to pass it out through the other end, is adorned with ornamental silverwork and is studded with gems and other precious stones. Usually the horn of a bull or rhinoceros is employed for this purpose. The *dhārābhiṣeka* which follows immediately after this is a kind of shower bath, and is arranged by pouring water into a broad-bottomed vessel with many perforations,[435] which is held over the image. The *śaṅkhas*, which are already installed and worshipped, are brought to the place of bathing and their contents are poured over the image. The *pradhāna-śaṅkha* is the last to be used, and is attended by great pomp and grandeur. After a processional *pradakṣiṇā* around the temple, the contents of this *śaṅkha* are poured over the image accompanied by loud music and the recitation of praises for the goddess. This marks the end of the *abhiṣeka*. Then follows the drying of the goddess with a towel (*udvartana*). Her limbs are then besmeared with unguents like *mṛgamada*, *candana* and *kastūri*, and she is decorated with *alaṁkāras*. The goddess is clad in a silken saree, worn in various styles. *Ābharaṇas* of different types are assigned to her various limbs. *Stotras* are recited during the *alaṁkāra* hour. The rite of *alaṁkāra* ends with her decoration with garlands.

The close of the *abhiṣeka* ceremony usually coincides with the *madhyāhna-pūjā*. The goddess is then fed an elaborate meal which contains all the six *rasas* in abundance. Curries, *pāyasa*, *māṣāpūpa* and curd are necessary constituents of this meal. The *dīpārādhana*,

---

[435] The structure of the vessel used or the *dhārābhiṣeka*, and the merit derived by having this *dhārābhiṣeka* performed is described as follows:
Sarvadoṣaharaṁ puṇyaṁ sarvatīrthaṁ tathaiva ca |
Sarvapāpaharaṁ caiva sahasradhārābhiṣecanam ||
Sauvarṇam uttamaṁ proktaṁ madhyamaṁ rājataṁ bhavet |
Adhamaṁ tāmrajam uktaṁ pūrṇacandravadākṛtiḥ ||
Tanmadhye padmapatraṁ ca dalānām aṣṭasaṁyutam |
suṣiraṁ sahasrasaṁyuktaṁ kalpayet tu vicakṣaṇaḥ ||
… … …
Sahasradhārām uddhṛtya liṅgasyordhve tu kalpayet |
Kāraṇa, I. 47.2-7.

arcanā, *Vedaghoṣa*, *āśīrvacana*, *drāviḍastotragāna*, as well as the distribution of the *prasāda*, which consists (among many other things) of the *tīrthodaka* or bath water, form the concluding items in the *abhiṣeka* ceremony.[436]

The goddess is then brought back to the *maṇḍapa* with such honours as the waving of chowries and such *upacāras* as *chatra*, *vyajana* and *tālavṛnta*. This procession back to her chamber, where she is to resume her sitting on her *siṁhāsana*, is very stately and imposing. The procession is conducted first to the accompaniment of *Vedaghoṣa*, then to the *maṅgalavādya*, then of other musical instruments such as *mṛdaṅga* and lute, then of Tamil devotional songs, then for some distance absolute silence (*mauna*) is maintained, and

---

436 The following *sūtras* from a ritual text dealing with the worship of Śakti mentions the sixty-four *upacāras*. Among these are mentioned the ornaments which are offered to the goddess:

Tritārīmuccārya pādyaṁ (1) *kalpayāmi namaḥ iti krameṇa ābharaṇāvaropaṇaṁ* (2) *sugandhatailābhyaṅgaṁ* (3) *majjanaśālāpraveśanam* (4) *majjanamaṇḍapa-maṇipīṭhopaveśanaṁ* (5) *divyasnānīyodvartanam* (6) *uṣṇodakasnānaṁ* (7) *kanakakalaśacyutasakalatīrthābhiṣekaṁ* (8) *dhautavastraparimārjanam* (9) *aruṇadukūlaparidhānam* (10) *aruṇakucottarīyam* (11) *ālepamaṇḍapapraveśanaṁ* (12) *ālepamaṇḍapamaṇipīṭhopaveśanaṇ* (13) *candanāgarukuṅkumaśaṅkumṛgama-dakarpūrakastūrigorocanādivyagandhasarvāṅgīṇavilepanaṁ* (14) *keśabharasya kālāgarudhūpaṁ* (15) *mallikāmālatījāticaṁpakāśokaśatapatrapūgakuḍmali-punnāgakalhāramukhyasarvartukusumamālāṁ* (16) *bhūṣaṇamaṇḍapapraveśanaṁ* (17) *bhūṣaṇamaṇḍapamaṇipīṭhopaveśanaṁ* (18) *navamaṇimakuṭaṁ* (19) *candraśakalaṁ* (20) *sīmantasindūraṁ* (21) *tilakaratnaṁ* (22) *kālāñjanaṁ* (23) *pāliyugalaṁ* (24) *maṇikuṇḍalayugalaṁ* (25) *nāsābharaṇaṁ* (26) *adharayāvakaṁ* (27) *prathamabhūṣaṇaṁ* (28) *kanakacintākaṁ* (29) *padakaṁ* (30) *mahāpadakaṁ* (31) *mukuṭāvalim* (32) *ekāvaliṁ* (33) *channavīraṁ* (34) *keyūrayugalacatuṣṭayaṁ* (35) *valayāvalim* (36) *ūrmikāvalim* (37) *kāñcīdāma* (38) *kaṭisūtraṁ* (39) *saubhāgyābharaṇaṁ* (40) *pādakaṭakaṁ* (41) *ratnanūpuraṁ* (42) *pādāṅgulīyakaṁ* (43) *ekakare pāśam* (44) *anyakare'ṅkuśam* (45) *itarakare puṇḍrekṣu* (46) *cāpam aparakare* (47) *puṣpabāṇaṁ śrīmanmāṇikyapāduke* (48) *svasamānaveṣā-bhirāvaraṇadevatābhiḥ saha mahācakrādhirohaṇam* (49) *kāmeśvarāṅka-paryaṅkopaveśanam* (50) *amṛtāsavacaṣakam* (51) *ācamanīyakaṁ* (52) *karpūra-vīṭikam* (53) *ānandollāsavilāsahāsaṁ* (54) *maṅgalārārātikaṁ* (55) *chatraṁ* (56) *cāmarayugalaṁ* (57) *darpaṇaṁ* (58) *tālavṛntaṁ* (59) *gandhaṁ* (60) *puṣpaṁ* (61) *dhūpaṁ* (62) *dīpaṁ* (63) *naivedyaṁ* (64) *kalpayāmi nama iti catuḥṣaṣṭyupacārān vidhāya*.

Paraśurāmakalpasūtra, (Gaekwad Oriental Series), p. 138-139.

finally she is borne to the accompaniment of all the *vādyas* and the *ghoṣas*. The goddess is again installed on the *siṁhāsana* and this marks the end of the programme for the morning.

The proceedings of the ceremony at night are equally elaborate, and extent over four to five hours. First, the *pūjā* of *Śrīcakra* installed in front of the goddess is performed. This *pūjā* is characterized by *bhūtaśuddhi*, *antaryajana*, *pañcāyatanapūjā*, *gurupādukāpūjā*, the *āvāhana* of the goddess (which, incidentally, marks the climax of the *cakrapūjā*), the *catuḥṣaṣṭyupacārapūjā*, and the *navāvaraṇapūjā*. The *cakra-pūjā* is followed by *Lalitāsahasranāmārcanā* and the *Lalitā-triśatī-arcanā*, which are performed by offering *sindūra* (not flowers) at the recital of each name, which is as usual appended with *namas*. *Stotras* are sung in praise of the goddess, and the *aparādhakṣamā-yācana* is performed. These are followed by an elaborate *dīpārādhana*, *Lalitāṣṭottara-arcanā*, the *mahānīrājana*, and of course by the *caturvedaghoṣa* and the singing of (Tamil) devotional songs. The whole programme is brought to a close with the distribution of the *prasāda*, which consists of *vibhūti*, *kuṅkuma*, *tīrtha*, *candana* and a portion from the *naivedya* offered to the goddess. The *abhiṣeka* in the morning and the *cakra-pūjā* in the night are repeated on each of the ten days including *Vijayadaśamī*.

A few temples in south India have priests who are not brāhmaṇas. Nevertheless, they receive formal initiation through the *dīkṣā* rites, and thus qualify to perform the *nitya* and the *naimittika* rites. Of course, the brāhmaṇa priests do not participate in any rituals in which these non-brāhmaṇa priests officiate. The non-brāhmaṇa priests do not employ any Vedic *mantras*, but confine themselves to the non-Vedic sections of the Āgamic *mantras*. It is, however, highly significant that the *mantras* used by these priests outside the pale of brāhmaṇic orthodoxy are entirely in Sanskrit. Only the *Tevārams* or the devotional songs are in Tamil, and they are sung exactly in the same manner as in the temples in which brāhmaṇa priests officiate.

A brief survey of Śaiva temples and temple worship would lead one to the following conclusions: the temples of south India are structurally similar in their essence. The scenes portrayed on the domes of all the temples, as well as those depicted on some pillars and walls, are derived from Epic and Purāṇic sources. The *pūjā* ritual, consisting of the offering of flowers, *candana*, incense, *abhiṣeka*, etc., represents but the elaboration of the *pūjā* described in the *Purāṇas*. It is based directly on the *Āgamas*, which have carried out such elaboration to the utmost degree. For their rituals, the priests in Śaiva temples employ *mantras* taken from the *Āgamas* and *Vedas*, which are assigned a high status among the religious texts. It should therefore be seen that, except for some minor differences which are bound to exist due to a lack of facilities or other circumstances, the Śaiva rituals are similarly performed from temple to temple in south India.

A note on the important Śaiva vratas

Among the various forms of worship prevalent in India today, the *vrata* alone can be shown to have maintained particularly close connections with its Purāṇic roots. *Pūjā*,[437] certainly the most popular form of worship, developed independently into the elaborate rituals of the temple worship. In a sense, therefore, *vrata* may be said to form a connecting link between earlier forms of worship like *tapas* [438] and *tīrtha* [439] and the fully developed Āgamic system [440] characterized by elaborate rites classified into *karṣaṇa*, *pratiṣṭhā*, *utsava* and *prāyaścitta*. The *vrata* cult has maintained its individuality right from the beginning. It is entirely Purāṇic in character. This is indicated, among other things, by the fact that the authoritative works on *vratas* refer to the *Purāṇas* as their source texts.[441]

437 See chapter VI.

438 See chapter VI.

439 See chapter VI.

440 See chapter VI.

441 The *Caturvargacintāmaṇi* of Hemādri is the most popular treatise on the *vratas*. This author has been assigned to the latter half of the 13th century (Keith, *History of Sanskrit Literature*, p. 448). The *Vratacuḍāmaṇi*, an equally popular but a more simplified exposition of this subject, is of much later date. This latter refers liberally to the former work.

To begin with, it may be pointed out that *vrata* is essentially a domestic ritual. It contains various elements of the *pūjā*, such as the installation of the *pratimā*, *dhyāna*, *abhiṣeka*, *vastra-samarpaṇa*, *naivedya* and *arcanā* with flowers, but for obvious reasons, all these rites are performed in a simple and unelaborated manner. The domestic *vrata* originally had no connection whatsoever with temple worship. This is clearly indicated by the fact that temples are not mentioned at all in connection with the observance of *vratas*; on the contrary, the place where the *vrata* is observed is temporarily converted into a temple. An image is installed and *pūjā* is offered to the image on a less elaborate scale, and the image is discarded at the end of the *vrata*. Over the course of time, however, *vratas* came to be associated with temples. For instance, it has now become more or less customary for the observants of *vratas* to visit temples for the *darśana* and worship of the gods enshrined in them. The god in whose honour a particular *vrata* is observed becomes the center of attraction on the days of the observance of that *vrata*. In Srilanka, the practice is prevalent to observe fasts on the days when the *brahmotsava* or other such special celebrations are being held in the local temples. Such *vratas* have never been prescribed in the *Purāṇas* or in later works dealing with the *vratas*.

The etymology of the word *vrata* [442] implies will, command, rule or conduct; it also means manner, ordinance, or custom. Secondarily, the term assumed the sense of a religious vow or practice. It ultimately came to indicate any pious observance. *Vrata* is a meritorious act of devotion or austerity. It is a solemn vow, a holy practice, and often involves fasting and continence. The texts dealing with *vrata* explain it as being a vow essentially connected with mental resolve. It is a religious rite which is characterized by physical and spiritual discipline. Like other rituals, *vratas* are also of two types, *nitya* (those which are obligatory) and *kāmya* (those which are

[442] For the word *vrata* and its implications, see Apte, *BDCRI*, 3; *QJMS*, 47,49; Kane, *JBRAS*, 29; Schmidt *Vedisch vrata usw*, Hamburg.

performed for a specific purpose). The times for the observance of the various *vratas* are fixed and are indicated in the annual almanacs.

Hemādri's *Caturvargacintāmaṇi* and Viśvanātha's *Vratacūḍāmaṇi* are the most popular and elaborate treatises on the subject of *vrata*. Both these works are replete with Purāṇic citations.[443] The *Purāṇas* are, indeed, the earliest texts to have recorded the *vrata* traditions and the rules relating to the practices of the *vratas*. One may account for the important place which the *Purāṇas* seem to assign to the *vratas* in the scheme of religious practices by the fact that the *vratas* are usually observed in honour of one of the three gods celebrated in these texts. Actually, the *vratas* only relate to two of them, Śiva and Viṣṇu. Brahmā is rarely thought of in this connection, but some ancillary divinities of Śaivism, like Gaṇeśa, Kārttikeya, and Śakti are at times worshipped through *vratas*. It may be further pointed out that the *pratimās* prescribed for worship in connection with the *vratas* conform to the descriptions of the particular gods and goddesses given in the *Purāṇas*.[444] Even the *dhyāna-mantras* present the gods in a characteristically Purāṇic form. To a certain extent, this would account for the fact that, barring certain peculiarities arising from local traditions (*deśācāras*), the practices of the *vratas* were more or less essentially similar.

The holy places scattered throughout Bhāratavarṣa have been proclaimed to be the fittest places in which *vratas* may be observed. Various mountains, sacred rivers, oceans and forests are mentioned in this connection. Special and frequent mention is, however, made of Gayā, Gaṅgā, Kāśī (Benares), Kurukṣetra, Naimiśāraṇya, Prayāga, Jambukeśvara, Kedāra, Puṣkara, Someśvara, and Vindhya. Among such places are also included the dwelling places usually assigned to

---

[443] *Cf. Srīmadvyāsamaharṣir adbhutatarāṇy ādau purāṇāntare*
Yāny āha vratarūpakāṇi bhagavatpūjādikarmāṇy api |
Tāny ādāya videśaśiṣṭacaritāny ekatra saṁyojyate
Cakre tadvratarājam ity abhinavaṁ śrīviśvanāthaḥ kaviḥ ||
Vratacūḍāmaṇi, p. 1.

[444] *Matsya P.*, 257 ff; *Bhaviṣya P.*, II.12.

Kārttikeya. All this would clearly show how the *tīrtha* cult and the *vrata* cult are mutually related.

The most significant feature of the *vrata* cult is that it can be freely practiced by all castes.[445] In this context it may also be pointed out that one of the reasons for the wide prevalence of the cult of *vratas* is that even women are authorized to practice it.[446] A few *vratas* are, indeed, meant exclusively for women.[447] It is, however, interesting to note that women are required to obtain the permission of their husbands before they undertake any *vrata*.[448] Some special requirements expected of the observants of the *vratas* are enumerated. First and foremost among these is adherence to the code of conduct prescribed for the caste to which he belongs. Purity of mind, absence of greed, truthfulness, and a kind disposition towards one's fellow beings are some of the other requisites. Also mentioned are faith, aversion to sin, and hatred for pomp and pride. But more than anything else, it is unflagging devotion that is proclaimed to be indispensable

---

[445] The *Vratacūḍamaṇi* reproduces the following extract from the *Devī-purāṇa*:
Brāhmaṇāḥ kṣatriyāḥ vaiśyāḥ śūdrāścaiva dvijottama |
Arcayanti mahādevaṁ yajñadānasamādhibhiḥ ||
Vratopavāsaniyamaiḥ homasvādhyāyatarpaṇaiḥ | (p. 6).

The cult of *vratas* is, according to some authorities, extended even to the *mlecchas*.

[446] The section entitled "Strīṇāṁ vratādhikāraḥ" (p. 6) in the *Vratacūḍāmaṇi*, deals with this topic. For a contrary view, Cf. *Manusmṛti*, V.155:
Nāsti strīṇāṁ pṛthagyajño na vrataṁ nāpy upoṣaṇam |
Bhartuḥ śuśrūṣayāvaitad lokān iṣṭān vrajanti tāḥ ||

"For women there is no worship apart of their husband, nor vow, nor even fast. They go to the desired upper worlds only by obedience to their husband."

[447] See the *vratas* described on subsequent pages as follows:
Maṅgalagaurī-vrata, p. 447.
Bhakteśvara-vrata p. 451.

[448] The *Vratacūḍāmaṇi* observes as follows (p. 7):
Kāmaṁbhartur anujñātā vratādiṣvadhikāriṇīti. Śaṅkho pi 'kāmaṁ bharturanujñāya vratopavāsaniyamāḥ strīdharmāḥ iti.

Hemādri is quoted here in the course of the discussion:

Nārī khalv ananujñātā bhartrā pitrā sutena vā viphalaṁ tad bhavet tasyā yat karoty aurdhvadaihikam
Iti mārkaṇḍeyokteḥ pitrādyājñayā tasyā adhikāraḥ iti Hemādrih.

for the practice of *vratas*. Some general rules which relate to the conduct of the practitioner during the observance of any *vrata* may also be mentioned here. He is to practise *kṣamā*, *satya*, *dāna*, *śauca*, *indriyanigraha*, and *steyavarjana*. Among the religious acts he is to perform are *devapūjā*, *agnihavana*, *japa* and *homa*, although the last is only prescribed by a few authorities.[449] Such acts of personal discipline as lying on a bare floor and charitable acts like distribution of *dānas* at the end of the *vrata* or honouring brāhmaṇas with *dakṣiṇā* are also recommended to the *vratin*.[450]

Saṁkalpa marks the beginning of a *vrata*. This consists of a lengthy formulaic proclamation of the person's intention to observe the *vrata* in question. He is to take bath, abstain from food and generally renounce all comforts which are likely to be pleasurable to the *indriyas*. One authority seems to prescribe abstinence only from the morning meal. According to other teachers, however, a fast is to be observed on *vrata*-days. The rule regarding abstinence from the morning meal applies to the day previous to the one of complete abstinence; on that day, a single meal is the rule.[451]

A *vrata*, once undertaken, is not to be abandoned under any circumstances. One is reborn a *caṇḍāla* if he violates this rule. As a matter of fact, he is to be treated as a *caṇḍāla* henceforth in this very life. Exception is, however, made in the case of individuals who are

---

449 *Kṣamā satyaṁ dayā dānaṁ śucam indriyanigrahaḥ |*
Devapūjāgniharaṇaṁ santoṣo'steyam eva ca ||
Sarvavrateṣv ayaṁ dharmaḥ sāmānyo daśadhā smṛtaḥ |
Agni P., 175. 10-11.

450 Cf. *Snātvā vratavatā sarvavrateṣu vratamūrtayaḥ |*
Pujyāḥ svarṇamayādyāḥ śaktyā vai bhūmiśāyinā ||
Vratacūḍāmaṇi, p. 9.

451 *Saṁkalpaṁ ca yathā kuryāt snānadānavratādike iti anantarakṛtyamāha madanaratne Devalaḥ:*
Abhuktvā prātarāhāraṁ snātvācamya samāhitaḥ |
Sūryāya devatābhyaśca nivedya vratam ācaret || iti
... pūrvadine prātarāhāram abhuktvā arthād ekabhaktaṁ kṛtvā snātvācamya vratādikaṁ kuryāt.
Vratacūḍāmaṇi, p. 8.

prevented from continuing by illness. *Vratas* may also be suspended on instructions from the *guru*.[452] Further, there is provision for the interrupted *vratas* being atoned for through suitable expiation rites. For instance, the interruption caused by hunger or greed could be made good by a fast of three days' duration. A complete shaving of the head is sometimes prescribed as an expiatory punishment.[453]

As a matter of fact, *upavāsa* is closely connected with *vrata*. This term has lost its etymological significance. It has now come to mean a complete fast. *Upavāsa* has been defined as abstinence from all comforts, pleasures, and enjoyments.[454] *Japa*, *yajña*, *dhyāna* and *kathāśravaṇa* (possibly of stories relevant to the *vrata* observed) are the religious acts expected of one who observes *upavāsa*. Similarly, his conduct is expected to be characterized by compassion for all beings, forbearance, purity and absence of greed.

The following prohibitions are to be heeded on *vrata* days. The cleaning of teeth is to be avoided. Some authorities interpret this injunction as only the prohibition of cleaning the teeth with tree twigs. In one context it is stated that, whenever cleaning of the teeth is not possible, one should rinse his mouth twelve times, with one mouthful of water each time.[455] Repeated drinking of water is precluded. Chewing of betel, sleeping during the daytime and sexual intercourse are strictly forbidden. The *Purāṇas* also refer to these and various other prohibitions.[456] It is, however, to be noted that under special

---

[452] Cf. *Tathā ca Hemādrau Skānde*
Sarvabhūtabhayaṁ vyādhiḥ pramādo guruśāsanam |
Avrataghnāni paṭhyante sakṛd etāni śāstrataḥ iti ||
Vratacūḍāmaṇi, p. 9.

[453] *Krodhāt pramādāllobhād vā vratabhaṅgo bhaved yadi* |
Dinatrayaṁ na bhuñjīta muṇḍanaṁ śiraso'tha vā iti ||
Ibid., p. 10.

[454] *Upāvṛttasya pāpebhyo yastu vāso guṇaiḥ saha* |
Upavāsaḥ sa vijñeyaḥ sarvabhogavivarjitaḥ ||
Agni P., 75.5-6.

[455] *Vratacūḍāmaṇi*, p. 11.

[456] *Kāṁsyaṁ māṁsaṁ masūraṁ ca caṇakaṁ koradūṣakam* |
Śākaṁ madhu parānnaṁ ca tyajed upavasan striyam ||

circumstances some relaxation of these strict rules is allowed. In this connection, the verdict of the *guru* and the pronouncement of brāhmaṇas are to be regarded as the guiding principles. At the same time, as indicated above, various expiation rites can be prescribed to counteract any deficiencies in the observance of the *vratas*. These might consist of *japa*, flower offerings, or of oblations to Agni. In a few cases, such measures as additional fasts of a severe type are prescribed.[457]

As *naimittika* rites, *vratas* are always preceded by the *nitya* rites. These latter are the rites which the participant is obliged to perform daily.

In exceptional cases, one is permitted to delegate another person to observe *vratas* on one's behalf. A pregnant woman, a woman who has just delivered a child, a woman with an illness and a woman in menarche are mentioned in this connection.[458] Though such persons are authorized to depute others to perform a part of their *vratas*, they are still expected to observe the normal rules of spiritual discipline. This kind of delegations is usually for the offering of *pūjā* and *homa*. No deputy is ever permitted for the *vratas* undertaken for the fulfillment of specific desires (*kāmyavratas*).[459]

Havis is prepared and offered on *vrata*-days. Though *havis* originally denoted an offering to be made to the fire for some specific god, that term has over time acquired a wider sense, and now denotes also the cooked offerings made to god as *naivedya*. Various restrictions have been laid down with regard to the preparation of *havis* to be

---

Puṣpālaṅkāravastrāṇi dhūpagandhānulepanam |
Upavāse na śasyanti dantadhāvanabhañjanam ||
… … …
Asakṛjjalapānācca tāmbūlasya ca bhakṣaṇāt |
Upavāsaḥ praduṣyeta dive svapnāc ca maithunāt ||
Agni P., 157.6-9.

Also cf.
Varjayet pāraṇe māṁsaṁ vratāhe 'pyauṣadhaṁ sadā |
Viṣṇudharma P., 11.

[457] *Vratacūḍāmaṇi*, p. 12. [458] *Ibid.*, p. 13. [459] *Ibid.*, p. 14.

offered at *vratas*. The cereals, condiments, and vegetables to be used for the cooking of the *havis* are all enumerated. Simplicity and absence of richness of any kind are to be the characteristics of this food. The observant is allowed to eat portions of this *havis* on *vrata*-days.

The performance of a *vrata* begins with the appointment of a *ṛtvik* who officiates at the various rites for the performer or assists the performer in connection with the *pūjā*.[460] Equipped with the requisites already described and purified by the observance of the various disciplinary restrictions, particularly of *upavāsa*, the performer engages himself in the worship of the deity in whose honour the *vrata* is being undertaken. In this context, *pratimās* made of gold and decked with gems are often mentioned. At the end of the *vrata*, these are to be handed over to a brāhmaṇa along with some *dakṣiṇā*. The worship of the *pratimā* forms the most important event in the *vrata*. Various articles are prescribed for use over the course of the *pūjā*. They include the five gems, gold, silver and diamonds. Whenever precious gems are not available, gold may be used as a substitute. For this *pūjā*, one can use such items as the sprouts of five trees, namely *aśvattha*, *udumbara*, *plakṣa*, *cūta* and *nyagrodha*, *pañcagavya*, consisting of cow urine, cow dung, milk, curd, and ghee, *pañcāmṛta*, consisting of *dadhi*, *madhu*, *ghṛta*, *śarkarā* and *payas*, the six *rasas*, namely, *madhura*, *amla*, *lavaṇa*, *kaṣāya*, *tikta* and *kaṭuka*, and *candana*, consisting of a mixture of *kastūrī*, *keśara* and *karpūra*. The *pratimā* is set on a *kumbha* (*kalaśa*) which is filled with water and decked with the tender sprouts of the trees already mentioned, particularly the *cūtapallavas*. The various *upacāras* are offered to the *pratimā* in which the immediate presence of the deity is definitely assumed. *Maṇḍalas* are sometimes substituted for the *pratimās*.[461] The *pūjā* begins with purificatory rites. Then follows the *prāṇapratiṣṭhā*,[462] a rite which infuses the image with life. The various acts and items mentioned below may be said to constitute the entire procedure of the *pūjā*:

---

460 *Vratacūḍāmaṇi*, p. 22. 461 *Ibid.*, pp. 22-29. 462 *Ibid.*, p. 31.

1. *Āvāhana*	Invocation to the deity to be present in the image.
2. *Sthāpana*	The deity is established in the image.
3. *Āsana*	A seat is offered.
4. *Pādya*	Water is provided for washing the feet.
5. *Arghya*	Water with costly ingredients mixed into it is offered.
6. *Madhuparka*	A mixture of ghee, honey and milk is offered.
7. *Snapana*	Bathing with various prescribed articles.
8. *Vastra*	Clothes are offered for after the bath.
9. *Yajñopavīta*	The sacred thread is offered.
10. *Sindūra*	Red powder for the *tilaka* mark on the forehead.
11. *Vilepana*	Unguents for the body.
12. *Akṣata*	Unbroken rice (coloured with saffron).
13. *Puṣpa*	Flowers, fragrant and of variegated colours.
14. *Aṅgapūjā*	The offerings (of flowers etc) to the limbs of the god or goddess. This is done to the accompaniment of the recital of the names of the presiding deity of each limb.
15. *Dhūpa*	Incense
16. *Dīpa*	Waving of lamps.
17. *Naivedya*	Offerings of cooked food.
18. *Pānīya*	Water for drinking.
19. *Uttarāpośana*	The sipping of water at the close of a meal.
20. *Mukhaprakṣālana*	The washing of the mouth after a meal.
21. *Karodvartana*	Cleaning of the hand.
22. *Phala*	Fruits
23. *Tāmbūla*	Betel and other such articles.
24. *Bhūṣaṇa*	Ornaments and jewels.
25. *Nīrājana*	The waving of the *nīrājana*, usually consisting of lit camphor.
26. *Pradakṣiṇa*	Circumambulating the image clockwise.

27. *Mantrapuṣpa*	Flowers offered to the accompaniment of (*Veda*) *mantra.*
28. *Dakṣiṇādāna*	The distribution of *dakṣiṇā.*
29. *Pratimādāna*	Handing over the *pratimā* soon after the *visarjana.*

The *Purāṇas*, which have devoted a considerable portion to a detailed description of the *vratas*, have in many cases recounted the circumstances leading to the coming into vogue of these *vratas*. In this, they follow the tradition of the *Brāhmaṇa* texts, which have provided aetiological legends to explain the genesis of the various sacrifices or sacrificial rites. A greater number of the *vratas* mentioned in the *Purāṇas* are connected with Viṣṇu. Of course, Śiva also has not a few *vratas* dedicated to him. The *vratas* connected with Śakti, Gaṇeśa, and Kārttikeya, are, however, much less in number.

The annual Hindu almanacs mention the specific dates on which different *vratas* are to be observed.[463] The *vratas* specifically relating to Gaṇeśa are (as mentioned above) comparatively few, although each *vrata*, like every other domestic rite, must begin with the worship of Gaṇeśa. The *Agni Purāṇa* mentions the *Vināyaka-vrata*,[464] while the *Bhaviṣya Purāṇa* refers to the *caturthī-vrata*. The *Gaṇeśa Purāṇa* also mentions the *caturthī-vrata* and the *saṅkaṣṭacaturthī-vrata*. The only *vrata* which is specifically associated with Kārttikeya is *Skanda-saṣṭhī*. To Umā is assigned the *Navarātri*, which consists of the *Mahā-navamī*. Many *vratas* are observed in honour of Śiva; of these, the *Mahāśivarātrī-vrata* is the most important. The *pradoṣa-vrata*, connected with Śiva, is of fortnightly occurrence. Other *vratas* connected with Śiva may be mentioned the *somavāra-vrata*, the *caturdaśī-vrata* and the *pāśupata-vrata*. The *vratas* in which worship is simultaneously offered to Śiva and Umā are the *Umāmaheśvara-vrata* and the *Kedāreśvara-vrata*.

---

463 Even from among the *vratas* mentioned in the almanac, only a few are now actually prevalent. Others are gradually passing out of vogue.

464 The places where the various *vratas* are mentioned in the *Purāṇas* are cited when each *vrata* is taken up for a detailed description later.

Below are described some of the *vratas* relating to Śiva and his ancillary divinities which are most commonly observed in India and Srilanka. The normal rules regarding the observance of a *vrata* that have already been mentioned above are naturally also applicable to the *vratas* described below. The *pūjās* performed in connection with the different *vratas* are also characterized by more or less similar details. Only the *mantras* vary with various divinities.[465] Thus, for instance, whenever the *upacāras* are offered, the appellations used change from deity to deity. Apart from this, there are a few other special characteristics which distinguish one *vrata* from another. Only such differences are indicated below.

Vināyakacaturthī-vrata [466]

This *vrata* is to be observed on the *caturthī*, the fourth day of the bright half of the month of *Śrāvaṇa*. The *caturthī* of the bright half of the month of *Kārttika* is also prescribed by some authorities as the day on which the *caturthī-vrata* is to be observed. A golden *pratimā*

---

[465] The *Vratacūḍāmaṇi* (p. 38) gives the *mantras* relating to the gods propitiated in the various *vratas*. Some of the *mantras* are Vedic, while others are non-Vedic. The *āvāhana* is to be performed with the first verse of the *Puruṣasūkta*. (*Sahasra-śīrṣāpuruṣaḥ sahasrākṣaḥ sahasrapāt sa bhūmiṁ viśvato vṛtvā atyatiṣṭhad daśāṅgulam*) The following non-Vedic *mantra* is also prescribed in this connection:

Āgacchāgaccha deveśa tejorāśe jagatpate
Kriyamāṇāṁ mayā pūjāṁ gṛhāṇa surasattama

Each of the 29 rites in the *pūjā* mentioned above has a specific *mantra* prescribed for it. It is to be noted that in these *mantras* as well as in the *mantras* given in the *Vratacūḍamaṇi* (p. 38), the specific characteristics of the particular god concerned are not necessarily mentioned. When, however, each *vrata* is described in detail, separate *mantras* are given which refer to the special characteristics of the god in whose honour that *vrata* is to be observed. For instance, in the *Siddhivināyaka-vrata* the following *āvāhana-mantra* is prescribed, and it reveals the features of Gaṇeśa, who is propitiated:

Ekadantaṁ śūrpakarṇaṁ gajavaktraṁ caturbhujam |
Pāśāṅkuśadharaṁ devaṁ dhyāyet siddhivināyakam ||

"One should meditate on Siddhivināyaka, who has one tusk only, ears like winnowing baskets, the head of an elephant, four arms, holding noose and elephant goad."

[466] *Agni P.*, 178 ff. *Skanda P.*, IV.2.80 mentions the *vrata* called *Gaurīvināyaka-vrata*.

of Gaṇeśa is made and provided with a pedestal which is also made of gold. A *kalaśa* is installed, and on it is set the *pratimā* of Gaṇeśa. The *pratimā* is sanctified by purificatory rites. The other rites such as *sthāpana*, *āvāhana* etc., are performed in their usual order. Red flowers, leaves, (*patrāṇi*), *bilva* and *dūrvā* are the articles prescribed in connection with this *vrata*. The *naivedya* should mainly consist of *modaka* as well as *jambūphala*. The *pūjā* is concluded with the following verses, which, incidentally, indicates the purpose for which the *vrata* is observed:

Vināyaka gaṇeśāna sarvadevanamaskṛta |
Pārvatīpriya vighneśa mama vighnaṁ vināśaya ||[467]

"O Vināyaka, Lord of Gaṇas, hailed by all the gods, dear to Pārvatī, Lord of obstacles, discard obstacles from me."

Siddhivināyaka-vrata [468]

This *vrata* is observed in the month of *Bhādrapada*. The *tithi* is expected to extend at least up to midday. The *vrata*, which generally conforms to the rules already mentioned, has a few special characteristics of its own. The image obtained for installation is made of clay. *Dūrvā* is specially mentioned as being offered along with other flowers and leaves. There is a legendary account which explains the greatness (*māhātmya*) of this *vrata*. Kṛṣṇa is said to have instructed the Pāṇḍavas about this *vrata*; they observed it and as the result always succeeded in their warlike undertakings. The sight of the moon is strictly forbidden on the day of this *vrata*.[469] A mere glance at the moon not only rids one of all the merits of the *vrata*, the act actually brings him woe, misery and complete ruin.[470]

---

[467] *Vratacūḍamaṇi*, p. 66. [468] *Ibid.*, p. 71.

[469] The *Purāṇas* narrate a legend to account for this prohibition. Cf. *Gaṇeśa P.*, I.61.

[470] *Kanyāditye caturthyāṁ ca śukle candrasya darśanam* |
Mithyābhiduṣaṇaṁ kuryāt tasmāt paśyenna taṁ tadā ||
Vratacūḍāmaṇi, p. 73.

"When the sun is in the Virgo, on the fourth day in the bright fortnight, looking at the moon will cause opposite fruit and ruin. Therefore one should not see the moon at that time."

The *Syamantakopākhyāna* recounts in detail the events leading to the peculiar attitude shown to the moon on this *vrata*-day. The story concerns the gem called *syamantaka*. After severe *tapas*, Satrājita is said to have secured this jewel from the Sun god, who had himself been wearing it. The gem was granted to him on the condition that he maintains absolute purity, and the slightest sign of impurity would result in the loss of the gem. Over the course of time, however, the gem fell into the hands of king Jāmbavān. Jāmbavān later offered it, along with his daughter Jāmbavatī, to Kṛṣṇa. Kṛṣṇa, who now became the possessor of the gem, had a quarrel with his brother Balarāma about it. The latter left his home in anger, and went on a pilgrimage. At Vārāṇasī, he met Nārada, who told him that all this trouble had arisen because, despite the prescribed convention, he had glanced at the crescent moon on a *caturthī* day. Nārada related to Balarāma how Candra had once mocked at Gaṇeśa for his queer appearance. The god cursed the moon to become unfit to be seen. Candra later realized his folly and repented for his mistake by observing the *Caturthī-vrata*. The curse was, therefore modified, and Gaṇeśa decreed that the moon ought not be seen only on the *caturthī*-day.[471]

Saṅkaṣṭagaṇapati-vrata

In its details, this *vrata* agrees for the most part with the *vratas* described earlier. The *pratimā* for this *vrata* is made of gold. On the completion of the *vrata*, the *pratimā* is given over to a brāhmaṇa along with the relevant *dakṣiṇā*.[472]

---

[471] *Bhaviṣya P.*, III.32 and 33; *Varāha P.*, 23.19-38.

[472] The following verses from the *Vratacūḍāmaṇi* (pp. 63-64) proclaim at length the results which follow the *saṅkaṣṭa-vrata*:

Kṛtaṁ yudhiṣṭhireṇaitad rājyakāmena vai dvija |
Tena śatruṁ nihatyājau svarājyaṁ prāptavān svayam ||
Tasmāt sarvaprayatnena vrataṁ kāryaṁ vicakṣaṇaiḥ |
Yena dharmārthakāmāś ca mokṣaś cāpi bhavet kila ||
Yaḥ karoti vrataṁ viprah sarvakāmārthasiddhidam |
Sa vāñchitaphalaṁ prāpya paścād gaṇapatiṁ vrajet ||
Yadā yadā varaṁ vipraḥ naraḥ prāpnoti saṅkaṭam |
Tadā tadā prakartavyaṁ vrataṁ saṅkaṣṭanāśanam ||

Skandaṣaṣṭī-vrata

This *vrata* is popular in south India and Srilanka. However, only incidental references have been made to it in the *Purāṇas* and the texts dealing with the *vratas*.[473] The *ṣaṣṭhī-vrata* begins the day after *Dīpāvalī* and continues for six days. The last day of this *vrata* is celebrated in the temples of Kārttikeya in Srilanka and south India with the *Sūrasaṁhāra* festival.[474]

Sarasvatī-pūjā

Sarasvatī-pūjā is one of the *vratas* observed in honour of Śakti. It occurs on the seventh day of the bright half of the month of *Āśvina*. It is laid down that the *saptamī-tithi* should pervade the early morning hours of the day on which the *vrata* is to be observed. The details of worship are the same as those already described. No special rites relating to this *vrata* have been given in the *Vratacūḍāmaṇi*.

Durgāṣṭamī-vrata

The texts dealing with *vratas* mention two such *aṣṭamīs*. One is celebrated as the birthday of Umā, and falls on the eighth of the month of *Caitra*. The rites in this *vrata* are for the most part the same as those mentioned earlier. The other *aṣṭamī* occurs on the eighth of the bright half of the month of *Āśvina*. This is also known as *Mahāṣṭamī*. No details are given of this *vrata* in the *Vratacūḍāmaṇi*.

... ...
Vidyārthī labhate vidyāṁ dhanārthī dhanam āpnuyāt |
Putrārthī putram āpnoti rogī rogāt pramucyate ||

473 The *Agni Purāṇa* (181) makes a casual reference to this *vrata*. The *Bhaviṣya Purāṇa*, (I.45 and 46) describes in a few verses the details of this *vrata*. The *Varāha Purāṇa* (25.49-51) refers to the *Ṣaṣṭhī* as the day on which Skanda was installed the commander of the army of the gods. The method of observing the *vrata* and the consequent results are briefly mentioned in a couple of verses:
Svayaṁ Skando mahādevaḥ sarvapāpapraṇāśanaḥ |
Tasya ṣaṣthīṁ tithiṁ prādād abhiṣeke pitāmahaḥ ||
Asyām phalāśane yastu pūjayed yatamānasaḥ |
Aputro labhate putram adhano'pi dhanaṁ labhet ||
Varāha P., 25.49-50.

474 See chapter VI, p. 424.

Maṅgalagaurī-vrata

This *vrata* is observed on all Tuesdays in the month of *Śrāvaṇa*. The peculiarity of the *vrata* lies in its being confined only to women. In connection with this *vrata*, *dīpa* is substituted for the *pratimā*. Other *pūjā* details are the same as described above. Distributions of sweets at the end of the *vrata* is also prescribed. Brāhmaṇas, young girls, and the mother of the *vrata* performer are declared to be the most suitable persons to receive these gifts. Worship with sixteen *dīpas* and the feeding of sixteen girls are also prescribed. This *vrata* is performed with a view to obtaining prosperity. As this is possible for women only so long as their husbands live, all this ultimately amounts to asking for longevity for their husbands.

Amuktābharaṇa-vrata [475]

This is performed on the *saptamī* of the bright half of the month of *Bhādrapada*. The *vrata* is observed in honour of Śiva. The details of the *pūjā* performed over the course of the *vrata* are the same as mentioned earlier. The speciality of this *vrata* lies in the tying of a thread around the wrist of the performer.

The following legend is narrated relating to the *vrata*.[476] Vasudeva and Devakī lost every child born to them due to the hostility of Kaṁsa, the brother of Devakī. Once they met the sage Romasa, who casually told about this *vrata*. As the result of the observance of this *vrata* long before, Bhuṣaṇā had won longevity for her children. The worship of Śiva and wearing that thread on this *vrata* day would bring the desirable outcome. The thread is to be made of silver or cotton. Clothes are to be distributed to brāhmaṇas. The performer has to keep awake the whole night, and throughout must engage himself in the worship of Śiva. *Homa* is prescribed, and oblations to Śiva are offered on the fire. The oblations are to consist of *tila*, *akṣata* and ghee. Devakī and Vasudeva are said to have observed the *vrata*, and this later resulted in the birth of Kṛṣṇa. Kṛṣṇa lived a long life, and one of his great exploits was to have chastised Kaṁsa, who was a terror to everyone.

---

[475] *Vratacūḍāmaṇi*, p. 107.

[476] *Ibid.*, 109 ff.

Pakṣapradoṣa-vrata [477]

This *vrata* is of a fortnightly occurrence. The following verse proclaims the merits which this *vrata* brings to the performer:

Pakṣe vaidikasya pradoṣe śivapūjanam |
Agnihotraṁ yathā nityaṁ pāpaghnaṁ mokṣadāyakam || [478]

"The worship of Śiva at sunset every fortnight, always destroys sins and give liberation, like the *agnihotra* sacrifice."

Whoever undertakes to observe this *vrata* in honour of Śiva should abstain from food until the end of the day. He should take a bath two *ghaṭikās* before sunset. He should wear a white garment. *Sandhyā* and *japa* are to be performed as usual. This is to be followed by *Śiva-pūjā* in the manner laid down in the *Āgamas*. Ganeśa should be installed on the right and Skanda on the left of Śiva. Śakti also is to be worshipped. *Nyāsa* [479] and *sohaṁbhāvanā* [480] are specifically mentioned. At the end of the *pūjā*, there is to be *nṛtta*, although this is rarely practised. The importance of this *vrata* has been summarised in the following verse:

Brahmahatyā śataṁ vāpi śivapūjā vināśayet |
Mayā kathitaṁ etat te pradoṣaśivapūjanam ||

"The worship of Śiva will destroy even one hundred murders of brahmins. This has been told by me as the sunset worship of Śiva."

The following verses relate in detail the results which follow this *vrata*:

Etanmahāvrataṁ puṇyaṁ pradoṣe śaṅkarārcanam |
Dharmārthakāmamokṣāṇāṁ yadetat sādhanaṁ param ||
Jñānārtham ṛṣayaḥ prāñcaḥ dhanārthaṁ ca dhanārthinaḥ |

---

477 *Skanda P.*, III.3, chapters 6 and 7. *Somapradoṣa* is described in chapter 8.

478 *Vratacūḍāmaṇi*, p. 211.

479 For *nyāsa* rites see earlier p. 388.

480 *Sohaṁbhāvanā* is the ritual assumption on the part of the performer of a complete identity of himself with the god or goddess in whose honour the *pūjā* is performed. When Śiva is the object of such worship this process is termed *Śivohambhāvanā*.

Jayādhikārasiddhyartham indropendrapurogamāḥ |
Vidyārthino'pi vidyārthaṁ sutārthaṁ putrakāṅkṣiṇaḥ ||
Ārogyārthaṁ ca rogārtāḥ cakruḥ etadvratottamam |
Brāhmaṇānām idaṁ mukhyaṁ viseṣāt kalitārakam || [481]

"This great, meritorious vow, worship of Śaṅkara at sunset is the supreme means to realise *dharma*, *artha*, *kāma* and *mokṣa*. The ancient sages have performed it for knowledge, those who desire fortune for fortune, Indra, Viṣṇu and other gods to achieve their function of victory, those desiring knowledge for knowledge, those desiring a son for a son, those afflicted by disease for health. For Brahmins this excellent vow is the main, especially to cross the Kali age."

Śanitrayodaśī-vrata

The *Śanitrayodaśī-vrata* [482] is said to be observed when *trayodaśī* and the *Śanivāra* are on the same day. It is also called *Śanipradoṣa*. Special significance is attached to the *Śanipradoṣa vrata* occurring in *Śrāvaṇa* and *Kārttika*. In this *vrata*, Śiva is worshipped in the *liṅga* form. Midday worship is prescribed. Later in the evening commences the *pūjā* of the *liṅga*. *Tila* and *āmalaka* are specially mentioned for use in this *vrata*. Among the *liṅgas* recommended for worship are mentioned the self-produced *liṅga* (*svayaṁbhū*) and *liṅgas* installed in forests, outside the village, on mountaintops or in the penance groves. The *Śivaliṅgas* installed in Kāśī are, of course, given the greatest importance in this connection. Thirty-two *dīpamālās* and a thousand lights are to be provided. The one hundred names of Rudra are also to be recited.

The following story is told about this *vrata*:[483] King Citraka of the Vidyādharas once visited Kailāsa. There he derided Śiva, who was seated amidst his family. Umā was greatly annoyed by the discourteous remarks made by the king. She therefore cursed him that he would be hurled into the world of the mortals. He was, accordingly, born as the demon Vṛtra. Indra is said to have performed

---

481 *Vratacūdāmaṇi*, p. 221.   482 *Ibid.*, p. 208.   483 *Ibid.*, p. 202.

Śanipradoṣa-vrata, and as the result of it to have acquired enough strength to easily vanquish this demon.

Somavāra-vrata [484]

The *somavāra-vrata* is observed in honour of Śiva. The following *somavāravrata-kathā* is narrated in the *Vratacūḍāmaṇi*.[485] Once there lived in Āryāvarta a king named Citravarman. He had a son and a daughter. The soothsayers predicted that the daughter had a bright future before her. One of them, however, boldly declared that she would become a widow in her fourteenth year. The wife of the sage Yājñavalkya taught her the details of the *Somavāra-vrata*. Thereupon she began to perform that *vrata* regularly. Over the course of time, Citravarman gave his daughter in marriage to Indrasena. Once, while Indrasena was going out on a sea journey, the ship in which he was sailing was upset and he was drowned. The princess thus became a widow, but she still kept her observance of the *vrata*. This had the desired effect: she regained her husband. Thereafter, both of them lived long and ruled their country for many years.

Amāsomavāra-vrata [486]

The *Amā-somavāra-vrata* is to be observed on a Monday which coincides with the new moon day. In this *vrata*, *pūjā* is offered to the *aśvattha* tree, although Śiva and Viṣṇu receive greater attention. The various *upacāras* are offered to both these gods. The purpose of this *vrata* is said to be ridding oneself of sins and ensuring the continuity of one's family. This *vrata* is also said to prevent widowhood in this and subsequent births.

A story which glorified the *Amāsomavāra-vrata* was narrated by Bhīṣma to Yudhiṣṭhira.[487] There once lived a king by name Ratnasena. In his kingdom there lived a brāhmaṇa called Devasvāmin, who had Dharmavatī for his wife. The couple was blessed with seven

---

[484] *Skanda P.*, VI. 1.24.

[485] *Vratacūḍāmaṇi*, p. 349.

[486] *Ibid.*, p. 311.

[487] *Ibid.*, p. 314.

boys and one daughter. One day, when the seven brothers offered alms to a brāhmaṇa, they were suitably blessed by him and thus became endowed with *saubhāgya* (fortune). The daughter, however, was not blessed at that time, and was accordingly doomed to *vaidhavya*. Nevertheless, it was made known that *soma* brought from Saiṁhala would help her out of her misfortune. The brothers, therefore, crossed the ocean and brought back the *soma* with the help of an eagle that lived in a huge tree standing on the shore of the sea. This *vrata* was practised by the girl and her *vaidhavya* was removed.

Bhakteśvara-vrata [488]

This *vrata* is to be observed on full moon days. It is especially recommended for barren women. There is the normal *vrata-pūjā*, wherein the offering of *arghya* is specially emphasized. As for the genesis of the *vrata*, the *Vratacūḍāmaṇi* narrates the following story:[489]

Candra Pāṇḍya, the ruler of Madura, and his queen Kumudvatī, were for a long time without any issue. They therefore retired into the wilderness and performed *tapas*. Thereupon Śiva manifested himself before them and offered them a strange boon: they would have either a long-lived but widowed daughter, or a short-lived but wise and highly endowed son. The king, of course, chose the latter alternative. In due course, the king married his son to the daughter of king Mitrasahasra and the queen Kalāvatī. The daughter observed the *Bhakteśvara-vrata*. As the result of this, when the destined hour of the death of her husband approached, the god of death was overpowered and the prince of the Pāṇḍya kingdom and his bride lived happily for a long life.

Kedāreśvara-vrata [490]

This *vrata* is to be observed on the new moon day of the month of *Āśvina*. In connection with the *vrata-pūjā*, the tying of *sūtra* (*dorabandhana*) and the distribution of sweets are mentioned.

---

[488] *Vratacūḍāmaṇi*, p. 293. [489] *Ibid.*, p. 296. [490] *Ibid.*, p. 302.

The following story [491] is told to glorify this *vrata*. Once, at *Kailāsa*, Śiva was seated among his attendants, and much dancing was going on. The sage Bhṛṅgin also danced in great ecstacy, but his dance was quite irregular and unrythmic. This caused an outburst of laughter. Śiva, however, was much pleased with Bhṛṅgin and granted him special favours. Elated by this incident, the sage resolved to worship Śiva exclusively. Accordingly, he purposefully kept Umā out when he made his circumambulation of Śiva. Umā, who was distressed by what was happening, left Kailāsa and went to the hermitage of Gautama. There the sage imparted to her the knowledge of the *Kedāra-vrata*. Thereupon, Umā undertook to observe the *vrata*, and this had the desired effect; soon after, Śiva appeared before the goddess and offered her half of his body. This was obviously intended to render the circumambulation of Śiva alone impossible. Puṇyavatī, the wife of Citrāṅga, is also said to have observed this *vrata* and to have thereby had all her desires fulfilled.

Umāmaheśvara-vrata [492]

The *Umāmaheśvara-vrata* is said to be observed on the *caturdaśī* of the bright half of the month of *Bhādrapada*. The *pūjā* is performed as usual. A peculiarity of the *vrata* is that it has to commence not on the day of the *vrata* itself but on the day previous to it.[493] The performer takes a bath in the morning of that day and then goes through the rite of *anujñā* whereby permission of the god is sought to observe the *vrata*. The following verse is recited in this connection with that rite:

Śvaḥ kariṣye vrataṁ yatnād umāmaheśvarābhidham |
Ājñāṁ dehi mahādeva soma somārdhaśekhara || [494]

"To-morrow, I shall perform with effort the vow called Umāmaheśvara. Give me the permission, o Mahādeva, accompanied by Umā, you whose diadem is the halfmoon."

---

[491] *Vratacūḍāmaṇi*, p. 305.

[492] *Matsya P.*, 55; *Skanda P.*, III.3.18; *Padma P.*, I.25.

[493] *Vratacūḍāmaṇi*, p. 286. [494] *Ibid.*, p. 286.

Arcanā of the god is to be performed at midday. At night, the observant can sleep only in the direct presence of the god. On the following morning the *vrata-pūjā* commences immediately after the performance of the daily rites. The worship of Śiva in this *vrata* is characterized by elaborate *dhyānas*. There are the usual *āvāhana*, *pādya*, and *arghya*, and the normal *upacāras* are performed. This is followed by the tying of a thread (*doraka*) around the wrist of the performer. Complete fasting is prescribed for the day.[495] The performer keeps awake through the whole night listening to religious stories and performing *pūjā* at the end of each *yāma* of the night. *Agnikārya* and offerings to Agni are also prescribed.

The following legend [496] is narrated by the sage Gautama to glorify this *vrata*. One day, Durvāsas went to Viṣṇu and presented to him a *bilva-mālā*, which he casually placed on his Garuḍa. The sage naturally got enraged at this and cursed Viṣṇu that he would be deserted by Lakṣmī, Garuḍa, and even Vaikuṇṭha. Thereupon, Bṛhaspati advised Viṣṇu to observe the *Umāmaheśvara-vrata*, which he did. This enabled Viṣṇu to regain all that he had lost, including Vaikuṇṭha.

Śivarātri-vrata [497]

This is by far the most important of the *vratas* observed in honour of Śiva. Accordingly, this *vrata* has acquired wide popularity. In Srilanka it is scrupulously observed by all staunch adherents of Śaivism.[498] The day assigned for the observance of this *vrata* is the *caturdaśī* in the dark half of the month of *Māgha*.[499] The *tithi* is required to extend up to the midday. This day, it is said, was the day

---

495 Milk is sometimes allowed to be taken in the night only.

496 *Vratacūḍāmaṇi*, p. 291.

497 *Agni P.*, 193; *Skanda P.*, III.3.4; IV.1.13; IV.P.67; VI.266; VII.1.39; VII.2.16; *Garuḍa P.*, 124.

498 The importance of this *vrata* may be judged from the fact that the day of the *vrata* is declared a public holiday both in India and Srilanka.

499 *Vratacūḍāmaṇi*, p. 262.

on which Śiva assumed the *liṅga* form for the first time. The *vrata-pūjā* is performed as usual. *Upavāsa* and *jāgaraṇa* are also undertaken. *Pūjā* is performed at the end of each *yāma* of the night, and *arghyas* are also offered each time. The *vratapāraṇam* is performed on the following day.

It is said about this *vrata* that if one happens to fast and keep awake on the night of the *caturdaśī* in the dark half of the month of *Māgha*, even unintentionally, he is bound to be endowed with the merit ensuing from the regular observance of the *Śivarātrī-vrata*. The following story is recounted in the *Vratacūḍāmaṇi* in confirmation of this belief.[500] Once there lived a hunter who mercilessly killed every animal which he came across in the forest. One day, he came to a *bilva* tree; there he saw a deer, and prepared to kill it. Just at that moment, the deer made an appeal to the hunter in a human voice. It said that it would go to its mate, bid her farewell, and then return and offer itself to the hunter. The latter felt so much assured by the sincerity of the beast that he granted its request. He then climbed the *bilva* tree, and in order to keep himself occupied while awaiting the return of the deer, he plucked the leaves of the tree one by one and dropped them down. Soon the mate of the deer herself came to the spot in search of her master. The hunter mistook her for the deer who had promised to return and was about to discharge his arrow. Seeing this, the doe also spoke in a human voice and requested the hunter to spare her until she returned after having met her husband. The hunter agreed and continued to wait for the return of the deer, plucking the leaves of the *bilva* tree and dropping them down as before in order to divert himself. Thus the hunter was engaged — albeit unintentionally — in the acts of keeping awake through the night and dropping the *bilva* leaves on a *liṅga* that happened to be under the tree. He was

[500] *Vratacūḍāmaṇi*, pp. 268 ff. The *Garuḍa P.*, I.124.1-12, gives a slightly different version of this story. The *Agni Purāṇa* (193.6) makes only a casual reference to this popular story. The *Skanda Purāṇa* narrates in six places (III.3.4; IV.1.13; IV.2.67; VI.2.66; VII.1.39; VII.2.16) six different stories, and each of them speaks about the greatness of the *vrata* in its own way.

also forced by the circumstances to go without food. And the day on which all this happened was the fourteenth day in the dark half of the month of *Māgha*. The hunter had thus observed, though unknowingly, the *Śivarātri-vrata*. He therefore became entitled to the fruits of the regular observance of that *vrata*. Accordingly, on the following morning, the Śiva *gaṇas* appeared on the scene and led him to the world of Śiva, with all the honours due to divine beings.

Besides these *vratas* which are more commonly observed, some other *vratas*, such as the *Śivacaturdaśī-vrata*,[501] the *Anaṅgatrayodaśī-vrata*,[502] and the *Pāśupata-vrata*,[503] are mentioned in the *Purāṇas*. As, however, these latter *vratas* do not enjoy wide prevalence, they are not treated here.

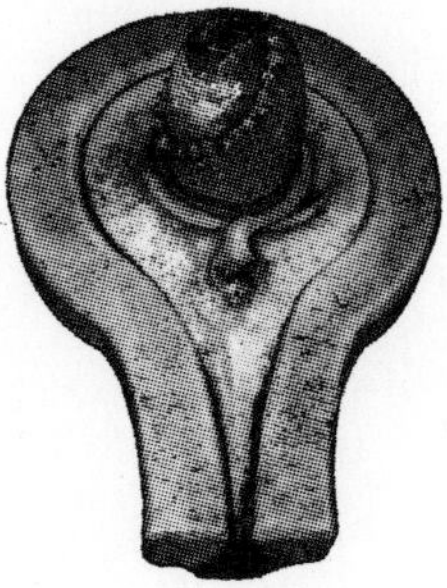

[501] *Matsya P.*, 95.

[502] *Padma P.*, III.24.

[503] *Brahmāṇda P.*, 27.116-123; *Vāyu P.*, I.30.190-194; *Kūrma P.*, II.39.32 ff; *Liṅga P.*, II.9.

Chapter VII

The Ancillary Cults

As has been already pointed out, a survey of the Śaivite religion of the Āgamic, Epic and Purāṇic periods will not be complete without a study of the cults of the deities ancillary to Śiva. These ancillary cults, which seem to have originally been independent religious cults, were over time absorbed into the more pervasive and influential religion of Śiva, and soon became vital aspects of that religion. Among these cults, special attention needs to be paid to the worship of Śakti, Kārttikeya and Gaṇeśa. Of course, in view of the limited scope of this work, these three cults have been dealt with here in their bare outlines and with regard to the extent to which they are helpful in our understanding of the religion of Śiva.

However, before proceeding to deal with these ancillary cults, a few general observations on the nature and functions of ancillary deities in general may not be out of place. To begin with, it may be pointed out that some traces of the worship of ancillary deities may be seen in the *pañcāyatana-pūjā*.[1] From among the five gods Gaṇeśa, Sūrya, Viṣṇu, Śiva and Śakti worshipped in the *pañcāyatana*, he or she who is the chosen deity of the individual worshipper becomes the principal center of worship, while the others are assigned subordinate places. Far more relevant from our point of view, however, is the *āvaraṇa-pūjā* which is a special feature of the Śaiva ritual, although it is held in common with Śaktism. In this context, the *āvaraṇa* implies a gathering of attendant deities around the chief deity.

---

[1] In the *Śiva Purāṇa* (*Jñāna-saṁhitā*, 32) the *sūta* explains to the sages how the *pañcayatana-pūja* came into vogue.

Nine *āvaraṇas* are referred to in connection with the Śākta ritual.[2] The Śaiva ritual texts, on the other hand, prescribe only five *āvaraṇas*.[3] The invocation of Śiva with the *āvaraṇas*, as well as the fixed plan of the *yāga-śālā* according to which the different ancillary deities are installed in fixed places, indicate how vitally the ancillary cults are connected with Śaiva ritualism. It should be remembered in this context that the elaborate worship of Śiva in any form, particularly according to the Southern Āgamic tradition, does not begin or end abruptly with the worship of Śiva alone. The worship is always preceded by an invocation of Gaṇeśa and is concluded with an obeisance to Caṇḍeśa. Over the course of the *pūjā*, other ancillary deities are worshipped at the appropriate time.

A study of the structure of a temple of Śiva in South India will also help us to understand the significance of the attendant deities. Śiva, as the chief god, is installed in the central shrine of the temple. The temples in the South maintain uniformity in this respect, and the convention relating to the allocation of the positions in the temple to the subordinate deities is uniformly maintained.[4] Gaṇeśa is installed on the right [5] and Kārttikeya on the left of the central shrine.[6] The place assigned to Umā in the temple is always to the left of Śiva,[7] and this goddess, in most cases, faces towards the south. Nandin is set up outside the central shrine and faces Śiva.[8] Immediately behind Nandin is the *dhvajastaṁbha*. Bhairava, who is also known as Kṣetrapāla, is the sentinel god, and since his is the responsibility to guard the temple he is assigned a place close to the main entrance (*gopura*) between the north and the north-east. This guardian god also faces towards

---

[2] Cf. *Paraśurāmakalpasūtra*, pp. 150-186. While commenting on the opening word of the first *sūtra* in the fifth *Khaṇḍa*, the commentator observes: *Atha iti navāvaraṇapūjādhikāradyotakam*

[3] *Śivaliṅgapratiṣṭhāvidhi*, pp. 119-123.

[4] See Fig. 15: Structural plan of a typical south Indian temple.

[5] See Fig. 15, no. 17

[6] See Fig. 15, no. 23.

[7] See Fig. 15, no. 5.

[8] See Fig. 15, no. 9.

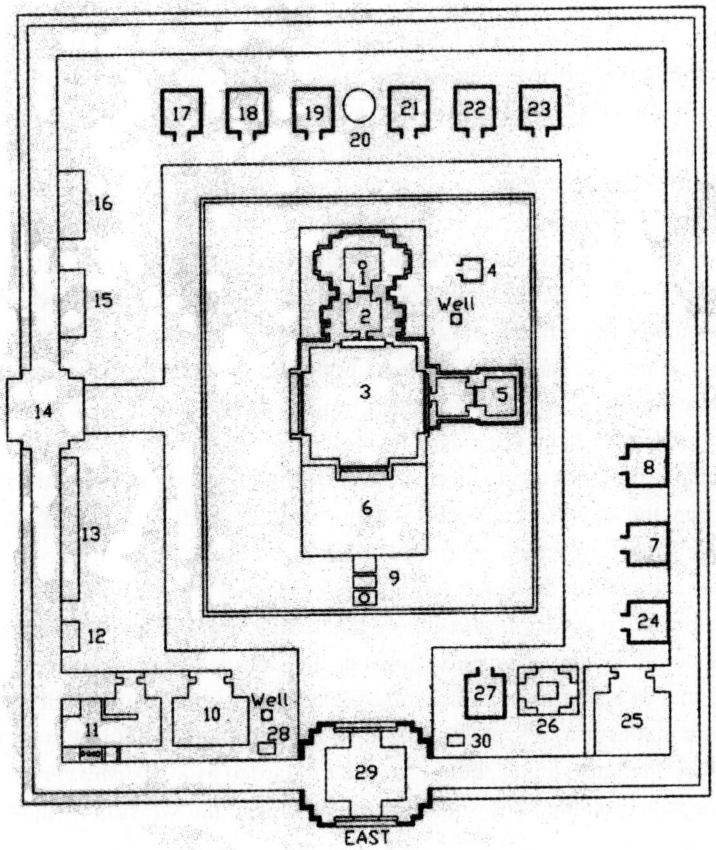

Fig. 15: Structural plan of a typical south Indian temple.

1. Garbhagṛha
2. Mukhamaṇḍapa
3. Mahāmaṇḍapa
4. Caṇḍeśvara shrine
5. Śakti shrine
6. Nṛttamaṇḍapa
7. Naṭarāja shrine
8. Śayanagṛha
9. Nandin, Balipīṭha, Dhvajastambha
10. Store room
11. Pākaśālā
12. Śaiva devotees
13. Śaiva devotees
14. Gopuram, leading to Śakti shrine
15. Samaya gurus
16. Samaya-gurus
17. Gaṇeśa shrine
18. Somāskanda shrine
19. Mahāviṣṇu shrine
20. Mahāliṅga
21. Pañcaliṅga
22. Mahālakṣmī, Jyeṣṭhā, Mātṛkās
23. Kārttikeya shrine
24. Alaṃkāramaṇḍapa
25. Ābharaṇaśālā
26. Yāgaśālā
27. Bhairava shrine
28. Sūrya shrine
29. Rājagopuram (main entrance)
30. Candra shrine

the central shrine, though he is stationed far from where Nandin is stationed. Caṇḍeśvara, another attendant god, is installed very close to the outer walls of the innermost shrine, always to the left to the central image.[9] This god is supposed to bestow upon the worshippers the merits of *Śiva-pūjā*. Each *pūjā* offered to Śiva and the other attendant deities is concluded with an offering of *Śiva-nirmālya* to this deity and a prayer to him to render the worship fruitful. A large number of *parivāradevatās* must, indeed, be regarded as a special feature of the religion of Śiva.[10]

It may be incidentally pointed out that these deities, even after they became ancillary to the religion of Śiva, continued to be worshipped as chief deities in their own right. Accordingly, one finds separate temples erected for Gaṇeśa,[11] Kārttikeya and for the goddess. Even the different aspects of Umā such as Kālī and Durgā are worshipped in separate temples. Attention must be drawn to the fact that all such temples are modeled on a Śiva temple. There are the respective *parivāradevatās*, though naturally fewer in number. In the place of Nandin, *mūṣaka* is shown as the *vāhana* of Gaṇeśa, *mayūra* as that of Kārttikeya, and *siṁha* as that of Śakti.[12] It is interesting to note that Śiva too is, at times, installed in the temples of Gaṇeśa and other ancillary deities, but he is never regarded as a *parivāradevatā*, nor is he assigned any subordinate position in the worship of those deities.

---

9 See Fig. 15, no. 4.

10 About the location of the ancillary deities, the *Kāraṇāgama*, I.60.9-12 prescribes as follows:

Sthāpayed vṛṣabhaṁ pūrve tv agastyaṁ vahnigocare
Yāmye kātyāyanīproktaṁ nairṛtyāṁ tu gaṇeśvaram
Brahmāṇaṁ vāruṇe deśe vāyavyāṁ caiva ṣaṇmukham
Keśavaṁ saumyadigbhāge aiśānyāṁ bhāskaraṁ tathā
Maṇḍapaṁ tu caturdvāraṁ kartavyaṁ vṛṣabhālayam
Pākālayaṁ pāvake tu durgālayaṁ ca svastikam
Gajapṛṣṭhe tu nairṛtyāṁ brahmaṇaḥ pūrvato mukham

11 See Appendix 6, p. 551.

12 In temples where Umā is presented as subordinate to Śiva, Nandin is always installed and not *siṁha*.

There is another interesting point which may be noted here. While describing a temple of Śiva, it has been noted that Śiva is invariably represented by a *liṅga* in the central shrine. This *liṅga* is made of stone, and is permanently fixed to the *āsana-śilā*. At the same time, other anthropomorphic representations of Śiva may well be installed at various points in the temple. Most of such images of Śiva are made of bronze. The positions assigned to these images in the temple and the treatment given to them in the rituals clearly indicate that these images, though intended to be representations of Śiva himself, are regarded as ancillary in relation to the *liṅga* in the central shrine. The *liṅga* is the *mūla-mūrti* or the *mūla-vigraha*, and it is in respect of the *liṅga* alone that all the important rites are performed.

Returning to the ancillary cults of the Śiva religion, it may be pointed out that the *Purāṇas* and the Epics are perhaps the earliest literary texts that celebrate such deities as Kārttikeya, Gaṇeśa and Śakti. At the same time, it has to be noted that these texts have throughout stressed the ancillary character of these deities, care being always taken to place Śiva on a higher level.

Śakti

The cult of Śakti or the Mother Goddess [13] can be traced back to the Mohenjodaro period. The large number of terracotta figurines discovered at different sites in the Indus valley clearly indicate not only the importance which must have been attached to female divinities in the Indus valley religion,[14] but also the wide prevalence of the cult of the Mother goddess in that civilization. It must be presumed that the coexistence of the Mother goddess cult and the

[13] For a detailed statement on the subject, see: Dandekar, "Rudra in the *Veda*", *JUPH*, no. 1, pp. 143 ff. Also see J.N. Banerjea, "Some Aspects of Śakti worship in India", *Pr.Bh.*, 59,227-32; S.K. Das, *Śakti or Divine Power*, Calcutta, 1935.

[14] Goddesses, on the whole, occupy a very subordinate position in the Vedic pantheon. As wives of the great gods they play an insignificant role and are devoid of any independent character. Indeed, hardly anything is mentioned about them except their names, and even these are formed from the names of their male consorts by means of feminine suffixes.

Śiva cult was a special feature of the proto-Indian religion. Over time, the Mother goddess cult merged into the Śaiva religion,[15] and it is with the period subsequent to this merger that we are really concerned. However, it seems that even after its merger with the Śiva religion the cult of Śakti continued to be regarded as an independent and influential religious cult. Śaktism represented the Goddess as supreme. In the Śākta texts, she is often referred to as *Parābhaṭṭārikā* and *Mahātripurasundarī*. She is *Mahārājñī* and *Jaganmātā*.[16] All the gods of the Hindu pantheon are said to be subordinate to her.[17] Epithets like *pañcapretāsanāsīnā* [18] are significant in this connection.[19] Even within the *ardhanārī* representation, which is obviously a result of the amalgamation of the cults of Śiva and Śakti, the goddess shares equal honours with her counterpart.[20] Furthermore, the Śakti cult seems to have vitally influenced the Śiva religion, as indicated by the infiltration of several Śākta elements into the Śaiva ritual.[21]

---

[15] The concept of Tryaṁbaka-Rudra is perhaps one of the results of this merging of the two cults.

[16] See also *Kūrma P.*, I.12.7-15.

[17] This idea is clearly indicated by several *stotras* still sung in praise of the goddess, one of which is cited below:

Tanīyāṁsaṁ pāṁsuṁ tava caraṇapaṅkeruhabhavam
Viriñciḥ sañcinvan viracayati lokān avikalam |
Vahatyenaṁ śauriḥ kathamapi sahasreṇa śirasām
Haraḥ saṁkṣudyainaṁ bhajati bhasitoddhūlanavidhim ||

Saundaryalaharī, verse 2.

"Collecting the tiniest dust from the lotus of your foot, Brahmā creates the worlds without defects; Śauri carries it with great difficulty on a thousand heads, Hara reduces it to ashes and enjoys the process of rubbing ashes on himself."

[18] *Lalitāsahasranāma*, p. 126.

[19] In Bengal and adjoining areas, the worship of Śakti as an independent cult is very popular even to this day. In the South, too, the worship of Śakti, particularly in her dreadful aspects, prevails to a certain extent. This is attested by separate temples being assigned to such aspects of the goddess as Kālī, Durgā and Mahāmārī. However, it is Śakti, subordinated to Śiva, who is the most commonly worshipped.

[20] Also cf. *Śivaḥ śaktyā yukto yadi bhavati śaktaḥ prabhavitum*
Na cedevaṁ devo na khalu kuśalaḥ spanditum api |

Saundaryalaharī, 1st verse.

"Śiva is able to rule, if he is united with Śakti. Otherwise he is incapable of even a stir."

[21] Among these may be mentioned *kuṇḍas*, *maṇḍalas*, *yantras*, *mantras*, *mudrās* and rites such as *nyāsa* and *bhūtaśuddhi*. See chapter VI.

The *Purāṇas* describe the goddess as the most powerful being, and at the same time as the consort — and subordinate — of Śiva.[22] By and large, however, it is the latter aspect of the goddess which is more commonly represented in those texts.

The *Purāṇas* speak of two distinct existences of the goddess. To begin with, she was the daughter of Dakṣa.[23] At Brahmā's suggestion, her father gave her in marriage to Śiva,[24] who showed no respect to his father-in-law. As a result, Śiva was not honoured at a sacrifice performed by Dakṣa. The goddess, unhappy about this, herself appeared on the scene of the sacrifice. Unable to bear the indignities which her husband had to suffer, she decided to break all connections with her father. She even resolved to disown her name Dākṣāyaṇī which she had acquired from her father. She, therefore, incinerated her body with *yogāgni*, and was reborn as Pārvatī, Haimavatī, the daughter of Himavat, the king of the mountains. Thus the goddess had two existences, one as Dākṣāyaṇī and the other as Haimavatī. In both these manifestations, she had Śiva as her husband.[25]

---

22 *Cf. Ekā sarvagatānantā kevalā niṣkalā sivā |*
Ekā śaktiḥ śivaiko'pi śaktimān ucyate śivaḥ ||
Śaktayaḥ śaktimanto'nye sarve śaktisamudbhavāḥ |
Śaktiśaktimator bhedaṁ vadanti paramārthataḥ ||
Abhedaṁ cānupaśyanti yoginas tattvacintakāḥ |
Śaktayaḥ girijā devī śaktimān atha śaṅkaraḥ ||
Viśeṣaḥ kathyate cāyaṁ purāṇe brahmavādbhiḥ |
Kūrma P., I.12.26-29.

"Unique is the all-pervading, limitless, single, unmanifest Śivā. Śivā is the Śakti, unique. Though one, Śiva is called 'Endowed with Śakti'. All other Śaktis and possessors of śakti are born from Śakti. The yogins who meditate on reality speak of difference of Śakti and possessor of Śakti and in ultimate truth see non-difference. The goddess Girijā is all the Śaktis and Śaṅkara is endowed with Śakti. This difference is narrated in Purāṇas by the *brahmavādins*."

Also cf. *MBh*, III.404; III.41.19 & 25; III.217.5; III.220.

23 *Brahmāṇḍa P.*, III. 10.1 ff.

24 *Bhāgavata P.*, IV.2.4 ff.

25 *Kūrma P.*, I.14 and 15; *Brahmāṇḍa P.*, I.13; *Vāyu P.*, I.30; *Liṅga P.*, I.96 and also I.100; *Śiva P.*, *Jñāna-saṁhitā*, 7; *ibid.*, *Vāyu-saṁhitā*, chapters 15-20; *Brahma P.*, I.32, also 37; *Vāmana P.*, 5; *Varāha P.*, 21; *Garuḍa P.*, I.5.35-58; *Skanda P.*, I.3 and 4; *Harivaṁśa*, III.32. *Kālikā P.*, 17; *MBh*, X.18.1-26, also XIII.160.24.

The goddess is often represented in the *Purāṇas* as being dark-complexioned. This gave her the name Kālī. At the same time, she is often referred to as Gaurī, a name which indicates that she is fair in complexion. The *Purāṇas* repeatedly narrate how the goddess became enraged when Śiva teased her by calling her Kālī, the Dark One. Petulantly, she left her home and retired to a secluded spot to perform *tapas*. Brahmā, in whose honour the *tapas* was performed, manifested himself before her and granted her the light complexion she desired. Henceforward she came to be known as Gaurī.[26]

The *Purāṇas* have portrayed the goddess as the destroyer of demons. Mahiṣa, Raktabīja, Śumbha, Niśumbha, Bhaṇḍāsura and several others were destroyed by her at the request of the gods. It is in such contexts that the goddess is conceived as being endowed with several arms carrying in them dreadful divine weapons. Even her vehicle the lion [27] conformed to the needs of the situation; the *Purāṇas* narrate how the lion was only a manifestation of the anger of the goddess herself. (Fig. 16)

The *Devībhāgavata-Purāṇa* accords the goddess a very high status, which at times is superior to that of Viṣṇu or even Śiva. Viṣṇu proclaims the dependence of the three gods on Śakti.[28] Once she is described as having only become manifest in order to enable the three gods to discharge their respective functions.[29] At the same time, in

---

[26] *Vāmana P.*, 54; *Matsya P.*, 157; *ŚivaP.*, *Vāyu-saṁhitā*, 21 and 22; *Skanda P.*, I.2.28.

[27] *Tatra sthāpya harir devīṁ dattvā siṁhaṁ ca vāhanaṁ |*
Bhavāmarārihantrī cetyuktvā svargamupāgamat ||
Vāmana P., 54.28.

[28] *Nāhaṁ svatantra evātra na brahmā na sivas tathā |*
Nendrāgnir na yamas tvaṣṭā na sūryo varuṇas tathā ||
Devībhāgavata P., IV.18.

Elsewhere the goddess remarks:
Aśaktaḥ śaṅkaro hantuṁ daityān kila mayojjhitaḥ |
Śaktihīnaṁ naraṁ brūte lokaś caivātidurbalam ||
Rudrahīnaṁ viṣṇuhīnaṁ na vadanti janāḥ kila |
Śaktihīnaṁ yathā sarve pravadanti narādhamam ||
Ibid., III.17.18-19.

[29] *Druhiṇe sṛṣṭiśaktiś ca harau pālanaśaktitā |*
Hare saṁhāraśaktiś ca sūrye śaktiḥ prakāśikā ||
Ibid., I.8.28-19.

Fig. 16: Durgā and siṁhavāhana, Kailāsanātha Temple at Kanchipuram.

another context, it was said that all the gods gave forth their energies, which combined and gave rise to Caṇḍikā.[30] They also made their weapons available to her and thus enabled her to destroy the demon Mahiṣa.[31] Elsewhere we are told that it was Rudra's Śakti which, assuming the forms of Vaiṣṇavī and Cāmuṇḍī, destroyed the demon Mahiṣa;[32] another Purāṇic account [33] narrates how a young female being was born out of the glances exchanged by Brahmā and Rudra; to the perplexed gods she revealed her identity as the manifestation of the *śakti* of those gods themselves. She became the protector of the worlds and the destroyer of the demons.[34] She chastised the demons Mahiṣa, Śumbha, Niśumbha, Caṇḍa, Muṇḍa and Raktabīja.[35] Once she is said to have commanded her subordinate Durgā to destroy Mahiṣa.[36] On the eve of this battle, the goddess is said to have worship-

---

Cf. also: *Brahmā sṛjati lokān vai viṣṇuḥ pāty akhilaṁ jagat* |
Rudraḥ saṁharate kāle traya ete ca kāraṇam ||
Ekā murtiḥ trayo devāḥ brahmaviṣṇumaheśvarāḥ |
Rajaḥsatvatamobhiś ca saṁyutāḥ kāryakārakāḥ ||
Ibid., I.7.3-4.

[30] *Mārkaṇḍeya P.*, 82.8-18. See also: S.B. Das Gupta "A Historical Study of Candī", *BRMIC*, 10, pp. 138-43.

[31] *Mārkaṇḍeya* P.,82.19-31.

[32] *Padma P.*, I.36

[33] *Varāha P.*, 90.

[34] The goddess is said to have remarked:
Kiṁ māṁ na vettha suśroṇiṁ svaśaktiṁ parameśvarīm |
Tato brahmādayaste ca tasyās tuṣṭāḥ varaṁ daduḥ ||
... ...
Evam uktā tadā devaiḥ sākarot trividhaṁ tanum |
... ...
Yā sā brāhmī śubhā mūrtis tasyāḥ sṛjati vai prajāḥ |
... ...
Śaṅkhacakradharā devī vaiṣṇavī sā kalā smṛtā |
Sā pāti sakalaṃ viśvaṁ ...
... ...
Yā sā kṛṣṇena varṇena raudrā mūrtis triśūlinī |
Daṁṣṭrākarālinī devī sā saṁharati vai jagat ||
Varāha P., 90.22-29.
See also 96.60-64.

[35] *Vāmana P.*, 55 and 56.

[36] *Skanda P.*, I.3.2.19.

ped Viṣṇu in order to gain the necessary strength.[37] After destroying the demon, the gods showered their praises upon her. She gave them the boon that she would always befriend them if they recalled her to mind in times of calamity.[38]

This goddess, who forms part of Śiva,[39] also bears close relationship to Viṣṇu;[40] it is for this reason that she is called Nārāyaṇī. She is sometimes also called Padmanābhasahodarī.

As has been already pointed out, the goddess was well-known for her remarkable capacity to practise *tapas*. In an earlier chapter she is shown to have excelled all others — gods, demons, and mortals — in this respect. Even as a child she practised severe penance, despite her mother's constant attempts to dissuade her from her self-mortification. According to one *Purāṇa*,[41] it was this episode which gave the goddess the name of Umā.

It should be noted that Umā is mentioned in the *Kena-Upaniṣad*[42] as the teacher of a significant philosophical doctrine. This philosophical aspect of the personality of Umā is also reflected in the *Purāṇas*; in the *Kūrma Purāṇa*,[43] for instance, she is represented as preaching philosophical doctrines to her father Himavat. This philosophy bears close resemblance to the philosophy of the *Bhagavadgītā*, both in language and content.[44] In this passage of the *Purāṇa*, Umā speaks of herself as the highest godhead.

---

[37] *Garuḍa P.*, I.14.12-13.

[38] *Mārkaṇḍeya P.*, 84.29.

[39] *Tatra yā sā mahābhāgā śaṅkarasyārdhakāminī* |
Vāyu P., I.9.75.

[40] In this connection, the following pronouncement made by Śiva may be noted:
Ayaṁ nārāyaṇo gaurī jaganmātā sanātanaḥ |
Vibhajya saṁsthito devaḥ svātmānaṁ bahudheśvaraḥ ||
Na me viduḥ paraṁ tattvaṁ devyāś ca na maharṣayaḥ |
Eko'yaṁ veda viśvātmā bhavānī viṣṇureva ca ||
Kūrma P., I.16.158-160.

[41] *Bhaviṣya P.*, III.14.67.

[42] *Kenopaniṣad*, III.25 ff.

[43] *Kūrma P.*, I.12.

[44] Cf. *Divyaṁ dadāmi te cakṣuḥ paśya me rūpam aiśvaram* |
... ...

Himavat gave his daughter Umā in marriage to Śiva. The *Purāṇas* describe in detail the wedding ceremony.[45] It is these descriptive accounts in the *Purāṇas* which gave rise to the installation of Śiva as Kalyāṇasundaramūrti.[46] In this, Umā figures as the bride given by Himavat to Śiva. Obviously, her role here is subordinate to that of Śiva. The *Purāṇas* portray Umā as the mother of two sons; Gaṇeśa is the elder son and Kārttikeya the younger.[47] Vīrabhadra and Bhairava also are spoken of as her sons,[48] but these two latter are actually different manifestations of Śiva himself.[49] Even Gaṇeśa is represented in the *Purāṇas* not as having been born of Umā, but as having been adopted by her; Kārttikeya was also not born from Umā's womb.[50]

Though there was sometimes the tendency to portray Śakti as the all-powerful divinity subordinating various other gods to herself,[51] Śiva does not seem to have been subjected to this treatment in every

---

Evaṁ rūpaṁ darśayāmāsa divyaṁ tat pārameśvaram ||
Koṭisūryapratīkāśaṁ tejobiṁbaṁ nirākulam |
... ...
Divyamālyāṁbaradharaṁ divyagandhāṇulepanam |
Sarvataḥ pāṇipādaṁ tat sarvato'kṣiśiromukham ||
Sarvam āvṛtya tiṣṭhantīṁ dadarśa parameśvarīṁ |
Kūrma P., I.12.51-59.

"I give you a divine eye, see my lordly form ... Thus he saw the divine form of the supreme goddess, shining like crores of suns, a pure circle of light ... wearing divine garlands, anointed with divine perfumes, having feet and arms on all sides, eyes and heads in all directions. He saw the supreme goddess standing, pervading everything."

It may be pointed out, in this connection, that the *Kūrma Purāṇa* contains a section which is called *Īśvaragītā*, obviously in imitation of the *Bhagavadgītā*.

[45] *Matsya P.*, 154.423-494; *Śiva P.*, *Jñāna-saṁhitā*, 15-18; *Padma P.*, I.43; *Bhaviṣya P.*, III.14.67; *Varaha P.*, 22.

[46] See Chapter V, pp. 262-263.

[47] Chapter IV, p. 194.

[48] Moore, *Hindu Pantheon*, p. 61.

[49] See Chapter V, pp. 272, 274.

[50] The details regarding the birth of Gaṇeśa and Kārttikeya are related elsewhere in the present chapter.

[51] The following reference from a *stotra* reflects this tendency:
Īśānādipadaṁ śivaikaphalakaṁ ratnāsanaṁ te śubham
Mantramātṛkāpuṣpamālāstava, verse 3.

such reference. It is significant that the Śākta texts and the *Purāṇas* do not ever mention Śakti alone. The former, in particular, invariably associate her with her consort Kāmeśvara, who is no other than Śiva himself, the highest of all beings.[52] The *Purāṇas* seem to portray an even later stage, in which the goddess is not only described as the spouse of Śiva, but is also assigned a position which is clearly subordinate to his. She recognizes Śiva as the highest godhead, and accordingly practises *tapas* in his honour.[53] It is this Purāṇic tradition which is reflected in the religious practices prevailing in the South, as even where a separate place is assigned for installation of the goddess, stress is always laid on the fact that she is second to Śiva in importance. This impression is sought to be created by focusing all attention on Śiva who is installed as the central deity. A similar attitude governs the elaborate system of the rituals. In the *ardhanārīśvara* form,[54] Śiva and Śakti are shown to be sharing equal honours. According to this concept, the two divinities were regarded as equal in status and inseparable, if not one in essence.[55] When the *ardhanārīśvara* concept relates to the representation of Śiva as a *liṅga*, the lower part or the base is identified with Śakti, and the upper part (*liṅga*) with Śiva.[56] There are also instances where anthropomorphic images of Śiva and Śakti are installed separately, but side by side on equal footing.[57]

The goddess' *stotras* describe her as having eight arms, benign, and thrusting her spear into the demon lying close to her feet; it is this aspect of the goddess which is commonly represented in Chola architecture. A reference may also be made to other aspects of the

---

[52] Cf. *Brahmāṇḍa P.*, *Lalitopākhyāna*, 10.

[53] *Skanda P.*, I.1.21; I.3.1.3.; I.3.1.9; I.3.1.10; *Kālikā P.*, 45; *Vāmana P.*, 51; *Matsya P.*, 154.273-300.

[54] Cf. *Kūrma P.*, I.11.1-13.

[55] Cf. *Bhāgavata P.*, IV.6.1-53; *Śiva P.*, *Vāyu-saṁhitā*, II.5.

[56] The *Purāṇas* have referred, in clear terms, to the contribution of Umā to the *liṅga* concept.

[57] See chapter V, pp. 262-263, 282-286.

goddess, such as Kālī, Durgā [58] and Caṇḍikā, by which she is widely worshipped even today. There are also other aspects which are worthy of our attention. The Saptamātṛkās and Jyeṣṭhā [59] are assigned a distinctive but subordinate place in the temples. The local village deity Māriamman, who also represents a minor aspect of the goddess, commands great popularity among the masses. The anger of this deity, who is at times called Mahāmārī, is greatly dreaded, and it is believed to manifest itself in the form of pestilence. Small pox is particularly associated with her, and special offerings are made to placate Māriamman and thereby get rid of this frightful disease.

For the purpose of worship, Śakti is always featured with a single head and two arms, one of which holds a lotus, the other hanging down (Fig. 17).[60] This portrayal is interpreted as expressive of the subordinate nature of Śakti. Śakti portrayed with four arms, on the other hand, assumes an independent status. She is *svatantra*-Śakti and is regarded as a very powerful goddess. In her four arms she wields a bow, an arrow, a noose and a goad,[61] symbolic of her main functions. However, only in a few temples is Śakti installed along with Śiva in this form, the other type with two arms being more common.

A few general observations may now be briefly made about some of the other more common representations of the goddess installed and worshipped in various parts of the country.

---

[58] See C. Chakravarti, "The Worship of Goddess Durgā", *BRMIC* 9, 81-87; N.N. Choudhuri, "Mother Goddess Durgā", *PO* 15, 32-38.

[59] See Fig. 15, no. 22. Here, Jyeṣṭhā and the Mātṛkās are assigned their places.

[60] Cf. the following description of the goddess:
Śyāmā dvinetrā dvibhujā tribhaṅgī |
Savyāpasavyasthitakuñcitānghriḥ ||
Savyotpalā sakanakastanāḍhyā |
Hastāvalaṁbā Parameśvarī sā ||
Kāraṇa, I.90.3.

[61] Cf. the following description in the *Lalitāsahasranāma*, (53-54):
... ...
Rāgasvarūpapāśāḍhyā krodhākārāṅkuśojjvalā |
Manorūpekṣukodaṇḍā pañcatanmātrasāyakā ||
"She holds a noose which is desire a goad which is anger, a sugar-cane bow which is the mind and arrows which are the five objects of senses."

Fig. 17: Śakti, bronze from Tamil Nad.

Gaurī

As Gaurī, the goddess is represented with two arms. Her complexion, contrary to what is implied by her name, is prescribed to be dark. She holds a lotus in her right hand. She is crowned with *karaṇḍamakuṭa* and decked with every ornament. Usually, she is featured as a subordinate deity of Śiva, as his Śakti.[62]

Parameśvarī

In this aspect also the goddess is portrayed as dark-complexioned. She has two arms, and is represented in the *tribhaṅga* pose. She holds a lotus in her right hand and her left hand hangs downwards. Her right leg is planted erect on a lotus seat, and the left is slightly bent. Her breasts are prominently displayed.[63]

Manonmaṇī

The goddess is portrayed here as having a complexion like the colour of the moon. Other salient features of this representation are three eyes, *jaṭāmakuṭa*, and ornaments of various kinds. Out of her four arms, two are in the *abhaya* and the *varada* positions. The third arm holds the lotus while the fourth hangs down.[64]

Cāmuṇḍā

As Cāmuṇḍā, the goddess wears a garland of skulls, and serpents around her neck. Her left foot is planted on the demon Raktabīja. The goddess is adorned with a crescent moon. She is dark-faced and a frightening expression is seen in her eyes. The usual *prabhāmaṇḍala* is displayed around the figure. In the image, Cāmuṇḍā may be either standing or sitting. She may even be represented as mounted on a corpse. Four arms are optionally prescribed; in this case, *pāśa*, *ḍamaru*, *śūla* and *kapāla* are assigned to them respectively.[65]

---

62 *Kāraṇa*, II.84.7-13; also *ibid* I.90.2.

63 *Ibid.*, I.90.3.

64 *Ibid.*, I.90.6-10.

65 *Agni P.*, 261.33-37.

Durgā

The installation and worship of the goddess as Durgā is prescribed in the *Āgamas*. The details relating to the form and the construction of the image are, however, not given. The *Āgamas* only mention that the image should be made of *śilā* or *loha* and that it should be constructed as has been stipulated.[66]

Mahāmārī

The goddess is declared to have destroyed the demon called Mārāsura, and thenceforth she was known as Mahāmārī. Mahāmārī is three-eyed and four-armed, and has a peaceful expression. She is shown with flames shooting upwards as her hair. Red-complexioned, she wields *kapāla*, *khaḍga*, *pāśa* and *ḍamaru*. Her left leg is planted on the seat and the right one hangs down. Clad in a dark garment and wearing a serpent as her *yajñopavīta* and *tāṭaṅka* as her left earring, the figure is encircled by the *prabhāmaṇḍala*.[67]

It will be seen that the representations of the goddess described above are based on the Purāṇic depictions of the goddess. In the same way, the worship of the goddess, which had its roots in the early form of both *vāma* and *dakṣiṇa* Śākta rituals, also underwent various changes and adjustments over time to suit the character of the goddess as portrayed in the *Purāṇas*. By and large, it was brought in line with the worship of Śiva; it is this modified form of the worship of Śakti which is prevalent among the Śaivites. This form of worship has eliminated the abhorrent practices of the *vāmamārga*, though it has preserved several essential elements of the old traditional Śaktism.

Insofar as the traditions prevailing in the South are concerned, the details of ritual relating to Śakti as worshipped along with Śiva do not differ widely from those mentioned in connection with Śiva alone. Rites like *karṣaṇa*, *pratiṣṭhā*, *utsava* and *prāyaścitta* [68] are performed even for the worship of the goddess. A reference may, however, be

---

[66] *Kāraṇa*, I.98.

[67] *Ibid.*, II.95.

[68] See chapter VI, p. 351 and *passim*.

made to certain specific traditions of early Śākta worship, which have been preserved and which have influenced the Śaiva ritual traditions. In its early stages, the worship of the goddess was associated with the five *makāras*: *madhu*, *matsya*, *māṁsa*, *maithuna* and *mudrā*. This form of worship is clearly evidenced by most of the *Tantras*. Over time, the ritual texts themselves began to speak of two forms of Śakti worship and the *makāra* form came to be known as the *vāma-mārga*. It was suggested that this form was fit to be adopted only by a select few who are mature enough to practise it. The other form came to be known as the *dakṣiṇa-mārga*. Broadly speaking, it is the latter set of rites that have been assimilated by Śaiva ritualism. The *upāsanā* of the goddess is called *śrīvidyopāsanā* or *śrividyā-saparyā*; for the most part, this consists of the worship of the *śrīcakra* depicted in three ways.[69] Over time, *Kalpasūtras* [70] and several *Paddhatis* [71] were composed, embodying instructions to the *upāsaka* regarding the details of the worship of the goddess in the *cakra*. *Arghya-sādhanā*, *mudrās*, *bhūtaśuddhi*,[72] *nyāsa* [73] and *gurupūjā* form the characteristic elements of the *Śakti-pūjā*. These have been freely incorporated into the Śaiva ritual.

---

[69] Chapter VI, p. 361.

[70] In a discussion with the priests officiating at the Kamākṣi temple at Kanchipuram, it was revealed that the rites performed in that temple are strictly in adherence to the *Kalpasūtra*, the authorship of which is attributed to Durvāsas. The *Kalpasūtra* quoted in the present work is the *Paraśurāmakalpasūtra*; this is widely popular among the Śāktas. The following extract from the preface to the first edition of the *Paraśurāmakalpasūtra* (Gaekwad Oriental Series, no. XXI) speaks about the nature of this work: "The *Kalpa-sūtra* is a digest of Śrīvidyā system of Divine Mother's worship compiled by one Paraśurāma from the several systems of the same which prevailed in his day. This only is one of the many forms now in vogue, though it is tersest and perhaps the best arranged one of them all. It seems very hard to make out in what sense the author can be identified with Paraśurāma of the *Rāmāyaṇa* as is done in the colophons of the several sections of the Sūtra." See *Paraśurāma-kalpasūtra*, pp. 111-4 for detailed information about the *Kalpasūtra*.

[71] The *Śrīvidyāsaparyāpaddhati* and the *Śrīvidyā-nityāhnika* edited by Subramaniya Ayyar (Balamanorama Press, Madras) are *Paddhatis* based on the *Kalpasūtra*. The *Varivasya-rahasya* of *Bhāskararāya* (edited by the same author) and his expositions in Tamil of the rituals relating to the worship of Śakti entitled *Śrīvidyāsaparyā-vasāna* are very informative.

[72] For detailed comments see Arthur Avalon, *Principles of Tantra*, Part III, pp. 365 ff.

[73] See Avalon, *op.cit.*, pt. II, pp. 373 ff.

A devotee desirous of worshipping Śakti cannot do so directly even if he has both the genuine desire and the means of doing so. He must first get himself properly initiated through the rite of *dikṣā*. *Gaṇeśa-pūjā*, *Ṣaḍaṅga-pūjā*, *āvāhana*, *upacāras*, *maṅgalārāti*, *āvaraṇapūjā*, *dhūpa*, *dīpa*, *bali*, *pradakṣiṇa*, are among the main constituents of the Śakti-worship. The worship of Gaṇeśa is first as is the case in every Hindu ritual. The *Kalpasūtras* describe every rite in detail and in order, beginning with the daily duties enjoined on the *upāsaka*. After rising early in the morning, he begins by cleansing himself of all sin by paying obeisance to his *guru*.[74] Thereafter, such rites as *snāna* and *sandhyā* are performed.[75] The *upāsaka* then enters the *yāgamandira* to perform the *cakra-pūjā*.[76] The *dīpa* [77] is ceremonially installed, lit and worshipped. This is followed by *prāṇāyāma* and the dispelling of obstacles (*vighnotsāraṇa*);[78] then comes the *nyāsa* and preparing the *arghyapātras* (like the *pātrasādhana*),[79] filling them with sanctified water and the *arghya* ingredients (*arghya-dravyas*). The *āvāhana* [80] which follows is a very important rite, for it marks the entry of the goddess into the *yantra*. The goddess, who was until now enshrined in the heart-lotus (*hṛdaya-kamala*) of the worshipper, is led out by the *sādhaka* with an invocation for her to take her seat in the *yantra*. This seat is, in fact, the centralmost point of the *cakra*, known as the *baindavasthāna*. Having taken her seat, the offering of the sixty-four *upacāras* is performed,[81] and the nine *mudrās* are practised.[82]

The *ṣaḍaṅga* and the *nitya-pūjās* are performed in honour of the attendant deities. These are followed by the *āvaraṇa-pūjā*, [83] which is offered to the attendant deities associated with Śakti who are conceived as surrounding the central deity in nine circles (*āvaraṇas*).

---

[74] *Paraśurāmakalpasūtra*, p. 87.
[75] *Ibid.*, p. 88.
[76] *Ibid.*, pp. 92-98.
[77] *Ibid.*, p. 99.
[78] *Ibid.*, pp. 101 f.
[79] *Ibid.*, p. 105.
[80] *Ibid.*, pp. 134-136.
[81] *Paraśurāmakalpasūtra*, pp. 137-139.
[82] *Ibid.*, 142. See also pages 608-656, where the *mudrās* are described at great length.
[83] *Ibid.*, pp. 142-166.

The *bindu* at the center is the seat of the goddess. This is enclosed on all sides by a *trikoṇa*, *aṣṭakoṇa*, *antardaśāra*, *bahirdaśāra* and *manvasra* (a fourteen-cornered figure). The *aṣṭadala*, *ṣoḍaśadala* and *bhūpuratraya* also characterize the *yantra*. The *parivāradevatās* are invoked to take their seats at the points surrounding the *bindu* where Śakti is believed to be enthroned in all her majesty. The *āvaraṇa-pūjā* is followed by *dhūpa*, *dīpa ārati*, *bali*, and *pradakṣiṇa*. The *pūjā* is concluded with the withdrawal of the goddess from the *cakra* and leading her back into the heart-lotus.

Gaṇeśa (Fig. 18)

Gaṇeśa holds a unique position in the religious ideology of the Hindus. As a rule, all religious rites must begin with the worship of this god. His place in the religion of Śiva is particularly significant. Śiva is portrayed in the *Purāṇas* as being waited upon by a large groups of attendants,[84] the leader of which receives the appellation *gaṇapati*. Gaṇapati is also the son of Śiva. Emerging out of the fusion of the two concepts of son of Śiva and leader of the *gaṇas*, the cult of *Gaṇapati* was firmly established and has maintained its importance in the religious ideology of Śaivism. However, as both the son of Śiva and as the chief of the *gaṇas* who attend on him, Gaṇeśa is presented to us in the *Purāṇas* as a subordinate of Śiva and he remains such throughout the Śaivite religion.

The early history of Gaṇeśa is shrouded in darkness. Aravamuthan [85] regards Gaṇapati neither as a *yakṣa*, as Coomaraswamy has done,[86] nor as a totemic or agrarian god as suggested by Foucher,[87] but assumes for that god an exclusively Vedic provenance. He thinks that Gaṇapati is a conglomerate of Bṛhaspati and the Vedic Maruts. Heras, on the other hand, is equally emphatic in suggesting that there

[84] The *gaṇas* are called *pramathas*. They are the special attendants of Śiva. Cf. Pramathāḥ. *Amarakośa*, *svargavarga*, verse 35.

[85] T.G. Aravamuthan, Gaṇeśa: "Clue to a Cult and a Culture", *JORM* 18, 221-245.

[86] A.K. Coomaraswamy, *Yakṣas*, Washington, 1931.

[87] *In Gaṇeśa* by A Getty, pp. xxi-xxii.

Fig. 18: Dancing Gaṇeśa, Hoysaleśvara Temple at Halebid.

is no basis in the *Veda* for the elephant-headed Hindu god. A more or less mystic interpretation of the origin and nature of this god is offered by Alain Daniélou,[88] according to whom Gaṇeśa is the 'Lord of the Numbered' through whom the identity between macrocosm and microcosm is represented. Interesting and thought-provoking as they are, [89] we should not concern ourselves with these theories in the present context, but rather restrict ourselves to the consideration of this god as portrayed in the Epics and the *Purāṇas* in his aspect as an ancillary deity of Śiva.[90]

The name Gaṇeśa [91] is indicative of the primary function of this god, which is clearly of Purāṇic origin. This god is the leader of the *gaṇas*, the attendants of Śiva. This leadership seems to have been assigned to two gods of a subordinate nature. One of them is Nandin,[92] whom the *Purāṇas* often call Ganapati. He maintains his individuality and figures as a god quite distinct from Gaṇeśa the son of Śiva. The other is Vīraka, who is also a recipient of the appellation Gaṇapati.[93] Moreover, Vīraka is represented in the *Purāṇas* as having been adopted by Umā as her son, and she is said to have developed for him a particularly great affection.[94] It would thus appear that the fusion of the two concepts of the son and of the leader of the *gaṇas* was a

---

[88] A. Danielou, "The meaning of Gaṇapati", *ALB* 18, 106-119.

[89] See also: Renou, "Note sur les origines vediques de Gaṇeśa", *JA* 229 (1937). Lacchmidhar Sastri, "Is Gaṇeśa originally a corn-deity?" Ninth *AIOC* (1937).

[90] The earliest recorded reference to the worship of Gaṇeśa in the South belongs to the seventh century AD. An inscription mention a hero by name Parañjoti usually identified with Ciruttodar, who was a Śaiva devotee of great repute and was engaged in the worship of Gaṇeśa. He had brought an image of that god from Vātāpi and had installed it at a place called Kaṇapatīccuram. See Cuppiramaniyam Pillai, *History of Tamil Literature*, pt. II, pp. 310-311.

[91] The god is known in Tamil as Pillaiyār. *Pillai* is the Tamil word for child and Pillaiyār means 'noble child'. Bagchi is of the opinion that *pillai* originally meant the young of the elephant, for the Pali word *piḷḷaka* has the significance of a young elephant. Cf. "Some Linguistic Notes", *IHQ* IX, no. 1, 1933.

[92] *Liṅga P.*, I.44.30-46.

[93] *Padma P.*, I.43.

[94] *Matsya P.*, 155.33-34.

common feature in the *Purāṇas*. The *Purāṇas* often emphasize the immense capacity of Gaṇeśa to remove obstacles.[95] To him is always assigned the first and foremost place in every Śaiva rituals.[96] The *smārtas* from the South also recommend first worshipping Gaṇeśa during any ritual. He is is sought to remove all obstacles before beginning the rites.[97]

Gaṇeśa is usually represented in the *Purāṇas* as the son of Gaurī.[98] Gaṇeśa is further represented as having the head of an elephant.[99] The following story is narrated in the *Varāha Purāṇa* to explain this phenomenon.[100] Śiva once cast a loving glance at Umā, as the result of which was born a child with all the lovely features of Rudra himself. Accordingly, as soon as he was born he attracted all the gods towards him on account of his remarkable personality. As was but to be expected, Umā also gazed at the child affectionately — however, this enraged Śiva. Consequently, he pronounced a curse that the child would lose all his attractive features. So, the newborn god received the head of an elephant, a protruding belly, and the *upavīta* of a serpent.

A different account is narrated in some *Purāṇas* relating to the birth of Gaṇeśa.[101] Soon after the child had been born, he was clad in a variegated dress, and was decked with beautiful ornaments. He adored his parents. Specific duties were assigned to him, such as destroying the demons and protecting the gods.[102] He was also empowered by Śiva to remove all obstacles that stood in the way of men

---

[95] *Liṅga P.*, I.103.

[96] *Śiva P.*, *Vidyeśvara-saṁhitā*, 16.98-129; *Padma P.*, I.65; 1-35; *Skanda P.*, I.10 and 11; *ibid.*, III.2.12; *Varāha P.*, 23.19-38.

[97] Cf. the following verse which is usually recited in the South at the commencement of the ritual:
Vighneśvara mahādeva sarvalokanamaskṛta |
Mayārabdham idaṁ karma nirvighnaṁ kuru sarvadā ||

[98] *Padma P.*, I.65.1-35.

[99] *Liṅga P.*, I.103.

[100] *Vārāha P.*, 23.1-18.

[101] *Liṅga P.*, I.105.1-30; I.104.1-28; I.103.1-81.

[102] *Ibid.*, I.105.1-30.

and mortals.[103] At the same time, he could create obstacles for those who failed to propitiate him at the commencement of any undertaking.[104] Whosoever may be the god to whom the main *pūjā* is to be offered, this remover of obstacles must be the first to be invoked.

A reference may be made to still another Purāṇic account about the birth of this god.[105] Umā was childless. She was exhorted to observe the vow of *puṇyaka*, in which Kṛṣṇa was the object of adoration. Umā duly observed that vow, and as a result, Kṛṣṇa himself was born as her son. Kṛṣṇa, the lord of all gods born in this manner came to be known as Gaṇeśa. Mere remembrance of this deity was supposed to remove all obstacles. Gaṇeśa was born as the result of the *puṇyaka* vow, in connection with which the stomachs of one's every guest was to be stuffed full with food; hence, the child who was born as the result of that vow obtained the name Lambodara. People offered him worship at the very commencement of all religious rites, for it was believed that unless he was worshipped first, the worship of any other god would be rendered futile.[106]

A strange account about the birth of Gaṇeśa is narrated in some other *Purāṇas*. It was time for Pārvatī to take her bath. She wanted one of her own associates to wait at the entrance while she bathed. As none was at hand at that time to do the job, she collected all the dirt from her body and fashioned a being out of it. To the being so created was entrusted the responsibility of guarding the entrance to her bath. Later, that being was adopted by Śiva and Umā and came to be known as Gaṇeśa.[107] Elsewhere we are told that Pārvatī collected dirt from her body and out of it shaped Gaṇeśa, who over time became the leader of the *gaṇas* and caused great worry to the *asuras*. Śiva later recognized him as his son. Slightly different is the account [108]

---

[103] *Liṅga P.*, I.105.

[104] *Ibid.*, I.105.

[105] *Brahmavaivarta P.*, III.8.

[106] *Padma P.*, V.61.20.

[107] *Śiva P.*, *Jñāna-saṁhitā*, 32-36.

[108] *Vāmana P.*, 54.56-78.

according to which Umā collected the dirt on her body and fashioned out of it a male human being with an elephant's head. His body began to grow immensely. He was glorified as Gāṅgeya, and to him was assigned the leadership of the *gaṇas*.

Gaṇeśa is also designed as Vināyaka. His name implies that he has no one above him as his controller, and also that he is the leader of all, particularly of the *gaṇas*.[109] The *Mahābhārata* mentions the Gaṇeśvaras and Vināyakas as acting like men pervading every quarter.[110] In the same work, they are also described as removing all difficulties coming in the way of their devotees when they are praised.[111] The *Atharvaśiras Upaniṣad* identifies Rudra with Vināyaka.[112] A reference may also be made in this connection to a spirit going by the name of *vināyaka*.[113] The *Mānavagṛhyasūtra* mentions four types of this evil spirit,[114] and rites have been prescribed to be performed on behalf of those who are found to be possessed by it.[115]

Once, when Śiva shook his body through anger, the hairs on his body became coated with perspiration. Out of that perspiration arose numerous *vināyakas*. The gods felt anxious at the sight of these *vināyakas*, for they feared that these creatures would cause disaster to the world. At that moment, Brahmā appeared and assured the gods that they were indeed fortunate, since they had actually been favoured by Śiva. Those newly-created beings were to be the attendants of Gaṇeśa. Brahmā further announced that Gaṇeśa deserved worship at the very beginning of every religious ceremony, and warned that this god might put obstacles in the way of that ceremony were he not honoured. Śiva himself performed the *abhiṣeka* which marked the installation of Gaṇeśa as the leader of the *gaṇas*, and he then also proclaimed him as his son.[116] We are told in the *Brahma Purāṇa* that,

---

[109] *Padma P.*, I.65.1-35.

[110] *MBh*, *Anuśāsana-parvan*, 151.26.

[111] *Ibid.*, 57.

[112] *Atharvaśiras*, 1.

[113] *Garuḍa P.*, I.100.1-17.

[114] *Mānavagṛhyasūtra*, II.14.

[115] Bhandarkar, *op.cit.*, p. 147.

in a sacrifice performed by the gods on the banks of the Gaṅgā, they first prayed to Vināyaka and consequently achieved their objects without hindrance.[117] In the *Tripuradāha* episode, Vināyaka is said to have pointed out to the gods that they were bound to meet with obstacles in their enterprise because they had failed to worship him with an offering of *modakas*.[118] Similarly on another occasion, when the gods set out to fight the demons without having first worshipped Gaṇeśa, Nandin warned them they were likely to encounter difficulties to do so; from this arose a description of the various details of the *Gaṇeśa-pūjā*.[119] Even Kārttikeya once became a victim of the anger of Gaṇeśa, who is said to have broken his tusk and attacked his brother. Their parents, however, interfered and brought about peace.[120]

In the *Purāṇas*, Gaṇeśa is represented as a great foe of demons. Traipura, who wanted to avenge his father's death, challenged Gaṇeśa to a combat. A severe battle followed in which Gaṇeśa was ultimately victorious.[121] Gajāsura, who had come to the assistance of Traipura, was also destroyed.[122] As a matter of fact, the tradition in the South makes this Gajāsura the chief enemy of Gaṇeśa, who is often described as having broken one of his tusks and used it as a weapon to destroy the demon. This episode, which is believed to have a Purāṇic background, is annually celebrated in South India through a religious dramatization.[123]

---

[116] *Varāha P.*, 23.19-38.

[117] *Brahma P.*, II.44.

[118] *Liṅga P.*, I.72.45-50.

[119] *Padma P.*, I.67.

[120] *Bhaviṣya P.*, I.24.1-51.

[121] *Padma P.*, I.76.

[122] Cf. "A South Indian legend gives another version of the absence of the tusk and accounts for the presence of the rat which usually accompanies Gaṇeśa: There was once a giant-demon with the face of an elephant unconquerable either by god or by man ... At their first encounter the giant-demon Gajamukhāsura broke off Gaṇeśa's right tusk, but Gaṇeśa caught his broken tusk and hurled it at the demon, who instantly turned into a rat, whereupon Gaṇeśa took him into his service as *vāhana*." Getty, *Gaṇeśa*, p. 15.

[123] See Ch. VI, p. 401.

Perhaps the most outstanding feature of Gaṇeśa is his wisdom. There was once arranged a competition between Gaṇeśa and Kārttikeya to find out which of them could go around the world in the shortest possible time. Kārttikeya mounted his peacock and set out immediately; Gaṇeśa, who was noted for his wisdom, quietly got up and walked around his parents. Circumambulating one's parents was always regarded as being as meritorious as circumambulating the whole world. Accordingly, Gaṇeśa was declared to have been the victor.[124]

As mentioned above, Gaṇeśa is the son of Śiva. As such, his image, as is often that of his brother Kārttikeya, is prominently installed and worshipped in almost all the temples dedicated to Śiva. But the rank assigned to him is a distinctly subordinate one. One also notices in South India the practice of worshipping this god under large trees in various parts of a village. Temples solely dedicated to this deity where he is installed as the chief god are also not wanting.[125] In such temples the *mūṣaka* takes the place of Nandin, and the same is chosen as the crest for his banner. According to the tradition of South India, Gaṇeśa is a bachelor; otherwise, Siddhi and Buddhi (the latter is also called Ṛddhi) are often mentioned as his wives.[126] Yet it is rare to come across instances where Gaṇeśa is being portrayed in the company of his two wives.

All the main features which characterize the later portrayal of this god, such as the elephant's head, four arms, three eyes (like his father), one tusk, a fondness for *modaka*, having a rat as his vehicle, etc., are clearly derived from the various Purāṇic accounts. For instance, the *Āgamas* have laid down the rules relating to the construction of the image of Gaṇeśa, which closely conform to the Purāṇic description.[127] The verses from the *Kāraṇa-Āgama* quoted below are

---

[124] *Padma P.*, V. 61.7-20.

[125] See Appendix 6, p. 551-552.

[126] *Siddhibuddhiyuto bhāti Gaṅgomābhyāṁ yathā śivaḥ* | *Gaṇeśa P.*, II.14; also *Siddhiparājaya*, *ibid.*, II.66, and *Buddhiparājaya*, II.65; *Śiva P.*, *Jñāna-saṁhitā*, 36.

[127] *Kāraṇa*, II.92.

quite significant in this connection. In them is made a reference to his human form, his head and ears which resemble those of an elephant, his prominent belly and huge body, his one tusk, his frightful eyes, his protruding lips, and the serpents used by him as *yajñopavīta* and *karaṇḍamakuṭa*. He is also described in these verses as wearing ornaments of various kinds, and wielding *aṅkuśa* and *danta* in the right hands and *pāśa* and *laḍḍuka* in the left. With his trunk, he snacks upon a *laḍḍuka* he carries in one hand:

Gaṇeśaṁ puruṣākāraṁ gajakarṇaṁ gajānanam |
Mahodaraṁ bṛhatkāyam ekadaṁsṭraṁ trilocanam ||
Raudraṇetraṁ tu laṁboṣṭhaṁ nāgayajñopavītinam |
Karaṇḍamakuṭopetaṁ sarvābharaṇabhūṣitam ||
Caṭurdordaṇḍasaṁyuktaṁ dakṣiṇe'ṅkuśadantadhṛk |
Pāśaṁ ca laḍḍukaṁ caiva vāmabhāge tu dhāriṇam ||
Karasthalaḍḍukenaiva gajahastāgrasaṁyutam | [128]

Gaṇeśa is Śiva's son. Presumably on account of this, the *Āgamas* assign to him many physical features of his father. We accordingly come across images of Gaṇeśa intended for installation and worship showing the god with five heads (each with the elephant's face) and ten arms, with two eyes per face. His complexion is red, and he has large ears, a big belly, a snake *yajñopavīta* and *karaṇḍamakuṭa*. The left leg hangs down and the right one is folded on the seat. In the image, the god is depicted as seated on the *padmāsana*. In his ten hands he holds the following ten objects: *danta*, *kuṭhāra*, *pāśa*, *cakra*, *musala*, *apūpa*, *ṭaṅkā*, *śūla*, *dhvaja*, and *musala*.[129] One face, sixteen arms, and an elephant's trunk in the middle of his face are mentioned as the distinctive features of yet another type of the image of Gaṇeśa prescribed for worship. In his arms the god is shown as holding *pāśa*, *aṅkuśa*, *kuṭhāra*, *bīja*, *daṇḍa*, *musala*, *ghaṇṭā*, *bhiṇḍipāla*, and *nāga*. With one hand he embraces his consort, who is depicted as being seated on his lap.[130] The commonest *mūrti*, prescribed by the *Āgama*,

[128] *Kāraṇa*, I.57.54-57. [129] *Ibid.*, II.92.2-7. [130] *Ibid.*, II.92.8-11.

however, has four arms and an elephant's face. Here, he has the complexion of the moon, and wields *pāśa*, *aṅkuśa*, *danta* and *āmra* respectively in his four arms.[131]

No other god among the ancillary deities in Śiva's religion can claim a wider popularity than Gaṇeśa, from the point of view of worship and ritual. It has been already pointed out that, as the god is specifically celebrated as the remover of obstacles, he must be invoked by the worshippers at the beginning of every undertaking.[132] In almost every *gṛhya* rites Gaṇeśa is invoked and prayed to for the removal of obstacles. After the performance of the *saṁkalpa*, however, he is implored to retire from the scene. It is after such an *udvāsana* that the rest of the ritual is continued and brought to perfection. All the religious rites described elsewhere in connection with the worship of Śiva are performed in honour of Gaṇeśa as well. Thus there is the usual offering of flowers, *naivedya*, *candana*, *dhūpa*, *dīpa*, and *nīrājana* made to that god. Generally speaking, when Gaṇeśa is installed as the main deity in the temple,[133] he is worshipped in the same way as is Śiva when the latter is the central deity. The necessary modifications are of course made, such as that the *mūṣaka* takes the place of Nandin, and the *aṅkuśa* replaces the *triśūla* of Śiva.

The coconut is the special offering that is made to Gaṇeśa.[134]

---

[131] *Ibid.*, II.92.12.

[132] Cf. *Vidyārthī labhate vidyāṁ dhanārthī vipulaṁ dhanam |*
Iṣṭakāmaṁ tu kāmārthī dharmārthī mokṣam akṣayam ||
Vidyārambhe vivāhe ca praveśe nirgame tathā |
Saṅgrāme saṅkaṭe caiva vighnas tasya na jāyate ||
Bṛhatstotraratnākara, pt. I, p. 29.

[133] The following remarks by Getty is relevant to the present context: "Temples were erected to him alone, with his *vāhana*, the rat, guarding the entrance as did Nandi, the bull, the temples dedicated to Śiva. The largest one built in honour of Gaṇeśa was a rock-cut temple near Trichinopoly known as Ucchi-pillayār kovil." Getty, *op.cit.*, p. 5.

[134] Cf. *Praharen nālikeraṁ tu gaṇeśanikaṭopale |*
Prādeśamātram aunnatyaṁ Tryaṁbakeṇa mantrataḥ ||
Ekaprahāramātreṇa dvibhāgaṁ samam udbhavet |
Kāraṇa, I, p. 335, verses 7-8.
Pages 334-336 describe in detail the method of offering the coconuts and the results which follow as a consequence.

This seems to be a characteristically South Indian custom. The coconut is broken before the god. When shattered thus, it is believed that the various obstacles in the way of the devotees also break in a similar manner.[135]

Gāṇapatya is often mentioned as the highest rank to which Śiva raises his devotees when found deserving a promotion.[136] In his *Śaṅkaradigvijaya*, Ānandagiri refers to six varieties of the *Gāṇapatya* sect.[137] The worship of *ucchiṣṭa-gaṇapati* is discussed in connection with Śaṅkara's attitude towards it. There is also mentioned a left-handed way of Gaṇeśa worship, which had presumably arisen in imitation of the *vāmamārga* of the Śāktites. An obscene form of Gāṇapati is chosen for this worship. No distinction of caste or sex is observed among the adherents of this sect. Like the Śāktites, the followers of this sect wear a red *tilaka* mark on their forehead. Śaṅkara is said to have denounced this form of worship as vehemently as he did the *vāma-mārga* of the worshippers of Śakti.

Kārttikeya (Fig. 19)

It may be presumed that the cult of Kārttikeya or the Kaumāra cult had once existed independently.[138] Kārttikeya is prominently mentioned in the *Rāmāyaṇa* and the *Mahābhārata*,[139] but, there, as in the *Purāṇas*, he is usually represented as the son of Śiva and as ancillary within the Śiva religion. Śaivism, especially Purāṇic Śaivism which is best reflected in the temple cults of the South, considers Skanda worship as one of its integral parts.[140] However, as will be

[135] When the coconut is broken, the pieces are studied by soothsayers with a view to foretelling the fortune of the devotee.

[136] *Liṅga P.*, I.100.1-52; I.93.1-26; *Matsya P.*, 95.35; *ibid.*,180.55-99; *Kūrma P.*, I.18.1-7; I.35.1-11.

[137] Bhandarkar, *op.cit.*, p. 149.

[138] Sukumar Sen suggests (*Indo Iranica* 4, p. 27) that Kumāra mentioned in *ṚV*, X.135, is the prototype of post-Vedic Kumāra and a counterpart of the Iranian Sraoṣa.

[139] In this respect, he is to be contrasted with Gaṇeśa, who figures rarely in the Epics.

[140] There is hardly any Śaiva temple of importance in South India, which has not assigned, in its system of worship, a significant place to Kārttikeya. This applies to Gaṇeśa as well.

Fig. 19: Subrahmanya, Hoysaleśvara Temple at Halebid.

shown afterwards, Kārttikeya does have his own special importance in the religious ideology of South India.

The Epics and the *Purāṇas* present elaborate but diverse versions of the account of the birth of Kārttikeya. The common motif in all these accounts is this: the gods were oppressed by the demons under the leadership of Tāraka. They therefore complained to Brahmā and sought his help in the matter of overcoming Tāraka. Brahmā told them that it was the son to be born to Śiva and Umā who alone would be capable of destroying the demon king; it was thereby necessary for the gods to bring about the marriage of Śiva and Umā. Madana, the god of love, was urged by the gods to bring Śiva, who was engaged in *samādhi*, under the spell of love and draw him towards Umā. Enraged at being disturbed from his *samādhi*, the great god burnt Madana to ashes, but the latter's mission was nevertheless successful and the union of Śiva and Umā did indeed materialize. The son for whom the gods were so anxiously waiting was at last born to the divine couple. This is the general outline of the legend of the birth of Kārttikeya; there are, however, several variations in the details. The *Skanda Purāṇa*, for instance, narrates the following legend. After their marriage, when Śiva and Umā were enjoying themselves privately, the gods urged Agni to enter their apartment and find out what was going on there. Thereupon Agni entered their bed chamber with the guise of a parrot. Greatly disturbed by his presence, Śiva cursed him that he would be the bearer of the semen which was about to be discharged; it would be Agni's responsibility to hold that semen until it matured. Umā, on her part, cursed the gods who had instigated Agni to cause the disturbance that they would be devoid of issue. This episode, which frequently occurs in the *Purāṇas*, seems to suggest in clear terms that Kārttikeya was not born from the womb of Umā, yet everywhere he claims to be her son. Agni received the *retas* of Śiva and carried it about for sometime, but being unable to bear that lustrous burden for a long time, he deposited it in Gaṅgā, at a spot overgrown with *śara* reeds. At last the child was born. The six Kṛttikās appeared on the scene and breastfed the baby, nurturing him with great care. Eventually Śiva and Umā came to that spot, embraced the child, and blessed him.[141] In this connection, the *Purāṇas* also tell us how Umā was fully engaged in severe *tapas* and could not suckle her own child Skanda, and how, on account of this, the goddess came to be known as *apītakucā*.[142]

According to another version, Kārttikeya was the son not of Śiva and Umā, but of Agni and Svāhā.[143] However, in that context, Agni is identified with Śiva and Svāhā with Umā.[144] Yet another version tells quite a different story about the birth of Kārttikeya. It speaks of six children, born separately, having been ultimately joined into one. Svāhā, the wife of Agni, was anxious to fulfil her husband's longfelt desire to unite with the wives of the seven sages. She, therefore, assumed the form of each of them, one by one, and cohabited with Agni, who had already received from Śiva his *retas*. However, Svāhā could do this only six times, because, when the turn came for her to impersonate Arundhatī, who was particularly noted for her chastity, she could not succeed.[145] Every time Svāhā united with Agni, the latter transferred Śiva's *retas* into her womb, but each time Svāhā discarded that *retas* in a place overgrown with *śara*-grass, resulting in six babies coming into being. They were later joined together and became Kārttikeya. Elsewhere in the *Skanda Purāṇa* we are told that, when the six Kṛttikās were in the proximity of Agni, the *retas* of Śiva, which Agni had been bearing, subtly entered their bodies. Out of fear of being suspected, they discharged it into Gaṅgā, which was full of *śara* reeds. There Ṣaṇmukha was ultimately born.[146]

A reference may be made at this stage to the account in the *Matsya Purāṇa* which compares the birth of Kārttikeya with the production of fire from *araṇis*.[147] An allegorical interpretation of the birth of Kārttikeya is given in another *Purāṇa*. Viṣṇu, identified with Śiva, is Puruṣa, and Umā, who is none other than Śrī, is Avyakta or Prakṛti.

[141] *Skanda P.*, I.2.29.
[142] *Ibid.*, I.3.2.21.
[143] *MBh*, III.220.
[144] *Ibid.*, III.217.5.
[145] *Skanda P.*, I.2.29.
[146] *Ibid.*, I.27.

From their union was produced Ahaṁkāra, and this was Kārttikeya. A strong need was felt at that time for the birth of such a god, for a leader had to be appointed to command the army of the gods.[148] The *Purāṇas* also mention that Brahmā and Viṣṇu were born respectively as Heraṁba and Ṣaḍānana,[149] thereby suggesting the identity of Kārttikeya with Viṣṇu.

The Epics and the *Purāṇas* present Kārttikeya as having six heads and twelve arms.[150] At one place, he is described to have divided himself into six forms, with a view to satisfying the maternal instinct of the six Kṛttikās, each of whom herself wanted to suckle the child.[151]

Elsewhere the god is said to have assumed four different forms to serve four different purposes. As Kumāra, he brought great joy to Śiva. As Viśākha, he was the sole delight of Umā. To Kuṭilā (Gaṅgā) and Agni, who also were in their own way responsible for his birth, he was Śākha and Naigameya respectively.[152] The picture of the god usually presented in the *Purāṇas* is that of a child or a youth. Skanda, even when only a child, could destroy the demon Tāraka. Based on this Purāṇic ideology, Skanda is often worshipped as a child, or as a hero endowed with youth and exquisite beauty. For the South Indians he is Murukan, an embodiment of beauty.[153]

The Epics and the *Purāṇas* have attributed to Kārttikeya the function of leading the army of the gods.[154] As has been mentioned earlier, the gods had no suitable commander to lead their army against the demons. Therefore, on the advice of Brahmā, they brought about the birth of Kārttikeya. The great pomp and pageantry which accompanied the installation of this god as the leader of the army are

---

[147] *Matsya P.*, 154.52-53.

[148] *Varāha P.*, 25.1-43.

[149] *Skanda P.*, I.3.2.17.

[150] *MBh*, III.214.1-21.

[151] *Brahmāṇḍa P.*, III.10.40-51.

[152] *Vāmana P.*, 57.1-59.

[153] *Matsya P.*, 158.39-41.

[154] *Vāmana P.*, 21.1-22; *ibid.*, 57.50-102; *Skanda P.*, I.2.30.

described in detail in the *Mahābhārata* [155] and *Purāṇas*. The *Mahābhārata* recounts how Indra offered to renounce his sovereignty and expressed his desire to install Skanda in his place as the king of the gods; Skanda declined the offer but readily consented to take the leadership of the army.[156] It is interesting to note that both sons of Śiva have been assigned more or less similar functions as leaders — one became *gaṇapati*, the leader of the *gaṇas* [157] and the other became *devasenāpati*, the commander of the gods' army.[158]

The various Purāṇic accounts about the god have contributed to the shaping of the popular present concept of the god, Skanda. *Śakti* is the special weapon of this god, and it was by means of this weapon that he vanquished the demon Tāraka.[159] It was, again, by means of *śakti* that he split the mountain Krauñca into two.[160] *Mayūra* is often mentioned as the vehicle of Skanda;[161] *Kukkuṭa* also is associated with him, sometimes as his vehicle.[162] In later mythology it was displayed as the crest on his banner. The goat also is connected with the god.[163] All these are mentioned in the *Purāṇas* as having been presented to Skanda when the gods celebrated his birth.

The various names by which Skanda is celebrated reflect the various features of his character and personality as depicted in the *Purāṇas*. The *retas* of Śiva borne by Agni was deposited in a pond in which *śara* grass grew in abundance; Kārttikeya was thus born in the *śaravaṇa*, and he accordingly came to be known as Śaravaṇabhava or Śarajanmā.[164] He was brought up by the six Kṛttikās and therefore received the name of Kārttikeya. He was also called Ṣāṇmātura

---

155 *MBh*, III.218.25.
156 *Ibid.*, III.218.21.
157 *Matsya P.*, 154.544-47; *Kūrma P.*, II.43.42.
158 *Brahmāṇḍa P.*, III.10.40-51.
159 *Vāyu P.*, I.54.24; *Matsya P.*, 160.1-25.
160 *Vāmana P.*, 58.1-21.
161 *Vāyu P.*, I.54.19.
162 *Varāha P.*, 24.1-45; as a toy: *Matsya P.*, 159. 4-11.
163 *Brahmāṇḍa P.*, III.10.40-51.
164 *Matsya P.*, 6.27.

because he was nurtured by the six Kṛttikās as mothers. Kṛttikāputra is another name of Kārttikeya.[165] When Agni was unable to bear the *retas* of Śiva and deposited it in the river Gaṅgā, the river retained it and the child was ultimately born from her. This accounts for Skanda's other name, Gāṅgeya.[166] Because six babies, originally born separately, were merged together into one (*skanna*), the god received his name Skanda.[167] The god is often described as having six faces, and is therefore, known as Ṣaṇmukha [168] or Ṣaḍānana. As a continuous source of delight to Pārvatī, he is Pārvatīnandana.[169] His names Agnibhū, Pāvakeya and Pāvaki point to the part played by Agni in the matter of the birth of this god.[170] Viśākha is another name which occurs in the *Purāṇa*.[171] He is Śikhivāhana because he rides on a peacock.[172] As the commander of the armies of the gods he is Mahāsena and Senānī.[173] Ascetics had their own way of propitiating the god by enshrining him in their heart; presumably on account of this the god received the name *guha*, which means 'the heart' in philosophical terminology.[174]

We come across two diametrically opposite pictures of Kārttikeya in the *Purāṇas*. One presents him as a bachelor god,[175] while the other presents him as a young hero married to two wives.[176] Both traditions are prevalent in the country. In Mahārāṣṭra, for instance, Kārttikeya is regarded as a confirmed bachelor. Even the mere appear-

---

[165] *Matsya P.*, 6.27.

[166] *MBh*, I.127.13.

[167] *Brahmāṇḍa P.*, III.10.40-51; *Rāmāyaṇa*, I.37.24-32.

[168] *Varāha P.*, 25.44-49; *Vāmana P.*, 57.46.

[169] *Vāyu P.*, I.54.20-21.

[170] *MBh*, I.127.13.

[171] *Matsya P.*, 6.26.; *ibid.*, 159.1-3; according to *Varāha P.*, 25.1-43, Śākha and Viśākha are his attendants.

[172] *Vāyu P.*, I.154.24.

[173] *Varāha P.*, 25.1-17; *Vāyu P.*, I.54.20.

[174] *Vāmana P.*, 58.1-121.

[175] *Brahma P.*, II.11.

[176] See below.

ance of women in his temples is strictly prohibited.[177] In contrast, in the temples of the South he is shown with two wives, Vallī and Devasenā. There are, however, some temples where the god is also depicted as a *saṁnyāsin*. The *Śiva Purāṇa* mentions Gajavallī as the wife of Skanda.[178] The *Purāṇas* and also the *Mahābhārata* describe Skanda's marriage with Devasenā in detail. Devasenā obviously represents a figurative personification of the army of the gods. As the leader of the gods, Indra is said to have given her in marriage to Kārttikeya.[179] The characterization of this god as a bachelor has also a Purāṇic background. The *Brahma Purāṇa*, for instance, narrates the following legend: Kumāra was deeply addicted to sensual pleasures and he often enjoyed the company of divine damsels. Once, however, he suddenly discovered in these damsels a resemblance to his mother; this recognition fundamentally changed his attitude towards women in general.[180]

About Skanda, Bhandarkar has made the following observation: "Another god whose worship was extensively practised in ancient times, but is now rare, is Skanda or Kārttikeya." [181] Obviously, inasmuch as South India is concerned, this observation is quite unwarranted. As a matter of fact, it may be pointed out that among the Hindu gods, Kārttikeya possibly claims the largest number of devotees in the South. The ancient Tamil literary works present us quite a wealth of information about this god.[182] In Tamil Nadu Kārttikeya is celebrated as Murukan, a name which denotes a youth with exquisite beauty. Being such an embodiment of beauty, Murukan is always regarded as a standard of comparison in that respect. This appellation has its equivalent in the Sanskrit name Kumāra; he is also known as Kumārasvāmin for this reason. Another name prominently ascribed

[177] Such is the rule, for instance, at the Kārttikeya temple on Pārvatī Hill near Poona.

[178] *Śiva P.*, *Kailāsa-saṁhitā*, 7.40 and 64.

[179] *Matsya P.*, 4. 11.

[180] *Brahma P.*, II.11.

[181] Bhandarkar, *op.cit.*, p. 150.

[182] See Appendix 3, p. 516.

to this god in the South is Vēlan, implying that he is a wielder of a lance; almost identical is the implication of the Sanskrit name Śaktidhara. He is Sēyōn, which means one of red complexion. He is the lord of *kuruñci* or mountainous regions. In this regard, it is significant that most of the temples exclusively assigned to this god are situated on hilltops. Curiously enough, Tamil literary works speak of young girls as being at times possessed by Murukan. Under such circumstances, the god was to be propitiated by magic spells. The same idea seems to be reflected in the reference to an evil spirit as a *skandagraha*.

In conformity with the Purāṇic portrayal of Skanda, the *Āgamas* and the *Kumāratantra* have prescribed the construction of the image of Kārttikeya in various poses for the purpose of installation and worship. Of these, the one portraying the god with six faces and twelve arms may be said to be the most significant. Provision is also made for images with six heads and two arms, another with one head and eight arms, and still another with one head and two arms.

The Ṣaṇmukha image, as the name implies, shows Skanda with six faces and twelve arms. His faces have two eyes each. The splendour of the moon and the thirty-two auspicious marks are displayed in the image. Both ankles are adorned with anklets. The peacock is displayed in the background. Ten out of the twelve arms are depicted as wielding the *śakti*, *śara*, *khaḍga*, *dhvaja*, *gadā*, *cāpa*, *kuliśa*, *kheṭaka*, *śūla*, and *paṅkaja* weapons. The other two hands are in the *abhaya* and the *varada* poses. The Ṣaṇmukha image is also shown as mounted on the peacock, whereby the left leg drops down, and the right one is folded at the knee and lies on his vehicle. The image portrayed on the *padmapīṭha* is in a standing pose with both feet placed evenly.[183] If six arms are featured, the weapons held in four of his hands are the *nāga*, *vajra*, *śakti* and arrow; the other two hands are in the *abhaya* and the *varada* poses.[184] The image with six faces and two arms is depicted as wielding the *vajra* and *śakti*. On the left is represented

[183] *Kāraṇa*, II. 93.2-5.

[184] *Ibid.*, verse 6.

Devasenā and on the right Vallī, both of whom are featured as carrying lotuses in their left and right hands respectively. The other two hands of these two consorts of the god are shown as hanging down.[185]

A mention may be made at this stage of a peculiar portrayal of the god which is fairly common in the South but which cannot be directly related to any Purāṇic tradition, wherein Skanda is presented as an ascetic, unattached to worldly life. A shaven head, a rosary, a staff, and coloured robes befitting a *saṁnyāsin* are the salient features of this image. Skanda is also featured in sculpture as *gurumūrti*, where he is shown as imparting higher knowledge to his father Śiva, who as a *śiṣya* sits at his feet with all the humility befitting a pupil.[186] Another representation peculiar to the South is based on the account which is given in the Tamil rendering of the *Skanda Purāṇa*, but which is not traceable in the original; therein Skanda is portrayed as chastising Brahmā, the creator, because the latter had failed to explain to him the meaning and significance of the *praṇava*.[187] Mention should also be made in this connection of the Somāskanda form of Śiva, already described.[188] Here, Skanda is depicted as a child in the company of Śiva and Umā.

The rituals performed in the worship of Kumāra are, for the most part, similar to those performed for the worship of Śiva, the difference lying only in the substitution of the appropriate subordinate deities and weapons. Nandin is thus replaced by *mayūra*, and the *triśūla* of Śiva is substituted by the *śakti* or a lance. That the worship of Skanda gained great popularity in the South — certainly greater than that of any other ancillary god of Śaivism — is indicated by the fact that only in connection with the worship of Skanda was an independent text needed for instructing worshippers about the various rituals. Apart from what is laid down in this *Tantra*, each temple of Skanda in the South has evolved its own tradition. The god enshrined in the temple

185 *Kāraṇa*, verses 9-12.

186 *Kantapurāṇam* (Tamil rendering in verse), *Ayanaicciraipuripaṭalam*, pp. 500-508.

187 *Ayanaicciraipuripaṭalam*, pp. 508-522.

188 Chapter V, pp. 284-285.

at Palani, for example, is presented as an ascetic, though neither the *Purāṇas* nor the *Tantras* support this.

One finds the worship of his *śakti* prevailing in some temples. This *śakti*, a weapon of Skanda shaped like a lance, is made of bronze or silver or gold and is installed in the place of the image of the god. The rituals relating to the installation and worship of the *śakti* and the treatment which this object of veneration receives clearly imply the complete identification of it with Skanda.

Nandin

The *Purāṇas* have assigned to Nandin a very prominent place among the ancillary deities of Śaivism. His importance is duly emphasized in the *Purāṇas* as well as in the scheme of entire Śaiva worship prevalent in the South. In every temple of Śiva, the images of Nandin are invariably installed. Some temples actually have more than one image of Nandin, and many of them are quite colossal. Nandin is almost always represented with the features of a bull, although he is sometimes also shown as having the face of a monkey. He himself explains that he had to assume the features of a monkey as the result of a curse uttered by Rāvaṇa.[189]

The *Rāmāyaṇa* and the *Purāṇas* refer to Nandin as a great devotee and attendant of Śiva, and he is presented in these works as devoutly discharging the function of guarding the entrance of the abode of Śiva.[190] Whenever the gods assembled at Kailāsa, they first approached Nandin and obtained his permission to enter into the inner abode of Śiva.[191]

Nandin is the leader of the *gaṇas*.[192] He is said to have led the army against the demon Vidyunmāli who ruled over the three cities.[193] Vīraka, a leader of the *gaṇas*, is separately mentioned in the *Purāṇas*.

---

189 *Rāmāyaṇa*, VII.16.13-22.

190 *Liṅga P.*, I.80.44.

191 *Ibid.*, I.80.

192 *Ibid.*, II.44.30-46; *Padma P.*, I.101.1-31.

193 *Matsya P.*, 155.1-63.

He was adopted by Śiva and Umā as their son, and was given a boon by Umā that he would be reborn as Nandin.[194] An account of the early life of Nandin before he became the chief of the *gaṇas* is recounted in the *Purāṇas*. Śilāda, who was a great devotee of Śiva, was practising penance. The god appeared before him as the result of his *tapas* and granted him a son who equaled him in all respects. Soon after, Śilāda found a child while he was ploughing the field. He took up the child and brought him up. The child learnt the *Vedas* and became a great devotee of Śiva. Once, when the boy was worshipping Śiva, he performed *japa* marked by the repetition of the name of Śiva ten million times. The god became manifest to him and asked him to choose a boon. The boy prayed to Śiva that he be granted enough strength to once again repeat the name of Śiva another ten million times. Each time the god appeared before him, he asked for the same boon. After this happened five times, Śiva was sufficiently pleased with his devotion to elevate him to the highest rank of the leader of the *gaṇas*. Thus he became not only *gaṇapati*, the leader of the *gaṇas*, but also the son of Umā. The *Liṅga Purāṇa* mentions Nandin as the son of Śilāda and relates how Śiva himself became manifest in that form.[195]

An elaborate description of Nandin's installation as the chief of the *gaṇas* is given in the *Purāṇas*.[196] All the gods assembled to grace the occasion. Brahmā himself is said to have performed the ceremony, and Viṣṇu to have assisted him.[197] Nandin's knowledge about Śiva and his religion was unequalled.[198] The sage Maṇikaṅkaṇa once requested him to proclaim to him the *Śiva-dharma* as taught in the *Āgamas*. Nandin's mastery over the *Āgamas* was perfect and he was often referred to as an authority on them.

---

[194] *Ibid*, 155.33-34; *Padma P.*, I.43.

[195] *Liṅga P.*, I.43; also *Kūrma P.*, II.43.

[196] *Kūrma P.*, II.43.19-42.

[197] *Liṅga P.*, I.44.30-46.

[198] *Liṅga P.*, II.20.13-15. Nandin is also said to have explained the details of Gaṇeśa-*pūjā* (*Padma P.*, I.67).

Other Ancillary Deities

Viṣṇu

Viṣṇu is sometimes installed as a subordinate deity in the temples of Śiva.[199] In this regard it is interesting to note that Śiva is never represented as an ancillary deity in Viṣṇu temples. The *Śaiva Āgamas* have laid down detailed rules regarding the installation of the image of Viṣṇu in the Śiva temples.[200] They have prescribed that the *garbha-gṛha* in which the image of Viṣṇu is to be installed should be constructed according to the Vaiṣṇava traditions. They further recommend the worship of Viṣṇu, in all such cases, being performed in the manner prescribed by the *Pāñcarātra Āgama* of the Vaiṣṇavites.[201] Representations of Viṣṇu are also displayed on the *gopuram*, walls, pillars, and domes of the temples of Śiva — the most prominent parts of these places being always reserved for the Śiva images, of course. In such portrayals of Viṣṇu, his position as a subordinate god — in receiving his *cakra* from Śiva, for instance — is invariably emphasized.

Brahmā

In the actual practice of worship prevalent in the Śiva temples, Brahmā has no place.[202] Nevertheless one does come across some representations of him in Śiva temples.[203] Of course, as in the case of Viṣṇu, Brahmā's position also is shown to be quite subordinate. His image enjoys little prominence, and is usually installed in one of the niches on the side walls of the central shrine of Śiva.

---

[199] For instances of such worship, see Appendix 6, p. 554.

[200] *Kāraṇa*, I.99. For rules regarding the installation of Lakṣmī, the consort of Viṣṇu, see chapter 100 of that *Āgama*.

[201] *Mayā saṁkṣepataḥ proktaṁviśesaṁ pāñcarātravat* |
Pāñcarātrakrameṇaiva homādīny āsamācaret ||
Kāraṇa, I.99.20.

"In short I have prescribed the special features as in the Pāñcarātra. One should perform *homa* and other rituals according to the course of Pāñcarātra."

[202] *Śiva P.*, *Vidyeśvara-saṁhitā*, 5 and 6.

[203] The temples at Tirukkaṇḍiyūr and Tiruppāṇḍikkoḍumudi in South India (see Appendix 6, pp. 529, 542), for instance, have images of Brahmā installed in them.

Caṇḍeśvara (Fig. 20)

The place of Caṇḍeśa in the temple worship of the Śaivites of the Southern tradition is as important as that of Gaṇeśa. Indeed, in several respects, Caṇḍeśa can be regarded as a regular counterpart of Gaṇeśa. Gaṇeśa is worshipped at the beginning of all rituals, while Caṇḍeśvara is worshipped at their end.[204] The former removes the obstacles in the way of the worshippers and helps them to perform their religious duties without let or hindrance; the latter helps them to enjoy the fruits of their religious performances.[205] Śiva himself is said [206] to have proclaimed that the worship offered to him would be ineffective if due obeisance was not paid to Caṇḍeśvara. To Caṇḍeśvara are to be offered the Śiva-*nirmālya*, the remnants of all that has been already offered to Śiva.[207] Because this god is always depicted as being fully engaged in meditation on Śiva, his worshippers approach him and clap their hands to draw his attention. The image of Caṇḍeśvara is installed in close proximity to the central shrine of the temple where Śiva is installed.

Sūrya and Candra

On either side of the inner main entrance are installed the images of Sūrya and Candra. These are installed in such a manner that the

---

[204] *Agni P.*, 76.

[205] The following invocation is made to Caṇḍeśa at the end of the *Śivapūjā*:
Jñānato'jñānato vāpi yannyūnādi kṛtaṁ mayā |
Tatsarvaṁ pūrṇam evāstu sutṛpto bhava sarvadā ||
Yāvat tisthati gehe'smin devadevo maheśvaraḥ |
Tāvat kālaṁ tvayā deva sthātavyaṁ śivasannidhau ||
Śivaliṅgapratiṣṭhāvidhi, II, p. 386.
"That which is missing etc., being committed by me consciously or unconsciously, may all that be completed. Be always well-satisfied. As long as the god of gods Maheśvara stays in this temple, you must stay, o God, in the presence of Śiva."

[206] *Śiva P.*, *Kailāsa-saṁhitā*, 7.12.

[207] Cf. *Kāraṇa*, I.59.230:
Caṇḍeśaṁ pūjayitvā tu nirmālyaṁ tu nivedayet.
"After worshipping Caṇḍeśa, one should offer him the remnants of offerings."
See also *Agni P.*, 76.

Fig. 20: Caṇḍeśvara, Bṛhadīśvara Temple at Gangaikondacolapuram.

two deities are made to face Śiva. The main *pūjā* of the day begins with the worship of Sūrya, and that of the night with that of Candra.

Bhairava

Bhairava is assigned a place by the side of the outer main entrance. This deity is believed to act as the watchman of the temple. He is shown naked and has a dog for his vehicle. The representation of Bhairava is usually characterized by a predominantly frightful aspect.[208]

Jyeṣṭhā

The goddess Jyeṣṭhā is the veritable embodiment of bad luck, misery and poverty, and is always depicted as possessing undesirable characteristics. She too has a place assigned to her in Śiva temples; this is invariably a deserted corner of the temple. Jyeṣṭhā is believed to be the elder sister of Śrī, the goddess of wealth, and is usually shown by the side of the latter. It is believed that the wealth of those who censure Śiva passes on to Jyeṣṭhā.[209]

Navagraha

The worship of the nine planets possesses much significance in Śaiva ritualism. These planets (Sūrya, Śani, Candra, Budha, Śukra, Maṅgala, Bṛhaspati, Rāhu and Ketu) known as the Navagrahas have a distinct place assigned to them in the temples of Śiva.[210] Devotees

---

[208] *Nīlanibhavedakaravahninayanaṁ syāc*
Chūlakapālaḍamarupāśakaradharam
Nagnanīlaśunavāhanakiṅkiṇī
Vibhūṣyam ūrdhvagatikeśadharasarpadharaḥ
Kāraṇa I. 103.64.

"He should be of dark colour, having four arms, with three eyes, holding a pique, a skull, a drum and a noose, naked, with a black dog as mount, decorated with small bells, with uprising hair, holding serpents."

[209] *Liṅga P.*, II.6.85-88. See also verses 12-29 in that chapter.

[210] In the Śiva temples at Tiruṭṭeṅkūr and Tiruvallam in South India, the worship of the Navagrahas is particularly prominent. The nine *grahas* are celebrated individually in some other temples also. For *pratimālakṣaṇa* of the *navagrahas*, see *Agni P.*, 51.

often worship them to avert any evil influence which they would otherwise display. The status of these planetary deities is sometimes greatly elevated as the result of their being identified with gods of a high rank. For instance, Aṅgāraka (Maṅgala) is identified with Skanda, Budha with Nārāyaṇa, and so on. *Navagraha-pūjā* and *Navagraha-homa* are mentioned in the *Purāṇas*.[211] It is said that the planets were installed for worship by the great gods Brahmā and Śiva themselves.[212] The worship of the planets has found a definite place even in the present system of ritual in the Śiva temples; for instance, the *Navagrahamakha* is one of the preliminary rites of the *pratiṣṭhā* ritual.[213]

The Devotees of Śiva, Śivabhakta (Fig. 21)

The ritual of Śaiva temples in the South is greatly enriched through the incorporation into it of the worship of mortal devotees of Śiva, who were more or less deified. The exclusive basis of this worship is a Tamil *Purāṇa* entitled *Periyapurāṇam* which is also noted for its literary merits, and contains the accounts of sixty-three saints, all of whom hail from the South. These Nāyanmārs belonged to different castes — some of them even to the lowest. The life of each of these saints is depicted in the *Purāṇa* as having been distinguished by some deed characterized by great religious merit and deep devotion to Śiva. The images of these saints are installed for worship in the places expressly assigned to them in the temples.[214]

Reference may now be made to a few other ancillary deities of the Śaiva religion whose images are never installed for worship in the Śaiva temples, but who, all the same, have a distinctive place assigned to them in the system of Śaiva ritual. These mostly comprise the *āvaraṇa-devatās*, and their presence is always to be mentally assumed at the time of worship. Among them are Ananta, Sūkṣma,

---

[211] *Matsya P.*, 93.

[212] *Liṅga P.*, I.60.1-6; also verses 38-39.

[213] *Śivaliṅgapratiṣṭhāvidhi*, II, p. 60-81.

[214] See Appendix 2, p. 510, App. 3, pp. 513-516, App. 6, p. 523 (no. 12), 545 (no. 225).

Fig. 21: Śivabhakta, Amṛtaghaṭeśvara Temple at Melakadambur.

Śivottama, Ekanetra, Ekarudra, Trimūrti, Śrīkaṇṭha, Śikhaṇḍin, Nandin, Mahākāla, Bhṛṅgin, Vināyaka, Vṛṣabha, Skanda, Devī, and Caṇḍa. The eight *dikpālakas* (Indra, Agni, Yama, Nirṛti, Varuṇa, Vāyu, Kubera and Īśāna) also fall within this category. Further, the weapons of these eight gods along with those of Brahmā and Viṣṇu are deified and included in the list of the *āvaraṇa-devatās*. Whenever these deities are invoked over the course of the ritual, the *dhyānaśloka* gives a detailed description of each to facilitate the worshipper's ability to meditate on them, as they are not usually prominently depicted in sculptural representations.

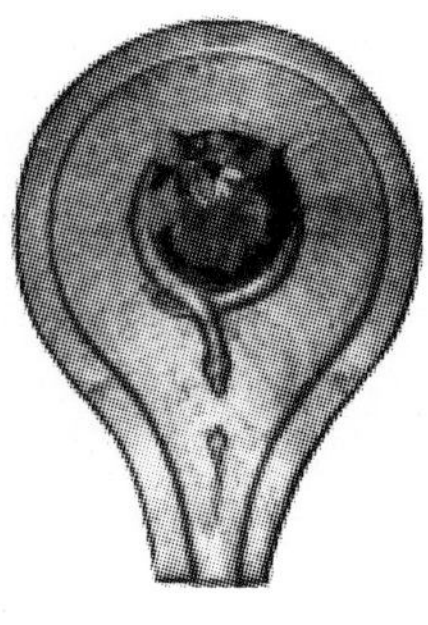

Appendix 1

A Brief Account of a Few Texts Mentioned in this Work

Some editions of these texts are printed in the *nagarī* script. Those in the *grantha lipi* are not easily available.

Āgamas

Āgamas are Śaivite texts, said to have been written by Śiva himself soon after the creation of the world. Each *Āgama* has a number of *Upāgamas*. The dates assigned to these religious texts by scholars vary from the first to the seventh century AD. According to Schomerus,[1] the *Āgamas* were used by Tirumūlar and other Tamil poets as far back as the first or the second century AD, and therefore must have originated in the early years before the common era. The generally accepted view, however, is that these poets actually belonged to the seventh or eighth century AD. In the Kailāsanātha temple of Kanchipuram we have the earliest inscriptional record of the twenty-eight *Āgamas*, in which the Pallava king Rajasimhavarman affirms his faith. That inscription is said to belong to the end of the sixth century AD.

These are the twenty-eight *Āgamas*:

1. Kāmika
2. Yogaja
3. Cintya
4. Kāraṇa
5. Ajita
6. Dīpta
7. Sūkṣma
8. Sahasra

[1] Winternitz, *HIL*, vol. I, p. 588. fn. 2.

9. Amśumān
10. Suprabheda
11. Vijaya
12. Niśvāsa
13. Svāyambhuva
14. Āgneya
15. Vīra
16. Raurava
17. Makuṭa
18. Vimala
19. Candrajñāna
20. Mukhabimba
21. Prodgīta
22. Lalita
23. Cintya
24. Santāna
25. Sarvokta
26. Pārameśvara
27. Kiraṇa
28. Vātula

Among these, the best known are the *Kāraṇa* and the *Kāmika Āgamas*.

Available in print are only a few *Upāgamas*, like the *Mṛgendra*, *Pauṣkara*, *Matangapārameśvara*, *Rauravottara*, *Sārdhatriśatī*, *Kālottara*, as well as the main *Āgamas*: the whole of the *Kāraṇa*, *Kāmika*, *Kiraṇa*, *Ajita*, *Raurava* and *Suprabheda Āgamas*. Of the other *Āgamas*, a few have survived in fragments, but many parts are entirely lost to us.

In the present work, we have often spoken of the traditional religious practices of south India, and the principal authority for this has always been the *Āgamas*. These works contain detailed account of the rituals, and it is to these works that any adherent of Śaivism look to for guidance when in doubt.

Every temple of the South conforms to the rules laid down in the *Āgamas*. These rules relate to the various details regarding the temple, its images, and the rites performed daily and on special occasions.

The information in the *Āgamas* is arranged under the following four headings: *Caryā*, *Kriyā*, *Yoga*, and *Jñāna*, and they are always discussed in this exact order. If this order is adhered to, the process is known as *saṁhāramārga*; the reverse order is called the *sṛṣṭimārga*. Every *Āgama*, however, does not deal with all these four topics as a rule; each *Āgama* is noted for the specific examination of one of these topics. In the *Kāraṇa* and the *Kāmika*, only the *kriyā* (that is, the second of the four topics) is discussed in detail; it is for this reason that we had to depend more particularly on these two works. The *Suprabheda* deals with all four topics, but this *Āgama*, as it has become available to us, is of a small size. *Raurava* and *Ajita* have less details than *Kāmika* and *Kāraṇa*. *Mṛgendra* and *Matangapārameśvara* do not deal with temple rituals. The various topics falling under *kriyā* are divided into four categories, *karṣaṇa*, *pratiṣṭhā*, *utsava* and *prāyaścitta*.

Paddhatis

The *Paddhatis* are ranked next in importance to the *Āgamas*. These are handy manuals of Śaiva ritual practice. They were obviously to serve the needs of the Śaiva worshippers. The *Āgamas* deal with the rituals in great detail, but the information relating to the various rites given in them is not likely to be accessible to the worshipper. The *Paddhatis*, therefore, cater to the needs of such worshippers by giving only the *prayoga* of the application of the rules rather than a detailed account of everything that concerns the rite in question. As mentioned above, the authorship of the *Āgamas* is traditionally ascribed to Śiva himself. The creation of *Paddhatis*, on the other hand, is attributed to human authors. Pious men with considerable ritual experience are said to have composed the *Paddhatis* for the benefit of the Śaiva devotees. All the material is derived from the *Āgamas* themselves, but it is rearranged in a more practical form. There is no doubt that the *Paddhatis* are governed by the *Āgamas*. They only indicate the actual form (*Paddhati*) to the worshipper. Among the *Paddhatis* now available, the *Somaśambhu-paddhati*, the *Īśānaśivagurudevapaddhati*, the *Rāmanāthapaddhati*, the *Īśānaśivācāryapaddhati*, the *Sadyojātaśivācāryapaddhati* and the *Aghoraśivācāryapaddhati* enjoy wide currency across the country.[2] In the present work, however, we have quoted profusely from the *Śivaliṅgapratiṣṭhāvidhi*.

[2] For a complete list of the *Paddhatis* see above p. 355.

Kumāratantra

This is actually a miniature *Āgama*, for though this work does not get the appellation *Āgama*, it bears all its characteristics in a small scale. The *Kumāratantra* deals with the worship of *Kārttikeya*, and is generally classed with *tantra* works. However, it should not be confused with the *Śākta Tantras*. Though in the *Kumāratantra* we have a work dealing with the worship of one of the ancillary deities of the Śaiva religion, we do not find similar works dealing with the worship of Devī or of Gaṇeśa. As far as the worship of these other deities is concerned, we have to depend on what the Śaiva *Āgamas* themselves have to say on the subject. The *Kumāratantra* consists of fifty-one chapters. Among the topics discussed in this work are *mantra, śauca, snapana, nityapūjā, naivedya, agnikārya, kuṇḍa, maṇḍala, dīkṣā, utsava, prāyaścitta, jīrṇoddhāra, vāstuśānti, pratimālakṣaṇa, garbhanyāsa, tailābhiṣeka, aṇkurārpaṇa*, as well as the rites relating to the installation of Mahāvallī and Devasenā.

Appendix 2

Śiva and his Ancillary Deities as Depicted in the Ancient Tamil Works

The ancient literary works in Tamil clearly indicate in what form the religion of Śiva had once been prevalent among the Tamils. An attempt is therefore made to summarize the typical descriptions which are found scattered in those works.

Śiva

The *Tolkāppiyam* is considered to be the oldest work available in the Tamil language. Though a treatise on grammar, occasional references are made in it to the religious faiths that were prevalent at the time of its composition. Murukan, Koṟṟavai, Kaṇṇan, Initiran and Varuṇan are the five gods mentioned; the absence of Śiva is conspicuous.

The collection of eight major works called *Eṭṭuttokai* and the ten songs called *Pattuppāṭṭu*, both of which are assigned to the Saṅgam period, are the oldest poems available in Tamil. References are found in these works to Śiva, but the name Śiva as such does not occur in them. References are made to the matted hair of the god, his three eyes, and his blue neck. He is the ancient one, and has assigned one half of his body to the blue-complexioned damsel (Umā). He carries a cloud on his head. He rides a bull. He is also described as being seated under a banyan tree. He wears the *konṟai* flowers in his matted hair, as well as the crescent moon and the river Gaṅgā. The *Vedas* reside in his mouth, and he taught them to the brāhmaṇas. He is eight-armed and is clad in the skin of a tiger. He performs *tapas*. He is the protector of all beings and the destroyer of the three worlds.

He covers his body with ash. He performs the dance of destruction called *koṭukoṭṭi*, and the dance called *Pāṇṭaraṅgam* was also performed by him when he destroyed the three worlds. He carries the *kapāla* of Brahmā in his hands, and performs the dance called *Kāpāla*. Himavat is his mountain abode.

The absence in these works of even the slightest indirect hint of *liṅga* worship deserves to be noted. The *Cilappatikāram* and *Maṇimēkalai* make positive references to Śiva. Among the gods mentioned in these works, Śiva occupies a prominent place. He is distinguished as the one with an eye on his forehead, and as the one free from birth. The *Cilappatikāram* refers to Ceran Ceṅkuṭṭuvan as a devotee of Śiva. The word 'Śaivam' occurs only once in the *Maṇimekalai.*

In the literary works of the subsequent Pallava and Chola periods, we see the Śaiva religion portrayed in its most developed form. The literature of these periods, the contents of the *Tirumuṛai* in particular, present to us an elaborate picture of this Śaivism. The Nāyanmārs who propagated the Śaiva faith during this time were responsible for the prosperous conditions under which Śaivism flourished. The connections which the Śaivism taught by these religious teachers maintained with the *Purāṇas* are given in Appendix 3. Through the colosssal temples they built, the Pallavas and their successors gave a prominent expression to what these Nāyanmārs actually taught, by representing Śiva and the ancillary deities as reflecting the descriptions and portrayals presented in the devotional literary works they had written.

Śakti

Like Śiva, Śakti is not assigned any distinctive place in the ancient system of worship as revealed in the ancient Tamil works.

Śakti is referred into ancient poems as Koṟṟavai. She is the goddess of victory, celebrated as the mother of Murukan. Heroes pay her homage on the eve of their departure to the battlefield. *Balis* were offered to her on such occasions in order to win her favour.

Gaṇeśa

In light of the available literary evidence, the worship of Gaṇeśa does not seem to have had early provenance in the Tamil country. Vināyaka cannot, accordingly, be proclaimed to be a Tamil god. Murukan had found a distinctive place in the Sangaṁ works, but not Gaṇeśa. The worship of Gaṇeśa is widely prevalent among the people of Maharashtra. This country was ruled by the Cāḷukyas while the Tamil country was governed by the Pallavas. When Ciṟuttoṇḍar, a Tamil chieftain, took Vātāpi, the capital of the Cāḷukyas, he must have brought this new god along with him when he returned to his country. The god was installed for worship and his temples received the name Kaṇapatīccuram. This is presumably the god who finds mention in the *Tēvāram* songs of Saṁpantar. Gaṇeśa is represented in the later Tamil works as the son of Śiva and Umā. He is the leader of the *gaṇas* and the remover of obstacles. He is always worshipped first. Every Śiva temple in the South has assigned a separate shrine for this god.

Murukan or Kārttikeya

Murukan is presented in Tamil literature as the lord of the land known as Kuriñci. This includes the mountainous regions of the Tamil land. Murugan is depicted as a great hero. Koṟṟavai is his mother. He wears the garland of *kaṭaṁpam* leaves and flowers. He is warlike. His anger is proverbial, for it always constitutes the standard comparison employed while describing the anger to which a warrior king is roused in the peak of battle. In the Saṅgam works, the very word *muruku* stands for the god. That word is interpreted by commentators to mean both divinity and beauty. Lovesick girls are described as being possessed by Murukan. Raising a rooster banner smeared with ghee and mustard, girls offer garlands and burnt incense to Murukan. They also offer him oblations of balls of cooked rice smeared with goat's blood.

The Murukan presented in the *Tirumurukāṟṟuppaṭai* shows a close likeness to the Kārttikeya described in the Epics and the *Purāṇas*.

Likewise is the picture given in the *Paripāṭal*. This work describes him as the child of the six Kṛttikā deities. He is said to have vanquished the demon Sūran. He is portrayed as a child with twelve arms, and also as the commander of the armies of the gods. Sometimes, he is said to be the chief of the three gods. He is the husband of Vallī and Devasenā. The *Tirumurukāṟṟuppaṭai* says that Murukan is the son of the god seated under the banyan tree (Śiva). The peacock is the emblem on his banner. Below is reproduced in translation an extract which contains characteristic descriptions of the god: "In the minds of the sages who, with unfaltering devotion, follow their own life, visions arise of his glorious faces. One face spreads afar rays of light, perfectly illuminating the world's dense darkness; one face with gracious love grants the prayers of his beloved devotees; one face watches over the sacrificial rites of the peaceful ones who fall not from the path of the scriptures; one face searches and pleasantly expounds upon hidden meanings, illumining every quarter like the moon; one face with overwhelming countenance and impartial wrath, cleanses the field of his foes and celebrates sacrifice; one face dwells, smiling, with the slender-waisted Vedda maid, the pure-hearted Valli." [3]

Viṣṇu

The protector god Viṣṇu is known in ancient Tamil works as Māl, Tirumāl and Māyon. The name Viṣṇu does not occur in the ancient Tamil works, but the descriptions of Māyon and Tirumāl easily lead us to the conclusion that it is Viṣṇu who is indicated by these descriptions.

His complexion is spotlessly blue. He carries a banner with the *garuḍa* as its emblem on it. He carries *śaṅkha* and *cakra*. On his breast he bears the goddess of fortune. He has also the mark *śrīvatsa* on his chest. He is pictured as reclining on a serpent couch. He has given birth to the god with four heads. He also measured the three worlds with three steps.

---

[3] Aruṇacalam, *op. cit.*, pp. 141 f.

Appendix 3

Some Purāṇic Episodes Relating to Śiva which Are Mentioned in the Tēvāram Texts

The literary works of the Saṅgam period present the god Śiva as possessing qualities and features which are akin to those that are ascribed to him in the Epics and the *Purāṇas*. During the Pallava regime, Śaivism flourished to a remarkable extent. The great religious teachers known as Nāyanmārs lived during that period. Their service to Śaivism is unparalleled, for without their devoted efforts, the religion would have been overpowered by Buddhism and Jainism. These Nāyanmārs have composed the *Tēvārams*, hymns in honour of Śiva. These were composed on various occasions, mostly during their pilgrimages to places of religious importance. They were marked by the glorification of Śiva as a performer of various exploits — each of these being associated with some locality in the South. Most of these exploits are derived from the *Purāṇas*. It is from the Nāyanmārs that we hear for the first time of such associations of Purāṇic episodes with shrines in south India. This gave rise to the belief that these episodes actually ocurred in these very places. A few relevant references from the *Tēvāram* are given below:

Śiva sharing half his body with Umā

(Sampantar) I.97.2; III.35.6; II.87.3.

(Appar) IV.2.7; IV.6.3; IV.8.2; IV.8.10; IV.22.6; IV.40.3: IV.40.9; IV.73.1; IV.103.2.

Śiva sharing half his body with Viṣṇu

(Sampantar) I.97.2; II.87.3; III.35.6.

(Appar) IV.22.4; IV.24.7; IV.37.7; IV.43.7; IV.40.5; IV.66.8; IV.78.7.

Śiva having a thousand names

(Saṁpantar) I.56.11; II.59.2; II.94.5; III.7.5; III.26.5; III.27.7.

(Appar) IV.4.8; V.65.1; VI.21.8.

The destruction of Kāma

(Saṁpantar) I.66.3; III.103.2.

(Appar)IV.68.3;IV.102.5;VI.36.10; VI.8.4; V.63.9; VI.69.4.

Wearing the skin of an elephant

(Saṁpantar) I.75.1.

(Appar) IV.73.6.

The destruction of Jalandhara

(Saṁpantar) III.122.2.

(Appar) VI.54.1.

The destruction of Dakṣa's sacrifice

(Saṁpantar) I.20.3; I.131.3; III.118.5; III.33.3.

(Appar) VI.96.9.

The destruction of the three cities

(Saṁpantar) I.11.6; I.11.7; I.69.1.

(Appar) V.72.5; VI.64.4; VI.86.9.

Drinking the world-poison

(Saṁpantar) I.22.1.

(Appar) IV.65.2; V.33.6; VI.99.2.

Śiva grants the *cakra* to Viṣṇu in exchange for his eye

(Sampantar) III.119.7.

(Appar) IV.14.10; IV.49.5

Granting longevity to Mārkaṇḍeya

(Sundarar) VII.1.63; VII.1.243.

(Saṁpantar) I.20.7.

(Appar) IV.14.6; IV.31.9; IV.49; IV.64.1.

Cutting off Brahmā's head
(Saṁpantar) I.30.7; I.131.7.

Brahmā and Viṣṇu searching for Śiva
(Saṁpantar) I.48.9.

Granting boons to Viṣṇu as Varāha
(Saṁpantar) I.21.7.

Favouring Bhagīratha with Gaṅgā
(Saṁpantar) III.69.6.
(Suntarar) VII.7.5.

Granting boons to Nandin
(Appar) VI.41.5.

Granting the Pāśupata weapon to Arjuna
(Saṁpantar) I.20.6; I.48.6; I.62.5.
(Appar) IV.7.10; IV.50.1;VI.83.5
(Suntarar) VI.2.154; VII.4.64; VII.6.119; VII.7.2444.

Appearing as a child of Pārvatī
(Appar) IV.88.1.

Śiva as a dancer
(Appar) IV.3.6; IV.2.8; IV.68.8; V.85.2; VI.4.5; VI.44.5.

Śiva performs the five acts
(Appar) IV.4.2; VI.11.5; VI.23.8;
(*Pañcakṛtya*) VI.44.1; VI.44.4.

Śiva's eight great achievements and the places concerned
(Appar) VI.71.2.

Śiva blesses Paraśurāma
(Suntarar) VII.3.150.

Śiva grants a boon and a sword to Rāvaṇa
(Saṁpantar) II.63.8.

(Appar) IV.14.11; V.87.10; VI.79.10.

Śiva frees Rāma from *brahmahatyā*
(Saṁpantar) III.10.2.

Upamanyu giving milk
(Saṁpantar) II.65.9.
(Appar) IV.107.6; V.65.6.

References to Gaṇeśa
(Saṁpantar) I.115.2; I.123.5; II.96.3.
(Appar). IV.2.5; VI.13.10; VI.53.4; VI.65.9; VI.74.7; VI.77.8.

References to Murukan (Kārttikeya)
(Saṁpantar) I.12.20; I.115.3; II.62.1; II.63.6; II.73.1; II.74.6; II.87.2; II.115.9; III.35.6; III.113.1.
(Appar) IV.18.6; IV.43.2;IV.43.8; IV.60.3; IV.75.4; IV.104.5; V.16.7; V.19.9; V.64.10; V.84.6; VI.32.1; VI.5.10; VI.6.1; VI.13; VI.18.4; VI.23.4; VI.42.6; VI.53.6; VI.65.9; VI.74.7; VI.75.7; VI.89.2.

APPENDIX 4

THE PURĀṆAS AND THE SOUTH

Among the languages spoken in India today, Tamil seems to have once shown a special predilection towards *Purāṇa*-styled compositions. Consequently, no language in India can boast of a richer collection of Purāṇic works than Tamil. As a matter of fact, the number of the *Purāṇas* written in Tamil exceeds the number of those originally composed in Sanskrit. From among the eighteen principal *Purāṇas* in Sanskrit, there is hardly one which can claim to display all the five traditional *lakṣaṇas* of a *Purāṇa*, namely *sarga*, *pratisarga*, *vaṁśa*, *manvantara* and *vaṁsānucarita.* The Tamil authors have faithfully followed the Sanskrit model, accordingly, the Tamil *Purāṇas* also have failed to strictly conform to the definition of *pañcalakṣaṇa.*

The Tamil *Purāṇas* may be classified into two types. To the first type belong the *Purāṇas* which are free renderings — either in prose or verse, but usually in verse — of the Sanskrit originals. The other type of *Purāṇas* is of an entirely independent origin. For instance, the Tamil *Kantapurāṇam* belongs to the first category, as it is only an adapted rendering of one section of the Sanskrit *Skanda Purāṇa.* Composed in verse, it is a free rendering which differs in many details from the Sanskrit original. The *Periyapurāṇam*, on the other hand, is completely original, and is composed to celebrate the glorious deeds of the Śaiva saints of the South. The work is full of literary embellishments, and is rightly regarded as a model of *kāvya.* The case of the *Tiruviḷaiyāṭal Purāṇam* is peculiar. This Tamil work narrates in glorious terms the deeds of Śiva enshrined in the temple at Madura. Over time, it was rendered into Sanskrit so that it should gain a wider recognition. The Sanskrit rendering is known as *Hālāsyamāhātmya.*

The study of the Tamil Purāṇic literature is a field which has not been fully explored; as such, it is not possible to give a complete account of all the *Purāṇas* composed in Tamil. A list of a few *Purāṇas* which can claim wide currency is, however, given below:

Periya-Purāṇam
Tiruvilaiyāṭal-Purāṇam
Kanta-Purāṇam
Kāñcī-Purāṇam
Taṇikai-Purāṇam
Śivarāttiri-Purāṇam
Śiva-Purāṇam
Tiruvātavūraṭikaḷ-Purāṇam
Sētu-Purāṇam
Koyiṛpurāṇam
Tirukkuṭantai-Purāṇam
Dakṣiṇakailāsa-Purāṇam
Tirunākaikkāroṇa-Purāṇam
Tiruvārūr-Purāṇam
Tiruttaṇikai-Purāṇam
Tiruccentūr-Purāṇam
Viṣṇu-Purāṇam
Vināyaka-Purāṇam
Śrī-Purāṇam
Brahmottarakāṇṭam
Kāśikāṇḍam

It must be repeated that this list is certainly not exhaustive; perhaps it is not even thoroughly representative. In certain parts of the South the tradition still prevails of competent *paurāṇikas* who give recitals and expositions of the *Purāṇas* before a gathering of devotees. Mention may also be made in this regard of the fact that, besides these works, each temple in south India has its own private Purāṇa which goes by the designation *Sthala-Purāṇa.*

Appendix 5

Temple-Building in South India

The art of building temples had developed to a remarkable extent in south India. The colossal temples of the South with their tall *gopurams* and pinnacles of the central shrines are distinctive representatives of temple architecture in India. The Tamils seem to have been interested in the art of temple building from very early times. The descriptions in the Saṅgam works are very significant in this regard. The *Cilappatikāram* makes positive references to temples. The achievement of the Pallavas in this field is outstanding. It was during their regime that a distinct pattern of temple architecture had evolved. Before the time of the Pallavas, materials such as bricks, lime, timber and various metals were used for building purposes. In an inscription dated 615 AD, the Pallava Mahendra claims to have built a stone temple. The Cholas who succeeded the Pallavas (AD 900-1300) also had made very remarkable contributions to the art of building temples. To them goes the credit of replacing old temples with new ones built exclusively from granite stones. They not only repaired old temples in this manner, but also expanded their size.

The nucleus of the structure of the temple is the central shrine. At first this shrine would be encircled by an outer wall. Extensions began to be added in stages, resulting in both enlargement of the structure and in the enrichment of the fortunes of the ancillary deities. For instance, the image of the goddess (which originally had found a place in the same shrine as Śiva) began to be installed in a separate shrine; the same happened in the case of Gaṇeśa and Kārttikeya. Caṇḍeśa also got a shrine for himself outside the central shrine. This was ultimately followed by the assignment of either separate rooms or specified places to all the ancillary deities, including Sūrya, Candra, and even Jyeṣṭhā.

Great elaboration began to characterize the *stūpa* or the *vimāna* erected atop the central shrine. Over time, *gopurams* were constructed in such a way that they surpassed the *vimānas* in height. Parks were laid and tanks were constructed in the vicinity of the temple, and huge walls were built around the temple providing for paths and roads. *Maṇḍapas* came to be added according to need.

It may be pointed out that the kings of old were not content merely by building temples of this calibre; they also made adequate provisions for their proper maintenance.

Appendix 6

Śiva Temples in South India

Name & Location of the Temple
Names of the god & goddess
Tīrtha and Tree
Comments, Purāṇic or otherwise, if any.

1. **Akattiyānpaḷḷi** (close to Vedāranyam)
   Akattīccurar Pakaṁpiriyānāyaki
   Agnitīrtha
   The place where Śiva is said to have revealed himself as Kalyāṇasundara to Agastya.

2. **Acciṛupākkam** (59 miles away from Madras)
   Pakkapureśar Sundaranāyakī
   Devatīrtha Konṛai
   When Śiva set out to destroy the three cities, the devas failed to worship Gaṇeśa. As a result, the axle of the chariot in which Śiva rode broke here.

3. **Añcaikkaḷam** (about 15 miles from Coranur Railway Station)
   Añcaikkaḷattīccurar Umaiyammai
   Śivagaṅgai
   Paraśurāma is said to have worshipped in this temple to wipe off the sin incurred by the murder of his mother.

4. **Aṇṇāmalai** (42 miles from Viluppuram Railway Station)
   Aruṇācaleśvarar Uṇṇāmulai
   Brahmatīrtha Makiḷ
   Brahmā and Viṣṇu are said to have searched here for the top and bottom of the tejoliṅga of Śiva.

5. **Atikai** (close to Panrutti Railway Station)
Vīraṭṭeśvarar Tripurasundarī
Keṭilanadī
Śiva enshrined here is celebrated as the destroyer of the three cities. This Purāṇic event is believed to have taken place here.

6. **Amparpperuṁtirukkōyil** (close to Peralam Junction)
Brahmapurīśvara Pūnkuḷalammai
Brahmatīrtham Punnaivṛkṣam

7. **Amparmākālam** (close to No. 6)
Kālakaṇṭheśvara or Mahākālanātha Pakṣanāyakī
Mākāḷatīrtha
Kālī worshipped Śiva in this temple and wiped off the stain she accrued when she destroyed Aṁbāsura.

8. **Aracili** (close to Putucceri and Tindivanam)
Aracilinātha Periyanāyakī
Aracaṭitīrtha Aracaṭitīrtha

9. **Arataipperuṁpāli** (close to Saliyamangalam in Tanjore)
Pātāleśvara Alaṁkāranāyakī
Brahmatīrtha
Śiva subdued Viṣṇu in his varāhāvatāra, broke his tusk and wore it as a trophy.

10. **Aricirkkaraipputtūr** (close to Kumbhakonam)
Svarṇapurīśvara Āḷakāmbikā
Aricilāṟu

11. **Avaḷivaṇallūr** (close to Salliyamangalam at Tanjore)
Sākṣināyakeśvara Saundaranāyakī
Candrapuṣkaraṇi
Viṣnu is said to have been subdued by Śiva in his varāha form here. Śiva broke his tusk, and Viṣṇu thereafter worshipped Śiva in this temple.

12. **Avināsi** (close to Tiruppur Railway Station near Erode)
Avināsīśvara Karuṇāmbikā
Pātirivṛkṣa
Pārvatī is portrayed as performing tapas under a tree here. The sixty-three devotees are also prominently installed here. The Nandi of this temple is huge.

13. **Tēraḷuntūr** (close to Kurnalam near Mayavaram)
Vedapurīśvara Saundarāmbikā
Vedatīrtha
The Vedas, the gods, and the eight directional guardians are said to have worshipped here.

14. **Aṛaiyaṇinallūr** (close to Tirukkovalur Railway Station)
Araiyaṇinatha Aruḷnāyaki
Peṇṇaiyāṛu
The temple is situated on a hilltop. Close to the tank is a cave associated with the Pāṇḍavas.

15. **Anekataṅkāpatam** (difficult to locate; probably in North India)
Aruṇmanneśvara Manonmaṇī
Gaurī is said to have performed tapas here. Sūrya and Candra are depicted as worshipping Śiva.

16. **Anpilālanturai** (close to Dālkuti)
Satyavāgīśvara Saundaranāyakī
Koḷḷiḍanadī
Brahmā and other sages are said to have worshipped here.

17. **Anniyūr** (close to Māyavaram)
Āpatasahāyeśvara Periyanāyakī
Varuṇatīrtha
Varuṇa is said to have worshipped in this temple.

18. **Ākkūr** (close to Māyavaram)
Svayaṁbhunātheśvara Vāṇeṭuṅkaṇṇi

19. **Ātānai** (44 miles from Manamadurai)
Āṭānainātha Snehavallī
Sūryatīrtha
Sūrya worshipped Śiva in this temple.

20. **Āppanūr** (close to the Madurai temple)
Āppanūriśvara Aṁbikā
Vṛṣabhatīrtha
Both bronze and stone images of Natarāja are found installed here.

21. **Āppāṭi** (close to Aduturai)
Pālukantheśvara Periyanāyakī
Maṇṇiyāṛu Āttivṛkṣa
Caṇḍeśvara is depicted as worshipping Śiva here.

22. **Āmāttūr** (close to Viḷuppuram)
Abhirāmeśvara Muktāmbikā
Paṁpānadī Vahnivṛkṣa
Rāma worshipped Śiva here.

23. **Tiruvārūr** (14 miles away from Nāgapaṭṭinam)
Valmīkanātha Alliyaṅkōtai
Vahnivṛkṣa Kamalālaya
The liṅga installed in this temple is celebrated as Pṛthvīliṅga.

24. **Ārūraraneṛi** (near Tiruvārur)
Akhileśvara Bhuvaneśvarī

25. **Ārūrpparavaiyuṇmaṇḍaḷi** (near Tiruvārur)
Durvāseśvara Pañcimellaṭiyammai
The sage Durvāsas worshipped here

26. **Tiruvālaṅkāṭu** (40 miles from Madras)
Ūrdhvatāṇḍaveśvara
Muktitīrtha Panasavṛkṣa.
Ratnasabhā (one of the pañcasabhās) is found here.

27. **Tiruvālampoḻil** (in the vicinity of Tanjore)
Ātmanātheśvara Jñānāṁbikā
Kāverītīrtha Vaṭavṛkṣa
The eight Vasus worshipped here.

28. **Tiruvālavāy** (Madura Temple is known by this name)
Sundareśvara Mīnākṣī
Poṟṟāmarai Vaikaiyāṟu Kaṭampavṛkṣa

29. **Tiruvāvaṭuturai** (11 miles away from Māyavaram)
Māsilāmaṇīśvara Oppilāmulaiyammai
Gomuktitīrtha Paṭararasuvṛkṣa.
Tirumūlar is believed to have composed his Tirumantiram here.

30. **Āvūr** (8 miles from Kumbhakonam)
Paśupatīśvara Maṅgalanāyakī
Brahmatīrtha

31. **Tiruvānaikkā** (close to Śrīraṅgam)
Jaṁbukeśvara Akhilāṇḍanāyakī
Kāverī Jaṁbuvṛkṣa
This is the Āpoliṅga, one of the pañcabhūta-liṅgas

32. **Ituṁpāvanam** (close to Tirutturaippūṇḍi)
Satkuṇanātheśvara Maṅgalanāyakī

33. **Iṭaiccuram** (5 miles from Chengleput)
Iṭaiccuranātha Imayamaṭakkoṭi

34. **Tiruvidaimarutūr** (5 miles from Kumbhakonam)
Mahāliṅgeśvara Perunalamāmulai
Kāverī Marutavṛkṣa

35. **Iḍaiyāṟu** (3 miles from Tiruvennainallur)
Iḍaiyāṟrīśvara Ciṟriḍaināyakī
Peṇṇainadī

36. **Intiranīlaparuppatam** (not identified; probably in North India)
Nīlācalanātha Nīlāṁbikā
Indratīrtha

37. **Rāmanadīśvara** (4 miles from Nannilam)
Rāmanātheśvara Karuvārkuḷali
Rāmatīrtha
Rāma is said to have worshipped in this temple.

38. **Rāmeśvara**
Rāmanātheśvara Parvatavardhanī
Dhanuṣkoṭi
Rāma installed a Śiva-liṅga in this temple.

39. **Iruṁpūḷai** (close to Nīḍāmaṅgalam)
Araṇyeśvara Elavārkuḷali
Viśvāmitra and other sages worshipped here.

40. **Iruṁpaimākāḷam** (5 miles from Putucceri)
Mahākāleśvara Kuilmoḷi

42. **Innaṁpar** (4 miles from Kumbhakonam)
Eḷuttaṛinātheśvara Saundaranāyakī

43. **Īṅkōymalai** (close to Trichi)
Marakatācaleśvara Marakatavallī
Tintṛṇīvṛkṣa

44. **Ucāttānam** (close to Muttuppettai Station)
Mantrapurīśvara Priyanāyakī
Rāma received instructions in mantras in this temple before he proceeded to Laṅka.

45. **Tiruvūṛal** (close to Takkōlam Station)
Umāpatīśvara Umā

46. **Etirkoḷpāṭi** (close to Kuṛṛālam Station)
Airāvateśvara Malaṛkuḷalmātu

47. **Erukkattaṁpuliyūr** (close to Tirumutukunṛam, No. 237)
Nīlakaṇṭheśvara Nīlamalarkaṇṇammai
Veḷḷerukkuvṛkṣa

48. **Tiruveṛuṁpiyūr** (close to Trichy)
Eṛumpīśvarar Nāṛuṅkuḷalnāyakī

49. **Tiruvēṭakam** (close to Madura)
Eṭakanātheśvara Sugandhakuntalāṁbikā
Vaikai

50. **Tiruvaiyāṛu** (close to Tanjore)
Pañcanadeśvara Dharmasaṁvardhanī
Kāverī
Indra and Vālin are said to have worshipped in this temple.

51. **Tiruvoṛṛiyūr** (close to the Station)
Ādipurīśvara Tripurasundarī
Brahmatīrtha Bakulavṛkṣa

52. **Tiruōṇakāntantaḷi** (near Kanchipuram)
Ōṇakānteśvara Kāmākṣī

53. **Ōttūr** (near Kanchipuram)
Vedanātheśvara Iḷamulaināyakī
Seyāru Panaivṛkṣa

54. **Ōmāṁpuliyūr** (20 miles from Chidambaram)
Tuyartīrttanātha Pūṅkoṭināyakī
Koḷḷidanadī
Śiva showered his blessings on a hunter who was engaged in unintentional liṅga worship the whole night.

55. **Kaccianēkatāṅgāpatam** (Kanchipuram)
Anekataṅkāpateśvara Kāmākṣī

56. **Kacciēkaṁpam** (Kanchipuram)
Ekāṁpareśvara Kāmākṣī
Kaṁpanadī Āmravṛkṣa

57. **Kaccineṛikkāraikkāṭu** (Kanchipuram)
Kāraittirunākeśvara Kāmākṣī
Indratīrtha

58. **Kaccimēṟṟaḷi** (Kanchipuram)
Tirumēṟṟaḷinātha Kāmākṣī
Viṣṇutīrtha
Viṣṇu performed tapas and attained the sārūpya of Śiva.

59. **Tirukkaccūr** (Chengleput)
Viruntiṭṭa-Iśvara Umā
Kūrma-tīrtha

60. **Kañcanūr** (Narasighanpeṭṭai)
Agnīśvara Kalpakanāyakī
Agnitīrtha

61. **Kaṭampanturai** (20 miles from Trichy)
Kaṭampavanātha Muṟṟilāmulai
Kāverī Kaṭampavṛkṣa

62. **Kaṭampūr** (Ōmāmpuliyūr)
Amṛtaghaṭeśvara Cōtiminnammai

63. **Tirukkaṭavūr** (close to Māyavaram)
Amṛtaghaṭeśvara Śivagaṅgā
Śiva chastised Yama for interfering with Mārkaṇḍeya when the latter was engaged in his worship.

64. **Kaṭavūrmayānam** (Tirukkaṭavūr)
Brahmapurīśvara Malarkulaḷminnammai
Kāśitīrtha
This is the place where Śiva authorized Brahmā to create the universe.

65. **Kaṭikkuḷam** (Tirutturaippūnti)
Kalpeśvara Saundaranāyakī
Vināyakatīrtha

66. **Kaṭuvāykkaraipputtūr** (close to Nidamangala)
Svarṇapurīśvara Śivāṁbikā

67. **Kaṭaimuṭi** (near Ānandatandavapuram)
Kaṭaimuṭinātheśvara Abhirāmī

68. **Kaṇḍiyūr** (close to Tanjore)
Viraṭṭeśvara Maṅgalanāyakī
Kāverī
Śiva cut off Brahmā's fifth head; the temple celebrates this event annually.

69. **Kaṇṇārkoyil** (close to Vaittīśvaran Koyil)
Kaṇṇāyirēśvara Murukuvaḷarkōtai
Indratīrtha
It was here that Indra's curse was modified and he was thereafter endowed with a thousand eyes.

70. **Śrīkailāsa** (probably in North India)
Kailāsanātha Pārvātī

71. **Karavīra** (7 miles away from Tiruvarur)
Karavīreśvara Pratyakṣaminnammai

72. **Karukāvūr** (close to Aiyyampeṭṭai Station)
Mullaivaneśvara Garbharakṣakī
Mullaivṛkṣa

73. **Karukkuṭī** (close to Kumbhakonam)
Brahmapurīśa Kalyāṇī
A saikata liṅga installed here; Rāma and Brahmā are said to have worshipped in this temple.

74. **Karuppariyalūr** (5 miles from Vaittīśvaran Koyil)
Kuṟṟaṁporuttanātheśvara Kōlvaḷaiyam
Indratīrtha

75. **Karuvili** (6 miles from Kumbakonam)
Saṛkuṇanātheśvara Sarvānganāyakī

76. **Karuvūr** (45 miles from Trichi)
Paśupatīśvara Saundaryanāyakī
Āṁprāvatīnadī Vañci

77. **Kalayanallūr** (close to Kumbhakonam)
Amṛtakaleśvara Amṛtavallī

78. **Kalikkāmūr** (13 miles from Sīkali)
Sundareśvara Aḷakuvanamulai

79. **Kaḷippālai** (7 miles from Chidambaram)
Pālvaṇṇanātheśvara Vedanāyakī
The sage Vālmiki is said to have worshipped here.

80. **Kaḷukkunṛam** (close to Chengleput)
Vedagirīśvara Peṇṇinallāḷammai

81. **Kaḷar** (9 miles from Tirutturaippūṇḍi)
Pārijātavaneśvara Alakeśvarī
Durvāsatīrtha
The sages Parāśara and Durvāsas worshipped here.

82. **Kaḷḷil** (22 miles from Madras)
Śivānandeśvara Ānandavallī

83. **Kaṛkuṭi** (close to Trichy)
Kalpakanātha Añjanākṣī

84. **Kanrāppūr** (close to Tiruvarur)
Naṭutaṛiyappar Mātumaiyammai

85. **Kāṭṭuppaḷḷi** (8 miles from Siyali)
Āraṇyasundareśvara Akhilāṇḍanāyakī
The gods worshipped here so Indra might be set free from the brahmahatyā incurred by killing Vṛtra.

86. **Kāṭṭuppaḷḷi** (16 miles from Tanjore)
Tīyāṭiyappar Saundaranāyakī
Kāverītīrtha

87. **Pallavanīccuram** (10 miles from Siyali)
Pallavaneśvara Saundaranāyakī
Kāverītīrtha

88. **Kali** or **Śrīkāli Cīyāḷi** (11 miles from Chidambaram)
Brahmapurīśvara Tirunilaināyakī
Brahmātīrtha
Brahmā is said to have worshipped Śiva in this place.

89. **Kālatti** or **Kālahasti** (away from Reniguntha)
Gaṇanātha Jñānappūṅkotai
Ponmukariyāṟu Kallālavṛkṣa
The liṅga installed here is Vāyuliṅga, one of the pañcabhūtaliṅgas. A spider, a snake and an elephant are said to have worshipped Śiva in this temple.

90. **Kārāyil** (away from Tiruvarur)
Kaṇṇāyiranātheśvara Kailaināyakī
Indratīrtha

91. **Kānappar** (39 miles from Madura)
Sundareśvara Mīnākṣī
Yānaimaṭutīrtha

92. **Kānāṭṭumuḷḷūr** (18 miles from Chidambaram)
Patañjalinātheśvara Kānārkuḷali

93. **Kānūr** (7 miles from Putalur)
Semmeninātheśvara Sivayoganāyakī
Koḷḷiṭanadī
Umā performed tapas in this temple; Śiva became manifest in the form of Agni and granted her desires.

94. **Kīḻvelur** (7 miles from Tiruvarur)
Akṣayaliṅgeśvara Vanamulaināyakī
Saravaṇappoykai Ilantaivṛkṣa
The images of Indra and Kubera, who worshipped Śiva in this temple, are installed.

95. **Kuṭantaikkāroṇam** (close to the banks at Kumbhakonam)
Viśvanātha Viśālākṣī

96. **Kuṭantaikkīḻkkōṭṭam** (Kumbhakonam)
Nageśvarasvāmi Periyanāyakī

97. **Kuṭamūkku** (the largest temple of Śiva at Kumbhakonam)
Kuṁbhesvara Maṅgalanāyakī
Kāverītīrtha Mahāmakhatīrtha

98. **Kuṭavāyil** (32 miles from Tanjore)
Koṇeśvara Periyanāyakī

99. Kurakkukkā (close to Tiruppariyalur)
Kuntaḷeśvara Kuntaḷanāyakī
Hanumān worshipped Śiva here.

100. **Karaṅkaṇimuṭṭam** (6 miles from Kanchipuram temple)
Vālīśvara Iṛaiyārvaḷaiyammai

101. **Kuraṅkātuturai** (North) (17 miles from Kumbhakonam)
Kulaivaṇankīśvara Aḷakucaṭaimuṭiyammai
Kāverītīrtha

102. **Kuraṅkatuturai** (South) (close to Tiruvitaimarutūr)
Āpatsahāyeśvara Pavaḷakkoṭiyammai
Kāverī
Sugrīva is said to have worshipped here.

103. **Kurukāvūr** (4 miles from Siyali)
Veḷḷaṭainātha Kāviyaṅkaṇṇiyammai

104. **Kuṛukkai** (10 miles from Mayavaram)
Vīraṭṭeśvar Jñanāṁbikā
Kāma, the god of love, was reduced to ashes here.

105. **Kuṛṛālam** (Tirunelveli)
Kuṛumpalāvīśvara Kuḷalvāymoḷi
Citrānadī Panasavṛkṣa
Citrasabhā, one of the five sabhas is found here.

106. **Kūṭalaiyāṛṛūr** (14 miles from Vṛddhācalam)
Neṛikāṭṭunāyakar Purikuḷalāṁbikai
Maṇimuktānadī

107. **Kedāra** (Himālaya)
Kedāreśvara Kedāragaurī
Pārvāti worshipped here and attained the ardhanarīśvara form

108. **Tirukketīśvara** (Srilanka)
Ketīśvara Gaurī
Pālāvi
The demon Malayavān is said to have worshipped here.

109. **Kaiccinam** (close to Tiruvārur)
Kaiccinanātheśvara Velvalaiyammai
Indratīrtha
The Dakṣiṇāmūrti installed here is very prominent.

110. **Koṭimāṭacceṅkunṛūr** (Salem District)
Ardhanārīśvara Pākaṁpiriyāḷammai

111. **Kotuṅkunṛam** (57 miles from Madura)
Ugragirīśvara Amṛteśvarī

112. **Koṭṭaiyūr** (close to Kumbhakonam)
Kotīśvara Pantāṭunāyakī

113. **Koṇṭīccuram** (3 miles from Nannilam Station)
Paśupatīśvara Śāntanāyakī

114. **Koḷḷampūtūr** (close to Nidamangalam)
Bilvavaneśvara Saundarāṁbikā

115. **Koḷḷikkāṭu** (close to Tiruvārur)
Agnīśvara Mṛdupadāṁbikā
Agni worshipped in this temple, and Śani is prominently installed here as well.

116. **Gokarṇa** (Karnataka)
Mahābalanātha Gokarṇanāyakī
Koṭitīrtha

117. **Koṭi-Kuḷakarkoyil** (in the vicinity of Vedaranya)
Amṛtaghaṭeśvara Maiyārtaṭaṅkaṇṇi
The image of Subrahmaṇya installed here has a single face and six hands.

118. **Koṭikā** (vicinity of Tiruviḍaimarutūr)
Trikoṭīśvara Vaḍivāṁbikai
Kāverītīrtha

119. **Tirukkōṭṭāru** (vicinity of Tiruvaiyyaru)
Airāvateśvara Vaṇḍamarpūṅkuḷali

120. **Koṭṭūr** (10 miles from Mannarkuti)
Koḷuntīśvara Madhuravacanāṁbikā
Vahnivṛkṣa

121. **Koṇamalai** (Srilanka)
Koṇeśvara Mātumaiyāḷammai

122. **Kōyil** or **Chidambaram**
Tirumūḷanātha Umaiyammai
Śivagaṅgā
This temple at Chidambaram has the kanakasabhā, the most famous of the five sabhās. In this temple is installed the ākāśaliṅga, one of the pañcabhūtaliṅgas.

123. **Kōlakkā** (close to Sīyāḷi)
Saptapurīśvara Ōsaikoṭuttanāyakī

124. **Kōvalūr**
Vīraṭṭeśvara Śivānandavallī
Peṇṇainadī
The destruction of Andhaka is said to have taken place here.

125. **Koḷaṁpam** (close to Narasinganpeṭṭai)
Kokileśvara Saundaranāyakī

126. **Kōḷili** (close to Velur)
Kōḷilināthe śvara Vantārpūṅkuḷalammai
Brahmatīrtha
Brahmā is said to have worshipped here.

127. **Cakkirappaḷḷi** (close to Aiyyampeṭṭai)
Paśupatināyakeśvara Alliyaṅkōtai
Kāverītīrtha
Viṣṇu worshipped Śiva and obtained cakra

128. **Cattimuttam** (close to Kumbhakonam)
Śaktivaneśvara Periyanāyakī
Śūlatīrtha

129. **Cāttamaṅkai** (5 miles from Tirunaḷḷāru)
Ayavantīśvara Malarkkaṇṇammai

130. **Cāykkāṭu** (9 miles from Siyali)
Cāyāvaneśvara Kuyilunalmoḷiyammai
Kaverītīrtha
The sage Upamanyu worshipped here.

131. **Cikkal** (close to Nagapatanam)
Veṇṇayiliṅgeśvara Vēneṭuṅkaṇṇiyammai

132. **Tirucciräppalli**
Tāyumāneśvara Maṭṭuvārkuḷalammai
Kāverī

133. **Civapuram** (close to Kumbhakonam)
Śivapuranātha Siṅgāravallī
Campakavṛkṣa

134. **Cirukuṭi** (close to Peralam)
Maṅgaleśvara Maṅgalanāyakī

135. **Ciṟṟemam** (close to Tirutturaippūṇḍi)
Caturvedapurīśvara Vedanāyakī

136. **Cuḷiyal** (38 miles from Madura)
Tiruměninātheśvara Tuṇaimālaiyammai
Pārvatī performed tapas with a request to Śiva to accept her as his wife.

137. **Ceṅkāṭṭaṅkuṭi** (away from Nannilam)
Kaṇapatīccurar Tirukkuḷanāyakī
Āttivṛkṣa
Ganeśa worshipped Śiva in order to be cleansed of the sin incurred by the destruction of Gajāsura.

138. **Cemponpaḷḷi** (near Semponnārkoyil)
Svarṇapurīśvara Sugandhavananāyakī
Indra and Kubera worshipped here.

139. **Cēyjñalūr** (12 miles from Kumbhakonam)
Satyagirīśvara Sakhīdevī
Maṇṇinadī
Skanda worshipped here before he set out to fight a demon.

140. **Ceṟai** (away from Kumbhakonam)
Conneṟiyappar Jñānavallī

141. **Gopuram** (8 miles from Kutalur)
Gopuranātha Gopuranāyakī

142. **Coṟṟutturai** (away from Tanjore)
Otavaneśvara Annapūraṇī
Kāverīnādī

143. **Taṇṭalainīṇeṛi** (close to Tirutturaippundi Station)
Nīnerināthesvara Jñānāmbikā
Viṣṇu in his kūrmāvatāra was punished by fire here.

144. **Tarumapuram** (near Karaikkāl)
Yāḷmūrināthesvara Sadāmadhurāṁbikā
Brahmā and Yama are said to have worshipped here.

145. **Talaicceṇkātu** (near Ākkūr Station)
Saṅkaruṇāthesvara Saundaranāyakī
Kāverī-Tīrtha
Viṣṇu worshipped Śiva and obtained the conch Pāñcajanya.

146. **Talaiyālaṅkātu** (close to Kūṭavayil)
Āṭavallavīśvara Tirumaṭantai
The demon Muyalakan was directed against the god by the sages of Dāruvana; Śiva subdued the demon and danced upon him.

147. **Tiruntutēvankuṭi** (5 miles from Kumbhakonam)
Karkaṭakesvara Arumaruntammai

148. **Tilataippati** (close to Peralam Station)
Muktīśvara Poṛkoṭiyammai
Candratīrtha

149. **Tinainakar** (in the vicinity of Cudalore)
Tirundīśvara Oppilānāyakī
Konṛaivṛkṣa

150. **Turutti** (close to Māyavaram)
Vedesvarar Mukiḷāmbikai
Kāverītīrtha

151. **Tuṛaiyur** (5 miles from Paṇṛuṭṭi Station)
Paśupatīśvara Pūṅkotaināyakī
Peṇṇainadī

152. **Teṅkūr** (close to Tirunellikkā)
Veḷḷimalainātha Periyanāyakī
Lakṣmī and the navagrahas are said to have worshipped Śiva in his liṅga form here.

153. **Teḷiccēri** (Karaikkāl)
Parvateśvara Saktiyammai

154. **Tenkuṭittiṭṭai** (close to Tanjore)
Paśupatīśvara Ulakanāyakī

155. **Tevūr** (9 miles from Nagapattinam)
Tevapurīśvara Madhurabhāṣiṇī
Kadalīvṛkṣa

156. **Naṇā** (close to Erode)
Śaṅkhamukhanātheśvara Vedāṁbikā
Bhavānītīrtha

157. **Nallam** (close to Tiruvidaimarutūr)
Umāmaheśvara Maṅgalanāyakī

158. **Nallūr** (near Kumbhakonam)
Kalyāṇasundareśvara Kalyāṇasundarī
Saptasāgara-tīrtha

159. **Nallūrpperumaṇam** (3 miles from Koḷḷidam)
Śivalokatyāgeśa Naṅgaiyumai

160. **Nallāṛu** (3 miles from Kāraikkal)
Darbhāraṇyeśvara Pokamārttapūṇmulaiyammai
Nalatīrtha
An image of Śani is installed here. Nala worshipped Śiva and freed himself from the influence of Kali.

161. **Nāṛaiyūr** (away from Kumbhakonam)
Cittanātheśvara Alakāṁbikā

162. **Nanipaḷḷi** (8 miles from Māyavaram)
Naṟṟuṇaiyappar Parvatarājaputrī

163. **Nannilam** (3 miles from Nannilam Station)
Madhuvaneśvara Madhuvananāyakī

164. **Nakēccuram** (4 miles from Kumbhakonam)
Caṁpakāraṇyeśvara Kunṛāmulaināyakī

165. **Nākaikkāroṇam** (Nagapaṭṭanam Station)
Adipuraneśvara Nīlāyatākṣī
Āmravṛkṣa

166. **Nāṭṭiyattānkuṭī** (6 miles from Tiruvārūr)
Ratnagirīśvara Maṅgalanāyakī

167. **Naraiyūr** (11 miles from Chidambaram)
Saundareśvara Tripurasundarī
The Gaṇeśa installed here is called Pollāppiḷḷaiyār. Gaṇeśa worship is very popular here.

168. **Nālūr mayānam** (10 miles from Kumbhakonam)
Palāśavaneśa Periyanāyakī

169. **Nāvalūr** (away from Viluppuram)
Nāvaleśvara Saundaranāyakī

170. **Ninṛiyūr**
Mahālakṣmīsvara Ulakānāyakī

171. **Nīdūr** (close to Mayāvaram)
Cananṛtteśvara Atikanti
Makiḷavṛkṣa

172. **Nīlakkuṭi** (away from Aduturai Station)
Nīlakaṇṭheśvara Umā

173. **Netuṅkuḷam** (7 miles from Eruṁpiyūr Station)
Nityasundareśvara Oppilānāyakī

174. **Neittānam** (close to Tiruvaiyāṛu)
Neyyātiyappar Balāṁbikā
Kāverītīrtha

175. **Nellikkā** (away from Tiruvārur)
Āmalakeśvara Maṅgalanāyakī

176. **Nelvāyil** (Sivapuri) (away from Chidambaram)
Uccinātheśvara Kanakāṁbikā

177. **Nelvāyil** (Aratturai) (3 miles from Pennatakam Station)
Arattuṛaināttha Ānandanāyakī
Veḷḷāṛutīrtha

178. **Nelveṇṇai** (4 miles from Uluntuppeṭṭai Station)
Veṇṇaiyappar Nilamalarkkannammai

179. **Nelveli** (Tinneveli)
Nellaiyappar Kāntimatī
Tāmbraparṇi
In this temple is found the tāmrasabhā, one of the five sabhās.

180. **Paṭṭīccuram** (4 miles from Kumbhakonam)
Paṭṭīśvara Paivaḷaināyakī
Jñānatīrtha Vahnivṛkṣa

181. **Pantaṇainallūr** (6 miles from Tiruviḍaimarutūr)
Paśupatīśvara Kāṁpanatōḷi

182. **Payaṛṛūr** (10 miles from Tiruvārūr)
Payaṛṛīśvara Kāviyaṅkaṇṇi

183. **Paraṅkuṇṛu** (4 miles from Madura)
Paraṅgirinātheśvara Āvuṭaināyakī
Saravaṇatīrtha

184. **Parāyttuṛai** (away from Trichy)
Paraytturaināttha Ponmayilāṁbikā
Kāverī
Indra, Kubera and the seven sages are said to have worshipped here.

185. **Paritiniyamam** (away from Tanjore)
Paritiyappeśvara Maṅgalanāyakī
Sūryatīrtha

186. **Paruppatam** (Śrīśaila) (North India)
Parvateśvara Parvatanāyakī

187. **Paḷanam** (close to Tiruvaiyyāṛu)
Āpatsahāyeśvara Periyanāyakī
Kāverī

188. **Paḷuvūr** (10 miles from Tiruvaiyyāṛu)
Vaṭamūlanātheśvara Aruntavanāyakī
Koḷḷiḍanadī

189. **Paḷaiyārai** (away from Paṭṭīśvaram)
Someśvara Gaurī
Somatīrtha

190. **Paḷḷiyinmukkūṭal** (3 miles from Tiruvārur)
Mukkoṇanātheśvara Maimmevukaṇṇi

191. **Pariyalūr** (away from Māyavaram)
Vīraṭṭeśvara Iḷaṅkoṭiyammai
The destruction of Dakṣa's sacrifice took place here.

192. **Panaṅkāṭṭūr** (away from Kanchipuram)
Panaṅkāṭṭīśvara Amṛtavalli
Panaivṛkṣa

193. **Panantāl** (10 miles from Kumbhakonam)
Saṭaiyappeśvara Periyanāyakī

194. **Panaiyūr** (away from Tiruvārur)
Saundaryanātha Maimmevukaṇṇī

195. **Pacūr** (31 miles from Madras)
Pacūrnātheśvara Paśupatināyakī

196. **Pāccilāccirāmam** (away from Tiruvanaikka)
Māṟṟarivarata Bālasaundarī
Vannivṛkṣa

197. **Pāṇḍikkoṭumuṭi**
Makuṭeśvara Tripurasundarī
Kāverī Vannivṛkṣa

198. **Pātāḷeccura** (close to Rajamannār Station)
Sarpapurīśvara Amṛtanāyakī
Sage Dhananjaya worshipped here; the image is endowed with two faces.

199. **Pātirippuliyūr** (away from Cuddalore)
Pātaleśvara Periyanāyakī
Keṭilanadī Pātirivṛkṣa

200. **Pāmpuram** (close to Peralam)
Pāmpureśvara Vanḍārpūṅkuḷali
Vannivṛksa
Nāgarāja is said to have worshipped here.

201. **Pālaitturai** (close to Kumbhakonam)
Pālaivananātheśvara Tavaḷeṇṇakai
Kāverī
Śiva tore the skin from a tiger which had been sent against him by the sages of Dāruvana.

202. **Pāṟṟuṟai** (5 miles from Tiruvanaikka)
Mūlanātheśvara Mekhalāṁbikā

203. **Pukalūr** (4 miles from Nannilam Station)
Agnīśvara Karuntāḷkuḷali
Agnitīrtha Punnaivṛkṣa
The image of Candraśekhara installed in this temple is a great attraction.

204. **Pukalūr** (close to 204)
Vardhamāneśvara Karuntāḷkuḷali
Agnitīrtha Punnaivṛkṣa

205. **Puttūr** (38 miles from Madura)
Puttūrīśvara Sivakāmi
Sītaḷitīrtha Konṛaivṛkṣa
Bhairava is particularly worshipped here. The temple has assigned a separate shrine for Viṣṇu.

206. **Puḷḷamaṅkai** (Pasupati Station)
Paśupatinātheśvara Alliyaṅkōtai
Kāverīnadī
The temple is associated with the Purāṇic episode of Śiva drinking the poison.

207. **Puḷḷirukkuvēḷūr** (close to Vaittīśvaran Koyil Station)
Vaidyanātheśvara Taiyalnāyakī
Veṁbuvṛkṣa Siddhāmṛtatīrtha

208. **Puṛaṁpayam** (6 miles from Kumbhakonam)
Sākṣinātheśvara Ikṣuvāṇi
Vahnivṛkṣa
The images of Dakṣiṇāmūrti and Gaṇeśa are famous in this temple.

209. **Puṛavārpanaṁkāttūr** (5 miles from Viḷuppuraṁ)
Netroddhāraṇa Satyāṁbikā
Tālavṛkṣa

210. **Punavāyil** (30 miles from Arantanki)
Paḷaṁpatinātheśvara Periyanāyakī
Punnaivṛkṣa

211. **Punkūr** (5 miles from Pattisvaran Koyil)
Sivalokanātha Sokkanāyakī
Puṅgavṛkṣa

212. **Pūnturutti** (2 miles from Tirukkaṇḍiyūr)
Puṣpanātheśvara Aḷakālamarntanāyakī

213. **Pūvanam** (12 miles from Madura)
Pūvaṇanātheśvara Minnanaiyāḷammai
Vaikainadī Palāvṛkṣa

214. **Pūvanūr** (close to Nīḍāmaṅgalam)
Puṣpavaneśvara Rājarājeśvarī

215. **Peṇṇāṭakam** (Peṇṇātakam Station)
Cuṭarkkoḷuntīśvara Kaṭantaināyakī

216. **Peruṁpuliyūr** (close to Tiruvaiyāru)
Vyāghrapurīśvara Saundaranāyakī
Kāverī
Vyāghrapāda is said to have worshipped in this temple.

217. **Peruvēlūr** (close to Tiruvārūr)
Piriyā-īśvara Minnanaiyāḷ

218. **Pēṇuperunturai** (7 miles from Kumbhakonam)
Praṇaveśvara Maṅgalanāyakī

219. **Pēreyil** (close to Kuḷikkarai)
Jagatīśvara Jagannāyakī
Agnitīrtha

220. **Painnili** (away from Trichy)
Nīlakaṇṭheśvara Viśālākṣī
Kalvāḷai

221. **Maṅgalakkuṭi** (close to Tiruviḍaimarutūr)
Prāṇavaradeśvara Maṅgalanāyakī
Kāverī
Kālī, Sūrya, Viṣṇu, Brahmā and Agastya are said to have worshipped at this temple.

222. **Maṇanderi** (away from Māyavaram)
Arulvaḷḷanayakeśvara Yāḷinmeymoḷiyammai

223. **Maṇṇippaṭikkarai** 6 miles from Vaittīśvaran
Nīlakaṇṭheśvara Amṛtakaravalli
Drinking the poison is also believed to have taken place at this temple.

224. **Mayilātuturai** (close to Māyavaram)
Māyūranātheśvara Abhayāṁbikā
Kāverī
Gaṇeśa is prominently installed here and he goes by the name Mukkuṛuṇipiḷḷaiyār. The Dakṣiṇāmūrti installed here is a great attraction.

225. **Mayilāppūr** (Madras)
Kapālīśvara Kalpakavalli
Punnāgavṛkṣa
The festival of the Nāyanmārs is celebrated here in a grand scale every year.

226. **Mayentirappalli** (away from Chidambaram)
Tirumēniyaḷakar Vadivāmbikai
Sūrya, Candra, Brahmā and Indra are said to have worshipped here.

227. **Marukal** (7 miles from Nannilam Station)
Māṇikkavaṇṇeśvara Vanṭārkuḷalammai

228. **Maḷapāṭi** (away from Tiruvaiyaru)
Vajrastaṁbheśvara Aḷakammai
Koḷḷiḍanadī Panaivṛkṣa
Viṣṇu and Indra are said to have worshipped here. Nandin's wedding is annually commemorated here as well. A stone image of Somāskanda is installed here.

229. **Maraikkāṭu** (Vedāraṇyam Station)
Vedāraṇyeśvara Yāḷaippaḷittamoḷi

230. **Mākaṛal** (10 miles from Kanchipuram)
Akattīśvara Tribhuvaneśvarī
Indra is said to have worshipped here.

231. **Māṇikuḷi** (3 miles from Tirupāttirippuliyūr)
Māṇikkavarada Māṇikkavallī
Kēṭilnadī
Viṣṇu as Vāmana is said to have worshipped Śiva here. The curtain of this temple is never removed.

232. **Mānturai** (close to Trichy)
Āmravaneśvara Aḷakāṁbikā
Āmravṛkṣa

233. **Māṛpeṛu** (close to Kanchipuram)
Maṇikaṇṭheśvara Añjanākṣī
Pālāṛu Bilvavṛkṣa
In this temple Viṣṇu is said to have plucked his eye and offered it to Śiva in place of a lotus. He obtained a cakra from Śiva. The Nandin of this temple is depicted in a standing pose.

234. **Mīyaccūr** (close to Peraḷam)
Muyarcinātheśvara Saundaranāyakī
Sūryapuṣkaraṇi Bilvavṛkṣa
Śiva and Umā in this temple are depicted as mounted on an elephant. Sūrya is said to have worshipped here.

235. **Mīaccuṛ** (Iḷaṅkoyil) (close to No. 234 above)
Bhuvaneśvara Mekhalāṁbikā

236. **Munḍīśvaram** (close to Tiruvennainallur)
Śivalokanātha Saundaryanāyakī
Brahmā and Indra are said to have worshipped here.

237. **Mutukunram** (Vṛddhācalam) (Vṛddhacalam Station)
Vṛddhācaleśvara Periyanāyakī
Maṇimuktānadī Vahnivṛkṣa

238. **Murukanpūṇti** (away from Erode)
Murukanātheśvara Muyaṅkupūṇmulai

239. **Mullaivāyil** (North) (away from Madras)
Māsilāmaṇīśvara Koṭiyiṭaināyakī

240. **Mullaivāyil** (South) (9 miles from Siyali)
Mullaivananātha Koṭiyiṭaiyammai

241. **Mukkīśvara** (away from Trichy)
Pañcavarṇeśvara Kāntimatī

242. **Vakkarai** (7 miles from Maiyilam)
Candraśekhara Vadivāṁbikai
Śiva is depicted here with three faces, the first for Candra, the second for Brahmā and the third for Viṣṇu. Viṣṇu also has a shrine assigned to him.

243. **Vaṭukūr** (12 miles from Putucceri)
Vaṭukeśvara Vaṭuvakiṛkkaṇṇi
Bhairava as Vaṭuka is worshipped in this temple.

244. **Valañcuḻi** away (from Kumbhakonam)
Kalpakanātheśvara Periyanāyakī
Special significance is attached to Gaṇeśa installed here.

245. **Valaṁpuram** (8 miles from Siyali)
Valaṁpurinātha Vaṭuvakiṛkkaṇṇi
Viṣṇu worshipped here and obtained a conch from Śiva.

246. **Valitāyam** (Madras)
Valitāyanātha Tāyammai

247. **Valivalam** (6 miles from Tiruvarur)
Manattuṇainātha Māḷaiyaṅkaṇṇiyammai
Punnaivṛkṣa

248. **Vallam**
Vallanātha Vallāṁbikai
The Navagrahas are worshipped here.

249. **Vanniyūr** (2 miles from Tiruviḷimiḷalai)
Agnīśvara Pārvatī
Agnitīrtha

250. **Vāñciyaṁ** (11 miles from Tiruvarur)
Vāñciliṅgeśvara
Guptagaṅgātīrtha
Viṣṇu worshipped here, and as a consequence reunited with Lakṣmī. Yama also is assigned a shrine in this temple.

251. **Vāṭpōkki** (6 miles from Kulittalai)
Ratnagirīśa Curuṁpārkuḷali
Kāverītīrtha Veppavṛkṣa

252. **Vāymūr** (15 miles from Tiruvarur)
Vāymūranātha Pālinunanmoḷi
Eight images of Bhairava are believed to have originally been installed here, but only seven can be found.

253. **Vāḷolipuṟṟūr** (5 miles from Vaittīśvaran Koyil)
Māṇikkavāṇar Vanṭārpūṅkuḷāli

254. **Vānmiyūr** (3 miles from Mayilapur)
Amṛteśvara Sokkanāyakī
Vālmīki is said to have worshipped here. Vālmīki is also installed in this temple.

255. **Vicayamaṅkai** (10 miles from Kumbhakonam)
Vijayanātha Maṅgaināyakī
Arjunatīrtha

256. **Viyalūr** (close to Kumbhakonam)
Purātaneśvara Saundaranāyakī

257. **Vilanakar** (close to Māyavaram)
Uśiravaneśvara Vaṁsabhujāṁbikā
Kāverītīrtha

258. **Vilamar** (away from Tiruvārūr)
Patañjalimanohara Yāḷinumenmoḷi
Agnitīrtha
The images of Patañjali and Vyāghrapāda are depicted here as engaged in the worship of Śiva.

259. **Viṛkuṭi** (close to Tiruvārūr)
Vīraṭṭāneśvara Elavūrkuḷali
The demon Jhalandhara is said to have been destroyed here.

260. **Viṛkkōlam** (6 miles from Kaṭampattūr Station)
Tripurāntaka Tripurāntakī
Śiva is depicted here as wielding a bow, and is shown as being ready to set out for the destruction of the three cities.

261. **Viḷimiḷalai** (away from Māyavaram)
Netrārpaneśvara Sundarakucāṁbikā
Viṣṇutīrtha Bilvavṛkṣa

262. **Vencamākkūṭal** (close to Karuvur)
Vikṛtanātheśvara Vikṛtanāyakī

263. **Veṇkāṭu** (7 miles from Siyali)
Śvetāraṇyeśvara Brahmavidyānāyakī
Somasūryāgnitīrtha
The images of Vīrabhadra, Naṭarāja and Kālī are great attractions in this temple.

264. **Veṇṭurai** (close to Tanjore)
Veṇṭurainātha Venetuṅkaṇṇiyammai
Bhṛṅgi, who is noted for the hatred he had for Umā, assumed the form of a bee and pierced through the middle of the Ardhanārī and completed the circumambulation of Śiva avoiding thereby the circumambulation of Umā.

265. **Veṇniyūr**
Ikṣupurīśvara Aḷakiyanāyakī
Nandyāvarttavṛkṣa

266. **Veṇṇainallūr** (close to the station)
Kṛpāpurīśvara Maṅgalāṁbikā
Peṇṇainadī

267. **Veṇpākkam** (35 miles from Madras)
Tyāgeśvara Minnaloḷiyammai
Ilantaivṛkṣa

268. **Vēṭkaḷam** (2 miles from Chidambaram)
Pāśupatīśvara Nallaināyakī
It is here Śiva is believed to have granted the Pāśupata weapon to Arjuna.

269. **Vēṭṭakkuti** (6 miles from Karaikkal)
Tirumēniyaḷakar Sāntanāyakī
Śiva appeared before Arjuna in the form of a hunter.

270. **Vētikuṭī** (away from Tanjore)
Vedapuriśvara Maṅgayaṛkkaraci

271. **Veḷvikkuṭi** (away from Māyavaram)
Kalyāṇasundareśvara Parimalasundaranāyakī

272. **Veṛkātu** (away from Madras)
Vedapurīśvara Veṛkaṇṇiyammai

273. **Vaikanmāṭakkōyil** (close to Aduturai Station)
Vaikanātha Vaikalāṁbikā

274. **Vaikāvūr** (away from Kumbhakonam)
Bilvavaneśvara Sarvajanarakṣakī
Yamatīrtha Bilvavṛkṣa
Śiva became manifest to the hunter who had mounted a bilva tree out of fear of a tiger which was chasing him. This episode is connected with the Śivarātrī vrata.

Temples Dedicated to Gaṇeśa

Special name given to Gaṇeśa	*Temple*
1. Aḷakiyavināyakar	Tiruvāvaḍuturai
2. Āṇṭapiḷḷaiyār	Naṟaiyūrcittīccuram
3. Ātivināyakar	Tiruvaiyāṟu
4. Uccippiḷḷaiyār	Tirucciräppaḷḷi
5. Kaṅkaikkaṇapati	Kuṭantaikkīḷkoṭṭam
6. Kaṭukkāyppiḷḷaiyār	Tirukkāṟāyil
7. Karukkaṭivināyakar	Tirukkaccūr
8. Kaḷḷavāraṇappiḷḷaiyār	Tirukkaṭavūr
9. Kaṟppakkappiḷḷaiyār	Kaṭikkuḷam, Tirukkarukāvūr
10. Kūppiṭupiḷḷaiyār	Tirumurukanpūṇḍi
11. Kaikāṭṭivināyakar	Tirunāṭṭiyattānkuṭi
12. Koṭivināyakar	Koṭṭaiyūr
13. Cintāmaṇikaṇapati	Tirumaṟaikkāṭu
14. Sundarakaṇapati	Kīḷveḷūr, Tirumaḷapāṭi
15. Cūtvanappiḷḷaiyār	Tiruvucāttānam
16. Cevicāyttavināyakar	Anpilalanturai
17. Corṇavināyakar	Tirunaḷḷāṟu
18. Tālamūlavināyakar	Tirukkaccūr
19. Tunaiyiruntavināyakar	Tiruppanaiyūr
20. Nākaparaṇavināyakar	Nākaikkāroṇam
21. Nirttanavināyakar	Innampar
22. Paṭikkācuvināyakar	Tiruvīḷilimilaḷai
23. Paṭitturaivināyakar	Tiruviṭaimarutūr
24. Piraḷayaṅkāttavināyakar	Tiruppuṟampayam
25. Poyyāvināyakar	Tirumākaṟal
26. Pollāppiḷḷaiyār	Tirunāraiyūr
27. Mavaṭippiḷḷaiyār	Nākaikkāroṇam
28. Māṟṟuraittapiḷḷaiyār	Tiruvārūr

29. Mukkuṛuṇippiḷḷaiyār	Ālavāy, Koyil, Māyūram
30. Veracittivināyakar	Tiruvallam
31. Valaṁpurivināyakar	Tirukkaḷar
32. Vātāpikaṇapati	Tiruppukalūr
33. Vīrakattivināyakar	Tirumaṛaikkāṭu
34. Veḷḷaivināyakar	Tiruvalañcuḷi
35. Vētappiḷḷaiyār	Tiruvētikuṭī

Temples dedicated to Kārttikeya

Temples	*Location*
1. Tiruttaṇikai	Cittūr
2. Tiruvēṅkaṭam	Cittūr
3. Vaḷḷimalai	Cittūr
4. Veḷḷikaram	Cittūr
5. Viriñcipuram	North Arcot
6. Kacci Kumarakōṭṭam	Chengelput
7. Taccūr (Andāḷkuppam)	Chengelput
8. Kōṭainakar (Vallakkōṭṭai)	Chengelput
9. Tiruppōrūr	Chengelput
10. Uttaramērūr	Chengelput
11. Sēyūr (Ceyyūr)	Chengelput
12. Pēṛainakar (Peruṁperu)	Chengelput
13. Mayilam	South Arcot
14. Vaittīśvaran Koyil	Tanjore
15. Tiruviṭaikkaḷi	Tanjore
16. Kantankuṭi	Tanjore
17. Cikkal	Tanjore
18. Eṭṭikkuṭi	Kilvelur
19. Eṇkaṇ	Tirumatikunṛam
20. Svāmimalai	Kumbhakoṇam

21. Vayalūr	Tiruccirāppaḷḷi
22. Virālimalai	Tiruccirāppaḷḷi
23. Tirucceṅkōṭu	Cēlma
24. Cennimalai	Kōyamuttūr
25. Marutamalai	Kōyamuttūr
26. Kāṅkeyam Paṭṭāli, Sivamalai	Kōyamuttūr
27. Tirupparaṅkunṛam	Madurai
28. Paḷamutircōlai (Kallalakarkovil)	Madurai
29. Paḷani	Paḷani
30. Kunṛakkuti	Kāraikkuṭi
31. Koṭuṇkunṛam	Rāmanathapuram
32. Koṭumaḷūr	Rāmanathapuram
33. Kaḷukumalai	Tirunelvēli
34. Ilañci	Tenkāci, Tirunelvēli
35. Tirumalai	Tirunelvēli, Tēnkāci
36. Valliyūr	Tirunelvēli
37. Tiruccentūr	Tirunelvēli

Temples in which the Goddess is prominently installed and worshipped

Place	*Name of the goddess*
1. Tiru Ānaikkā	Akhilāṇḍeśvarī
2. Kāñci	Kāmākṣī
3. Tiruvaṇṇāmalai	Uṇṇāmulai
4. Avināci	Karuṇāmbikai
5. Tiru Āmāttūr	Muktāṁbikā
6. Tiru Ārur	Kamalāṁbikai
7. Tiru Ālavāy (Madurai)	Mīnākṣī
8. Tiru Aiyāṛu	Dharmasaṁvardhanī

9. Tiruvoṟṟiyūr	Vaḍivuṭaiyammai
10. Tirukkaḷukkunṟam	Tripurasundarī
11. Tirukkāḷatti	Jñānappūṅkotai
12. Kuṭamūkku	Maṅgaḷanāyakī
13. Kuṟṟālam	Kuḷalvāymoḷi Ammai
14. Tiruccirāppaḷḷi	Maṭṭuvārkuḷaliyammai
15. Tirunaḷḷāru	Pōkamārtapūṇmulaiyammai
16. Nākai	Nīlāyatākṣī
17. Tirunelvēli	Kāntimatiyammai
18. Tiruppātirippuliyūr	Periyanāyakī
19. Puḷḷirukkuvēlur	Taiyalnāyakī
20. Tirumaṭaikkāṭu	Yāḷaippaḷittamoḷiyammai
21. Tirumullaivāyil	Koṭiyiṭaināyakī

Temples of Śiva in which a place is assigned to Viṣṇu

Temple	*Special name of Viṣṇu installed therein*
1. Tiruvōttur	Ādikecavapperumāḷ
2. Kacciēkampam	Nilāttuṇḍapperumāḷ
3. Koṭimāṭaccenkunṟūr	Ādikesavapperumāḷ
4. Koyil (Chidambaram)	Govindarājapperumāḷ
5. Sikkal	Kōlavāmanapperumāḷ
6. Tirunaṇā	Ādikeśavapperumāḷ
7. Tirunāvalūr	Varadarājapperumāḷ
8. Tirunelvēli	Nellai Kōvindar
9. Tiruppaḷanam	Nellaikovindar
10. Pāṇḍikkoṭumuṭī	Araṅganātar
11. Tirupputtūr	Araṅganātar
12. Tiruvakkarai	Araṅganātar

A few temples with images of Śiva and his ancillary gods which have Purāṇic significance

Images	*Location*
Andhakāsurasaṁhāramūrti	Tirukkōvalūr
Arjuna	Tiruvēṭkaḷam
Ardhanārīśvara-vigraha	Kuṭantaikkīḻkkōṭṭam
Indra	Kīḻvēḷūr
Kālasaṁhāramūrti	Tirukkaṭavūr
Kālī (installed and worshipped with great significance)	Ambarmākāḷam
	Tiru ālaṁkāṭu
	Tiruvakkarai
Kubera	Kiḷveḷūr
Śani	Koḷḷikkāṭu
	Tirunaḷḷāṟu
Candraśekhara	Tiruppukalūr
Śivakāmi (*śilāvigraha*)	Āppanūr, Kañjanūr, Tirupputtūr, Tiruppūvaṇam
Somāskandamūrti (*śilāvigraha*)	Tirumaḷapāṭi
Dakṣiṇāmūrti (standing pose)	Tiruneyttānam
Durgā	Vētāraṇyam
Naṭarāja (this image as a rule is installed in all temples. Yet the temples mentioned here are celebrated for the great significance of each Naṭaraja image installed)	Tiruvālaṅkāṭu
	Tiruvālavāy (Madura)
	Tirukkaḷar
	Kuṟṟālaṁ
	Chidambaram
	Tirunaḷḷam
	Tirunelvēli
	Tirumurukanpūṇḍi
	Tiruveṇkāṭu
Naṭarāja (*śilāvigraha*)	Tiruppūvaṇam
	Kañcanūr
	Tirupputtūr

Nandikeśvara (standing pose)	Tirumālppeṛu
Nāgarāja	Tiruppāṁpuram
Paraśurāma	Tiruppaḷuvūr
Yama	Tiruvāñciyam
Vālmīki	Tiruvānmiyūr
Bhairava	Tirupputtūr

Temples of Śiva in the South which present the ancillary gods as engaged in the act of worshipping Śiva

Ancillary gods	*Location of temple*
Gaṇeśa	Kaccianēkataṅkāppatam
	Kaṭikkuḷam
	Tirucceṅkāttaṅkuṭi
Kārttikeya	Tirukkaṭaṁpantuṛai
	Kīḷvēḷūr
	Sēynallūr
	Puḷḷirukkuvēḷūr
	Pēṇuperuntuṛai
	Tirumurukanpūṇṭi
	Vaṭatirumullaivāyil
	Erukkattaṁpuliyūr
Umā	Tiruvaṇṇāmalai
	Anēkataṅkāpatam
	Tiruvānaikkā
	Kacciēkampam
	Tirukkāṇūr
	Kuṭantaikkārōṇam
	Tirukkētāram
	Tiruccattimuṭṭam
	Turccuḷiyal
	Pēṇuperuntuṛai
	Mayilāḍutuṛai

Viṣṇu	Avalivaṇallūr
	Tirueṛumpūr
	Tiruveṭakam
	Kaccūr
	Cakrappaḷḷi
	Sivapuram
	Talaiccaṅkāṭu
	Tirunelvēli
	Tirumaṅgalakkuṭi
	Tirumaḷapāṭi
	Tirumāṇikuḷi
	Tirumālppeṛu
	Tiruvakkarai
	Tiruvalampuram
	Tiruvāñciyam
	Vaḷolipuṟṟūr
	Tiruvīḻimiḻalai
Brahmā	Anpilālanturai
	Tiruveṛumpūr
	Kañcanūr
	Kaṭaimuṭi
	Tirukkarukkuṭi
	Sīkāli
	Tirukkoḷili
	Tirucciṟṟēmam
	Tarumapuram
	Tirunellikkā
	Tirunelvēli
	Tiruppūvaṇam
	Pēṇupeṛunturai
	Tirumaṅgalakkuṭī
	Mayēndirapaḷḷi
	Tirumunṭīccuram
	Tirumūkkīccuram
	Tiruvakkaṛai

The eight guardians of the world /

Indra	Tiruvaḷuntūr
	Indranīlaparuppatam
	Tiruvaiyāṛu
	Kaccineṛikkāraikkāṭu
	Tirukkaṭampūr
	Kaṇṇārkōyil
	Karuppariyalūr
	Karuvili
	Kāḷatti
	Kārāyil
	Kiḷvēḷūr
	Kaiccinam
	Semponpaḷḷi
	Tiruccoṛṛutturai
	Tēvūr
	Tirunīḍūr
	Tirupparāytturai
	Tiruppūnturutti
	Mayēntirappaḷḷi
	Tirumaḷapāṭi
	Tirumākarai
	Tirumuṇḍiccuram
	Tirumullaivāyil
	Tiruvalañcuḷi
	Vāṭpōkki
	Tiruveṇkāṭu
Agni	Kañcanūr
	Koḷḷikkāṭu
	Tiruppukalūr
	Tiruvanniyūr
Yama	Tarumapuram
Varuṇa	Anniyūr
	Tirunīlakkuṭi

Vāyu	Tiruvāṭpōkki
Kubera	Kaccianēkataṅkāpatam
	Kiḷvēḷūr
	Tiruccemponpaḷḷi
	Tevūr
	Tirunaṇā
	Tirupparāyttuṛai

The Navagrahas

The Navagrahas . . .	Tiruttenkūr
	Tiruvallam
Sūrya	Anēkataṅkāpatam
	Aṭānai
	Kuṭaṇṭaikkiḷkkottam
	Tiruccōṛṛuttuṛai
	Tiruṭṭuṛaiyūr
	Nannilam
	Tirunākeccuram
	Tirunīḍūr
	Tirunellikkā
	Paritiniyamam
	Puḷḷirukkuvēḷūr
	Puṛavār
	Panaṅkāṭṭūr
	Tirumankalakkuṭi
	Mayēntirappaḷḷi
	Tirumaḷapāṭi
	Tirumākaṛal
	Tirumīyaccūr
	Tirumunṭīccuram
	Valivaḷam
	Tiruvāṭpokki
	Tiruvāymūr
Candra	Anekataṅkāpatam

	Karukāvūr
	Tilataippati
	Tirunākeccuram
	Tirunīṭūr
	Palaiyāṛai
	Mayēntirappaḷḷi
	Tirumālpeṛu
	Tiruvakkarai
Aṅgāraka (Kuja) . . .	Ciṛukuḍi
Guru (Bṛhaspati) . . .	Teṅkuṭittiṭṭai
	Tiruvalitāyam
Śukra	Tirunāvalūr

Other gods

Bhairava	Vatukūr
Kālī	Ambarmākāḷam
	Tiruniḍūr
	Tirumangalakkuḍi
	Mīyaccūr
	Ilaṅkovil
Nandideva	Tirupparupatam
Vedas	Tiruvaḷuntur
	Tiruccirremam
	Tirumaraikkāṭu
	Tiruvetikuṭi
	Tiruvēṛkātu
Madana	Tirumanañjeri
Varuṇa	Tiruvāṭānai
Rāma	Ramanādiccuram
	Rāmeśvaram
	Tiruvucāttānam
	Karukkuḍi
	Kālatti
	Paṭṭīccuram

Paraśurāma	Tiruvañcaikkaḷam
Lakṣmaṇa	Tiruvusāttānam
	Kuraṅkukkā
	Vatakuraṅgātuṭuṛai
	Tiruvalitāyam
Pāṇḍavas	Araiyaṇinallūr
Bhīma	Kōḷili
	Tirutturaiyūr
Arjuna	Vāḷolipuṛṛūr
	Vijayamaṅgai
	Tiruvēṭṭakuṭi

Asuras

Kara	Kaṛkuṭi
Jalandhara	Ōṇakāntantaḷi
Triśira	Tirucirāppaḷḷi
Vakrāsura	Tiruvakkarai

Appendix 7

Construction of Images

While constructing any image, the *śilpin* or sculptor must adhere to the various details of measurements etc. prescribed in the relevant texts. The *śilpin* employs two measurements — one is *aṅgula* and the other is *tāla*. The length of the face is called *tāla*. One twelfth of a *tāla* is one *aṅgula*. *Aṅgula* are of four kinds: *berāṅgula*, *mānāṅgula*, *mātrāṅgula* and *dehalabdhāṅgula*. *Berāṅgula* is measured in terms of the finger of the image. *Mānāṅgula* is the *aṅgula* as it is normally understood (i.e. $1/12^{th}$ of a tāla). The *mātrāṅgula* is the measure of the finger of the *yajamāna* who commissioned the image. The *dehalabdhāṅgula* is $1/124^{th}$, $1/120^{th}$ or $1/116^{th}$ of the full height of the image under construction. We give below three tables giving the details of the measurements of the *tālas* with which the images are constructed.

Daśatāla and its detailed measurements
(The numbers indicate the *aṅgulas*)

Parts of the body	*Uttama*	*Madhyama*	*Adhama*
The *uṣnīṣa*	1	1	1
Hair (*keśa*)	3	3	3
Face	13	13	12.5
Chin to throat	1/2	-	-
Neck	4	4	4
From neck to chest	13.5	13	12.5
From chest to navel	13.5	13	12.5
From navel to *meḍhra*	13.5	13	12.5
From *meḍhra* to thigh	27	26	25
Kneecap	4	4	4
Jaṅghā	27	26	25
Jaṅghā to *pāda*	4	4	4

Navatāla, details of measurements

Parts of the body	*Uttama*	*Madhyama*	*Adhama*
Crown	1		
Hair	3	3	
Face	12	12	
Neck	4	3	
Up to the chest	12	12	
Up to the navel	12	12	
Up to the *meḍhra*	12	12	
Thigh	24	24	
Knee	4	3	
Leg	24	24	
Feet	4	3	
	112	108	

Pañcatāla and its measurements

Parts of the body	*Uttama*	*Madhyama*	*Adhama*
Crown	-	1	
Hair	3	2	
Face	12	7	
Neck	2	2	
From neck to chest	11	8	
Up to navel	12	9	
Up to *meḍhra*	6	7	
Thigh	6	10	
Knee	3	2	
Leg	6	10	
Feet	3	2	
	64	60	56

The following scheme is generally adhered to for determining the *tāla* for the image in question:

Uttamadaśatāla	Sabhāpati
	Rudra
	Viṣṇu
	Kaṅkāla
	Dakṣināmūrti
	Lakṣmīnārāyaṇa
	Varāhamūrti
	Brahmā
	Narasiṁha
Madhyamadaśatāla	Rāma
	Gopāla
	Paraśurāma
	Bhadrakālī
	Durgā
	Lakṣmī
	Bhūdevī
	Ṣaṇmukha
	Īśvarī
Adhamadaśatāla	Subrahmaṇya
	Sūrya
	Indra
	Candra
	Ādityas (twelve)
	Rudras (eleven)
	Vasus (eight)
Aṣṭadala	Śaktis of various gods
Saptatāla	Vetāla
Saṣṭhatāla	Preta
Pañcatāla	Vināyaka, Kṛṣṇa
Caturthatāla	Vāmana

The Poses of the Hands

The hands of the image are shown in various poses. The following are a few of the fairly important poses:

Varada-hasta	The fingers of the left hand point downwards. This *hasta* indicates the fact that the deity concerned is ready to bestow boons on the devotees.
Abhaya-hasta	The fingers of the right hand point upwards.
Kaṭaka-hasta	In this pose the fingers of the right hand are folded into a loose fist, and the half-folded fingers point upwards. The goddess is invariably portrayed with her hand in this pose.
Lola-hasta	The fingers of the left hand of the image of the goddess in the standing pose are represented in this pose.
Gaja-hasta	The left hand of Naṭarāja is shown in this pose, which bears a resemblance to the trunk of an elephant.
Ardhacandra-hasta	This is the position in which the hand of Naṭarāja which carries fire is depicted.
Ḍamaru-hasta	This is the pose of the hand that carries the drum (also for Naṭarāja)
Siṁhakarṇa-hasta	This is a hand carrying a lotus. The goddess is always presented in this pose.
Tripatāka-hasta	A hand wielding a weapon is generally depicted in this pose. The two fingers which are featured gripping the weapon bear a resemblance to *patāka*. This is displayed in the representations of Candraśekhara and Subrahmaṇya.
Sūci-hasta	This resembles the *kaṭaka-hasta*, but the forefinger points straight upwards.
Añjali-hasta	The palms are joined together with the forefingers pointing upwards. Devotees are shown in this pose.

Appendix 8

Śaiva Tīrthas

Below is given a list of *tīrthas* connected with Śiva and his ancillary deities Śakti, Gaṇeśa and Kārttikeya. The *tīrthas* in this list are arranged in alphabetical order, and their occurrences in the Epics and the *Purāṇas* are indicated. It will be seen that the *tīrthas* have derived their names from their geographical location or from the gods with whom they are specially associated.

The *Skanda Purāṇa* and the *Padma Purāṇa*, particularly the former, have devoted a considerable part of their texts to descriptions of the *tīrthas*. Other *Purāṇas* confine themselves more to their enumeration rather than to any detailed description. The *Skanda Purāṇa*, on the other hand, actually devotes one chapter for each of the various *tīrthas*.

It may be pointed out here that the list of *tīrthas* presented by P.V. Kane in his *History of Dharmaśāstra* is (in the words of the author) "comprehensive enough and far longer and more informative than any list of *tīrthas* presented by any scholar so far." In a sense, however, that list of *tīrthas* is incomplete, because the compiler has not paid sufficient attention to the *Skanda Purāṇa*, which is especially concerned with Śiva. In this regard Kane observes: "The *Skanda Purāṇa* has been a source of great trouble and labour. Owing to the limited time at my disposal, I have not been able to digest thoroughly the ninety thousand odd verses of that *Purāṇa*, though I have very carefully gone into the *Kāśī* and some other *Khaṇḍas*." [4] An attempt has been made in this appendix to rectify that deficiency, at least to

[4] Kane, *History of Dharmaśāstra*, vol. IV, p. 724.

some extent, by including in this list most of the *tīrthas* mentioned in that *Purāṇa*. The chapters of the *Skanda Purāṇa* relating to the *tīrthas* are only informative to a limited extent. No doubt, they give detailed accounts of the *tīrthas* and their glories, but they lack in other information which would help in the identification of these *tīrthas*. Of course, in the matter of the correct identification of the various *tīrthas*, one would do well to heed the following observation made by Kane: "Many of the doubts and difficulties about the identification of the *tīrthas* can, if at all, be solved only by means of actual journeys to various places and investigations on the spot. That is a task which would require for its accomplishment a team of workers. A single individual can hardly attempt such a task with his own resources." [5]

1. A List of the Tīrthas Connected with Śiva

ABHAYEŚVARA	*Skanda P.*, V.1.37; V.2.48.
ACALEŚVARA	*Liṅga P.*, I.92.165; *Skanda P.*, VI.13; VII.3.4-7.
ĀDITYEŚVARA	*Matsya P.*, 191.5; *Padma P.*, I.18.5; *Skanda P.*, V.3.153; VII.1.43.
AGĀREŚVARA	*Matsya P.*, 190.9.
AGASTYA	*MBh*, III.118.4.
AGASTYEŚVARA	*Matsya P.*, 191.5; *Padma P.*, I.18.16; *Skanda P.*, V.1.20; V.1.35; V.2.1; V.3.64.
AGHOREŚVARA	*Skanda P.*, VII.1.92.
AGNIPĀLEŚVARA	*Padma P.*, VI.134.26.
AHALYĀTĪRTHA	*Kūrma P.*, II.41.43; *Matsya P.*, 191.90-92. *Padma P.*, I.18.84.
AHILYEŚVARA	*Skanda P.*, V.3.136; VI.208.
AIRAṆḌITĪRTHA	*Matsya P.*, 191.41.
AJAPĀLEŚVARA	*Skanda P.*, VI.95.
AJĪGARTEŚVARA	*Skanda P.*, VII.1.191.

[5] Kane, *op.cit.*, p. 727.

AJOGANDHEŚVARA	*Skanda P.*, VII.1.294.
AKHAṆḌEŚVARA	*Skanda P.*, V.1.68.
AKRŪREŚVARA	*Skanda P.*, V.2.39.
AKṢAMĀLEŚVARA	*Skanda P.*, VII.1.129.
ALIKEŚVARA	*Skanda P.*, V.3.225.
AMALEŚVARA	*Skanda P.*, V.3.213.
AMARAKAṆṬHA	*Skanda P.*, IV.2.74.
AMARAKAṆṬHAKA	*Kūrma P.*, II.40.36; *Matsya P.*, 188.79; 188.84-87. *Padma P.*, I.15.68-69.
AMAREŚVARA	*Liṅga P.*, I.92.151; *Matsya P.*, 188.93; *Skanda P.*, V.3.28; VI.145 and 146; VII.1.194.
AMATAKEŚVARA	*Padma P.*, I.33.33.
AṄKUREŚVARA	*Skanda P.*, V.3.168.
ĀMRĀTAKEŚVARA	*Matsya P.*, 22.51; 181.28.
AMṚTAKEŚVARA	*Matsya P.*, 190. 5.
AMṚTEŚVARA	*Skanda P.*, IV.2.94.
AMṚTODBHAVA	*Skanda P.*, V.1.51.
ĀNĀDIKALPEŚVARA	*Skanda P.*, V.1.20.
ĀNANDABHAIRAVA	*Skanda P.*, V. 1.68.
ĀNANDEŚVARA	*Skanda P.*, V.1.31; V.2.33; V.3.65.
ANAṄGEŚVARA	*Skanda P.*, VII.1.158.
ANARAKEŚVARA	*Skanda P.*, V.2.27; V.3.159; VII.1.225.
ANARAKA	*MBh*, III.81.149.
ANARTAKEŚVARA	*Skanda P.*, VI.65.
ANARTEŚVARA	*Skanda P.*, VII.1.151.
AṄGĀRAKEŚVARA	*Kūrma P.*, II.41.7; *Skanda P.*, V.2.43; VII.1.45.
AṄGĀREŚVARA	*Matsya P.*, 190.9; *Padma P.*, I.17.6. I.18.56.
AṄGIRASA	*Kurma P.*, II. 41.31-33; *Padma P.*, I.18.50.
ANILEŚVARA	*Skanda P.*, VII.1.109.
AṄGAPĀDA	*Skanda P.*, V.1.27.
AṄKUŚEŚVARA	*Matsya P.*, 194.1.

APASAREŚVARA	*Skanda P.*, V.2.17.
APSAREŚA	*Matsya P.*, 194.16.
ARGHYEŚVARA	*Skanda P.*, VII.1.66.
ARUṆĀDITYA	*Skanda P.*, IV.2.51.
ARUṆEŚVARA	*Skanda P.*, V. 2.76.
ASALIṄGA	*Liṅga P.*, I.92.148.
AṢṬAKULEŚVARA	*Skanda P.*, VI.1.162.
AṢṬAṢAṢṬITĪRTHA	*Skanda P.*, VI. 108.
AŚVATTHATĪRTHA	*Kūrma P.*, II.35.38; *Vāmana P.*, 36.40.
AŚVINEŚVARA	*Skanda P.*, VII. 1.164.
AṬEŚVARA	*Skanda P.*, VI. 128.
AVANTĪ	*Agni P.*, 109.24; *Brahma P.*, 43.24; *Brahmāṇḍa P.*, II.16.29; *Matsya P.*, 114.24; *Nārada P.*, II.78; *Skanda P.*, V.1.42; *Vāmana P.*, 45.98.
AVIMUKTA	*Agni P.*, 109.18; 112.2 and 4; *Liṅga P.*, I.53.12-14; *Matsya P.*, 22.7; 181 (the entire chapter); *Padma P.*, I.33.31; *Skanda P.*, IV.1.26; IV.1.39.
AVIMUKTEŚVARA	*MBh*, III.84.79-80; *Skanda P.*, V.2.78; *Viṣṇu P.*, V.39.30 & 43.
AVIYUKTEŚVARA	*Skanda P.*, VII.3.57.
BAḌAVEŚVARA	*Skanda P.*, VII.1.65.
BAHUSVARṆEŚVARA	*Skanda P.*, VII.1.355.
BALABHADREŚVARA	*Skanda P.*, VII.1.227.
BALĀKEŚVARA	*Matsya P.*, 191.19.
BĀLAPENDRA	*Padma P.*, VI.145.
BĀLASAKHYA	*Skanda P.*, VI.21.
BALEŚVARA	*Liṅga P.*, I.92.148; *Skanda P.*, VII.1.289.
BĀṆATĪRTHA	*Brahma P.*, 123.214; *Kūrma P.*, II.41.9.
BHADRATĪRTHA	*Brahma P.*, 165.1; *Matsya P.*, 22.50; *Padma P.*, I.18.54; I.33.33.
BHADRAKĀLEŚVARA	*Matsya P.*, 22.74.

BHADRAKARṆA	*Agni P.*, 109.17; *Padma P.*, I.33.22; I.33.33; *Skanda P.*, VII.3.8.
BHADRAKARṆEŚVARA	*MBh*, III.82.35; *Kūrma P.*, II.20.35; *Skanda P.*, VII.1.8.
BHADRAVAṬA	*MBh*, III.80.69; *Padma P.*, I.12.10; *Varāha P.*, 51.2.
BHADREŚVARA	*Kūrma P.*, II.41.4; *Matsya P.*, 22.25; *Padma P.*, VI.129.13.
BHĀGĪRATHĪ	*MBh*, III.80.12; *Matsya P.*, 121.41.
BHAIRAVEŚVARA	*Liṅga P.*, I.92.137; *Skanda P.*, VI.41; VI.94; VII.1.63; VII.1.149; VII.1.228.
BHAIRAVAKṢETRA	*Skanda P.*, VI.151.
BHAṄGATĪRTHA	*Matsya P.*, 191.51.
BHĀRABHŪTI	*Matsya P.*, 194.18.
BHARATEŚVARA	*Skanda P.*, VII.1.172.
BHARGALEŚVARA	*Skanda P.*,V.3.152.
BHĀRGAVEŚVARA	*Skanda P.*, VII.1.178.
BHAṬṬIKA	*Skanda P.*, VI.117.
BHILLATĪRTHA	*Brahma P.*, II.99.
BHĪMEŚVARA	*Kūrma P.*, II.41.20; II.44.15; *Matsya P.*, 22.46; 22.75; 191.5; 191.27; *Padma P.*, I.18.5; I.18.28; *Skanda P.*, V.1.25; V.3.77; VI.40; VII.2.3.
BHṚGUTĪRTHA	*Kūrma P.*, II.42.1-6; *Matsya P.*, 193.46-58; *Padma P.*, I.20; *Skanda P.*, V.3.181.
BHṚGUKACCHA	*Skanda P.*, V.3.182.
BHṚKUṬEŚVARA	*Skanda P.*, V.3.128.
BHRŪṆAGARTA	*Skanda P.*, VI.53.
BHŪTANĀTHEŚVARA	*Skanda P.*, VII.1.117.
BHŪTEŚVARA	*Kūrma P.*, I.35.10; *Padma P.*, I.37.13; VI.158; *Skanda P.*, V.3.177; *Vāmana P.*, 34.36.
BHŪTEŚĀRŪDRA	*Skanda P.*, VI.87.
BILVAKA	*Padma P.*, VI.129.11.

BILVAVANA	*Varāha P.*, I.153.
BILVEŚVARA	*Skanda P.*, V.2.83.
BRAHMAKEŚVARA	*Agni P.*, 116.24.
BRAHMAKUṆḌA	*Skanda P.*, III.1.14; VII.2.3; *Varāha P.*, 141.4-6; 151.71; *Vayu P.*, 110.8.
BRAHMATĪRTHA	*Agni P.*, 115.36; *Bhāgavata P.*, X.78.19; *Brahma P.*, 113.1 & 23; *Brahmāṇḍa P.*, III.13.56; *Kūrma P.*, I.35.9; II.37.28; *Nārada P.*, II.45.102; *Padma P.*, I.37.9-12; *Skanda P.*, V.3.129.
BRĀHMAṆĪTĪRTHA	*Skanda P.*, VI.198.
BRAHMASARAS	*MBh*, III.93.10.
BRAHMEŚVARA	*Kūrma P.*, II.41.18; *Skanda P.*, V.2.65; VII.1.150; VII.1.245; VII.1.248; VII.1.317; VII.2.3.
BṚHADEŚVARA	*Skanda P.*, VII.1.46.
BṚHASPATĪŚVARA	*Skanda P.*, VII.1.47.
CAMASĀ	*MBh*, II.80.118; *Padma P.*, I.25.8.
CANDANEŚVARA	*Padma P.*, VI.142.
CAṆḌĀDITYATĪRTHA	*Skanda P.*, V.3.91.
CANDEŚVARATĪRTHA	*Agni P.*, 112.4.
CAṆḌĪŚA	*Skanda P.*, VII.1.42.
CAṆḌĪŚVARA	*Skanda P.*, V.1.25; VII.1.34.
CANDRABHĀGĀ	*Kūrma P.*, II.41.35; *Matsya P.*, 191.64; *Nārada P.*, II.60.30; *Padma P.*, I.18.62; VI.148.12; VI.149.
CANDRĀDITYEŚVARA	*Skanda P.*, V.2.72.
CANDRAHĀSA	*Skanda P.*, V.3.121.
CANDRAPRABHĀSA	*Skanda P.*, VIII.3.20.
CANDREŚVARA	*Padma P.*, VI.149; VI.162; *Skanda P.*, V.1.31.
CANDREŚVARAKĀLAKUṆḌA	*Skanda P.*, VII.1.342.
CARMA	*Kurma P.*, I.35.4.
CARMAṆVATĪ	*MBh* III.80.73; *Agni P.*, 109.10; *Padma P.*, I.24.3.

CARMAMUṆḌA	*Skanda P.*, VI.54.
CHĀYĀLIṄGA	*Skanda P.*, VII.1.263.
CINTĀṄGATEŚVARA	*Padma P.*, I.37.13; *Skanda P.*, VI.144.
CITRĀṄGADEŚVARA	*Padma P.*, I.37.14; *Skanda P.*, VII. 1.122.
CITREŚVARA	*Skanda P.*, VI.35; VII.1.142.
CŪḌĀMAṆĪŚVARA	*Skanda P.*, V.1.25.
CYAVANEŚVARA	*Skanda P.*, VII.1.280.
CYAVEŚVARA	*Skanda P.*, V.2.30.
DADHISKANDA	*Skanda P.*, V.3.79.
DĀKṢĀYAṆĪŚVARA	*Skanda P.*, IV.2.67.
DAKṢEŚVARA	*Skanda P.*, IV.2.87. *Vāmana P.*, 34.20.
ḌAMARUKEŚVARA	*Skanda P.*, V.1.20; V.2.4.
DĀRUKĀ	*Liṅga P.*, I.2.9.
DĀRUVANA	*Brahmāṇḍa P.*, 27.79; *Kūrma P.*, II.39.66.
DAŚARATHEŚVARA	*Skanda P.*, VII.1.171.
DASĀRṆA	*Kūrma P.*, II.37.35-36; *Matsya P.*, 22.34; *Vāyu P.*, 45.99; 79.93.
DAŚĀSVAMEDHIKA	*Brahmāṇḍa P.*, III.13.45; *Kūrma P.*, II.37.26; *Matsya P.*, 185.68; 106.46; *Skanda P.*, V.3.180; VII.1.234.
DEVADĀRUVANA	*Kūrma P.*, II.37.53; *Liṅga P.*, I.3.1-4; *Padma P.*, VI.129.27.
DEVAHRADA	*MBh*, III.83.18; *Varāha P.*, 145.71.
DEVAPATHA	*MBh*, III.83.46; *Padma P.*, I. 39.42.
DEVARĀJEŚVARA	*Skanda P.*, VII.1.217.
DEVIḲA	*MBh*, III.80.111
DHANADA	*Skanda P.*, 7.3.68.
DHANADEŚVARA	*Skanda P.*, VII.1.36.
DHANUḤSAHASREŚVARA	*Skanda P.*, V.2.63.
DHANUṢKOṬI	*Skanda P.*, III.1.31.
DHARMĀRAṆYA	*MBh*, III.80.65; *Agni P.*, 115.34; *Nārada P.*, II.45.100; *Skanda P.*, III.2.1.
DHARMARĀJEŚVARA	*Skanda P.*, VI.138.39.
DHARMEŚVARA	*Skanda P.*, IV.2.78.

DHAUTAPĀPA	*Skanda P.*, V.3.184.
DHAVALEŚVARA	*Padma P.*, VI.144.
DHRUVEŚVARA	*Skanda P.*, VII.1.131.
ḌHUṆḌHEŚVARA	*Skanda P.*, V.1.20; V.2.3.
DHUNDHUMĀREŚVARA	*Skanda P.*, VI.38.
DĪPEŚVARA	*Kūrma P.*, II.41.25-27; *Matsya P.*, 191.37.
DṚMI	*MBh*, III-80. 88-89.
DUGDHEŚVARA	*Padma P.*, VI.148.
DUḤSĪLEŚVARA	*Skanda P.*, VI.274.
DURDHARṢEŚVARA	*Padma P.*, VI.146; *Skanda P.*, V.2.70.
DURVĀSEŚVARA	*Skanda P.*, VI.274; VII.1.236.
VĪREŚVARA	*Padma P.*, I.18-38.
EKĀDAŚARUDRA	*Skanda P.*, VI.277.
EKĀDAŚARUDRALIṄGA	*Skanda P.*, VII.1.362.
EKADHARA	*Padma P.*, VI.136.12-15.
EKASĀLAḌIṆḌIMEŚVARA	*Skanda P.*, V.3.212.
EKAŚṚṄGA	*Varāha P.*, I.81.
ELĀPURA	*Matsya P.*, 22.50.
ERAṆḌITĪRTHA	*Matsya P.*, 191.42; 193.65; *Padma P.*, I.18.44.
GAJAKARṆA	*Matsya P.*, 22.38.
GAṆATĪRTHA	*Matsya P.*, 22.73; *Padma P.*, VI.133.24-37.
GĀṆAPATYA	*Padma P.*, VI.163; also VI.129.26.
GAṄGĀ	*MBh*, III.83.63; *Vāyu P.*, I.42.36-40.
GAṄGĀDHARA	*Skanda P.*, VII.3.56.
GAṄGĀDVĀRA	*MBh*, III.80.13; *Agni P.*, 4.7; *Kūrma P.*, II.44.13; *Matsya P.*, 22.10.
GANDHARVASENEŚVARA	*Skanda P.*, VII.1.27.
GANDHARVEŚVARA	*Skanda P.*, VII.1.26 & 30; VII.1.56; VII.1.302.
GANGĀHRADA	*MBh*, III.81.85 and 153; *Padma P.*, I.27.63.
GAṄGĀPAKṢAGAṄGEŚVARA	*Skanda P.*, VII.1.267.

GAṄGĀVĀHAKA	*Skanda P.*, V.3.178.
GAṄGEŚVARA	*Matsya P.*, 191.81; also 193.14; *Nārada P.*, II.49.46; *Skanda P.*, V.1.25; V.2.42; VII.1.250; VII.1.285; VII.1.289; VII.2.5.
GAṄGEYEŚVARA	*Skanda P.*, VI.58.
GĀRGEŚVARA	*Matsya P.*, 191.82; *Skanda P.*, VII.1.173.
GARUḌEŚVARA	*Skanda P.*, VII.1.156.
GAUṚĪŚVARA	*Skanda P.*, VII.1.69.
GAUTAMATĪRTHA	*Padma P.*, VI.129.7.
GAUTAMEŚVARA	*Kūrma P.*, II.42.6-8; *Matsya P.*, 22.70; *Padma P.*, I.20.58; *Skanda P.*, VI.208; VI.267; VII.1.80; V.3.74; VII.1.216.
GAUTAMI	*Brahma P.*, II.105.
GĀYATRĪŚVARA	*Skanda P.*, VII.1.54.
GAYĀ	*Garuḍa P.*, 74; *Kūrma P.*, II.35.0; *Nārada P.*, II.67. *Padma P.*, I.33.2; I.37.5.
GHAṆṬEŚVARA	*Matsya P.*, 22.70; *Skanda P.*, V.2.57; VII.1.254.
GHARGHARA	*Matsya P.*, 22.35; *Padma P.*, II.39.43.
GHAṬEŚVARA	*Padma P.*, VI.159.
GODĀVARĪ	*MBh*, III.118.3; *Matsya P.*, 22.57.
GOKARṆA	*MBh*, III.83.22; *Brahmāṇḍa P.*, III.51.58; *Kūrma* P., II.35.30-31; *Nārada P.*, II.74; *Matsya P.*, 22.38; 181.25; *Liṅga P.*, I.33.33; I.77.37-47; *Padma P.*, I.39.22; VI.129.11; *Skanda P.*, VI.26.
GOKARṆEŚVARA	*Vāraha P.*, I.213; I.215.118.
GOLAMEŚVARA	*Skanda P.*, V.3.179.
GOMATI	*Matsya P.*, 22.13. *Skanda P.*, VII.4.4.97-98; 85.32.
GOMUKHATĪRTHA	*Skanda P.*, VI.93.
GONIṢKRAMA	*Varāha P.*, I.147.
GOPAKA	*Padma P.*, VI.129.11.
GOPAREŚVARA	*Skanda P.*, V.3.73.

GOPEŚVARA	*Skanda P.*, V.3.162; V.3.174.
GOPĪŚVARA	*Skanda P.*, VII.1.120; *Vāyu P.*,III. 35-37.
GOPRAKHYA	*Kūrma P.*, I.35.33.
GOPYĀDITYEŚVARA	*Skanda P.*, VII.1.118.
GOVATSALIṄGA	*Skanda P.*, III.2.27.
GṚDHRAVAṬA	*MBh*, III.82.79; *Agni P.*, 116.12; *Nārada P.*, II.44; *Padma P.*, I.38.11.
GṚDHREŚVARA	*Agni P.*, 116.11. *Nārada P.*, II.47.78.
GUHEŚVARA	*Skanda P.*,V.2.2; VII.1.253; VII.3.56.
GUPHEŚVARA	*Skanda P.*, VII.1.253.
HAṀSEŚVARA	*Skanda P.*, V.3.221.
HANUMANTEŚVARA	*Skanda P.*, V.1.21; V.3.83
HANUMATKEŚVARA	*Skanda P.*, V.2.79.
HARASIDDHI	*Skanda P.*, V.1.19.
HARIHARAPRABHĀ	*Varāha P.*, I.144.
HĀṬAKEŚVARA	*Skanda P.*, VI.1; *Skanda P.*, VII.1.346; *Vāmana P.*, 63.78.
HIMĀLAYA	*Kūrma P.*, I.35.13.
HIMAVAT	*Brahmāṇḍa P.*, 22.1-81; *Liṅga P.*, I.6.6.
HIRAṆYĀTUṆḌAPURAGHARGHARAHRADAKANDEŚVARA	*Skanda P.*, VII.1.363.
HIRAṆYEŚVARA	*Skanda P.*, VII.1.153.
HUṄKĀRASVĀMI	*Skanda P.*, V.3.157.
IKṢUNADĪ	*Matsya P.*, 191.48; *Padma P.*, I.18.47; *Vāyu P.*,45.96.
INDRATĪRTHA	*Brahma P.*, 96.1; *Skanda P.*, V.3.118.
INDRADYUMNEŚVARA	*Skanda P.*, I.2.13-209; V.2.15; VI.271.
INDREŚVARA	*Liṅga P.*, I.92.152; *Skanda P.*, V.2.35; VII.1.224; VII.1.295; VII.2.3.
ĪŚĀNA	*Padma P.*, I.33.33.
ĪŚĀNADHYUṢITA	*MBh*, III.82.7.
ĪŚĀNAŚA	*Padma P.*, I.18.27.
ĪŚĀNEŚVARA	*Skanda P.*, V.2.16.
JĀBĀLEŚVARA	*Skanda P.*, IV.2.65; VI.144.

JĀGEŚVARA	*Skanda P.*,VI.78.
JAIGĪṢAVYEŚVARA	*Skanda P.*, VII.1.14.
JĀLANDHARA	*Brahmāṇḍa P.*, IV.44.95; *Matsya P.*, 13.46; 22.64; *Padma P.*, VI.4.19-20; VI.129.26.
JALAPRABHĀSALIṄGA	*Skanda P.*, VII.1.196.
JĀLEŚVARA	*Kūrma P.*, II.40.22; II.40.35; *Matsya P.*, 181.28; 186.15 and 38; 188.90; *Padma P.*, I.14.3; I.14.15; *Skanda P.*, V.3.26; VII.1.338.
JĀLPEŚVARA	*Skanda P.*, V.2.66.
JĀMADAGNYEŚVARA	*Skanda P.*, V.3.218; VII.1.122; VII.1.197.
JAMBUKEŚVARA	*Kūrma P.*, I.35.4; *Liṅga P.*, I.92.107; *Nārada* P., II.50.67; *Padma P.*, I.37.4.
JANAKEŚVARA	*Skanda P.*, VII.1.113.
JANMEŚVARA	*Matsya P.*, 22.42.
JAPYEŚVARA	*Agni P.*, 112.4; *Kūrma P.*, II.43.17.
JARADGAVEŚVARA	*Skanda P.*, VII.1.344.
JAṬEŚVARA	*Skanda P.*, V.2.28.
JAYANTEŚVARA	*Skanda P.*, III.2.19.
JAYEŚVARA	*Skanda P.*, V.1.28.
JVĀLĀMĀLEŚVARA	*Vāmana P.*, 34.36.
JVĀLEŚVARA	*Matsya P.*, 188.80 and 94-95; *Padma P.*, I.15.69, 77 and 78; *Skanda P.*, VII.1.271.
JVARAGHNI	*Skanda P.*, V.1.49.
JYEṢṬHEŚA	*Skanda P.*, IV.2.63.
JYOTIRŪPEŚVARA	*Skanda P.*, IV.2.94.
KAILĀSA	*Brahma P.*, II.6.7; *Bhāgavata P.*, IV.6; *Brahmāṇḍa P.*, 25.24-40; *Liṅga P.*, I.51.20-30; *Vāyu P.*, I.30.94-104; I.41.1-13.
KĀLA	*MBh*, III.83.11; *Kūrma P.*, I.35.2.
KĀLABHAIRAVA	*Liṅga P.*, I.92.132; *Skanda P.*, V.1.64.
KĀLABHAIRAVAŚMAŚĀNA	*Skanda P.*, VII.1.201.
KĀLĀGNI-RUDRA	*Skanda P.*, V.3.187.
KĀLAKĀLEŚVARA	*Skanda P.*, V.2.18; V.3.154; VII.1.75.

KĀLAKEŚVARA	*Kūrma P.*, I.35.7.
KĀLAÑJARA	*Brahma P.*, 146.1; *Kūrma P.*, II.36.11; *Padma P.*, I.37.15.
KALAŚEŚVARA	*Skanda P.*, VI.49-51.
KĀLEŚVARA	*Liṅga P.*, I.92.136; *Matsya P.*, 191.85; *Padma P.*, I.18.80; *Skanda P.*, VI.13.
KALHOḌĪTĪRTHA	*Skanda P.*, V.3.93; V.3.119.
KĀLAÑJAREŚVARA	*Matsya P.*, 181.27.
KĀMATĪRTHA	*Garuḍa P.*, I.81.9; *Kūrma P.*, II.41.58; *MBh*, III-80.113.
KAMBALEŚVARA	*Skanda P.*, VII.1.310.
KĀMBODIKEŚVARA	*Padma P.*, I.18.60.
KAMBUKEŚVARA	*Skanda P.*, V.3.120.
KĀMEŚVARA	*Padma P.*, I.25.12; *Skanda P.*, IV.2.85; V.1.25; V.2.13; VII.1.96; VII.1.67; V.3.71; VII.3.40; *Vāmana P.*, 35.42.
KAṀSAREŚVARA	*Skanda P.*, VI.176.
KĀÑCĪ	*Brahmāṇḍa P.*, IV.5.6-10; *Padma P.*, I.17.8; *Vāyu P.*, 104.76.
KANAKHALA	*Agni P.*, 109.17; *Kurma P.*, II.37.10.
KANAKHALEŚVARA	*Skanda P.*, V.3.186.
KANAKHALABHAIRAVAKṢETRAPĀLA	*Skanda P.*, VII.1.137.
KANDARPEŚVARA	*Padma P.*, I.34-10.
KANDUKEŚVARA	*Skanda P.*, IV.2.65.
KANTAKEŚVARA	*Skanda P.*, V.2.54.
KAṆṬHADEŚVARA	*Skanda P.*, V.2.34.
KAPĀLAMOCANA	*MBh*, III.81.118; *Agni P.*, 109.19; *Kūrma P.*, I.35.15; *Padma P.*, I.37.18; I.27.26; VI.129.28; VI.132.3-4; *Skanda P.*, II.3.6; IV.1.31.
KAPĀLAMOKṢA	*Bhaviṣya P.*, III.14.67-117.
KAPĀLAMOKṢAṆA	*Skanda P.*, V.1.6.
KAPĀLEŚVARA	*Skanda P.*, V.1.20; V.2.8; VI.269; VII.1.103.

KAPĀLĪŚVARARUDRA	*Skanda P.*, VI.1.89.
KAPĀLĪŚA	*Skanda P.*, V.1.2.
KAPARDĪŚVARA	*Kūrma P.*, I.32.12; I.33.4; *Padma P*; I.35.1; *Skanda P.*, VII.1.38.
KAPILATĪRTHA	*Kūrma P.*, II.41.93-100; *Matsya P.*, 193.4; *Skanda P.*, IV.2.62.
KAPILAHRADA	*MBh*, III.82.69.
KAPILEŚA	*Agni P.*, 116.5.
KAPILEŚVARA	*Skanda P.*, V.3.88; V.3.175; VII.1.343.
KAPĪŚVARA	*Padma P.*, VI.136.5-11.
KARABHEŚVARA	*Skanda P.*, V.1.28; V.2.73.
KARAÑJEŚVARA	*Skanda P.*, V.3.40.
KARKARĀJA	*Skanda P.*, V.1.69.
KARKATEŚVARA	*Skanda P.*, V.2.22; V.3.157.
KĀRKOṬAKA	*Padma P.*, VI.129.13.
KĀRKOṬAKEŚVARA	*Matsya P.*, 191.35; *Skanda P.*, V.2.10.
KARMADEŚVARA	*Skanda P.*, V.3.123.
KĀRMUKA	*Padma P.*, VI.129.7.
KARṆAHRADA	*Padma P.*, I.32.4.
KAROḌĪŚVARA	*Skanda P.*, V.3.62.
KARUṆEŚVARA	*Skanda P.*, IV.2.94.
KĀŚĪ	*Agni P.*, 112.3; *Bhavisya P.*, II.13.1-9; *Nārada P.*, I.29.48.
KĀŚĪKṢETRA	*Skanda P.*, IV.1.6.
KĀŚIKĀ	*Skanda P.*, IV.1.40.
KĀŚĪŚVARA	*Padma P.*, I.26.53.
KAŚMĪRA	*Kūrma P.*, II.43.4; *Padma P.*, I.25.1.
KĀŚYAPEŚVARA	*Skanda P.*, VII.1.213.
KATESVARA	*Skanda P.*, VII.3.62.
KAṬHEŚVARA	*Matsya P.*, 191.62.
KAUŚIKEŚVARA	*Skanda P.*, VII.1.214.
KAUŚIKĪ	*Matsya P.*, 194.40.
KAUṬUMBIKEŚVARA	*Skanda P.*, V.1.10.

KĀVERĪ	*MBh*, III.83.22; *Kūrma P.*, II.37.16.19; II.40.40; *Matsya P.*, 22.64; *Padma P.*, I.39.20; VI.24.34; *Vāyu P.*, 45.104.
KĀVERĪSAṄGAMA	*Matsya P.*, 189.14; *Agni P.*, 113.3.
KĀYĀVAROHAṆA	*Kūrma P.*, II.4[illegible]7-8; *Matsya P.*,13.48; 22.30; 181.26.
KĀYĀVAROHAṆEŚVARA	*Skanda P.*, V.2.82.
KĀYAVARṢANA	*Kūrma P.*, II.44.7.
KEDĀRA	*MBh*, III.81.59; III.83.16-17; *Agni P.*, 112.5; *Kūrma P.*, I.35.12; II.41.7-8; *Matsya P.*, 22.11; 181.29; *Liṅga P.*, I.77.37-47; I.92.7-13; *Padma P.*, I.26.69; I.33.32; I.37.15; VI.129.10; *Skanda P.*, VI.121; *Vāmana P.*, 36.16; 36.26.
KEDĀRANĀTHA	*Agni P.*, 115.53; *Skanda P.*, V.1.28; V.1.31; IV.2.77; V.2.67; V.3.183; VII.1.39; VII.3.9.
KEDĪŚVARA	*Skanda P.*, VII.1.51.
KHAṆḌEŚVARA	*Skanda P.*, V.2.31.
KHAḌGADHAREŚVARA	*Padma P.*, VI.147.
KHAḌGATĪRTHA	*Padma P.*, VI.140.
KILIKILĪŚA	*Agni P.*, 116.31.
KOHANAŚVA	*Skanda P.*, V.3.122.
KOKAMUKHA	*Padma P.*, I.33.33; I.38.65.
KOSEŚVARA	*MBh*, III.81.46.
KOTĪŚA	*Agni P.*, 116.6; *Kūrma P.*, II.41.33.
KOṬITĪRTHA	*MBh*, III.80.68; III.82.24; III.83.59; *Agni P.*, 119.10; *Matsya P.*, 191.55; 191.7; *Padma P.*, I.18.8; I.12.9; I.VI.129.17; *Skanda P.*, III.1.27; *Vāmana P.*, 55.63; 84.11.
KOTĪŚVARA	*Liṅga P.*, I.92.157; *Matsya P.*, 191.9; *Padma P.*, 26.4; *Skanda P.*, VII.1.104; VII.1.357; VII.3.11; *Vāmana P.*, 34.28; 36.65.

KOṬIKEŚVARA	*Padma P.*, I.18.36.
KOṬIHRADAMANDAKEŚVARA	*Skanda P.*, VII.1.361.
KOTĪŚVARATĪRTHA	*Skanda P.*, V.3.96; V.3.224.
KṚTTIVĀSEŚVARA	*Padma P.*, I.34.10; *Skanda P.*, IV.2.68.
KRATVĪŚVARA	*Skanda P.*, VII.1.212.
KṚMICAṆḌEŚVARA	*Matsya P.*, 181.29.
KṚṢṆATĪRTHA	*Skanda P.*, VII.3.34; *Vāmana P.*, 36.9.
KṢEMAṄKARIRAIVATEŚVARA	*Skanda P.*, VI.118.
KṢEMAṄKAREŚVARA	*Skanda P.*, VII.1.127.
KṢEMEŚVARA	*Skanda P.*, VII.1.323.
KṢETRAPĀLEŚVARA	*Skanda P.*, VII.1.181.
KUBJĀMRA	*Padma P.*, I.33.33.
KULĪŚA	*Skanda P.*, VII.1.76.
KUKKUṬEŚVARA	*Skanda P.*, V.2.21.
KUMĀREŚVARA	*Skanda P.*, V.3.63; VII.1.73; VII1.215.
KUMBHEŚVARA	*Skanda P.*, V.3.84.
KUMBHĪŚVARA	*Skanda P.*, VII.1.266; VII.2.3.
KUṆḌALEŚVARA	*Matsya P.*, 190.12; *Padma P.*, I.17.9; *Skanda P.*, V.3.41.
KUNDEŚVARA	*Skanda P.*, V.1.31; V.2.40.
KUÑJATĪRTHA	*Matsya P.*, 194.9-14.
KUÑJARAGIRI	*Varāha P.*, I.81.
KUNTEŚVARA	*Skanda P.*, VII.1.174.
KURU	*Padma P.*, I.27.54.
KURUKṢETRA	*Agni P.*, 119.14; *Liṅga P.*, I.77.37-47; *Padma P.*, I.33.33.
KUŚATĪRTHA	*Kūrma P.*, II.41.33.
KUŚAKEŚVARA	*Skanda P.*, VII.1.173.
KUŚASTHALĪ	*Skanda P.*, V.1.41.
KUŚEŚVARA	*Skanda P.*, VI.104.
KUSUMEŚVARA	*Matsya P.*, 191.111-112; 191.124; *Skanda P.*, V.1.28; V.2.38; V.3.150.
KUṬUṀBAKEŚVARA	*Skanda P.*, V.2.14.
KUṬUṀBEŚVARA	*Skanda P.*, V.1.67.

LAKṢMAṆATĪRTHA	*Brahma P.*, 123.215; *Skanda P.*, III.1.19; III.52.106-7.
LAKṢMANEŚVARA	*Nārada P.*, II.49.64; *Skanda P.*, V.3.84; VII.1.112.
LAKṢMĪŚVARA	*Brahma P.*, 137.1; *Skanda P.*, VII.1.64.
LAKULĪŚA	*Skanda P.*, VII.1.177.
LAKULĪŚVARA	*Skanda P.*, VII.1.79.
LĀṄGALA	*Padma P.*, I.18.51.
LAVEŚVARA	*Skanda P.*, VI.104.
LIṄGAVARĀHA	*Skanda P.*, V.3.149.
LOKAYAṢṬI	*Skanda P.*, VI.94.
LOKAPĀLEŚVARA	*Skanda P.*, V.2.12.
LOLĀRTHA	*Kūrma P.*, I.35.14; *Padma P.*, I.32.17; *Vāmana P.*, 15.58-59.
LOMAŚEŚVARA	*Skanda P.*, VII.1.136.
LOṬANEŚVARA	*Skanda P.*, V.3.220.
LUMPEŚVARA	*Skanda P.*, V.2.41.
LUṄKEŚVARA	*Skanda P.*, V.3.67.
MADHYAMEŚVARA	*Kurma P.*, I.32.12; I.34.1-2; *Liṅga P.*, I.92.151; *Padma P.*, I.34.10; I.36.
MADOTKAṬA	*Padma P.*, VI.129.9.
MAHĀBALA	*Padma P.*, I.33.32.
MAHĀBHAIRAVA	*Kūrma P.*, II.44.3; *Matsya P.*, 181.29.
MAHĀKĀLA	*MBh*, III.80.68; *Brahma P.*, 43.66; *Kūrma P.*, II.44. 11; *Liṅga P.*, I.92.137; *Matsya P.*, 13.41; 22.24; 179.6; 181.26; *Padma P.*, I.12.0; VI.129.21; *Skanda P.*, IV.1.91; V.1.7.
MAHĀKĀLEŚVARA	*Skanda P.*, V.1.39.
MAHĀKALEŚVARATĪRTHA	*Skanda P.*, VI.46; VII.1.93.
MAHĀLAYA	*Brahmāṇḍa P.*, III.13.62-84; *Kūrma P.*, II.37.1.*Matsya P.*, 181.25; *Padma P.*, I.37.16; *Vāmana P.*, 90.22.
MAHĀLAYEŚVARA	*Skanda P.*, V.2.24.

MĀHEŚVARA	*Matsya P.*, 188.2; *Padma P.*, I.15.2; VI.129.21.
MAHEŚVARAKUṆḌA	*Varāha P.*, I.151.
MĀHEŚVARAṀ STHĀNAM	*Matsya P.*, 188.2.
MAHEŚVARAPADA	*MBh*, III.82.103; *Padma P.*, I.38.36.
MAHIṢATĪRTHA	*Skanda P.*, VI.119.
MAHIṢAKUṆḌA	*Skanda P.*, V.1.9.
MAITREYEŚVARA	*Skanda P.*, VII.1.173.
MALLIKEŚVARA	*Padma P.*, I.18.6.
MĀNASA	*Matsya P.*, 194.8. *Padma P.*, VI.128.7.
MĀNASASARAS	*Matsya P.*, 22.23.
MANAVEŚVARA	*Skanda P.*, VII.1.218.
MANDĀRA	*Nārada P.*, II.60.22; *Vāmana P.*, 51.74; *Varāha P.*, I.78.
MĀṆḌAVYEŚVARA	*Skanda P.*, VI.2.65; VII.1.179.
MADHUSKANDATĪRTHA	*Skanda P.*, V.3.79.
MAṄGALATĪRTHA	*Skanda P.*, III.1.12.
MAṄGALEŚVARA	*Padma P.*, II.92.33; *Skanda P.*, V.3.69.
MAṆIKAṄKA	*Kūrma P.*, I.35.8.
MAṆIKARṆIKEŚVARA	*Skanda P.*, VII.3.16.
MAṆIMATĪRTHA	*Vāmana P.*, 90.7.
MAṆIMATTĪRTHA	*MBh*, III.80.109.
MAṆINĀGEŚVARA	*Skanda P.*, V.3.72.
MAṄKANAKEŚVARA	*Skanda P.*, VI.40.
MAṄKEŚVARA	*Skanda P.*, VII.1.270.
MAṄKĪŚVARA	*Skanda P.*, VII.1.184; VII.1.203.
MANMATHEŚVARA	*Skanda P.*, V.5.102.
MANDĀREŚVARA	*Matsya P.*, 190.1.
MĀRKAṆḌEŚVARA	*Skanda P.*, VII.1.360.
MĀRKAṆḌEYEŚA	*Skanda P.*, V.3.100.
MĀRKAṆḌEYEŚVARA	*Agni P.*, 116.11; *Nārada P.*, II.55.18-19; *Skanda P.*, IV.33.154-155; V.1.28; V.2.36; V.3.167; VII.1.209.
MARKAṬEŚVARA	*Skanda P.*, V.1.12.

MĀSEŚVARA	*Padma P.*, I.18.77.
MĀTAṄGEŚA	*Agni P.*, 115.35.
MĀTAṄGEŚVARA	*Skanda P.*, V.2.60.
MATHURĀ	*Brahma* P., 14.55-56; *Nārada P.*, II.79.20-21; *Varāha P.*, I.168; *Vāyu P.*, 99.382-3.
MEGHANĀDEŚVARA	*Skanda P.*, V.2.23.
MEGHANĀTHA	*Skanda P.*, V.3.35.
MEGHEŚVARA	*Skanda P.*, VII.1.226.
MERU	*Liṅga P.*, I.48; 22-29; I.6. *Varāha P.*, I.77.
MIṢṬĀNNADEŚVARA	*Skanda P.*, VI.141.
MOKṢATĪRTHA	*Skanda P.*, V.3.160.
MOKṢEŚVARA	*Skanda P.*, III.2.15.
MṚGATĪRTHA	*Skanda P.*, VI.23.
MṚGAŚṚṄGODAKA	*Varāha P.*, I.215.
MṚTYUÑJAYA	*Skanda P.*, VII.1.95.
MUKTIKṢETRA	*Varāha P.*, I.144.
MUKTĪŚVARA	*Skanda P.*, V.2.25.
MUÑJAVAṬA	*MBh*, III.81.18; *Padma P.*, I.39.63; *Vāmana P.*, 34.38.
MUÑJIVAṬA	*Padma P.*, I.26.19.
NĀGATĪRTHA	*Brahma P.*, III.1; *Kūrma P.*, I.35.7; *Matsya P.*, 22.23; *Padma P.*, I.28.33; *Skanda P.*, VI.31.
NĀGACAṆḌEŚVARA	*Skanda P.*, V.2.19.
NĀGAREŚVARA	*Skanda P.*, VI.164.
NĀGEŚVARA	*Matsya P.*, 191.82; *Padma P.*, I.18.7; *Skanda P.*, 7.3.99; V.3.131; VII.1.186.
NAGODBHEDA	*MBh*, III.80.118; *Agni P.*, 109.13; *Padma P.*, I.25.28.
NAIMIŚA	*Kūrma P.*, II.20.34; II.43.12-15; *Matsya* P., 22.12;109.3; *Padma P.*, VI.129.6.
NAMIŚĀRAṆYA	*Padma P.*, I.33.32.
NAITARAṆI	*MBh*, III.81. 70-71.
NAKULEŚA	*Matsya P.*, 22.77; *Matsya P.*, 7.26.

NAKULEŚVARA	*Kūrma P.*, II.44.12.
NALEŚVARA	Skanda P., VI.55; VII.1.345.
NANDITĪRTHA	*Kūrma P.*, II.41.90; *Matsya P.*, 191.37; *Padma P.*, I.18.32.
NANDIKEŚA	*Matsya P.*, 191.6.
NANDIKEŚVARA	*Skanda P.*, V.3.80; V.3.94.
NANDĪŚA	*Padma P.*, I.18.37.
NANDĪŚVARA	*Matsya P.*, 191.36.
NĀRADATĪRTHA	*Kūrma P.*, II.41.16-17; *Padma P.*, I.18.24.
NĀRADEŚVARA	*Matsya P.*, 191.5; *Skanda P.*, V.3.78; VII.1.152; VII.1.347.
NARADĪPA	*Skanda P.*, V.1.36.
NARĀDITYEŚVARA	*Skanda P.*, VI.60.
NARMADĀ	*MBh*,III.80.71; *Kūrma P.*, II.40.7; *Matsya P.*, 180.10; 190.25; 194.34; *Padma P.*, I.13; I.33.33; *Vāyu P.*, 71.32.
NARMADĀTAṬA	*Matsya P.*, 191.113.
NARMADEŚA	*Matsya P.*, 191.72.
NARMADEŚVARA	*Matsya P.*, 194.2; *Padma P.*, I.18.69; *Skanda P.*, IV.2.92; V.3.38; V.3.124.
NĀSATYEŚVARA	*Skanda P.*, VII.1.165.
NĪLAGANDHAVATĪ	*Skanda P.*, V.1.16.
NILAKAṆṬHATĪRTHA	*Padma P.*, VI.168.
NĪLAKAṆṬHEŚVARA	*Skanda P.*, VII.1.219.
NĪLARUDRA	*Skanda P.*, VII.1.88.
NIṀBEŚVARA	*Skanda P.*, VI.275.
NĪRAJEŚVARA	*Padma P.*, I.18.6.
NŪPUREŚVARA	*Skanda P.*, I.34.1.
OṀKĀRA	*Padma P.*, I.34.1.
OṀKĀREŚVARA	*Kūrma P.*, I.32.1-11; *Liṅga P.*, I.92.137; *Matsya P.*, 22.27; 186.2; *Padma P.*, I.92.32; VI.131; *Skanda P.*, IV.2.73; V.5.37; V.2.52.
PAMPĀ	*Matsya P.*, 22.50; *Padma P.*, I.26.20-21; *Vāmana P.*, 90.16.

PAÑCATĪRTHA	*Brahma P.*, II.32; *Brahmāṇḍa P.*, IV.40.59-61.
PAÑCAKROŚA	*Varāha P.*, I.147.
PAÑCANADA	*MBh*, III.81.14; *Agni P.*, 109.12; *Kūrma P.*, II.44.1; *Liṅga P.*, 43.47-48; *Padma P.*, I.24.31; I.26.14; *Vāmana P.*, 34.27.
PAÑCANADĪTĪRTHA	*Skanda P.*, IV.2.59.
PAÑCAPRABHĀSA	*Skanda P.*, VII.1.198.
PAÑCAVAṬA	*MBh*, III.81.141-42; *Padma P.*, I.27.50; *Vāmana P.*, 41.11.
PĀPANĀŚINĪ	*Padma P.*, VI.1.50.
PĀṆḌAVEŚVARA	*Matsya P.*, 191.61-62; *Padma P.*, I.18.58; *Skanda P.*, VII.1.86; VII.1.233.
PARĀŚAREŚVARA	*Skanda P.*, IV.2.65.
PAREŚVARA	*Skanda P.*, V.3.76.
PĀRTHEŚVARA	*Skanda P.*, VII.3.33.
PĀRVATĪŚA	*Skanda P.*, IV.2.90.
PĀŚURATA	*Matsya P.*, 22.56.
PAŚUPATĪŚVARA	*Skanda P.*, V.1.28; V.2.64; VII.1.130.
PATREŚVARA	*Padma P.*, I.17.1; *Skanda P.*, V.2.52.
PAULASTYA	*Brahma P.*, I.27; I.97.
PAULOMĪŚVARA	*Skanda P.*, VII.1.125.
PAUṆḌHRA	*Padma P.*, VI.129.27
PAUṢPA	*Padma P.*, VI.129.27.
PAVANAHRADA	*Vāmana P.*, 37.1.
PIṆḌĀRAKA	*MBh*, III.80.62.
PIṄGATĪRTHA	*MBh*, III.80.76.
PIṄGALEŚVARA	*Kūrma P.*, II.41.21; II.42.35; *Matsya P.*, 191.31; *Padma P.*, I.18.32; VI.129.24; *Skanda P.*, V.2.81; V.3.86; V.3.176.
PIPPALĀDA	*Padma P.*, VI.150
PIPPALĀDEŚVARA	*Skanda P.*, V.3.42.
PIPPALEŚA	*Matsya P.*, 190.13.
PIPPALEŚVARA	*Brahma P.*, II.40; *Padma P.*, I.17.10.

PIŚĀCAMOCANA	*Padma P.*, I.35.2; VI.250.62-63.
PIŚĀCAMOCANI	*Skanda P.*, IV.2.54.
PIŚĀCEŚVARA	*Skanda P.*, V.2.68.
PRABHĀSA	*MBh*, III.80.77; III.118.15; *Agni P.*, 116.15; *Garuḍa P.*, I.4.81; *Kūrma P.*, I.35.16; II.35.16; *Nārada P.*, II.70.1-95; *Padma P.*, I.37.5; I.33.33; VI.129.23; *Skanda P.*, V.3.98; VII.1.2.44-53; *Vāmana P.*, 84.29; *Vāyu P.*, 108.16; 109.14.
PRABHĀSAKA	*Agni P.*, 109.10.
PRABHĀSAKAKṢETRA	*Skanda P.*, VII.1.2.
PRABHĀSEŚA	*Agni P.*, 116.13.
PRABHĀSEŚVARA	*Skanda P.*, VI.110.
PRATĪHĀREŚVARA	*Skanda P.*, V.2.20.
PRATYUṢEŚVARA	*Skanda P.*, VII.1.108.
PRAYĀGA	*MBh*, III.93.10; *Agni P.*, 109.19; *Kūrma P.*, I.35.16; *Matsya P.*, 110; *Padma P.*, I.37.1; I.33.32; VI.129.6.
PRAYĀGEŚVARA	*Skanda P.*, V.2.58; V.2.71.
PṚTHVĪŚVARA	*Skanda P.*, VII.1.98.
PṚTHUKEŚVARA	*Skanda P.*, V.2.49.
PULAHEŚVARA	*Skanda P.*, VII.1.211.
PULASTYEŚVARA	*Skanda P.*, VII.1.210.
PUṆḌARĪKAPURA	*Matsya P.*, 22.77; *Nārada P.*, II.73.45.
PUṢKARA	*Agni P.*, 109.5; *Padma P.*, IV.129.5; VI.129.23; I.12; I.33.32.
PUṢKARAṆI	*MBh*, III.80.65; *Kūrma P.*, II.41.10; *Skanda P.*, V.3.59.
PUṢKAREŚVARA	*Skanda P.*, VII.1.115; VII.1.173.
PUṢPADANTEŚVARA	*Skanda P.*, V.2.77; VII.1.180.
PUṢPEŚVARA	*Skanda P.*, VII.1.294.
PŪTIKEŚVARA	*Skanda P.*, V.3.89.
RĀGHAVEŚVARA	*Matsya P.*, 22.60.
RĀGHVEŚVARA	*Skanda P.*, VII.1.50.

RĀJASTHALA	*Skanda P.*, V.1.14.
RAJASTHALEŚVARA	*Skanda P.*, V.2.74.
RĀMANĀTHA	*Skanda P.*, III.1.13.
RĀMANĀTHALIṄGA	*Skanda P.*, III.1.44.
RĀMEŚA	*Agni P.*, 116.24.
RĀMEŚVARA	*Garuḍa P.*, I.81.9; *Matsya P.*, 22.50; *Nārada P.*, II.76; *Skanda P.*, V.1.31; V.2.29; V.3.84; V.3.133; VI.101; VII.1.111; VII.1.202.
RASĀVARTANA	*Vāmana P.*, 36.47.
RATHACAITRAKA	*Padma P.*, VI.129.9.
PADMEŚVARA	*Skanda P.*, IV.2.67; VII.1.153.
RĀVAṆEŚVARA	*Matsya P.*, 191.25; *Skanda P.*, VII.1.123.
RAVITĪRTHA	*Skanda P.*, V.3.34; V.2.125; V.3.70.
REVĀTĪRTHA	*Bhāgavata P.*, V.19.18; *Skanda P.*, V.3.60.
REVANTHĪŚVARA	*Skanda P.*, V.2.56.
ṚṆATĪRTHA	*Kūrma P.*, II.41.19 and 29; *Matsya P.*, 191.26.
ṚṆAMOCANEŚVARA	*Skanda P.*, VII.1.221.
ṚṆATRAYAVIMOCANA	*Skanda P.*, V.3.87.
ṚṢABHATĪRTHA	*Agni P.*, 109.21; *Kūrma P.*, I.35.3; *Padma P.*, I.37.3.
ṚṢIKOṬI	*MBh*, III.80.124; *Padma P.*, I.25.25.
ṚṢITĪRTHA	*Padma P.*, I.18.22.
RUDRAHRADA	*Skanda P.*, VII.3.55.
RUDRAKARṆA	*Matsya P.*, 181.25.
RUDRAKARṆAHRADA	*Padma P.*, I.37.15.
RUDRAKOṬI	*MBh*, III.80.124-128; III.81.63; *Kūrma P.*, II.36.1-4; *Matsya P.*, 181.25; *Padma P.*, I.25.25; VI.129.13; *Skanda P.*, VI.52; *Vāmana P.*, 36.22-23.
RUDRAMAHĀLAYATĪRTHA	*Padma P.*, VI.139.
RUDRAPADA	*Agni P.*, 115.48; *Padma P.*, I.26.94; *Vāyu P.*, III.64-67.
RUDRASARAS	*Matsya P.*, 22.23; *Skanda P.*, V.1.22.

RUDRAŚĪRṢA	*Skanda P.*, VI.78.
RUDRĀVARTA	*Padma P.*, I.32.2.
RUDRAVEDI	*Padma P.*, I.27.58.
RUDREŚA	*Agni P.*, 116.24.
RUDREŚVARA	*Skanda P.*, V.1.28; VII.1.39; VII.1.188.
RUKMAVAṬEŚVARA	*Skanda P.*, VII.1.222.
RŪPATĪRTHA	*Skanda P.*, VI.153.
RŪPEŚVARA	*Skanda P.*, V. 2.62.
SĀGAREŚVARA	*Matsya P.*, 194.41.
ŚAILESVARA	*Liṅga P.*, I.92.86; *Nārada P.*, II.50.57; *Skanda P.*, IV.2.65; IV.33.145; *Varāha P.*, 215; 216.23.
ŚAIVATĪRTHEŚVARA	*Matsya P.*, 22.78.
ŚAKRATĪRTHA	*Brahma P.*, II.39; *Kūrma P.*, II.41.11-12; *Matsya P.*, 22.29; 22.73; *Padma P.*, I.24.29; *Varāha P.*, 126.81.
ŚAKREŚVARA	*Skanda P.*, V.3.61; V.3.138
SĀLAṄKA	*Liṅga P.*, I.77.37-47.
SAMVARTEŚVARA	*Skanda P.*, VII.1.364.
SĀMBĀDITYEŚVARA	*Skanda P.*, VII.1.101.
SAṄGAMEŚVARA	*Kūrma P.*, II.41.36; *Liṅga P.*, I.92.88; *Matsya P.*, 191.73; *Nārada P.*, II.50.63-64; *Padma P.*, I.18.53; VI.138; *Skanda P.*, VII.1.249.
SAṀVAREŚVARA	*Skanda P.*, V.3.164.
ŚANAIŚCAREŚVARA	*Skanda P.*, VII.1.49.
ŚĀṆḌILYEŚVARA	*Skanda P.*, VII.1.126.
SAṄGAMEŚVARA	*Kūrma P.*, II.41.36; *Matsya P.*, 191.54; *Padma P.*, I.18.53; *Skanda P.*, V.2.69; V.3.158; VII.1.327.
SAṄGALEŚVARA	*Skanda P.*, VII.1.300.
ŚĀKALYEŚVARA	*Skanda P.*, VII.1.74.
ŚĀṄKARA	*Matsya P.*, 22.43; *Padma P.*, VI.129.25.
ŚAṄKARAVĀPI	*Skanda P.*, V.1.15.

ŚAṄKHATĪRTHA	*Kūrma P.*, II.42.17; *Skanda P.*, VI.10.
ŚAṄKHACŪḌĀTĪRTHA	*Skanda P.*, V.3.75.
ŚAṄKUKARṆESVARA	*MBh*, III.80.87; *Kūrma P.*, I.33.48; *Liṅga P.*, I.92.135; *Matsya P.*, 181.27; *Nārada P.*, II.48-19-20.
SAPTASĀRASVATA	*MBh*, III.81.114. *Kūrma P.*, II.35.44; *Padma P.*, I.27.4; *Vāmana P.*, 38.22-23.
SAPTARṢI	*Skanda P.*, VI.32.
SARAKA	*Nārada P.*, II.65.62-63; *Padma P.*, I.26.76; *Vāmana P.*, 36.22-23.
SARASVATĪ	*Skanda P.*, VI.46; *Vāmana P.*, 3.8.
ŚARMIṢṬHATĪRTHA	*Skanda P.*, VI.61.62.
SARPATĪRTHA	*Skanda P.*, V.3.161.
SARVATĪRTHA	*Skanda P.*, III.1.29; *Padma P.*, II.92.4 & 7.
ŚAŚAYANA	*MBh*, III.80. *Padma P.*, I.25.20.
ŚATAMEDHĀDILIṄGA	*Skanda P.*, VII.1.235.
SATĀNANDEŚVARA	*Skanda P.*, VI.208.
SATĪŚVARA	*Skanda P.*, IV.2.93.
SATYABHĀMEŚVARA	*Skanda P.*, VII.1.157.
SATYASANDHEŚVARA	*Skanda P.*, VI.126.
SAUBHĀGYEŚVARA	*Skanda P.*, V.2.61; VII.1.24.
SAVITRĪSVARṆABHAIRAVA	*Skanda P.*, VII.1.151.
SIDDHATĪRTHA	*Brahma P.*, II.73.
SIDDHEŚVARA	*Agni P.*, 116.24; *Brahma P.*, 128.1; *Matsya P.*, 22.43; 43.181; 181.25; 191.121; *Padma P.*, I.18.100; I.18.114; II.20.34; *Skanda P.*, V.1.20; V.2.11; V.2.59; V.3.135; V.3.147; V.3.165 and 166; VI.29 and 30; VI.267; VII.1.14; VII.1.52; VII.1.175; VII.1.260; VII.1.301; VII.3.14; VI.3.43; *Vāmana P.*, 46.34.
SIMHEŚVARA	*Skanda P.*, V.3.55.
SIPRAGUMPHEŚVARA	*Skanda P.*, V.1.20.
ŚĪTALA	*Skanda P.*, V.1.12.

ŚIVATĪRTHA	*Padma P.*, VI.129.14; *Skanda P.*, III.1.24; III.2.20; V.3.145.
ŚIVADHARA	*Matsya P.*, 22.48
ŚIVAGAṄGĀKUṆḌA	*Skanda P.*, VII.3.38.
ŚIVALIṄGAMAHEŚVARA	*Skanda P.*, VII.3.39.
ŚIVEŚVARA	*Skanda P.*, V.2.37.
ŚIVODBHEDA	*Padma P.*, I.25.19; I.25.78; *Skanda P.*, III.80.118.
SOMATĪRTHA	*Kūrma P.*, II.41.47; I.35.7; *Matsya P.*, 191.29; 191.93; *Padma P.*, I.26.14; I.18.29; I.27.3; I.30; VI.154; I.37.7; *Skanda P.*, V.3.121; V.3.139; *Vāmana P.*, 41.4; *Varāha P.*, I.140.26; I.154.
SOMANĀTHA	*Agni P.*, 109.10; 116.23; *Padma P.*, VI.196.37; *Skanda P.*, VII.1.290.
SOMANĀTHEŚVARA	*Skanda P.*, V.3.85.
SOMAVATILIṄGA	*Skanda P.*, V.1.28.
SOMEŚA	*Skanda P.*, VII.1.8.
SOMEŚVARA	*Kūrma P.*, II.35.20; *Padma P.*, VI.129.25; *Skanda P.*, V.1.28; V.2.26; VI.63; VII.1.25; VII.1.44; VII.2.14; *Vāmana P.*, 34.34; *Varāha P.*, I.144.
ŚOṆATĪRTHA	*Matsya P.*, 22.35.
ŚRĪKAṆṬHA	*Liṅga P.*, I.48.22-29.
ŚRĪKAPĀLATĪRTHA	*Skanda P.*, V.3.214.
SṚṄGĀREŚVARA	*Skanda P.*, VII.1.359.
SṚṄGEŚVARA	*Skanda P.*, VII.1.356; VII.1.359; *Varāha P.*, I.215.
ŚRĪPARVATA	*MBh*, III.83.16-17; *Agni P.*, 112.4; 113.4; *Kūrma P.*, II.37.13; *Liṅga P.*, I.77.37-47; I.92.147-166; *Padma P.*, I.39.16; *Matsya P.*, 13.31; 181.28;188;79. *Vāyu P.*, 77.28.
ŚRĪŚAILA	*Matsya P.*, 22.43; *Padma P.*, I.33.32; VI.129;12.

SRĪBILVAVANA	*Varāha P.*, I.80.
STAṀBHA	*Padma P.*, I.18.93.
STHĀNEŚVARA	*Liṅga P.*, I.92.136; *Matsya P.*, 13.3; *Padma P.*, VI.129.11.
STHĀVAREŚVARA	*Skanda P.*, V.2.50.
STHĀNUVAṬA	*MBh*, III.81.155.
ŚUDDHEŚVARA	*Skanda P.*, V.3.173.
ŚŪDRAKEŚVARA	*Skanda P.*, VI.65.
ŚŪDRĪTĪRTHA	*Skanda P.*, VI.198.
ŚUKLATĪRTHA	*Kūrma P.*, II.69-79; *Matsya P.*, 192.1-22; *Padma P.*, I.19; *Skanda P.*, I.2.3.5; VI.123.
ŚUKREŚVARA	*Kūrma P.*, I.35.15; *Liṅga P.*, I.92.93; *Nārada P.*, II-50.65; *Padma P.*, I.37.18; VI.129.23; *Skanda P.*, V.1.25; VII.1.48; VII.1.247; VII.3.15.
ŚŪLABHEDATĪRTHA	*Kūrma P.*, II.41.12-14; *Matsya P.*, 191.3; *Padma P.*, I.18.3. *Skanda P.*, V.3.45-46.
ŚŪLEŚVARA	*Skanda P.*, V.2.51; V.3.198.
SURABHIKEŚVARA	*Padma P.*, I.18.36.
SUREŚVARA	*Matsya P.*, 191.35.
SUSIDDHEŚA	*Agni P.*, 115.35.
SVARṆĀKṢA	*MBh*, III.82.16-19; *Kūrma P.*, II.35.19; *Matsya P.*, 181.25.
SVATANTREŚVARA	*Matsya P.*, 191.6.
SVAPNEŚVARA	*Skanda P.*, V.2. 80.
SVARGADVĀRALIṄGA	*Skanda P.*, V.2.9.
SVARṆATĪRTHA	*Agni P.*, 109.16; *Padma P.*, I.29.19; I.28.19.
SVARṆAJĀLEŚVARA	*Skanda P.*, V.1.20; V.2.6.
ŚVETATĪRTHA	*Padma P.*, VI.133.15-23.
ŚVETADVĪPA	*Garuḍa P.*, I.81.7; *Kūrma P.*, II.35.33; I.49.40; *Vāmana P.*, 25.16; 60.56.
TALATĪRTHA	*Padma P.*, I.37.2.

TĀMRAPARṆI	*Brahma P.*, 27.36; *Brahmaṇḍa P.*, III.13.24; *Kūrma P.*, II.37.21-22; *Matsya P.*, 22.48; 114.30; *Vāyu P.*, 45.105 and 77.
TĀPASEŚVARA	*Kūrma P.*, II.41.66; *Padma P.*, I.18.96.
TAPEŚVARA	*Matsya P.*, 191.104; *Skanda P.*, V.3.141.
TILODEŚVARA	*Skanda P.*, V.2.222.
TRYAṀBAKA	*Kūrma P.*, II.35.18; *Matsya P.*, 22.47; 191.19; *Padma P.*, I.18.112; *Skanda P.*, VII.1.91.
TRIBHUVANEŚVARA	*Matsya P.*, 188.57.
TRILOCANA	*Kūrma P.*, I.35.14; *Padma P.*, I.37.17; *Skanda P.*, IV.2.74; IV.33.120; V.3.117.
TRILOCANEŚVARA	*Skanda P.*, V.2.45.
TRIṆETREŚVARA	*Skanda P.*, VII.1.275.
TRIPURALIṄGA	*Skanda P.*, VII.1.272.
TRIPUṢKARATĪRTHA	*Skanda P.*, VI.45.
TRIŚŪLAKHĀTA	*MBh*, III.82.10.
TRIVIṢṬAPA	*Padma P.*, I.26.79.
TRIVIṢṬAPEŚVARA	*Skanda P.*, V.2.7.
TṚṆABINDVĪŚVARA	*Skanda P.*, VII.1.138 and 142.
UDDĀLAKEŚVARA	*Skanda P.*, VII.3.42.
UDUṀBARAVANA	*Varāha P.*, I.80.
UGRASENEŚVARA	*Skanda P.*, VII.1.129.
UJJAYINĪ	*Skanda P.*, V.1.43.
UMĀMAHEŚVARA	*Skanda P.*, VI.48; VII.3.58.
UṢEŚVARA	*Skanda P.*, VII.1.71.
UTTĀNAPĀDEŚVARA	*Skanda P.*, V.3.57.
UTTANKEŚVARA	*Skanda P.*, VII.1.77.
UTTAREŚVARA	*Skanda P.*, V.2.4; V.2.84; VII.1.303.
VAḌALEŚVARA	*Skanda P.*, V.2.75.
VAIŚVANAREŚVARA	*Skanda P.*, VII.1.78.
VAITARAṆĪ	*MBh*, III.81.70-71.
VAIDYANĀTHA	*Matsya P.*, 22.24; *Padma P.*, VI.160.
VĀLAHOṬI	*MBh*, III. 93.4.

VAIVASTATEŚVARA	*Skanda P.*, VII.1.169.
VAJREŚVARA	*Skanda P.*, VII.1.237.
VALMĪŚVARA	*Skanda P.*, V.3.82.
VĀLMĪKEŚVARA	*Skanda P.*, V.1.24.
VĀMANEŚVARA	*Padma P.*, I.18.26.
VĀRĀṆASĪ	*MBh*, III.82.69; *Agni P.*, 119.18. *Kūrma P.*, I.30.32; I.35; *Liṅga P.*, I.92; I.108; I.105.75-76; I.77. 37-47; *Matsya P.*, 22.7; *Padma P.*, VI.129.5.
VARĀROHEŚVARA	*Skanda P.*, VII.1.57.
VĀRUṆEŚVARA	*Matsya P.*, 191.6; *Skanda P.*, V.3.81; VII.1.70; *Padma P.*, I.18.6; I.18.29; I.27.52.
VĀSEŚVARA	*Skanda P.*, V.3.223.
VASTRAPADA	*MBh*, III.80.108.
VAṬEŚA	*Agni P.*, 109.20.
VAṬEŚVARA	*Agni P.*, 115.73; *Kūrma P.*, II.41.19; *Matsya P.*, 22.9; 191.26 and 53; *Nārada P.*, I.47.59; I.56.28; *Padma P.*, I.18.27; I.18.51; I.38.46.
VAṬIKEŚVARA	*Skanda P.*, VII.148.
VICITREŚVARA	*Skanda P.*, VII.1.143; VII.1.244.
VIDŪREŚVARA	*Skanda P.*, VI.59.
VIDYĀDHAREŚVARA	*Kūrma P.*, I.35.11; *Padma P.*, I.37.14.
VIHAṄGEŚVARA	*Padma P.*, I.21.
VIJAYATĪRTHA	*Kūrma P.*, II.35.21; *Padma P.*, I.33.33.
VIMALEŚVARA	*Kūrma P.*, II.41.15; II.42.36; *Matsya P.*, 22.8; 190.14; 194.38; *Padma P.*, I.17.11; VI.131.50; *Skanda P.*, V.3.43; V.3.226; VII.1.55; *Vāmana P.*, 34.15.
VINDHYAPĀDA	*Kūrma P.*, II.37.24.
VĪRABHADRA	*Skanda P.*, V.1.20.
VĪREŚVARA	*Skanda P.*, V.1.64; V.2.46.
VIŚVAKARMEŚVARA	*Skanda P.*, IV.2.86; VII.1.192.

VIŚVAKĀYA	*Padma P.*, VI.129.8.
VIŚVĀMITRAKUṆḌA	*Skanda P.*, VI.44.
VIŚVĀMITREŚVARA	*Brahma P.*, 93.4. and 27; *Padma P.*, I.27.28; *Skanda P.*, VII.1.289.
VISVANĀTHA	*Skanda P.*, IV.2.91.
VIŚVARŪPA	*Kūrma P.*, I.35.2; *Padma P.*, I.37.2.
VIŚVARŪPAKA	*Padma P.*, VI. 129.14.
VIŚVEŚVARA	*MBh*, III.82.116; *Kūrma P.*, I.32.12; I.35.18.II.41.60; *Nārada P.*, II.51.4; *Padma P.*, I.34.10; I.38.51; VI.129.10; *Skanda P.*, IV.2.82.
VṚDDHAPRABHĀSALIṄGA	*Skanda P.*, VII.1.195.
VṚṢADHVAJA	*Kūrma P.*, I.35.13; *Liṅga P.*, I.92.106; *Nārada P.*, II.50.48.
VṚṢABHADHVAJEŚVARA	*Skanda P.*, VII.1.220.
VṚṢABHEŚVARA	*Skanda P.*, VII.1.90.
VṚṢAPRASTA	*MBh*, III.93.4.
VYĀGHREŚVARA	*Kūrma P.*, I.35.14; *Liṅga P.*, I.92.109; *Nārada P.*, II.50.56; *Padma P.*, I.37.17.
YĀJÑAVALKYEŚVARA	*Skanda P.*, VI.175.
YAMAHĀSYA	*Skanda P.*, V.3.92.
YAMEŚVARA	*Skanda P.*, V.1.22; VII.1.12; VII.1.144; VII.1.193.
YAYĀTĪŚVARA	*Skanda P.*, VI.39.
YOGEŚVARA	*Skanda P.*, VII.1.97.
YOJANEŚVARA	*Skanda P.*, V.3.143.

2. A List of Tīrthas Connected with the Ancillary Deities

Name of Tīrtha	*Deity concerned*	*References*
AJĀDEVI	Śakti	*Skanda P.*, VII.1.59.
AJAPĀLEŚVARĪ	Śakti	*Skanda P.*, VII.1.58.
AMBĀREVATĪTĪRTHA	Śakti	*Skanda P.*, VI.116.
ASAPURAVIGHNARĀJA	Gaṇeśa	*Skanda P.*, VII.1.341.
BHADRA	Śakti	*Padma P.*, I.18.54.
BHADRAKĀLI	Śakti	*Skanda P.*, VII.1.292.
BHAVĀNĪVANA	Śakti	*Vāmana P.*, 35.29.
BRĀHMĪMAṄGALADEVĪ	Śakti	*Skanda P.*, VII.1.60.
CAMATKĀRIDURGĀDEVĪ	Śakti	*Skanda P.*, VI.64.
CAṆḌIKĀ	Śakti	*Skanda P.*, V.1.20; VII.3.36.
CATURMUKHAVINĀYAKA	Gaṇeśa	*Skanda P.*, VII.1.309.
CITREŚVARĪPĪṬHA	Śakti	*Skanda P.*, VI.154.
DEVAMĀTṚGAURĪ	Śakti	*Skanda P.*, VII.1.185.
DEVIKĀ	Śakti	*Agni P.*, 109.12; *Varāha P.*, 144.83.
DUḤKHĀNTAKARIṆĪ	Śakti	*Skanda P.*, VII.1.135.
DURGAKŪṬAGAṆAPATI	Gaṇeśa	*Skanda P.*, VII.1.349.
DURGĀTĪRTHA	Śakti	*Brahma P.*, 132.8; *Vāmana P.*, 42.14-15.
GAṆAPATITRAYA	Gaṇeśa	*Skanda P.*, VI.142.
GAURĪŚIKHARA	Śakti	*Matsya P.*, 22.76.
GAURĪTĪRTHA	Śakti	*Kūrma P.*, I.35.3; *Matsya P.*, 22.31; *Padma P.*, I.37.3.
JALAVĀSAGAṆAPATI	Gaṇeśa	*Skanda P.*, VII.1.72.
KAKAŚILĀ	Kārttikeya	*Agni P.*, 116.4.
KALAŚĪDEVĪ	Śakti	*Vāmana P.*, 36.19.
KARṆOTPALA	Śakti	*Skanda P.*, VI.127.
KĀRTTIKEYA	Kārttikeya	*Agni P.*, 116.23.
KĀRTTIKEYAKUṆḌA	Kārttikeya	*Varāha P.*, I.151.

KĀRTTIKEYASTHĀPITAŚAKTI	Śakti	*Skanda P.*, VI.71.
KĀTYĀYANĪ	Śakti	*Skanda P.*, VII.3.24.
KETĪŚVARĪ	Śakti	*Skanda P.*, VI.150.
KOṬITĪRTHA	Kārttikeya	*Padma P.*, I.19.
KUMĀRADHARA	Kārttikeya	*Brahmāṇḍa P.*, III. 13.94,95; *Kūrma P.*, II.37.20-21; *Vāmana P.*, 84.23.
KUMĀRAKOṬI	Kārttikeya	*Agni P.*, 109.13; *Padma P.*, I.25.23.
KUMĀRĪMĀHĀTMYA	Śakti	*Skanda P.*, VII.1.242.
KUMĀRATĪRTHA	Kārttikeya	*Brahma P.*, II.11.
MAHĀKĀLIPĪṬHA	Śakti	*Skanda P.*, VII.1.133.
MARUDĀRYĀDEVĪ	Śakti	*Skanda P.*, VII.1.315.
MANDRAVIBHŪṢAṆAGAURĪ	Śakti	*Skanda P.*, VII.1.348.
MĀTṚGAṆABĀLADEVĪ	Śakti	*Skanda P.*, VII.1.170.
MĀTṚGṚHA	Śakti	*Matsya P.*, 22.66.
MĀTṚTĪRTHA	Śakti	*Brahma P.*, II.42; *Vāmana P.*, 35.43.
NAGARĀDITYAŚĀKAṂBHARĪ	Śakti	*Skanda P.*, VI.164.
PAÑCAPIṆḌIKĀGAURĪ	Śakti	*Skanda P.*, VI.131; VI.178.
PRATHŪDAKA	Kārttikeya	*Padma P.*, I.27.31.
ṚṆATĪRTHA	Kārttikeya	*Kūrma P.*, II.41.28-31; *Matsya P.*, 191.27.
ŚĀKAMBHARĪ	Śakti	*Skanda P.*, VI.275; *Padma P.*, I.29.19.
ŚAKTIBHEDA	Śakti	*Skanda P.*, V.1.34.
SAṄGINĪ	Śakti	*Vāmana P.*, 35.34.
ŚAṄKHODAKAKUṆḌEŚVARAGAURĪ	Śakti	*Skanda P.*, VII.1.117.
SIDDHALAKṢMĪPĪṬHA	Śakti	*Skanda P.*, VII.1.132.

ŚĪTALAGAURĪ	Śakti	*Skanda P.*, VII.1.135.
SKANDATĪRTHA	Kārttikeya	*Matsya P.*, 191.49; *Padma P.*, I.18.49; *Skanda P.*, V.3.111.
SKANDAVANA	Kārttikeya	*Skanda P.*, IV.1.25.
ŚRĪKAPARDIVINĀYAKA	Gaṇeśa	*Agni P.*, 116.21.
ŚRĪMATA	Śakti	*Skanda P.*, VII.1.
ŚRĪMĀTĀDEVĪ	Śakti	*Skanda P.*, III.2.17.
UMĀTUṄGA	Śakti	*Kūrma P.*, II.37.32-33; *Vāyu P.*, 77.81.
UMĀKUṆḌA	Śakti	*Varāha P.*, I.151.64.
UMĀSTANAKUṆḌA	Śakti	*Varāha P.*, I.215.
UMĀTĪRTHA	Śakti	*Padma P.*, VI.129.20.
UNNATAVINĀYAKA	Gaṇeśa	*Skanda P.*, VII.1.329.
VAIŚĀKHA	Skanda	*Liṅga P.*, I.92.156.
VAIṢṆAVĪ	Śakti	*Skanda P.*, VII.1.61.
VARARUCIGAṆAPATI	Gaṇeśa	*Skanda P.*, VI.131.
VASTUPADATĪRTHA	Śakti	*Skanda P.*, VI.132.
VIGHNARĀJATĪRTHA	Gaṇeśa	*Varāha P.*, I.154.
VAINĀYAKATĪRTHA	Gaṇeśa	*Garuḍa P.*, I.81.8; *Matsya P.*, 22.32.
VINĀYAKA	Gaṇeśa	*Padma P.*, VI.129.20
VINĀYAKATĪRTHA	Gaṇeśa	*Brahma P.*, II.44.
YOGĪŚVARĪ	Śakti	*Skanda P.*, VII.1.75.

Main Śaiva Tīrthas

The following tabulated list seeks to give further details about some of the more important *tīrthas* which are held sacred to Śiva and the ancillary gods of Śaivism.

Name of Tīrtha
Textual references
Legendary background and other details, if any

Ambārevatītīrtha
Skanda P., VI.116
A female serpent, Revatī by name, was cursed that she should constantly commit the sin of devouring her kith and kin. She bit Bhaṭṭikā, a sister of Kratha. Revatī was thereafter born a human being, and she propitiated Devī. The goddess as Ambā revealed herself. The *tīrtha* was set up in order to free her from her miseries, and was named after her as *Ambārevatītīrtha*. This *tīrtha* is connected with Sakti.

Avimukta
Agni P., 109.18; 112.2 and 4; *Liṅga P.*, I.53.12-44; *Matsya P.*, 22.7, also chapter 181 ff; *Padma P.*, I.33.31; *Skanda P.*, IV.1.26; IV.1.39.
Oppressed with *brahmahatyā* incurred by severing Brahma's fifth head, Śiva roamed about and finally arrived at Kāśī, where he was freed from the sin. Śiva fixed his abode permanently at this place. Since Śiva has never forsaken this place (*avimukta*), the *tīrtha* came to be known by this name. This *tīrtha* is identical with Kāśī. Although Kāśī, Varāṇasī and Avimukta are used as synonyms in the *Purāṇas*, distinction is sometimes made between them as to their size and limits.

Brahmatīrtha
Agni P., 115.36; *Bhāgavata P.*, X.78.19; *Brahma P.*, 113.1 and 23; *Brahmāṇḍa P.*, III.13.56; *Kūrma P.*, I.35.9; II.37.28; *Nārada P.*, II.45.102; *Padma P.*, I.37.9-12; I.38.69; *Skanda P.*, V.3.129.
A demon named Puloma went to the ocean abode of Viṣṇu and challenged him to combat. On seeing this, Brahmā went to

Mahākālavana and performed *tapas*. This resulted in the victory of the gods over the *asuras*. In this regard Brahmā is said to have installed the *liṅga* which came to be known as Brahmeśvara. This *tīrtha* is connected with Śiva.

Candrabhāgā

Kūrma P., II.41.35; *Matsya P.*, 191.64; *Nārada P.*, II.60.30; *Padma P.*, I.18.62; VI.148.12; VI.149.

The sacred river Candrabhāgā has a *liṅga* on its banks called Candreśvara. Soma, the Moon god, is said to have performed *tapas* on this spot, and the *liṅga* was installed by him.

Caturmukhavināyaka

Skanda P., VII.1.309.

This *tīrtha* is mentioned in the *Prabhāsa-khaṇḍa*. At Prabhāsa, to the north of Caṇḍīśa, is enshrined Vināyaka, who is featured with four faces. His worship consists of the offerings of flower, incense and *modaka*; this leads to the removal of obstacles.

Citreśvarīpīṭha

Skanda P., VI.154.

In the *Nāgarakhaṇḍa* of the *Skanda Purāṇa* are described the shrines located at Hāṭaka. The *Citreśvarī-pīṭha* mentioned therein is a great seat of Śakti worship. A bath in the *Gaurī-kuṇḍa* and the *Vijayakuṇḍa*, both of which are connected with this *tīrtha*, brings immense merits and is particularly noted for removing barrenness.

Dhanuṣkoṭi

Skanda P., III.1.31.

In response to Vibhīṣaṇa's request, Rāma is said to have drawn a line with the edge of his bow, even diving deep into the sea and drawing the line there, destroying a bridge. Asvatthāman is said to have bathed here and to have been relieved of the *brahmahatyā* incurred by killing the young sons of the Pāṇḍavas.

Dharmāraṇya

Mahābhārata, III.80.65; *Agni P.*, 115.54; *Nārada P.*, II.45.100; *Skanda P.*, III.2.1.

Dharma once performed *tapas* in the midst of *pañcāgni*. Śiva became manifest to him and granted the boons he had requested. The place where he performed *tapas* came to be knwon as Dharmāraṇya. Dharma, thereafter installed a *svayaṁbhū-liṅga* and named it Viśvesvara. One full *khaṇḍa* consisting of forty chapters is devoted to this *kṣetra* and all the shrines connected with it.

Gaṇapatitraya

Skanda P., VI.142.

This sacred *tīrtha* is connected with Gaṇapati. The creation of Gaṇapati from the dirt collected off Umā's body by the goddess herself is told. The three Gaṇapatis mentioned in this connection are Īśānagaṇapati, Heraṁba and Martyada. The *tīrtha* is situated at Hāṭakeśvara. The worship of this god leads to the removal of obstacles.

Gaṅgeśvara

Matsya P., 191.82.139.14; *Nārada P.*, II.49.46; *Skanda P.*, V.2.42; VII.1.250, VII.1.285; VII.1.289; VII.2.5.

When the celestial river Gaṅgā began to flow earthwards with great speed, Śiva checked her flow and received her within the meshes of his matted hair. Later on, by a request from Bhagīratha, he let the river flow. Bhagīratha installed a *liṅga* in recognition, which came to be known as Gaṅgeśvara.

Gautameśvara

Kūrma P., II.42.6-8; *Matsya P.*, 22.70; *Padma P.*, I.20.58; *Skanda P.*, V.3.74; VI.208; VI.267; VII.1.80; VII.1.216.

Rāma restored Ahalyā to her former position by the touch of his feet. He instructed her husband Gautama to install a *liṅga* which later received the name Gautameśvara.

Gokarṇeśvara

Varāha P., I.213; I.215.

On instructions from their master, the *dūtas* of Yama took the brāhmaṇa Gokarṇa to the world of Yama. The god of death granted his request and described to him the twenty-two kinds of hell. On Yama's advice, Gokarṇa thereafter went to Camatkāra, and installed Gokarṇeśvara on the bank of the river.

Hāṭakeśvara

Skanda P., VI.1.

Unable to bear the pangs of separation from Umā, Śiva wandered near the *āsramas* in which some sages lived with their wives. Enraged at this, the *ṛsis* cursed Śiva and caused his *liṅga* to fall. When propitiated by Brahmā, Viṣṇu and other gods, Śiva instructed them to worship the *liṅga*. The *liṅga*, accordingly, was installed at Hāṭa-keśvara.

Jambukeśvara

Kūrma P., I.35.4; *Liṅga P.*, I.92.107; *Nārada P.*, II.50.60; *Padma P.*, I.37.4.

A demon named Jambuka was destroyed by Śiva. In connection with this, a *liṅga* was installed there for worship, and came to be known as Jambukeśvara. One of the *pañcabhūtaliṅgas* is found at Jambukeśvara situated near Srīraṅgam.

Kailāsa

Bhāgavata P., IV.6; *Brahma P.*, II.6.7; *Brahmāṇḍa P.*, I.24.40; *Liṅga P.*, I.51.20-30; *Vāyu P.*, I.30.94-104, also I.41.1-13.

The Epics and the *Purāṇas* demonstrate many clear connections of Śiva with mountains. Śiva is known as Girīśa and also Giriśa. Kailāsa is specified as his special abode, though other mountains are also mentioned in this regard. The *Liṅga Purāṇa* describes Kailāsa and Gaṅgā which flows in that region. Śiva is described as residing there in the company of his attendants.

Kāmeśvara

Padma P., I.25.12; *Skanda P.*, IV.2.85; V.1.25; V.2.13; V.3.71; VII.1.67; VII.3.40; *Vāmana P.*, 35.42.

In Vārāṇasī, Durvāsas installed a *liṅga* and performed *tapas* in honour of Śiva. As there was no sign of Śiva's manifestation, the sage with his characteristic choleric temper was about to subject the entire city of Kāśī to a dreadful curse. Śiva therefore appeared before him and granted all his desires. For this reason, the *liṅga* came to be known as Kāmeśvara.

Kāñci

Brahmāṇḍa P., IV.5.6-10; *Padma P.*, I.17.8; *Vāyu P.*, 104.76.

Kāñci is one of the seven holy cities of the Hindus. It was once the capital of the Cholas, and is still celebrated as one of the great Śakti pīṭhas. It is both a Śaivite and a Vaiṣṇavite centre. Temples of Śiva, Viṣṇu, Śakti and Kārttikeya are found here.

Kapālamocanatīrtha

MBh, III.81.18; *Agni P.*, 109.19; *Kūrma P.*, I.35.15; *Padma P.*, I.37.18; I.17.26; VI.129.28; VI.132.3-4; *Skanda P.*, II.3.6; IV.1.31.

Śiva assumed the Kālabhairava form and severed Brahmā's fifth head. The *kapāla* stuck fast to his hand despite all his efforts to be free from it. Afflicted with *brahmahatyā*, he wandered throughout the world and eventually reached this *tīrtha*. He was immmediately absolved from the *brahmahatyā* sin and relieved of the *kapāla*. Thereafter, he fixed his abode at this place. The *tīrtha* came to be known as Kapālamocanatīrtha.

Karṇotpalātīrtha

Skanda P., VI.127.

Karṇotpalā performed *tapas* to win herself a husband. Devī manifested herself and directed her to bathe in this *tīrtha*, which she did. As a consequence, she became young and beautiful. On seeing her, Kāma fell in love with her, and her father gave her in marriage to him. The *tīrtha* was named after her.

Kāśī

Agni P., 112.3; *Bhaviṣya P.*, II.13.1-9; *Nārada P.*, I.29.48.
Hindus consider Kāśī to be the most sacred city. This city is still a centre of religious and cultural activities. The river Gaṅgā flowing through the city, the sacred *liṅgas* installed there, and the strong belief that people who die there attain *mokṣa* are some factors which rank Kāśī as the most sacred *tīrtha* in India.

Kātyāyanītīrtha

Skanda P., VII.3.24.
After the destruction of the demon Niśumbha, the goddess is said to have fixed her abode at Arbudācala, one of the *Śakti-pīṭhas*. The goddess worshipped here is called Kātyāyanī.

Kāverītīrtha

MBh, III.83.22; *Kūrma P.*, II.37.16-19; II.40.40; *Matsya P.*, 22.64; *Padma P.*, I.39.20; VI.224.3, 4 and 19.
This river flows in south India. Its source is in the Sahya mountains. The river is glorified as Dakṣīṇagaṅgā, and is considered as one of the seven great rivers of India of religious importance.

Kedāratīrtha

MBh, III.81.59; III.83.16-17; *Agni P.*, 112.5; *Kūrma P.*, I.35.12; II.41.7-8; *Liṅga P.*, I.77.37-47; I.92.7; I.134; *Padma P.*, I.26.69; I.32.32; I.37.15; VI.129.10; *Skanda P.*, VI.122; *Vāmana P.*, 36.16; 36.26.
Oppressed by the demon Hiraṇyākṣa, the gods gathered before Śiva and appealed for his protection. Śiva assumed the form of a buffalo and went about shouting "Whom shall I tear to pieces?" (Ke dārāyāmi?). The god, thereafter was installed and worshipped as Kedāreśvara.

Kelīśvarītīrtha

Skanda P., VI.150.
Kelīśvarītīrtha is mentioned in connection with Andhaka's obtaining a boon from Kelīśvarī, who was invoked in a sacrifice by Śukra, the

preceptor of the demons. This was a consequence of the defeat which Andhaka sustained in an encounter with Śiva.

Koṭitīrtha

MBh, III.60.68; III.82.24; III.83.59; *Agni P.*, 119.10; *Matsya P.*, 191.55; 191.7; *Padma P.*, I.12.19; I.18.8; I.26.14; I.26.95; I.33.33; VI.129.7; *Skanda P.*, III.1.27; *Vāmana P.*, 55.53; 84.11.

After the destruction of Rāvana, Rāma reached the Gandhamādana island situated in the southern sea. He installed the *Rāmanāthaliṅga* at Rāmeśvara and worshipped Śiva there to free himself from the *brahmahatyā* sin. Soon after the installation, Rāma felt the desire of the waters of the sacred Gaṅgā to also bathe the *liṅga*. He pierced the earth with the end of his bow and thereby allowed Gaṅgā to flow from the netherworld. This *tīrtha* was thereafter called Koṭitīrtha.

Mahākāla

MBh, III.80.68; *Brahma P.*, 43.66; *Kūrma P.*, II.44.11; *Liṅga P.*, I.92.137; *Matsya P.*, 13.41; 22.24; 178.5.181.26; *Padma P.*, I.12.9; VI.129.21; *Skanda P.*, IV.1.91; V.1.17; VII.1.326.

The fight of Śiva with the demon Andhaka took place in the Mahākāla-vana in Avantī. The Mahākālatīrtha commemorates this event. This is the special name of Śiva enshrined at Ujjain, one of the twelve *jyotirliṅgas*.

Mahākālīpīṭha

Skanda P., VII.1.133.

This *pītha* is situated at Prabhāsa. The worship of Devī in the brighter half of the month of Āśvina during the first nine days is mentioned.

Mānasatīrtha

Matsya P., 194.8; *Padma P.*, VI.128.7.

This is the name of a lake in the Himālayas, between Kailāsa to the north and Gurla to the south.

Maṇikarṇikeśvara

Skanda P., VII.3.16.

A woman named Maṇikarṇikā wanted her ugly appearance removed. She came to this *tīrtha* and bathed in it. Soon after, she found herself in the possession of a beautiful appearance. The *tīrtha* thereafter came to be known as Maṇikarṇikā.

Nāgeśvara

Matsya P., 191.82; *Padma P.*, I.18.78; *Skanda P.*, V.3.99; V.3.131; VII.1.186.

Kṛṣṇa's death occurred closely after the destruction of the Yādava race. Balabhadra went to Prabhāsa and installed there a *liṅga*. Thereafter, he assumed the form of a *nāga* and entered the netherworld through a hole. The *liṅga* installed by Balabhadra whilst assuming his *nāga* form came to be known as Nāgeśvara.

Narmadeśvara

Matsya P., 194.2; *Padma P.*, I.18.69; *Skanda P.*, IV.2.92; V.3.124.

Revā, aslo known as Narmadā, was disappointed with Brahmā's denial to grant her parity with Gaṅgā. She installed a *liṅga* at Kāśī and performed *tapas* in honour of Śiva, who became manifest to her and granted her requests. The *liṅga* installed by her came to be known as Narmadeśvara.

Oṁkāreśvara

Skanda P., IV.2.73; V.5.37; V.2.52.

The sacred syllable *oṁ* was first pronounced from the mouth of Śiva. The god proclaimed that this *liṅga*, a manifestation of the *praṇava*, be installed and worshipped as Oṁkāreśvara.

Pañcanada

MBh, III.88.14; *Agni P.*, 109.12; *Kūrma P.*, II.44.1; *Liṅga P.*, I.43.47-48; *Padma P.*, 24.31; I.26.14; *Vāmana P.*, 34.27.

The five rivers in Punjab are often mentioned in the *Purāṇas*. The five rivers mentioned in the Vedic texts are the Śutudrī, Vipāś, Paruṣṇī,

Asiknī and Vitastā. In modern times they are known as the Sutlej, Bias, Ravi, Chenab, and Jhelum.

Piṅgaleśvara

Kūrma P., II.41.21; *Matsya P.*, 191.31; *Padma P.*, I.18.32; *Skanda P.*, V.3.176.

An orphan girl called Piṅgalā repented the sins she had committed during her previous birth. With permission from the god of death, she went to Mahākālavana and installed a *liṅga* which was named after her. She was absolved thereby of her sins.

Prabhāsa

MBh, III.80.77; III.118.15; *Agni P.*, 116.15; *Garuḍa P.*, I.4.81; *Kūrma P.*, I.35.16; *Nārada P.*, II.70.1-95; *Padma P.*, ***I.37.5; I.33.33***; *Skanda P.*, V.3.98; *Vāmana P.*, 84.29; *Vāyu P.*, 108.16; 109.14.

The importance of this *tīrtha* is described in the chapters which constitute one full *khaṇḍa* entitled *Prabhāsakhaṇḍa*. This section of the *Skanda Purāṇa* mentions all the shrines of Śiva found at Prabhāsa.

Prayāga

MBh, III.93.10; *Agni P.*, 109.19; *Kūrma P.*, I.35.116; *Matsya P.*, 110; *Padma P.*, I.37.1. I.33.32; VI.129.6.

Śantanu and Gaṅgā had many children. In order to free herself from the pollution caused by her having served as the source of human beings, Gaṅgā visited Prayāga. On Nārada's advice, she propitiated Prayāgeśvara and was freed from all impurities.

Rāmanātheśvara

Skanda P., III.1.44.

After the destruction of Rāvaṇa, Rāma halted at Gandhamādana on the way back to Ayodhyā. Agastya and a few other sages visited Rāma there and advised him to install a *liṅga* at Rāmeśvara, and thereby wipe the *brahmahatyā* with which he was then afflicted. Hanumān, who had gone to Kailāsa to bring the *liṅga*, was delayed. As the auspicious hour had approached, a *liṅga* was made from sand on the beach. The *liṅga* installed by Rāma was known thenceforth as Rāmanātheśvara.

Rāmeśvara

Garuḍa P., I.81.9; *Kurma P.*, II.30.23; *Matsya P.*, 22.50; *Nārada P.*, II.76; *Skanda P.*, V.1.31; V.2.29; V.3.84; V.3.133; VI.101; VII.1.11; VII.1.20.

The *tīrtha* renowned as Rāmeśvara is associated with Rāma, the hero of the *Rāmāyaṇa*. The *Purāṇas*, however, speak of another Rāmeśvara which is connected with Bhārgava Rāma, also known as Paraśurāma. After the destruction of the *kṣatriya* race, he installed a *liṅga* and worshipped Śiva for the removal of *brahmahatyā*. The *Skanda Purāṇa* speaks of yet another Rāmeśvara, installed by Rāma the hero of the *Rāmāyaṇa* at Hāṭakeśvara.

Rudrakoṭi

MBh, III.80.124; III.81.63; *Kūrma P.*, II.36.1-4; *Matsya P.*, 181.25; *Padma P.*, I.25.25; VI.129.13; *Skanda P.*, VI.52; *Vāmana P.*, 36.22-23.

Śiva is said to have assumed a crore of Rudra forms to satisfy the longings of a crore of Ṛṣis who had for long been anxious to see the god's manifestations. The *tīrtha* connected with this incident is known as Rudrakoṭi.

Sākambharī

Padma P., I.29.19; *Skanda P.*, VI.275.

Duḥśīlā was a forester. Instructed by his preceptor Nimbaśuka, he installed for worship a *liṅga* which came to be known as Nimbeśvara. His wife Sākambharī installed Devī for worship and the *tīrtha* is known as Sākambharītīrtha.

Skanda-Pura

Skanda P., VI.71.

Soon after the destruction of Tāraka, Kārttikeya is said to have installed his *śakti* (a deified form of his own energy). Worship of this form of Skanda on the sixth day of the brighter half of the Caitra month is prescribed.

Skandavana

Skanda P., IV.1.25.

The sage Agastya is said to have circumambulated Śrīparvata in the company of his wife. He entered Skandavana and worshipped Kārttikeya enshrined there.

Someśvara

Kūrma P., II.35.20; *Skanda P.*, V.1.28; V.2.26; VI.63; VII.1.23; VII.1.44; VII.2.14; *Padma P.*, VI.129.23; *Vāmana P.*, 34.34; *Varāha P.*, I.144.

Dakṣa pronounced a curse on the Moon god. Romaka advised Soma to install and worship a *liṅga* at Hāṭaka; this he did and was freed from the effect of the curse. The *liṅga* was thereafter known as Someśvara.

Śrīparvata

MBh, III.83.16-17; *Agni P.*, 112.4; 113.4; *Kūrma P.*, III.37.13; *Matsya P.*, 13.31; *Liṅga P.*, I.77.37-47; *Padma P.*, I.39.16; *Vāyu P.*, 77.28.

The hill is also known as Śrīśaila and is situated on the southern side of the Kṛṣṇā river. There are many famous *liṅgas* in this *tīrtha*, including Mallikārjuna, one of the twelve *jyotirliṅgas*. This is considered to be one of the eight *sthalas* held most sacred to Śiva.

Tryambakeśvara

Kūrma P., II.35.18; *Matsya P.*, 22.47; 191.19; *Padma P.*, I.18.112; *Skanda P.*, VII.1.91.

This *kṣetra* is located near Nasik, quite close to the source of the Godāvarī river.

Unnatavināyaka

Skanda P., VII.1.329.

At Prabhāsa, towards the north of Devakula is located the famous *tīrtha* known as Unnatasthāna. The Vināyaka enshrined in this *tīrtha* is celebrated for removing the obstacles confronting his worshippers. His worship on the *caturthī* day is especially prescribed.

Vaidyanātha

Matsya P., 13.41; 22.24; *Padma P.*, VI.160.

The temple of Vaidyanātha has a *liṅga* which is celebrated as one of the *jyotirliṅgas*.

Vārāṇaśī

MBh, III.82.69; *Agni P.*, 119.18; *Kūrma P.*, I.30.32; *Matsya P.*, 22.7; *Padma P.*, VI.129.5.

This *tīrtha* is also known as Kāśī. The *Matsya Purāṇa* has devoted five chapters (180-85) to the description of this *tīrtha* in every detail. This *tīrtha* has many other names besides Vārānaśī, like Kāśī, Avimukta, Ānandakāraṇa and Mahāśmaśāna.

Vararuciganapati

Skanda P., VI.131.

At Hāṭakeśvara is situated a *tīrtha* dedicated to Ganeśa. Vararuci, the celebrated grammarian also known as Kātyāyana, is said to have worshipped this god with a view to acquiring knowledge. The worship of the god on the fourth day of the bright half of the month is prescribed.

Bibliography

I. Source Texts

Epics

Mahābhārata	*Parvans* I to VIII and *Parvan* XII, Critical edition, published by the Bhandarkar Oriental Research Institute, Poona.
All other *Parvans*	Chitrasāla edition, Poona.
Harivaṁśa	Chitrasāla edition.
Rāmāyaṇa	In two volumes, edited by Krishnamācharya and published by T.K. Venkobhacarya, Madhvavilas Book Depot, Kumbhakonam, 1929.

Purāṇas

Agni Purāṇa	Laksmivenkatesvar Steam Press, Bombay.
Bhāgavata Purāṇa	Gita Press, Gorakhpur
Bhaviṣya Purāṇa	Lakshmivenkatesvar Steam Press, Bombay
Brahma Purāṇa	Laksmivenkatesvar Steam Press, Bombay
Brahmāṇḍa Purāṇa	Laksmivenkatesvar Steam Press, Bombay.
Brahmavaivarta Purāṇa	Laksmivenkatesvar Steam Press, Bombay
Devibhāgavata Purāṇa	Laksmivenkatesvar Steam Press, Bombay
Gaṇeśa Purāṇa	Laksmivenkatesvar Steam Press, Bombay
Garuḍa Purāṇa	Laksmivenkatesvar Steam Press, Bombay
Kālikā Purāṇa	Laksmivenkatesvar Steam Press, Bombay
Kūrma Purāṇa	Laksmivenkatesvar Steam Press, Bombay
Liṅga Purāṇa	Laksmivenkatesvar Steam Press, Bombay

Mārkaṇḍeya Purāṇa	Edited by Vidyasagar, Sarasvati Press, Calcutta, 1879.
Matsya Purāṇa	Venkatesvar Steam Press, Bombay
Nārada Purāṇa	Laksmivenkatesvar Steam Press, Bombay
Padma Purāṇa	Laksmivenkatesvar Steam Press, Bombay
Śiva Purāṇa	Ganapat Krishnaji edition [1]
Skanda Purāṇa	Laksmivenkatesvar Steam Press, Bombay
Vāmana Purāṇa	Laksmivenkatesvar Steam Press, Bombay
Varāha Purāṇa	Laksmivenkatesvar Steam Press, Bombay
Vāyu Purāṇa	Laksmivenkatesvar Steam Press, Bombay
Viṣṇu Purāṇa	Laksmivenkatesvar Steam Press, Bombay
Sūta saṁhitā	Ānandāśrama series, Poona.

II. (a) Sanskrit Texts consulted

Aghoraśivācāryapaddhati, edited by Sadyojātaśivācārya. Lakṣmīvilas Press, Trichi (granthalipi).

Aghorasivācāryapaddhati Utsavavidhi, Sivajñānabodham Press, Madras (Kali eta, 4994).

Aitareya Brāhmaṇa, Ānandāśrama ed.

Aitareya Upaniṣad, Ānandāśrama ed.

Amarakośa, O.B.A., Poona, 1941.

Aṣṭādhyāyī, Nirṇayasāgar ed.

Āśvalāyana Gṛhyasūtra, ed. Stenzler, Leiptzig, 1864.

[1] There are evidently two editions of this *Purāṇa*. The one which belongs to the Bhandarkar Collection of the B.O.R. Institute, and which is used for the present book, is published by Ganapat Krishnaji. It contains six *saṁhitās*, namely *Jñāna Vidyeśyara*, *Kailāsa*, *Sanatkumāra*, *Vāyu*, (*pūrvardha* and *uttarārdha*) and *Dharma*. The other edition is published by the Venkatesvar Press, Bombay. This also contains six *saṁhitās*, namely *Vidyeśvara*, *Rudra*, *Śatarudra*, *Koṭirudra*, *Kailāsa* and *Vāyu* (*pūrvārdha* and *uttarārdha*). On comparison of the two editions, it is seen that three *saṁhitās*, *Vidyeśvara*, *Kailāsa*, and *Vāyu* are common to both editions (though their order is not the same in the two, and there is a slight difference in the length of these *saṁhitās*). The remaining three *saṁhitās* in the Ganapat Krishnaji edition have nothing in common with the remaining three *saṁhitās* in the Venkatesvar Press edition.

Atharvaveda, Aundh ed.
Bhagavadgītā, Critical ed. Poona.
Bṛhadāraṇyaka Upaniṣad, Ānandāsrama ed.
Bṛhastotraratnākara, Nirṇayasāgar ed. (in two volumes).
Caturvargacintāmaṇi, Biblioteca Indica, Calcutta, 1879.
Chāndogya Upaniṣad, Ānandaśrama ed., Poona.
Gaṇeśasahasranāmastotra, Kumbhakonam ed. (grantha-lipi).
Hālāsyamāhātmya, Kumbhakoṇam (granthalipi).
Hiraṇyakeśin Gṛhyasūtra, ed. Kirste, Vienna, 1889.
Īśādyaṣṭottaraśatopaniṣad, Nirṇayasāgar ed.
Kāmikāgama, Śivajñānabodham Press, Madras (granthalipi).
Kaṭha Upaniṣad, Ānandāśrama ed.
Kiraṇāgamamahātantra, Published by Śivāgamasiddhānta-paripālanasaṅgam 1932, (granthalipi)
Kriyākramadyotikā, Jñānasaṁbandhavilāsa Press, Chidambaram, 1927 (grantha-lipi).
Kumārasaṁbhava, Nirṇayasāgar Press, Bombay.
Kumāratantra, Sivajñānabodham Press, Madras, Kali 5006 (grantha-lipi).
Kuṇḍaratnāvalī, Nirnayasāgar Press, Bombay, 1919.
Lalitāsahasranāma, Theosophical Society ed., Madras.
Mānavagṛhyasūtra, Gromingten Batavia, Wolters Uitgevers, 1941.
Māṇḍūkya Upaniṣad, Ānandāśrama ed.
Manusmṛti, Nirnayasāgar ed., Bombay.
Meghadūta, Kale ed., Bombay.
Muṇḍaka Upaniṣad, Ānandāśrama ed., Poona.
Pañcaviṁśa Brāhmaṇa, Bibliotheca Indica, Bengal, 1931.
Paraśurāmakalpasūtra, Gaekwad Oriental Series, XXII, 1950.
Praśna Upaniṣad, Ānandāśrama ed., Poona.
Raghuvaṁśa, Nirnayasāgar ed. Bombay.
Ṛgveda, Vaidika Samsodhan Mandal, Poona.
Śāṅkhāyana Brāhmaṇa, Ānandāśrama ed., Poona.
Śāṅkhāyana Śrauta Sūtra
Śatapatha Brāhmaṇa, Calcutta, Bengal Asiatic Society ed., 1902.

Saundaryalaharī, University of Mysore Oriental Library, Public. 11/ 86, 1945.
Siddhāntasārāvalī, Śivajñānabodham Press, Madras (grantha-lipi).
Śivaliṅgapratiṣṭhāvidhi, Kalānidhi Press, Point Pedro, Ceylon, Part I and II (grantha-lipi).
Śivārcanācandrikā, Kumbhakoṇam, ed. 1922.
Somaśaṁbhupaddhati, Śivāgamasiddhāntaparipālana Publication, Trivandrum, 1931.
Suprabhedāgama, Śivajñānabodham Press, Madras (grantha-lipi).
Śvetāśvatara Upaniṣad, Ānandāśrama ed., Poona.
Tāṇḍyamahābrāhmaṇa, Kāśī Sanskrit Series, No. 105.
Taittirīya Saṁhitā, HOS series Vol. 18 and 19, 1914.
Taittirīya Brāhmaṇa, Ānandāśrama ed., Poona, 1934.
Taittirīya Upaniṣad, Ānandāśrama ed., Poona.
Vāmakeśvaratantrāntargata-nityāṣoḍaśikārṇava, Ānandāśrama ed.
Viṣṇusahasranāma stotra, Adyar Theosophical Society, Madras, 1927.
Vratacūḍāmaṇi, Kumbhakoṇam ed. 1933 (grantha-lipi).
Yājuṣamantraratnākara, Kumbhakoṇam ed. (grantha-lipi).

(b) Pāli Texts

Dhammapada, PTS ed. O.U.P. 1914.
Dīghanikāya, PTS ed. O.U.P. 1890- 1903-
Majjhimanikāya, PTS ed. 1889.
Saṁyuttanikāya, PTS ed. 1884-1904.

III. General Literature

Aravamuthan, T.G., *Some Aspects of Harappa Culture*, Bombay, 1942.
Arbmann, *Rudra Untersuchen Zun Altindischen Glauben*, Upasala, 1922.
Arunacalam, P., *Studies and Translations Philosophical and Religious*, Colombo, 1937.
Barth, A., *Religions of India*, Trubner's Series, London, 1889.
Banerjea, R.D., *The Development of Hindu Iconography*, Calcutta, 1956.

Bhandarkar, R.G., *Vaiṣṇavism Śaivism and Minor Religious Systems*, Verlag Von Karl, Trūbner Strassburg, 1913.

Bhāratīya Itihāsasamiti 1). *Vedic Age*, George Allen Unwin, London, 1951. (2) *The Age of the Imperial Kanauj*.

Chaterji, *Kashmir Śaivism*, Śrīnagar, 1914.

Cartman, *Hinduism in Ceylon*, Colombo 1957.

Chanda, Ramaprasad, *The Indus Valley in the Vedic Period*, Calcutta, 1926.

Childe, V. Gordon, *New Lights on the Most Ancient East*, London, 1935.

Coomaraswamy, Ananda K. 1) *History of Indian and Indonesian Art*, London, 1927. 2) *The Dance of Shiva*, Asia Publishing House, 1956.

Das, A.C., *Ṛgvedic India*, Calcutta, 1925.

Das Gupta, *Indian Philosophy*, Vol.V.

Diehl, *Instrument and Purpose, Studies on Rites and Rituals in South India*, Gleerup, London, 1956.

Diksitar, V.R.R., *Studies in Tamil Literature and History*, Madras, 1942.

Deussen, P., *The Philosophy of the Upaniṣads*, Edinburgh, 1908.

Dubreuil, Jouveau, 1. *Dravidian Architecture*, Madras, 1917. 2. *Iconography of Southern India*, Paris, 1937.

Elliot, Charles, *Hinduism and Buddhism*, Vols.I-III, London, 1921.

Eggeling, Julius, *Śatapatha Brāhmaṇa*, Translation, (SBE) Oxford Clarendon Press, 1897.

Elmore, Wilber, T., *Dravidian Gods in Modern Hinduism*, Madras, 1925.

Farquhar, J.N., 1). *A Primer of Hinduism*, Christian Literature Society, 1922.

2) *Outlines of Religious Literature of India*, O.U.P., 1920.

3) *The Crown of Hinduism*, OUP, 1920

Fergusson, James, *Tree and Serpent Worship*, London, 1910.

Getty, Alice, *Gaṇeśa*, OUP, 1936

Gonda, Altind, *Pratisara sraj und Viṣṇuism*

Gonda, *Medieval Religious Literature in Sanskrit.*

Gonda, *Aspects of Early Viṣṇuism*, Utrecht, 1954.

Gopinath Rao, *Elements of Hindu Iconography*, Vols. I and II, Madras, 1914.

Griswold, H.D., *The Religion of the Ṛgveda*, OUP, 1923.

Heras, H., *Studies in Proto-Indo-Mediterranean Culture*, Bombay, 1953

Hopkins, E.W. 1) *Epic Mythology*, Strassburg, 1915.
2) *The Religion of India*, Boston, 1908.
3) *Origin and Evolution of Religion*, Yale Univ. Press, 1923.

Hunter, G.R., *The Script of Harappa and Mohenjodaro, and its Connection with other Scripts*, London, 1934.

Jagathisa Iyer, 1) *South Indian Festivals*, Higginbothams Ltd., Madras, 1921.
2) *South Indian Shrines.*

Kanagasabai, V., *The Tamils Eighteen Hundred Years Ago*, Śaivasiddhānta Publishing Works Society, 1956.

Kane, P.V., *History of Dharmaśāstra*, Bhandarkar Oriental Research Institute, Poona.

Karmarkar, A.P., *The Religions of India*, Vol.I., Lonvala, India, 1950.

Keith, A.B., *The Religion and Philosophy of the Veda and the Upaniṣads*, Vols. I and II, (HOS. Vols. 31 and 32), Cambridge, 1925.

Kenneth Morgan, *The Religion of the Hindus*, New York, 1953.

Levi, S.J., Przyluski, and Bloch, *Pre-Aryan and Pre Dravidian in India.*

Macdonell, A.A., 1) *History of Sanskrit Literature*, London, 1900
2) *Lectures on Comparative Religion*, Calcutta, 1925.
3) *Vedic Mythology*, Strassburg, 1897.

Mackay, E.J.H., 1) *Early Indus Civilisation*, London, 1933.
2) *Further Excavations at Mohenjodaro*, Vols.I and II, Delhi, 1938

Martin, E.O., *The Gods of India*, London, 1914.

Max Müller, *History of Sanskrit Literature*, 1860.
Mendis, G.C., *The Early History of Ceylon*, Calcutta, 1951.
Minaksi, C., *Administration and Social Life under the Pallavas*, Madras, 1938.
Monier Williams, 1) *Brāhmanism and Buddhism*, London, 1891.
2) *Hinduism*, London, 1881.
Moor, T., *The Hindu Pantheon*, Madras, 1864.
Muir, J., *Original Sanskrit Texts*, Vols.I -V, London, 1872-1884.
Nivedita, Sister and Coomaraswamy A.K., *Myths of the Hindus and the Buddhists*, New York.
Narayana Ayyar, C.V., *Origin and Early History of Śaivism in South India*, Madras, 1936.
Pattabhiramin, P.Z., *Trouvailles de Neḍuṅgadou Tāṇḍavas de Śiva*, Pondichery, 1956.
Payne, Ernest A., *The Śāktas*, Calcutta, 1933.
Poornalingam, *Tamil Literature*, Tinneveli, 1929.
Potdar, K.R., *Sacrifice in the Ṛgveda*, Bombay, 1953.
Pusalker, A.D., *Studies in Epics and Purāṇas of India*, Bombay, 1953.
Radhakrishnan, S., *Indian Philosophy*, Vols.I and II, Allen and Unwin, London 1948.
Ramakrishna Centenary Committee, *The Cultural Heritage of India*, Vols. I-IV, Calcutta.
Rapson, E.J., *Cambridge History of India*, Vol.I., *Ancient India*, Cambridge University Press, 1922.
Renou, Louis, *Religions of Ancient India*, London, 1953.
Rose, E., *Beitrage zur Kenntnis des Śivaitischen Namenglaubens nach den Purāṇen*.
Sakhare, *Lingārcanācandrikā*, Belgaum, 1942.
Sankarananda, *Rgvedic Culture of the pre-Historic Indus*, Calcutta, 1946.
Sesa Iyengar, *The Ancient Dravidians*, Madras, 1925.
Scott, George R., *Phallic Worship*, London, 1941.
Shivapadasunderam, S., *Śaiva School of Hinduism*, George Allen and Unwin, London, 1934.

Somasunderam, J.M., *University Environs*, Annamalai, 1955.
Srinivasa Iyengar, P.T., *History of the Tamils*, Madras, 1929.
Slater, Gilbert, *Dravidian Element in Indian Culture*, London, 1934.
Subramaniam, K.V., *The Origin of Śaivism and its History in the Tamil Land*, Madras, 1929.
Thomas, P., *Hindu Religious Customs and Manners*, Bombay.
Tylor, E.B., *Anthropology*, A Thinker's Library Series, London, 1946.
Vaiyyapuri Pillai, S., *History of Tamil Language and Literature*, Madras, 1956.
Venkataramanayya, N., 1. *Rudra-Śiva*, Madras University 1941.
2. *Origin of the South Indian Temple*, Madras, 1930.
Whitney, W.D., *Atharvaveda*, Translation, HOS vols. 7 and 8.
Wilkins, W.J., *Hindu Mythology*, London, 1913.
Winternitz, M., *History of Indian Literature*, Calcutta, 1927.
Woodroffe, John 1. *Shakti and Shakta*, Madras, 1929.
2. *Varṇamālā*, Madras 1951.
3. *Principles of Tantra*, Madras, 1952.
Zimmer, Henrich, *Myths and Symbols in Indian Art and Civilisation*, Bollingen Series, New York, 1953.
2. *The Art of Indian Asia*, Bollingen Series (2 Vols.) New York, 1955.

IV. Reference Books

Apte, V.S., *Sanskrit English Dictionary*, Delhi, 1959.
Dandekar, R.N., *Vedic Bibliography*, Bombay, 1946.
Encyclopaedia of Religion and Ethics.
Kauśītakībrāhmaṇāraṇyaka Viśvakośa, Compiled by Kevalananda Sarasvati, 1954.
Macdonell, A.A., and Keith, A.B., *Vedic Index* (2 vols.)
Stenzler, A.F., *Wortverzeichniss zu den Hausregeln von Āśvalāyana, Pāraskara, Śāṅkhāyana, und Gobhila*, Leipzig, 1886.
Visvanbandhu Sastri, *Vaidikapadānukramakośa*.
Williams Monier, *Sanskrit-English Dictionary*, Oxford.

V. Commemoration Volumnes etc.

Belvalkar Commemoration Volume
D.R. Bhandarkar Volume
Dr. C. Kunhanrajah Presentation Volume
Kane Commemoration Volume
Jha Commemoration Volume
B.C. Law Commemoration Volume
Dr. S. Krishnaswamy Iyengar Commemoration Volume
Sukthankar Commemoration Volume
Gopalakrishnamachariar Commemoration Volume
Winternitz Memorial Number, ed. N.N. Law, 1938.

VI. Journals, Periodicals etc.

Annals of the Bhandarkar Oriental Research Institute
All India Oriental Conference Proceedings
Ancient India
Annals of the Oriental Research University of Madras
Ceylon University Reviews
Indian Antiquary
Indian Historical Quarterly
Indian Culture
Journal of the Bihar and Orissa Research Institute
Journal of the Department of Letters, University of Calcutta.
Journal of the American Oriental Society
Journal of the Anthropological Society
Journal of the Annamalai University
Journal of the University of Poona
Journal of Indian History
Journal of the Ganganath Jha Research Institute
Journal of the Royal Asiatic Society
Kalyāṇakalpataru
Madras University Journal
New Review
Prācyavāṇī

Quarterly Journal of the Mythic Society
Tanjore Art Exhibition Souvenir, 1955.
Tamil Culture
Wiener Zeitschrift für die Kunde des Morgenlandes

VII. Tamil Texts Consulted

Akanānūru, Śaivasiddhānta Works Publishing Society Madras, 1957.
Aiṅkurunūru, Annamalai University, 1957.
Appar Tēvāram, Śaivasiddhānta Mahāsamājam, Madras, 1941.
Cilappatikāram, Saminathiyar ed., Madras, 1927.
Kalittokai, Śaivasiddhānta Publishing Society, Madras, 1938.
Kantapurāṇam, Tiruppanantāḷ Maḍam ed., 1952.
Maṇimēkalai, Saminathiyar ed. Madras, 1931.
Narriṇna, Śaivasiddhānta Publishing Society, Madras, 1956.
Paripāṭal, Saminathaiyar ed. Madras, 1935.
Patirruppattu, Saminathaiyar ed. Madras, 1941.
Pattuppāṭṭu, Saminathiyar ed. Madras 1956.
Puranānūru, Saminathiyar ed. Madras, 1935.
Sampantar Tēvāram, Śaivasiddhānta Mahāsamājam, Madras, 1937.
Suntarar Tēvāram, Śaivasiddhānta Mahasamājam, Madras, 1935.
Sūtasaṅkitai, Addison Press, Madras, 1914.
Tirumantiram, Śaivasiddhānta Publ. Society, Madras, 1957 (2 vols.)
Tiruppukāḷ, Gopalakrishnakone, Madura, 1955.
Tiruvācakam, ed. G.U., Pope, Oxford Clarendon Press, 1900.
Tolkāppiyam, Kanecaiyyar ed. Jaffna, 1938.
Uṇmaiviḷakkam, Tiruppanantāḷ ed., 1954.

VIII. General Literature in Tamil

Cuppiramaniya Pillai, *Ilakkiya Varalāru* (2 Parts), Śaivasiddhānta Publishing Works, Madras, 1958.
Duraisamy Pillai, Auvai, *A History of Tamil Śaivasiddhānta Literature*, Annamalai University, 1958.
Sadasiva Pandarathar, *A History of Tamil Literature*, Annamalai University Tamil Series, 1957.

Srinivasa Pillai, K.S., *Tamil Varalāru*, Tanjore 1957.
Raghavaiyangar, R., *Tamil Varalāru*, Annamalai University, 1952.

IX. Journals, Periodicals etc., in Tamil.

Kalaimagal
Sentamil
Sentamil Selvi
Elakesari Jubilee Volume

Index

Other books of related interest
published by **INDICA BOOKS**:

- **THE APHORISMS OF SIVA**
  trans. with exposition and notes
  by Mark S.G. Dyczkowski
- **THE STANZAS ON VIBRATION**
  The Spandakārikā with Four Commentaries
  trans. with introduction and exposition
  by Mark S.G. Dyczkowski
- **A JOURNEY IN THE WORLD OF THE TANTRAS**
  by Mark S.G. Dyczkowski
- **ASPECTS OF TANTRA YOGA**
  by Debabrata SenSharma
- **ABHINAVAGUPTA'S COMMENTARY ON THE BHAGAVAD GITA**
  Gītārtha Saṁgraha
  trans. with introduction and notes
  by Boris Marjanovic
- **VIJÑANA BHAIRAVA**
  THE PRACTICE OF CENTRING AWARENESS
  trans. and commentary
  by Swami Lakshman Joo
- **THE HINDU PANTHEON IN NEPALESE LINE DRAWINGS**
  Two Manuscripts of the Pratiṣṭhālakṣaṇasārasamuccaya
  compiled by Gudrun Bühnemann
- **SELECTED WRITINGS OF M.M. GOPINATH KAVIRAJ**
- **आगम-संविद्** **Āgama-Saṁvid** (Sanskrit) डॉ. कमलेश झा
- **स्पन्दप्रदीपिका** ***Spandapradīpikā*** (Sanskrit)
  A Commentary on the Spandakārikā by
  Bhagavadutpalācārya Edited by Mark S.G. Dyczkowski
- **मीमांसा-पदार्थ-विज्ञानम्**
  काशीनाथ न्यौपाने (Sanskrit & Hindi)